CSWE EPAS 2015 Core Competencies and Behaviors in This Text

Competency	Chapter
Competency 1: Demonstrate Ethical and Professional Behavior	
Behaviors:	
Make ethical decisions by applying the standards of the NASW *Code of Ethics*, relevant laws and regulations, models for ethical decision-making, ethical conduct of research, and additional codes of ethics as appropriate to context	3, 6, 8, 13, 15
Use reflection and self-regulation to manage personal values and maintain professionalism in practice situations	1, 3, 4
Demonstrate professional demeanor in behavior; appearance; and oral, written, and electronic communication	6
Use technology ethically and appropriately to facilitate practice outcomes	10
Use supervision and consultation to guide professional judgment and behavior	1, 13, 16
Competency 2: Engage Diversity and Difference in Practice	
Behaviors:	
Apply and communicate understanding of the importance of diversity and difference in shaping life experiences in practice at the micro, mezzo, and macro levels	2, 6, 9, 13
Present themselves as learners and engage clients and constituencies as experts of their own experiences	4, 7, 14
Apply self-awareness and self-regulation to manage the influence of personal biases and values in working with diverse clients and constituencies	3
Competency 3: Advance Human Rights and Social, Economic, and Environmental Justice	
Behaviors:	
Apply their understanding of social, economic, and environmental justice to advocate for human rights at the individual and system levels	5
Engage in practices that advance social, economic, and environmental justice	4
Competency 4: Engage in Practice-Informed Research and Research-Informed Practice	
Behaviors:	
Use practice experience and theory to inform scientific inquiry and research	15
Apply critical thinking to engage in analysis of quantitative and qualitative research methods and research findings	9, 15
Use and translate research evidence to inform and improve practice, policy, and service delivery	2, 10
Competency 5: Engage in Policy Practice	
Behaviors:	
Identify social policy at the local, state, and federal level that impacts well-being, service delivery, and access to social services	14
Assess how social welfare and economic policies impact the delivery of and access to social services	1, 5, 14
Apply critical thinking to analyze, formulate, and advocate for policies that advance human rights and social, economic, and environmental justice	9, 11

Competency	Chapter
Competency 6: Engage with Individuals, Families, Groups, Organizations, and Communities	
Behaviors:	
Apply knowledge of human behavior and the social environment, person-in-environment, and other multidisciplinary theoretical frameworks to engage with clients and constituencies	7
Use empathy, reflection, and interpersonal skills to effectively engage diverse clients and constituencies	5, 7, 12
Competency 7: Assess Individuals, Families, Groups, Organizations, and Communities	
Behaviors:	
Collect and organize data, and apply critical thinking to interpret information from clients and constituencies	7, 9
Apply knowledge of human behavior and the social environment, person-in-environment, and other multidisciplinary theoretical frameworks in the analysis of assessment data from clients and constituencies	2, 10
Develop mutually agreed-on intervention goals and objectives based on the critical assessment of strengths, needs, and challenges within clients and constituencies	5, 8, 11
Select appropriate intervention strategies based on the assessment, research knowledge, and values and preferences of clients and constituencies	8, 10, 11
Competency 8: Intervene with Individuals, Families, Groups, Organizations, and Communities	
Behaviors:	
Critically choose and implement interventions to achieve practice goals and enhance capacities of clients and constituencies	8, 12
Apply knowledge of human behavior and the social environment, person-in-environment, and other multidisciplinary theoretical frameworks in interventions with clients and constituencies	1
Use inter-professional collaboration as appropriate to achieve beneficial practice outcomes	13, 16
Negotiate, mediate, and advocate with and on behalf of diverse clients and constituencies	6, 12
Facilitate effective transitions and endings that advance mutually agreed-on goals	16
Competency 9: Evaluate Practice with Individuals, Families, Groups, Organizations, and Communities	
Behaviors:	
Select and use appropriate methods for evaluation of outcomes	15
Apply knowledge of human behavior and the social environment, person-in-environment, and other multidisciplinary theoretical frameworks in the evaluation of outcomes	2
Critically analyze, monitor, and evaluate intervention and program processes and outcomes	11
Apply evaluation findings to improve practice effectiveness at the micro, mezzo, and macro levels	3

Adapted with the permission of Council on Social Work Education

EIGHTH EDITION

Generalist Social Work Practice

An Empowering Approach

Karla Krogsrud Miley
Black Hawk College

Michael W. O'Melia
St. Ambrose University

Brenda L. DuBois
St. Ambrose University

PEARSON

Boston Columbus Indianapolis New York San Francisco Hoboken
Amsterdam Cape Town Dubai London Madrid Milan Munich Paris Montreal Toronto
Delhi Mexico City São Paulo Sydney Hong Kong Seoul Singapore Taipei Tokyo

VP and Editorial Director: Jeffery W. Johnston
Senior Acquisitions Editor: Julie Peters
Program Manager: Megan Moffo
Editorial Assistant: Pamela DiBerardino
Executive Product Marketing Manager:
  Christopher Barry
Executive Field Marketing Manager: Krista Clark
Team Lead Project Management: Bryan Pirrmann
Team Lead Program Management: Laura Weaver
Procurement Specialist: Deidra Skahill
Art Director: Diane Lorenzo

Art Director Cover: Diane Ernsberger
Cover Design: Carie Keller, Cenveo
Cover Art: Shutterstock
Media Producer: Michael Goncalves
Editorial Production and Composition Services:
  Lumina Datamatics, Inc.
Full-Service Project Manager: Murugesh Rajkumar
  Namasivayam
Printer/Binder: LSC Communications
Cover Printer: LSC Communications
Text Font: Dante MT Pro

Library of Congress Cataloging-in-Publication Data
Miley, Karla Krogsrud, 1942-
  Generalist social work practice : an empowering approach / Karla Krogsrud Miley, Black Hawk College,
Michael W. O'Melia, St. Ambrose University, Brenda L. DuBois, St. Ambrose University. – 8 Edition.
    pages cm
  Revised edition of the authors' Generalist social work practice, 2013.
  Includes bibliographical references and indexes.
  ISBN 978-0-13-394827-1 (alk. paper) – ISBN 0-13-394827-7 (alk. paper) 1. Social service. 2. Social case work. I.
O'Melia, Michael. II. DuBois, Brenda, 1949- III. Title.
  HV40.M5223 2015
  361.3'2–dc23

                                                                    2015030088

Student Edition
ISBN-10: 0-13-394827-7
ISBN-13: 978-0-13-394827-1

eText
ISBN 10: 0-13-394832-3
ISBN 13: 978-0-13-394832-5

Package
ISBN 10: 0-13-440334-7
ISBN 13: 978-0-13-440334-2

PEARSON

Contents

PART II: ENGAGEMENT: THE DIALOGUE PHASE

16. Intervention: Integrating Gains 408

Preface

The approach to social work practice presented in this text acknowledges our interdependence and celebrates the resources that collaboration creates. It reflects a broad-based view of human functioning and explores processes for activating resources in people and their environments. Moreover, it specifically focuses on the nature of the helping relationship itself as a resource for both workers and client systems. Collaboration is the heart of this empowering approach. We believe in the creative synergy of collaborative processes. It's how we wrote this book.

New to This Edition

This eighth edition of *Generalist Social Work Practice: An Empowering Approach* provides updated information about topics in generalist social work practice and integrates additional pedagogy to support student learning. The authors have incorporated new material relevant to contemporary trends in social work practice, offered revisions to critical thinking questions consistent with the Council on Social Work Education's (CSWE) current core competencies and practice behaviors, and added links to e-resources to promote student learning and assessment. Specifically, this edition does the following:

- Better prepares students for present-day generalist social work practice by offering *new material* about biological influences on behavior, trauma theory, trauma-informed practice, and evidence-based practice
- Ensures extensive coverage of required outcomes identified by CSWE in 2015, with revised critical thinking questions that target the current core competencies and associated practices behaviors
- Uses a new full-length case example in Chapter 2 that demonstrates how a generalist social worker applies key theoretical perspectives to her work with a veteran reintegrating into civilian life after combat
- Adds to students' professional foundations by including the National Association of Social Work's (NASW) strategies for professional action through 2020 and revisions to material based on current NASW policy statements as well as the current International Federation of Social Workers' (IFSW) definition of social work
- Promotes students' self-assessment by using formative essay assessments at the end of each major section (Assess Your Understanding) and summative multiple-choice assessments at the end of each chapter (Evaluate Your Competence)
- Facilitates an interactive learning experience throughout the Pearson eText by integrating e-resources including links to a glossary of key concepts; and video assets integrated into the text presentation
- Uses carefully crafted case examples to illustrate the core competences of social work practice across a wide range of practice settings

- Updates demographic information to ensure currency
- Supports students' inquiry into specialized topic areas with updated bibliographic references and text citations throughout
- Improves readability by fine-tuning the organization of material in many chapters

Organization of This Book

This book organizes material into four parts. Part I creates a perspective for empowerment-oriented generalist social work practice. Parts II, III and IV articulate processes for generalist social workers to apply with clients at the micro- mezzo-, and macrolevels of practice.

Part I, "Social Work Practice Perspectives," describes how generalist social workers using an empowerment-based approach can meet the core purposes of social work to enhance human functioning and promote social justice.

Chapter 1, "Generalist Social Work Practice," overviews the profession of social work, including its value base and purpose. This chapter defines generalist social work, delineates roles for generalist practitioners, and introduces the empowering approach to generalist practice featured in this text.

Chapter 2, "Human System Perspectives," considers the importance of theoretical frameworks for practice. It describes the key perspectives of ecosystems, feminist theory, critical and critical race theories, social constructionism, biology and behavior, and a trauma-informed perspective. This chapter also discusses useful concepts about human systems and proposes an ecosystems framework to apply these perspectives in practice.

Chapter 3, "Values and Multicultural Competence," explores the various filters through which we experience the world, including expectations, values, and culture. It describes how practitioners can infuse professional values and cultural competence into their practice.

Chapter 4, "Strengths and Empowerment," introduces the strengths perspective, describes the principles of empowerment, and discusses the implications of these orientations for social work practice.

Chapter 5, "An Empowering Approach to Generalist Practice," integrates the various perspectives offered in Part I to create an empowerment-based generalist practice model and extensively applies it to examples at the micro-, mezzo-, and macrolevels of practice.

Part II, "Engagement: The Dialogue Phase," describes the practice processes related to constructing and maintaining empowering client–worker relationships, communicating effectively with diverse clients about their situations, and defining a purpose for the work.

Chapter 6, "Engagement: Forming Partnerships," examines the social worker–client system relationship and the qualities necessary for building professional partnerships. To ensure a social justice perspective, this chapter also discusses how to relate with clients who are culturally different, oppressed, or reluctant to participate.

Chapter 7, "Engagement: Articulating Situations," discusses dialogue skills. It emphasizes how social workers respond proactively to clients in ways that clarify their challenges, validate their feelings, and respect their perspectives on the presenting situation.

Chapter 8, "Engagement: Defining Directions," explains how social workers reorient clients and constituencies away from describing what is wrong toward creating a vision of how they would like things to be. It also discusses how to increase client motivation, collaborate with clients who resist, partner with involuntary clients, and take priority actions in response to crisis situations.

Part III, "Assessment: The Discovery Phase," presents solution-oriented processes to identify client system strengths and environmental resources as preliminary to developing a plan of action.

Chapter 9, "Assessment: Identifying Strengths," describes how social workers orient their conversations with clients to uncover strengths and potential solutions. Specifically, this chapter helps practitioners locate strengths through solution-focused dialogue, exploration of clients' cultural memberships, and clients' responses to adversity.

Chapter 10, "Assessment: Assessing Resource Capabilities," offers processes and tools for social workers and clients at all system levels to discover their own abilities and the resources of their environments.

Chapter 11, "Assessment: Framing Solutions," describes planning processes in which clients and social workers collaborate to look at situations in strength-focused ways, set concrete goals and objectives, and generate possible strategies for change.

Part IV, "Intervention and Evaluation: The Development Phase," features generalist social work skills for implementing, evaluating, and stabilizing change efforts.

Chapter 12, "Intervention: Activating Resources," describes intervention activities to empower clients with their own capabilities and increase access to the resources of their environments. Social workers implement processes to enhance interactions, develop power, change perspectives, manage resources, and educate clients.

Chapter 13, "Intervention: Creating Alliances," explores ways to initiate alliances in support of client systems' change efforts. All new relationships with clients and their constituencies have potential benefits, including such examples as empowerment groups, natural support networks, and service delivery alliances.

Chapter 14, "Intervention: Expanding Opportunities," examines possibilities for resource expansion through social reform, policy development, legislative advocacy, and community change. These activities fulfill the professional mandate to ensure a just distribution of societal resources.

Chapter 15, "Evaluation: Recognizing Success," discusses how to monitor the success of the social work effort in order to maintain client motivation, determine effective strategies, and recognize successful outcomes. Specifically, this chapter describes practice evaluation, social work research, single-system design, and how an empowerment perspective influences research processes.

Chapter 16, "Intervention: Integrating Gains," focuses on closure processes. Social workers use skills to complete contracts with clients, make necessary referrals, stabilize the progress achieved, and resolve the emotional elements of the relationship. Endings with larger systems receive special attention.

Instructor Resources

Prepared by the authors and available online, the Instructor's Manual contains comprehensive resources for each chapter, including an overview, student learning outcomes, detailed outlines, discussion questions, in-class activities, out-of-class assignments, and multiple choice and short answer essay test items. To supplement these materials, the authors also offer a full-length generalist-focused case study that coordinates with each of the four parts of the book as well as tables to encapsulate the social service agencies and social workers in the fictitious Northside Community examples that are featured throughout the text.

Acknowledgments

We are thankful for the encouragement and support offered by our colleagues, friends, and families. We also express appreciation to Julie Peters, Megan Moffo, and Andrea Hall for their guidance on this project; to Doug Bell for his thoughtful direction and support; to Murugesh Rajkumar Namasivayam for careful editing; and to all for their diligent work during various stages of production. We also thank the reviewers who provided useful comments as we engaged in preparing the eighth edition:

Tina L. Jordan, Delaware State University; Katy Miller, Western New England University; La Tonya Noel, Florida State University; and Karen Zellmann, Western Illinois University.

1

Generalist Social Work Practice

BLEND IMAGES/SHUTTERSTOCK

"What's working well that you would like to see continue?" With this question, Andrea Barry, a family preservation worker, shifts focus in her work with the Clemens family. She carefully studies the reactions to her question on the faces of the family members who are gathered with her around their kitchen table. She reads caution, apprehension, maybe even a little anger, and yes, there it is, a growing sense of surprise, of intrigue with her approach. As a social worker with the family preservation program of Northside Family Services, Andrea has seen this before. Preparing to fend off the blame of abuse or neglect, families involved with the program are often taken off guard by the careful, nonjudgmental phrasing of her questions. With the query about "what's working well," Andrea recognizes family strengths and looks toward the future, toward things families can still do something about. In other words, she sets the stage for empowering families by focusing on their strengths and promoting their competence.

Andrea's question embodies her view of how families might find themselves in this predicament. To continue to focus on "What are your problems?" doesn't make sense to Andrea, who sees family difficulties arising from the challenge of scarce resources rather than resulting from something that the family is doing wrong. As reflected in her question, Andrea believes that even those families referred by the Child Protective Unit for work with the family preservation program are actually doing a lot right. She regards families as doing the best they can with currently available resources. So, of course, in trying to overcome their present difficulties, the subsequent question becomes, "What can we do to build on your strengths?" rather than "What else is wrong?" Her approach presumes that all families have strengths and are capable of making changes; it prompts them to collaborate with her as partners in the change process.

Andrea has learned from experience that different families benefit from different constellations of resources for optimal functioning. Some family members need to understand themselves and each other better. Others need information about how to cope with the inevitable, and also the unexpected changes that occur throughout their lives. Often, isolated families benefit from connections to the support of interpersonal relationships. Still other families need to access resources from within the community. Andrea teams with families to manage a network of social services, selecting among possibilities ranging from housing assistance to job training to crisis child care to child abuse prevention.

Andrea also recognizes that to serve their best interests, she must broaden her focus and look beyond the needs of individual families. Many times, families confined by forces they consider to be beyond their personal control seek a professional voice to speak for them at the levels of government, policy, and resource allocation. They certainly need power and resources to take charge of their own direction in a world that continues to grow more complex and confusing.

As Andrea provides opportunities for the members of the Clemens family to respond to her questions she reminds herself that this family is unique. She knows to attend to the ways that her clients are similar as well as to the ways they are different. As an African American woman, Andrea herself is sensitive to the confinement of prejudgments. The strengths the Clemens family members have to offer and the challenges they face are particular to their own situation. Demonstrating her cultural competence, Andrea thoughtfully examines the assumptions she makes about people based on their obvious similarities so that she will not ignore their inevitable differences.

Clients have taught Andrea that individual differences themselves can be the key to solutions. Social work practitioners accept the challenge of enabling each client system to access its own unique capabilities and the resources of its particular context. Andrea's role in the professional relationship is that of a partner to empower families with their own strengths, not to overpower families with her own considerable practice knowledge and skills. Andrea has learned to depend on each family system's special competencies to guide her in this empowering process.

Even though Andrea considers the Clemens family as a whole, she will not neglect her professional mandate to act in the best interest of the Clemens children. Ethical considerations and legal obligations compel Andrea to protect the children in this family. However, family service social workers simultaneously focus on the preservation of families and the protection of children. Andrea sees the needs of families and children as convergent.

What benefits the family will help the children's development. What benefits the children will contribute to the cohesiveness of the family. Theoretically, she sees the whole family system as her client and knows that any change in the family system will create changes for individual family members.

Andrea's work with the Clemens family reinforces her opinion that social policy that aims to keep families together is good policy. She always feels best when implementing a policy that reflects a professional philosophy that so neatly fits her own values. The policy of family preservation makes sense in Andrea's practice experience as well. She has observed the trauma for families and children when children at risk are removed from their own homes. Reuniting them, even after positive changes occur, always seems to be a difficult transition. Research in the field of child welfare confirms Andrea's practice observations and lends support to the current policy of family preservation. Andrea believes that keeping families together makes good economic sense, too. She suspects that economic considerations are a major force motivating the development of policies that favor family preservation.

"What's working well that you'd like to see continue?" This is a simple question, yet it reflects Andrea Barry's empowerment orientation toward social work practice. Andrea has learned that even simple questions can have dramatic effects. Simple questions set the tone, bond relationships, and lead to successful solutions.

This overview of social work practice describes the underlying values, purposes, and perspectives that contribute to the empowering approach used by Andrea Barry and articulates what generalist social workers do. The outcome is a foundation on which to build an understanding of social work practice from a generalist perspective.

SOCIAL WORK VALUES AND PURPOSE

Andrea Barry practices in family services—one of the many fields of **social work**. Other practice arenas include school social work, medical social work, probation and other criminal justice services, mental health, youth services, child welfare, community organizing, and housing and urban development, to name a few. The predominant fields of social work practice, representing more than 70 percent of the professional workforce, are mental health, medical health, child welfare, and aging services (Whitaker et al., 2006).

All social work practitioners, regardless of their particular field of practice, share a common professional identity and work toward similar purposes. The National Association of Social Workers (1999), in its *Code of Ethics*, defines this unifying purpose, or mission, of all social work as "to enhance human well-being and help meet the basic human needs of all people, with particular attention to the needs and empowerment of people who are vulnerable, oppressed, and living in poverty" (Preamble). To meet this purpose, social workers recognize that personal troubles and public issues are intertwined.

Thus, social workers strive to both strengthen human functioning and promote the effectiveness of societal structures. This simultaneous focus on persons and their environments permeates

Ethical and Professional Behavior

Behavior: Use reflection and self-regulation to manage personal values and maintain professionalism in practice situations

Critical Thinking Question: Human dignity and worth along with social justice are the two cornerstone values of the social work profession. In what ways are these professional values consonant (or not) with your personal values?

all social work practice. As a social worker, Andrea Barry works with the Clemens family to facilitate the adaptive functioning of their family and preserve its unity. She also works to create a resource-rich and responsive environment that will contribute to the development and stability of the Clemens family. Both of these activities reflect Andrea's integration of the fundamental values of the social work profession. The overarching values of **human dignity and worth** and **social justice** shape her attitudes; the purpose of the profession directs her actions.

Human Dignity and Worth

Valuing the inherent human dignity and worth of all people reflects a nondiscriminatory view of humankind. The *Code of Ethics* (NASW, 1999) ensures social workers treat clients with respect, attend to individualization and diversity, promote self-determination, strengthen clients' capacities and opportunities for change, and responsively resolve conflicts between the interests of clients and those of society. Similarly, in their joint statement on ethics in social work, the International Federation of Social Workers (IFSW) and the International Association of Schools of Social Work (IASSW) affirm that human rights follow from respect for the inherent dignity and worth of all people. As such, social workers are expected to defend and uphold the physical, psychological, emotional, and spiritual integrity and well-being of all persons by

1. Respecting the right to self-determination—Social workers should respect and promote people's right to make their own choices and decisions, irrespective of their values and life choices, provided this does not threaten the rights and legitimate interests of others.

2. Promoting the right to participation—Social workers should promote the full involvement and participation of people using their services in ways that enable them to be empowered in all aspects of decisions and actions affecting their lives.

3. Treating each person as a whole—Social workers should be concerned with the whole person, within the family, community, societal and natural environments, and should seek to recognise all aspects of a person's life.

4. Identifying and developing strengths—Social workers should focus on the strengths of all individuals, groups, and communities and thus promote their empowerment. (IFSW & IASSW, 2004, Sec. 4.1)

Respectful interaction with others affirms a person's sense of dignity and worth. Social workers treat people with consideration, respect their uniqueness, appreciate the validity of their perspectives, and listen carefully to what they have to say. Ultimately, according people dignity and worth affords them the opportunities and resources of a just society.

Social Justice

Social justice describes circumstances in which all members of a society have equal access to societal resources, opportunities, rights, political influence, and benefits (DuBois & Miley, 2014; Healy, K., 2001). Social justice prevails when all members benefit from the resources that a society offers and, reciprocally, have opportunities to contribute to that society's pool of resources.

The philosophy of social justice is deeply rooted in the social work profession; however, political realities and ethical dilemmas confound workers' attempts to apply the principles of social justice in practice. For example, Reisch (2002) describes two problems associated with relating social justice principles to the social policy debates taking place in today's political and economic environment. First, Reisch notes a paradox of defining justice principles based on a socio-political-economic system that for the most part perpetuates injustice. Additionally, Reisch highlights the tension between asserting individual rights and advancing the common good in allocating societal resources. Group and individual interests do not always converge. Clearly, social workers face dilemmas when choosing actions in practice that promote a social justice ideal. The International Federation of Social Workers and International Association of Schools of Social Work (2004) detail the fabric of social justice:

Social justice describes circumstances in which all members of a society have equal access to societal resources, opportunities, rights, political influence, and benefits.

1. Challenging negative discrimination—Social workers have a responsibility to challenge negative discrimination on the basis of characteristics such as ability, age, culture, gender or sex, marital status, socio-economic status, political opinions, skin colour, racial or other physical characteristics, sexual orientation, or spiritual beliefs.

2. Recognising diversity—Social workers should recognise and respect the ethnic and cultural diversity of the societies in which they practise, taking account of individual, family, group and community differences.

3. Distributing resources equitably—Social workers should ensure that resources at their disposal are distributed fairly, according to need.

4. Challenging unjust policies and practices—Social workers have a duty to bring to the attention of their employers, policy makers, politicians and the general public situations where distribution of resources, policies and practices are oppressive, unfair or harmful.

5. Working in solidarity—Social workers have an obligation to challenge social conditions that contribute to social exclusion, stigmatisation, or subjugation, and to work towards an inclusive society. (Sec. 4.2)

Social injustice prevails when society infringes on human rights, holds prejudicial attitudes toward some of its members, and institutionalizes inequality by discriminating against segments of its citizenry. Encroachments on human and civil rights deny equal access to opportunities and resources, limiting full participation in society. Collectively, the injustices enacted by advantaged groups create conditions of discrimination and oppression for disadvantaged groups. Members of oppressed groups often personally experience dehumanization and victimization. Social workers understand the consequences of injustice and intervene to achieve individual and collective social and economic justice.

Defining Social Work

Social work is a profession that supports individuals, groups, and communities in a changing society and creates social conditions favorable to the well-being of people and society. Social workers strive to create order and enhance opportunities for people in an increasingly complex world. The social work profession charges its members with the responsibility of promoting competent human functioning and fashioning a responsive and just society. To achieve these goals, social workers require a clear understanding of the way things are and a positive view of the way things could be. Social work practitioners fine-tune their vision by incorporating professional perspectives on human behavior, cultural diversity, social environments, and approaches to change. The International Federation of Social Workers (2014) defines social work as:

> a practice-based profession and an academic discipline that promotes social change and development, social cohesion, and the empowerment and liberation of people. Principles of social justice, human rights, collective responsibility and respect for diversities are central to social work. Underpinned by theories of social work, social sciences, humanities and indigenous knowledge, social work engages people and structures to address life challenges and enhance wellbeing. (Global Definition section, ¶ 1)

Similarly, the Council on Social Work Education (CSWE), which accredits undergraduate and graduate social work programs, describes the dual focus of the social work profession as promoting the well-being of individuals and the collective betterment of society through the "quest for social and economic justice, the prevention of conditions that limit human rights, the elimination of poverty, and the enhancement of the quality of life for all persons, locally and globally" (2015 , p. 1).

Framing social work's commitment to respect the dignity and worth of all people and the profession's quest for social justice, the **core values of the social work** profession also set the standards for what is desirable in practice. Based on the National Association of Social Workers' *Code of Ethics* (1999), the professional values that guide social work practice include:

- Service—Helping people and solving social problems
- Social justice—Challenging injustices
- Dignity and worth of the person—Respecting inherent dignity
- Importance of human relationships—Recognizing the importance of belongingness
- Integrity—Being trustworthy
- Competence—Practicing competently

Achieving the Purpose of Social Work

Social work focuses on releasing human power in individuals to reach their potential and contribute to the collective good of society; it emphasizes releasing social power to create changes in society, social institutions, and social policy, which in turn create opportunities for individuals (Smalley, 1967). This view conceptualizes the **purpose of social work** in relation to both individual and collective resources. The trademark of the social work profession is this simultaneous focus on persons and their impinging social and physical environments.

To this end, practitioners work with people in ways that strengthen their sense of competence, link them with needed resources, and promote organizational and institutional change so that the structures of society respond to the needs of all societal members (NASW, 1981). Additionally, social workers engage in research to contribute to social work theory and evaluate practice methods. To achieve these purposes, social workers engage in a variety of activities.

First, social work practitioners engage with clients to assess challenges in social functioning, process information in ways that enhance their ability to discover solutions, develop skills to resolve problems in living, and create support for change.

Second, social workers link people with resources and services, a vital strategy in any change effort. More than simply connecting people with services, workers advocate optimal benefits, develop networks of communication among organizations in the social service delivery network, and establish access to resources. When necessary resources do not exist, practitioners generate new opportunities, programs, and services.

Third, the NASW charges practitioners to work toward a humane and adequate social service delivery system. To accomplish this, social workers champion the planning of pertinent programs by advocating client-centeredness, coordination, effectiveness, and efficiency in the delivery of services. Importantly, they strengthen lines of accountability and ensure the application of professional standards, ethics, and values in service delivery.

Fourth, social workers participate in social policy development. In the arena of social policy, workers analyze social problems for policy ramifications, develop new policies, and retire those that are no longer productive. They also translate statutes, policies, and regulations into responsive programs and services that meet individual and collective needs.

Finally, practitioners engage in research to further the knowledge and skill base of social work. Effective and ethical social work depends on practitioners using research-based theory and methods as well as contributing to the knowledge base of the profession through their own research and evaluation activities.

> ▶ Watch this video where work students describe their "fit" with the social work profession. In what ways do their ideas reflect social work's core purposes and values? How do you describe your own fit with the social work profession?
> www.youtube.com/watch?v=iPw9LZOCG0o

> ❓ Assess your understanding of the values and purpose of social work by taking this brief quiz.

GENERALIST SOCIAL WORK

Generalist social work provides an integrated and multileveled approach for meeting the purposes of social work. Generalist practitioners acknowledge the interplay of personal and collective issues, prompting them to work with a variety of human systems—societies, communities, neighborhoods, complex organizations, formal groups, families, and individuals—to create changes that maximize human system functioning. This means that generalist social workers work directly with client systems at all levels, connect clients to available resources, intervene with organizations to enhance the responsiveness of resource systems, advocate just social policies to ensure the equitable distribution of resources, and research all aspects of social work practice.

The generalist approach to social work practice rests on four major premises. First, human behavior is inextricably connected to the social and physical environment. Second, based on this linkage among persons and environments, opportunities for

Policy Practice

Behavior: Assess how social welfare and economic policies impact the delivery of and access to social services

Critical Thinking Question: Generalist social workers practice in the context of personal and collective issues. In what ways does policy practice impact their work with clients in direct practice?

enhancing the functioning of any human system include changing the system itself, modifying its interactions with the environment, and altering other systems within its environment. Generalist practitioners implement multilevel assessments and multimethod interventions in response to these possible avenues for change. Third, work with any level of a human system—from individual to society—uses similar social work processes. Social work intervention with all human systems requires an exchange of information through some form of dialogue, a process of discovery to locate resources for change, and a phase of development to accomplish the purposes of the work. Finally, generalist practitioners have responsibilities beyond direct practice to work toward just social policies as well as to conduct and apply research.

Levels of Intervention in Generalist Practice

Generalist social workers look at issues in context and find solutions within the interactions between people and their environments. The generalist approach moves beyond the confines of individually focused practice to the expansive sphere of **intervention at multiple system levels**. In generalist social work, the nature of presenting situations, the particular systems involved, and potential solutions shape interventions, rather than a social worker's adherence to a particular method.

The perspective of generalist social work is like the view through a wide-angle lens of a camera. It takes in the whole, even when focusing on an individual part. Workers assess people in the backdrop of their settings, and interventions unfold with an eye to outcomes at all system levels. They visualize potential clients and agents for change on a continuum ranging from micro- to mezzo- to macrolevel interventions, small systems to large systems, including the system of the social work profession itself (Figure 1.1). Generalist social workers view problems in context, combine practice techniques to fit the situation, and implement skills to intervene at multiple system levels.

Microlevel Systems Intervention

Microlevel intervention focuses on work with people individually, in families, or in small groups to foster changes within personal functioning, in social relationships, and in the

Figure 1.1
System Levels for Social Work Intervention

ways people interact with social and institutional resources. Social workers draw on the knowledge and skills of clinical practice, including strategies such as crisis intervention, family therapy, linkage and referral, and the use of group process. For instance, in this chapter's introductory example, Andrea Barry could work with Mr. and Mrs. Clemens to improve their parenting skills or refer them to a parent support group.

Although microlevel interventions create changes in individual, familial, and interpersonal functioning, social workers do not necessarily direct all their efforts toward changing individuals themselves. Workers often target changes in other systems, including changes in the social and physical environments, to facilitate improvement in an individual's or family's social functioning. These activities involve work with systems at other levels.

Mezzolevel Systems Intervention

Mezzolevel intervention creates changes in task groups, teams, organizations, and the network of service delivery. In other words, the locus for change is within organizations and formal groups, including their structures, goals, or functions. For example, if, in working with the Clemens children, Andrea learns of their embarrassment at receiving lunch subsidies because the school physically segregates the "free lunch" students from the "full pay" students in the cafeteria, she can help them and other families who report similar concerns by working directly on the school's policy. Andrea's work with the school to address this demeaning and discriminatory practice represents a mezzolevel intervention. Effecting change in organizations requires an understanding of group dynamics, skills in facilitating decision making, and a proficiency in organizational planning. Working with agency structures and the social service delivery network is essential for developing quality resources and services.

Macrolevel Systems Intervention

Macrolevel intervention addresses social problems in community, institutional, and societal systems. At this level, generalist practitioners work to achieve social change through neighborhood organizing, community planning, locality development, public education, policy development, and social action. A worker's testimony at a legislative hearing reflects a macrolevel strategy to support a comprehensive national family welfare policy. Working with neighborhood groups to lobby for increased city spending on police protection, street repair, and park maintenance is another example of a macrolevel intervention. Social policy formulation and community development lead to macrosystem change.

Generalist social workers look at issues in context and find solutions within the interactions between people and their environments.

Professional-Level Intervention

Finally, when working with the social work profession, generalist practitioners address issues within the system of the social work profession itself. These **professional-level intervention** activities project a professional identity, define professional relationships with social work and interdisciplinary colleagues, reorient priorities within the social work profession, or reorganize the system of service delivery. For instance, by supporting social work licensure and the legal regulation of practice, practitioners use their collective influence to ensure the competence of those persons who become social workers. Standard setting and accountability call for social workers to be actively involved in the system of the social work profession.

Policy and Generalist Practice

Social policy determines how a society distributes its resources among its members to promote well-being. Social policies direct the delivery of health and human services, including mental health, criminal justice, child welfare, health and rehabilitation, housing, and public assistance. Social workers press for fair and responsive social policies that benefit all persons and advocate changes in policies affecting disenfranchised and oppressed groups whose dignity has been diminished by injustice.

Social welfare policies affect all facets of social work practice (Schorr, 1985). First, value-based policies implicitly guide how we orient social workers to the profession, the ways we educate workers for practice, and the choices we make to define the dimensions of practice activities. Second, policy shapes bureaucracy and the structure of agency practice—a culture that ultimately defines who gets services and what services they get. And, finally, in their own practice activities, social workers unavoidably make policy judgments by attending to or overlooking constantly changing social realities. To this list, Specht (1983) adds other major policy decisions that arise in the sociopolitical context of social work practice. These policy choices determine eligibility requirements, the array of programs and services offered, the structure of the social service delivery system, financing for health and human services, the form and substance of educating social work practitioners, and the regulation of social work activities.

To understand the impact of social policies on social work practice, consider how policy affects all aspects of Andrea Barry's practice in family preservation. Social policies, framed at the legislative level in the amendments to the Social Security Act and implemented through state administrative procedures, define the goals and processes that Andrea implements in family preservation. Agency-level policy to design programs and services consistent with empowering principles and a strengths perspective further refines Andrea's approach to working with families. As a professional social worker, Andrea's direct practice with families falls within the policy guidelines established by the NASW standards for child protection. Policy choices at many levels—federal, state, agency, and worker—influence the day-to-day practice of social work.

> ▶ Observe how the social worker in this video advocates to assist prison inmates placed in segregation. Which levels of intervention does the social worker use?

Research in Generalist Practice

Research is a method of systematic investigation or experimentation, the results of which can enrich theory and refine practice applications. When clients are integrally involved in designing and implementing research, research processes themselves empower clients. Research informs social work practice in several ways. It contributes to the theoretical base for understanding human behavior and change. Further, research is a tool for designing intervention strategies, measuring intervention effectiveness, and evaluating practice. Research is essential for program development and policy analysis. Aware of the integral relationship between theory and practice, generalist social workers use research-based knowledge to support practice activities and directly conduct their own research and analysis. The press for evidence-based practice attests to the importance of the research–practice connection. The goal of evidence-based research is to identify effective intervention strategies and robust program models. Based

Box 1.1   Professional Image and a Social Justice Identity: A Policy–Practice Connection

The social work profession today faces a confusing and inaccurate public image, an image perpetuated by the portrayal of social work in the media (Freeman & Valentine, 2004; Zugazaga et al., 2006). To address this concern about image, social work professionals may need to look inward. The bifurcation of the social work profession into two mutually exclusive divisions, one focusing on clinically based (micro) practice and the other on policy-oriented (macro) practice, dilutes the social justice image of social work (Dennison et al., 2007; Dessel et al., 2006; Olson, 2007; Reisch & Andrews, 2004; Specht & Courtney, 1994). Social workers debate questions that reinforce the notion of a dichotomy in social work practice. Should social work's emphasis be clinical work or policy practice? Does facilitating individual adaptation mean succumbing to social injustice? Do the long-range solutions of macropractice address the immediate needs of social work clients? Are social work solutions best found at the microlevel or macrolevel?

The past several decades have shown social work leaning more toward clinical than political practice, leading Karger and Hernandez (2004) to suggest that the profession has abandoned its engagement in public discourse, social commentary, political and social activism, and intellectual life. As a result, social workers "have little influence on the pressing issues of the day" (p. 51), particularly with respect to policy concerns about social justice. Searing (2003) charges social work "to reclaim its radical tradition. This asserts that the assessment of clients' 'needs' should not only be driven by the availability of resources but should also be concerned with the reduction of inequality and social justice" (¶ 4). Furthermore, "if we want the profession of social work to pursue a social justice mission, which our official and espoused position suggests, then we need to take steps to ensure that the way we frame and conceptualize our practice is congruent with, and furthers, social justice principles" (Hawkins et al., 2001, p. 11).

A generalist, empowerment method bridges the micro–macro split within the social work profession; it frames social work practice to meet the social justice mandate based on the following principles:

- The unifying purpose of social work is to enhance human well-being and to promote a mutually beneficial interaction between individuals and society.

- The social work profession maintains an integrated view of persons in the context of their physical and social environments.

- Social workers practice at the intersection of private troubles and public issues.

- Social workers work with people to enhance their competence and functioning, to access social supports and resources, to create humane and responsive social services, to influence social policy, and to expand the structures of society that provide opportunities for all citizens.

- Social workers have a partisan commitment to people who are vulnerable, oppressed, and living in poverty. The mandate of the social work profession is to ensure the fulfillment of the social justice contract between individuals and society, particularly for those groups that are disenfranchised.

- A just society is one in which all members of society share the same rights to participation in society, protection by the law, opportunities for development, and access to social benefits, and who, in turn, contribute to the resource pool of society.

- Empowerment social work is simultaneously clinical (personal) and critical (political) (Miley & DuBois, 2005).

on rigorous client outcome studies, best practices are emerging in all fields of social work practice.

Research enhances social work effectiveness, as illustrated in the example of Andrea Barry's work with clients in family preservation. Her coursework on empowerment-based practice, theories about families, and the dynamics of child abuse and neglect—all information rooted in decades of social work research—informs Andrea each time she interacts with her clients. Andrea regularly reads professional journals, especially *Social Work, Child Welfare, The Journal of Ethnic and Cultural Diversity in Social Work, The Journal of Evidence-Based Practice*, and *Families in Society*, to keep up with best practices within the field of child welfare. She also uses evaluation and research techniques to monitor her clients' progress toward goals and to assess her own practice effectiveness. Additionally, Andrea's work presents opportunities to add to the knowledge base of the profession as she and other family preservation workers carefully document the results of a new intervention program piloted by her agency. Research supports practice, and practitioners conduct research.

Advantages of a Multifaceted Approach

Because of their multidimensional perspectives, generalist practitioners are likely to uncover more than one possible solution for any given problem.

Social workers realize many advantages from their generalist practice approach. Inevitably, changes in one system ripple through other interrelated systems. In other words, a significant improvement in a client or environmental system might precipitate other beneficial changes. A single policy change may have far-reaching benefits for an entire society. Research demonstrating effective change strategies in one situation may lead to broader implementations to assist others in similar situations. Because of their multidimensional perspectives, generalist practitioners are likely to uncover more than one possible solution for any given problem.

? Assess your understanding of generalist social work by taking this brief quiz.

Generalist social workers see many possible angles from which to approach any solution. They analyze the many dimensions of any challenging situation to discover entry points for change. They also align the motivations and efforts of client systems with systems in their environments, synchronizing the movements of all involved to achieve the desired outcome. Generalist social work frames a way of thinking about both problems and solutions in context, and it describes a way of working with clients at a variety of system levels.

Generalist social workers use best practices with all families.

MONKEY BUSINESS IMAGES / SHUTTERSTOCK

SOCIAL WORK FUNCTIONS AND ROLES

Generalists work with systems at many levels, but what does that actually mean in their daily practice of social work? As a family preservation worker, Andrea Barry intervenes directly with individuals and families. She provides them with education, counseling, and linkage to needed community resources—activities associated with roles at the microlevel.

Yet, Andrea's work encompasses more than microlevel intervention. In her position, Andrea identifies gaps in the social service delivery network when resources families need are not available. As a result, she works with other professionals in child welfare to address social service delivery issues—a mezzolevel intervention. She and her inter-disciplinary colleagues are developing a community education plan to promote effective parenting—a macrolevel strategy. Finally, Andrea systematically evaluates the effective-ness of her work and keeps abreast of child welfare policy initiatives. In doing so, Andrea demonstrates the integration of research, policy, and multilevel intervention that charac-terizes generalist social work practice.

Activities of generalist social work practice fall broadly into three related functions: **consultancy, resource management**, and **education** (DuBois & Miley, 2014; Tracy & DuBois, 1987). Within each function are associated roles that explicate the nature of the interaction between clients and social workers at various system levels. These roles define responsibilities for both client systems and practitioners. Interventions designed within this model cover the range of issues presented to generalist social workers by clients at all system levels.

Consultancy

Through consultancy, social workers seek to find solutions for challenges in social functioning with individuals, families, groups, organizations, and communities. Within the roles of the consultancy function of social work, workers and clients confer and deliberate together to develop plans for change. Practitioners and clients share their expertise with one another for the purpose of resolving personal, family, organizational, and societal problems. Consultancy acknowledges that social workers and clients and constituencies bring information and resources, actual and potential, that are vital for resolving the issue at hand.

As a collaborative process, consultancy draws on the knowl-edge, values, and skills of social workers and clients to clarify issues, recognize strengths, discuss options, and identify potential courses of action. As consultants, social workers empower clients by re-specting their competence, drawing on their strengths, and working

Intervention

Behavior: Apply knowledge of human behavior and the social environment, person-in-environment, and other multidisciplinary theoretical frameworks in interventions with clients and constituencies

Critical Thinking Question: Social worker roles direct the nature of interaction between practitioners and client systems. How do these social work roles associated with the functions of consultancy, resource management, and education guide the process of intervention at various client system levels?

with them collaboratively to discover solutions. These consultancy activities cast workers into the roles of **enabler, facilitator, planner**, and **colleague** and **monitor** (Table 1.1).

Enabler Role

In the enabler role, social workers engage individuals, families, and small groups in coun-seling processes. An enabler encourages action by engaging in a helping relationship, framing solutions, and working toward constructive and sustainable change. In other words, enablers are change agents who "use varying approaches in order to provide the conditions necessary for clients to achieve their purposes, meet life challenges, engage in their natural life development processes, and carry out their tasks" (Maluccio, 1981, p. 19). In the context of work with groups, social workers enable supportive interactions

Table 1.1 Consultancy Roles

Level	Role	Strategy
Micro-	Enabler	Empower clients in finding solutions
Mezzo-	Facilitator	Foster organizational development
Macro-	Planner	Coordinate program and policy development through research and planning
Social Work Profession	Colleague/Monitor	Mentor, guide, and support professional acculturation

Based on the *Information Model for Generalist Social Work Practice* by B. C. Tracy and B. DuBois, 1987.

among group members to facilitate problem solving. As enablers, practitioners consult with individual and family client systems to improve social functioning by modifying behaviors, relationship patterns, and social and physical environments.

Facilitator Role

Through the facilitator role, social workers activate the participation of organizational members in change efforts. By facilitating group processes, social workers encourage competent group functioning, stimulate intragroup support, observe group interaction, offer constructive feedback, and share information about group dynamics. As facilitators, social workers enhance linkages within organizations and help them counteract apathy and disorganization. In this role, practitioners may even target their own agency settings to increase the cooperation of staff and ensure the effectiveness of social service delivery.

Planner Role

Social workers, in their planner role, understand community needs, recognize gaps and barriers in service delivery, and can facilitate a process for community-based or social change. Techniques to understand social problems and develop innovative solutions at the macrolevel include needs assessments, service inventories, community profiles, community inventories, environmental scans, and field research to understand social problems and develop innovative solutions at the macrolevel. As planners, social workers often participate in community organizing efforts to recommend changes.

Colleague and Monitor Roles

Through their colleague and monitor roles, social workers uphold expectations for the ethical conduct of members of their profession. Consultative relationships among social work practitioners lead to sound practice and professional development. As colleagues, social workers develop working partnerships with other practitioners through their participation in professional organizations such as the NASW and its local membership groups, and through their everyday contacts with other professionals. The *Code of Ethics* (NASW, 1999) specifically casts social workers as monitors, charging them to review the professional activities of peers to ensure quality and maintain professional standards.

Resource Management

In the resource management function, social workers stimulate exchanges with resources that client systems already use to some extent, access available resources that client systems are not using, and develop resources that are not currently available. Resources are sources of power and provide the impetus for change at any system level. Resources are found within individuals, in relationships, and in social institutions.

Resources are sources of power and provide the impetus for change at any system level.

Resources are not gifts bestowed by social workers. Instead, both social workers and clients play active roles in managing resources. Clients, as resource managers, take action to explore existing opportunities, activate dormant supports, and assert their rights to services. Social workers bring the resources of professional practice—the value imperative of equitable access to societal resources, the broad knowledge of the availability of resources, and a repertoire of skills to access and develop resources. Resource management is empowering when it increases the client system's own resourcefulness through coordinating, systematizing, and integrating rather than through controlling or directing. Social workers as resource managers function in the roles of **broker**, **advocate**, **convener**, **mediator**, **activist**, and **catalyst** (Table 1.2).

Broker and Advocate Roles

The professional mandate of the social work profession, to help people obtain resources, lays the foundation for the roles of broker and advocate. In the broker role, social workers link clients with available resources by providing information about resource options and making appropriate referrals. Competent brokers assess situations, provide clients with choices among alternative resources, facilitate clients' connections with referral agencies, and follow up to evaluate their efforts.

Social workers act as intermediaries between clients and other systems to protect clients' rights in their advocate role. Frequently, advocates function as spokespersons for clients in the bureaucratic maze of governmental structures. Advocates intervene with

Table 1.2   Resource Management Roles

Role	Strategy
Broker/Advocate	Link clients with resources through case management
Convener/Mediator	Assemble groups and organizations to network for resource development
Activist	Initiate and sustain social change through social action
Catalyst	Stimulate community service through interdisciplinary activities

Based on the *Information Model for Generalist Social Work Practice* by B. C. Tracy and B. DuBois, 1987.

social service delivery systems or policy makers on behalf of clients. Circumstances often press social workers to take on advocacy roles because the rights of social service clients have often been abridged.

Convener and Mediator Roles

Social workers often adopt convener and mediator roles with formal groups and organizations to coordinate the distribution and development of resources. Conveners promote interagency discussion and planning, mobilize coordinated networks for effective service delivery, and advocate policies that promise equitable funding and just service provisions. As conveners, social workers use networking strategies to bring together diverse representatives to address collective goals, such as in the examples of community task groups, interagency committees, and United Way panels. When controversy or conflicts of interest arise, social workers as mediators use their skills for negotiating differences and resolving conflicts. Conveners-mediators ally service providers in identifying service delivery gaps and encouraging proactive interagency planning, activities that are central to prevention efforts in social work.

Activist Role

Generalist social workers are in positions to identify societal conditions detrimental to the well-being of clients—a view that defines the social worker as activist. Strategies employed through the activist role include informing citizens about current issues, mobilizing resources, building coalitions, taking legal actions, and lobbying for legislative changes. Activists create just social policies as well as initiate new funding or funding reallocations that address their identified priority issues. Engendering community support, activists empower community-based efforts to resolve community issues, redress social injustice, and generate social reform.

Catalyst Role

Watch this video where social workers in various fields of practice describe what they do. What social work functions and roles occur in each of these practice settings? www.youtube.com/watch?v=77UGDj48oHs

The catalyst role implies a change motive that compels social workers to team with other professionals to develop humane service delivery, advocate just social and environmental policy, and support a worldview acknowledging global interdependence. Through professional organizations, social workers lobby at the state and federal levels and provide expert testimony. As catalysts, social workers initiate, foster, and sustain interdisciplinary cooperation to highlight client, local, national, and international issues.

Education

The social work function of education requires an empowering information exchange between a client system and a social work practitioner. Mutual sharing of knowledge and ideas is central to the educational function. Educational processes at all system levels reflect partnerships of co-learners and co-teachers. Collaborative learning presumes that client systems are self-directing, possess reservoirs of experiences and resources on which to base educational experiences, and desire immediate applications of new learning. The education function of social work respects the knowledge and experience that all parties contribute. Functioning as educators involves social work roles of **teacher**, **trainer**, **outreach**, **researcher**, and **scholar** (Table 1.3).

Table 1.3   Education Roles

Level	Role	Strategy
Micro-	Teacher	Facilitate information processing and provide educational programming
Mezzo-	Trainer	Instruct through staff development
Macro-	Outreach	Convey public information about social issues and social services through community education
Social Work Profession	Researcher/Scholar	Engage in discovery for knowledge development

Based on the *Information Model for Generalist Social Work Practice* by B. C. Tracy and B. DuBois, 1987.

Teacher Role

The teacher role in social work empowers client systems with information to stimulate competent functioning in all domains of living. Through teaching strategies, social workers strengthen clients with information to resolve current issues and to prevent other difficulties from emerging. To affirm clients' existing knowledge and skills, social workers select collaborative learning strategies to implement educational activities. Educational exchanges may occur in structured client–worker conferences, in formalized instructional settings, or in experiential exercises such as role plays.

Trainer Role

As educational resource specialists for formal groups, social workers in their trainer role make presentations, serve as panelists at public forums, and conduct workshop sessions. Sometimes, trainers are organizational employees; at other times, organizations contract with social workers to provide specific training experiences. Effective trainers select methods and resource materials based on research about adult education, attitude change, and learning modalities. Successful training strategies require a careful assessment of staff-development needs, clear goals of what the organization seeks, the ability to convey information through appropriate training formats, and a concrete evaluation process.

Outreach Role

In outreach roles, social workers inform a variety of audiences about social problems, describe social injustices, and suggest services and policies to address these issues. Workers disseminate information to inform the community about public and private social service organizations, thereby enhancing service accessibility. At the macrosystem level of community and society, the outreach role supports the prevention of problems. Increasing awareness of such issues as poverty, health care, disease control, stress, suicide, infant mortality, substance abuse, and family violence leads to early intervention and stimulates support for preventive actions. Using mass media, distributing posters and leaflets, conducting mailings, staffing information booths, and engaging in public speaking all bolster community members' awareness about programs and services. Sensitive to the unique needs of potential clients, outreach social workers provide multilingual, signed, Braille, and large-print announcements.

Ethical and Professional Behavior

Behavior: Use supervision and consultation to guide professional judgment and behavior

Critical Thinking Question: As illustrated in Table 1.4, generalist social worker Andrea Barry engages in the functions of consultancy, resource management, and education at all client system levels. Based on the knowledge, values, and skills that Andrea uses in this example, create a plan for your own continuing education for professional development and use of supervision to become an informed and effective generalist practitioner.

? Assess your understanding of social work functions and roles by taking this brief quiz.

Researcher and Scholar Roles

The social work *Code of Ethics* (NASW, 1999) specifically describes how professional knowledge and scientific research form the basis for practice. The *Code of Ethics* obligates social workers to contribute to the profession by conducting their own empirical research and sharing their findings with colleagues. Through researcher and scholar roles, professionals also critically examine the social work literature to integrate research findings with their practice. Social workers contribute to and draw on research related to human behavior and the social environment, service delivery, social welfare policy, and intervention methods.

Integrating Generalist Functions

In practice, social workers interweave the functions of consultancy, resource management, and education. For example, in addition to counseling, consultancy may involve linking clients with resources and teaching them new skills. Similarly, even though education is identified as a separate function, educational processes are inherent in all other social work activities as well. Rather than compartmentalizing these roles, this trilogy of social work functions provides an organizing schema for generalist social workers to construct and integrate multifaceted interventions. Table 1.4 offers examples of how family service worker Andrea Barry engages in consultancy, resource management, and educational interventions at all system levels.

Table 1.4   Family Service Interventions—Case Example: Andrea Barry

	Microlevel	Mezzolevel	Macrolevel	Social Work Profession Level
Consultancy	Counseling with families	Facilitating organizational change to prevent burnout in child protective workers	Participating in child welfare community planning	Addressing ethical and legal issues in mandatory reporting of child abuse and neglect
Resource Management	Linking families with additional community resources	Coordinating service delivery planning among local agencies	Developing a stable funding base for child welfare services	Stimulating interdisciplinary cooperation to develop resources
Education	Providing opportunities for learning anger control and positive parenting	Leading staff development training on mandatory reporting at local day care centers	Initiating public education regarding child protective resources	Presenting family preservation research at a regional conference

LOOKING FORWARD

Generalist social work describes a multifaceted approach designed to help people overcome challenges in their lives. Guided by the core values of human dignity and social justice, generalist practitioners perform many professional roles, apply and develop social work research, and improve social policy. Proficiency as a social worker requires a coherent practice framework and resourceful ways of looking at human systems to effect change in individual and social functioning. A competent generalist approach interweaves consultancy, resource management, and education strategies at all levels of practice (micro, mezzo, and macro) to enhance the lives of individual, family, group, organizational, community, and societal clients.

This book explains the processes essential for an empowerment-oriented method of social work. This first chapter provides an overview of the purposes and values of the social work profession and describes generalist social work. Chapter 2 discusses social work theory and articulates how various views, including the ecosystems perspective, biology, feminism, life course theory, and critical theory, support a generalist approach. Chapter 3 describes the ways in which values, expectations, and diverse cultural influences filter perceptions and affect social work practice. Chapter 4 explains how the strengths perspective and the ideal of human power shape an empowerment method of generalist practice.

Chapter 5 introduces this text's empowering method of social work practice framed within three concurrent phases—dialogue, discovery, and development—each explicated by discrete practice processes. Through dialogue (engagement processes), workers and clients develop and maintain collaborative partnerships, exchange relevant information, and define the purposes of the work. In discovery (assessment processes), practitioners and clients locate resources on which to construct plans for change. During development (intervention and evaluation processes), workers and clients activate resources, forge alliances with others, and create new opportunities to distribute the resources of a just society. Chapters 6 through 16 delineate each of these phases, examine each process in detail, and apply these processes at all levels of social work practice.

Evaluate what you learned in this chapter by completing the Chapter Review.

Human System Perspectives

ROB / FOTOLIA

Generalist social work, with its multileveled focus with clients and constituencies, requires extensive knowledge about the functioning of many types of human systems, and demands a multidisciplinary preparation for practice. Fundamental to a social work view, the **ecosystems perspective** offers an adaptable framework for integrating other useful views of human functioning. Practitioners need to understand the dynamics of human system behavior and the impact of the sociopolitical, economic, and physical environments. Competent social workers apply this enhanced ecosystems perspective throughout the practice process as they build relationships, assess client situations, and determine the most promising interventions to achieve desired outcomes.

KEY PERSPECTIVES FOR EMPOWERING PRACTICE

No single theory or perspective represents "the generalist social work view." Instead, social workers draw upon diverse theoretical perspectives to construct an integrated approach. Derived primarily from the social and behavioral sciences, theories about human systems provide a cogent understanding of how biological, environmental, psychological, social, cultural, economic, and political systems affect and are affected by human behavior and social structures. Effective social workers critically analyze the theories and perspectives they apply to client situations. To evaluate a theory's efficacy in practice, workers examine its relevance, universality, utility, reliability, integrity, and impact (Table 2.1). The choices social workers make about theory determine whether they function as agents of social control or empower clients to make changes in themselves, their situations, and social structures.

The choices made about theory determine whether social workers function as agents of social control or empower clients to make changes in themselves, their situation, and social structures.

The ecosystems perspective represents the predominant way generalist social workers frame their practice; however, it is frequently integrated with other useful views to support an empowering generalist social work practice method. Several key perspectives support empowerment based social work practice. Among these are **social constructionism**, the **feminist perspective**, **life course theory**, **critical theory**, including **critical race theory**, **biology and behavior**, and a **trauma-informed perspective**. A case example demonstrating how a social worker applies these theories in practice follows descriptions of these key perspectives.

Evaluation

Behavior: Apply knowledge of human behavior and the social environment, person-in-environment, and other multidisciplinary theoretical frameworks in the evaluation of outcomes

Critical Thinking Question: Social workers analyze the underlying assumptions of theories and practice frameworks they use. In what ways does this initial analysis inform the eventual evaluation of client outcomes?

Ecosystems

The ecosystems perspective centers on the exchanges between people and their physical and social environments by combining key concepts from ecology and general systems theory (Germain, 1979, 1983; Germain & Gitterman, 1996; Gitterman & Germain, 2008; Siporin, 1980). Ecological theory stresses the simultaneous nature of interaction between people and their environments. General systems theory offers principles about how human systems operate and interact with one another. Together, ecology

Table 2.1 Analyzing Theoretical Perspectives

Dimension	Key Questions
Relevance	What is the main focus of the theory? Is it relevant to the situation? To what system level does the theory apply?
Universality	Does the theory apply widely to diverse situations or narrowly to particular cases? Is the theory culturally sensitive? What is the differential impact of applying this theory to various cultural groups?
Utility	Does the theory further the worker's understanding of human system behavior or guide the worker's efforts in change activities?
Reliability	What research and evidence support the theory? Are the samples in the research studies representative of diverse groups or of only particular segments of the population?
Integrity	Is the theory congruent with the professional values and ethics of social work?
Impact	What assumptions does the theory make about clients, including their power, expertise, and roles?

and systems theory describe the functioning and adaptation of human systems in their social and physical environments.

In the ecosystems view, persons and environments are not separate but exist in on-going **transactions** with each other. We cannot simply add an understanding of persons to an understanding of environments. Instead, we must also examine the reciprocal interactions or transactions between the two. The ecosystems perspective describes the ways that environments affect people and the ways people affect their environments.

Three compelling reasons support an emphasis on the ecosystems view to frame generalist social work practice. First, because of its integrative nature, the ecosystems view draws on the strengths of many helpful theories to describe human behavior in all of its complexity. Second, it describes the interconnected functioning of individuals, families, groups, organizations, local communities, and international societies, thereby supporting the multilevel strategies of generalist social work intervention. Third, the ecosystems view clearly focuses on how people and their environments fit, rather than forcing social workers to place blame on either the person or **environment** for problems that arise (Gitterman & Germain, 2008). This accepting posture toward human behavior reflects the value base of social work; it directs workers and clients to join forces against the problematic fit of clients in situations rather than judge clients themselves to be deficient.

Social Constructionism

Social constructionism focuses on how people understand themselves and interpret what is happening in their lives. Each of us selectively attends to, interprets, and acts on our beliefs about ourselves and the world around us, a concept embodied in the theory of social constructionism. Social constructionism centers on how people construct meaning, emphasizing social meaning as generated through language, cultural beliefs, and social interaction (Gergen, 1994). Each person understands events only as they are filtered through the ecosystemic layers of the social and cultural environment.

More than the simple telling of one's story, discourse constitutes a process of continuous reinterpretation of the socially constructed meaning of that story as developed in conversation with others. Through such social exchanges, people expand their perspectives as they willingly incorporate divergent points of view and new ideas that validate their behaviors and perceptions, or they yield to pressure from others to adopt alternative interpretations.

Cultural identity and social position influence the person you believe yourself to be and therefore the way you interpret the events in your life. The privilege of membership in an advantaged group offers a sense of fit with the world; it reinforces well-being and validates feelings of control. Through social interaction, discourse becomes the means by which dominant groups promote self-serving ideologies, limit social participation, impose meaning, and construct "realities" for less powerful others. In contrast, members of cultural groups disadvantaged by oppression, prejudice, and stereotypes are likely to be encumbered by dominant cultural views. This control over norms held by the majority group is known as **hegemony**—an invisible force that offers privilege to dominant groups and maintains oppressive beliefs about nondominant groups (Mullaly, 2002). "Consequently, a person from an ethnic group in the minority may construct a sense of self that is influenced by this devaluation, lack of power, and discrimination in the societal context" (Greene et al., 1996, p. 2).

Applying a social constructionist view, social workers see two distinct intervention points in the lives of clients who are oppressed. First, workers can interfere with the internalization of disempowering beliefs by collaborating with clients to question socially generated "truths" and their relevance for the particular client. For example, the practitioner who questions how a female client's love of another woman can be "wrong" and validates the experience as "maybe something to celebrate" works to disable the heterosexist bias that undermines the client's emotional experience. Second, workers can advocate for social and political changes to liberate disadvantaged groups from the kind of oppressive belief systems and discriminatory laws that undermine this client's happiness. Interventions at both the individual and societal levels apply social constructionist thinking to overturn the hegemony that distorts the client's emotional reality and inhibits her free choice.

Similar to social constructionism, the psychological theory of constructivism questions the assumption of a fixed and objective reality. Constructivism holds that two people can interpret the same event very differently because each experiences a personalized, idiosyncratic view of what has occurred. Each person's unique perspective is rooted in individual history, current expectations, and sense of self. Like social constructionism, constructivism favors the idea of each individual's creation of a unique reality (Gergen, 1994). Both theories also view reality as maintained through language (Greene & Lee, 2002). In social work literature, the terms constructivism and social constructionism are frequently used interchangeably.

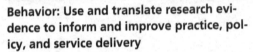
Research-Informed Practice

Behavior: Use and translate research evidence to inform and improve practice, policy, and service delivery

Critical Thinking Question: Social workers bring practice knowledge from research and professional experiences to the social work process, and clients bring their understanding of the events and experiences in their lives. How is the social work process affected by those who construct the meaning or define the problem or issue?

Feminist Perspective

A feminist perspective provides a political foundation for social workers striving to achieve a just society (Baines, 1997; Carr, 2003; Gutiérrez & Lewis, 1998; Saulnier, 1996; Turner & Maschi, 2015). Consistent with the ecosystems perspective, a feminist view concretely links individual experiences with social forces. In essence, gender is a defining factor in how power is distributed at all levels of society. From a feminist perspective, the personal is political. Social forces perpetuate the subjugation of women, and this oppression plays out in interpersonal relationships and interactions. The feminist perspective aligns with social constructionism, proposing that the oppressed position of women in our society results from a patriarchal construction of reality. To ignore this social reality is to participate in it. Feminism forces social workers to turn from a stance of neutrality to a position of advocacy for gender equality.

Feminism does not offer a singular view, but rather a set of perspectives that have a core consistency. In their review of the history of feminisms, Kemp and Brandwein (2010) note five prevalent themes: (1) efforts to include women in all aspects of society, (2) a goal of solidarity among women, (3) the elevation of women's perspectives and experiences in shaping a just society, (4) an emphasis on the intertwined nature of

This video focuses on gender identity. How do you understand the child's preference for male-associated toys when he was raised by two mothers?

personal and political experience, and (5) a focus on praxis, the process by which people take action, critically reflect on their experiences, and determine new strategies to advance personal and political goals.

Translating these ideas into practice, Bricker-Jenkins (1991) recommends that feminist practitioners "reflect and express ideologies, relations, structures of power and privileges, or other salient features of the cultural milieu" (p. 279). To align with the value placed on egalitarianism by feminists, Hyde (2008) states that tenets of feminist practice should include

- incorporating democratized processes and structures that promote collaboration, networking, and relationship building;
- extending the focus beyond gender and white middle-class perspectives to eliminate all forms of oppression; and
- understanding the transformational nature of change in social, economic, and political structures inherent in pursuing justice for all those who experience oppression and discrimination.

Disempowering views held toward women are rooted in the constructions of dominant groups who ignore the experiences of those who are disadvantaged. The social worker's task becomes one of "deconstructing" a disempowering reality for women and "reconstructing" a new one that is sensitive to diversity and honors unique experiences.

Life Course Theory

Life course theory emphasizes the influences of the sociocultural-historical contexts on human development. Founded on the work of sociologist Glenn Elder (1994, 1998, 2001), life course theory traces sociological influences on human development across the course of life. Historical contexts and events experienced throughout the life span ultimately shape life choices, social relationships, and resilience.

Four main themes frame life course theory: the historical influences on life course, timing of life events, linked lives, and human agency. A fundamental force, the *historical context* provides both opportunities and restraints that expand or limit life choices. Those born about the same time, or cohort groups, experience the influence of a similar sociopolitical-historical milieu throughout their lives. However, the individual life trajectories of cohort members may differ depending on the exact *timing of their life events*, such as marriages, deaths, births, education, employment, and retirement. Whether the timing meets the social expectations of "on time" or "off time" influences the individual's experience of the event. The theme of *linked lives* calls attention to how networks of social and intergenerational relationships influence human development. For example, the effects of family caregiving responsibilities for an aging parent reverberate throughout the family system. Finally, *human agency* highlights the power of personal decision making that gives direction to lives within the boundaries set by contextual opportunities and constraints.

Findings from large-scale longitudinal studies reveal many variations in life trajectories among cohort group members based on diversity in trajectories and the influence of risk and resilience (Hutchinson, 2005). For example, locale, gender, socioeconomic status, ethnicity, and immigration all generate differences in a person's sense of agency, potential choices, and opportunities, which, in turn, lead to differences in timing, linkages, and experiences of turning points. Finally, life course theory underscores the significance of protections or resilience for attenuating developmental risks and altering life course trajectories.

By emphasizing the integral relationship between the social and historical contexts and development over the life course, life course theory fits with social work's person: environment construct, extending our understanding of the dynamic elements involved in this reciprocal interaction. According to Hutchinson (2005), this theory may bridge the micro–macro divide, as it offers various vantage points from which to view both the microlevel event history of individuals and families, and the macrolevel influences of sociocultural-historical forces on entire cohorts and individual trajectories. Hutchinson recommends applying life course theory to social work practice at the microlevel by focusing on turning points in clients' lives that reset their trajectories and at the macrolevel by altering contexts to increase the prevalence of resources and opportunities.

Critical Theory

Critical theory directs practitioners to examine the significance of power differentials for clients in their lives and in their relationships with social workers. This theory examines the interconnections between people and their environments (Gray & Webb, 2013; Kondrat, 2002; Salas et al., 2010; Wheeler-Brooks, 2009). Adding a significant element to person–environment interactions, critical theory highlights how "everyday practices operating in multiple locations... enact relations of culture, power, identity, and social structure" (Keenan, 2004, p. 540). Some of these interactions serve as resources; others promote privilege and sustain oppression.

To apply critical theory, social work practitioners first acknowledge that the relationship between human actions and social structures is a recursive process in which each produces the other (Keenan, 2004). Second, workers recognize that repetitive actions can lead to stable social structural arrangements; some arrangements are good, some not so good. Shifts in detrimental patterns can lead to improvements in people's lives. Third, intercultural power relationships arise as products of many interactions. These interchanges elevate some beliefs to positions of truth and invalidate others. This system of beliefs about truth and reality is social construction, not reality. Critical theory offers a perspective for "examining institutional and social practices with a view to resisting the imposition of oppressive and dominant norms and structures" (Salas et al., 2010, p. 93).

Informed by critical theory, empowerment-oriented generalist practitioners take actions to collaborate with clients, thus asserting their human rights. Critical theory directs social workers to analyze the sociopolitical and economic arrangements that define human identity, beliefs, and interactions. A critique of these arrangements focuses on issues of hierarchy and privilege, class distinctions and distortions, definitions of power, and the culture of silence and domination (Baines, 2007; Fook, 2002; Gray & Webb, 2013; Williams, 2002). Critical questions for social work practitioners include the following:

- Who defines the structural arrangements?
- Who holds the power?
- Who controls the resources?

Informed by critical theory, empowerment-oriented generalist practitioners take actions to collaborate with clients, thus asserting their human rights.

- Which groups benefit or suffer?
- Whose voices are valued?
- Who has the most to gain or lose from changing the social arrangement?
- In what ways do various diversities influence structures?
- What actions can lead to change?

In effect, "critical reflection seeks to challenge the prevailing social, political, and structural conditions which promote the interests of some and oppress others" (Ruch, 2002, p. 205). Application of critical theory corresponds with the profession's core value of social justice and aligns with such practice strategies as anti-oppression, antidiscrimination, advocacy, human and social rights, democratic participation, and redressing social injustice.

Critical Race Theory

Closely related to critical theory, critical race theory emphasizes social structures and everyday patterns of action as forces behind racism. In essence, race defines access to resources and power. Tenets of critical race theory include the ideas that (1) racism is an ordinary, everyday experience of most people of color, originating in social interactions and embedded in the institutional structures of society; (2) interests of majority group members converge to maintain the status quo favoring those in positions of power; (3) race is socially constructed rather than biologically determined; (4) driven by self-interest and economics, dominant groups differentially racialize members of minority groups; and (5) no one has a singular identity that can be easily described (Delgado & Stefancic, 2007, 2012). Critical race theory challenges the myth of objectivity and "color-blindness" (Abrams & Moio, 2009). Social workers apply critical race theory to understand power, privilege, oppression, and diversity and to inform social work practice (Daniel, 2008; Kolivoski et al., 2014; Sisneros et al., 2008). Both critical race theory and critical multicultural social work see racism as embedded in racist social structures; they prompt social workers to take actions to redress these institutionalized injustices.

Biology and Behavior

For decades, social workers have claimed the biopsychosocial realm of human behavior as a foundation for understanding clients' situations but have generally emphasized psychosocial domains over biological determinants. However, emerging scientific evidence increasingly reveals the extensive biological underpinnings of behavior, pressing social work professionals to understand more fully the reciprocal interaction of behavior and biology. Occurring throughout the life span, biological effects on behavior can be positive or negative, subtle or dramatic, short or long term. Salient examples of the interdependence between biology and behavior include **epigenesis** and **stress**.

Epigenesis

Epigenesis describes how genetics and human behavior are connected. Recent research sheds new light on the ways physical and social environments influence physiological and behavioral adaptation through the **phenotypic expression** of a person's **genotype**.

Completed in 2003, the Human Genome Project mapped the genetic code, creating a representative blueprint identifying and sequencing the totality of genes in the human **genome** (NIH, 2015). Knowing the specific function of certain genes can predict genetic expression. Research on epigenesis, a biochemical process that regulates cells and their phenotypic expression without altering the genetic instructions on the DNA molecule, holds promise for understanding the impact of environmental influences on behavior (Combs-Orme, 2012; Cooney, 2007). Epigenetic changes may be inherited, or they can occur at any time during the life span, most likely during critical developmental phases such as prenatal development, growth spurts, or the slow-down of cell division associated with aging.

Features of both the physical and social environments fuel epigenetic changes that create vulnerability to risks or buffer resilience. Combs-Orme (2012) notes the epigenetic hazards in physical environments associated with inadequate nutrition and exposure to toxic chemicals and the social justice issues related to disadvantage, poverty, and discrimination. Social environmental factors such as nurturance and support for attachment during infancy, quality of interpersonal relationships, exposure to stress, and the experience of **trauma** can influence epigenetic change. Research reveals the genetic and epigenetic factors associated with many challenges social work clients encounter, including **fetal alcohol spectrum disorder** (Tunc-Ozcan et al., 2014), alcohol dependence (Diaz-Anzaldua, 2011), mental health (Sasaki et al., 2013), responses to stress (Radley et al., 2011; Tyrka et al., 2012), aging (Cortes & Lee, 2012), and health status (Gilbert, 2009; Kalil, 2015).

Stress

We are all likely familiar with some facet of stress. According to a recent large-scale survey conducted by the American Psychological Association (2015), Americans rank money, work, family responsibilities, and health concerns as the top four stressors. Overall reported stress levels are trending downward, with ratings of stress on a 10-point scale reported at 4.9 in 2014 as compared to 6.2 in 2007. However, stress levels remain higher among people with lower incomes, parents, those in younger generations, and persons reporting fewer sources of emotional support.

Although we often think of stress as problematic, it can actually have positive benefits. Moderate degrees of stress motivate us to complete our work and to initiate desired changes in our lives. However, stress resulting from overwhelming or threatening experiences has a negative impact that is amplified when stressful experiences are long-lasting, chronic, and/or compounded by other stressors. The more unpredictable and uncontrollable a situation seems, the more likely we are to perceive it as a major stressor. Usually affecting large groups of people, catastrophic stressors include such events as natural disasters, tornados, floods, and large-scale violence. Major life events, transitions, and the accumulation of daily hassles typify stressors in more personal circumstances. Qualities of physical environments such as noise, pollution, violence, food insecurity, impoverished resources, and safety issues likely exacerbate any experience of stress, personal or catastrophic.

How does stress affect us? Psychosocial signs may be irritability, sleeplessness, withdrawal, or moodiness. Biologically, our bodies show stress with increased heart rate and breathing, tense muscles, and elevated blood pressure, all of which are related to the evolutionary "fight or flight" survival response. These physiological responses to hormonal changes induced by our perception of stressors produce a cascading chain reaction. For example, the hormone cortisol functions effectively under "normal" conditions of stress but may cause harm when we experience chronic stress (Staufenbiel et al., 2013; Teixeira, 2015). High levels of cortisol increase susceptibility to disease, impede memory, and impair the hormonal feedback loop, which further stimulates the release of cortisol. A vicious cycle is set in motion in which stress affects biological, psychological, and social functioning. This in turn creates more stress. The reciprocal impact of biology and behavior continues.

Research provides evidence that chronic exposure to stress significantly affects health and wellness (Schneiderman et al., 2005) by contributing to obesity (Sominsky & Spencer, 2014; Talbot et al., 2013), drug and alcohol abuse (Rodrigues et al., 2011), mood disorders (Heim & Binder, 2012; Sousa & Almeida, 2012), posttraumatic stress disorder (Sareen, 2014), and cognitive issues such as Alzheimer's disease (Sotiropoulos, 2011).

Trauma-Informed Perspective

Stress elevates to the level of **trauma** when we experience overwhelming threats, with elements of terror, helplessness, and loss of control. Examples include military combat, rape, terrorism, disasters, forced migration, child maltreatment, sexual abuse, and violence. Trauma will likely interfere with a person's ability to cope with even mundane daily activities. Reactions to trauma can occur whether one has experienced it firsthand, vicariously as a witness, or by hearing others' personal accounts. The traumatic events experienced by clients may have far-reaching impact for both social workers and clients.

The cumulative effects of multiple experiences of trauma, sometimes called poly-victimization, increase vulnerability for longlasting physical and psychological effects (Finkelhor et al., 2011). To retrospectively assess **adverse childhood experiences (ACEs)** such as child abuse and neglect, sexual abuse, family dysfunction, and their relation to health and well-being in adulthood, a large-scale 1998 epidemiological study surveyed a predominantly White sample of late-middle-age, well-educated enrollees in a health maintenance organization (Felitti & Anda, 2010). Even in this privileged sample, two-thirds reported experiencing at least one ACE, one-fourth experienced substance abuse in their family of origin, and 10 percent tallied five or more ACEs (Anda, n.d.). Further analysis revealed that high ACE scores were associated with problems as adults such as health risks, addictions, psychiatric disorders, and shorter life expectancies (Felitti & Anda, 2010). Again, we see the connection between social experiences and biological outcomes.

Another comprehensive study, the National Survey of Children's Exposure to Violence, confirms that childhood exposure to violence is widespread (Finkelhor et al., 2009). When queried about their experiences in the past year in their homes, schools, and communities, more than 60 percent of respondents indicated they had directly or indirectly experienced violence. Forty percent reported multiple experiences of victimization. Because the development of the brain and neural pathways that regulate emotions and behavior are critical during early developmental stages, infants and children are particularly susceptible to the deleterious effects of chronic stress, adversity, and exposure to violence (NCSDC, 2005/2014; Putman et al., 2013; Thompson, 2014; Tyrka et al., 2013).

The adverse reactions to trauma vary considerably, depending on an individual's age, socioeconomic status, history of adversity, current life stressors, resiliency, coping capacities, optimism, and access to social support (Booth et al., 2012; Lai et al., 2015; Lee et al., 2014). Research provides evidence of **posttraumatic growth**, the potential of positive life trajectories, and resiliencies emerging from surviving trauma (Li et al., 2012; Rodgers, 2014).

A negative potential outcome of trauma is **posttraumatic stress disorder** (PTSD). The incidence of PTSD is increasing in the general population and occurs at an alarmingly high rate among military personnel and veterans. Results of a large-scale representative national survey indicate that 50 percent of adults in the United States have a history of trauma, with 25 percent experiencing more than one trauma event (Hamblen, 2013). Of this number, 7 percent develop PTSD, though the rate among male military combat veterans is much higher, at 39 percent. Four clusters of behaviors indicate PTSD: (1) reliving the trauma through spontaneous memories, recurrent dreams, and flashbacks; (2) avoidance of persons, experiences, places, and objects that are reminders of the trauma and trigger adverse reactions; (3) negative changes in mood and cognitions, such as distorted beliefs, self-blame, estrangement, and diminished interest in activities; and (4) changes in arousal and reactivity, including aggression, reckless behavior, sleep disturbances, inability to concentrate, hypervigilance, and an intensified startle response (American Psychiatric Association, 2013). PTSD is associated with an increased risk for depression, suicide, substance use disorders, impulsivity, and aggressive behavior (McGovern et al., 2015; Kotler et al., 2001; Olatunji et al., 2014; Oquendo et al., 2005).

People of all ages with histories of trauma are overrepresented in the various fields in which social work professionals practice (CSWE, 2012). For example, trauma, more likely than not, intersects with issues clients present in child welfare, criminal justice, family and aging services, mental health, school social work, employee assistance programs, public health, and social work in medical settings. Consequently, social workers need to tune in to the difficulties that trauma can engender. At the same time, workers should remain alert to client strengths and resilience, another potential outcome of trauma. Since they are vulnerable to secondary trauma as a result of their emotional reactions to working with traumatized clients, social workers should practice trauma-informed self-care (Salloum, 2015).

Applying Theory in Practice: A Case Example

Theory informs practice. When social workers critically examine client situations from relevant theoretical perspectives, they generate many potential approaches for assisting clients. Consider the example of social worker Megan Camden as she applies social work theory to guide her work with client Gero Hudson.

Megan is a social worker at the regional Veterans Administration (VA) treatment center located in the Northside community. Her client Gero is a veteran of Operation Enduring Freedom. After his second deployment to Afghanistan, Gero received an honorable discharge from military service, yet he struggles to reintegrate into civilian life. Previously, Gero intended to pursue a lifelong military career, so he has no plan for a postdischarge vocational alternative.

Gero seeks treatment for multiple problems, including nightmares, an inability to sleep, irritability accompanied by outbursts of anger and aggressiveness, and withdrawal from nearly all social activities. After administering an evidence-based structured interview called the CAPS-5, Megan concludes that Gero's symptoms fit the criteria for posttraumatic stress disorder (PTSD). Megan's comprehensive assessment also includes the VA screening for a history of sexual harassment and assault. Megan poses her interview questions with sensitivity, knowing that for male veterans, military sexual trauma (MST) carries a high degree of victim shame and social stigma. Although initially reluctant to self-disclose, Gero now shares that he once attempted to report his victimization and received a degrading response.

The complexity of working with veterans' issues is well known to Megan. The intense experience of combat, the separation from family and friends followed by the difficulty of reintegration, and the dissonance between military and civilian cultures—all present unique challenges to social workers and their military clients. In analyzing Gero's situation, Megan considers several theoretical perspectives that shape her practice approach.

Applied Ecosystems

As a social worker, Megan first looks at a client's situation through an ecosystems lens. Characteristic of an ecosystems view, the simultaneous focus on client and environment distinguishes social work from other helping professions. Megan will best understand what is happening when she puts the personal problems Gero is experiencing into an environmental context. An ecosystems view focuses on the interrelationships of social systems. Gero's reintegration into civilian life requires him to negotiate many levels of social interaction. He returned home to live with his wife, Renee, and their 2-year-old son, Niko. Gero's parents and extended family celebrated his return but express concern about his withdrawal. His previous friendships are strained by his irritability and increased consumption of alcohol. And although Gero is hailed as a hero by the community at large, he has yet to secure a job.

From an ecosystems perspective, Megan sees what is happening at each system level. Within the level of his immediate family, Megan recognizes three significant shifts. First, Renee was in charge and on her own with Niko during Gero's deployments. A shift in the family structure has occurred, leaving all family members to wonder what Gero's role should be, especially in light of his emotional and social withdrawal now that he is home. Second, Gero missed significant family events—Niko's birth, his first steps, holidays, and birthdays. Gero's son Niko bonds with his mother Renee but reacts to his father as somewhat of an outsider. Third, the intimacy that Renee and Gero previously experienced as a married couple has been shattered by Gero's pronounced irritability, outbursts of anger, and occasional aggressiveness toward Renee.

Extended family members also recognize changes in Gero. Their joy about his safe return from war transitioned to concern about his well-being. The previous closeness they experienced with him has dissipated. Megan knows that war changes everyone. The military experience shifts people culturally. Sexual assault assails identity. Gero, the man who went to war, is not the same man who has come home. Megan sees that her task is to help the family support the person that Gero has become, rather than to question the person they lost. Resolving the difficulty in relationships with family and friends will likely involve a remediation of Gero's PTSD symptoms, but it may also require their increased understanding about how trauma and combat exposure shift a person's worldview.

Communities appear to revere veterans, applauding them at airports and thanking them for their service. Yet, in contrast, community members also suspect veterans. Public knowledge about combat-related PTSD and **traumatic brain injury** (**TBI**) creates ambiguity about whether a particular veteran is psychologically okay and builds significant barriers to full social participation. Despite government programs to help veterans get jobs, the unemployment rate among veterans exceeds the average. Megan recognizes this paradoxical treatment of veterans by the community and assesses the impact of this bias with each of her clients. Supplementing her role as an interpersonal therapist, Megan acts politically to advocate support for veterans in the community at large.

Social Constructionism Applied

Social constructionism emphasizes how individuals interpret events and ascribe meaning to their personal experiences. When something happens, we interpret it, and that interpretation becomes a reality in our lives. Megan recognizes that both his combat-related and sexual assault traumas have shifted Gero's understanding of who he is. As a civilian, Gero always experienced himself as strong, a belief fueled by his accomplishments as an athlete in high school. As a soldier, Gero saw himself as tough, a combatant inured to battlefield injuries and death. Even the name Gero has roots in an African word meaning "fierce." As a victim of sexual assault, Gero now reexperiences himself as weak, not able to protect himself, less of a man. The assault casts doubts for him about his masculinity and toughness.

Gero's military training prepared him to engage in dangerous situations, and the military culture instilled a certain stoicism and machismo response to war experiences. In his civilian life, Gero is now expected to construct a new identity as a returning veteran with PTSD. Help-seeking behaviors are new to him. Gero learned to distrust authority after receiving a negative response when he divulged his sexual victimization, but he now needs to trust that Megan and other professionals at the VA have genuine concern for his well-being.

Feminist Perspective Applied

A feminist perspective definitively states that gender matters. Who you are as a woman or man makes a difference in how society treats you and how you view yourself and others. What Megan knows is that Gero is not alone in his sexual victimization. Even though women in the military are sexually harassed and assaulted at a much higher rate than men, numerically, more male than female veterans have been sexually assaulted during their service (Street, 2013).

Sexual assault is traumatic for all victims, male and female. However, because sexual victimization is so contrary to prescribed male gender roles, the experience is likely even more stigmatizing for men. Gero's response to victimization is not just personal, it is also contextual, rooted in the culture of military society. Even though they may experience more severe symptoms than women, in the warrior culture of the military, male victims of MST are more reluctant to divulge their trauma history or file official reports. In addition, because of the stoic expectations embedded in their military training, men are also less likely to seek professional help for behavioral health issues.

Life Course Theory Applied

Considering Gero's situation with respect to life course theory helps Megan recognize Gero's strengths. Life course theory postulates that current situations in people's lives are shaped by previous events, both personal and sociocultural-historical. Gero was born after the civil rights movement, so there was hope that he would have equal opportunities. He comes from supportive nuclear and extended families and a community that celebrates him as a high school athlete, all of which contribute to his resilience. His identity as African American—a source of pride to Gero—places him at risk in the larger environment. Megan acknowledges the discriminatory treatment of young African American males by schools, police, and courts. However, she understands that Gero has previously navigated these life challenges, a strength to build on in her work with him.

Critical Theory Applied

Critical theory postulates that all social structures and social relationships are inherently hierarchical. Any examination of social structure requires critical reflection to explore structural inequities and unjust practices. As a social institution, the military is notably characterized by a clear hierarchical structure of authority and power differential between ranks. But within troops, particularly those in combat, there is also an expectation for cohesion. Megan questions whether Gero's naming of a fellow serviceman in a sexual assault claim, given his vulnerable social position in a subordinate rank and the solidarity of his own troop, left him ostracized. She acknowledges there may be an unwritten code of silence about MST. Although Gero experiences his problem as an individual one, Megan knows the solutions may be structural. The challenge for Megan is how to empathize with the personal dilemma that Gero has experienced and also to advocate for him at the wider institutional level. From her understanding of critical race theory, Megan is also mindful of embedded racism in social structures and patterns of interaction. For that reason, she will be attentive to ensure that Gero's interactions with her and others in the VA system neither diminish nor oppress him.

Biological Perspective Applied

Megan acknowledges that Gero's current problems also spring from changes in biological functioning. Survival in war requires hyperarousal. One must stay alert, sleep lightly, and be prepared to fight at any moment. Suspicion of other people and situations is absolutely necessary to survive. These postures, adaptive in battle, set up Gero for difficulties in civilian life. His body is constantly on alert. He is vigilant and suspicious, leading to irritability and quick acceleration to anger. While deployed, Gero's body ran on adrenaline to keep him alert. Upon his return home, the desire for the rush of adrenaline and constant stimulation continues. Gero craves excitement and cannot sleep—problems he solves with alcohol to mitigate his tension and temper his need for adrenaline-fueled action.

Veterans who, like Gero, were deployed in Iraq and Afghanistan are also at risk for biomechanical trauma caused by explosions and blast waves. Severe trauma to the brain is termed traumatic brain injury (TBI). TBI and PTSD are often closely linked; even mild TBI elevates the risk of PTSD (Hurley, 2013). TBI is characterized by cognitive, emotional/behavioral, and somatic symptoms that include, for example, memory problems, irritability and impulsivity, and insomnia—many of the symptoms reported by Gero. Working with a multidisciplinary team that includes medical personnel, Megan knows that the effects of trauma physiology will impact any treatment intervention.

Trauma-Informed Perspective Applied

Trauma shapes subsequent experience. Gero is forever changed by his experiences of sexual victimization and on the front lines of war. All people interpret and respond to current events based on what they have experienced in the past. Persons exposed to trauma develop a heightened sense of threat, possibly overreading the danger of current events because of the harm they experienced in the past. Though protective at one level, this sensitivity can interfere with effective functioning overall. Gero has learned not to trust, especially people in power. He avoids situations where he might be alone with those who are more powerful and has withdrawn his trust from many people he formerly trusted.

Megan recognizes that some of Gero's seemingly maladaptive responses actually make sense in terms of the trauma he has experienced. As Megan explores his misperceptions, she will be patient as she helps him see more functional interpretations that lead Gero to more positive interactions with family, friends, and others in his community.

Applying Theories to Practice

In her role as a VA social worker, Megan comfortably melds the overarching ecosystems perspective with other practice theories and her extensive training on PTSD to assist military veterans. This integrated multitheoretical view fortifies Megan's practice with many intervention possibilities for her clients and their environmental systems.

> **?** Assess your understanding of key perspectives for social work practice by taking this brief quiz.

SOCIAL SYSTEMS

The systems with which practitioners work may be as small as a single element of the internal processes of one individual or as large as the entire human population. Generalist social workers develop skills to understand, support, and facilitate change at all system levels because **systems** at all levels are potential clients and targets for change.

System Defined

Technically speaking, a system is "an organized whole made up of components that interact in a way distinct from their interaction with other entities and which endures over some period of time" (Anderson et al., 1999, p. 294). More simply, a **social system** is a structure in which interdependent people interact. For example, groups of people are identified as systems because they interact with each other in some definable way or are associated with each other because of shared attributes. In other words, a pattern of relationships or shared characteristics separates one group from other groups. Note how this definition encompasses groups as different as a family, a street gang, residents of a nursing home, employees of a corporation, and social work professionals. These and all other social systems, small and large, share common features.

Systems as Holons

All social systems are **holons**, meaning that each system is a part of a larger system, while, at the same time, it is composed of smaller systems (Anderson et al., 1999). For example, a family is a social system that is only one part of the neighborhood suprasystem in which the family resides. Children and parents within this family are also systems themselves within the context of the larger family system. All of these systems—the children, the parents, the family, and the neighborhood—are holons that share systemic properties.

The family unit is a primary human system.

ANDRESR / SHUTTERSTOCK

Box 2.1   Opportunities, Risks, and Resilience: A Policy-Research-Practice Connection

No human system thrives in isolation. The successes or failures of individuals, families, groups, organizations, neighborhoods, and communities result from their unique interactions within their environments. The effective functioning of social systems is determined by the relative balance or imbalance of resources, opportunities, and demands within and between systems. Risks present within these interactions increase the likelihood of negative outcomes, whereas protective factors mitigate risks (Little et al., 2004).

Interestingly, research shows that even people who have experienced extreme difficulties have the capacity, or resiliency, to overcome them (Carp, 2010; Greene, 2010; Harris, 2008; Mancini & Bonanno, 2009). **Resilience** is the ability to manage positively, even in the face of adversity. Resilient people are characteristically hopeful; have a sense of mastery, self-efficacy, and meaning in life; and they are effective problem solvers. Based on a 20-year longitudinal study on competence and resilience, Masten (2005) identifies several environmental factors that enhance resilience in children. These factors include connections to adults who are competent and caring, connections with faith communities, availability of community resources, and educational opportunities.

The macrolevel environment is a source of both risks and opportunities (Garbarino, 1983). **Environmental opportunities** are those resources available to systems in their social and physical environments that foster well-being. Examples of such macrosystem opportunities include governmental assistance in times of emergencies, legislative support for social programs, and budgetary allocations for community infrastructures. In contrast, **environmental risks**, such as oppression and discrimination, disenfranchise many from society's

opportunity structures. Environmental risks are ideologies or cultural alignments that work against the well-being of individuals and society. Shortages and barriers in resource provisions, social inequities, and lack of opportunities create social problems and pose environmental risks. Other examples of such risks include national economic policies that create inequities and increase poverty for some, and social policies that magnify racism, sexism, or other discriminatory practices. Limiting environmental risks while expanding environmental opportunities promotes social justice and supports empowerment.

Creating responsive environments rich in opportunity is a policy issue. Access to health care, adequate education, technical training, child care, civil rights, jobs, transportation, and comprehensive community-based services all benefit individual citizens and contribute to the general good. The lives of individual clients cannot improve without the opportunities of resource-rich environments to contribute to their clients' sense of power and well-being. This posture "embodies the profession's mission to improve societal conditions and to enhance social functioning. A resilience-enhancing approach underscores the need to seek resources and sources of natural support within clients' environments" (Greene & Cohen, 2005, p. 369).

Perspectives on risk, opportunity, and resilience have both research and policy implications for social work practice. Informed by research evidence about risk and resilience factors in individuals, families, neighborhoods, faith communities, and schools, social workers craft strategies that span system levels (Corcoran & Nichols-Casebolt, 2004). With respect to policies, social workers draw on research evidence and practice experiences to advocate social policies that provide the infrastructures for resource-rich environments.

Subsystems and Environments

Two important concepts clarify the idea of systems within systems: **subsystem** and **environment**. Smaller systems within every system are subsystems. For example, children and parents make up subsystems of the larger family system. Similarly, each individual within a family is actually a subsystem. Conversely, the larger system that

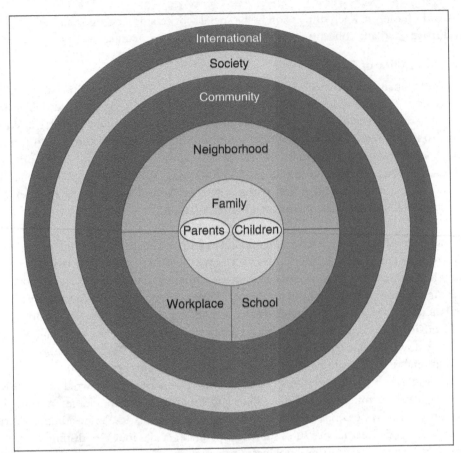

Figure 2.1
Subsystems and Environments
Whether social workers define a particular system as an environment or a subsystem depends on which system they identify as the focal system.

encompasses a social system is that system's environment, which influences and provides the context for the systems functioning within it. Schools, workplaces, and neighborhoods are all examples of a family system's social environment. Broadening the focus to an even larger picture, the community is the social environment for both neighborhoods and families (Figure 2.1).

All systems have subsystems and environments. All systems are also subsystems, while, at the same time, they are environments. For example, the family is a system itself, but, in switching the focus, this same family is also the environment of the children within it. Another perspective shift leads us to describe this family as a subsystem of the neighborhood in which it lives. Whether we label a system a "subsystem," a "system," or an "environment" is relative and changes as we shift our point of focus.

Dimensions of Systems

The complex behavior of human systems gives rise to several helpful ways for viewing them, including the system's **structure**, **interaction**, **biopsychosocial dimensions**, and

cultural elements. Each dimension helps social workers describe human behavior in productive ways and conceptualize creative possibilities for change.

Structural View of Systems

How individuals and subsystems within a system arrange themselves is the structure of the system. Structure is not actually visible; we discern it by observing two variables that characterize the structural arrangements of any system—closeness and power. Closeness refers to the closed or open nature of system **boundaries**, whereas the distribution of power aligns the system **hierarchy**. When we ask, "How close or distant are members?" we discover the boundaries of a system. When we ask, "Who's in charge?" we uncover the hierarchy for distributing power within a system. Considering both boundaries and hierarchies offers a complete picture of a system's structure.

Boundaries   Boundaries define systems. They distinguish the interior of the system from its environment. Boundaries vary in permeability or, in other words, in how many transactions they allow between systems. **Open systems** interact frequently and exchange resources with their environment, offering the potential for meeting systems' needs and the risk of being overwhelmed by demanding environments. Having no access to the environment, **closed systems** may seem protected, but they must meet all of their needs by drawing on resources from within their own systems. With such limited access to additional resources, closed systems may deplete their resources.

Boundaries also differentiate people within a given system. Internal boundaries, those that exist around various individuals and subgroups within a larger system, define subsystems. For example, for most social agencies, boundaries define administrative, supervisory, and direct service subsystems. Particular agencies may also distinguish other subsystems such as experts and novices; professionals, paraprofessionals, and clerical staff; or direct and indirect service providers. These internal boundaries have different degrees of permeability. Like boundaries that define systems, subsystems' boundaries vary on a continuum from open to closed. The level of closeness within a system is a significant element in understanding the system's structure.

Hierarchy   Hierarchy indicates which individuals and subsystems have status, privileges, and power within a particular system. Typically, hierarchy describes who is in charge. For example, organizational charts, formalized procedures, and position titles such as president, director, or supervisor clearly define hierarchy in formal organizational systems. Discerning hierarchy in other systems may be more difficult. Although titles such as mother, father, or ringleader may give clues about power and control within the system, these titles may not match the system's actual distribution of power. Observing who makes decisions and who initiates actions provides a more accurate picture of hierarchy.

Interactional View of Systems

In contrast to structure, which offers a static look at systems, the interactional view places the structure in motion. It examines the way in which people relate within a system and with their environments. The interactional perspective focuses on the ways systems maintain **equilibrium**, provide **feedback**, and understand **circular causality** and **wholeness**.

Equilibrium   Systems tend to interact in ways that maintain balance, or equilibrium. In collaboration with clients, social workers attempt to stabilize productive interactional patterns while interrupting those where difficulties reside. Events that temporarily knock a system out of balance leave it scrambling to regain its previous equilibrium or lead it quickly toward establishing a new one. For example, funding cuts require a social service provider's immediate response. Likely, the agency will first act to maintain the status quo by locating new funds. Otherwise, the agency may look internally, cutting staff positions and redistributing the workload to ensure the organization's survival and maintain system balance. Rebalancing can also occur if this agency system changes its relationship to the environment. The agency may decrease the services it offers to the community, thereby reaching a new balance without overloading the remaining staff. Whatever the agency does to regain equilibrium, one thing is clear—changes in funding, staffing, or programming create other changes in the internal functioning of the agency as well as in its ability to work successfully with clients.

Feedback   Feedback provides a continuous flow of information. Two forms of feedback exist—information that maintains the existing equilibrium and information that induces change toward a new equilibrium. First, some information fits neatly with the system's existing way of doing things. The system assimilates this feedback, reinforcing the current pattern. Second, incompatible information forces the system to change to accommodate the discrepancy. Social workers provide both kinds of feedback as they work toward desired goals. They offer reinforcing feedback to maintain the existing strengths and introduce system-altering feedback to disrupt problematic patterns, clearing the way for new possibilities.

Circular Causality   Human systems influence their environments and are influenced by them. One person does not directly cause the behavior of another; instead, behavior occurs as a response to multiple social and structural influences. This concept is described as circular causality. Although, theoretically, all system members share some responsibility for interactions within the system, there is an important note of caution here! Social workers remain particularly vigilant when weighing causality in relationships with large discrepancies in power among the players. Clearly, persons who are victimized hold no responsibility for the acts of others. The principle of circular causality does not free abusers from accountability for their own behaviors or blame victims for having no access to power.

Wholeness   Closely related to circular causality, the axiom of wholeness postulates that a change in one part of a system will precipitate changes in other parts and in the system as a whole (von Bertalanffy, 1968). In other words, altering one part of any person:environment transaction affects the other transactional elements. Prompting one productive change can initiate a cycle that may subsequently benefit the entire transactional system. This rule extends beyond the system's boundary to describe how a system changes in response to its environment, as well as how an environment responds to changes in those systems within it. Consider the previous example of the agency and its funding cuts. Reduced funding, a change in the environment, reverberates internally with changes throughout the agency system and subsequently reemerges to affect the environment in terms of the agency's abilities to serve its clients.

Biopsychosocial Dimensions

All social systems have distinctive human qualities based on the biological, psychological, social, cultural, and spiritual characteristics of their individual members. A biopsychosocial view of systems holds special significance for change processes. As thinking and feeling beings, humans have options and to some extent the power to choose responses to what is happening in their lives. These options may be limited by individual and environmental conditions, but, within a reasonable range, people are able to make choices about how they view themselves and interpret the events around them.

The biopsychosocial view applies to more than individual functioning in that multiperson systems, composed of thinking and feeling individual members, also have cognitive and affective dimensions that can lead to change. The neighborhood whose residents "believe" that a neighborhood watch program can ensure personal safety and property rights will activate and participate in such a program. Families who "feel" pride in their reputation and accomplishments will risk activities that have the potential to add to their accomplishments, further contributing to a greater sense of pride. This biopsychosocial view expands the options for social workers and clients to construct new ways of perceiving and responding to events.

> ▶ This video illustrates the many factors that determine how people choose to act. How do the biological, psychological, and social influences interact to determine human behavior?

Cultural Influences

Every human being identifies cultural memberships in multiple contextual systems. Race, ethnicity, gender, socioeconomic class, religion, sexual orientation, age group, geographic location, political affiliation, occupation, and lifestyle are several of the cultural dimensions that influence human behavior. Cultural influences are profound. Not only do we build our own identities around the various groups of which we are members, but frequently others also view us more in terms of our general cultural attributes than of our own unique identities.

Our cultural memberships affect the way others treat us. Human societies do not afford the same status and privileges across cultural categories. **Privileged groups** sometimes disenfranchise members of other cultural groups. For example, in the United States, someone identified culturally as male, White, and heterosexual simply has more opportunities and fewer constraints than someone whose cultural group memberships include female, African American, and lesbian.

Generalizations based on memberships in cultural systems also obscure individual differences. Although membership in a particular cultural group usually indicates certain similarities among group members, individual members hold other cultural group memberships as well. Add these multicultural influences to each person's unique physical, cognitive, and affective attributes, and the result is diversity among members within even the most influential of cultural groups. Simply put, no two people are alike! The multiple influences of simultaneously intersecting cultural contexts individuate even members of the same family.

> ### ✳ Diversity and Difference in Practice
>
> **Behavior: Apply and communicate understanding of the importance of diversity and difference in shaping life experiences in practice at the micro, mezzo, and macro levels**
>
> ---
>
> **Critical Thinking Question:** All human beings are shaped by the multiple cultures in which they hold membership. What effect does this cultural imprint have on how we regard and interact with others?

> **?** Assess your understanding of social systems by taking this brief quiz.

ECOSYSTEMS: PERSPECTIVE AND FRAMEWORK

The ecosystems perspective contributes to generalist social work practice in three major ways: It provides a way to comprehend human diversity and explicate the relationship between humans and their physical and social environments. Additionally, it offers an organizing framework for comprehensive assessment. Finally, social workers can use an ecosystems view to elucidate each phase of generalist practice processes.

 Watch this video that uses songs to illustrate social work theory. What elements of each song illustrate theoretical concepts that fit within an ecosystems perspective? www.youtube.com/watch? v=fWvfPhzXfZU

Ecosystems Perspective

The ecosystems perspective conceptualizes a dynamic view of human beings as systems interacting in **context**, emphasizes the significance of human system transactions, traces **evolutionary change** in systems over time, and describes current behavior as an **adaptive fit** of "persons in situations."

Humans in Context

The ecosystems perspective describes humans as multidimensional biological, psychological, spiritual, social, and cultural beings with thoughts, feelings, and observable behaviors. We are initiators within our environments as well as responders to those same environments. We create our own traditions and legacies just as we inherit and respond to our cultural and ethnic heritage. The ecosystems view acknowledges that we not only react consciously and intentionally but also act unconsciously and spontaneously. We are complex wholes with internal parts and, at the same time, we are parts or members of larger groups. In the ecosystems view, humans are neither completely powerful nor powerless. Instead, humans play an active role in creating events that shape their lives, a role tempered by environmental forces and conditions.

How we work with people and their situations logically follows from how we perceive human behavior. If we believe the ecosystems model cogently explains how people develop strengths and vulnerabilities, then the choices we make in supporting growth and change will reflect this perspective. Ecosystemically oriented social work practice centers on changing and maintaining both client and environmental systems.

Multiple Possibilities for Change   The interdependent functioning of human systems offers many entry points for social work intervention. Because altering one part of any person:environment transaction affects the other system elements, workers and clients may choose a particular strategy from among several intervention targets that may be most amenable to change or have the greatest potential benefits.

Consider the example of Dorothy Masters, a disgruntled resident of Northside Care Center. She complains about nearly every aspect of her care. Social worker Jan Kim sees several options for addressing Dorothy's concerns, including individual counseling support, family involvement to enhance the frequency and quality of family interaction, or social network intervention to help Dorothy find other residents who share her interests. When Dorothy chooses to organize a resident's council, a variety of related changes occur. Dorothy's mood improves as she redirects her energy toward relating with the other residents. Council members take charge of planning recreational and social events to match their own interests. The members also lobby the management team to change policies regarding menu choices and roommate assignments. Dorothy's son reports that he now enjoys his visits with Dorothy and will likely come more often. Count all of the positive changes! Recognize how these changes originated from interventions within Dorothy's ecosystem, efforts not simply focused on the "individual" issue of Dorothy's unhappiness. Prompting one productive change within an ecosystem initiates a cycle of changes that may have subsequent benefits throughout the entire system.

Focus on Transactions

Humans and their environments evolve in continuously accommodating responses to one another. Notice this two-way influence when you visualize the connection of a person interacting with the environment. These reciprocal interactions are transactions—"the processes by which people continually shape their environments and are shaped by them over time" (Germain, 1983, p. 115). The term "**person:environment**" symbolizes this mutual relationship (Gitterman & Germain, 2008). The colon emphasizes the dynamic interrelatedness of people in transaction with their social and physical environments. Productive transactions serve as sources of energy to sustain a system's functioning and fuel change. Deficient transactions inhibit growth and possibly even threaten basic sustenance.

Recognizing the significance of transactions reaffirms social work's traditional focus on social functioning—"people coping with life situations [or the] balance between demands of the social environment and people's coping efforts" (Bartlett, 1970, p. 130). This definition describes flexible people adapting to their demanding environments. An empowerment-based view of transaction increases the emphasis on the reciprocal dimension of social functioning, the notion that both people and environments can change. Not only do people respond to environmental demands, but environments must also adapt to the demands of people.

Development as Evolutionary Change

The ecosystems perspective views human development as evolutionary. It describes how individuals and other human systems change and stabilize in response to internal and external forces. As humans grow physically, emotionally, and intellectually, their behaviors reveal and respond to these internal changes. The changes within systems are not the only determinants of human behavior. Instead, these internal experiences themselves affect and respond to contextual events.

Development in Context   Individuals develop in a context in which other systems are evolving, too. Social groups, organizations, and societal and international institutions—entities that humans themselves help create—seem to take on lives of their own as they also grow and develop. These social systems act on and respond to individuals' behaviors. Neither the external nor the internal world has total responsibility for causing any particular human behavior. We create our world just as our world creates us.

When explaining human growth and development, certain contexts merit special note. Humans develop in societies that congregate individuals into categories and value certain group memberships over others. Cultural identities powerfully influence how we view ourselves and how others view us. Race, ethnicity, culture, and socioeconomic and gender contexts can be stepping stones to success for the power elite; however, they may function as roadblocks for those who are oppressed. Burdening individual development with stereotypic expectations denies overwhelming evidence of in-group diversity and ignores other environmental influences. Assumptions and expectations arising from membership in social groups influence self-perceptions, interactions with others, and access to social and economic resources.

Adaptive Fit

The ecosystems perspective explains behavior in terms of adapting to a situation. All individual and social systems evolve to fit the resources and demands of their worlds. How we interact at any specific time arises from a synthesis of what is happening in the world within us, what is happening in the world around us, and how we interpret those events. In the ecosystems view of dysfunction, the terms "maladaptive" and "dysfunctional" do not really apply. After all, if behaviors are adaptations to meet internal needs and the demands of environments, how can any behaviors be maladaptive? Even behaviors that are deemed unacceptable and have negative consequences make sense when considered in context. No human behavior occurs in isolation from other events. Rather, humans respond to multiple internal and environmental events simultaneously. In the world of gloves, we may be able to find that "one size fits all." However, in human behavior, we often find that a behavior that may be perfectly adaptive in one specific person:environment configuration is a mismatch in another. Describing a client's behavior as dysfunctional or maladaptive blames clients and neglects the reciprocal responsibility of environments for human behavior. The ecosystems view removes this blame from clients in favor of describing problems as transactional—a "fit" in a problem-producing context.

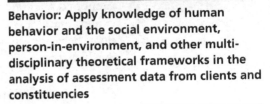

Assessment

Behavior: Apply knowledge of human behavior and the social environment, person-in-environment, and other multi-disciplinary theoretical frameworks in the analysis of assessment data from clients and constituencies

Critical Thinking Question: From an ecosystems perspective, all behaviors make sense to some degree when they are considered in the context of the impinging social environment. How does this understanding of behavior as a transactional experience inform how social workers assess clients and their situations?

Focus on Strengths   The ecosystems perspective offers many intervention possibilities, yet social workers move cautiously to initiate change. Because human beings naturally evolve to work in harmony with their environments, it is likely that client systems are actually doing a lot right. One ecosystems practice principle mandates that social workers build on the strengths and competencies clients already have available. A strengths orientation (described fully in Chapter 4) is an essential tool for successfully applying an ecosystems perspective.

Focus on the Environment   Whether difficulties arise when people encounter physical, intellectual, psychological, emotional, or situational challenges depends on the responsiveness of the environment and the strengths of the particular human system. A nurturing environment often compensates for a system's limitations, enabling the system to achieve the **goodness of fit** that characterizes the ecosystems view of competence (Germain, 1979). A resource-rich, **responsive environment** transforms persons who may otherwise be overwhelmed by challenges into contributors who can further enrich their environments. By considering the responsibility of environments, the ecosystems view precludes labeling individuals or social systems as dysfunctional or pathological in favor of recognizing that simply no goodness of fit exists. That which the system lacks, the environment is not providing. What the environment fails to provide, the system cannot compensate with its own resources. Even a good adaptation in one particular context may not work effectively in others. The ecosystems view concludes that dysfunctional behavior is transitory, changeable, and related to the responsiveness of the context in which it occurs.

Ecosystems Framework: As an Assessment Tool

How we work with people and their situations logically follows from how we perceive human behavior. If we believe the ecosystems perspective cogently explains how people develop strengths and vulnerabilities, then the practice choices we make and the processes we utilize will reflect this perspective. Ecosystemically oriented social work practice centers on changing and maintaining both client and environmental systems. A simple way to organize the ecosystems perspective into a user-friendly assessment framework for generalist social work practice involves a five-point schema (O'Melia, 1991):

Ecosystemically oriented social work practice centers on changing and maintaining both client and environmental systems.

- Identify the **focal system**.
- What's happening inside the system?
- What's happening outside the system?
- How do the inside and outside connect?
- How does the system move through time?

A closer look reveals the universality and usefulness of this simple framework (Table 2.2).

Identify the Focal System

All aspects of generalist practice involve human systems. Social workers practice within systems such as agencies, departments, institutions, and various other organizations.

Table 2.2   Ecosystems: Conceptual Practice Framework

Questions	Description
What's the focal system?	Identifies the system on which the ecosystems analysis will focus—can be an individual, family, group, organization, or community.
What's inside the system?	Explores the structure, interaction, biopsychosocial dimensions, and cultural features within the focal system.
What's outside the system?	Delineates the network of other systems and resources in the focal system's environmental context.
How do the inside and outside connect?	Examines the transactions between the focal system and systems in its context.
How does the system move through time?	Observes adaptation and changes occurring in the process of the focal system's development.

From *Generalist Perspectives in Case Coordination* by M. O'Melia (May 1991). Used with permission of the author.

Social workers interact with client systems, including individuals, couples, families, groups, organizations, and communities. Social workers also target changes in environmental systems to benefit their clients. Practitioners themselves are members of personal and professional systems that may support or inhibit their work. In effective generalist practice, workers understand the functioning of and resources within each of these systems, including their settings, their clients, their communities, and themselves.

The ecosystems view recognizes the complex configuration of these nested and interlocking systems. To ignore the multiple influences present in any situation is to offer only a partial account of why things are the way they are, what resources exist, and how things might change. Acknowledging these influences requires a step-by-step analysis that begins with a well-defined reference point, which we call the focal system. Any of these systems can be identified as the focal system.

What's Happening Inside the System?

After determining the focal system, we next analyze the system's internal functioning. A structural perspective offers information about the system's membership, boundaries, and hierarchies. Highlighting the interactional view provides information about how system members communicate, the patterns they develop, and the ways they maintain balance. Exploring biopsychosocial dimensions provides information about system members' physical health, thoughts, and feelings. Considering the cultural influences of values, beliefs, attitudes, communication patterns, and norms adds to our understanding of functioning inside the focal system.

What's Happening Outside the System?

All systems exist in the context of an ecosystem—a set of interconnected, interdependent, and interactive systems that affect one another. Identifying important environmental influences begins to explain the focal system's behavior and reveals possible targets for intervention. Because ecosystems are also systems, workers can describe and analyze ecosystems by applying the same perspectives used for describing any system—structural, interactional, biopsychosocial, and sociocultural.

Although many systems share aspects of the same environments, the particular ecosystem of any focal system is a unique configuration, idiosyncratic to that system. Consider the following examples of the ecosystems of potential client systems. For one 8-year-old child, relevant environmental systems may be the child's immediate family, extended family, peer group, neighborhood, school, and church. For a different 8-year-old child placed in foster care, relevant environments include the child's biological family, foster family, social worker, case management team, foster children's support group, and the family court system. On another level, significant contextual systems for a public housing project include the community, city government, local social agencies, and federal housing departments.

How Do the Inside and Outside Connect?

The viability of any human system depends on its success in interacting with its environment. For example, social workers need personal and professional backing. Clients need information, resources, and support. This interface of the system with the environment—the system:environment transaction—is a major target for assessment and intervention.

To illustrate how this relates to professional practice, consider the example of Tony Marelli. As a social worker for the Northside Addictions Recovery Center, Tony is experiencing feelings of burnout. Significant events in Tony's connections to his environment contribute to this situation. The Addiction Recovery Center's loss of a state grant has forced layoffs and a redistribution of work to remaining staff. Tony's workload has increased from 25 to 35 clients as a result. Normally, the agency has a supportive collegial and supervisory system with which Tony exchanges ideas about his experiences with clients, but the overload has sent everyone scrambling. Consequently, the workers hardly have time to talk to one another.

Look closely at the changes in Tony's connections to the world around him. The previous balance of Tony (the inside) with his clients and co-workers (the outside) is now skewed. His boundaries have opened wide to clients and have closed with respect to his professional support network. For Tony, more resources are going out, and fewer are coming in, obviously contributing to his burnout. This ecosystems analysis also points the way toward what might be done to ease Tony's situation. Changes in Tony's workload or his relationships with colleagues may be solutions. Analyzing Tony's transactions with his environment offers insights into what is currently happening and stimulates thinking about the possibilities for change.

How Does the System Move Through Time?

Systems at every level, from individual to society, move along their developmental paths in response to expected and unexpected events. Both kinds of events, predictable and surprising, affect systems. How systems negotiate these changes as they move through the context of time merits careful review. Social workers incorporate historical and developmental contexts by gathering enough information about the focal system to understand the system's evolution.

Many evolutionary changes occur naturally, including physical maturation and other developmental transitions. Erikson (1963) describes expected stages of psychosocial development for individuals. McGoldrick and colleagues (2015) expand this notion of developmental change to families and examine the mutual influences of individual and family life cycles. Another theorist describes the natural path of group development as sequential, passing through stages of forming, storming, norming, performing, and adjourning (Tuckman, 1965, as cited in Schriver, 2015). Systems at all levels evolve in predictable and adaptable ways.

Nodal Events   Other changes, some unexpected, can create temporary havoc in systems, leaving system members struggling to regain equilibrium. Consider how the sudden death of a child in a family system immediately disrupts the family's sense of how things should be and requires extensive adjustment in the way the family operates. These changes, called **nodal events**, have a dramatic effect on a system's development (Carter & McGoldrick, 2005). The addition or loss of a member or a significant change in a member's role profoundly affects the system as a whole. Such is the case in birth, marriage, death, and serious illness. Examples of nodal events in larger systems are organizational expansion and downsizing. In a community, nodal events can include a change in leadership, plant closings, or the receipt of federal grants. Nodal events can improve a system's functioning or challenge its capabilities.

Ecosystems Framework: As a Practice Model

As an assessment tool, this ecosystems framework provides ways for social workers to organize information about "what is" in a way that hints at "what might be." As a practice model, this framework guides practitioners as they build effective relationships with clients through dialogue, assess client functioning through discovery, and develop and implement change activities.

Dialogue: Building Relationships with Client Systems

By identifying the professional relationship as the focal system, workers can monitor how they relate to clients. The structural perspective allows workers to question issues of power and closeness: Does the client system have sufficient power in the relationship with the worker to ensure feelings of control, an experience of competence, and a guarantee of self-determination? Is the relationship sufficiently close to encourage an open and honest sharing of information yet distant enough to ensure professional integrity and encourage independence? By applying this framework, workers can construct empowering and respectful relationships with client systems.

This framework also helps workers monitor the effects of outside forces on their work with clients. Obviously, the relationships of social workers and clients respond to influences in their respective ecosystems. Cultural contexts are particularly important. Analyzing cultural dimensions can help workers recognize and confront their own biases and sensitize them to relate to clients in culturally appropriate ways.

Discovery: Assessing Functioning

The ecosystems framework is a tool for assessing a client's situation, regardless of the particular level of client system. Observing a system from structural, interactional, biopsychosocial, and cultural points of view offers considerable information for understanding individuals, families, groups, and communities. Assessing the client system's progress over time contributes additional clues about important historic events, the system's ability to adapt, and its future direction.

Development: Planning, Implementing, and Evaluating Change

Knowing the specific ways that systems function reveals multiple entry points for social workers and clients to initiate change. Altering internal aspects of a system's functioning, changing environments, or modifying the connections between the two all hold potential for creating change. Social workers and clients carefully analyze these possibilities to construct plans and carry out activities, enhance client competence, activate environmental support, create alliances, and expand opportunities.

> **?** Assess your understanding of the perspective and frameworks associated with ecosystems by taking this brief quiz.

LOOKING FORWARD

Human behavior theory guides and justifies actions that social workers take to help clients. Social work draws from many disciplines to flesh out an ecosystems view of human functioning. These perspectives include ecosystems, social constructionism, feminism, life course theory, a critical perspective, biology and behavior, and a trauma-informed view. The person:environment construct, a concept emphasizing the reciprocal relation-ship between persons and their impinging social and physical environments, remains central to social work practice. Social systems theory helps social workers decipher this symbiotic and evolutionary relationship. An ecosystems view provides a guiding frame-work for all social work activities from engagement through assessment, intervention, and evaluation.

Research-tested hypotheses are essential for establishing evidence-based practice. But ethical workers should take caution here—clients deserve their say. Favoring a professional view over a client's perspective may be oppressive, contradicting the key social work val-

Evaluate what you learned in this chapter by completing the Chapter Review.

ues of acceptance and client self-determination. Effective practitioners also recognize other important influences on interactions with clients. Chapter 3 describes how attitudes, expectations, values, and cultural identities affect pro-fessional practice. Social workers must inventory their own beliefs and cultural backgrounds to prepare for value-based, culturally competent practice.

3

Values and Multicultural Competence

R. GINO SANTA MARIA / SHUTTERSTOCK

By the first time social workers and clients actually talk together, both have already been formulating their expectations about each other and the work ahead. Each brings values, attitudes, and assumptions that will undeniably influence their interactions. Effective social workers acknowledge these existing **frames of reference**.

To create empowering experiences, practitioners examine their value base, develop their cultural competence, and even take it one step further to purposefully construct a set of presuppositions about clients that will influence their work productively. This chapter explores the ways that social workers prepare themselves both professionally and personally for relationships with clients, particularly in the areas of values and diversity. Using these skills, value-prepared, culturally competent social workers form relationships that activate clients' resources, respect clients' contributions, and maintain professional integrity.

PROFESSIONAL VALUES AND PRACTICE PRINCIPLES

Personal and professional values are a significant component of a social worker's frame of reference and have been since the beginning of the profession in the early twentieth century (Reamer, 2008). Through practice principles, values shape thinking and direct our actions as social workers, guiding the day-to-day practice of social work (Table 3.1). These principles include **acceptance**, **individualization**, **nonjudgmentalism**, **objectivity**, **self-determination**, **access to resources**, **confidentiality**, and **accountability**.

Acceptance

The principle of acceptance charges social workers to go beyond merely tolerating clients to regarding clients positively. Social workers demonstrate acceptance when they affirm clients' perspectives and value what clients contribute to the work. They treat clients with respect and dignity, realizing that clients have unique strengths and resources to offer. Acceptance facilitates change. According to Berlin (2005), "our attempts to assist the client to undertake positive change are most likely to be effective when the client feels both cared for and recognized as a free agent" (p. 485).

As existentialist theologian Paul Tillich (1962) wrote about the philosophy of social work, the type of love shown in acceptance is different from charity, as charity makes no critical demands. Instead, he associates acceptance with *agape* or *caritas*, the Greek and Latin words for love. The regard for others shown in *agape* or *caritas* is critical, accepting, and transformative. Social workers whose practice reflects acceptance authenticate the worth and dignity of client systems, expect clients to use their capacities for growth, and build on their strengths.

Individualization

Valuing individualization means recognizing that all humans have a right "to be individuals and to be treated not just as a human being but as this human being with personal differences"

Table 3.1   Social Work Practice Principles

Acceptance	Conveys positive regard for clients' strengths and potential for growth
Individualization	Affirms each client's unique and distinctive characteristics
Nonjudgmentalism	Maintains nonblaming attitudes toward clients
Objectivity	Promotes professional caring, concern, and commitment in working with clients
Self-determination	Upholds clients' rights to exercise their own decision making
Access to services	Promotes and fosters access to resources and opportunities
Confidentiality	Respects clients' rights to privacy
Accountability	Ensures competent professional conduct and comportment

(Biestek, 1957, p. 25). Although practitioners do rely on general information about human behavior gleaned from research, they carefully differentiate the distinctive qualities and unique circumstances of each client system. Social workers' sensitivity toward diversity prevents them from deducing too much about clients from background information, knowing that any cultural characteristic is only one of several individual and group identities clients hold. Individual members of any cultural group have distinctive stories to tell.

Oppression, discrimination, and stereotyping seriously impede individualization. The principle of individualization prompts social workers to customize their generalized view to accommodate individual differences. A social worker who individualizes clients, their situations, and their diversity resists applying labels or using stereotypes. Individualizing means focusing on each client's unique characteristics and treating clients as persons with rights and dignity rather than objects, cases, or the next appointment.

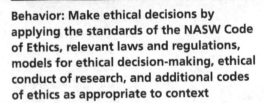

Ethical and Professional Behavior

Behavior: Make ethical decisions by applying the standards of the NASW Code of Ethics, relevant laws and regulations, models for ethical decision-making, ethical conduct of research, and additional codes of ethics as appropriate to context

Critical Thinking Question: Social work practice principles undergird professional standards and guide the day-to-day work of social workers. What conflicts arise as workers strive to uphold each practice principle in their ethical practice with clients?

Nonjudgmentalism

Think for a moment about conversations in which you feel blamed, evaluated, or condemned. Do you try to justify your behavior? Are you so aggravated that you stop listening? Do you feel as if the person with whom you are talking isn't really listening to you or understanding your situation? Judgmental attitudes and behaviors tend to shut down communication processes, create barriers to relationships, and cast doubts about abilities. "In situations where service users—and practitioners—feel defended, guarded, and self-protective, it can be difficult to establish a sound foundation on which to build future work" (Trevithick, 2003, p. 169). Nonjudgmental social workers neither blame clients nor evaluate them as good or bad. Rather, clients have rights to make their own value decisions.

Being nonjudgmental does not mean that social workers never make judgments about what clients are doing. Social workers inevitably filter what they learn about clients through their own professional and personal value screens, as all relationships are value based (Dolgoff et al., 2008). However, social workers are careful to help clients examine decisions through the clients' own value screens, not the workers'. Social workers applying an ecosystemic perspective readily recognize that diversity of choices is a natural result of the many influences that create human behavior. Culturally competent practice requires workers to avoid applying their own values and to suspend making judgments in favor of learning each client's worldview—a perspective in which the client's behavior makes sense. Adopting a nonjudgmental perspective, practitioners recognize circumstances that provoke judgment and blame, acknowledge that their personal values and beliefs are not likely to apply to the circumstances of others, and work to set aside their personal opinions.

Watch this video that illustrates how professional values frame actions taken by generalist social workers. How does the work of NASW Social Worker of the Year Marshall Wong reflect social work values and principles? www.youtube.com/watch?v=XPAotCc2ZWc

Objectivity

Objectivity, individualization, and nonjudgmentalism are all closely related. To ensure objectivity, practitioners separate their own personal feelings from a client's situation. They listen openly to avoid distorting a client's story with their own biases and refrain from prejudicially labeling the client. They also avoid the pitfalls of extreme reactions, responding neutrally with neither cold detachment nor emotional overidentification. Taken to an extreme, practicing objectivity devolves into being aloof, dispassionate, or indifferent.

Empathy expresses the objective caring and commitment that competent social work practice requires. A social worker's honest feedback that describes rather than evaluates a client's behavior reflects objectivity, too. Self-awareness helps sort out the worker's personal perspective and provides insight from which to draw for empathy with the client's situation. In keeping with the principle of objectivity, social workers invest themselves in their work with clients, yet maintain a professional perspective.

Self-Determination

The NASW's *Code of Ethics* (1999) upholds clients' rights to make their own decisions. This freedom to choose and decide reflects the principle of self-determination. Simply stated, self-determination is the freedom to make choices. Actualizing this freedom to choose depends on the presence of options and resources. Scarce resources limit opportunities for choice and, therefore, limit a client's potential for self-determination. Empowerment-based social work practice creates opportunities for clients to exercise choice and helps clients recognize their privilege to decide.

Although self-determination arises within, it can be stifled in a hierarchical relationship. For example, **paternalism** and **maternalism** both challenge clients' autonomy in social work practice. When social workers act paternalistically, they undermine autonomy by imposing their preferences and decisions on clients based on a belief that they "know best" or know what is in the best interest of the client. Also limiting clients' autonomy, maternalism is based on good intention gone awry—unintentional control exercised through overpowering caring behaviors. Collaborative social workers avoid skewed power relationships, freeing clients to define the direction of the change efforts. Involving social service consumers at all levels of decision making quells potential encroachments on client self-determination as well as paternalism or maternalism on the part of practitioners.

Self-determination also presupposes freedom from coercion. When social workers impose solutions, give direct advice, assume the role of expert, treat clients as subordinates, or in other ways control decisions, they thwart client self-determination. Upholding self-determination doesn't mean abandoning clients, abdicating responsibility, or failing to provide direction. Social workers committed to client self-determination actively guide rather than coercively direct the helping process. Social workers who advocate self-determination foster collaboration, affirm client strengths, activate resources, and expand opportunities.

Access to Resources

Without choices and resources, people lack power. Therefore, honoring dignity and self-determination hinges on clients having access to resources (Hopps et al., 1995). Guaranteeing clients' access to alternatives and opportunities is a fundamental practice principle and requisite of empowerment. The profession's *Code of Ethics* (NASW, 1999) mandates social workers advocate the development of opportunities for oppressed and disadvantaged populations and promote policy changes that improve social conditions. These efforts reveal workers' commitment to social justice and uphold client self-determination by providing rightful access to the resources that society offers.

To promote access to resources, social workers ensure that their practice settings demonstrate sensitivity to diversity. Workers urge their agencies to incorporate multicultural illustrations into their brochures, to provide multilingual staff and literature, to create information forms that are sensitive to lifestyle diversity, and to design office spaces that are comfortable and accessible to people with disabilities. Access to services is a reality only when clients can see that the agency is adapting to their styles and needs.

Confidentiality

All clients have a right to privacy, a right to have what they share held in confidence by the practitioner and protected by the agency. Confidentiality extends to all identifying information, case records, and professional opinions about clients' situations. As an ethical principle, confidentiality guides professional behavior and forms the basis for trustworthy professional relationships. Workers make exceptions only if clients give their express consent to disclose information or if laws compel workers to reveal information. Respecting privacy by maintaining confidentiality builds trust and demonstrates respect for client systems, two essential ingredients for developing collaborative partnerships.

Accountability

The *Code of Ethics* (NASW, 1999) clarifies professional roles and relationships at various levels of responsibility in relation to clients, colleagues, employers, employing organizations, the social work profession, and society. Our identities as social workers leave us accountable for our personal and professional conduct. Accountability requires that practitioners be proficient in the performance of professional practice. It means that workers regard the service obligation of social work as primary and, thus, prevent discriminatory and inhumane practices. To be accountable, social workers act with professional integrity and impartiality, and they use sound protocols in practice and research.

To meet the standards of accountability, social workers must know relevant laws and their implications for social work practice. Specifically, a continuum of legal technicalities—from the program and procedural requirements of policy initiatives to federal and state laws to the specifics of case law—applies to each particular field of social work practice. Social workers increase their professional accountability when they familiarize themselves with laws related to the general practice of social work as well as those related to their specific fields of practice.

> Watch this video that illustrates how value conflicts frequently arise in social work practice. What steps can social workers take to resolve conflicts between personal values and professional practice behaviors? www.youtube.com/watch?v=ptM-mvJVdp0

Value Conflicts in Practice

Values and principles guide professional behavior, yet making the most ethical choice is not always easy in practice. Value conflicts are frequent in social work, especially in practice with clients whom workers may feel the need to protect. When social workers experience these conflicts, they apply theories

> Assess your understanding of the values and purpose of social work by taking this brief quiz.

and principles for ethical decision-making; consult clients, colleagues, supervisors, and ethics committees; and sometimes obtain legal advice to make informed choices about their actions.

PERSONAL VALUES AND RESOURCES

A singular emphasis on having professional knowledge, techniques, and skills denies the importance of the "person" of social workers and their personal frames of reference. Personal attributes of warmth, honesty, genuineness, openness, creativity, sensitivity, commitment, and optimism are all assets for workers in engaging clients and building relationships. The personal values and resources of social workers can support the professional helping process.

Frames of Reference

Research documents that what people expect to happen influences how they respond, a phenomenon called the placebo effect. Experiments repeatedly demonstrate how positive changes in behavior result from participants' expectations that improvements will occur. Our expectations are influential in shaping how we understand experiences and in swaying our responses.

What others expect of us influences our responses, too. For example, a classic educational study found that a diverse group of children randomly labeled bloomers lived up to their teacher's expectations (Rosenthal & Jacobson, 1968). You can imagine the results if those same children had been labeled difficult or slow. Whether preconceived notions are positive or negative, their effects are often dramatic. What we expect powerfully shapes our sense of self, influences our behavior, and constructs the reality in which we interpret events.

Our values, **culture**, and patterns of thinking as well as our expectations of situations and others' expectations of us all contribute to our frames of reference. These factors serve as filters through which we view, interpret, and respond to our situations. For example, several people can witness the same incident, yet each perceives or explains the situation differently. Our actions and reactions to others reveal our frames of reference.

Your Frame of Reference Shows

Fundamentally, all social work activities, at any system level and in any field of practice, have a common core. Social work depends on interaction and communication with others. As social workers, we purposefully and spontaneously interact with clients. Within this interaction, our communication unavoidably and automatically reveals our frame of reference. Two facets of communication—its constancy and its influence on relationships—deserve careful attention when one is preparing for empowerment-based social work practice.

Communication Is Constant   Because assumptions influence outcomes, social workers should interact in ways that demonstrate positive expectations. They should communicate only messages that help clients accomplish their goals. This sounds simple enough, but the very nature of communication makes communicating productively a challenging task. As a matter of fact, "one cannot not communicate. Activity or inactivity, words, or silence all have message value" (Watzlawick et al., 1967, p. 42). Think about the implications of this simple concept. We are always communicating. In the way we look, the way we sit, the words we select, the information we choose to notice, and in countless other ways, we automatically send messages to one another.

Communication Defines Relationships   Messages are more than simple bits of information. Communication theorists believe that every communicated message has two sides: content and relationship. This means that a message both provides information and defines something about the relationship of the communicators. The relationship aspect of communication says, "This is how I see myself...this is how I see you...this is how I see you seeing me" (Watzlawick et al., 1967, p. 52).

Our values, culture, and patterns of thinking as well as our expectations of situations and others' expectations of us all contribute to our frames of reference.

Communicating in Empowering Ways   What social workers truly feel and sincerely believe about themselves and about clients emerges in social work interactions. Professionally constructed relationships are genuine relationships in which the values, beliefs, and opinions of social workers and clients show through. Empowering communication emphasizes the use of language and the influence of context in giving meaning to one's experiences and in defining one's place and value in those experiences. Language and context define self and social identity, assign social location, and channel individual access to resources. As such, there is power in both language and context. Power is evident in such examples as word usage, intonation, labels, nonverbal signals, body posturing, and the use of space.

The contextual power underlying discourse includes social structures, hierarchical relationships, economic privilege, ascribed social roles, dominant ideologies, and social institutions and the ways these dimensions have been socially constructed (Fairclough as cited in Webb, 2000). Sexism, racism, heterosexism, ageism, and ableism frame communication in ways that disadvantage vulnerable groups. If a worker's implicit or explicit messages reflect little confidence in a client or judgments about a client's culture, these messages undermine empowerment and countermand goals for promoting competence. Conversely, to the extent that social workers implicitly and explicitly relay messages of confidence, acceptance, and respect for diversity, their communication empowers.

Use of Self in Social Work

A repertoire of intervention techniques without positive personal qualities makes us merely technicians, not social workers, featuring the "science" of worker in our title rather than emphasizing the "art" of the social. Bringing one's self into relationships with clients is central to the art of social work. The **conscious use of self** as an expression of one's personal and practice style differentiates the work of one practitioner from another. Personal styles of practitioners are resources for working with clients. Reflective social workers inventory their personal values and resources as a way of preparing to work with clients. The conscious use of self requires **self-awareness** for practitioners to maintain professional boundaries in their work to benefit others.

Increasing Self-Awareness

Because so much of our personhood finds its way into practice, self-awareness is an essential quality for every social work practitioner.

Because so much of our personhood finds its way into practice, self-awareness is an essential quality for every social work practitioner. To prepare for practice, we identify and accept our own strengths and areas for growth. To heighten our self-awareness, we examine a broad range of personal characteristics, such as our lifestyle, moral codes, values, family roots, manner of meeting personal needs, attitude toward change, response to various life circumstances, and the personal biases and the stereotypes we hold (Johnson & Yanca, 2010). In addition, understanding our own cultural history and identity is a prerequisite for culturally sensitive social work. As practicing professionals, social workers refine their self-awareness through feedback from supervision, reviews by peers, team consultations, interactions with clients, and educational opportunities.

The Benefits of Self-Awareness

Our knowledge of "self" allows us to discern our inner core, our needs, thoughts, commitments, and values and, at the same time, to observe ourselves. Social workers learn to know themselves—their personal stories that reveal their attitudes, values, and beliefs—and step back and observe themselves to use themselves most effectively in the helping process. Social workers "always return to the need to be self-aware and self-knowing, for authentic dialogue with and true understanding of our clients, as well as for effective helping" (Siporin, 1985, p. 214).

When social workers are aware of their own perspectives, thoughts, and aspirations, they carry a supportive base of personal resources into each new relationship with a client. They acknowledge their own needs and actively pursue their own goals in their personal lives. In this way, social workers are able to enter and endure professional relationships in which their own needs are contained to work to benefit others.

Values and Principles in Action: A Practice Example

Personal qualities develop over a lifetime of relating, communicating, and reflecting. Expanding self-awareness of personal qualities blends with professional values, knowledge, and skills as social workers prepare to interact with clients. In the example that follows, consider how Paul Quillin reflects on his own readiness as he anticipates his work with a new client system. Follow Paul's thinking as he applies the professional practice principles of acceptance, individualization, nonjudgmentalism, objectivity, and self-determination while still maintaining his own personal values. Notice how he uses his self-awareness as a tool for empathy and as a way to build positive expectations about his clients.

Paul Quillin is one of several social workers at Northside Family Services (NFS) who gather weekly to share ideas and strategize new ways to deliver agency programs and services. The discussion at the last team meeting revealed that several gay and lesbian clients had expressed common concerns about parenting issues. In some ways, their issues include the usual parenting challenges; however, for these parents, the usual translates into complex realities made more difficult by the societal context of prejudice and discrimination. The workers concur that they have no easy answers for gays and lesbians in a homophobic society.

Brainstorming possible strategies, the workers report many examples of their clients' assertive, creative, and effective responses to the difficult situations. It seems only logical that these clients might benefit from the mutual support that group meetings could offer. When the social workers subsequently poll potential group members to determine their interest in a support group, they receive an enthusiastic, affirmative response. This sets the stage for Paul's work with the new support group for gay and lesbian parents.

Using Self-Awareness

As Paul reads through the referrals, he anticipates who the group's members might be and what he himself has to offer. Paul reflects on what he knows about people who are gay or lesbian. Narrow definitions of homosexuality lead to limited descriptions of sexuality. Understood more broadly in the context of social oppression, being gay or lesbian has dramatic implications. Paul realizes that each prospective group member is likely to experience the stress, anxiety, and fear that often accompany people's awareness that their sexual orientation evokes unpredictable responses from others. These responses range from acceptance to ignorance and misunderstanding, to imposing labels of pathology, to antagonistic acts of rejection, ridicule, and violence.

Paul's own identity as gay allows him to empathize with the struggles that are likely to characterize the life experiences of the support group members. Paul recognizes the strengths that he develops as he accepts and asserts his identity in the face of discrimination. Paul recounts that his own process of coming out increased his self-awareness, respect for human diversity, and ability to assert himself even when others disagree with his point of view. Although Paul knows that his own personal experiences will be helpful in his work with the support group, he tempers his thinking with the realization that his life doesn't actually match the lives of others. Similar sexual orientations do not mean that Paul and the support group members are all similar. Paul fully expects that group members have developed many distinctive personal strengths as a result of confronting the array of challenges in their own lives.

Respecting What Clients Bring

Consider the diverse array of resources that clients can offer to each other as the support group convenes. Members of the group will include Rita and Stephanie, who have been partners for 10 years. They met in graduate school when they were members of a lesbian activist group. They remain politically active. Both women have supportive extended families and friends. Rita's two children (Thomas, who is 11, and Ursala, who is 13) have always regarded Stephanie as a parent. They have grown up accepting their parents' lifestyle but now find themselves in uncomfortable struggles with their friends about their family. Previously, both parents had assertively intervened when the children reported incidents of discrimination against them. But lately, Ursala resists their assistance and keeps to herself. Both parents would like to reinitiate the support that was previously accepted by their daughter.

Ethical and Professional Behavior

Behavior: Use reflection and self-regulation to manage personal values and maintain professionalism in practice situations

Critical Thinking Question: Self-awareness is essential for practitioners to maintain professional boundaries and work to benefit others. How can overidentifying with the client's issues affect the professional relationship?

Vince has been a single parent to 8-year-old William since his wife abandoned the family shortly after William was born. Vince is quite accomplished as a single parent, balancing his job as an attorney with an active social life and responsible parenting. He has received much support and assistance from his family and friends in the care of his son. Currently, Vince is considering moving in with Andrew, with whom he has been in a committed relationship for 2 years. Although he is comfortable with this move for himself, he wonders about its effect on William. The three of them have fun together, but William isn't sure where Andrew fits into his dad's life. Vince wants to maintain an atmosphere of openness and honesty with his son but doesn't know what and how much to say. Vince is apprehensive about how to explain his decision to William, wonders about how to include Andrew in their daily family life, and is uncertain about the reactions of other family members and friends.

Barb teaches language arts and coordinates the reading program at the local middle school. Her divorce was a difficult one, finalized just a little more than a year ago after an extensive battle for custody of 6-year-old Carissa. Barb has gradually come to understand and accept her sexual orientation. At this time, she is open with only a few close friends. She has expressed many concerns about the consequences of others finding out that she is a lesbian. She worries about questions such as What about the custody of her daughter? Could her ex-husband use this against her? What about her her job?. The school district's policies are unclear about protection for employees, and her experiences with some of the parents make her cringe when she thinks about them finding out about her sexuality. Barb is looking forward to discussing these issues with other group members, but she is cautious with concerns about privacy and confidentiality.

Each person offers considerable resources that may be useful to the group and its members. Rita and Stephanie have successfully negotiated a working relationship as partners and parents. Vince may benefit from learning about their experiences. As an attorney, Vince has relevant knowledge for Barb. He may be able to inform her about the risks involved in coming out and the implications for her custody of Carissa and her employment as a teacher. Rita and Stephanie's openness about their sexuality may offer an experiential model for the transitions happening in Barb's life. Even Barb herself, although tentative in her decision to come out, clearly has important resources for the other group members. She brings a firsthand view of adolescence from her training and years of experience as a middle school teacher. Barb's insight into teenagers and their relationships may enlighten Rita and Stephanie as they struggle to cope with the changes in their parenting of 13-year-old Ursala. This list of potential resources is only a beginning. As the support group works together, its members will reveal again and again that they possess distinctive knowledge that is a reservoir of resources on which they can draw.

How Values Influence Practice

Paul's consideration of the support group members offers only general help in anticipating the exact value system that each new group member will bring. Being parents and gay or lesbian does not prescribe common beliefs or values. Differences within a group are often as striking as differences between groups. For example, members will likely have differing views on whether asserting one's identity as gay or lesbian is a personal or political matter. Each probably maintains different views on parenting, what is important for children to know, and how involved parents should be in their children's lives. Regardless of their particular beliefs, each has valid perceptions to support the way that he or she feels.

When the group convenes, Paul Quillin will consciously avoid imposing his own values on the group. Instead, he will identify and validate the value perspectives held by group members and encourage members to assert their unique views. Paul will

PHILIP DATE / SHUTTERSTOCK

help group members sort through and accept value differences as they form relationships, describe their perspectives, and develop solutions to their challenges.

Social workers support each other in increasing their self-awareness and multicultural competence.

Forming Relationships

Values influence the formation of professional relationships. Values often bond social workers with client systems when their respective value systems are similar. However, differing values may distinguish social workers from client systems. Differences test a worker's ability to demonstrate acceptance and affirm client self-determination. If Paul imposes his own values on the group, members will likely withdraw and fail to invest their resources in the group's efforts.

Also consider the interaction within the support group. Similar values among members will probably lead to cohesion, mutual respect, and congruent goals. Discrepant values among members may lead to disagreements and stalemates unless members can develop an atmosphere of acceptance and curiosity in which they question and enhance their own belief systems by incorporating the perspectives of other group members. The existing values of the support group members will intermingle to create group norms, which ultimately affect the behavior of each group member.

Viewing Situations

The way clients view their situations reveals their long-standing, deeply held beliefs and values. Often, the issues at hand are value laden and charged ethical dilemmas (Goldstein, 1987; Siporin, 1983, 1985). Frequently signaled by the word "should"—"What *should* I do?"—or denoted as a quandary about determining the right answer, these moral dilemmas are fraught with inner turmoil, intrapersonal conflict, and, sometimes, labels of immorality (Goldstein). Consider the support group members. Rita and Stephanie question how they *should* parent Thomas and Ursala. Vince is trying to decide how he *should* incorporate his partner Andrew into his family life. Barb is grappling with whether she *should* be open about her sexual identity. These issues all raise questions that have value issues at their core. Clients respond to challenges and solutions within the context of their values and beliefs.

Screening Possible Solutions

Clients screen options for change through the values they hold. What may be a viable solution for one may conflict with the values of another. Clients most readily apply change strategies that are congruent with their existing belief systems. An ethical social worker suggests options that are a good fit with clients' values or, as an alternative, guides clients to reconsider their value systems and broaden the range of acceptable solutions.

Values can change when people are exposed to different views. The dissonance that new information and perspectives creates can alter beliefs and lead to behavioral changes. For example, a father's newly acquired understanding of sexual orientation may change his perspective on whether he should welcome his gay son's life partner as a member of the family. Whatever beliefs currently guide a client system's behavior, perceptive social workers recognize that these beliefs inform a client's perspective, prescribe the dimensions of possible solutions, and influence the social worker–client relationship.

Values and Diversity

> **?** Assess your understanding of the influence of personal values and resources on practice by taking this brief quiz.

Values are not random; they develop over a lifetime. Each of us demonstrates values molded by family, friends, ethnic group, cohort group, neighborhood, region, and a host of other cultural influences. Recognizing and accepting a client's values requires social workers to be informed about human diversity.

MULTICULTURAL COMPETENCE

Social work values and principles are essential to working successfully with diverse clients, but good values alone are not sufficient for **multicultural social work** practice. Without ongoing efforts to develop capabilities in cross-cultural practice, even accepting, well-intentioned, and professionally principled practitioners make significant errors in relating to diverse clients. Putting social work values into practice requires knowledge of the dynamics of diversity and skills for working with diverse populations.

"Culture is the lens through which all things are viewed, and to a great extent culture determines not only how but what is viewed and how it is interpreted" (Briggs et al., 2005, p. 95). In essence, culture plays a pivotal role. It determines how clients "express and report their concerns, how they seek help, what they develop in terms of coping styles and social supports, and the degree to which they attach stigma" to their issues (Huang, 2002, p. 4). "Culturally different behaviors are not equivalent to social-skill deficits or behavior disorders" (Cartledge et al., 2002, p. 117). Coming from different worlds can lead to misunderstandings and leave workers and clients feeling alienated from one another—the antithesis of collaborative partnerships that characterize empowerment-oriented social work. Although both workers and clients experience difficulties in cross-cultural relationships, adjusting to those cultural differences is the responsibility of social work practitioners.

Diversity and Difference in Practice

Behavior: Apply self-awareness and self-regulation to manage the influence of personal biases and values in working with diverse clients and constituencies

Critical Thinking Question: The responsibility to resolve difficulties in cross-cultural relationships rests with social workers, not clients. How do social workers develop into competent multicultural practitioners?

Cultural Diversity and Social Work Practice

Cultural diversity, in its broadest sense, describes the phenomena of human differences as generated by membership in various identifiable human groups. Practice respecting client diversity requires a social worker to understand the complexity of cultural identity. Cultural identity is multidimensional, arising from the intersection of simultaneous memberships in various cohort groups including age, gender, gender identity, race, ethnicity, sexual orientation, ability, religion, socioeconomic status, and political persuasion.

Sometimes, social workers apply the term "diversity" more specifically to emphasize differences in race or ethnicity. As social constructed concepts, race refers to physical characteristics, with special attention to skin color and facial features, whereas ethnic group members share common cultural attributes such as language, ancestry, or religion. In a society that categorizes, segregates, and discriminates based on race and ethnicity, these differences may be especially difficult for social workers and clients to bridge.

None of us, regardless of our primary cultural identity, is monocultural. Our own **cultural uniqueness** derives from the intersections of memberships in multiple cultures such as cultures associated with gender, occupations, clubs and organizations, geographic regions, ethnicity, and religion, to name a few. Members of a group generally share some values or rules of behavior for participation and/or membership in that group. However, individual members of the same group also possess many qualities and behaviors that differentiate them from each other. If we consider the multitude of sociocultural variables affecting both workers and clients, we can unequivocally conclude that social work relationships are, in fact, multicultural.

> Watch this video and consider how Dr. Sue defines White privilege. What is the best advice for a social worker to heed about becoming culturally competent? www.youtube.com/watch?v=4sCvBIb6JP0

Considering cultural diversity and social work practice, Lee and Greene (1999), citing the works of others, distinguish between culturally competent and culturally sensitive approaches to multicultural practice. **Cultural competence** targets social workers' knowledge of development, focusing on culturally specific demographics, characteristics, values, and interventive techniques. In contrast, achieving **cultural sensitivity** is more value centered. Implementing a culturally sensitive approach requires a worker's genuine appreciation of the client's uniqueness and universalistic respect for the client's humanness. Expanding on the work of Lee and Green, a third possibility for success in multicultural practice is a skill-based approach we describe as **cultural responsiveness**. To be culturally responsive, social workers use dialogue skills that place the client's construction of reality at the center of the conversation. Clients take the role of cultural expert, leaving the worker as an inquisitive and respectful learner. A competent, sensitive, and responsive approach to multicultural practice is rooted in the knowledge, values, and skills of generalist social work; it is cultivated through years of experience interacting with those who are culturally different.

Cultural Competence

The NASW's (2001a) *Standards for Cultural Competence* indicate that cultural competence is the ability to engage in respectful and effective practice with diverse individuals, families, and communities, preserving their dignity and affirming their worth. This standard requires social workers to be aware of their own and their clients' cultural and environmental contexts, to value diversity, to continually refine skills that enhance the cultural strengths of others and draw on informal networks of support, and to advocate systems of service delivery that are culturally competent.

Identifying a client's strengths requires cultural competence; however, "cultural competence is never fully realized, achieved, or completed, but rather cultural competence is a lifelong process for social workers who will always encounter diverse clients and new situations in their practice" (NASW, 2001a, p. 11). Voluminous cultural knowledge is neither necessary nor sufficient to respond in a sensitive way to diverse clients. On the contrary, accepting one's own lack of understanding of socially, racially, and ethnically diverse groups and subsequently seeking knowledge directly from clients effectively positions workers to achieve cultural competence (Dean, 2001; Walker & Staton, 2000; Weick & Chamberlain, 2002). Culturally competent workers recognize strengths in the traditions, values, and beliefs from which cultural group members rely for shared identity, community belonging, and even survival. In short, cultural resources are strengths, and clients are the ultimate cultural experts on their own strengths—something to respect about clients.

Culturally competent workers recognize strengths in the traditions, values, and beliefs from which cultural group members rely for shared identity, community belonging, and even survival.

Cultural Sensitivity

Culturally sensitive practice shifts the emphasis from acquiring extensive knowledge about various cultural groups toward developing the worker's attitude of acceptance, respect, and appreciation for each client's cultural uniqueness. Practitioners who are culturally sensitive demonstrate social work values in action and display a willingness to learn about the cultural worlds of their clients. In maintaining an open and inquisitive style, workers become lifelong learners about human diversity, defining multicultural competence as a process of becoming rather than an achievement or end product (Castex, 1994; Green, 1999; Sue & Sue, 2013). Cultural sensitivity implies that social workers recognize that the multiple facets of clients' life experiences affect their values and priorities.

Cultural Responsiveness

A culturally responsive approach accentuates key practice skills as a method to achieve multicultural competence. Extensive knowledge about a client's culture is not the key. Rather, cultural responsiveness is the worker's abilities to frame the conversation without overriding the client's perspective. "The worker's expertise lies in applying the skills necessary to access the client's cultural expertise. The ability to elicit and accept client stories without imposing the worker's assumptions, biases, or interpretations is the starting point" (O'Melia, 1998).

? Assess your understanding of multicultural competence by taking this brief quiz.

A GENERALIST VIEW OF CULTURAL COMPETENCE

Social workers do not function in isolation; rather, they work in a professional context that includes colleagues, agencies, and the community in which they work. What happens in these contextual systems influences the capability of workers to practice in culturally sensitive ways. Cultural competence requires a systemic effort—the synchronization of values, knowledge, skills, and attitudes at the worker, agency, and service network levels—as well as the incorporation of these attributes

Box 3.1   Cultural Competence: A Research–Practice Connection

Culturally competent delivery of social services is essential to achieve the goals of the social work profession. Human differences rooted in gender, race, culture, ethnicity, age, sexual orientation, religion, varying abilities, and other dimensions demand that social workers transcend human differences in relating to diverse clients.

Contemporary research on multicultural competence reveals the difficulty of achieving cultural competence and shows that social workers and clients alike believe that workers fall short of realizing this goal. For example, in a survey of providers who serve Asian Americans with developmental disabilities and their families, 44 of the 112 workers who were surveyed reported significant barriers to delivering culturally appropriate services (Choi & Wynne, 2000). Obstacles included language differences resulting in communication difficulties, cultural variance in defining what it means to have a disability, and diverse expectations about the responsibilities of family members and social service providers. Another exploratory study of caregivers' perspectives on their workers' cultural competence provides mixed reviews (Walker & Cook, 2002). Although most respondents indicated that service providers had done fairly well in respecting clients' cultural values, nearly half of those respondents who were minorities described interactions with service providers as disrespectful. Their words echoed a need for service providers to be more aware of the realities of racism, oppression, and discrimination: "Don't say, 'Just put it behind you.' That does not validate the reality of what people of color experience with racial prejudice" (p. 36). Additionally, about 20 percent of respondents with low incomes reported instances in which they perceived a worker's disrespect, inferring it from such labels as lazy, loser, and trash.

Other studies provide guidance about the essential elements included in culturally effective practice. Based on a large-scale study of services in multiple Systems of Care sites, Gomez (2002) reports that respondents assessed workers' cultural competence based on perceptions of service providers' demeanor of caring and commitment: "Families judged the cultural competence of their providers in terms of the respect, honesty, trust, support, equality, acceptance, and mutual growth that their relationships engendered" (p. 13). Notably, those service providers judged less culturally competent had adopted a deficit view in their approach. Another study by Kulis and colleagues (2005) shows that program modifications to incorporate specific cultural elements have benefits. Their randomized control study evaluated the effectiveness of keepin' it REAL, a substance abuse prevention program that uses culturally grounded prevention strategies. Results indicate that "the Latino and multicultural versions of the intervention provided the clearest benefits to Mexican and Mexican American students" (p. 140).

Research also identifies areas for continued professional development. Based on her survey of Native American social workers and social work students, Weaver (1999) compiled results from many tribes to delineate key characteristics of cultural competence for working with First Nations people. Increased knowledge is necessary to recognize within-group diversity among Native Americans and to know both the history and contemporary realities of specific Native American clients. Weaver identifies developing patience for listening and tolerating silence as important skills, coupled with the expression of traditional social work values of respectfulness, nonjudgmentalism, and open-mindedness. Napoli (1999) expands this list, emphasizing trust, the role of spirituality, differing perceptions of time, variable meanings in communication, and the value of community over individuality as core components of culturally competent services for Native Americans.

The daunting need for cultural competence is transparent. Our success in meeting the need has been limited. Keeping informed of current research is one way in which social workers can develop their abilities to be culturally responsive and respectful in their practice with diverse populations.

The ability of workers to sort out differences among values and cultural dimensions begins with an intensive review and articulation of their own personal values and cultural heritage.

into practices, policies, services, institutions, and community functioning (Raheim, 2002). Multicultural social work practice begins at the worker's personal level and must be supported by both the agency and the community to sustain an ongoing and successful effort.

Practitioner-Level Cultural Competence

Workers themselves bear primary responsibility for developing competence in multicultural social work. Key elements of this practitioner level of competence include (1) self-awareness, both in terms of values and cultural background; (2) knowledge of other cultures coupled with the skill to adapt general knowledge to specific clients; and (3) the ability to identify and articulate the differentials of power and privilege that characterize intercultural relationships.

Becoming Self-Aware

To truly know others, you must first know yourself. The ability of workers to sort out differences among values and cultural dimensions begins with an intensive review and articulation of their own personal values and cultural heritage. Culturally competent social workers continuously refine their self-awareness. They acknowledge the ways in which their own biases influence their professional practice. Practitioners determine how similarities as well as differences between themselves and clients affect their perceptions and professional judgments. An extensive consideration of our own cultural identities is a requisite for developing a culturally competent repertoire of practices, including understanding your own ethnic identities and cultural memberships, spiritual beliefs and practices, knowledge of other cultural groups, and skills in cross-cultural relationships. Complete the cultural self-inventory in Figure 3.1 as a way to begin to envision the cultural lens through which you perceive the world and the clients with whom you will work.

Developing Awareness of Others

None of us enters any relationship without expectations about the cultures of those with whom we are about to relate. These presuppositions have many sources. Families, neighborhoods, the media, and history of experiences with others influence our knowledge about other cultures. Some of us have had extensive contact with people who are culturally different from ourselves, whereas others of us have been isolated in more secluded monocultural worlds. Whether diverse or narrow, our experiences leave us with preconceived notions, stereotypes, and prejudices that taint our views even when, as students of social work, we accumulate knowledge about others through academic preparation, volunteer work, and field experiences.

Identifying our views about others combined with acquiring more formal knowledge begins to build a more realistic understanding of cultural differences. The more we articulate and question our preconceived notions as we examine various cultures, the more we experience alternative ways of knowing, feeling, and behaving. However, no single practitioner can know all that is relevant to know about every cultural group. Instead, workers can initiate interactions with others in the community while systematically monitoring what they observe and how they react to their experiences.

Personal Identity
- What are your ethnic identities?
- Of which other cultural groups are you a member?
- Which cultural memberships are most influential in the way you define yourself?
- What characteristics or behaviors do you display that indicate the influences of these cultural identities?
- What values are associated with these cultural memberships?
- Do you feel positively or negatively about these identities?
- Have you ever experienced discrimination based on your cultural memberships?
- What privileges do your cultural memberships afford you?

Spiritual Beliefs
- What are your spiritual beliefs?
- What led you to these beliefs?
- How important are spiritual beliefs in your daily life?
- How do these beliefs influence the way you perceive others who hold different beliefs?
- How do your spiritual beliefs influence your choices and behaviors?

Knowledge of Others
- What other cultural groups are present in your community?
- What do you know about the beliefs, values, and customs of members of these other cultural groups?
- What is the source of this knowledge?
- Have your interactions with people from these cultures reinforced or altered this knowledge base?
- How do your cultural perspectives differ from those of your clients?
- What stereotypes or prejudices do you hold about other cultural groups?
- What is the source of your biases?
- What are you doing to increase your knowledge about people who are culturally different from you?

Cross-Cultural Skills
- Do you impose the dominant norm or honor the integrity of your clients' culture?
- Are you currently involved in relationships or activities in which you have ongoing interactions with people from other cultures?
- What is your comfort level while interacting with people who are culturally different from you?
- Are you able to talk with people who are culturally different from you about these differences?
- What languages do you speak other than your own primary language?
- What words, phrases, or nonverbal behaviors do you know that have different meanings in different cultures?

Figure 3.1
Cultural Self-Inventory

Recognizing Status and Privilege

Cultural group membership means more than differences of values, attitudes, and behaviors. Membership in some culture groups also confers differences in status and **privilege**. A socially and economically stratified society such as that of the United States does not afford all groups equal status. Many of us have the luxury of ignoring this fact.

To develop collaborative cross-cultural relationships, both workers and clients must neutralize the impact of the wider society related to whom society has granted greater status. For example, do you recognize the privileges or restrictions that society assigns you based on your own cultural identity? How might these privileges affect your practice with people from other cultures?

Certain cultural characteristics—such as race, gender, religion, and economic class—are weighted more heavily in determining social privilege and ranking societal status. Most Whites are oblivious to White privilege and the underlying racist ideologies inculturated in the institutional structures of society (McIntosh, 1998). Because those with privilege are often blind to both its existence and its effects, White privilege is particularly insidious.

Religion is often overlooked as a source of privilege; however, in the United States, those belonging to Christian religious groups are often rewarded with signs of status and power. Christian privilege is likely invisible to those who are Christian, virtually a nonconscious ideology. However, Christian privilege is transparent to those who profess a faith other than Christianity or no faith at all. People who are members of religious minority groups may feel that "their religious identity is not valued, and, subsequently, they feel discrimination and oppression because of their religious group membership" (Schlosser, 2003, p. 47).

History reveals a plethora of instances of gender-based privilege, including gender stereotyping, gender bias, and discrimination based on sex. "Hidden assumptions about sex and gender remain embedded in cultural discourses, social institutions, and individual psyches that invisibly and systematically reproduce male power in generation after generation" (Bem, 1993, p. 2). Bem calls the sexist assumptions of androcentrism (men are human, and women are "other"), gender polarization (men are masculine, and women are feminine), and biological essentialism (biological destiny) the lenses of gender. These lenses shape perceptions of social realities, embed themselves in social structures, and influence such day-to-day realities as unequal pay for equal work and inadequate social policies that support family life.

Sexism interacts with other types of oppression and exploitation such as racism, heterosexism, and classism. Women of color face the double jeopardy of racism and sexism. Lesbians must deal with the patriarchy inherent in sexism as well as in heterosexism and its corollary, homophobia. Classism multiplies the oppression and discrimination experienced by the expanding ranks of women who are poor.

Overcoming Microaggressions

Social workers need to recognize the insidious nature of **microaggressions**. Overt and covert microaggressions emanate from racism and other prejudices embedded in the structures and power differentials of society. We cannot live in a society in which isms are embedded in the fabric of society without reflecting those same prejudices in our own thoughts and communication patterns. In fact, common, everyday verbal and nonverbal communications may contain hidden messages that denigrate others whose status has already been marginalized by virtue of race, ethnicity, gender, sexual orientation, religion, disability, age, or class (Sue, 2010a, 2010b; Sue et al., 2007).

Types of microaggressions include microassaults, which are intentional assaults such as name-calling or discriminatory actions; microinsults, which include comments and behaviors that demean others; and microinvalidations, which are cues that devalue or exclude the feelings, beliefs, or capabilities of others. Exploring unintentional micro-aggressions, qualitative research conducted by Sue and colleagues (2008) reveals several themes, including assumptions about intellectual inferiority, second-class citizenship, criminal intent, inferiority, universality of experiences, and the superiority of White values and approaches to communication.

Among the consequences of microaggressions are emotional upheaval, sense of rejection and low self-esteem, disparities in opportunities, and ineffective communication. Although microassaults are intentional, microinsults and microinvalidations are typically delivered by unwitting individuals who are well-intentioned and unaware of the harmful consequences of their behavior. In fact, these individuals may erroneously believe they are totally unbiased or even "color-blind." If social workers will be effective communicators, they need to heighten their awareness of the presence of microaggressions and strive to communicate more respectfully.

Becoming a Competent Cross-Cultural Social Worker

In summary, learning to be competent in cross-cultural practice is an evolutionary process that begins with awareness and increases with each interaction with clients. Workers first attempt to understand their own cultural filters. Second, they build a knowledge base of other perspectives through literature reviews and field research. Third, workers analyze the impact of cultural identities on the power dynamics of the worker–client partnership. Finally, practitioners continue to fine-tune their cultural sensitivity through their ongoing practice experiences with unique client systems.

Agency-Level Cultural Competence

The agency setting is crucial in supporting workers' attempts to deliver culturally sensitive services. A culturally competent agency prepares its workers with the necessary training and skills for diversity-sensitive practice, and it promotes multicultural awareness and functioning in all aspects of its organizational structure and program delivery. Specifically, culturally competent agencies infuse multicultural influences into their policies, orientations to practice, structures, resource networks, and physical environments.

Evaluation

Behavior: Apply evaluation findings to improve practice effectiveness at the micro, mezzo, and macro levels

Critical Thinking Question: To improve practice effectiveness, agencies and other social service organizations need culturally responsive policies, practices, and services. How can agencies involve consumers in evaluating attempts to create culturally sensitive policies and deliver culturally competent services?

Agency Policies

Organizational policies guide an agency's operations, including hiring and training staff, evaluating program effectiveness, and defining criteria for eligibility for services. Reflected in these policies are cultural attitudes and assumptions. Agency policies may simply ignore diversity issues, adopting a dominant cultural perspective by omission, or these policies may reflect sensitivity to the cultural elements inherent in all human interaction.

Multiculturally sensitive administrators actively seek to employ a staff that reflects the cultural and social diversity of the community. This means hiring diverse staff at all levels of the agency, including administrative, supervisory, direct service, clerical, and maintenance personnel. Ideally, hiring policies and procedures ensure processes for actively recruiting culturally diverse staff members. Interviewers incorporate interview questions that evaluate the cultural sensitivity of prospective employees, and ongoing training provides opportunities for all agency personnel to develop the specific cultural knowledge and skills that are relevant to the community.

Eligibility guidelines can either enhance or restrict access to services. Culturally competent policies ensure the accessibility of services to all potential clients. Culturally sensitive agencies recognize the difficulty that many people, particularly those who have been historically disenfranchised, have in connecting to traditionally delivered social services. In response, an agency develops inclusive policies to promote access to diverse clients through the creative design of service delivery—such as locating services in various neighborhoods and offering concrete, pragmatic aid as part of its program (Lum, 2004).

Culturally aware agencies also structure their program evaluation methods for maximal participation by the consumers of their services. Evaluation procedures are most effective when they request input from clients through consumer satisfaction surveys, seek direct feedback from clients in other forums, and ask clients to provide specific information regarding their perceptions about the cultural sensitivity of the agency's practices.

Orientation Toward Practice

An agency's theoretical orientation affects the ways that workers view clients and their situations. In social constructionist terms, workers construct the world in which they interact with clients by selecting which theories and perspectives to apply. Not all of these choices are equal in terms of cultural sensitivity. For example, an agency that implements an intrapsychic approach may overlook the social etiology and ramifications of the clients' situations. Multicultural competence at the agency level means developing programs and services based on theories that place clients in cultural and social contexts. Competent agencies develop programs and procedures that focus on client strengths, use culturally sensitive assessment instruments, consider culture to be a resource, and make use of ethnically oriented indigenous helping networks (Miller & Gaston, 2003). Even when agencies serve clients primarily on the individual and family level, addressing macrolevel issues—including policy, social inequity, and the distribution of resources—is an essential ingredient of multiculturally sensitive practice.

Structures

The way in which an agency organizes itself, particularly in determining the roles that clients play and in ensuring direct linkages with local communities, affords opportunities to facilitate cultural competence. Involving diverse clients in all aspects of agency operations ensures synergistic multicultural interchanges in all aspects of agency functioning, operations, and governance.

The distribution of power within the agency is an important structural component. Traditional organizational paradigms maintain rigid vertical lines of authority, hierarchical structures that likely mirror the inequities of the larger society (Schriver, 2015). In contrast, a flatter organizational structure encourages the sharing of power through consensus-based decision making. It also enhances opportunities for mutual influence among management, direct service, and support staff. When the agency's organizational structure allows workers to have greater control over their practice, workers, in turn, are more likely to respond similarly with their clients, encouraging them to participate more fully in planning, evaluating, and developing services. When clients have a greater influence on services, agencies meet clients' needs more consistently, regardless of the variations in culture they represent.

Physical Environment

The culturally competent agency is accessible in every way. This means that it is physically accessible to persons with disabilities. It is verbally accessible to those who speak languages other than English. It also is conveniently located in neighborhoods where clients live, has offices on major public transit routes, offers clients transportation, or provides outreach services.

Even the ways that an agency decorates and furnishes its offices and promotes its programs affect whether clients will perceive the agency as culturally open or as an agent of majority control. See Figure 3.2 for a list of questions to evaluate the degree of an agency's cultural competence. These expressions of an agency's perspective can be critical to helping clients feel comfortable, or they can edge clients toward a more guarded mode of interaction.

Resource Networks

All social work organizations connect to a network of services, both to refer clients to services and to receive referrals from other agencies. For an agency to be considered culturally competent, this continuum also includes all of the indigenous resources for solving problems. Examples of indigenous resources include churches, schools, clubs, local healers, neighborhood leaders, and culturally oriented media.

Culturally responsive agencies are also active participants in their larger environments (Chow & Austin, 2008). Agencies need to connect with legislative bodies to

---

- Can persons with disabilities readily access the agency? Consider those with difficulties in walking, hearing, and seeing as well as those with intellectual and emotional challenges.
- Does the agency display artwork that is culturally diverse?
- Is the reading material available in waiting areas of interest to a variety of cultural groups?
- Do story books, games, dolls, and other toys appeal to both boys and girls as well as children from various cultural backgrounds?
- Are brochures and orienting information multilingual and do they contain pictures which reflect the diversity of the agency's clients? Are forms and brochures available in large print format?
- Are agency materials nonracist, nonsexist, and nonheterosexist?
- Do agency materials define concepts inclusively? For example, does its literature on family life define family to include blended families, extended families, and families with same-sex parents?
- Does the agency staff represent diverse cultural groups?

Figure 3.2
Cultural Inventory for Agencies

advocate clients' rights and social justice reforms. Agencies should also work to build coalitions with other community groups and organizations working toward social change.

Community-Level Cultural Competence

Both workers and clients respond to the same community context. In some ways, each cross-cultural practice relationship is a microcosm of the status of similar relationships in the community. A community that discriminates in housing, segregates its schools, and maintains separateness in cultural events fixes distinct boundaries between cultural groups—a chasm that workers and clients must bridge to form working partnerships.

A community that values pluralism, celebrates its diversity, promotes cross-cultural interactions, and works toward social justice facilitates the work of social workers and clients. Even practitioners working at the individual and family level can, in generalist fashion, play an activist role in the community-at-large to encourage cross-cultural interactions, awareness, and respect.

? Assess your understanding of a generalist view of cultural competence by taking this brief quiz.

LOOKING FORWARD

Professional practice principles, personal values, cultural attributes, individual beliefs, and expectations permeate the relationships of social workers and clients. The social worker–client relationship is potentially a complex web of personal–professional–relational transactions. Social workers must resolve conflicts between their personal values and professional obligations, between their cultural backgrounds and those of clients, between their own perspectives and their clients', and between the values of social work and those of society. Agency and community cultures also influence worker–client relationships.

Workers' expectations that develop from personal and professional preparation and their anticipation of what clients will bring to the process will influence the relationship. A positive view of clients, appreciation of cultural diversity, understanding of ethical principles, and heightened self-awareness prepare social workers to construct effective relationships with clients. These filters become increasingly important as practitioners engage clients in the social work processes explained in later chapters. These are not the only filters through which workers view clients and their situations. Chapter 4 discusses the strengths perspective and empowerment, which also orient a worker's views and approach to practice.

✓ Evaluate what you learned in this chapter by completing the Chapter Review.

4

Strengths and Empowerment

EDBOCKSTOCK/SHUTTERSTOCK

A good conference can be energizing, and this one, "Empowerment and the Strengths Perspective," is giving Mark Nogales a real boost. Mark's 8 years as an outreach worker in the Community Support Program of the County Mental Health Center sometimes leaves him in need of professional revitalization. Facilitating the community integrated living arrangements for persons with chronic mental illnesses has its challenges. But today's conference is crystallizing something for Mark that he has been sensing for some time now. People's lives get better when you focus on what they can do rather than on what they can't. Mark has learned that his clients, often identified more by their pathological labels and diagnoses than as the unique individuals that Mark knows them to be, bring considerable talents and skills to the challenges in their lives. Mark openly acknowledges and celebrates the diverse resources each client reveals. And now, this conference on the **strengths perspective** clearly says that the very process of activating client strengths is the quickest and most empowering path toward increasing client **competence**.

Mark's study of social work taught him to implement a process focused on solving problems. "Good social work practice," the words of his first social work professor still echo, "has a beginning, a middle, and an end." More specifically, Mark knew this professor was talking about a well-organized social work process that begins with a concrete definition of problems. Mark built his early practice by using this framework offered by experts in the field.

As a practicing social worker, Mark is learning from other experts in the field—his clients. These experts are teaching him to look beyond their presenting problems, to shift the attention of the work from solving problems per se to developing strengths and finding solutions. This gradual transition has been a natural evolution for Mark and his clients, a subtle—yet significant—shift in Mark's orientation toward practice.

Simply put, Mark sees the impossibility of trying to solve the problems of chronic mental illness, which are, by definition, unchangeable and lifelong. Besides, working closely with the people defined as his clients, Mark has discovered that the various labels of mental illness assigned to them hold little meaning to the relationships he forms with them. Each of his clients is unique. Mark's work with them reflects his awareness that diversity in approach is a natural response to a clientele so distinct in lifestyle, personality, and aspirations as to defy the deficiencies implied in the categories by which they are grouped.

The common message to Mark from his clients is consistent and clear. They respond in positive ways when Mark accepts their challenges and accentuates their talents. Mark is learning it. His clients are proving it. His practice experience is validating it. And now, at this conference, the "experts" in the social work field are promoting it. Practice processes that focus on client strengths rather than on deficits actualize **empowerment**.

Mark's orientation to strengths reveals his respect for his clients. He affirms their capacity and creativity to discover ways to manage their own challenges. When trying to accomplish something, it only makes sense to make use of all the resources available. Building on resources reflects the growing trend in social work to practice from a strengths perspective. When social workers incorporate the strengths perspective, their orientation simply represents a standard of excellence for empowerment-based social work practice.

Adopting an empowerment-based strengths perspective influences the ways that social workers view and involve clients in a change process. This chapter presents the strengths perspective and empowerment as the foundation for an empowering approach to generalist social work practice. Understanding the strengths perspective and empowerment prepares social workers to implement a social work practice approach that emphasizes clients' abilities and ensures their active **collaboration** in change processes.

STRENGTHS PERSPECTIVE

Client strengths are resources to use when working for change. The strengths perspective subscribes "to the notion that people have untapped, undetermined reservoirs of mental, physical, emotional, social, and spiritual abilities that can be expressed. The presence of this capacity for continued growth and heightened well-being means that people must be accorded the respect that this power deserves. This capacity acknowledges both the being and the becoming aspects of life" (Weick et al., 1989, p. 352).

Essentially, all people have a natural power within themselves that can be released (Weick & Chamberlain, 2002). When social workers support this inherent power, they enhance the probability for positive growth. People strive toward the development of their potential, mastery, and self-actualization. The strengths perspective is consonant with social work's fundamental values regarding human worth and social justice. A focus on strengths is essential to operationalizing social work's professional value base. By actualizing these fundamental values, social workers, in turn, heighten the strengths and capabilities of clients. Simply stated, applying a strengths perspective creates an atmosphere that accords client systems dignity and support and, combined with empowerment, directs actions that lead to a more just society.

Ethical and Professional Behavior

Behavior: Use reflection and self-regulation to manage personal values and maintain professionalism in practice situations

Critical Thinking Question: The strengths perspective assumes that every client has the capacity for growth and change. How can social workers reconcile the ethical conflict between the assumptions of the strengths perspective with their biases about clients who have a history of abusive behavior or other social deviances?

Practice Assumptions

Currently, the strengths perspective brings together principles and techniques that highlight the resources and promote the resourcefulness of clients (Saleebey, 2009). Strengths-oriented social workers believe that the strengths of all client systems—individual, familial, group, organizational, and societal—are resources to initiate, energize, and sustain change processes (see Figure 4.1). Workers draw on the resources available, both within client systems and in their environmental contexts, to promote more effective functioning.

Key Transitions

Words construct the meaning of our experiences. The particular words we use to describe social work, the metaphors we select to elaborate the process, and the labels we assign to categorize information are extremely significant. Words influence how we think, interpret situations, envision possibilities, and conduct day-to-day activities. The evolution of social work practice from "expert treatment" to a practice process that promotes strengths compels us to enrich our professional language to reflect these changes.

Social workers who subscribe to the strengths perspective:

- Acknowledge that clients have existing reservoirs of resources and competencies to draw upon
- Recognize that each client has a distinct capacity for growth and change
- Define problems as occurring within the transactions between systems rather than residing in deficient system functioning
- Hold that collaboration augments existing strengths to build new resources
- Affirm that clients know their situations best and, given options, can determine the best solutions for their challenges
- Maintain that positive change builds on a vision of future possibilities
- Support a process to magnify mastery and competence rather than correct deficits

---

Figure 4.1
Assumptions of a Strengths Perspective

One example of the paradigm shift is the movement toward asset-based assessments and planning. The asset-based approach shifts the focus away from identifying risk factors to promoting protective factors. This shift signals a move in thinking from problem-focused to strengths-based, from at-risk to resiliency, from individual to family and community context, from dependency to self-efficacy, and from alienation to connectedness (NASW, 2002). Social work that focuses on strengths and emphasizes collaboration transforms the way that professionals conceptualize their practice of social work. To apply the strengths perspective, practitioners need to reexamine their orientation to practice, their views of client systems, and their interpretation of the issues clients present. Practicing from a strengths perspective prompts social workers to examine two key transitions—the transitions from pathology to strengths and from a preoccupation with the past to an orientation toward the future.

Pathology or Strength?

When social workers orient their view of clients toward strengths, they question the centrality of focusing on pathology.

Social workers who focus on strengths do not ignore the difficulties that clients bring. The point is not whether problems are part of the helping process; they are. When social workers orient their view of clients toward strengths, they question the centrality of focusing on pathology. Narrowly focusing on problems and pathology blocks the ability to uncover strengths. Negative frames of reference obscure the unique capabilities of client systems. For example, the problem of "a half glass of water" is that the glass is half empty. If we fail to recognize that the glass is half full, we may go thirsty because of our oversight.

Good reasons exist for social work's long-standing focus on pathology. After World War I, the social work profession ushered in an era of practice based primarily on the psychoanalytic perspective and the medical model. This approach, replete with its own language set, served the profession well. Widely accepted, the model helped social work achieve professional status, gain society's sanction by providing psychiatric services to veterans and their families, and establish a definitive theoretical and technical base for practice. As its title implies, the medical model adopts the medical practice of predicating any prescriptive treatment on a diagnosis. Transposed to the arena of social work, the medical model views presenting problems as "pathologies" that require "diagnosis" by a social work "expert" to recommend and carry out the proper course of "treatment." Although helpful as an organizing framework for practice, the medical model falls short of acknowledging the reciprocal nature of human interaction in environmental context. Instead, the medical model presumes individual fault, failure, personal inadequacy, and deficiency.

Diagnosing "pathology" does more than obscure people's strengths. It creates labels that conveniently describe the presenting "pathological" behaviors. This may prompt social workers to move from the construct of a "person with a pathology" to the stigmatizing conceptualization of a "pathological person." Clients whose behavior society judges immoral—those involved in child abuse, domestic violence, incest, or other criminal acts—are themselves labeled immoral (Goldstein, 1987). Clients who have been victimized, and thus called victims, begin to take on the diminished, impotent persona of the victim role. When careless social workers belittle their clients by evoking labels such as welfare cases, those people, the handicapped, or run-down communities, even their images of clients become depersonalized and dehumanized.

Maligning clients with unfavorable and impersonal labels generates images of stagnation with no potential for regeneration, renewal, or change. The labels social workers use influence their sense of a client's worth and even shape their ideas about what course of action to take. Labeling has the potential to stereotype people and communities and to temper practitioners' inclinations toward **social action** (Breton, 2002). Pathological labels establish negative expectations that diminish the chances for positive change. Collectively, pejorative labels and stereotypes assign categorical meanings, block visions of potential, and constrict plans for service delivery and social policy. When social work practitioners shift their orientations to strengths, they escape the many pitfalls of focusing on pathology.

Past or Future?

The shift in perspective from problems to challenges also refocuses our view from a look at the past to an eye on the future. An intervention process based on the medical model searches the past to detect when, why, and how client systems went wrong. In contrast, strengths-oriented social workers explore the present to discover the resources that clients currently have that they can use to take charge of the future. Take careful note of this shift—*from the past to the future*. This change from *what was* to *what can* and *will be* reorients our thinking about the entire process of social work practice.

Life doesn't stand still. No matter how stuck we may feel, we have little choice but to go on, as life continues to present its challenges and possibilities. Clients have all gone on and are continuing on despite previous events that may have stretched their capabilities. The ecosystems perspective describes the ongoing evolution of human systems as they adapt to difficult circumstances in productive ways or even as they cope in ways that further complicate their situations. Regardless of its positive or negative direction, change is always occurring. When clients and social workers begin their work together, they can only influence the current situation and the direction of future evolution; they cannot alter past events. What's done is done. What's yet to come is still in question.

None of us can stop the clock or reverse time to rewrite an episode in our past. Our lives just keep happening. If we become mired in looking backward, we are likely to be blindsided to presently occurring events. As an alternative, if we face toward the future, we have opportunities to review what we currently know, apply skills we have developed, and determine what additional resources are available to meet upcoming challenges. No rules say that all past problems must be uncovered and resolved or all deficits erased to move forward. Focus instead on an approach that permits forging ahead to a more promising future in which past difficulties fade in the light of success.

Applying a Strengths Perspective

To apply a strengths perspective, practitioners need a clear understanding of how to focus on the present and to incorporate a vision of the future. Consider the example of how Olivia Adams builds on her present strengths to construct a workable future.

Olivia, a 24-year-old client of Mark Nogales, resides in a supportive living arrangement and attends a work activity program sponsored by the County Mental Health Center where Mark is employed. Olivia presents herself

Watch this video that illustrates how empowerment-oriented social workers build on clients' strengths. What elements of the strengths perspective are evident in this video? https://www.youtube.com /watch?v=Q6W5IrZH7tc&list =PLV96Vr0WaovR5MX_RU7_ Z1aKjpG5Lry-9 as withdrawn and socially awkward and seldom interacts with others at the center. Although she is very capable of performing her assigned tasks, she isolates herself. Mark could dwell on the etiology of Olivia's timorous behavior, but instead he uses a forward-looking perspective that considers what is, not what was.

Mark believes that the unique way that Olivia copes is a potential resource for directing the future. In withdrawing from social situations, Olivia shifts her attention away from others toward solitary activities. Olivia is gifted with incredible memory skills, especially remembering dates. Fascinated with holidays and celebrations, she can easily recite dates for every U.S., Mexican, and Canadian holiday and religious observance. Her interest also extends to significant dates in the lives of persons with whom she is acquainted. Olivia recalls birthdays and wedding anniversaries of everyone in her extended family. She reminds Mark on a weekly basis of the upcoming birthdays of clients and staff associated with the work activity program. Mark recognizes this significant strength in Olivia.

One of Olivia's goals is to develop her social support network. As a first step, Mark and Olivia plan a way to increase Olivia's contacts with friends at the center by building on Olivia's unique capacity for remembering dates. The work activity program has a policy of granting paid leave for both clients and staff on their birthdays. Olivia's new job will be to acknowledge each individual's birthday by personally delivering the agency's birthday greeting and the letter granting paid leave. One can easily imagine the positive exchange that accompanies this interaction. As Olivia uses her talents productively, she becomes more confident in interpersonal relationships and develops friendships through her contacts with co-workers.

In viewing client systems as resourceful, social work practitioners demonstrate their respect for what clients have to offer. Mark Nogales discovers and activates the strengths present in his clients' current situations and in their previous adaptations to life events. Mark and his clients draw on these strengths as well as the resources available in the community network to achieve their goals. This orientation toward client strengths and environmental resources is an essential backdrop for implementing practice processes that empower change.

> **?** Assess your understanding of the strengths perspective by taking this brief quiz.

EMPOWERMENT

Social work pioneers in the settlement house movement planted the seeds of empowerment. However, the problem-focused, medical genre of social casework practice overshadowed empowerment as a practice process in the decades after World War I. Today, the integration of empowerment into practice mandates social workers to move beyond diagnosing deficits toward emphasizing strengths and to create solutions that incorporate elements of social action.

By definition, empowerment is both a complex concept and a multisystem process that has personal, interpersonal, and sociopolitical implications (Parsons, 2008; Parsons & East, 2013; Swift & Levin, 1987). On a *personal level*, empowerment refers to a subjective state of mind, feeling competent and experiencing a sense of control; on an *interpersonal level*, empowerment refers to a sense of interdependence, support, and respected status; on a *sociopolitical level*, it refers to the objective reality of opportunities in societal structures and the reallocation of **power** through a modification of social structures. Empowerment is also a process of becoming, whereby individuals, families, organizations, communities, and societies increase their personal, interpersonal, and/or political power to realize improvements in their situations. Easily identified when not present in "powerlessness, real or imagined, learned helplessness, alienation, loss of a sense of control over one's life, [empowerment] is more difficult to define positively only because it takes on a different form in different people and contexts" (Rappaport, 1985, p. 16).

 Watch this video and listen to the social workers' stories about their work. What characteristics of empowerment-based practice do they describe?
www.youtube.com/
watch?v=M3hzv4z3aHQ

Personal Dimensions of Empowerment

Personal empowerment embodies our own sense of competence, mastery, strength, and ability to effect change. Essentially, people who experience personal power perceive themselves as competent. Competence is the ability of any human system to fulfill its function of taking care of itself, to draw resources from effective interaction with other systems, and to contribute to the resource pool of the social and physical environment.

A Transactional View of Competence

On the surface, words used to describe human competence, such as efficacy, mastery, and accomplishment, seem like self-appraisals. Without looking beyond individuals, we are left wondering, "Effective in what way?" "Mastery over what?" or "Accomplished in what endeavor?" Rather than being individually derived, feelings of competence arise from the goodness of fit between systems and their environments. In contrast, a sense of helplessness, ineffectiveness, or inadequacy results from the lack of fit between systems and their social and physical environments. It is not the system alone; rather, it is the system in the context of the environment that defines the competence.

From a transactional view, personal empowerment and, therefore, competence result from the interplay between a system's assets and needs and the environment's resources and demands. A sense of power results from a good fit between a system and its environment. A transactional view of human competence highlights the interdependence of individual, interpersonal, and environmental factors in competent system functioning.

Personal Competence in a Political Context

A transactional understanding of competence prompts social workers to design and implement empowerment-oriented strategies that deal with both internal and contextual barriers. However, competence is a necessary but not sufficient condition for empowerment: "When personal competence is isolated from the interpersonal, social and structural contexts in which it manifests, and when individual rights are not coupled with responsibilities towards others' rights, the outcome can be nefarious as often as it can be benign" (Breton, 1993, p. 31). Personal competence coupled with personal responsibility is not enough. Empowerment requires access to societal resources.

Human Rights and Justice

Behavior: Engage in practices that advance social, economic, and environmental justice

Critical Thinking Question: Feelings of competence derive from a goodness of fit between individuals and their social environments. What role does protecting human rights and promoting social, economic, and environmental justice play in achieving this goodness of fit for clients' well-being across the life span?

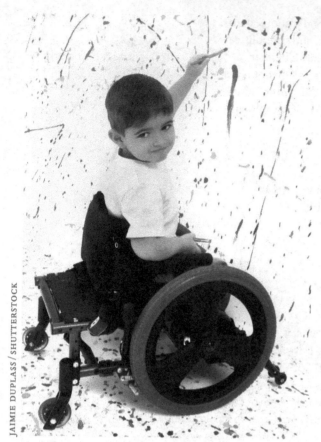

JAIMIE DUPLASS/SHUTTERSTOCK

Participating in recreational activities is a source of personal and interpersonal empowerment for all children.

Interpersonal Dimensions of Empowerment

Although we may experience empowerment as a feeling within, it emerges from our interactions with others. **Interpersonal empowerment** refers to our ability to influence others. Our successful interaction with others and the regard others hold for us contribute to our sense of interpersonal empowerment.

The social power of positions, roles, communication skills, knowledge, and appearance contribute to a person's feelings of interpersonal empowerment (Gutiérrez, 1991). Therefore, interpersonal power comes from two sources. The first source is power based on social status—for example, power based on race, gender, and class. The second is power achieved through learning new skills and securing new positions, key features of empowerment. Both reshaping the societal ascription of power and enhancing personal skills expand our experience of interpersonal power.

Sociopolitical Dimensions of Empowerment

Sociopolitical empowerment involves our relationships with social and political structures. When, as a result of interactions with environments, people increase their access to and control of resources, they experience empowerment (Leonardsen, 2007). This focus of empowerment at the structural level increases access to resources and opportunities, develops individual strengths, and accentuates interpersonal competence.

All human systems require an ongoing, expansive set of resource options to keep pace with constantly changing conditions. The more options available, the more likely systems can master their challenges. The fewer the options, the greater the vulnerability of systems. Competent social systems contribute to the effective functioning of their members and likewise function as opportunity structures for other systems in their environments.

Blocks to Sociopolitical Power

Power blocks at three levels deny access to opportunities and thereby undermine competent functioning (Solomon, 1976, 1987). First, power blocks deny accessibility to needed resources. For example, inadequate health care is a barrier to good health. A second power block barricades sources for learning technical and interpersonal skills; people fail to qualify for jobs or promotions as a consequence of inadequate educational opportunities. The third power block denies valued social roles. For example, with respect to employment practices, discrimination can impede the abilities of parents to support their children. Powerlessness usurps a system's energy and blocks access to a sufficient mix of personal, interpersonal, and contextual strengths, resources, and support to achieve empowerment.

To expect individuals to seek a higher "empowered state" without considering whether they have a minimal level of resources needed even to exercise choice mocks empowerment. However, even having access to resources is insufficient for empowerment, as people also need opportunities to contribute to their communities as respected citizens to experience empowerment fully (Breton, 1993). People are more likely to overcome barriers to power by making structural changes in political and social institutions than by changing themselves (Solomon, 1976). Achieving structural changes creates new opportunities to redistribute resources equitably and to give and take within a competent society.

> *To expect individuals to seek a higher "empowered state" without considering whether they have a minimal level of resources needed even to exercise choice mocks empowerment.*

Power

Having power means having access to information, choosing actions from many possibilities, and acting on one's choices. Power is the ability to obtain the resources one needs to influence others and to effect changes in how resources are distributed in such systems as families, organizations, or communities. Power is a dynamic inherent in all social interaction. The personal, interpersonal, and sociopolitical dimensions of power intertwine. The experience of power within one realm contributes resources for accessing power in another. Additionally, sharing power in relationships is generative; it unleashes the strengths and resources of participants and builds on and creates new energy and information through synergistic interaction.

Powerlessness

Like power, **powerlessness** is multidimensional. Personal, interpersonal, social, and political factors all contribute to the pervasive **oppression** of disenfranchised population groups, individually or in communities. Blocks to power at one level can impede access to power at another. Power imbalances deplete individual and relationship resources. In situations of oppression and domination, more powerful groups in society control access to power and opportunities, suppress beliefs of less powerful people about their capacity, and deny those oppressed their rights to exercise power, thereby wasting essential human potential to contribute to community.

Experiences of powerlessness generate a sense of self-blame, distrust, alienation, vulnerability, and disenfranchisement (Kieffer, 1984). However, hope exists. Someone who feels powerless is not empty of resources. Although feelings of powerlessness have muffled competencies, the advent of niches and opportunities gives rise to their appearance (Rappaport, 1981). Empowerment practice recovers this potential, emphasizing the critical use of power to achieve social rights and social justice, promote human well-being, and create a humane society.

Oppression

Powerlessness and oppression go hand in hand. As a structural source of powerlessness, oppression involves economic, social, and psychological exploitation of others—individuals, groups, social classes, religious groups, and nation-states (Hodge, 2007). Oppression results in injustice or "the consequences of domination and exploitation: multidimensional inequalities and development-inhibiting, discriminatory, and dehumanizing conditions of living" (Gil, 2002, p. 36). Such conditions include poverty,

Oppression may be the single most disabling social force affecting social work clients.

unemployment, inequitable access to housing, health care, and education. By imposing categorical judgments, dominant groups in society classify other groups as less worthy, affording them little prestige, few possibilities, and limited resources. Racism, classism, ableism, heterosexism, regionalism, sexism, ethnocentrism, and ageism are all interrelated expressions of oppression, exploitation, social exclusion, and injustice (Table 4.1). As a consequence of oppression, social exclusion severely damages individuals' aspirations and abilities (Ward, 2009; Washington & Paylor, 2000). In sum, oppression is the injustice that results from the domination and control of resources and opportunities that entitles favored groups and disenfranchises and excludes others. Oppression may be the single most disabling social force affecting social work clients.

Victim Blaming

Victim blaming compounds the insidious experience of oppression. According to Ryan (1976), in his book *Blaming the Victim*, victim blaming occurs in two different ways. One way labels victims as inferior, genetically defective, or unfit. The other casts blame for inferiority on environmental circumstances. Victim blaming casts aspersions on society's victim rather than holding society itself accountable for the social problem. Paradoxically, the victim then becomes the target of change, with "humanitarian" programs created to correct individuals. Although do-good helpers recognize the impact of social problems, they probe those who have the problem, designate them different from others, and label them incapable, unskilled, ignorant, and subhuman. People who subscribe to this view believe that changing "those people" is requisite to solving social problems. They unjustly blame those who experience the effects of social problems, rather than recognizing that these difficulties result from oppression, discrimination, and injustice. These are sociopolitical issues that require sociopolitical solutions.

Persons who experience blame, shame, and stigma often assimilate this negativity into their self-images (Link & Phelan, 2001). Self-blame generated by stigma may lead

Table 4.1   Prejudicial Attitudes Contributing to Oppression

Racism	Ideology often based on negative stereotyping that perpetuates individual and institutional discrimination against members of racial groups
Sexism	Based on sex role stereotyping and cultural beliefs that one sex is superior to the other
Classism	Elitist attitudes about persons based on their socioeconomic status or class
Heterosexism	Prejudice and discrimination directed against anyone who is not heterosexual
Ableism	Prejudicial attitudes and behaviors that result in unequal regard for persons because of their physical or mental disability
Ageism	Negative stereotyping of persons based on their age
Regionalism	Generalizations about the character of individuals or population groups based on the geographic region of their origin or residence
Ethnocentrism	Condescending belief that one's own ethnic group, culture, or nation is superior to others

people to feel incompetent, dependent, and rejected. Ironically, people who feel victimized may identify with the oppressors, conclude that these charges are accurate, and apply the derogatory labels to themselves. In general, feelings of powerlessness increase, often resulting in low self-esteem, alienation, and despair.

Empowerment Social Work and Oppression

Social work clients often find themselves trapped by powerlessness and oppression. In today's world, social workers likely deal with clients who are "profoundly vulnerable and disempowered...overwhelmed by oppressive lives, circumstances and events they are powerless to control" (Gitterman & Shulman, 2005, p. xi). Oppression, discrimination, injustice, and experiences of powerlessness are the very circumstances that call for the application of empowerment-based social work practice. Therefore, social workers confront the multiple dimensions of oppression present in society that discriminate by race, ethnicity, socioeconomic status, level of ability, gender, sexual orientation, age, health status, or any other status that is held in low regard by those who have privilege and power.

To address these issues of oppression, injustice, and powerlessness, strengths-oriented social work incorporates empowerment practice as concept, process, and outcome. As a concept, empowerment practice constructs a framework for understanding the personal, interpersonal, and sociopolitical dimensions of any given situation. **Empowerment as a concept** offers a perspective to assess the interconnections between personal circumstance and political realities.

Empowerment as a process describes how practitioners actually approach their work. The process of empowerment represents the ways by which systems—individuals, families, groups, organizations, and communities—gain control over their situations. In other words, empowerment is a process by which people procure personal, interpersonal, and sociopolitical resources to achieve their goals.

The outcome of acquiring power—that is, power achieved—does not necessitate a struggle or relinquishment of power by one group in favor of another. **Empowerment as an outcome** is a geometrically expansive rather than a zero-sum commodity. Empowering—the process of empowerment—means recognizing, facilitating, and promoting a system's capacity for competent functioning. Empowering also implies taking actions that respond to the linkages among the personal, interpersonal, and sociopolitical dimensions of empowerment.

 Assess your understanding of empowerment by taking this brief quiz.

EMPOWERMENT-BASED PRACTICE

Working toward the goal of empowerment significantly affects the way social workers practice. First, workers apply an ecosystems perspective and a strengths orientation in practice. This means that workers consider client situations in context, search for client strengths and environmental resources, and describe needs in terms of transitory challenges rather than fixed problems. Second, as generalists, social workers draw on skills for resolving issues at many social system levels and respond to the interconnections between personal troubles and public issues. Instead of dwelling on vulnerabilities, empowerment-based practice accentuates resiliencies. An empowering approach liberates client systems from the encumbrances of eliminating problems to the promises of generating solutions. Empowerment-based practitioners join with clients as partners and rely on clients' expertise and participation in change processes. They discern the interconnections between client empowerment and social change.

These changes are not trivial! They redirect every phase of the practice paradigm. Empowerment social work begins with a *way of thinking* about human systems, context, and oppression; applies a *way of doing* that incorporates processes that are collaborative, political, and action oriented; and results in outcomes that alter *ways of being* in personal, interpersonal and familial, and sociopolitical and organizational domains (see Table 4.2).

> ▶ Watch this video and analyze what the women from the United States say about their experiences working in India. What do they say that exemplifies empowerment? www.youtube.com/watch?v=qRlgdsnj_3w

The Paradox of an Empowering Process

Social workers empower clients toward feelings of competence and control of resources. Take note, however, social workers cannot bestow empowerment on other systems from star-tipped wands. Empowerment is not something one person can give to another. Only those seeking power can initiate and sustain the process.

Even if one could bestow power, bestowing power, in itself, would be disempowering! Empowerment-based social workers actively involve client-partners in collaborative processes to release the resources of change. Empowerment, by definition, requires the full participation of clients. Rather than given away, empowerment draws on both internal and external resources; it generates from within systems and their environments.

Collaboration and Partnership

An orientation toward strengths and empowerment compels social workers to redefine their relationships to embrace the notion of **collaborative partnership** with clients. Without this redefinition, overzealous social workers assume responsibility for solutions and often ascribe responsibility for failures to clients. Clients, too, may succumb to the notion of social workers as experts as a result of being socialized to the idea of professionals as authorities who take charge. Unfortunately, this has "the unintended side effect of ascribing to the professional an unrealistic amount of responsibility for the solution of the client's problems" (Lenrow & Burch, 1981, p. 243). Empowerment liberates social workers from an elevated status, emphasizes collaborative partnerships, and delineates mutual responsibilities.

For clients, collaboration is a resource for power. In his book, *Power and Innocence*, Rollo May (1972) identifies nutrient power or "power for the other" and integrative power or "power with the other" as positive manifestations of power. "Both of these positive expressions of power suggest collaboration in a common enterprise in which cooperation becomes a form of power" (Weick, 1980, p. 183). In other words, social workers who share power with clients free clients to access their own power; the cooperation within the professional relationship itself becomes a new source of power. Collaboration is the hallmark of empowerment (Figure 4.2).

Decisions made collaboratively by workers and clients and constituencies are not simple choices between what is right and what is wrong. Political realities, ethical

Table 4.2 Empowerment Social Work

Empowerment Social Work as a Way of Thinking

Focuses on context; human behavior is reciprocal and transactional

Links the personal with the political

Views all people and systems as having strength and potential

Considers the power of language in shaping realities

Elevates voices of clients

Deconstructs structural arrangements and their implications for human well-being

Attends to intertwining oppressions

Considers the intersectionality of social identities

Adopts the position that not questioning structural arrangements accepts the status quo

Empowerment Social Work as a Way of Doing

Builds on collaborative partnerships that ensure full participation by clients

Facilitates a climate of empowerment rather than bestowing power (paternalism) or taking care of others (maternalism)

Engages in critical reflection

Applies praxis—reflection, action, reflection

Engages in conscientization—making connections between personal and political

Takes action, working for justice and human rights

Empowerment as a Way of Being

Personal Empowerment

Heightened competence and mastery

Resilience

Feeling of control

Coping capacities

Raised consciousness

Balance of assets and needs with resources and demands

Interpersonal and Familial Empowerment

Positive interactions and relationships with others

Effective communication and support networks

Sense of connectedness and belonging

Respected status

Ability to influence others

Sociopolitical and Organizational Empowerment

Removes power blocks

Creates opportunities in social structures and resource systems

Ensures access to opportunities

Accords social and economic justice

Equalizes privilege and reduce status hierarchy

Protects civil and human rights

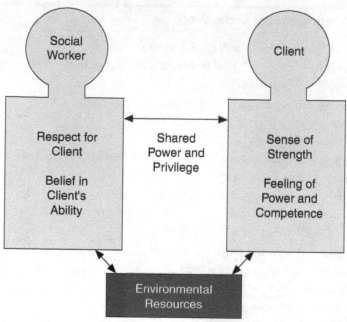

Figure 4.2
Elements of Empowerment in the Social Worker–Client Relationship
An empowering social worker–client relationship has personal, interpersonal, and sociopolitical elements.

![icon] **Diversity and Difference in Practice**

Behavior: Present themselves as learners and engage clients and constituencies as experts of their own experiences

Critical Thinking Question: Establishing a collaborative relationship between the social worker and client is the hallmark of the empowerment process. In what ways does engaging clients and constituencies as partners and experts about their own experiences in the intervention process enhance their sense of power in professional relationships?

contradictions, and systemic interaction complicate the simplest choices, leaving workers and clients to ponder the meaning and impact of what they are doing. Actions taken may define clients as powerful or vulnerable, may activate social and political forces opposing equity and change, or may lead to inequity or injustice for others.

Clients or Consumers?

The terms social workers use to describe their clients shape the expectations for their roles and define the nature of professional relationships. Over the years, practitioners have assigned many different labels to persons or groups who use social services, including supplicants, patients, and those receiving help. Each of these labels characterizes clients as "people who need fixing." Furthermore, these labels imply that professionals are experts who have the knowledge, power, and authority necessary to supply, heal, or treat, leaving receivers of services as have-nots who passively acquire supplies, healing, or treatment.

Some use the term "consumer" to emphasize a client's active role. Viewed as consumers, social work clients seek information, make choices, and contract for what they need from public or private organizations or corporations through fees, vouchers, or citizens' rights. "Consumerism offers a way that, in combination with other strategies for equalizing power and control between givers and receivers of services, can revitalize and relegitimate our social welfare institution" (Gummer, 1983, p. 934). Tower (1994) indicates that persons who experience difficulties understand the impact of issues with regard to age, health status, mental and physical disabilities, or economic circumstances more fully than their social workers. Clients' personal control expands when practitioners respect them as consumers of services rather than patients or recipients.

Others criticize the term "consumer" as conveying passive, compliant consumption. On the receiving end, those labeled consumers may believe they need to be on guard because "buyers must beware." "Consumer" may also imply a business marketing strategy of rationing services rather than an empowerment model of service user involvement (Vojak, 2009). In its most empowering construction, the concept of consumer conveys the idea that a person or other social system seeking services has both rights and responsibilities, yet negative connotations about consumerism restrain widespread use of this term in social work.

The use of the term client predominates social work literature, codes of ethics, and international documents. Numerous other professional groups apply the term "client" when referring to those who engage their services. Critics contend that this designation suggests a subservient position to the professional expert, thus lending too much power to the "expert" professional. However, in general use, the term "client" affords dignity. Consider the example of an international business client or the client of a corporate attorney. Only in relation to social work does the role of client seem to take on negative connotations. Perhaps, it's society's view of social work itself that taints any term we choose.

Today, several different terms are in vogue, depending on the context. Some alternatives used in agency practice include neighbors, participants, residents, parents, members, students, and citizens. Writers vary among the use of the term "client," which reflects a professional relationship; client system, which broadens the concept beyond individuals to include multiperson systems; consumers of social services, which emphasizes rights; and constituents to underscore stakeholder participation.

Carefully chosen words embody a sense of reciprocity. Any term chosen should clearly recognize that clients are people first, and our relationships with them should encompass the dignity and respect of collaborative partnerships. In this text, we use the terms *clients and constituencies* along with *client systems* to emphasize the various system levels in generalist social work and *partners* to acknowledge their collaborative participation. We also, without apology, refer to practitioners as social workers!

Ethical Preferences for Empowerment Social Work

Empowerment social work bridges the clinical (or personal) and the critical (or political) dimensions of practice. The simultaneous focus on human well-being and human rights is central to social work and should direct our thinking and doing in social work. A philosophical framework for empowerment social work necessarily include ethical preferences for both clinical and critical ways of thinking and doing (Miley & DuBois, 2004). To approach their clinical work, social workers adopt a mindset that includes the **ethic of care**, **ethic of autonomy**, **ethic of power**, and **ethic of change** and a practice orientation

Box 4.1   Empowerment: A Practice–Research Connection

Empowerment as a concept unites social workers in a shared vision of human competence in a just and resourceful world. Empowerment as a method is less universally understood or consistently practiced. Research demonstrates the viability of the empowerment-method (Parsons & East, 2013).

What are the similarities and differences in the ways workers implement an empowerment approach? In Ackerson and Harrison's (2000) qualitative study of eight seasoned social workers, respondents all described empowerment as microlevel intervention, including self-determination, choice, and the ability to act on choices; only half referred to macrolevel dimensions of empowerment in social, institutional, and political systems. These results support earlier evidence by Gutiérrez and colleagues (1995a) that practitioners were more likely to apply empowerment-based concepts in micro-focused ways. This limited focus on individual or psychological empowerment stands in contrast to the theoretical literature that defines empowerment as multidimensional with a full complement of social, political, and economic components (Breton, 1994; Rappaport, 1987). Theoretically, empowerment reaches beyond individual clients to include sociopolitical dimensions and the organizational context of practice (Cohen, 1998; Gutiérrez et al, 1995b). Empowerment in practice may fall short of this multidimensional ideal.

In what settings does an empowerment approach work best? Examples of research findings in child welfare, mental health, and aging services demonstrate the positive impact of empowerment methods. Meta-analytic research included a review of 56 studies of child welfare services to determine elements of program effectiveness with respect to family wellness and the prevention of child abuse (Macleod & Nelson, 2000). Those home visitation and intensive family preservation programs that achieved high levels of involvement by participants, incorporated empowerment strategies, and emphasized social support measures showed the best outcomes. A small-scale qualitative study analyzed the meaning of social support to participants in consumer-run mental health agencies (Hardiman, 2004). Analysis of the narrative themes uncovered personal agency, organizational empowerment, a shared sense of ownership, and a deeply felt sense of community in peer networks of caring as significant benefits to participants. In the context of aging services, an outcome evaluation study of a program providing support for African American grandmothers raising their grandchildren demonstrated shifts in participants' perceptions of personal empowerment and engagement in collection collective action and advocacy (Whitley, 2011).

What do clients tell us about empowerment? A qualitative study of psychiatric consumers found that empowering processes at multiple levels facilitated recovery (Nelson et al., 2001). Conditions identified as empowering included personal motivation; supportive relationships with mental health workers, in natural support networks, and self-help groups; responsive mental health agencies and receptive communities; advocacy for social change; and social policies that provide adequate mental health resources.

What benefits are there in a group approach to empowerment practice? Parsons (2001) gathered data through focus groups and intensive interviews with women involved in two social work groups, one focusing on domestic violence and the other on poverty. Despite differences in goals, members in both groups experienced similar benefits from group membership as they worked to "foster interdependence, interaction, and behaviors that facilitate changes, such as learning about the problem, acquiring new skills, having the courage to take risks, taking small steps, resolving conflict, and engaging in collective action" (p. 175). Another study examined the personal and group-level effects of participating in an art guild for older adults (Fisher & Gosselink, 2008). Results indicated that charter members experienced increased efficacy and empowerment through their participation in this successful organization, demonstrating the intertwining relationships among efficacy experienced personally and in the context of the group, engagement, empowerment, and a sense of well-being. Furthermore, the study demonstrates the power of achieving goals for promoting personal and collective efficacy. These studies confirm that personal well-being, efficacy fueled by successful accomplishments, and social action intersect. As these examples show, social workers advance the knowledge base of social work when they connect practice and research.

that includes the **ethic of respect**, **ethic of critical thinking**, **ethic of praxis**, and **ethic of discourse**. Engaging in political practice, social workers approach their work by focusing on the **ethic of critique**, **ethic of justice**, **ethic of contextual practice**, and **ethic of inclusion**. Ethical preferences for political interventions include the **ethic of anti-oppressive practice**, **ethic of advocacy**, **ethic of collaboration**, and **ethic of politicized practice**.

Ethic of Care

Embodying social work's concern with maximizing human potential, respecting human dignity, and treating each client as a unique individual, the ethic of care actualizes core social work values. Focusing on individual care without regard to ensuring a caring society abandons the core social work purpose of social justice.

Ethic of Autonomy

The ethic of autonomy recognizes personal initiative, free choice, voluntary action, and power and authority in governing one's life. For social workers, this maximizes self-determination and translates into a practice mindset that perceives clients as capable and into actions that promote voluntary participation by clients. The benefits of autonomy are evident only when genuine opportunities are available to clients.

Ethic of Power

In response to the ethic of power, empowerment social work practice provides perspectives and methods to assist people who are disenfranchised to access and exercise power in order to protect human rights and achieve social justice. The experience of worth and potential is prelude to personal change and social and political actions. The exercise of power requires attention to the environment because power can be sustained or diminished depending on interactions within the interpersonal, social, and cultural contexts.

Ethic of Change

From an empowerment perspective, change is continuous and multidimensional, as all humans experience the interplay of change and stability perpetuated through multisystemic interaction. Working together informed by the ethic of change, practitioners and clients deliberately interact with systems affecting clients' situations. The ability of clients to sustain progress depends on whether the desired changes were embedded in the ecosystem, including relevant organizational, community, policy, and institutional structures.

Ethic of Critique

The critique of social arrangements focuses on issues of hierarchy and oppression. To critique is to challenge assumptions and question the status quo—why something is arranged the way it is and why it should be different. The ethic of critique implies examining the "why" of a constructed social relationship, and the "why not" of alternatives involves questioning who holds the power, controls the resources, or has the most to gain or lose from changing the social arrangements. One cannot critically examine what one takes for granted.

Ethic of Justice

Empowerment-based social work practitioners confront issues of injustice and inequality. The guarantee of access to services, the opportunity to experience social and economic privilege, an awareness of due process, a voice in policy formulation and implementation, and the power to influence resource allocation—all are trademarks of justice-centered and empowerment-based social work practice.

Ethic of Contextual Practice

The empowerment paradigm underscores the importance of context by locating social work practice at the intersection of persons and their social, cultural, and physical environments. Context can be either oppressive or empowering. Empowerment-oriented workers widen their lens to identify and modify contexts that bind personal experience. The ethic of contextual practice directs empowerment strategies that extend beyond individual adaptation to creating change in social and political contexts.

Ethic of Inclusion

The long-standing principle of maximum feasible participation by clients is the bedrock for the ethic of inclusion. The ethic of inclusion presses empowerment-oriented social workers to redress issues of exclusivity in practice processes by working collaboratively with clients in all facets of practice, policy, and research. For example, inclusion extends to ensuring client voice in decision making about case plans, service delivery options, practice models, social policies, agency procedures, and evaluation designs.

Ethic of Respect

Expressing regard for clients embodies the core social work value of human dignity and worth. However, the ethic of respect means going beyond demonstrating mere acceptance of persons and situations to affirming qualities and strengths in all clients that can be genuinely and openly appreciated. When present in a relationship, genuine respect validates clients' identity and worth, facilitates communication, and encourages action.

Ethic of Critical Thinking

By definition, critical thinking leads to an examination of presenting issues as multidimensional. The reasoning process associated with the ethic of critical thinking opens many pathways to desired solutions by placing information in cultural, social, and political contexts. Social workers and clients reflect on the information they've gathered to achieve a diversity-sensitive appraisal of clients' situations and to estimate the capabilities of various environmental resources to respond to clients' needs.

Ethic of Praxis

Praxis involves a continuous process of reflection–action–reflection. In the context of empowerment, praxis is integral for practitioners and clients to develop a critical understanding about oppression and its impact (reflection) and to implement solutions for achieving social justice (action). The ethic of praxis does not denote a linear process with a defined end point; rather, it is a continuous looping of reflection–action–reflection as clients consider their situations, implement planned changes, and evaluate the outcomes.

Ethic of Discourse

Discourse is the exchange of ideas, beliefs, and practices that shape what we think is true or real about our personal and social situations. Through discourse, people tell and retell their stories, narrated with personally defined, culturally shared, and socially ascribed meanings, thus shaping views of themselves and their possibilities. The ethic of discourse embraces the notion of a network of social relations within which the communication and interchange of ideas occurs, a socially constructed context shaped by social inequality and privilege.

Ethic of Anti-Oppressive Practice

Distinguished by its actions to challenge exploitive relationships and alter power dynamics, anti-oppressive practice differs from antidiscriminatory practice. Embracing an ethic of anti-oppressive practice requires an understanding of how those in power use oppression to maintain the status quo as well as working to overturn power imbalances in personal interaction, professional relationships, and social structures. As such, social workers confront social inequality, advocate antidiscriminatory practices in policies and procedures, and practice from a value base of social inclusion.

Ethic of Advocacy

Among the most vulnerable populations and stigmatized groups of society, social work clients frequently have less leverage than others to obtain necessary resources and experience limited access to genuine opportunities. The ethic of advocacy means that social workers leverage professional resources as a way to champion the rights of individuals or causes. However, in the context of empowerment, advocacy as an ethical practice assumes social workers speak with, not for, others.

Ethic of Collaboration

The ethic of collaboration implies working in partnership with clients and establishing alliances within the social service delivery network to join power resources. Collaborating with clients as partners is foundational to microlevel empowerment practice with individuals, couples, families, and small group clients. Collaboration is also the guiding theme for working in concert with national and international organizations, professional groups, and local and world communities to facilitate macrolevel social change.

Ethic of Politicized Practice

Democratic principles, founded on maximizing participation, including the voices of all population groups in the democratic process, and exercising influence over political processes undergird the ethic of politicized practice. The charge for social workers to engage in policy practice is particularly important in times of policy devolution, managed care, new federalism, newly significant policy making at the state level, electronic advocacy, and the renewed emphasis in social work on social justice and macrolevel practice.

Characteristics of Empowerment-Centered Social Workers

Several characteristics distinguish empowerment-centered social workers, including their focus on context, affirmation of collaboration, emphasis on strengths and opportunities, integration of practice activities at multiple system levels, incorporation of a politicized approach, and commitment reflective practice.

Focusing on Context

Empowerment practice is based on a transactional view of human behavior, one that describes people in continuous interaction with the sociocultural, political, and physical environments. Focusing on context influences all facets of work. For example, in assessment, workers and clients identify the contextual elements that contribute to the problems that clients face. To intervene, workers can join with clients to block negative environmental influences, help clients to respond differently to environmental pressures, or directly address environmental challenges, thus creating benefits for specific clients and the community.

Affirming Collaboration

Collaboration is at the heart of empowering relationships, reflecting attitudes of mutual respect and modalities of shared power. In sharp contrast to the expert paradigm in which workers are expected to eliminate or control clients' problems, in the collaborative paradigm, workers and clients function interdependently to address challenges within a client's situation. Moreover, the collaborative quality extends beyond the worker–client relationship to define the structure of how the worker relates to colleagues, agencies, community, and society.

Emphasizing Strengths and Opportunities

A social work process that focuses on strengths activates resources rather than corrects deficits. The strengths perspective emphasizes the importance of envisioning a future goal and examining the present and the past to gather resources and create opportunities to reach that desired outcome. In dialogue with clients, workers respond in ways to re-center the view to highlight strengths, skills, solutions, and opportunities.

Integrating Practice Activities at Multiple System Levels

The systemic concept of wholeness states that a change in any part of the system can influence the situation and will likely reverberate throughout the system to create other changes. This implies that a problem experienced at the individual level may respond to changes in the environment. For maximal impact, workers and clients synthesize simultaneous interventions—in other words, they coordinate several forces at multiple levels to achieve a positive change. In sum, the empowerment method demands contextually framed generalist interventions when considering the multiple opportunities for change.

Incorporating a Politicized Approach

"The personal without the political is not empowerment" is the mantra of empowering social work. A political context constantly shapes the human condition. All human interaction is politicized by the implicit negotiation for power and privilege in meaning-making within relationships. Empowerment-based workers integrate a political perspective into direct practice, mobilizing clients through work in groups to initiate social action that addresses organizational, community, and social policy issues.

"The personal without the political is not empowerment" is the mantra of empowering social work.

Committing to Reflective Practice

To be reflective means to be perceptive and to exercise good judgment. Applied to social work, reflection involves a continuous cyclical process of thinking, doing, and reflecting—a process that incorporates feedback to garner insight and refine actions. In the context of empowerment, **reflective practice** involves exploring connections between personal troubles and public issues. Reflective practice not only fosters effective practice but also promotes ethical practice, including social justice realized through macrolevel change.

Empowerment-Oriented Strategies

Empowerment-oriented social workers assume that a client's issues reflect a lack of congruence between the system's capacities and environmental demands. They acknowledge the imbalance between the pool of personal, interpersonal, and societal resources and the system's need for these resources to meet the challenge. They select multilevel strategies that heighten the availability of personal, interpersonal, and sociopolitical resources. In the tradition of empowerment-based practice, this means selecting strategies that increase self-efficacy, develop skills, discern connections between personal difficulties and public issues, enhance collectivity, and take actions to create sociopolitical changes.

Integrating Clinical and Political Practice

The purpose of empowerment social work is to promote a just society in which all members share the same rights to participation in society, protection by the law, opportunities for development, and access to social benefits, and who, in turn, contribute to the resource pool of society. From an empowerment perspective, the mandate of the social work profession is to ensure the fulfillment of the social justice contract between individuals and society, particularly for those groups that are disenfranchised. The assessment of clients' "needs" should not only be driven by the availability of resources but also be concerned with the reduction of inequality and promotion of social justice. Empowering social workers are both clinical and political in their efforts to create social conditions favorable to the well-being of people and society (Miley & DuBois, 2007) (see Table 4.3).

Using Group Modalities

Many practitioners conclude that working with clients in groups maximizes empowerment and promotes social justice (Breton, 2004; Lee, 2001; Malekoff, 2008). Hearing others tell stories similar to one's own has a dramatic effect, particularly for those who have experienced oppression. Through the interactions with others, members of small groups are in a position to help others recognize issues of oppression, develop a critical consciousness, and collectively take action. The group process itself offers opportunities for mutual sharing that set the stage for looking outside oneself for both the causes of problems and the sources of solutions.

Developing a Critical Consciousness

Developing a **critical consciousness** about the interconnections of the personal and political is another essential component of empowerment-oriented practice (Hernandez et al., 2005; Nicotera & Kang, 2009; Sakamoto & Pitner, 2005; Wheeler-Brooks, 2009).

Table 4.3   Empowerment Social Work: Clinical and Political

Empowerment-oriented social workers are both clinical and political in their efforts to strengthen human functioning and relationships and to create conditions favorable to the well-being of people and society.

	Clinical Social Work	Political Social Work
Purpose	To ensure social participation	To protect social rights
Focus	The needs of the client	The rights of the client
Goal	Personal and interpersonal effectiveness	Socioeconomic-political justice
Strategies	Microlevel, direct practice, individual and family change	Macrolevel, indirect practice, social policy change, social and economic justice
Interventions	Counseling, casework, group work, case management	Advocacy, legislative initiatives, economic development, policy practice
Theme	Contributive justice: What a person owes to society • Contribute to the resource pool of society • Fully participate in society	Distributive justice: What a society owes its citizens • Provide resources and opportunities • Right to basic resources for living

Breton (2002) explains the interconnection: "Empowerment necessarily involves both conscientization (change at the personal level) and social action (change at the collective level)" (p. 26). Furthermore, Breton argues that private troubles and public issues are so intertwined that the process of conscientization necessarily addresses both. Through their work with groups, social workers implement consciousness-raising strategies, contextualize experiences, reduce self-blame, and provide opportunities for group members to evaluate and assume responsibility for the consequences of their choices. Furthermore, when this dialogue occurs in the context of a group, group members form a solidarity that can mobilize energy and lead to collective actions (see Figure 4.3).

Human Rights and Justice

Behavior: Engage in practices that advance social, economic, and environmental justice

Critical Thinking Question: Empowerment social work is both clinical and political. In what ways do these dual activities contribute to fulfilling the social justice contract between individuals and societies?

Incorporating Anti-Oppression

Anti-oppressive practice redresses oppression and social exclusion through its focus on the liberation, emancipation, and enfranchisement of members of vulnerable and oppressed groups (Baines, 2007; Cocker & Hafford-Letchfield, 2014; Hines, 2012; Strier & Binyamin, 2010). For social workers, key features of antioppressive practice include drawing on a foundation of theories and values that endorse egalitarian sharing of power, critically reflecting on one's social location and that location's influence on practice relationships, challenging exiting oppressive social structures and domination by powerful groups, and employing collaborative practice strategies that facilitate empowerment (Larson, 2008). Although the term "antioppressive practice" is not part of the language used in the NASW *Code of Ethics*

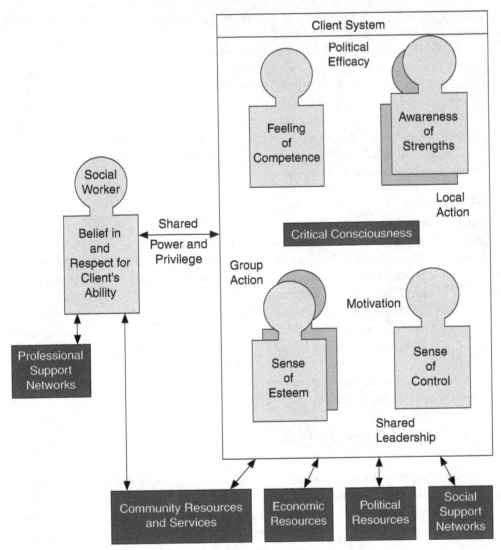

Figure 4.3
Developing a Critical Consciousness
Alliances among individuals create opportunities for developing social bonds, enhancing personal competence and political efficacy, and achieving a critical consciousness as requisites to collective social action.

(1999), it clearly reflects the social justice mandate. Antioppressive practice brings clarity in an actionable way to the social justice ideal.

Engaging in Praxis

Praxis involves cyclical processes of reflection, action, and reflection. Social workers and clients take actions and then pause to observe and reflect to guide the next step. As the work unfolds, reflection and action intertwine in praxis. According to Carr (2003), "empowerment is an inherently interpersonal process in which individuals collectively define and activate strategies to gain access to knowledge and power" (p. 18).

Praxis, with its alternating phases of collective dialogue and action, is a fundamental element of empowerment.

Applied in practice, praxis—or the continuous cycle of action–reflection–action—ensures that clients can describe their experiences with oppressive conditions through dialogue with others. Through this reflective discourse about their experiences, clients discover possible actions to take at the personal, interpersonal, and political levels. In this way, praxis "is used to consolidate and deepen the work of developing critical understanding and a vision for social change" (Lee, 2001, p. 89). Then, in implementation, clients and social workers initiate actions to achieve the vision and reflect on the processes and outcomes of the change effort.

Taking Action

Social action is the key to sociopolitical empowerment and is a legacy of the social work profession (Breton, 2006; Franco et al., 2007; Jacobson & Rugeley, 2007). Collective action strives to reallocate sociopolitical power so that disenfranchised citizens can access the opportunities and resources of society and, in turn, find meaningful ways to contribute to society as valued citizens.

Social action is not exclusively the domain of the macropractitioner. Generalist practitioners working primarily with microlevel clients also make efforts to improve conditions in communities, bureaucracies, and society. For example, they may act as advocates to speak out with clients at the institutional and political level to influence changes in social policies. In these ways, practitioners work in collaboration with clients to create social and political change.

> **?** Assess your understanding of empowerment-based practice by taking this brief quiz.

LOOKING FORWARD

Understanding diversity involves a process of critical questioning about issues of powerlessness, oppression, and discrimination. This approach goes beyond merely examining the demographic differences of diverse population groups to exploring the commonality of the experience of victimization and exploitation. Only in this way can social work practitioners step outside of their own perspectives into clients' worldviews.

When social workers view clients through the perspective of strengths and competence, they discover and appreciate the uniqueness and diversity inherent in all human systems. They affirm that client systems already have potential—knowledge, experiences, and resources—from which to draw. When social workers magnify client strengths, they heighten motivation and involvement as collaborative partners. When clients get in touch with their own strengths, they discover solutions in the personal, interpersonal, and sociopolitical dimensions of their situations.

> **√** Evaluate what you learned in this chapter by completing the Chapter Review.

As described in this chapter, an orientation to strengths and empowerment is essential to implement an empowering approach to generalist practice. Chapter 5 describes how social workers transform these perspectives on practice into a coherent approach that empowers clients at all system levels.

5

An Empowering Approach to Generalist Practice

MANDY GODBEHEAR/SHUTTERSTOCK

An empowerment orientation shapes the processes that structure social work practice. Empowering processes move clients to center stage—positioning them as the authors of their stories as well as the directors and producers of the action. This leaves workers in the roles of accentuating clients' "unique coping and adaptive patterns, mobilizing their actual or potential strengths, emphasizing the role of natural helping networks, and using environmental resources" (Maluccio & Libassi, 1984, p. 52). Changes accomplished by clients through such processes are likely to endure because they are "funded by the coin of their capabilities, knowledge, and skills" (Saleebey, 1992, p. 6).

The method of generalist practice described here empowers clients. Consistently, it demonstrates confidence in the abilities of client systems, builds solutions on their capabilities, and acknowledges the essential role of social and political change in empowerment. This approach also recognizes the incredible diversity of strengths that various client systems possess. This shift prompts social workers to view clients as capable, with the abilities to give voice to their own concerns and the potentials for finding solutions.

This chapter presents an overview of the **empowerment method** of generalist social work practice. When generalist practitioners use an empowerment approach, clients rediscover their own strengths and gain access to resources within their environments.

ELEMENTS OF AN EMPOWERING GENERALIST APPROACH

The empowerment method of generalist social work draws on the practice perspectives presented thus far. This approach applies the ecosystemic perspective and reflects social work values. It actualizes the strengths orientation through its assumptions of client expertise and consistent emphasis on collaborative roles for both clients and practitioners. Ultimately, it works to achieve empowerment for clients at the personal, interpersonal, and sociopolitical levels of human experiences.

Infusing an Ecosystems Perspective

The ecosystems perspective examines the interplay of human systems with their environments both to understand what is happening and to develop strategies for initiating change. Consistent with the ecosystems perspective, the empowerment method guides social workers and clients to view challenges and strengths in context, to identify the many possible paths to solutions, and to recognize that change in any given system reverberates through other system levels. Each phase of this approach accommodates the transactional nature of social work by considering the interaction of client systems in context. Informed by an ecosystemic perspective, workers are able to locate resources for change present in the entire ecosystem in which their relationships with clients exist.

Human Rights and Justice

Behavior: Apply their understanding of social, economic, and environmental justice to advocate for human rights at the individual and system levels

Critical Thinking Question: Empowerment social work reflects a commitment to social, economic, and environmental justice. What injustices and oppressive social conditions do social workers address in their quest for a just society?

Reflecting a Social Justice Commitment

All social work practice is political. Social workers participate in defining whether a society is just. If social workers impose dominant cultural views about human behavior, function to control deviance as defined by majority values, and offer expert solutions to client problems, they reinforce and perpetuate oppression. In contrast, if social workers align with client worldviews, define problems transactionally, and seek solutions in social and political change, they nudge society in the direction of social justice. Processes within this empowerment-oriented approach consistently reveal the requisite client-centeredness and focus on environmental conditions necessary to meet social work's commitment to social, economic, and environmental justice.

Applying a Strengths Orientation

As a lens for viewing clients, the strengths perspective shifts the view of clients from one of pathology toward one of potential. The fundamental question switches from "what is wrong" to "what is available" within clients and their environments to achieve desired changes. Strength-oriented social work processes describe methods for clients to discover what might be useful in the present for constructing a more positive future. Cultivating client strengths and resources throughout all phases of the practice process is essential for implementing an empowerment-based approach to social work practice. However, simply adopting a strengths perspective is insufficient in many situations. Activating client strengths becomes most effective in a socially and economically just environment in which opportunities are accessible to all.

Watch this video and examine the social worker's perspective on practice. How does this view reflect the tenets of an empowering generalist approach? www.youtube.com/watch?v=Uw5qLiQERBg

Collaborating with Clients and Constituencies

An orientation toward strengths redefines the social worker–client relationship. Recognizing client expertise, social workers partner with clients at all system levels. They collaborate to create a vision of what they hope to accomplish and then concentrate their efforts to search for resources to reach that goal. Collaboration entrusts clients with rights and responsibilities, encouraging clients to discover their own solutions and to remain in charge of their own changes. In an empowerment-focused approach, clients feel their own sense of power in the social work process and carry these feelings of competence and control beyond the boundaries of their relationships with social workers.

Constructing an Empowering Reality

Consistent with a social constructionist perspective, research demonstrates that a professional's prehelping attitudes and beliefs and the help-giving practices of social service programs influence a client's experience of empowerment (Dunst, 1993). This research also affirms that positive attributions and program orientations make a difference in a social worker's effectiveness. The empowerment method of practice introduced in this chapter consistently describes social work processes in language that frames a future-oriented, solution-saturated, and client-validating reality.

Effective social workers purposefully construct an empowering "practice reality" by orienting themselves toward client strengths, empowerment, and collaboration. They develop productive assumptions about clients and the practice process, including the following:

Assumptions About Human Systems

- All people deserve acceptance and respect.
- Clients know their situations best.
- All human system behavior makes sense in context.
- All human system behavior is motivated.
- Challenges emerge from transactions between human systems and their physical and social environments; the challenges do not reside within clients themselves.
- Strengths are diverse, including personal feelings of worth, cultural pride, successful relationships, and resourceful interdependence within a community.

Assumptions About Change

- Change is not only possible but also inevitable.
- A small change in one part of the ecosystem may initiate a chain of beneficial changes.
- Challenges are likely to have many solutions.
- One does not have to solve a problem to find a solution.
- Enduring change builds on strengths.
- Strengths and the potential for growth characterize all human systems.
- Given niches and opportunities, human systems cultivate competencies.
- Collaborative relationships stimulate feelings of power and lead to actions.
  - Cultural differences are resources offering broader perspectives, additional options, and possibilities of synergistic solutions.

When social workers believe that clients have the rights to their own beliefs, that they have made choices and can make new choices, and that they have the potential to achieve their goals, these expectations prepare workers to implement an empowering practice process.

> **?** Assess your understanding of the elements of an empowering generalist approach by taking this brief quiz.

PHASES AND PROCESSES OF EMPOWERING PRACTICE

Each of the various methods of social work practice describes a coherent framework to guide the progress of workers and clients as they strive to achieve desired goals. Likewise, this empowering approach offers an organized and deliberate, yet dynamic and flexible, structure for practice. The empowerment method frames practice as moving through phases of dialogue (engagement), discovery (assessment), and development (intervention and evaluation) and suggests specific activities to accomplish within each of these phases. Table 5.1 describes the engagement, assessment, and intervention and evaluation processes that comprise the dialogue, discovery, and development phases.

Engagement: The Dialogue Phase

Successful social work requires conversation, an ongoing dialogue with clients about their situations, goals, and strengths. Through this exchange, practitioners define their relationships with clients as a collaborative partnership to which both will contribute. In this phase of engagement, social workers and clients fully discuss the challenging situation and clarify the purpose of their relationship. In the **dialogue phase**, practitioners and clients collaborate to

- build partnerships based on acceptance, respect, and trust;
- define their respective roles;
- discuss clients' experiences with challenging situations;
- define the purpose of their work together;
- activate client motivation for change;
- address crisis needs.

Table 5.1   An Empowering Approach to Generalist Practice

Phase	Process	Activities
Dialogue as Engagement	Forming partnerships	Building empowering social worker–client relationships that acknowledge clients' privileges and respect their uniqueness
	Articulating situations	Assessing challenging situations by responding to validate clients' experiences, add transactional dimensions, and look toward goals
	Defining directions	Determining a preliminary purpose for the relationship to activate client motivation and guide the exploration for relevant resources
Discovery as Assessment	Identifying strengths	Searching for client strengths in general functioning, coping with challenging situations, cultural identities, and overcoming adversity
	Assessing resource capabilities	Exploring resources in clients' transactions with the environment, including connections to family, social groups, organizations, and community institutions
	Framing solutions	Constructing an achievable plan of action that utilizes client and environmental resources and leads toward desired goals
Development as Intervention and Evaluation	Activating resources	Implementing the action plan by mobilizing available resources through consultancy, resource management, and education
	Creating alliances	Forging empowering alliances among clients, within clients' natural support networks, and within the service delivery system
	Expanding opportunities	Developing new opportunities and resources through program development, community organizing, and social action
	Recognizing success	Evaluating the success of the change efforts to recognize achievements and inform continuing actions
	Integrating gains	Wrapping up the change process in ways that resolve the relationship, celebrate success, and stabilize positive changes

Adapted with permission of the authors from *Applying an Empowerment Process in Social Work Practice*, B. DuBois, K. Miley, & M. O'Melia, 1993. All rights reserved.

In the dialogue phase, workers and clients talk with one another to assess what is happening and develop a preliminary vision of the way clients and constituencies would like things to be. These engagement processes require open and respectful exchanges of information. Specific processes associated with this phase include **forming partnerships**, **articulating situations**, and **defining directions**.

In the dialogue phase, workers and clients talk with one another to assess what is happening and develop a preliminary vision of the way clients and constituencies would like things to be.

Forming Partnerships

Forming partnerships describes the process in which workers and client systems define their working relationship to reflect the purposes of social work and standards of ethical

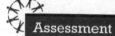

Assessment

Behavior: Develop mutually agreed-on intervention goals and objectives based on the critical assessment of strengths, needs, and challenges within clients and constituencies

Critical Thinking Question: The empowerment method of social work comprises activities for practitioners in the phases of dialogue, discovery, and development. What activities do clients and constituencies contribute in each process of the empowering method listed in Table 5.1?

codes (Chapter 6). For the process to be empowering, social workers and client systems resolve power and authority dilemmas to structure their relationship in an egalitarian way, maximizing their respective contributions. Social workers and clients become collaborators, working together to understand situations and accomplish change.

Articulating Situations

In the process of articulating situations, workers and clients develop a mutual understanding of what prompts clients to seek social work assistance (Chapter 7). To do so, social workers actively listen to what clients say and respond to both the information and feelings within these messages. They recognize cultural variations inherent in communication processes and place client perspectives at the center of the process. In work with larger systems, practitioners use group process techniques, surveys, and other tools to maximize the participation of and to ensure input from all members.

Defining Directions

In defining directions, practitioners and clients orient their work to achieve a specific purpose (Chapter 8). This concrete sense of direction determines which of the client's resources and strengths are useful in constructing solutions. Defining a desired direction motivates clients to participate. While clients are describing their situations and the outcomes they seek, alert social workers screen for issues requiring immediate attention such as trauma, homelessness, family violence, child abuse and neglect, substance abuse, and the threat of suicide.

Assessment: The Discovery Phase

During the **discovery phase**, clients and social workers continue to assess, systematically exploring resources on which to build solutions. These resources may be present within client systems or in the context of their social and physical environments. Working as partners, social workers and clients also organize the information gathered to develop plans for change. Specifically, they

- explore clients' strengths as resources for change,
- examine resource possibilities in clients' environments,
- collect relevant information from collateral sources,
- assess capabilities of available resource systems,
- specify outcome goals and concrete objectives,
- construct a plan of action,
- negotiate a contract for change.

In the discovery phase, client systems and practitioners explore personal and institutional resource systems to set goals and contract for change. Universally applicable to clients at all social system levels, discovery processes for assessment include **identifying strengths**, **assessing resource capabilities**, and **framing solutions**.

Identifying Strengths

The process of identifying strengths presumes that client strengths function as cornerstones for change and therefore should be noted early and often (Chapter 9). Exclusively focusing on problems traps workers and clients into thinking that nothing works. Scanning for strengths sets a positive tone and conveys expectations of success. Listening to clients describe their challenges with an ear for strengths leads workers to discover clients' abilities, resourcefulness, and creativity, as well as strengths found in interpersonal relationships, culture, organizational networks, and community connections. When workers accentuate strengths, clients experience hope and feel empowered to contribute as full partners to the change effort.

In the discovery phase, client systems and practitioners explore personal and institutional resource systems to set goals and contract for change.

Assessing Resource Capabilities

The process of assessing resource capabilities adds transactional dimensions to the understanding of clients' situations (Chapter 10). Workers and clients jointly assess personal, interpersonal, familial, group, organizational, community, societal, and political systems to detail a positive, broad-based view of the client system in transaction with its environment. Through this strength-oriented assessment, workers and clients discover what resource systems they might activate to reach the outcomes they seek.

Framing Solutions

The discovery phase culminates in framing solutions, a process in which social workers and clients develop plans for action (Chapter 11). Action plans contain explicit statements about what clients hope to achieve, as well as concrete strategies for achieving their goals and objectives. Developing this comprehensive plan signals the transition from understanding what is happening to acting on this information to make desired changes. A detailed action plan guides the implementation of activities throughout the development phase.

Intervention and Evaluation: The Development Phase

In the **development phase**, practitioners and clients intervene to activate interpersonal and institutional resources, create alliances with other systems, and expand opportunities through resource development. This approach empowers clients with their own abilities and the resource of their environments with a goal of recognizing and stabilizing the positive changes achieved. Together, workers and clients

- operationalize the plan of action,
- increase the experience of power within client systems,
- access resources necessary to achieve goals,
- create alliances among persons and organizations to accomplish the plan,
- enhance opportunities and choices by creating additional resources,
- evaluate ongoing progress and outcomes,
- identify and generalize achievements and gains,
- wrap up the professional relationship.

Major activities in the development phase work to organize and expand resources, reach outcome goals, measure achievements, and conclude the formal intervention process.

Major activities in the development phase work to organize and expand resources, reach outcome goals, measure achievements, and conclude the formal intervention process.

This intervention and evaluation phase includes the processes of **activating resources, creating alliances, expanding opportunities, recognizing success,** and **integrating gains.**

Activating Resources

In activating resources, workers and clients collaborate to put the agreed-on plan into action (Chapter 12). Clients make connections with necessary interpersonal and institutional resources, experiment with new behaviors and interactions, and carry out the tasks developed in their meetings with workers. Social workers organize and monitor intervention activities, motivate clients to participate in the plan, facilitate cooperative efforts in multiperson client systems, detail options and choices, and provide helpful feedback to clients. Workers play a variety of roles as they consult on strategies, work with clients to manage resources, and oversee educational activities.

Creating Alliances

Alliances generate new resources to fuel change. By creating alliances, social workers and clients align the efforts of clients in empowerment groups, strengthen the functioning of clients within their natural support networks, and organize the service delivery network (Chapter 13). These alliances bring emotional support to clients and build bases of power for social change efforts. Social workers also benefit from alliances through their collaboration with colleagues, supervisors, and professional organizations. Social workers who feel supported and experience their own power are most likely to engender these same feelings in their clients.

Watch this video and notice how the social workers have both similar and different experiences. What are the common elements portrayed across various fields of practice? www.youtube.com/watch?v=77UGDj48oHs

Expanding Opportunities

Generalist social workers understand the need to develop resources at all system levels. Through the intervention process of expanding opportunities, workers and clients work together to create resources that redress social injustice (Chapter 14). Possibilities for change in the service delivery network include refining access to existing social services and creating new programs. Practitioners and clients work to develop just social policy at the agency, local, state, and national levels; they use community organizing and social action strategies to inspire political reforms and legislative changes.

Recognizing Success

All effective plans of action include procedures for evaluation. The evaluation process of recognizing success highlights the numerous ways to measure the achievement of goals and evaluate service effectiveness (Chapter 15). Evaluating outcomes guarantees a worker's accountability to client systems and practice settings, credits clients with their contributions to the success, and functions as part of the process to bring closure to professional relationships. Measuring success gives clients and social workers a sense of their accomplishments and helps both clients and social workers generalize the success of a particular endeavor to cope with other situations that each will confront. Formal research increases the knowledge base and contributes to the development of the social work profession.

Integrating Gains

The final intervention process of integrating gains emphasizes that clients grow, develop, and change even after their efforts with social workers end (Chapter 16). The ultimate measure of the success of any social work endeavor is whether clients can independently continue the progress initiated within the professional relationship. To encourage continued success, workers facilitate a closure process that helps clients review the work, express their thoughts and feelings about ending, and recognize the transferability of the strategies implemented to managing other events.

The Recurring Nature of Dialogue, Discovery, and Development

Joining with others in support of a cause promotes social change.

Although this practice model provides a structure for engagement, assessment, and intervention and evaluation, it is nevertheless dynamic and flexible in its implementation. The processes recur and often occur simultaneously. The generalist practice model configured as the three phases of dialogue, discovery, and development—each involving several processes—gives the illusion that these components are distinct and arranged in sequential steps. However, in practice, the phases and processes overlap and interconnect, with workers interweaving the processes and moving freely among the phases as the situation warrants.

Consider the ways in which the phases of dialogue, discovery, and development interrelate. As strength-focused practitioners engage and build relationships with clients, a dialogue phase process, they unavoidably notice strengths, a process described as part of the discovery or assessment phase. While workers and clients implement intervention strategies for change, a development phase process, they continue to search for additional resources, a discovery phase activity. In practice, social workers move freely among various phases of practice over the course of the professional relationship and even within the same meeting with any client system. Because change in human systems is not likely to proceed in a lock-step fashion, social workers match what clients and constituencies need by implementing empowering processes flexibly.

Because change in human systems is not likely to proceed in a lock-step fashion, social workers match what clients and constituencies need by implementing empowering processes flexibly.

Application to Individual Sessions

Social workers can also use the recurring nature of the model of dialogue, discovery, and development to organize individual meetings with clients. In short, social workers ensure that each encounter provides clients with opportunities to reconnect with the worker, to share recent information, to evaluate progress, to discover resources, to plan new activities in pursuit of goals, and to leave each session with a clear idea about what happens next.

Box 5.1   Social Work Imperatives: A Policy–Practice Connection

In April 2010, the National Association of Social Workers convened the Social Work Congress 2010, Reaffirm, Revisit & Reimagine the Profession, in Washington, D.C. Cosponsored by a dozen social work organizations, the Congress brought together over 300 social work leaders to discuss professional issues and frame a response for the next decade. The participants adopted imperatives for professional action to inform social work strategies through 2020 (NASW, 2010). These imperatives set priorities to infuse business models into social work education and practice, including leadership development, and the recruitment and retention of social workers. Furthermore, the directives call on social workers to take actions to ensure professional competence, strengthen the influence of national social work organizations, and integrate technology in an ethical and responsible manner. In sum, the imperatives charge social workers to

- incorporate business and management practices into the social work profession;
- strengthen alliances among professional social work organizations to achieve shared advocacy goals;
- promote the knowledge, values, and skills of social work to prospective students;

- communicate the unique expertise and contributions of social work to policy makers and the general public;
- speak in concert about issues central to the mission of social work;
- incorporate leadership skill training into educational curricula for social work;
- promote the socioeconomic benefits of social work in recruitment efforts;
- strengthen retention activities, including mentoring, career advancement, and succession planning;
- increase financial incentives and advocate debt forgiveness supports for students and graduates of social work programs;
- incorporate supportive technologies in practice and education.

Clearly, the imperatives delineated by the Reaffirm, Revisit & Reimagine the Profession Congress demonstrate a heightened need to strengthen the profession through public awareness efforts; recruitment, education, and retention of social work students; and the business management of social work practice. Many opportunities will arise to promote the profession as social workers implement corresponding strategies.

Using the processes of the dialogue phase, when an individual session begins, practitioners engage clients to become comfortably reacquainted. From there, social workers and clients share updated information, report on pending activities, and clarify the direction and purpose of this particular meeting. For example, the meeting begins at the point of connection between the social worker and client: "Good morning, how are you doing today?" With contact reestablished, the partners bring each other up to date: "So maybe you can tell me what's been happening" and "I have some information to share with you, too." Shifting to the discovery processes, the practitioner and client then broaden their focus to explore and assess clustering events, search for resources, and develop options for activities, asking for example, "What else is going on? What kinds of things are you trying to do about it?" The partners do what they can within the meeting to develop goal-oriented activities and conclude by planning other activities to complete before the next session. Finally, social workers and clients summarize and point directly to the next step: "I'll follow up with my to-do list while you complete your tasks. Let's check back with each other next week to review our progress and plan the next steps."

Table 5.2   Empowering Processes and Traditional Problem Solving

Problem Solving	Empowering Processes
Engagement	Forming partnerships
Problem identification and assessment	Articulating situations
	Defining directions
	Identifying strengths
	Assessing resource capabilities
Goal setting and planning	Framing solutions
Intervention	Activating resources
	Creating alliances
	Expanding opportunities
Evaluation	Recognizing success
Termination	Integrating gains

From Solving Problems to Promoting Competence

This model for empowerment-based practice draws its organizational framework from the problem-solving model. Like problem solving, empowerment-based practice guides workers through activities of building relationships, defining purposes, assessing situations, planning, and implementing change. In contrast, however, the empowering approach reconstructs traditional problem solving into a process of seeking solutions, using language and concepts that emphasize strengths, empowerment, working in partnerships with clients at all system levels to promote competence, and facilitating macrolevel change (Table 5.2). This approach emphasizes strengths rather than deficits, solution seeking rather than problem detecting, competence promotion rather than prescriptive directives, and collaborative partnerships rather than professional expertise. It sets a different tone from deficit-based practice and reflects the contemporary paradigm shift in social work practice to strengths and empowerment.

? Assess your understanding of the phases and processes of empowering practice by taking this brief quiz.

PROCESSES IN ACTION: PRACTICE EXAMPLES

To understand the application of this empowering practice approach, read the following three examples carefully. Each example demonstrates the phases of dialogue, discovery, and development as applied to a different type of client system. Examine the actions of the social workers to discover the underlying theories, perspectives, competencies, and values that support their work. Specifically, look for generalist thinking, an ecosystemic perspective, respect for cultural diversity, and an orientation to strengths. Notice how the same processes apply at various client system levels, demonstrating the generalist application of this approach.

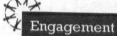

Engagement

Behavior: Use empathy, reflection, and interpersonal skills to effectively engage diverse clients and constituencies

Critical Thinking Question: Generalist social workers intervene at all system levels. What do Kay Landon, Margo Suarez-Rand, and Leon Casey, the three social workers in the generalist practice examples, have in common in terms of their professional skills and core values?

An Example at the Microlevel

On her way to the intake appointment, Kay Landon recalls her conversation with Helen Ingersoll. Helen sounded desperate when she made the appointment. Kay could hear the feelings of helplessness as Helen described events leading to her call. Helen's husband Jack is recovering from a work-related head injury that occurred 6 months ago. Things are not going well. Helen is overwhelmed. Jack's progress is slow, and the doctors are talking about "permanent disability." Helen is out of energy and nearly out of hope.

Kay empathizes, but she feels anything but hopeless. From Kay's experiences with other clients in Northside Prevention Services' Family Support Program, she knows that situations like these feel stressful. But, paradoxically, these challenges also bring out capabilities in clients they may not realize they have. Helen Ingersoll has been coping with this traumatic situation for 6 months with little assistance. She obviously has a great deal of strength. Kay is not willing to count Jack out either. The concept of permanent disability is one that Kay cannot quite grasp. Maybe Jack is not capable of things that he used to be able to do, but Kay will look for what he still can do. Kay has observed it so often that she assumes it: All clients bring strength to the social work process.

Engagement: Dialogue

When Kay arrives, she doesn't have to knock. Helen greets her at the door. Helen is clearly motivated. Once they are seated in the living room, Kay introduces herself and asks to meet Jack. Helen is unsure whether Jack should join them because he can be "unpredictable." Kay's response, "I guess we're all somewhat unpredictable at times," puts Helen at ease, and she leads Jack into the room. Kay begins the meeting by clarifying who she is, explaining what the Family Support Program has to offer, and answering the couple's questions about the services.

Next, it's the Ingersolls' turn to talk. Kay allows them to lead the way, responding attentively to encourage them to keep talking. She clarifies information that confuses her and reassures them that she understands what they say. Kay learns much as Helen and Jack describe their situation in their own way.

Only a few months ago, Helen and Jack Ingersoll were experiencing the kind of life they had planned. Having launched the second of their two children, they were settling into the "good life," relaxing with friends, pursuing individual interests, enjoying time together, and looking ahead to early retirement and travel. Jack was working at the power company and had only 3 years remaining to retire with full benefits. Helen worked part-time as a substitute teacher.

Then, the unexpected happened. Helen was stunned to receive the call about Jack's accident. He had slipped from a utility pole and fallen to the ground. The head and back injuries Jack sustained left him with numerous problems. Even now, his mobility remains limited, he requires assistance in many activities of daily living, and he has trouble remembering things. His condition requires Helen's constant care. This event reverberates throughout every aspect of the couple's lives.

As Kay gathers information, she readily identifies Helen's stress. The months of adjustment have taken their toll. Helen reels off a list of complicated issues. Tending Jack's needs leaves her exhausted. Even though she provides loving care, she endures Jack's frequent criticism and resistance, so uncharacteristic of his "old self." Helen doesn't understand Jack's angry outbursts and seeming lack of motivation to do things for himself. She feels confined to the house and socially isolated. She is frustrated by her inability to return to work and watching their bills pile up as their income decreases. Jack describes his feelings of depression and anger at his helplessness. He admits that he is sometimes difficult and that conflicts interrupt their previously tranquil relationship. For Jack and Helen, these problems seem insurmountable.

As Helen and Jack complete their story, Kay responds, "What resilience! How have you been able to make it this far?" At first, Helen and Jack hesitate. Then each begins to describe what has gotten them through the last few months. Helen talks about the emotional support that her children offer, even though they live out of state. She mentions a friend from church who stops by weekly with a covered dish. Jack credits Helen for her support and endurance. And he admits that occasionally there are good days; in fact, today is one of them. Sometimes, he believes that he just might get "back to normal." Both recognize their caring relationship as a source of strength throughout the entire ordeal. As the Ingersolls describe what is working, Kay notices a lightening of the mood and the looks of affection the couple exchange with each other.

When Kay asks, "So, what are you looking for from me?" Helen takes the lead. She explains that even though she knows things will never be the same, she still wants them back to the way they were. When Kay asks Helen to be more specific, Helen explains that she would like to be able to do some things on her own again. She wants greater financial stability, maybe even to return to work. Jack states that he would like to take care of himself better so that Helen can get out more. Kay believes these are workable goals and agrees to work with the Ingersolls to achieve them.

Assessment: Discovery

With a direction in mind, Kay continues her exploration to assess what resources the Ingersolls have to facilitate this effort. Having identified the Ingersoll couple as the focal system, she seeks additional information to discover what is happening inside the system. Previously, the Ingersolls enjoyed time together as well as maintaining their separate interests. Now, Jack's health care needs throw them together intensively around the clock. This circumstance blurs the boundaries that define them as distinct individuals. Consequently, each suffers a loss of independence and identity. The sense of equality and partnership previously characteristic of their marriage is disrupted. Jack feels dependent on Helen, and Helen feels trapped by the care Jack needs. Kay observes that both are held hostage by the challenge of Jack's physical condition. To Kay, the couple's depression and conflicts make sense in terms of their feelings of powerlessness. Kay also recognizes that in spite of their difficulties, they show genuine concern and care for each other.

What is happening outside of the system also influences this couple's experience. At first, the Ingersolls' family and friends showed support. Yet this support has dwindled over time. The couple's children are concerned, but they live out of state and can offer only long-distance support. Early on, numerous friends stopped by and called. Now, only one friend visits regularly. Kay notes that the potential for natural support exists but is not fully activated. Kay knows of several community programs that assist people in this situation, yet Helen and Jack have sought no other outside help. Finally, Kay discovers what contributes to the couple's financial instability. Disagreement over liability among the Ingersolls' insurance company, the manufacturer of the utility tower, and Jack's employer have stalled any kind of settlement for the injury.

How does the inside connect to the outside? Kay identifies that Jack's accident has initiated a sequence of events, isolating this couple from the resources of their environment. Before, the Ingersolls were free to work, interact with friends, and pursue individual interests. Now, Jack's injuries confine them to a shrinking world, just as their needs for outside support increases. The pressure builds for Jack and Helen as they run out of reserves.

The information Kay gathers shows that in the past, the Ingersolls had been artful in negotiating life's expected transitions. Not every family system progresses through time with the success evident in this couple's affection, achievements, and accomplishments. Kay sees this adaptability as a strength the couple has yet to rediscover.

Together, Kay and the Ingersolls analyze this information. They identify the power that Jack's health holds over the couple. They recognize the financial bind imposed by Helen's lack of opportunity to work and the unresolved insurance claim. They acknowledge the significance of the disruptions in their relationships with family and friends, and they note the absence of helpful social services. All agree to focus on these issues as they plan a strategy for change.

Building on this analysis, Kay helps Helen and Jack set concrete goals to guide their work together. They decide to stabilize their financial situation by resolving the insurance claim and freeing Helen to return to work. They also will access community services to lighten Helen's responsibilities, giving her more time to spend with friends and for herself. Finally, they will coordinate a network of health-related services to improve Jack's physiological functioning. As they articulate each phase of this plan, Kay works with Helen and Jack to generate specific objectives and activities to pursue each of these goals.

Intervention and Evaluation: Development

Kay and the Ingersolls collaborate to get things moving. Kay provides information about available resources, and the Ingersolls take charge of contacting and organizing the services they select. They access in-home physical therapy. A respite worker comes 1 full day each week, allowing Helen time for her own pursuits. Helen uses part of this time to attend a Northside Hospital mini-course on caring for persons with head injuries. She talks with others having similar experiences and learns about people recovering from head trauma. Helen also spends time with friends; she comes home with renewed energy and more patience for Jack. As Helen feels better, Jack's mood improves. He no longer feels stuck. He participates in rehabilitation activities and a support group for persons with head injuries. He develops new skills in self-sufficiency, which restore some feelings of control and reduce Helen's caregiving duties.

The goal of financial stability requires Kay to seek additional help. She locates a trained legal advocate, Quyen Nguyen of the Center for Citizens' Rights, who works to resolve the intersystem conflict over liability for Jack's accident. Quyen facilitates the flow of information among Jack's doctors, the insurance company, Jack's employer, the manufacturer of the utility tower, and the Ingersolls. Through advocacy and mediation, Quyen influences the participants to negotiate an acceptable settlement and avoid a lengthy court process.

Kay encounters obstacles in her efforts to assist Helen back to work. She finds no respite services that provide care on short notice to match Helen's unpredictable work schedule as a substitute teacher. The only respite care in Northside has few openings and limits regularly scheduled care to a maximum of 1 day per week. Kay reports this gap in service to the Northside Network, a consortium of social service providers in the Northside community, to encourage resource-development efforts to increase respite services.

While implementing the plan, Kay and the Ingersolls monitor the progress they are making. Kay emphasizes the success the Ingersolls are achieving. The Ingersolls have regained their momentum. In meetings with Kay, they now report their progress rather than request assistance. Kay realizes that the Ingersolls are planning a future again rather than looking back at what they have lost. Although their lives have changed course, they have overcome many hurdles and have the power to continue on their own. Kay wraps up her work with Helen and Jack by reviewing their success and celebrating their achievements.

An Example at the Mezzolevel

Mezzolevel practice focuses on change within organizations and formal groups. Such change may be initiated internally by workers who are part of the organization or by persons outside of the organization functioning as consultants or educators. Social worker Margo Suarez-Rand functions at the mezzolevel in her role as training director for the Area Association for People with Disabilities (APD). As part of her job, Margo is responsible for planning and implementing the initial orientation and training for direct service personnel in the agency's residential and day programs, as required by state regulations and as part of the agency's mission to provide quality care. Although Margo's training program has developed over a number of years and is approved by state regulators, Margo questions the effectiveness of the training in teaching the skills and attitudes necessary for working with APD's clients.

Recently in monthly meetings with frontline supervisors, Margo has heard complaints about the lack of readiness of newly hired direct service staff, most of whom have no previous work or life experience with people with disabilities. Margo cringes to hear reports that some direct service personnel are treating clients in demeaning ways, using discriminatory language, or ridiculing their behaviors, and others abandon programs designed to teach clients life skills in favor of doing things for clients because "it's just easier." To Margo, this anecdotal information suggests that even though the training program teaches a philosophy of client empowerment and includes clear instruction on how to implement this perspective in client treatment, the training may not be producing the outcomes that she seeks. She sees it as her responsibility to check into this situation further.

Although Margo operates within the overriding mission of APD and shares the vision of improving the quality of life for the individuals APD serves, her "client system" is really the agency system itself. As a social worker, Margo functions at the mezzolevel, working to strengthen the organization and its response to its clientele. Margo's organizational client system benefits from processes similar to those used with clients at other system levels. In the example that follows, note how Margo (like microlevel social worker Kay Landon in the previous example) guides her mezzolevel client thought phases of dialogue, discovery, and development as she works to achieve the desired outcomes.

Engagement: Dialogue

At this point, Margo has only a vague idea that the training program may not be working well. Her current concerns are based on conversations with a few frontline supervisors. She recognizes that although this information is useful, it does not represent the full view. Margo will need to establish some sort of *dialogue* that accesses a more complete picture of what is currently happening before she can move to assess what part of the training works and what should change.

Dialogue at the individual and family level usually involves a direct in-person exchange with the people involved. Dialogue at the organizational level is more complex, involving more people with differing perspectives. Margo must plan carefully to get a comprehensive and useful view. With whom should she talk? What methods would be best to ensure a productive and open exchange of information that fully articulates the current situation and defines a direction for improvement?

A systemic view guides Margo's decisions about whom to talk with and how to get information. Because her agency client is composed of several subsystems, Margo considers newly hired and recently trained staff, their immediate supervisors, and more experienced staff as useful subsystem perspectives. Margo's empowerment orientation also leads her to explore the client viewpoint. After all, who can better assess how staff members improve the quality of life for clients than the clients themselves?

Margo currently uses written surveys to evaluate trainees' perceptions of the training, and many trainers use written tests to measure learning. In mezzolevel social work, social workers frequently use assessment instruments such as surveys and tests to generate and exchange information. At ADP, these surveys report positive outcomes, but Margo believes that she does not receive the depth of information about the training she needs to refine. She determines that a series of focus groups may be a way to understand the situation better.

A focus group is a facilitated small group discussion centered on key questions of interest. To identify salient issues and conclusions, facilitators record and analyze responses from recipients. Acknowledging that the quality of information accessed through focus groups partly depends on participants' comfort in openly sharing their views, Margo looks for group facilitators who are neutral to the process. How free would various stakeholders in the program be to share opinions about the training when talking to the training director? So, Margo partners with faculty and students from a social work program at a nearby university.

The student facilitators begin by holding informal discussions with selected members of the constituent groups, including representatives of recently trained staff, supervisors, experienced staff, and clients. Through this initial dialogue with key informants and discussions with Margo, a series of key questions takes shape that will guide the focus group discussions. What current training content is most useful? What learning processes work most effectively? What do trainees actually learn that they are able to apply directly in their new positions?

During the focus group sessions, student facilitators use responding skills to fully articulate the thoughts and feelings of participants. They formulate well-phrased questions to access more complete and concrete information, and they encourage widespread participation among group members. Later, the students transcribe audio recordings of the meetings to allow a qualitative analysis of key themes and issues. These focus groups provide a forum for Margo's dialogue with her mezzolevel client system, that is, a way for Margo to discover the strengths of the existing training program and lend direction to plans for improvement.

Assessment: Discovery

A social service agency is a human system that has structures, functions, and policies that affect the transactions within it. An agency has its own culture that shapes rules, norms, and interactions within the agency system. Significantly, an agency also functions within an environmental context that influences its internal operations. Questions addressed within the focus groups help Margo gather internal and contextual information on agency functioning as well as assess how these dynamics affect the training program's effectiveness. Margo will combine conclusions drawn from the focus groups with other assessment measures to provide a comprehensive view.

The focus groups help Margo answer the assessment question related to *what's happening inside the system*. She notes the strengths of the training program, as indicated by the qualitative analysis of the group discussions. Most new and experienced frontline staff report the training program's success in orienting them to the state-mandated documentation and reporting requirements as well as the agency's personnel policies. Frontline supervisors agree with the conclusion that staff are proficient in paperwork and procedures. Staff participants also concur that the training helps to develop skills in providing personal care for clients, teaches them basic signs to communicate with clients who use American Sign Language, and prepares them with self-defense responses in case of aggressive client behaviors.

The focus group discussions also reveal significant challenges. Newly trained staff report that a lot must be accomplished without enough time to do everything. They turn to the more experienced staff for guidance, and they quickly learn to "document, document, document." To keep your job on the front lines, experienced workers say you need to stick to procedures. It's not so much what you do but your ability to keep supervisors and the state people off your back that is necessary to succeed in direct service. This bureaucratic culture predominates; when choices must be made, client care takes a back seat. New workers also report that it is a big adjustment to learn to relate to clients with developmental disabilities. Workers reveal their fears about what clients "might do," and they describe how their friends and families wonder how they can work with "those people."

To understand this focus group information further, Margo broadens her analysis to examine *what's happening outside the system* and how this affects transactions within the agency staff system. The clients' focus group reports are the first place she looks. Clients describe that staff are frequently hard to find because they are always "hanging out in the office" rather than in the program areas. Clients also report that staff members are unresponsive to their requests and sometimes irritable, saying they "are too busy right now" to deal with clients. Clients also report that staff sometimes hurt their feelings, treating them like "little kids."

Continuing her assessment, Margo examines the context to consider other influences. The emphasis placed on administrative work at the expense of client programs leads her to examine the increase in state requirements and the close scrutiny by state inspectors of client files and agency procedures. She takes a historical view to examine changes in the system over time and recognizes that as the state worked to deinstitutionalize services in favor of community-based care, much of the state's complex bureaucracy followed clients to community agencies. State functions have evolved from direct service to agency monitoring. Inspectors focus more on documentation than on client services and quality-of-life measures.

Margo looks directly to the training modules she teaches and notes that to meet state mandates, she has increased the content on paperwork and procedures, leaving her less opportunity to teach about program philosophy and treatment. Further discussion with other trainers leads Margo to conclude that this shift is common across many aspects of the training. Margo recognizes the issue of "goal displacement," a common organizational problem that develops over time. As more attention is given to the functioning and the survival of the agency, the client-centered mission begins to fade from view.

Turning her attention to the staff members' fears and client complaints about staff insensitivity reminds Margo that oppression is a daily experience for the clients of ADP. Stereotypic views, discrimination, and prejudice about people with developmental disabilities is rampart in the culture at large. Newly hired staff bring these cultural biases in with them, and the initial training may not be doing enough to confront these oppressive views and guide people to a more sensitive response. Interestingly, the focus groups of experienced staff and supervisors revealed little fear or bias. Margo concludes that daily interaction with clients over time cultivates new attitudes, as reflected in one supervisor's statement that "working here has opened me up to how beautiful all people are—I can't imagine working anywhere else."

To begin her planning process, Margo reviews all of the information she has gathered and summarizes the key strengths and needs of the training program. She focuses on three areas in setting goals. First, she decides to shore up the current strengths of the program by setting a goal to maintain the high level of staff compliance with paperwork and procedures. Margo doesn't want to change something that works as she makes attempts at improvement.

Second, Margo sets a goal to increase the successful implementation of client-centered programming by direct service staff. Two objectives flesh out this goal. The first objective—to maintain the existing training approach in teaching personal care for clients and sign language—is based on the assessment of these as existing strengths in staff functioning. The second objective within this goal—to increase the implementation of client developmental programs—will require modification in the training approach and additional emphasis. Some redistribution of workload requirements may also be necessary to optimize the chances for success.

Finally, Margo sets a goal to increase the humane treatment of agency clients by newly hired workers. She immediately sees the significant challenge associated with success in this arena because social injustice toward people with developmental disabilities is deeply ingrained in the wider society. But if all people committed to social justice avoided the difficult goals, society would never have achieved the gains of the civil rights and women's movements. Besides, Margo recognizes that she is not alone in this endeavor. The more experienced staff and the clients themselves are resources to assist her in addressing the wider social issue of oppression of people with disabilities.

Intervention and Evaluation: Development

Within the development phase, social workers and clients collaborate to implement the action plan. Margo and her agency client launch a multifaceted strategy to achieve the goals and objectives specified in the discovery phase and to evaluate the impact of their efforts.

The first goal—to maintain staff expertise with paperwork and procedures—is the easiest to achieve. To discover what works and continue it is always easier than to acknowledge a failure and guess how to improve things. To meet this "stay-the-course" goal, Margo needs only to activate existing resources. She teams with other agency trainers to identify those parts of the training program focused on paperwork and procedure and identifies strengths of the training program to ensure that upcoming changes will not interfere with their current success in these areas.

The second goal—to increase the successful implementation of client-centered programming—requires more work. Margo convenes the same group of trainers to enlist their expertise in this effort. She challenges them to improve training on the programmatic aspects of agency functioning. She structures the intervention for success by asking each trainer to convene a team of experts—an alliance of training instructor, experienced staff, supervisor, new direct service employee, and client—to redesign the content of each targeted training module. Margo knows that creating such an alliance will give voice to the differing perspectives, leading to changes that will benefit all stakeholders. Margo takes the responsibility to discuss with her own supervisor a possible redistribution of workload requirements to free direct service personnel for more client interaction and programming.

Margo also addresses the goal of creating a more affirming environment for agency clients. She implements a two-pronged approach aimed both at new employees and at the wider community pool of potential employees. She accesses experienced direct service employees as training "associates" to talk about their transformation in attitude toward clients. Margo encourages each to tell his or her personal story of professional and personal development within ADP and share his or her feelings about agency clients. Margo also seeks clients as experts to train new hires about who clients are and what they expect from staff.

The clients are a key resource in another arena to address the social justice goal. As part of an ADP community integration program, a group of clients has formed a "Speak Up" group—a social action coalition of clients who present information about people with developmental disabilities to community groups, issue press releases to local media, and offer training to individuals with disabilities in public speaking and legislative testimony. She asks this client group to join with ADP's employee recruitment and hiring efforts to initiate a resocialization process about persons with developmental disabilities from the first point of entry into the ADP system. Because her assessment showed clearly that interaction with clients was effective in reducing bias, Margo figures the sooner the better for employees to begin to relate positively to the clients they will serve.

As Margo coordinates this agency-wide effort to improve the training program, she continually evaluates the process and the progress. She meets regularly with those involved to monitor the impact of the changes she has initiated. Each group with whom she meets identifies what is working and should continue and also notes what is not working and should be modified. Changes in training judged to be effective are written into the training program modules, thereby institutionalizing them into the agency's culture and functioning.

As time goes on and the stakeholders begin to agree that "they are getting it right," Margo moves to wrap up this particular intervention with the training program. She recognizes that the procedural changes in hiring, the changes in the training content and process, and the cultural changes in agency atmosphere will work to stabilize the improvements initiated during this concentrated effort. Deciding to add periodic focus groups to the ongoing evaluation of the training program will give Margo another tool she needs to monitor the effectiveness of the training program as it evolves.

An Example at the Macrolevel

Leon Casey's job as a community prevention specialist at the Neighborhood Development Association (NDA) prompts him to keep abreast of community issues. At first, the neighborhood conflict between a Caucasian resident and his new African American neighbor seemed to Leon like an isolated incident. But when subsequent events occur—fights between groups of Latino and Caucasian students at the high school, a charge of police brutality by an Asian American claiming racial discrimination, and now a cross burning on the front lawn of Northside's only synagogue—a trend emerges. After the civil rights commission contacts Leon with the same concerns, Leon directs his efforts toward the simmering ethnic and intercultural tensions in his client system—the Northside community.

Engagement: Dialogue

Leon quickly convenes a meeting of relevant community members to function as key informants about this challenging issue. Participants include the community liaison from the police department, the chairperson of the Civil Rights Commission, the current president of the Ecumenical Council, the director of the Gay and Lesbian Alliance, a representative from United Way, the chairperson of a neighborhood action council, and the rabbi from the site of the cross burning. Each participant offers additional examples of cultural intolerance, and the group members agree that the Northside community must promote a greater acceptance of diversity.

Participants agree to work together to reduce intercultural tension. They form themselves into a steering committee to assess the situation further and develop a strategy for change. Leon facilitates this committee, exploring ways to articulate this challenging situation in more detail. Members agree to host community forums at their respective sites to encourage citizen participation in the assessment process. Leon's role is to coordinate the scheduling of these events. He will use the outreach capabilities of NDA to announce these forums to the public. Leon also trains forum observers to record information offered by citizens at the various meetings and to compile the results for the steering committee's consideration.

Assessment: Discovery

Leon facilitates the steering group's assessment processes, helping them complete a strengths-based ecosystemic assessment. This means Leon guides the group to look for strengths and resources within the community rather than focusing solely on its challenges. Leon also orients group members to consider the community's interactions with its environment as potential resources for change.

The community forums help Leon understand *what is happening inside the system.* Citizens report additional acts of racial and cultural hatred. Observers note several angry interchanges at the forums among citizens from different cultural groups. On the positive side, citizens describe several exceptions to these problems—successful cross-cultural community events and acts of kindness and friendships among diverse people, which counteract the trend toward intolerance. Those attending the forums want the community to respond quickly before the incidents "get out of hand" or "somebody really gets hurt."

Leon leads the steering group to consider *what's happening outside the system* and *how the inside is connecting to the outside.* Group members are all familiar with national events that create a context of racial and cultural divisiveness. An anti-immigration sentiment pervades national opinion, homophobia leads to regressive social policies and laws, White supremacy groups grow in popularity, and movements promoting English as the only language evidence the trend away from cultural pluralism.

Conversely, not all that is happening in the environment of the Northside community is bleak. Other cities, responding to the same pressures, have begun efforts to increase cultural acceptance in their communities. In a phone survey of similar-sized municipalities, Leon learns of several strategies used in other areas that are yielding positive results. He carefully records the information and asks these municipalities to send pamphlets, brochures, newspaper articles, program evaluation results, and other written information about their efforts.

Compiling the information obtained from the community forums and the telephone survey, steering committee members work together to construct a plan of action. They confirm their original purpose by setting a goal to increase acceptance of cultural diversity in the Northside community. To meet this goal, they articulate two objectives: (1) to form a Quick-Response Team to deal with hate crimes and (2) to establish a mediation center. These objectives are concrete steps toward the goal of cultural tolerance.

Intervention and Evaluation: Development

Steering group members divide up their efforts to achieve both objectives simultaneously. Some members complete activities to form the Quick-Response Team. After studying the composition of such teams in other locations, steering group members determine criteria for team membership. Qualifications include skills in crisis response, conflict resolution, bilingualism, and cultural competence. Subsequently, steering committee members poll social service agencies and other community organizations to see whether they have qualified personnel and whether they are willing to donate their resources.

In response to these inquiries, the Quick-Response Team begins to take shape. A large pool of team members assembles. Each individual response team includes at least one representative from the police department, a person skilled in mediation and conflict resolution, and a person or persons fluent in the languages and familiar with the cultures of the citizens involved. Other members from the larger pool of volunteers stand available to supplement teams as necessary in specific situations.

Leon's own agency takes a coordinating role with the team. The Northside Development Association uses its resources to supply office space and an emergency phone line. NDA will also serve as the location or the ongoing recruitment and training of the response team members.

Other steering committee members work on the second objective. They secure a site for the Northside Mediation Center when the rabbi volunteers space at the synagogue. They also visit other mediation centers in nearby communities to gather ideas for how to organize the Mediation Center. Once they develop a tentative plan for the center, the steering committee holds a public meeting at the proposed site to elicit additional input.

The steering committee integrates the information gathered from other mediation centers, adds perspectives from the citizen's forum, incorporates its own ideas, and then proposes a model for organizing and operating the Mediation Center. Members vote to approve the proposal and then focus their efforts on launching the new program. Steering group members use their community networks to locate both private and public sources of support, including technical expertise, funding, and volunteer mediators.

Finally, steering committee members combine their efforts to determine the interface between their respective projects. Clearly, the Quick-Response Team and the Mediation Center have complementary roles. Committee members negotiate a service agreement by which the Quick-Response Team focuses on crisis situations and refers citizens to the Mediation Center for more lasting solutions to their conflicts.

Once the team and the center are operational, the committee seeks ways to end its work and ensure that both services remain established as ongoing programs in the community services network. The Quick-Response Team will continue to function as part of the Northside Development Association. The Mediation Center will remain at the synagogue and be governed by a board of directors that includes some members from the original steering committee and other volunteers recruited from the community.

? Check your understanding of social work values and purpose by taking this brief quiz.

The steering committee also agrees to follow up on its work. At 6-month intervals, they will review evaluations of the two new programs and examine police reports to assess whether cultural tolerance is increasing.

MULTILEVEL PRACTICE IN GENERALIST SOCIAL WORK: AN INTEGRATIVE CASE EXAMPLE

Even when specializing at a particular level of practice, a generalist social worker will recognize viable interventions in other domains. Consider the following example of Alisha Shelton, a school social worker at Northside Elementary, who, while working with first-grade student Benita Alvarez, extends beyond the microlevel of practice to intervene at the mezzo- and macrolevels as well. Generalist social workers see multiple opportunities for change and sometimes intervene at all levels of practice to maximize potential benefits for clients and achieve social justice.

Social Work Practice at the Microlevel

In response to teacher Dorothy Campbell's concern, school social worker Alisha Shelton meets with Benita Alvarez, a first-grade student who has recently enrolled in Northside Elementary. The referral stems from Benita's reticence. According to Mrs. Campbell, Benita "hasn't said a word" in the 2 weeks she has attended the school. Mrs. Campbell sees Benita as compliant with instructions but thinks that Benita may have hearing loss, autism, or some kind of cognitive or speech difficulty. Perhaps she is simply shy or not fluent in English. Benita nods or shakes her head in response to questions or instructions given by Mrs. Campbell. She stays isolated from the other students and converses with no one.

Policy Practice

Behavior: Assess how social welfare and economic policies impact the delivery of and access to social services

Critical Thinking Question: Policy implications are evident in the micro-, mezzo-, and macrolevels of social work practice. What policy threads are woven in the practice example of school social worker Alisha Shelton that could form the basis for collaboration for effective policy action?

Before meeting with Benita, Alisha checks with school administrators. She learns that Benita transferred to Northside 3 weeks after the term began. Benita's mother Isabella Alvarez, together with a friend, had registered Benita, but Isabella had produced no school records or offered any information about previous school attendance. Isabella spoke only Spanish, and her friend, Ann, translated during the registration process. When asked about previous school experience, Isabella's response was evasive, saying the family had recently moved around a lot.

After registration, the school nurse coordinates with the Northside County Health Department for a physical exam and the immunizations required for school enrollment. Benita was placed in Mrs. Campbell's first-grade class based on her chronological age and her mother's report that first grade is the appropriate level. Mrs. Campbell receives instructions to assess Benita carefully to determine whether placement in the first grade is appropriate. Observing Benita's 2 weeks of silence leads Mrs. Campbell to question the placement, precipitating the referral to Alisha.

Benita behaves predictably in her first meeting with the social worker. Alisha does most of the talking, with Benita nodding occasionally or whispering a brief response. It seems to Alisha that Benita hears her well and also understands English, yet she demonstrates considerable shyness or a great need for privacy. Benita offers little information about her life or her family, but she does respond to direct questions, indicating that "things are OK" with school, Mrs. Campbell, and the other students. Alisha knows she needs to access other perspectives on Benita to determine what might help Benita at school. She decides to make a home visit.

Because no phone is listed on Benita's record, Alisha drops by the Alvarez home to schedule an appointment. Alisha intends to bring an interpreter to the family appointment but decides she knows sufficient Spanish to set a meeting time. Isabella answers the door cautiously and does not invite Alisha in. Standing on the front step, Alisha introduces herself to Isabella, describes her role and relationship to Benita, and clarifies the purpose of the proposed meeting. They agree to a time for Alisha to return with an interpreter.

Returning for the appointment with interpreter Carmen Mendes, Alisha is greeted at the door by Isabella's friend Ann. Ann explains that she knows Isabella from church, and Isabella has asked her to be present. Isabella and Benita are waiting in the kitchen.

Through the interpreter, Alisha again explains who she is and the purpose of the visit. Alisha notes that although Carmen translates everything to Isabella, Isabella frequently looks to her friend Ann for reassurance about what she is hearing. From this observation, Alisha concludes that language is not the only obstacle to communication. A great need exists on Isabella's part to include someone she trusts in the discussion. With Ann to offer reassurance, Isabella grows more comfortable. Isabella begins to talk about Benita more freely, and Alisha is able to do a brief assessment of Benita's developmental functioning.

At home, Alisha observes a very different Benita. As Isabella grows more trustful, Benita becomes more animated. Benita converses readily with her mother in Spanish and talks intermittently with Ann in English. Clearly, Benita is bilingual and not really shy at all in the comfort of her own home. As Alisha queries Isabella about Benita, the two tease one another playfully. Alisha sees the affection. She also notes that Benita will answer some questions herself without waiting for Carmen to translate and then will share the content with her mother. Benita is beginning to look like a typical first grader to Alisha. Perhaps the adjustment to school will come more easily as Benita's comfort increases. Alisha refocuses her efforts in this familiar setting to build an easy rapport with Benita, hoping to bridge that same level of comfort to school.

Next, Alisha shifts her assessment to the family. Immediately, Alisha notices uneasiness once again invade the conversation. Alisha learns that Benita is Isabella's only child and that Isabella's husband Roberto is at work. Isabella reports that the family originated in Guatemala and migrated to the Northside community, drawn by the promise of employment at a local food-processing plant. Although Alisha seeks more detailed information, none is forthcoming. Isabella remains silent about how long the family has lived in the United States and their path from Guatemala to Northside.

Noting the modest living situation, Alisha expects that Benita may qualify for the subsidized school lunch program. She explains how Isabella can apply by simply offering some proof of the family's income. Isabella resists, saying that whatever help she needs she can get from the church. Then Isabella stands up, indicating that she is ready to end the meeting. Alisha honors the preference and arranges to meet with Isabella again in a couple of weeks to help facilitate Benita's transition to the new school.

Back at school, Alisha reflects on her conversation in the Alvarez home and develops both a hypothesis about what is going on and a plan of action. She first notes the strengths. Benita is developmentally appropriate, perhaps gifted. She is bilingual and likely understands what others are saying to her in class. She lives in an affectionate household, and her mother, Isabella, shows both motivation and ability to parent in an uplifting way. An obvious goal is to generalize Benita's feelings of comfort and competence at home to the school environment.

Alisha also notes areas of concern. A significant difference appears between Benita at home and Benita at school. What is inhibiting Benita's integration into the classroom? Alisha believes that Isabella's pattern of sharing information in their meeting provides some clues. Isabella is very cautious, especially when talking about anything not directly related to Benita's performance at school. Perhaps a family rule exists about sharing too much. Could it be that Benita is permitted to be herself in the family setting but instructed to keep to herself in the outside world?

It strikes Alisha that she has seen this caution before in other immigrants. Many tread carefully when interacting with those they perceive to be authorities. Some bring memories of oppressive actions by officials in their countries of origin. Others fear that their status in the United States leaves them vulnerable to prosecution. Alisha recalls a previous student who was born in the United States but whose parents had entered the country without proper documentation. She respected the resistance the parents showed, recognizing the risks if their immigration status were discovered: deportation and possibly losing their child to state custody. The situation of the Alvarez family feels similar to her. Are concerns about immigration status the central theme that affects both Isabella's reluctance to share information and Benita's behavior at school?

Alisha concludes that Benita is probably appropriately placed and simply needs to gain comfort in the school environment to activate her potential. So Alisha develops a three-part plan. First, she places Benita in Alisha's first-grade girls' group, a group designed to help members develop social skills and build self-esteem. Second, she meets with Mrs. Campbell and Benita together to help Benita feel safe in the classroom and also to help Benita and Mrs. Campbell develop a more comfortable relationship. Alisha feels that she already relates effectively with Benita and hopes to help Mrs. Campbell do the same. Third, Alisha continues to visit with Benita and Isabella at home as a way to sustain a comfortable rapport with the family and to update Isabella on Benita's progress.

In many ways, this intervention plan is successful. Benita blossoms in the girls' group. Her comfort increases, and she makes friends. Isabella remains dedicated to her daughter's success, keeping regular appointments with Alisha and supporting Benita. But the goal of assisting Mrs. Campbell to relate well with Benita falters. Benita remains detached in class. Alisha earlier recognized that progress in the classroom could be slow. When first responding to the plan, Mrs. Campbell had said, "I don't know why I should have to take time to meet with her individually. Students like her take up way too much of my time. All this effort, and in 6 weeks they'll be moving away. That's just how those people are."

Noting Mrs. Campbell's resistance, Alisha determines two things. She will need to move cautiously with Mrs. Campbell not to alienate her further. Alisha remembers a former professor's advice that astute social workers respect a client's resistance and work to understand it before rushing ahead with a plan. Second, Alisha must craft an appropriate response to what Mrs. Campbell is saying. The teacher's words are likely rooted in bias, but exactly who does Mrs. Campbell mean by "those people," and what can Alisha do about it?

Social Work Practice at the Mezzolevel

Within the next week, Alisha gets her answer when she walks into the teachers' lounge. Mrs. Campbell is there, as are other teachers. The conversation is about immigration, specifically illegal immigration. Many teachers are siding with Mrs. Campbell, saying "those people" should be stopped at the border because they are taking American jobs and using up social and educational resources without contributing anything. Other teachers are expressing different views, saying things like, "but we all come from immigrants," "diversity in the United States is a good thing," and "they are doing jobs no American will take."

Alisha moves further into the room and joins the conversation. She refrains from offering her own opinions, responding instead to what others are saying, helping the teachers articulate their views. Participating in this dialogue, Alisha begins to understand that Benita's experience in the classroom may not be an isolated one. Several teachers express their desire to withhold efforts from "undeserving" students who they presume to be undocumented immigrants. Alisha realizes that this negative preconception is likely affecting Benita's comfort in the classroom, and she recognizes that other students at Northside Elementary may have similar disempowering experiences as well.

Frequently, when an individual client's behavior is viewed in context, a different perspective emerges. Rather than focusing exclusively on the individual needs of Benita, Alisha now sees the need for intervention at a different level—the mezzolevel of practice. Mezzolevel practice addresses challenges within the functioning of formal groups and organizations. Northside Elementary is such a system. Alisha can see the benefits that would accrue for Benita and others if teachers' views were more empathic.

Alisha takes her concerns to the school administration, saying that teachers need a better understanding of the changing demographics of the student population, particularly the needs and experiences of those who have immigrated. The timing for this discussion is good. The building principal mentions that school personnel are planning the next in-service day, and they are exploring various topics around the theme of student diversity. A focus on the experiences and rights of immigrant students is timely. He asks Alisha to join the in-service planning committee and share her ideas.

The in-service planning committee is a district-wide task group responsible for organizing relevant training for staff and teachers in the school system. They are receptive to Alisha's thoughts about immigration issues yet are unsure how to proceed. Alisha volunteers to develop a survey to assess the learning needs of those who will attend. The results will help the committee plan an event and suggest which expert presenters might speak directly to the concerns and attitudes of those who will attend. Alisha develops a brief survey and pretests it with a few staff in her building. She also develops a cover letter explaining the purpose of the survey and its confidential nature. Finally, she distributes sufficient copies of the survey and cover letter to each building in the district for teachers and staff to complete.

Frequently, assessment at the mezzolevel requires social workers to use such tools as surveys to access accurate assessment information. After compiling the results and analyzing the survey data, Alisha returns to the in-service committee with the concrete information necessary to plan a relevant and useful training event. The survey shows that school personnel are generally aware that all immigrants, documented and undocumented, have rights to school attendance. Beyond that fact, their knowledge is limited.

Very few understand what rights immigrants have to access other community and social services. Even fewer show knowledge of the larger social issues that have increased
the flow of immigration in recent times. Many teachers express resentment about increasing class size and the specialized instruction sometimes required to accommodate
foreign-born students.

These data lead the committee to plan a two-pronged event. First, an immigration attorney will explain the legalities of immigration. The attorney will also discuss
the rights of immigrant families and how immigration status determines eligibility
for community services and social benefits. Second, an immigration rights activist
will discuss the global social and economic dynamics contributing to the current immigration wave. The aim is to enlighten attendees on the possible motivations and
experiences of recent immigrants by using current research and facts to examine the
validity of myths and biases pervasive in the popular media. Perhaps this will lead to
greater empathy and understanding by school personnel for the students with whom
they work.

The in-service is a success, according to the attendees' evaluation forms and comments. Alisha herself learns much. From the attorney, she learns that immigration is a
complex issue. Those immigrants who are undocumented are entitled to very little ex-
cept public education and necessary medical care. Even those who have legally migrated
to the United States and are on a direct path to citizenship are prohibited in many states
from accessing certain social welfare benefits such as Temporary Assistance to Needy
Families (TANF). Alisha hears that the rights of legal immigrants vary tremendously
depending on their particular immigration status. For example, Alisha is surprised to
learn that undocumented immigrants arrested for violation of immigration law are not
guaranteed legal representation.

The immigration rights activist offers a powerful message to those attending. One
by one, the activist presents common myths about immigrants and dispels them with
current research and facts. Two misconceptions stand out in Alisha's mind—that undocumented immigrants don't pay taxes and that immigrants in general draw more from
the U.S. economy than they contribute. Neither is true. All immigrants do pay taxes
in the form of income, property, and sales taxes at the state and local levels—the very
taxes that pay Alisha's salary in the Northside school system. Moreover, through their
employment and entrepreneurship, immigrants likely contribute more to the American
economy than they ever recoup in public benefits. Many immigrants arrive during prime
working age and enter the U.S. workforce without ever having drawn on the resources
of the public educational system. Even undocumented workers receiving paychecks contribute to Social Security and Medicare funds from which they will never be able to draw
benefits.

Why is there such a wave of immigration at this time? The social activist points to
recent international trade agreements such as NAFTA as a primary cause. Just as the
movement of jobs to Mexico has depleted many employment opportunities in the United
States, the subsequent movement of jobs from Mexico to the cheaper labor pool in China
has brought increased unemployment to Mexico and other Latin American countries.
Loss of family farms to corporate agricultural conglomerates has similarly affected both
the United States and Mexico. Individuals seeking to support their families are not to

Watch this video and observe how problems that clients experience as personal might be solved by targeting changes in larger systems. What strategies are available at larger system levels to address personal problems? www.youtube.com/watch?v=vjRlFCgQ1e8

blame for the immigration controversy. Globalization, corporate interests, and trade agreements may be creating some of the circumstances that disenfranchise working people in both North and South America.

Alisha feels increased empathy for all of those affected by the immigration issue. Importantly, the in-service changes the conversation in the school environment. Several teachers thank Alisha for broadening their understanding. Even Mrs. Campbell's demeanor seems gentler when Alisha stops by to monitor Benita's progress in the classroom. The intervention at the school-system level seems to have trickle-down benefits for individual students.

Social Work Practice at the Macrolevel

The positive impact of the in-service gives Alisha a feeling of accomplishment. She feels proud that she has met the ideals of the social work profession by recognizing opportunities for change, both in the person and in the environment. Yet, what Alisha learns that day also leaves her with an unsettled feeling. Her work is not finished. The situations in which immigrants such as Benita find themselves seem fundamentally unfair. To Alisha, the treatment of immigrants is more than a legal issue; it is a human rights issue. Laws governing immigration should change. The societal response to immigrants—whether documented or undocumented—should be brought into line with global economic and social realities. Alisha feels strongly about these convictions.

Alisha realizes that intervention on a broader scale than is possible in her position as a school social worker is necessary to ensure the well-being and to respect the human dignity of clients like the Alvarez family. Although Alisha recognizes the need for change at the macrolevel, she must honor the boundaries of her professional position. A political stance about immigration falls outside her contracted role with the school system, yet Alisha's professional identity as a social worker extends beyond her job. She feels the pull of social justice and seeks to expand her efforts beyond her work environment.

Alisha is a member of two professional organizations—the National Association of Social Workers (NASW) and the School Social Worker Association (SSWA). Both groups serve multiple functions for their members and their clients. They implement social action efforts and employ lobbyists to press for legislation that benefits social work practice. Alisha specifically remembers the attention given to the rights of immigrant students at the last SSWA annual program meeting. SSWA is the place to start, so Alisha contacts the political action committee of the SSWA.

The response from the political action committee is immediate, informing Alisha that they are recruiting members for a newly formed subcommittee on immigration. Clearly, Alisha is not the only school social worker interested in the immigration issue. They invite Alisha onto the subcommittee, and she readily accepts. Attending her first meeting, Alisha realizes that considerable progress has already been made. They have completed many elements of the dialogue and discovery phases by researching current laws about immigration, surveying their own members about issues and preferences regarding their work with immigrant students, talking with congressional representatives about immigration reform, and looking broadly at the social policies of other countries to assess how they answer questions posed by immigration.

Alisha sees that immigration is a complex issue affected by both state and federal laws. The subcommittee recognizes this complexity and forms task groups to work toward goals at both governmental levels. At the state level, the group decides to focus on extending social service eligibility to all residents regardless of citizenship. At the federal level, they agree to support a humane path toward citizenship for undocumented current residents who intend to remain in the United States. Current laws criminalize the lack of documentation. The subsequent prosecution and deportation for those convicted frequently leads to community turmoil and family disruption. The subcommittee decides to support a program of amnesty for current residents and emphasize community preservation and family well-being in any immigration reform.

To achieve these goals, subcommittee members develop a multifaceted plan. Taking action at the federal level, the SSWA lobbyist will work to influence members of Congress to fashion an accessible and fair legalization process for undocumented residents. Some subcommittee members will organize an email and letter writing campaign in support of this new federal legislation. At the state level, other members of the subcommittee will contact their own state representatives, pressing them to introduce legislation to offer social welfare benefits to all residents without regard for immigration status. Still other members will recruit key informants and prepare them to participate in state legislative hearings when the legislation comes to the floor.

Alisha helps those preparing for the legislative hearings. She works to locate professional experts who will present evidence to prove the benefits of the proposed changes. She also seeks to identify clients who are willing to offer their perspectives about the detrimental impact of current laws. Finally, Alisha prepares to speak about her experiences as a school social worker in seeking to support the humane treatment of children adversely affected by the current policies.

Subcommittee members know that this will be a lengthy process. Such a complex problem as immigration reform will require a complex solution that accounts for many conflicting views and attitudes. Meanwhile, interested school social workers will continue their efforts at the microlevel by supporting individual students and at the mezzolevel by creating affirming school environments until such a time as a public solution at the macrolevel can be achieved.

 Assess your understanding of multilevel practice by taking this brief quiz.

LOOKING FORWARD

The approach to generalist practice presented in this chapter emphasizes empowering processes applicable to working with clients at all system levels. These processes incorporate a holistic view of clients' situations, a partnership view of the social worker–client relationship, and a solution-focused view of outcomes. The consistent application of the ecosystems perspective in unison with a strengths orientation structures this empowering generalist social work approach.

The empowerment paradigm frames practice within three continuous phases of dialogue (engagement), discovery (assessment), and development (intervention and evaluation) and distinguishes empowering processes to implement in each. Practitioners can apply this model to all levels of client systems, with the option of effectively integrating interventions within several spheres for maximum benefit. Adept workers maintain flexibility in implementation to account for the focal system, cultural diversity, and the particulars of clients' situations.

The remaining chapters comprehensively describe and exemplify this empowering approach to generalist social work practice. Each chapter presents an empowering process, explores its conceptual base, delineates collaborative roles for workers and clients at all levels, considers cultural diversity, and highlights ethical considerations. The first phase of dialogue describes the ways that social workers engage to understand clients and their situations. Chapter 6, "Engagement: Forming Partnerships," analyzes the dynamics of social worker–client relationships and suggests specific guidelines for transforming positive expectations about clients into empowering partnerships with them.

Evaluate what you learned in this chapter by completing the Chapter Review.

6

Engagement: Forming Partnerships

HELDER ALMEIDA/SHUTTERSTOCK

Relationships between social workers and clients are fundamentally relationships between human beings. Whether working with an individual or a whole community system, social workers are connecting with other humans to achieve mutual purposes. The relationships formed by social workers and clients differ from social relationships. Although they are friendly, social workers and clients are not friends. Although these relationships are genuine, they have designated purposes and defined endings. In addition to being spontaneous and personable, social work relationships are deliberate and professional. Successful professional partnerships are complex and directed toward goals. Social workers and clients carefully construct and monitor their relationships to ensure that they meet the purposes for which they exist.

Within the helping relationship, participants establish trust, sort out their respective roles and responsibilities, and develop patterns of interaction necessary to engage in a process for change. To the extent that this relationship nurtures and encourages mutual participation, it is empowering. Practitioners and clients work together as collaborative partners, with each serving as a resource for the other.

When developed as a partnership, the social worker–client relationship itself becomes an empowering resource for change. To achieve this partnership, workers need a conceptual understanding of the relationship, effective communication and interpersonal skills, abilities to relate cross-culturally, and social work ethics and values to guide transactions. This chapter prepares practitioners to develop collaborative relationships with clients. Ultimately, practitioners who put these concepts into practice will build partnerships with clients, collaborations that achieve cooperation and synergy throughout all phases of the change process.

ENGAGING WITH CLIENTS

Forming partnerships is the hallmark of engagement with clients. A respectful, collaborative relationship between a worker and client is the core of any social work endeavor. Whether client systems are individuals or larger groups, social workers must establish an atmosphere of trust and a sense of purpose to ensure an open sharing of relevant information.

Collaboration and Partnership

In the spirit of collaboration and partnership, social workers move quickly to engage clients in a focused dialogue that clarifies challenging issues and defines the purpose of their work together. The success of this dialogue depends on the practitioner's professional skills and interpersonal qualities. Working with clients as collaborative partners is grounded in the tradition of the social work principle of self-determination. Empowerment-based social workers respect what clients and constituents already know and can do. In short, they recognize client strengths and competence. Graybeal (2007) says that "the art of collaboration depends on finding ways to acknowledge, understand, and incorporate the client's world view into every aspect of practice" (p. 519).

The phrase "begin where the client is" expresses a fundamental social work practice imperative. Strengths-focused social workers interpret "begin where the client is" as a charge to discover potential strengths and resources, support developing competencies, and base constructive solutions on what already works for the client. This mindset has profound implications for developing relationships between social workers and clients.

The Dilemma of Social Workers as Experts

Reverence toward social workers as experts fabricates a hierarchy of haves and have-nots. In this view, proficient social work experts have knowledge, insight, and ideas to bestow on inept clients who lack these qualities. Proactive professionals take charge of passive clients. Masterful social workers commence action, and ineffectual client systems are acted on. Interpreted bluntly, the expert professionals are the champs, and the clients are the chumps!

Social workers beware! Traps exist in this definition of social workers as experts and clients as passive recipients, so no successful way out is available. If clients do not improve, then, of course, social workers are to blame. If clients get better, then social workers get the credit along with the responsibility of being the champion of keeping clients' lives on track. Ultimately, when expert social workers win, passive clients lose their sense of competence and independence. The insidious nature of this dependency subverts clients' power to define their own realities.

This configuration depicts a hierarchy of power and authority. The worker is the expert authority with decision-making power, and the client comes to depend solely on the power resources of the social worker or struggles with the worker to gain a share of the power. A one-sided perspective on expertise is the antithesis of empowerment!

The Rewards of Clients and Constituencies as Experts

Social workers bring professional expertise about change processes to the relationship, but they are not the sole experts. Social workers who practice from an empowerment perspective realize that social workers and clients and constituencies have complementary roles, each bringing valuable experiences and competencies. Clients bring their own assets and potentialities, whereas social workers contribute knowledge about strategies to facilitate change and information that will assist clients in making choices and achieving their goals. An empowerment view summons social workers to suspend any tendency to disbelieve clients and to acknowledge clients' expertise. Clients and constituencies are the most qualified experts about their own situations. Quite simply, they know their situations and capabilities best.

Social workers who practice from an empowerment perspective realize that social workers and clients and constituencies have complementary roles, each bringing valuable experiences and competencies.

The Social Worker's Roles

Viewing clients as experts about their own situations directs workers to redefine their roles in more egalitarian and consultative ways. Informed by an egalitarian view, social workers take on the roles of working in partnerships with clients, whereas, from a consultative view, social workers act as mentors in their interactions with clients. Social work clients in Cohen's (1998) study varied in their preferences for partnerships and mentorships. Some liked a more *client-directed* approach, as reflected by the partnership agreement. Others preferred a *client-centered* approach in which practitioners more actively advise and direct clients. Significantly, all clients in Cohen's study expressed dissatisfaction with authoritarian workers. Clients clearly wanted to be in charge of what happened in the relationship, even when that meant they could decide when they wanted workers to be in charge.

Clients' power in defining the relationship is central to an empowerment approach. Well-meaning professionals who control the helping process and make decisions for their clients undermine clients' efficacy. Paternalistic actions impede empowerment! To this end, workers continually monitor their behavior for paternalistic tendencies such as not fully listening to clients, discounting client perspectives, being nonreceptive to client feedback, using language infused with professional jargon, rushing clients, underestimating clients' capabilities, and focusing on deficits rather than strengths (Simon, 1994).

Empowerment demands the centrality of the perspectives of client systems in all aspects of social work practice. Collaborative social workers not only begin where the client is, but they also continue to stay with the client system's perspective throughout all phases of the change process.

Agency Influences on Worker–Client Relationships

The organizational context influences the degree to which social workers and clients can achieve a true partnership. Cohen (1998) questions whether this partnership can be achieved in the context of agencies dominated by hierarchical structures that prescribe the power imbalances in practitioner–client relationships. Workers may need to intervene within their own agencies to ensure that they have the necessary power to share with clients. Agencies can provide support through policies favoring collaborative methods, staff development training designed to equip workers with partnership skills, and initiatives that involve clients in various aspect of program development and evaluation. Only when social workers, themselves, experience empowerment in their professional lives can they implement an empowering approach to practice.

Making Initial Contacts

Effective social workers begin immediately to promote a client's hopes and active participation and consistently act in empowering ways from the outset. Practitioners encourage clients to become full partners by responding to clients with reflective listening skills, offering clients assistance that corresponds to their perceived needs, and encouraging their active participation in all facets of decision making. Even in the apparently routine tasks of beginning the relationship, workers and clients are already setting patterns that will influence the success of their work.

Early interactions reveal more than a worker's expectations for success. How the worker organizes the meeting around the client's experience and what the worker discusses about the client's responsibility in the process also begins to shape the degree to which the client collaborates. A worker who commandeers the early phases of the relationship may initiate a cycle of dependency throughout the work. In contrast, a worker who openly discusses the need for the client's active participation invites the client's expertise and elicits the client's perspective sets a pattern for partnership. Practitioners launch empowering relationships within the first meeting when they communicate positive expectations about success and accentuate the need for client participation.

Recognizing What Clients Bring

Clients experience a variety of thoughts and feelings as they enter working relationships with social workers. Perhaps clients have had previous relationships with helping professionals. Maybe they have specific knowledge about the agency, social workers, or the type of service, predisposing them to trust or resist services. Many clients are directed to social workers by others. The way that clients feel about these referral sources also influences their preconceptions. Each of us approaches new relationships based on our previous experiences. With clients, whatever stories precede their entry into a professional social work relationship inevitably define that partnership.

Now classic research examined clients' perceptions at the time they initiated contact with a family service agency. As might be expected, these new clients reported feelings of distress, discomfort, and confusion. Additionally, they described feelings of hope for finding quick solutions (Maluccio, 1979). Interestingly, clients also reported that they received encouragement from other professionals or family friends who prompted their contact with the worker. Clients' initial expectations reflect discouragement about their own abilities to overcome their problems combined with optimism and encouragement about working with social workers.

Other commentary on clients' perspectives emphasizes the significance of effective communication and interpersonal ambiance. After reflecting on the stigma and dehumanizing effects of chronic and persistent mental illness, consumers indicated that social workers were more helpful "when they could convey optimism and belief in the consumer's abilities, when they asked consumers for their ideas and opinions about what might help a particular problem, and they gave consumers choices and options" (Scheyett & Diehl, 2004, p. 443). In a study of family resource center service delivery strategies, O'Donnell and Giovannoni (2006) found that the highest client satisfaction ratings reflected clients' perceptions of the warmth and interpersonal relationship skills of staff. Engaging clients in respectful conversations sets the stage for collaborative partnerships.

Social workers should take heart, as many clients do enter professional relationships with seeds of trust and hope. Even clients whose lives have predisposed them to distrust and suspicion often remain alert to clues that this professional relationship may hold promise. The fact is that ambivalence characterizes most people's approach to any new relationship. It makes sense that we should begin with a "maybe yes" and "maybe no," or a "wait and see" attitude. Social workers cannot predetermine the expectations of clients or head off their feelings of ambivalence; however, social workers can influence first impressions, either reinforcing hope or inadvertently accentuating negative feelings. Workers must examine their own predisposition toward clients and construct productive assumptions about client potential if they wish to reveal optimism and confidence from the moment of the first contact.

A worker who openly discusses the need for the client's active participation invites the client's expertise and elicits the client's perspective sets a pattern for partnership.

Watch as a social worker meets with a new client. What professional qualities and skills does the social worker in this video demonstrate while engaging her client? www.youtube.com/watch?v=mwKnqvlGLaI

Beginning Steps: A Practice Example

During their first meeting with a client, workers have much to accomplish. Tasks include making a personal connection, clarifying the purpose of the meeting, describing the worker's role, exploring the client's issues, and wrapping up the meeting with a clear direction that defines the next step. Shulman (2012) also stresses the need for workers and clients to discuss issues related to power and authority. Workers use their natural abilities to implement these processes flexibly to match the unique characteristics of each client system. As an example of this beginning process, Karen McBride, a case manager at the Northside Hospital Outreach Program, goes through the steps of initiating a relationship with the Fuentes family, her newest client.

The Referral

The medical social worker in the emergency room at Northside Hospital referred the Fuentes family to Karen McBride only a few days before. Doctors there had treated Juanita Fuentes for a broken leg—which was injured while Juanita was helping her mother, Rosa Hernandez, down from their second-floor apartment to a taxi waiting below. Mrs. Hernandez herself was not injured. But Juanita, even while being treated for her own injuries, talked about her concern for how she would manage to take care of her mother while her leg mended. Her own daughter, Nora, was not that helpful.

And her husband? Well, Humberto had to work; sometimes, he was away from home for days at a time. Karen's job as case manager would be to discover with the Fuentes family how best to meet the needs of Mrs. Hernandez and ensure the well-being of the family while Juanita's leg healed.

Thinking Ahead

As Karen walks up the street to the Fuentes family's apartment, she can feel her anxiety increase. The relative quiet she left in her office has given way to throngs of people, aromas of spicy food, and the sounds of Latin music—it's all a bit strange to Karen. Her pace quickens. Her eyes focus straight ahead. Karen realizes that she is clutching her briefcase tightly. She has to admit it. She feels uncomfortable—out of her culture, so to speak. It makes sense that she would feel this way in a place so different from her own suburban home and even different from the quiet city street where her office is located.

Karen recognizes that her feelings of strangeness might approximate the feelings of the Fuentes family members when she, a 28-year-old White, suburban social worker arrives at their door. Logically, they might be uncomfortable or have doubts about whether someone who is so young and from a different culture can really understand and respect their situation. Karen will have to work quickly to help the family feel comfortable with her as a person and a professional. Karen's own feelings will help her empathize with the family's response to her.

Karen also contemplates the purpose of her visit and the family's potential reactions. Even though the intent of the outreach program is to help families cope effectively with their medical difficulties, not all clients begin as eager participants. Karen wonders if Mrs. Fuentes will see this visit as an intrusion into her private affairs or as a threat to her way of caring for her mother. Karen doesn't yet know what previous experiences this family may have had with outside assistance, but this will certainly affect their initial comfort with her, too.

As a case manager, Karen has initiated relationships with many clients before. All are strangers to her at first, but they soon become people that she likes, respects, and often admires. But bridging that initial distance between having no relationship and forming a working partnership characterized by mutual respect, trust, and effective communication is no small leap, especially across a cultural gap. Working together with the Fuentes family will again test Karen's abilities to clarify the boundaries of the professional relationship, accept views and lifestyles other than her own, and give clients the freedom to move in directions that work best for them.

Diversity and Difference in Practice

Behavior: Apply and communicate understanding of the importance of diversity and difference in shaping life experiences in practice at the micro, mezzo, and macro levels

Critical Thinking Question: Social workers and clients are likely to differ in many ways. How might differences in culture, life experience, and privilege affect a worker's ability to partner with clients and constituencies?

Telephone Work

The receptionist at Northside Hospital's Outreach Program scheduled this appointment. The hospital social worker referred Juanita while she was still at the emergency room because the Fuentes family had no phone, and subsequent contact would be difficult. When Karen schedules appointments herself, she directly and succinctly identifies who she is, where she works, and why she is calling. She states her purpose and clearly outlines the client's privileges of how to respond.

With the Fuentes family, Karen would have described her purpose as helping the family discover ways to care for Mrs. Hernandez while Juanita recovered. She would have assured the family that they were in control. For example, she would have told them that setting an appointment with her was completely their choice and, even if they met with her once, they were under no obligation to continue to see her or to do what she might suggest. Karen attends to power issues with each client, from the first phone call to the last contact. She treats clients as partners from the beginning to the end of their work together.

Meeting and Greeting Clients

Without the advantage of an initial phone contact, Karen will have to work quickly to orient the Fuentes family to the purpose of her visit. This family needs to know who she is and what she is doing there. When Juanita Fuentes opens the door, Karen is direct: "Mrs. Fuentes? I'm Karen McBride from the Northside Hospital Outreach Program. We have an appointment, arranged the day you were at the hospital." Juanita obviously is expecting her. Karen follows as Juanita maneuvers on crutches through the kitchen to the living room, where Mrs. Hernandez is waiting. As Juanita introduces Karen to her mother, Karen again explains her presence to the older woman. If Karen expects Mrs. Hernandez to be a contributing partner to their discussion, she has to include her in the conversation from the outset.

Within this brief introductory interchange, Karen learns two important aspects of relating to this family. She notes that Mrs. Hernandez speaks halting English. Karen will need to speak clearly and concretely to facilitate Mrs. Hernandez's participation. Karen also learns to call Juanita by her first name after Juanita requests that she do so. A respectful relationship always begins by addressing people in the ways they prefer.

Physical Arrangements

Juanita's choice to meet in the living room is a good one. Everyone seems comfortable, and Karen can easily interact directly with either Juanita or Mrs. Hernandez. If this had not been the case, Karen would have requested a rearrangement. Building relationships with a family or group requires direct interactions with each member. When conducting a meeting in a client's home, Karen balances her respect for the family's style, property, and privacy with her own preferences for an arrangement that facilitates family involvement. Karen wants all relevant family members in the room and actively participating. She finds it more empowering to talk with people than about them.

When Karen asks Juanita's permission to turn off the television, she completes her physical preparation for the session. Karen's comment—"I want to make sure I can hear everything you have to say, and the TV may be distracting. Would you mind if we turned it off?"—shows her respect for the family. Karen consistently defines the meeting as work that requires the client's full attention. In her own office, she doesn't take phone calls or interact with other staff when meeting with clients. Families have her full attention, and likewise, she wants theirs. In home visits, Karen also wants the meeting to be focused and productive. When phone calls or visitors interrupt home meetings, Karen lets clients handle the interruption but then discusses the need to control interruptions and focus on the meeting, or reschedule if necessary.

Karen accepts the cup of coffee that Juanita offers. Her agency's previous policy restricted workers from accepting gifts of any kind from clients. Now, they have the flexibility to accept gifts of hospitality in culturally appropriate and friendly ways. Clients have their own traditions of initiating relationships with workers, and Karen is sensitive to defining relationships mutually rather than rigidly structuring the visit to meet her own needs. With the Fuentes family, Karen briefly socializes, describing her trip over from the office and inquiring about Juanita's leg before getting down to business. Her experience has taught her that it is culturally appropriate with most Latino clients to establish social contact first.

Getting Down to Business

After the brief social exchange, Karen proceeds with the task at hand. Karen never assumes that clients know all about the social service network. Even with an insider's view, Karen still finds it confusing. For Juanita and Mrs. Hernandez, the connections between Karen's visit, Juanita's trip to the hospital, and her need for assistance in caring for Mrs. Hernandez may be hazy. Again, Karen repeats her name as she hands each of the women one of her business cards. She describes her role and the purpose of the agency for which she works. She clearly traces how she comes to be with them on this day. She recounts Juanita's conversation with the hospital social worker, the worker's call to the Northside Hospital Outreach Program, the appointment made by the receptionist, the information passed on to Karen, and her arrival at their door. Karen wants to demystify the social work world for this family, a world she hopes they will learn to activate for themselves.

When both women indicate they understand who Karen is, she hands them each a brochure describing her program's services. Karen is pleased that the pamphlet is multilingual. She notices that Mrs. Hernandez follows along in the Spanish language section as Karen highlights important features of the program. Karen stresses that participating in these services is voluntary and has no direct costs to clients. She also talks about confidentiality, assuring the family that she keeps their information private as long as no one in the home is in danger. Karen points out the guarantee of confidentiality and the exceptions as stated in the program brochure. When she completes her explanations, she asks the women if they have questions. Both agree that they understand. Karen notices that their nonverbal messages also indicate they are clear on what she is saying.

Respecting the Client's Perspective

Having completed this general business, it's time to get down to specifics, and that means Karen turns over the dialogue to Juanita and Mrs. Hernandez. Her simple statement of "Now, it's your turn" immediately activates both women, who relate their own parts of the story of Juanita's injury and the difficulties they are having. Karen is careful to respond to each woman, validating their different views and encouraging their continued sharing. Karen has dual goals—to understand the specifics of this family's situation and, simultaneously, to initiate a supportive relationship. To do so, she responds with warmth, acceptance, **respect**, and empathy.

Karen even attends to building relationships with family members who are not present in the room. When Juanita defends her husband, Humberto, as hardworking and caring, yet unable to help with her mother, Karen accepts her view. When Juanita describes her 17-year-old daughter Nora, who still lives at home, as unwilling to help,

Karen's neutral response—"So Nora doesn't think that her help is the answer here"—reveals a nonjudgmental acceptance of the choices that Nora is making while indicating to Juanita that she is listening. Karen knows that families work in the ways they do for good reasons. When building relationships with new clients, Karen accepts their current functioning as workable under the present circumstances. She also makes sure that she allies herself with every family member—even those not in the room—because a working relationship with each member of the client system will most likely elicit everyone's best cooperation and contributions.

Continuing the Relationship Work

The initial interchange between Karen and the Fuentes family focuses on launching and defining the social worker–client relationship. However, the dialogue of the first few minutes does not complete the work of building the relationship. Within this first meeting, Karen will continue to shape the partnership as she talks with them to understand their challenges, identify their existing resources and strengths, and clarify the purpose of their work together. In subsequent meetings, Karen will maintain her focus on the quality of the relationship so that the family continues to feel comfortable enough to share their thoughts, express their feelings, and assert their priorities. No matter what phase of the work she is engaged in, Karen will integrate her professional skills with her personal qualities to ensure that her relationship with the Fuentes family remains a resource for its members.

 Check your understanding of engaging with clients by taking this brief quiz.

QUALITIES OF PROFESSIONAL PARTNERSHIPS

With whom do you find yourself talking freely, sharing your innermost thoughts, and revealing the depth of your feelings? Whom do you trust? What characteristics draw you to others? What makes some people approachable and others not? Personal qualities and communication styles can enhance or detract from interpersonal relationships. Likewise, social workers' personal qualities either support or inhibit their success in developing and maintaining empowering relationships with clients.

Research validates the importance of personal qualities in building professional relationships. In his book *Learning from Clients*, Maluccio (1979) reports that clients appreciate personal qualities more than technical expertise. Those personal qualities most valued by clients include empathy, **genuineness**, acceptance, objectivity, and concreteness. Others agree that social workers need to invest themselves in their relationships with clients in genuinely caring ways. For example, results of a study by Hopps, Pinderhughes, and Shankar (1995) indicate that workers' attributes of caring and flexibility supported positive outcomes with clients.

At its essence, "social work is social caretaking" (Weick, 2000, p. 401). To care is to feel interest or concern, to provide encouragement or guidance, or to render some assistance. Caring feelings and actions characterize all supportive interpersonal relationships, and they are appropriate qualities in social worker–client relationships as well. Ethically based and reflective caring does more than support clients as they take risks to improve their situations. Caring stirs workers and clients to take action. Take note—the ethic of care is not separate or distinct from justice; rather, it is an integral component of

Competent and caring social workers successfully blend their personal characteristics with professional skills when they respond with genuineness, acceptance, respect, trustworthiness, empathy, sensitivity to diversity, and purposefulness.

just social work practice (Orme, 2002). Competent and caring social workers successfully blend their personal characteristics with professional skills when they respond with genuineness, acceptance, respect, **trustworthiness**, empathy, **cultural sensitivity**, and **purposefulness**.

Genuineness

Social workers seek to create a comfortable atmosphere in which clients can "be themselves." Certainly, clients are most likely to do so if workers are doing the same. When workers are genuine, they initiate authentic relationships with their clients. Drawing on the definitive works of Truax, Mitchell, Carkhuff, and Rogers, Fischer (1978) describes genuineness as a characteristic that facilitates communication and builds open relationships. Genuineness refers to social workers "being 'real.'...In fact, genuineness may be best understood as the absence of phoniness, as nondefensiveness, as congruence, and as spontaneity" (p. 199). Who social workers are as people shows through and enhances their professional roles. Disingenuous workers come across as distant, indifferent, and contrived and, as a result, are likely to fail to connect with clients in productive ways.

When Karen McBride interacts with Juanita Fuentes and Mrs. Hernandez, she does so honestly as a concerned person rather than a mechanical professional. When Mrs. Hernandez remarks, "Well, you know, that's the Mexican way," Karen responds with "I'm not really sure—could you explain it to me?" Karen is aware of herself, her similarities and differences from her clients, and her clients' reactions to her. She openly acknowledges these differences rather than distancing herself from the interaction to appear "professional."

Genuineness is different from total honesty. Being genuine does not mean that workers disclose everything they are thinking and feeling about clients. In addition, being genuine is not the same as being personal, as professional relationships differ from social relationships. Although social workers are friendly and genuinely interested in their clients, they find other ways to expand their networks of friends. In responding genuinely to clients, social workers maintain the qualities of purpose and standards of ethics that define relationships as professional.

Acceptance and Respect

Social workers draw on their personal qualities of acceptance and respect when building relationships with clients. Workers who demonstrate acceptance affirm the worth of others while at the same time holding them accountable for the consequences of their behaviors. Respectful social workers regard clients as partners, listen to their opinions, communicate cordially, honor cultural differences, and credit clients as having strengths and potential.

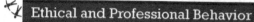

Ethical and Professional Behavior

Behavior: Demonstrate professional demeanor in behavior; appearance; and oral, written, and electronic communication

Critical Thinking Question: Social workers represent the social work profession. What are the defining professional qualities of social work and professional demeanors that practitioners demonstrate in their relationships with diverse client systems?

Acceptance leads social workers to regard clients as having knowledge about their own situations and as contributing as full partners. Berlin (2005) cautions that acceptance is neither passive nor placating; rather, acceptance accords dignity and respect, precipitates advocacy efforts regarding clients' human rights, and promotes access to resources. The strengths orientation provides direction to practitioners to achieve genuinely respectful interactions. By recognizing that all people possess strengths and innate power that can be tapped (Weick & Chamberlain, 2002) and that they have latent potential and creativity (Maluccio, 1981), social workers acknowledge that clients have qualities that merit respect. When you discover people's capabilities and talents, respect follows. Moreover, workers demonstrate acceptance and respect without expecting anything in return. Experience confirms that when social workers consistently treat clients in accepting and respectful ways, clients respond in kind.

A positive view of humankind makes it easier to accept and respect others. The ecosystems perspective offers such a view. As you will recall from Chapter 2, this framework explains all human behavior as evolutionary, adaptive, and functional in context. Social workers appreciate and even admire the unique and creative ways clients match their particular resources with the demands of their environments.

The ways that social workers communicate with clients reveal their acceptance and respect. Accepting workers restrain from asking judgmental "why questions" that critique clients' previous choices. Instead, workers use words such as "what, who, when, where, and how" to arrive at a mutual understanding of events without leaving the impression that clients are doing something wrong. Acceptance means that social workers listen carefully to comprehend rather than to critique what they see and hear. Respect means that social workers recognize clients are doing the best they can under their present circumstances.

Genuineness, trustworthiness, acceptance, and respect are essential qualities in helping relationships.

IOFOTO / SHUTTERSTOCK

Names and Respect

One concrete way of showing respect can be seen in the way social workers treat clients' names. Some workers address all members of client systems by their first names in an attempt to create a friendly atmosphere. Workers are free to address clients other than in the more formal style of using last names in instances in which clients specifically request workers to call them by their first names or nicknames. However, social workers should be cautious because in cross-racial and cross-cultural relationships, using first names may be perceived as disrespectful and insulting.

Examining naming practices in describing groups of people is also imperative. Do clients prefer to be described as African American or Black? Hispanic, Latino, or the more specific Mexican American? Weaver (2000) provides another example when she describes the significant distinction in meaning for indigenous people between their identification as part of a tribe or a nation, noting "the term 'tribe' has been used to minimize the social structures and civilizations" of American Indians while "the term [nation] carries with it a stronger sense of sovereignty" (p. 8). Culturally competent ways of relating to clients require sensitivity to the meanings associated with naming practices and honors clients with the privilege of naming themselves.

Trustworthiness

The presence or absence of trust or the ability to take risks in the context of interpersonal relationships affects the social worker–client relationship. To reach goals, clients must feel comfortable enough to exchange something that they know for some new way of doing things that has unknown potential. Taking these risks requires trust. Trustworthiness is a multidimensional personal quality based on the client's perception of the worker's reliability, honesty, credibility, sincerity, and integrity. It springs from a nonthreatening and open personal approach nestled in the context of professional expertise.

Many factors contribute to developing trust. Trust is reciprocal. In other words, "to get it, you must give it." For clients to trust social workers, social workers must trust clients. Social workers trust clients to be experts about their own situations, as open and honest as is currently possible, and motivated to make necessary changes. Each of us knows our own experience best. When others recognize and validate our experience, we begin to trust their value and to see the potential rewards of a relationship with them. Clients who experience a social worker's trust are more likely to trust the resources the worker has to offer.

Interactions influence the movement of trust along a continuum from no trust to complete trust. As social workers follow through on their own commitments, meet a client's expectations, and demonstrate their acceptance of a client's perspectives, trust increases. When social workers violate a client's developing sense of trust through what the client perceives to be distortion, insensitivity, or betrayal, trust plummets and struggles to recover. Trust builds slowly over time through repeated trustworthy acts but plunges in the blink of an eye. Parents can tell you that it takes a lifetime of relating to build enough trust to give their teenager the keys to the car and only one night of drinking and driving to have to start building trust all over again.

Each social worker–client relationship begins with a different level of trust. Individual differences depend on preconceived notions, personality variables, and cultural norms. A client's previous experience with trusting others influences how trust in the worker evolves. Perceived similarities and differences between clients and social workers as well as current levels of comfort or stress also affect a client's capability to trust. Wherever on the continuum trust begins, it evolves continuously in the relationship. Trust increases or decreases with respect to the experiences of clients and social workers within and outside of professional relationships. Practitioners develop trusting relationships with clients purposefully, by deliberately behaving in trustworthy ways.

> ▶ Watch this video that illustrates how trust between social workers and their clients is essential for effective practice. What does the experience of this social worker from the United Kingdom say about building trust? www.youtube.com/watch?v=_4BsyZOdNXc

Empathy

Clients experience support and trust when social workers respond with empathy. Empathy is "the helper's ability to perceive and communicate, accurately and with sensitivity, the feelings of the client and the meaning of those feelings" (Fischer, 1973, p. 329). For a client to experience the worker's empathy, a worker must accurately distinguish the client's situation and simultaneously "feel with the client, understand how his or her own feelings are different from the client's and hold in abeyance any cognitive distortion such as stereotyping or value judging" (Pinderhughes, 1979, p. 316). Empathic communication reflects respect and nonjudgmental acceptance.

Empathy differs significantly from both pity and sympathy. To understand this difference, visualize a response showing pity. Do you see someone patting another on the head while lamenting, "Poor you"? Responses flavored with pity suggest others are helpless and incapable. Feeling sorry for someone clearly indicates pity. Likewise, sympathy grows from viewing others as weak and vulnerable. Showing pity and sympathy defines a hierarchy of those who are competent and capable and those who are unfortunate and needy. When social workers express pity or sympathy, they disempower clients.

In contrast, when social workers respond with empathy, they validate the perspectives of clients. Clients experience the affirmation of having someone join with and understand their thoughts and feelings. Empathy communicates that social workers are with clients. Empathic support brings the power of affiliation to clients who are struggling to meet life's challenges. "Empathy is being able to finish a [client's] sentence. Being empathic, though, is not finishing that sentence" (Book, 1988, p. 423). Empathy is an act of loving imagination (Keith-Lucas, 1972) that empowers clients to work toward goals while they experience their competence, efficacy, and responsibility.

Cultural Sensitivity

With so many systems involved on both sides of this transactional relationship, social workers and clients find much in common as well as much that is different. Successfully responding to both similarities and differences is central to building cross-cultural relationships. Social workers should maintain an openness to cultural similarities and differences without judging attitudes, values, or behaviors as either inherently right or wrong. Perceived similarities lead to a sense of understanding, empathy, and trust. Similarities bond relationships and establish rapport. Sharing such characteristics as race, ethnicity, religion, or other defining characteristics may create commonalities that contribute to, but in no way ensure, a cognitive match (Walker, 2001).

Discussing Cultural Differences

Discovering differences is inevitable. The ways workers and clients differ are infinite; possibilities include gender, age, race, ethnicity, lifestyle, socioeconomic status, religion, and values. With larger client systems, differences multiply geometrically. These differences affect the dynamics of the helping relationship. Perceived differences may lead to questions about the ability to achieve a mutual understanding. Social workers acknowledge differences directly and respect clients' worldviews. Rather than viewing cultural differences as threatening, empowering social workers explore these differences as resources for generating culturally relevant solutions.

Accepting cultural differences is not as easy as we might like it to be. Cultural memberships define the very ways that we view the world. Western thinking tends to value human control over nature, an orientation to the future, individual autonomy, competition, and the work ethic. In contrast, ethnic minorities often have a non-Western perspective that values the natural environment, links to the past, community well-being, and extended family (Lum, 2004).

These differences in values, perspectives, and experience are enormous. They make cross-cultural relationships vulnerable to miscommunication and conflicting goals. Bridging cultural gaps requires appreciation of diversity, client-focused responding, and open communication. Practitioners may hesitate to ask direct questions about cultural background, racial identity, sexual orientation, prejudice, or discrimination, out of concern they might offend clients or appear incompetent (Woody & Green, 2001). However, research on cross-cultural communication has found that clients are more likely to respect workers who are able to talk openly about cultural differences. Research demonstrates that levels of rapport with clients increase when workers acknowledge and speak directly with clients about their difficulties in comprehending cultural differences or life circumstances presented by the client (Proctor & Davis, 1994).

Purposefulness

In her classic book *Social Casework: A Problem Solving Process*, Perlman (1957) defines the benchmark of a professional relationship as its conscious purposefulness. Social work relationships are grounded in the values and purpose of the profession. In general, social work relationships strive to fulfill the profession's mission to improve quality of life by achieving a goodness of fit between persons and their physical and social environments. In particular, each unique client guides the direction and defines the parameters of the relationship with the social worker.

> ? Assess your understanding of the qualities of professional relationships by taking this brief quiz.

Box 6.1　Relationships and Effectiveness: A Research–Practice Connection

What works in helping clients reach their goals? What techniques have proven effective? The press for accountability by workers and services to achieve desired outcomes propels social work researchers to investigate what works. Contemporary research reinforces the conclusions of past studies that a strong and positive helping alliance, that is, a close and respectful relationship between worker and client, is the key to effectiveness, possibly exceeding the importance of the particular change strategies implemented. This conclusion generalizes across fields of practice.

In the field of child welfare, studies reveal the pivotal role relationships play in achieving successful outcomes. Iachini and colleagues (2015) differentiated two clusters of relationship behaviors that promote engagement in treatment—developing practitioner–client alliances and collaborating with clients. With respect to building alliances with

clients, noteworthy practice behaviors include listening respectfully, responding nonjudgmentally, and fostering motivation. Collaborative behaviors include practitioners' sensitivity to diversity, willingness to share information, and ability to link clients with relevant community resources. Focusing on parents' perceptions of effectiveness in a family-centered approach to child welfare, another recent study underscored the central importance of establishing positive supportive relationships with clients (Fuller et al., 2015). Dawson and Berry (2002), too, identified factors from child welfare research shown to successfully engage parents in helping processes, lead to successful outcomes, and prevent out-of-home placements of children. Interestingly, worker behaviors associated with honoring client preferences and increasing client skills have the most positive effects. These behaviors include "setting of mutually satisfactory goals, providing services that clients find relevant and helpful, focusing on client skills rather than insights, and spending sufficient time with clients to demonstrate skills and provide necessary resources" (p. 312).

Studies conducted with parents of children with disabilities as well as with clients in mental health services also point to worker–client collaboration as central to effective helping. Itzhaky and Schwartz (2000) found that a partnership relationship, as defined by the parents' participation in decision making at the case and organizational levels, was a key element in producing a positive outcome. Dunst and colleagues (2002) also concluded that the benefits of participatory help giving, including strategies that facilitate clients' active involvement in identifying goals and planning courses of action, are more significant than specific strategies in promoting client empowerment. When comparing client outcomes in family-centered programs in the United States and Australia, Dempsey and Dunst (2004) reached a similar conclusion. Family members in both countries underscored the significance of both the relational and participatory dimensions of help giving for family empowerment. Likewise, a study of client engagement in mental health services concludes that a professional relationship demonstrating responsiveness to clients' priorities and offering support for dealing with day-to-day challenges is essential (Davies et al., (2014).

A large-scale qualitative study of clients' perceptions of the significant aspects in their relationships with social workers in hospice settings draws similar conclusions (Beresford et al., 2008). Respondents emphasized the significance of working in partnership with social workers, remaining in charge of their own decision making, and having someone available to be with them on their journey. In addition to social workers' personal qualities of caring and compassion, clients identified specific skills evidenced by social workers that supported professional relationships, including listening effectively and nonjudgmentally, treating clients respectfully, being responsive to clients' needs and reliable in following up on details, and drawing upon expert knowledge about networks of services.

Research also shows the power of relationships in group work practice, both worker–member relationships and member–member relationships. In her research, Parsons (2001) identified key elements associated with relationships in women's groups—support through acceptance, validation, and interdependence. Parsons notes that even though one worker in her study clearly defined her role as a consultant on strategies for social change, members of the social action group still valued their relationship with the worker highly, identifying her as "someone who was there for us."

For nearly a century, the social work profession has placed relationship at the heart of social work practice. Current research now validates this tradition, proving the importance and the power of the relationship between practitioners and clients in achieving successful outcomes.

CONSTRUCTING EMPOWERING RELATIONSHIPS

To the extent that social workers and clients are able to achieve a true partnership, the relationship empowers. This type of partnership develops when both partners have control over their own lives. Each can choose to behave in ways that are congruent with their own particular beliefs and intent at any given time. Freedom springs from mutual respect, acceptance, and a constant sense of permission to "be who you are." Achieving this openness ensures equality and leads to an unguarded dialogue in which new perspectives, options, and choices surface continually. With such relationships come rights, responsibilities, and considerations of power.

Recognizing Rights

Being partners guarantees certain rights and privileges. Partners have permission to view situations in their own ways along with the privilege to cooperate with or resist others' viewpoints or requests. For example, considering a client's point of view does not require social workers to sacrifice their own integrity, value base, or professional roles. In other words, social workers' acceptance, respect, and nonjudgmentalism do not signify their approval of a client's behavior. Neither is the client under any mandate to accept the view of the social worker as anything but information on how someone else sees things.

Inside empowering social worker and client relationships is a shared belief in equality and common goals, yet freedom to hold differences in perspective.

All clients have rights (Figure 6.1). Even clients coerced into social work services maintain their privileges to think the way they think, feel the way they feel, and, to the extent that their behavior doesn't hurt themselves or others, behave the way they choose. Inside empowering social worker and client relationships is a shared belief in equality and common goals, yet freedom to hold differences in perspective.

Taking Responsibilities

Responsibilities accompany privileges. Credible social workers bring professional ethics, knowledge, and skills to their partnerships with clients. They take care of their own needs and wants outside the context of professional relationships. Within professional relationships, they work in an efficient and goal-directed manner, using practice-tested, research-based, and ethically sound strategies.

Clients, too, take responsibility. They are responsible for deciding what goals to select and for approving what strategies to use. When clients have control, the choices

---

Clients have rights:

- To be treated with dignity and respect
- To privacy through confidentiality
- To participate as collaborative partners in the change process
- To receive culturally sensitive treatment
- To have an equitable share of societal resources
- To view their challenges from their own perspective
- To participate in gathering and analyzing information
- To set their own goals
- To resist what social workers want
- To choose from among the various alternative interventions
- To negotiate the distribution of roles and responsibilities for themselves and the social worker
- To collaborate on evaluation processes
- To help determine time frames and know costs involved

Figure 6.1
Client Rights

they make belong to them, along with credit for their success. Clients' active involvement in decision making not only leaves them accountable but promotes their sense of competence as well (Dunst, 1993).

Avoiding Dual Relationships

Serious problems and ethical issues arise when social workers assume secondary roles or **dual relationships** with clients, including such things as personal and business relationships. Examples include friendships, sexual relationships, business partnerships, affectionate communications, and gift giving. Boundary violations may also occur unintentionally as workers seek to fulfill their own emotional needs or altruistic motivations by becoming too emotionally invested or overly helpful in their work with clients. Other examples of potential boundary violations derive from roles social workers and clients may share as members of the same faith communities, residents of the same small towns or rural locales, or participants in the same civic organizations or social media networks. Dual relationships also extend beyond relationships with individual clients. For example, social workers who work with macrosystem clients as consultants, grant writers, board members, and volunteers also need to attend to issues of conflict of interest.

The NASW *Code of Ethics* (1999) explicitly condemns dual relationships and places the full responsibility for setting clear boundaries on social workers. Practitioners who engage in dual relationships risk disciplinary hearings and sanctions by the NASW and state licensing boards. Practitioners who commit sexual misconduct may find themselves subject to criminal action or a civil suit for malpractice. Moreover, because insurance companies consider sexual misconduct a flagrant breach of professional conduct, these practitioners may find themselves without the benefits of liability insurance coverage. In any form, dual relationships have the potential to exploit clients, cloud professionals' judgment, and result in charges of professional misconduct.

Discussing Rights and Responsibilities

When social workers openly take their own responsibilities and privileges seriously and leave space for clients to do the same, they begin to balance and distribute power in the relationship. Empowering social workers directly state their philosophy of practice, clarify their perceptions about the corollary roles of social workers and clients, and talk specifically about their confidence in clients' abilities to reach their own goals. Discussing approaches and roles enlightens clients as to the expectations of the relationship and frees them to contribute to the process.

All social workers make conscious and deliberate choices about how to practice; however, these practice theories, principles, and intervention strategies are not their private domain. Clients have the right to know the approach of the particular professional with whom they are working. Practitioners should prepare an understandable explanation of their practice philosophy to share directly with clients. If workers' approaches and clients' preferences are a "mismatch," clients can seek to work with other professionals who practice in ways clients prefer.

When social workers formulate a clear picture of what they do, their blueprint clarifies the roles of "worker" and "client." In the example that follows, note how one social worker explains the collaborative process of an empowering practice approach:

CLIENT: I'm here to find out what you think I should do.

WORKER: Okay, but I need your help. The way I see things, you have a lot to offer to what we are going to be doing. In fact, you know your situation best. I count on you to let me know what's happening in your life outside of this relationship, tell me where you want to end up, and make choices about what you think might work best.

CLIENT: Sounds like I'm doing all the work. What will you be doing?

WORKER: We both have responsibilities. You can count on me to help you make sense out of what we discover and locate resources that you might need. You bring the expert knowledge about your life. I'll be a guide who, hopefully, can work with you to put it together in a way that will get you where you want to go. Does that make sense to you?

Empowerment-based, strengths-focused social workers convey the expectation that clients are active participants. When clients indicate that they want to sit back and let social workers do all the work, empowering social workers take time to explain the logical impossibility of this approach. Workers openly discuss the implications of dependency, reveal their belief in clients' strengths, and candidly admit that they are unable to implement the social work process without clients' contributions.

Augmenting Power

Collaborative partnerships evolve. Many clients enter social work relationships humbled by their perceived inability to handle challenges on their own. Some clients initially expect to give over their power to social workers. Social workers report that clients often request "answers" to their dilemmas even before the social workers have any realistic possibility of understanding their difficulties. Developing solutions takes work, not magic.

"Social worker as magician" is a fictitious role that has no roots in empowering social work practice. Social workers resist the temptation to take over clients' situations by offering quick fixes, standard cures, or free-flowing advice. Only when clients explore and discover their own power and options does the social work relationship engender maximal benefits. Even when clients enter the relationship and relinquish their power, social workers move quickly to shift the locus of power from worker-centered to client-controlled. Ultimately, successful clients conclude their work with practitioners with both the responsibility and the credit for the choices they made. The best preparation for enhancing competence is a growing pattern of control by clients that increases over the duration of the professional relationship.

Power differentials in the social worker–client relationship can, in and of themselves, oppress clients (Sakamoto & Pitner, 2005). Social workers actively guard against the temptation to take over the process. Social workers who seek to empower rather than to dazzle client systems restrain themselves from trying to solve clients' problems, be experts, and perform extraordinary feats. Being obsessed with expert knowledge blocks social workers from comprehending clients' actual real-life experiences. Rather than imposing their own standards of what is best, social workers should respect and appreciate the diverse solutions selected by clients.

One way to help clients experience equality within the social work relationship is with the worker's selective use of self-disclosure. Workers who expect clients to be trusting and open may need to risk demonstrating these qualities first. To be culturally competent, social workers need to be open to the expectations of some cultural groups for shared disclosure.

When Clients Feel Powerless

Rarely do clients engage social work services with the sense that they are in charge of their environments. Their feelings and thoughts are evident when clients say things like, "The world is getting me down." or "Nothing I do seems to make a difference." Admittedly, in the early phases, the power dynamics of clients and their situations are often skewed against clients. Clients exhibit feelings of powerlessness in various ways, including anger, guardedness, self-hatred, aggression, passivity, humor, or manipulation (Pinderhughes, 1995).

Clients may perceive themselves as being carried along by external events rather than actively shaping their futures. Social workers accept the challenge of reversing this trend. They strive to build relationships in which clients recognize and use strengths to take charge of themselves and change their situations.

Clients view their roles in the social worker–client relationship in different ways. Some may be ready to operate as full partners in the process; others feel beaten down and dependent, and they look for social workers to lead the way. Long-standing research helps us understand why some clients feel helpless and disempowered when they enter relationships with social workers (Abramson et al., 1978; Dunst & Trivette, 1988; Seligman, 1975). Simply, experience has taught them to be helpless because their previous attempts have failed. People who learn that their efforts make little or no difference lose motivation. They give up and turn over the responsibility for decision making to someone else or to chance. When social workers yield to the temptation to rescue those who appear dependent and helpless, they often create harmful effects in their attempts to be helpful. Indeed, they add to clients' experiences of helplessness.

Many times clients approach social workers dependently because their previous experiences with other helping professionals have convinced them that their role is one of passive acceptance of assistance. Help can backfire in four ways and set up clients to be helpless:

- Help undermines clients' competence when it lessens their control over their lives.
- Help reduces clients' abilities to acquire new skills.
- Help seekers often lower their opinions of themselves and their capabilities in response to receiving help because needing to "have help" implies incompetence.
- Help erodes clients' sense of competence for solving problems.
  (Coates et al., 1983)

To be "helpful," workers guide clients to their own power to help themselves.

Collaborating with Oppressed Clients

Many social work clients enter the relationship burdened by the experience of oppression. When oppression denies people their own dignity and access to the resources of society, they feel disempowered. These feelings interfere with the development of a working partnership, especially when clients view workers as similar to their oppressors.

Ultimately, social workers and clients may choose to work on oppression as a goal of the relationship, but what can workers do to get over this initial hurdle? Dean (1993) advises that no way is known for social workers to ignore the power that they hold in these situations, even if it is subtle and implied in dominant cultural values and prejudices. Rather than denying them, workers do best by acknowledging these difficult issues and incorporating dialogue about them into the conversation.

Intervention

Behavior: Negotiate, mediate, and advocate with and on behalf of diverse clients and constituencies

Critical Thinking Question: Many social work clients are members of oppressed groups. What advocacy actions can social workers take individually and collectively to advance the social, economic, and political rights of these clients?

The goal of any social work relationship is simple—it's for clients and social workers to resolve difficult situations. Clients are supposed to take charge of their own worlds in enlightened and fruitful ways. Social workers should be proficient in networking resources, advocating **clients' rights**, and creating macrolevel changes. Establishing an equal partnership is challenging for workers relating to clients who feel helpless, coerced, or oppressed. However, effective collaboration helps clients realize their goals.

Voluntary and Involuntary Clients

The client system's status as voluntary or involuntary profoundly affects the relationship dynamics of power and closeness. **Voluntary clients** choose to participate freely, based on their perceived notion that social work assistance will help. **Involuntary clients** are forced by others who hold enough power over them to insist on involvement in social work services (Ivanoff et al., 1994; Rooney, 1992; Trotter, 2004). Examples of involuntary clients include persons convicted of crimes, parents ordered to receive services to regain custody of their children, and those whose use of substances necessitates mandated treatment. In some ways, all clients are involuntary. Would people decide to seek social work assistance if they weren't stuck on something that they would have preferred to solve on their own?

Although clients who are voluntary may choose social work services in desperation, they do participate with the power of choice to address their challenges in their own ways. They can choose to work with this particular social worker, shop for another, or try a totally different approach. They have choices to remain or to leave the relationship, and they are free to behave in openly powerful ways. Collaborative partnerships are easier to form with clients who are voluntary, as their voluntary status places them on more equal footing as partners from the outset.

In contrast, consider clients who are coerced into social work services because they have infringed on the rights of others. In these instances, social workers function as agents of social control as well as advocates for clients' rights. Clients begin the relationship in a "one-down" position, feeling more like prisoners than partners. To develop partnerships with involuntary clients, social workers quickly move to offer them honest and direct information about the structure of the helping relationship and their privileges within it.

Owning up to the reality of the coercive nature of the relationship reflects the social worker's genuineness and trustworthiness. Acknowledging that mandated clients still maintain rights shows the worker's acceptance, objectivity, and respect. This open discussion about limits and privileges is a beginning step toward ensuring equal footing for clients. Chapter 8 provides more extensive information about how workers develop and maintain collaborative relationships with mandated clients.

Partnerships with Larger Systems

Forming empowering relationships with larger client systems—such as groups, organizations, and communities—draws on all the skills already described and more. Building trusting relationships with program participants and members of organizations, neighborhoods, and communities is as important as building trust in work with individuals, families, and groups (Gutiérrez et al., 2005). Workers also assist clients and constituencies to maximize power by encouraging cohesive development and distribution of leadership. This means that workers facilitate feelings of power in as many members of the system as possible, including those members who may initially feel that their contributions are insignificant.

Workers guide group interactions so that a particularly powerful member does not overshadow the worker's efforts to form working partnerships with other members of the client system. Similar to when a social worker's directive approach inhibits the contributions of clients, dictatorial members of larger group systems are likely to stifle the contributions of other group members. Therefore, with multiperson client systems, workers make direct connections to each group member, seek and accept the contributions of both active and less active members, and encourage each member to take part.

> **?** Assess your understanding of constructing empowering relationships by taking this brief quiz.

RESPECTING CONFIDENTIALITY

Workers promote a client's power when they maintain confidentiality. In fact, confidentiality is central to developing trust in the social worker–client relationship. Generally, confidential information is information that is deemed private. To maintain confidentiality, workers refrain from disclosing information about clients to others. Fulfilling the ethical obligations of confidentiality demonstrates respect for clients and builds trust. Ethical codes and legal requirements prescribe the nature of confidentiality in professional social work practice. The NASW *Code of Ethics* (1999) obliges social workers to respect clients' right to privacy and maintain the obligatory standards of confidentiality. Furthermore, laws at the federal, state, and local levels regulate professional responsibility for confidentiality. The following section explores differences between **absolute confidentiality** and **relative confidentiality**, consents for releasing confidential information, and instances and implications of violating confidentiality.

Ethical and Professional Behavior

Behavior: Make ethical decisions by applying the standards of the NASW Code of Ethics, relevant laws and regulations, models for ethical decision-making, ethical conduct of research, and additional codes of ethics as appropriate to context

Critical Thinking Question: Ethical social workers respect a client's right to confidentiality. However, the promise of confidentiality is not absolute. What situations affect a client's confidentiality rights?

- Evidence of child abuse or neglect
- Legal mandates for reporting elder abuse or neglect
- Threats by clients to harm themselves or others
- Clients' needs for emergency services
- Guardianship hearings or committal procedures requiring information
- Quality assurance procedures, internal audits, or peer reviews of nonidentifiable case records
- Consultation with colleagues, consultants, and attorneys
- Lawsuits filed against social workers by clients
- Other exceptions, as prescribed by laws and regulations

Figure 6.2
Exceptions to Confidentiality

Absolute and Relative Confidentiality

Given the significance of privacy for the sanctity of professional relationships, many conclude that confidentiality is unconditional; yet, usually limits exist to confidentiality in social work practice. However, we can distinguish two types of confidentiality, absolute and relative. With absolute confidentiality, professionals never share information in any form with anyone. Workers neither record information about clients in any type of report nor orally share information about clients with supervisors, agency-based colleagues, or any other professional. Few circumstances afford absolute confidentiality. More likely, the principle of relative confidentiality guides practice. Relative confidentiality allows sharing of information within agencies, such as in supervision, case conferences, and team meetings. However, relative confidentiality still presumes that, with some exceptions, workers do not share information outside the agency context without the explicit permission of the client (Figure 6.2).

Violations of Confidentiality

Too often, social workers unwittingly violate client confidentiality and expose themselves to liability. For example, a common violation results when practitioners discuss client or work setting situations with their own family and friends under the misconception that not using names or identifying details protects anonymity. Family and friends are under no legal or professional constraint to keep shared information confidential. Even informal sharing with colleagues in public settings such as social gatherings, coffee break rooms, or restaurants also presents serious problems, as these conversations may be overheard by others. Additionally, inappropriate remarks, such as judgmental comments about other practitioners or agencies, may irrevocably damage working relationships. Although not necessarily revealing confidential information, phone calls or text messages taken during sessions with clients not only are distracting but also raise the potential for divulging privileged information. The accidental or careless revelation of records or identities occurs in numerous ways, including leaving confidential records unattended on a desk or in an unlocked file, working on records in public places, greeting a client by name in a public place, discarding unshredded records and notes, or even taking work home. Finally, using unprotected means of communication, such as cell phones, voicemail, fax machines, email, or any social networking websites can result in breaches of confidentiality.

If social workers break confidentiality, they seriously violate standards of professional ethics. In many states, if social workers violate confidentiality, they break the law. Possible consequences include professional sanctions and disciplinary actions, loss of professional licenses and certifications, misdemeanor charges, and civil lawsuits.

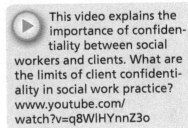

This video explains the importance of confidentiality between social workers and clients. What are the limits of client confidentiality in social work practice? www.youtube.com/watch?v=q8WIHYnnZ3o

Informed Consent for Releasing Information

Clients can grant a worker permission to release confidential information through a process called **informed consent**. For a client's consent to be "informed," the worker must fully reveal the conditions, risks, and alternatives of sharing information. However, obtaining consent for the release of information is not without controversy. Questions arise such as, What constitutes a valid consent? Is it ever appropriate to use a blanket consent? Is it appropriate to respond to a client's request for immediate disclosure if time constraints preclude having a written consent in hand? Do circumstances ever not require social workers to obtain informed consent?

Reamer (2003) notes additional concerns about third-party requests for information. For example: Is a social worker obligated to inform clients of the results of a request for information or of the potential consequences of not agreeing to sign the form? Can clients withdraw their consent?

Social workers also consider other factors when seeking informed consent. State and federal statutes, regulations, and policies, as well as court decisions and case law, stipulate the parameters for disclosing information. Additionally, cultural values influence clients' conceptualization of confidentiality and the propriety or even obligation to release information to others (Meer & VandeCreek, 2002; Palmer & Kaufman, 2003).

Consent forms clearly detail the nature of the information exchange. Informed consent implies that clients have been deemed competent to give consent; received full disclosure about the nature of the expected treatment, including the risks and benefits; and signed the consent to release form. Workers should make copies of the completed and signed consent form for the client's case file, the client, and the professional requesting the information.

Privileged Communication

Privileged communication provides the legal ground for upholding confidentiality in legal proceedings (Corey et al., 2015). Legal privilege protects a client's private communication with a social worker by prohibiting the professional from divulging information in court. As legally established, privilege belongs to the clients, not practitioners. Simply put, when clients claim legal privilege, ethical social workers respect confidentiality. If the client waives privilege, then practitioners have no legal ground for withholding information. Privilege often involves the following elements:

- The client invokes privilege to prevent the social worker's testimony or records from being used as evidence in a court of law.
- The social worker claims privilege at the client's request.

- If a client waives this right, the social worker is not legally bound to maintain silence in court.
- When privilege has been waived, practitioners are obligated to reveal only what is necessary and sufficient to meet the client's request to disclose information.
- The judge considers relevant statutory and case laws, principles of judicial proof, and client waiver and entitlement to determine whether privilege applies.
- In the absence of privilege, court officials compel social workers to testify and document their evidence with written records.

Safeguarding confidentiality conscientiously protects a client's legal right to privilege. However, privileged communication does not afford the absolute protection of privacy, as numerous exceptions exist, even in states that grant the status of privilege to clients of social workers.

Statutory Provisions

Federal, state, and local laws, which may or may not agree, stipulate conditions of confidentiality and privilege. In regard to federal cases, a U.S. Supreme Court ruling in *Jaffee vs. Redmond* indicates that clients can now claim protection from disclosure of confidential exchanges with licensed social workers in federal courts (NASW, 2005c). It also offers full protection to social workers who practice on Native American reservations with clients who face lawsuits or charges in federal courts.

All states have some legal definition of client privilege, but these statutes vary in the extent of confidentiality accorded and in the identification of types of practitioners covered. Typically, for clients to establish privilege, the social worker involved must either be licensed or registered, or be supervised by someone who is. In some states, privilege extends to social work students; in other states, it does not. Because laws stipulate conditions required for privilege to apply, social workers should learn the implications of the laws governing their specific area of practice. The serious legal implications of these issues press social workers to familiarize themselves with situations in which privilege applies, as well as with the exceptions.

Various laws regarding licensure, professional regulation, and human-service activities designate conditions for confidentiality and privileged communication. In general, stipulations for federal funding restrict social workers from disseminating records and other information in such practice areas as education, medical and health care, criminal justice, and other public services. With respect to health-related fields, regulations under the **Health Insurance Portability and Accountability Act of 1996 (HIPAA)** clearly delineate procedures for protecting clients' files. More specifically, in the public service arena, restrictions apply to child abuse, foster care, adoption, family preservation, Temporary Assistance to Needy Families (TANF), child support, and child custody. Other areas protected by privilege often include work in parole and probation, services to persons with developmental disabilities, practice in home health agencies, and services for persons with AIDS and HIV-related disorders. Federal laws regulating substance abuse treatment stipulate strict confidentiality, forbidding staff from even revealing whether someone is a client and mandating a secure record-keeping system.

Exceptions to Privilege

Like other laws, privilege laws contain exceptions. Based on the Association of Social Work Boards' Model Social Work Practice Act (2012), social workers may voluntarily disclose information obtained from clients or professional consultants in the following circumstances:

1. Informal reporting or consultation with administrators, colleagues, or consultants who are also bound by confidentiality or privilege

2. With the written consent of the client or consultant

3. With the written consent of the representative or beneficiary of a client who is deceased or disabled

4. In situations of duty to warn or forestall a threat to public safety

5. When privilege is waived by a client who is bringing public charges against the worker

Social workers are often called to testify in court proceedings such as child custody disputes, commitment hearings, child abuse and domestic violence cases, and malpractice suits. Subpoenas mandate disclosure of confidential client records (*subpoena dues tecum*) or mandate oral court testimony (*subpoena ad testificundum*); however, the legal requirement to provide that information ultimately rests with the judge (NASW, 2009b). Search warrants, on the other hand, require immediate compliance, although ways may exist to persuade law enforcement officers to wait for a court ruling.

In addition, privilege does not apply when clients know from the outset that social workers may be called on to testify. Frequently, this is the case with involuntary clients. For example, various situations—such as family violence, child custody disputes, criminal activity, or mental health issues—in which social workers gather information on behalf of the court exclude privilege.

Balancing Accountability and Privacy

Numerous factors influence the extent to which social workers maintain confidentiality. Rarely is confidentiality absolute. Codes of ethics and standards for professional practice emphasize that confidentiality is necessary to create the atmosphere of trust in which clients are free to reveal their situations. Statutory regulations, case law, judicial interpretations, and agency policies and procedures provide guidelines that support confidentiality. However, these same guidelines demand that professionals balance matters of privacy with the requisites of accountability and the rights of others. For example, in the managed care environment prevalent in many fields of practice, social workers should provide only that information necessary to make funding decisions. The same is true when protecting privacy rights in electronic record keeping; workers should limit access to only those persons who have a "need to know." Similarly, social workers balance the privacy of mandated clients with practitioners' obligation to provide the referral agency with a report of client compliance with the program expectations by limiting these reports to the bare essentials.

 Assess your understanding of confidentiality by taking this brief quiz.

LOOKING FORWARD

Social work ethics mandate that people be treated with acceptance and respect. The shift toward a more egalitarian and consultative partnership between social workers and client systems actualizes this value, overturning the social worker's role as sole expert. To maximize clients' participation and experience of power, workers allow space for active client participation, encourage open sharing, and honor client perspectives. Workers use their personal qualities and professional expertise when developing this relationship. Ethical practitioners also maintain the integrity of the relationship by orienting it to the goals that clients seek and by maintaining clients' rights to confidentiality.

Although social workers define the professional partnership in direct ways, clients likely experience the relationship most profoundly in dialogue about their situations. Chapter 7 details the processes that social workers use to talk with clients about the challenges they face in ways that respect client expertise, access useful information, and solidify the partnership relationship.

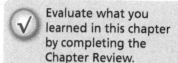

Evaluate what you learned in this chapter by completing the Chapter Review.

Engagement: Articulating Situations

TCSABA / SHUTTERSTOCK

Effective communication skills are the basis for engaging with clients to describe presenting issues and underlying concerns. While articulating situations, clients and social workers develop a mutual understanding of what they are getting together to do. An open and respectful dialogue identifies the issues clients confront and elucidates the contexts in which these difficulties occur. During this mutual exchange, clients and social workers define and strengthen their working partnership.

Social workers and clients share responsibility in articulating situations. Clients take the lead in telling their stories. Social workers respond to clarify and organize the information clients offer. By choosing responses to determine goals and to locate resources for change, social workers infuse purpose into the dialogue while demonstrating respect for clients' expertise and privilege of self-definition. This exchange requires a delicate power balance between social worker and client, made more complex in the context of social work with larger systems, such as organizations and communities.

An effective social worker focuses the information exchange with a client to describe what is currently happening, to determine goals, and to locate resources for change. This chapter describes effective ways for social workers to engage with clients to access their perspectives on their situations. Practitioners implementing these client-focused dialogue skills are able to initiate and maintain empowering relationships with diverse clients.

EMPOWERING DIALOGUE

A man, recently paroled and saddled with a felony record, can't find a job. A girl refuses to return to school after her fight with a teacher. A downtown redevelopment group wants to attract customers to its revitalized town center, an area that has become a gathering place for people who are homeless. A public housing project's reputation for crime and drug trafficking complicates a cycle of low occupancy rates, reduced income, and spotty maintenance, further decreasing the attractiveness to potential residents. Each of these client systems faces very different situations that challenge their capabilities to resolve issues.

In articulating the significant dimensions of any of these situations, social workers face choices of how to respond. What information is most relevant? Which avenues of exploration will be productive in leading toward desired goals? What kind of conversation will work best to guide the change process and to establish a working partnership that merges social worker and client expertise?

Active Listening and Proactive Responding

Social workers are active participants in conversations with clients, focusing their attention to understand and articulate the meanings clients intend. Using **active listening** skills, workers listen carefully and then respond directly to access a clear image of the client's world and to communicate interest, appreciation, and concern. The best comments by social workers build on and validate what clients have shared. Clients experience a worker's empathy and respect if the worker can describe the situation as the client sees it. Practitioners learn how to respond to clients by listening to them first.

Social workers demonstrate their acceptance of clients and foster collaboration when they emphasize responding. By using **proactive responding** skills, workers hold their own views in check in favor of eliciting the client's perspective. Responding in a client-focused dialogue is a culturally responsive way to interact, leaving to the client the role of cultural expert. When clients take the lead, they set a cultural tone for the work by revealing their language, style, hopes, and beliefs. Encouraged by a social worker's responses, clients disclose their own theories about events as well as their motivations and priorities.

A social work professional has a responsibility to maintain the defined purpose of any relationship with a client. Social work practice is best when it is client focused and goal directed. In conversations with clients, social workers deliberately choose responses that are useful in meeting the purposes of the relationship. To assist workers in conversations with clients, proactive responding weaves three related dialogue skills:

1. Responses to articulate the current situation and its impact from the client's perspective,

2. Responses to define a positive outcome to direct the work, and

3. Responses to identify strengths and resources available for goal achievement. (O'Melia, 1998, p. 2)

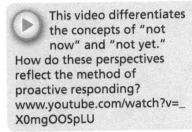

This video differentiates the concepts of "not now" and "not yet." How do these perspectives reflect the method of proactive responding? www.youtube.com/watch?v=_X0mgOOSpLU

These proactive responses maintain the client's central position as expert on the situation while allowing the worker to infuse a strengths orientation into the process. These responding skills assist clients to describe their current situations, to refine the goal direction, and to locate existing strengths and resources.

Proactive Responding: Describing the Current Situation

Clients and their situations make the most sense when social workers view them from the client's point of view and in context. A social worker's responses to access the client's unique perspective and relevant contextual information reflect the integration of two theoretical views: social constructivism and the ecosystems perspective. A social worker's best responses are to elicit clients' realities and validate their experiences and to expand clients' views about their difficulties by describing the transactional nature of their situations.

Eliciting the Client's Reality

We have already discussed the difficulty of anticipating another's experience. Inevitable differences in perspectives arise, generated by cultural group memberships and individual uniqueness. The differing realities between social workers and clients press workers to withhold their views in favor of eliciting the client's perspective. The worker takes on the role of learner to be educated rather than an expert on either culture or the client's situation. As a learner with respect to the client's construction of reality, the worker responds reflectively with interest and curiosity until achieving a mutual understanding.

Clients and their situations make the most sense when social workers view them from the client's point of view and in context.

Discussing the Transactional Nature of Situations

The social justice imperative directs workers to explore the social, institutional, and political contexts of client situations. Workers examine the goodness of fit of persons and their environments rather than investigate failures in the functioning of client systems themselves. When clients say they have failed, a worker immediately responds to link this "failure" to its context, in which other explanations of the client's experience become evident.

Placing a situation in its systemic context has two major advantages. First, this view assumes no fault or inadequacy on the part of clients. A gap simply exists between what client systems currently need and what their environments presently offer. Removing the need to pinpoint blame frees clients to cooperate rather than fend off the perception of judgment and blame. Second, when we describe situations transactionally, we scan the entire ecosystem in developing resources for change.

Examining the transactional or contextual features of situations reveals targets for solutions. Consider the girl who refuses to return to school after a fight with her teacher. A linear view looks first to the child and second to the teacher to see what and who is wrong. In contrast, the transactional view explores other elements of the ecosystem that may be supporting the transaction. Perhaps the girl has concerns about her elderly grandmother's health. Maybe she is reluctant to admit that she is having difficulty reading. Possibly her teacher is succumbing to pressures of increased class size and decreased student support services. Perhaps racial and ethnic bias is predisposing other children in the class to pick on her. Events happening within the ecosystem provide clues for assessment and focus for solutions.

Situations involving larger client systems also have transactional dimensions to explore. For example, the task group seeking to revitalize the downtown area looks beyond the immediate concern of a few businesses and a few customers to understand the issue more fully. A social worker would guide group members to examine the impact of the city's investment in a new shopping mall on the other side of town, the loss of jobs created when the area's major employer consolidated and moved its operations to another state, the influx of people who are homeless into the downtown area drawn by the empty buildings, and the shifts in population from the town center to suburban areas. When social workers respond to describe situations in concrete transactional terms, the area in which they search for solvable problems expands.

Proactive Responding: Orienting Toward Goals

The second important response by a social worker shifts the conversation to refine the direction of the work. When clients present their problems, social workers respond by asking how this problem gets in the way. This takes a first step toward defining where clients would like to go (see Chapter 8).

To shift the focus toward the future, social workers frame clients' situations in terms of challenges, rather than problems. Challenges differ significantly from problems; challenges orient us toward the future. Consider Zeb, a client recently paroled and looking for employment. The problem Zeb presents is his felony record. This fact about his past will not change. Focusing on this problem engenders feelings of guilt and powerlessness. However, Zeb's challenge is getting a job. Notice the perspective shift from what's wrong to what should happen. Despite Zeb's past, finding a job is still a future option. Similar to how you would assist any recent college graduate seeking a job, the social worker assesses Zeb's motivation and interests, defines his current capabilities, and determines his needs for additional job skills to increase his marketability in the eyes of potential employers. There may be no way to expunge the problem of a criminal record, but multiple approaches exist to the challenge of securing employment.

The concept of challenge steers workers away from the notion of eliminating a problem fixed in the past toward overcoming or avoiding hurdles in the pathway leading to a future goal. Previous problems are significant only if they interfere with achieving a desired future. Examine this shift in perspective: The concept of challenge reorients workers to move quickly beyond talking about what is wrong. Instead of dwelling on past problems, social workers encourage clients to articulate where they are going (goals) and what might help them get there (strengths and resources).

Proactive Responding: Searching for Strengths and Resources

A third effective response by social workers pivots toward a discussion of client strengths and environmental resources available to achieve goals. Social workers consistently choose responses that direct attention to what clients are doing right, what they have accomplished, and what resources may contribute to the effort (see Chapters 9 and 10).

Consider the example of an aging public housing project. The social worker's conversation with residents identifies their sense of helplessness about their situation—a reality of substandard living conditions, neglect by the housing authority, and periodic incidents of violence. But as the worker responds to reorient the conversation to how residents cope with their situation, a new picture emerges. Through this shift in direction, the social worker learns that the difficult conditions have contributed to a strong sense of community; some residents have researched their rights as tenants and are poised to assert themselves at the next meeting of the housing authority, and other residents have organized a neighborhood watch program. These newly articulated strengths of the neighborhood can contribute to achieving the solutions that residents seek.

Human system behavior adapts in context. Likely something works in each client's situation. Always finding it more empowering to validate and improve than to denigrate and redirect, social workers respond to clients with positive possibilities in mind. What's good about what clients are doing? The answer is "probably a lot."

Accessing the Client's Perspective

Central to success in any social work endeavor is an exchange of information that describes the client's situation in a useful way. With individual, family, and small-group clients, this exchange takes the form of conversation. Social workers and clients talk directly with each other. With formal systems, organizations, and communities, workers implement other methods to articulate the situation. Dialogue with larger systems may involve formal meetings, public forums, focus groups, or written surveys.

No matter what form this exchange of information takes, two key purposes orient the conversation. First, workers seek to articulate the situation as the client sees it. The idea is to access the client's perspective, untainted by the worker's biases. Second, workers nudge the conversation toward a broader view, broad enough to place situations in environmental context and to reveal strengths and resources for change.

In successful conversations, workers learn what clients know and, in the process, help clients organize and understand this information in useful ways. To accomplish this, workers listen carefully to what clients say and encourage them to say more.

Clients constantly communicate verbally and behaviorally, telling and showing workers how they think and feel. This abundance of information forces social workers to respond selectively. Empowering social workers choose responses that demonstrate acceptance and respect while encouraging clients to more fully articulate their situations. Through their responses, social workers send their own messages, explore what clients are thinking, and reflect what clients are feeling.

Sizing Up Situations

Only clients truly know their situations. As clients share, workers respond to articulate more fully the client's perspective and structure the dialogue. Social

> **?** Assess your understanding of empowering dialogue by taking this brief quiz.

Proactive responses maintain the client's central position as an expert on the situation while allowing the worker to infuse a strengths orientation into the conversation. Social workers using proactive responding combine attentive listening with reflections, clarifications, summaries, and occasional questions to access information about what is going on, to define what the client hopes will happen, and to locate resources available to assist in the effort. Specifically, proactive responding weaves three related dialogue skills, including:

Responses to articulate the current situation
- What is happening from the client's point of view
- Other associated events that may be related
- Other people involved in or affected by the current situation
- The impact the events are having on the client's life
- How the client makes sense out of what is happening

Responses to define a positive direction
- How the client would like it to be instead
- What it would look like if things were working in that way
- Indicators that would signal that things are beginning to improve

Responses to identify strengths and locate available resources
- Times in the past when things were working in the desired way
- Times currently when things are working best or even a little better than usual
- What the client sees as personal strengths, specifically those related to goals
- What is available in the environment that could be a resource
- Other people who might contribute to the effort and what they could do
- Coping methods the client uses to manage the situation
- Client's ideas about what others might do in a similar situation

Source: Adapted with permission of the author from "Proactive Responding: Paths Toward Diverse Strengths" by M. O'Melia (1998). All rights reserved.

Figure 7.1
Proactive Responding

workers respond proactively to access clients' thoughts and feelings, consider issues with respect to goals, and locate strengths and resources for solution development (Figure 7.1).

APPLYING MODELS OF COMMUNICATION

By definition, all communication processes involve exchanges of information between senders and receivers (Figure 7.2). Senders **encode messages**. In this process, senders consider their thoughts and feelings and symbolically represent them in words and actions. The actual verbal and nonverbal delivery of these words and actions transmits a message to the receiver. Receivers, in turn, interpret or **decode messages** they receive based on their perception of the message. When receivers respond to a sender's

Dialogue Information Loop

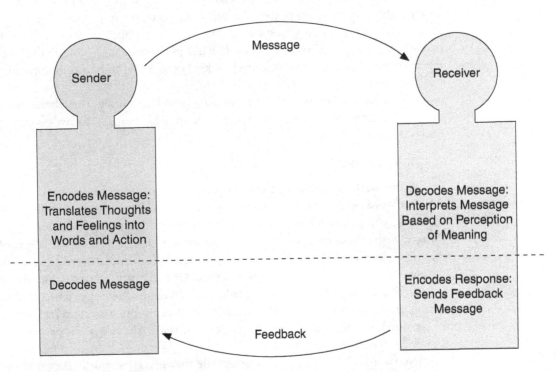

Figure 7.2
Communication Processes

message with messages of their own, a dialogue begins. As conversations unfold, receivers become senders, and senders become receivers, trading roles as they respectively encode, transmit, and decode messages. Communication is effective to the extent that senders clearly transmit and receivers accurately understand messages. Successful communication depends on the active participation and cooperation of both senders and receivers.

Communication is effective to the extent that senders clearly transmit and receivers accurately understand messages.

Verbal Communication

Several theorists contribute to our understanding of the human experience of remembering and reporting events (Bandler & Grinder, 1975; Johnson, 2014). When something happens, we perceive it and tuck it away in our minds for future reference, but already the event that actually occurred and the representation we store in our memory differ, as our attention is selective. The complexity of events defies our capabilities to absorb all the details. We see what we see, hear what we hear, and feel what we feel—and we remember it selectively. Others witnessing identical events do the same, resulting in a different perception of the events. Each of us constructs idiosyncratic memories, unique compilations of events as we perceive them.

Memory stores general information rather than precise, meticulous details. Then when we retrieve information, we fill in the gaps to reconstruct events logically, as we expect they would have happened (Loftus, 1979). In other words, when we report these events from memory, we are likely to leave out significant features or even embellish the details. Moreover, we can't possibly share everything we are thinking; there wouldn't be enough time. Most likely, we tailor our remarks to the requisites of specific conversations. Our motives for presenting information, the effect we seek, and our feelings further influence the choices we make in what and how to share. Rather than report our entire memory of events, we selectively delete, generalize, and distort information as we pass it along.

When clients express their thoughts about events, naturally, they share only bits and pieces of their stories. Social workers respond to help clients rediscover events in fuller, more productive detail.

Words Are Ambiguous

In talking with clients about their situations, workers choose their words carefully, as words either facilitate partnerships or block communication processes. For example, when social workers use jargon, technical terms, and vocabulary unfamiliar to clients, these esoteric words elevate social workers into expert roles and leave clients feeling as if they have nothing to offer. When social workers use complex, enigmatic terminology, they puzzle clients. One client who participated in a focus group for a child welfare research project talked about the importance of communicating on a level with clients this way: "I mean being personal and friendly and just being down on our level or whatever. It's just really the most important thing they can do" (Drake, 1994, p. 598).

Even when clients and social workers use the very same words, they may not mean the same thing. For example, the words, "eligibility," "referral," and "privacy" can invoke disparate meanings and reactions. Even common words such as "soon," "later," "possibility," and "likely" leave room for alternative interpretations. Workers choose words with an ear for what fits naturally with the world of the client system and continually check in with clients to ensure mutual understanding.

Nonverbal Communication

Words are only part of the messages we communicate. When we talk, we also send nonverbal messages. Humans rely heavily on **nonverbal communication** to convey and interpret meaning (Knapp et al., 2014). Nonverbal messages accompany every verbal expression and sometimes stand on their own. Body posture, facial expressions, eye contact, head and body movements, and other attending behaviors, as well as voice tone, inflection, and intensity, all contain nonverbal messages.

Nonverbal communication can be purposeful, but generally it is spontaneous. Nonverbal messages often communicate information that would otherwise go unsaid. Long-standing research indicates that nonverbal behavior influences communication processes more prominently than do verbal messages, generating about two-thirds of any communication's meaning (Birdwhistell, 1955). What you think and how you feel shows through in how you behave.

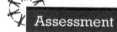

Assessment

Behavior: Collect and organize data, and apply critical thinking to interpret information from clients and constituencies

Critical Thinking Question: Effective communication is essential for successful social work practice. What is effective communication, and how does a social worker achieve it?

Social workers encourage or inhibit clients by their nonverbal responses to them. Nonverbal messages qualify otherwise neutral information. How we say words conveys information about our attitudes, making nonverbal messages particularly important in cross-cultural work. When there's a mismatch between verbal and nonverbal messages, we tend to believe the nonverbal ones.

Watch how body language affects how others see us and may also change how we see ourselves. Research proves that nonverbal communication is more influential than what you say. What do you need to do to fine-tune your nonverbal communication skills for success in professional social work practice?
www.youtube.com/
watch?v=Ks-_Mh1QhMc&index=107&list=PLAC463A2B6B-2CEC7F

Influences on Communication Processes

A number of factors influence communication processes by creating lenses through which we view and interpret messages. These include culture, assumptions, expectations, emotions, and distractions.

Culture

Culture powerfully influences communication processes. Consider the example of a social worker asking a client the simple question, "What does your family think about this?" Who pops into your mind as you consider your family's reaction? If you are Latino, you might think of your extended family, including your godparents (Falicov, 1996). If you are Asian American, you probably consider your extended family with an emphasis on your husband's or father's side (Nakanishi & Rittner, 1992). If you are Native American, you may think about a multihousehold, extended kinship network with tribal connections, including those in areas far away (Limb et al., 2008). If you are African American, you might include blood relatives and longtime friends in the community network as part of your family (Stewart, 2008). If you are European American, you probably flashed on an image of your nuclear family (McGoldrick, 1989). Cultural backgrounds trigger differences in meaning that confound social workers in their attempts to communicate effectively with clients, and they create communication gaps among members of multiperson client systems.

Culture influences some facets of nonverbal communication, whereas other facets are universally expressed and understood. For example, classic cross-cultural research discovered that people from different cultures usually interpret certain facial indicators of emotion—surprise, disgust, anger, fear, sadness, and happiness—similarly (Ekman & Friesen, 1975). This research reported remarkable agreement across cultures about communicating and interpreting these facial expressions of emotion. However, cultural differences prescribe variations in the meaning of other types of nonverbal behaviors.

People from varying cultures attribute different meanings to gestures, eye contact, and even voice intonation. For example, many North American cultural groups interpret direct eye contact as a sign of support, interest, and respect, yet others may interpret direct eye contact as rude and intrusive. Necessarily, social workers must be cautious about overgeneralizing because in a changing and assimilating society, there are exceptions to most cultural "rules."

Additionally, some cultural groups, emphasizing high context, are more sensitive to contextual features of communication in their interpretations of messages. Influential factors include nonverbal nuances of language and speech, as well as where the dialogue takes place, and inherent elements of hierarchy in the relationship between communicators. Given this variability in cultural meaning, social workers must decipher what verbal communications and nonverbal behaviors will work with each client system.

Assumptions

Social workers' assumptions may interfere with their understanding of clients' messages. For example, a practitioner working in foster care observed sparse interaction between a mother and her children during a supervised visit and assumed that the mother's behavior was aloof and disinterested. Talking with the mother after the visit, the social worker learned that the mother wanted to be "a good mom," so she let the kids play video games but was disappointed in her lack of opportunity to interact with them. "There's always the danger when we don't check things out, that we may think we understand a client's meaning and act as if we do, when we are actually not at all in accord" (Dean, 1993, p. 137). Careful clarification circumvents the pitfalls of assuming meanings.

Diversity and Difference in Practice

Behavior: Present themselves as learners and engage clients and constituencies as experts of their own experiences

Critical Thinking Question: Social workers use responding skills to access a client's perspective and to learn about cultural meanings from their clients and constituencies. What factors make these skills especially important for situations in which clients are culturally different from social workers?

Expectations

Past experiences create expectations that filter perceptions of here-and-now situations. Both workers and clients hold expectations for the helping encounter. A client may negatively interpret a social worker's message simply based on bad experiences with other helpers. Or, a social worker who observes particular patterns of communication in a single-parent family may presume that these patterns apply to all single-parent families, overlooking individual differences. Bits and pieces of past experiences influence how people send, receive, and interpret messages. Unchecked, categorical generalizations distort information and severely restrict social workers' ability to communicate effectively. To counteract the effect of negative expectations, social workers listen carefully and consciously send messages of acceptance and respect.

Emotions

Communication also involves emotional elements. Frequently, emotions affect how we send, receive, and remember information. For example, emotion-laden stress narrows our focus, distracts our attention, limits our ability to recognize alternatives, and increases our inaccuracies and misinterpretations (Wade et al., 2015). Research indicates that our moods may even influence our ability to recall information. For example, in an experiment on emotions and memory, Robinson and Rollings (2011) found participants' visual recognition and recall memories were more robust when their mood during "input" matched their mood during "retrieval." Other research suggests that acute stress triggers hypervigilant processing that amplifies stress-related memories (Henckens et al., 2009).

On the receiving end, strong emotions may blur our ability to listen accurately. Overidentifying with emotions confuses our own stories with those of the message sender. We project our own circumstances into our understanding of the messages we receive. In other words, caught up with personal emotions, we may interpret information through the masks of our own emotions. Most communication conveys emotion, but strong emotions held by either senders or receivers can undermine the effective sharing of information. Social workers take extra caution to communicate effectively in emotionally charged interchanges.

Distractions

Distractions confound communication processes. For example, background noise interrupts concentration, covers up softly spoken messages, and hinders communication with persons who have a hearing loss. Repetitive sounds, such as the ticking of a clock, accentuate silence. Odors, too, may distract us. Certain odors evoke deeply imbedded

---

Box 7.1   Social Work with Immigrants and Refugees: A Research–Practice Connection

By the end of 2014, there were nearly 19.5 million refugees and 1.8 million asylum seekers in the world (UNHCR, 2015). In addition, nearly 38.2 million people are displaced within their own countries because of civil wars, famine, and natural disasters.

Social workers in all fields of practice are likely to work with immigrants and refugees. Additionally, specialized immigrant services such as neighborhood centers, case management services, and refugee resettlement programs continue to emerge to meet the increased demand. In contrast to the century-old settlement house emphasis on assisting immigrants to assimilate into "American ways of life," the contemporary goal balances assimilation with respect for an immigrant's culture of origin. To this end, social workers encourage immigrants to draw on the resources and strengths of their own culture, while at the same time assisting them in transitioning to life in American society (Balgopal, 2000).

Research highlights a variety of communication challenges in working with immigrants and refugees. Trust building is often difficult because many immigrants are survivors of war and torture (Behnia, 2004). Successful cross-cultural communication is also important. In a study by Russell and White (2001), "all immigrant clients interviewed indicated that the ability to communicate innermost feelings was essential in remedying their sense of social isolation" (p. 81), yet to achieve such an intimate level of communication, workers and clients must overcome language and cultural barriers.

In a survey of 226 Asian Indian immigrants age 50 and older, Diwan and colleagues (2004) discovered factors mitigating stress in adjusting to life in the United States. Protective factors emerged from the immigrants' cultural contexts, including the bonds of friendships, a secure cultural identity, religious faith, and personal sense of mastery. The

researchers conclude that practitioners should promote social integration, spiritual well-being, and personal efficacy to assist immigrant clients.

Ely's (2004) review of the literature on domestic violence among immigrant women in the United States reveals the complexities faced by social workers. She found, for example, that "humiliation and dishonor are perceived by many immigrant women to be more harmful than enduring domestic violence" (p. 227), leaving these women reluctant to disclose the violence to social workers. In addition, not knowing exceptions in immigration law, these women fear that sharing information may jeopardize their immigration status. The social isolation that often accompanies abuse in any culture makes it less likely these women will know about available resources or protections against deportation under the Immigration Act of 1991 and the Violence Against Women Act of 1994. Ely recommends that social workers develop culturally competent education and advocacy programs that foster open communication and a safe environment for self-disclosure.

Because of ethnic strife in their own country, most Ethiopians of Jewish descent have immigrated to Israel. Stress, low self-esteem, and intergenerational conflicts often mark their acculturation experiences. Ringel and colleagues (2005) report that Ethiopian adolescents' integration into Israeli culture is complicated by cultural and generational differences in communication styles. They report that Ethiopian culture emphasizes nonverbal communication in contrast to an Israeli culture that prizes verbal exchange.

These research studies demonstrate the necessity and challenge of effective communication when working with immigrants and refugees; workers must understand the nuances of language, silence, context, and meaning.

? Assess your under-standing of models of communication by taking this brief quiz.

memories and shift our attention away from the present to the past of our own personal associations. Interruptions such as telephone calls, intercom messages, and requests to step outside suggest to clients that they are of sec-ondary importance. In home visits, distractions such as radios and televisions, neighbors dropping by, or other household activities may interrupt the flow of communication. When social workers feel the press of their own agenda or envi-ronmental distractions interfere, they take steps to remove the distractions to facilitate productive conversations.

RESPONDING TO WHAT CLIENTS SAY

In everyday conversations, we may share our thoughts and feelings freely, trying to get others to understand our points of view. In professional conversations, social workers initially withhold their thoughts in favor of learning about the client's expe-rience. Social workers deliberately offer responses to guide clients to describe their situations in concrete and transactional terms. A social worker's purposeful selection of responses

- helps workers clearly comprehend clients' challenges,
- promotes clients' understanding of their own situations,
- pursues information relevant to clients' goals,
- develops and maintains a respectful partnership that gives clients control over their own directions, and
- encourages all members of multiperson client systems to share their views.

In professional conver-sations, social workers initially withhold their thoughts in favor of learning about the client's experience.

Workers can choose from a continuum of responses that range from nondirective to fo-cused questions. As a general rule, social workers use the least intrusive responses when clients concretely describe events in context and consider them in the light of their goals. Social workers use more direct strategies for responding when clients remain ambiguous or repeat information.

Responses that elicit the client's perspective without imposing the worker's view in-clude **allowing space**, **nonverbal responses**, **single-word responses**, **verbal utterances**, **restatements**, **clarifications**, **summary clarifications**, **requests to continue**, and **ques-tioning** (Figure 7.3). These responding skills are useful for person-to-person interactions at all levels of social work practice.

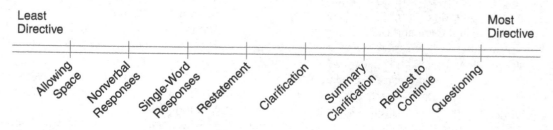

Figure 7.3
Response Continuum for Generalist Social Work

Allowing Space

If you want to hear what clients have to say, give them the space to talk. The dialogue between social workers and clients includes moments of silence. Quiet spaces give clients chances to formulate words to express their thoughts and feelings.

Allowing space may prove difficult. Most of us are socialized to fill the gaps in conversations. Add these personal tendencies to our pride in professional expertise, and we may feel the pressure to have answers. To allow space, social workers resist the temptation to describe what they see or what they can guess in favor of giving clients opportunities to express their own thoughts and feelings.

Multiperson Client Systems

Allowing space has special significance in working with multiperson client systems. Here, social workers do more than control their own contributions in ways that leave individual clients with opportunities to talk. Workers actually temper the contributions of actively verbal members to create space for more cautious members to contribute. Frequently, less talkative members of a system have the greatest impact. People who aren't talking have opportunities to observe and think. People who participate less frequently have the most new information to offer. Recognizing the potential resources of all members of a multiperson client system, practitioners work to create space to ensure that all members have chances to contribute.

Nonverbal Responses

Just as social workers observe clients carefully to see what they are saying nonverbally, clients pay attention to social workers' faces, hands, and bodies. The ways workers sit, the looks they give, and how they express themselves send messages to clients. Workers can show empathy, support, and comprehension through nonverbal responses while clients talk.

Nonverbal responses send powerful yet ambiguous messages. Each of us may interpret them differently. For example, an attentive posture may encourage clients to continue to articulate their views. A hand gesture in the direction of a member of a client system who is not contributing may invite his or her participation. However, members of some cultural groups may view close attention or gestures as threatening or demanding. To discover whether a client receives the intended message, social workers screen their nonverbal behavior for cross-cultural meanings and observe how clients react.

Single-Word Responses

Sometimes it doesn't take much for social workers to keep people talking about their situations informatively. Simple single-word responses or even verbal utterances convey an attentive and accepting tone and keep clients talking. Examples include

- Mmhmm...
- Okay
- Yes!
- All right
- Aaah...

When social workers use simple phrases with positive connotations, they nonjudgmentally validate what clients are saying and encourage clients to continue sharing.

Restatement

Social workers can respond by repeating a client's last few words or a significant phrase. This restatement functions as a perception check, verifying that workers have listened and understood. Even when social workers misunderstand what clients are talking about, restatements encourage clients to modify their messages, clarify, and continue to add more information.

Sometimes restatements cast information in a new light. In offering restatements, social workers select certain parts of the client's message. In this way, workers use restatements purposefully to develop a transactional view, provide glimpses of strengths, and forge a sense of direction toward goals.

CLIENT: I don't know what to do. Seems like every time I take him to the store, he throws a fit.

WORKER: Every time you take him to the store...

* * *

CLIENT: Sometimes I can handle it, sometimes I can't.

WORKER: Sometimes you can handle it.

With restatements, workers can also guide the focus of the conversation by emphasizing parts of the response with voice inflections or by adding an inquisitive tone.

CLIENT: My mom always complains, nags, and picks on me.

WORKER: Your mom always picks on you?

* * *

CLIENT: I've been thinking about what I need to do to make a career change.

WORKER: You're thinking about a career change?

Social workers use restatements sparingly. This type of response may fail to move conversations forward. Stringing together several restatements parrots the client and may be irritating or even sound sarcastic. Social workers select restatements to emphasize clients' conclusions and ensure they are hearing what clients are saying.

Restating what clients say is particularly important with multiperson client systems. This response inserts conversation breaks and discourages any one member from monopolizing exchanges, especially when the worker looks around at other members while restating the contribution. Restating what one member says emphasizes information clearly for other members of the client system to consider. When social workers use restatements, they demonstrate respect, model effective listening skills, and give other members of the client system the opportunity to respond.

Good listening skills prompt clients to engage in dialogue about their situations.

LISA F. YOUNG/FOTOLIA

Clarification

Clarification is a more active way for social workers to check their understanding. Here social workers may say, "So, what I hear you saying is..." followed by their best attempt to paraphrase and simplify what the client has just shared.

> **CLIENT:** You can't imagine the burden I feel caring for my father who has Alzheimer's. I never get out anymore. He needs around-the-clock care, can't find his way around the house, repeats the same question again and again, and doesn't sleep much. I'm afraid he's going to get out when I'm not looking, but I just can't keep my eyes on him 24 hours a day.
>
> **WORKER:** So, what I hear you saying is that you are having a tough time caring for your father 24 hours a day.

Clarifying what clients say has positive effects. It lets clients know that social workers are listening and understanding. Clarification can also add to clients' understanding of their situations.

Conversely, a client may think the clarification off base. This challenges clients to try again to explain their thoughts.

> **CLIENT:** Men just always want to be in charge.
>
> **WORKER:** So, men are controlling your life.
>
> **CLIENT:** Not really. I do what I want. But my husband never listens to my opinions about how he should handle the kids even though what I do works better.
>
> **WORKER:** Oh, I see. You're talking about your husband and how he relates to the kids. You would like him to handle them the way you do.
>
> **CLIENT:** That's right.

Clearly there are benefits when clients discover new ways to comprehend and explain their situations. When social workers respond by clarifying, clients and workers begin to see the situation more clearly.

Engagement

Behavior: Use empathy, reflection, and interpersonal skills to effectively engage diverse clients and constituencies

Critical Thinking Question: A social worker's genuine engagement with clients and constituencies is an ongoing dynamic process that may strengthen or weaken as the relationship progresses. What interpersonal skills work best to strengthen engagement during the information gathering phase?

Summary Clarification

When social workers identify important themes or clusters of information, they pull this content together to summarize as well as clarify. To use the summary clarification technique, social workers say things such as the following:

- Let me see if I'm getting this all right. There seem to be three common issues that the residents are most concerned about.

Or, in keeping with a strengths-oriented perspective:

- So, it seems like each time your boss confronts you, you find ways to respond assertively yet respectfully.

In each response, the worker does two things: groups information in a logical way and uses words other than the client's to frame the situation. Summary clarifications organize the work, prioritize the activity, and develop a focus on goals.

Watch this video that shows how every interaction that social workers have with clients reveals skills, values, and perspectives. What dialogue skills, professional values, and practice principles are highlighted in this supervision session?

Requests to Continue

Sometimes the best response is simply to ask clients to keep talking. Politely, many clients pause for the worker to talk, to make a contribution. When social workers sense that it's their turn to talk, they do so without interrupting clients' thinking. When needed, workers can unobtrusively request clients to continue by using short prompts or requests to continue such as the following:

- Go on...
- Tell me more...
- Please, continue...
- So...
- And, then...
- Anyone else want to comment...

When clients are doing a good job of expressing and organizing what they want to say, social workers do less so as not to interfere with the flow of information.

Workers sometimes respond with requests for more specific information:

- Tell me more about the time when things were getting better.
- I'd like to talk about parts of your life other than school.
- It does seem like the move to the new neighborhood was significant. Please talk more about that.
- Let's explore the economic and political ramifications of the policy proposal.

Note that when asking for specific information, social workers guide clients to focus on either important issues or areas that seem confusing:

- I'd like to understand better about what you were doing differently.
- Please help me understand specifically what is happening at work.
- I want to hear more about the recreation resources for community youths.
- Help me clear up my confusion about the task force's definition of homelessness.

Requests to continue also give workers direct opportunities to highlight strengths and help clients consider areas of resources that may lead to solutions:

- Could you go over that part again about the new approach you tried?
- So, you're a successful student. Tell me more.
- Let's focus on the steps the neighborhood watch has taken that seem to be working.

Additionally, social workers broaden descriptions by requesting that clients discuss contextual elements:

- I'd like you to tell me what else is happening in your life at this time.
- So, could you list for me who else attended the public forum?
- Tell me more about the new policies your agency developed.

Emphasizing certain topics as important makes these requests for specific information powerful responses. When social workers choose this type of response early in their work with a client, they strive to focus on issues the client presents, rather than leap away from the client's agenda.

Questioning

Questioning functions to open new areas of exploration or to pursue more specific, detailed information. As responses, questions merely follow up on what clients have already said. Well-framed questions invite clients to survey what they know rather than confess how they have failed. Specific questions can help clients focus directly on their strengths. When social workers construct their questions carefully, they can elicit important information and still let clients lead the way.

Well-trained social workers know that respecting clients' power while asking questions is a practice skill requiring extensive preparation. Envision what it's like to be questioned. Do hot lights and smoke-filled rooms spring to mind as you are being interrogated and forced to justify yourself to the uniformed figures circling around you? Certainly, this is not the atmosphere that social workers want to create as they gather information from clients. Experienced practitioners use questions selectively and phrase them carefully!

Phrasing Questions Is Important

Depending on how social workers ask questions, clients experience them as intrusive and confrontational or as interested and supportive. Questions that seek descriptive information begin with words such as "who," "what," "when," "how often," and "in what way." These questions lead to important concrete and contextual information. In contrast to the judgmental message of "why" questions, "who," "what," "when," "how often," and "in what way" questions seek readily available information that increases understanding.

Social workers avoid questions beginning with "why." "Why" questions force respondents to account for their behavior, although often people do not know "why" they've acted as they have. When social workers use "why" questions, they cast doubts on the choices clients have made and produce defensive postures. Consider how the following questions elicit a greater understanding of what clients are saying. When a client says, "He always lets me down," social workers can respond by asking the following questions:

- Who is the "he" that you're talking about?
- In what way does he let you down?
- How does this interfere with what you are trying to accomplish?
- What do you think is getting in his way?
- Always? Is there ever a time when he doesn't?

Notice the common elements of these questions. Each question follows up directly on the client's assertion. Each seeks to elicit concrete information about the client's thinking and the events that are occurring. The worker doesn't search for whom to blame, look for why the behavior occurs, or question whether the representation of the event is "really" true. Each question demonstrates acceptance of the client's experience and the associated feelings. Questions work best when they relate directly to what clients say and when answers will add new information.

Combining Responses

In practice, social workers weave combinations of these responses together to articulate a client's thoughts fully. Some clients offer considerable information with little prompting. Others need more direct approaches to explain their situations in concrete and helpful ways. Empowering social workers choose the least directive responses possible that still keep the conversation on track. The more clients offer on their own, the less directive social workers become.

Practice Example

Learning responding skills prepares practitioners to talk with clients. Review the following dialogue to see such skills and to discover the orientation to the future, transactional focus, positive tone, and variety of responses with which Alex Anderson, a practitioner from Northside Prevention Services, responds to Don, who calls their telephone hotline.

ALEX: Hello. This is the Listening Line. I'm Alex.

DON: Hi. I'm Don.

ALEX: Hi, Don. (allows space for client to continue)

DON: You probably want to know why I'm calling.

ALEX: Whatever you'd like to tell me.

DON: Well, I've got this problem.

ALEX: OK.

DON: You see, I'm the child of an alcoholic.

ALEX: Uh-huh.

DON: And my life is a mess.

ALEX: In what way, a mess?

DON: I can't seem to get anywhere.

ALEX: Some place specific in mind?

DON: Yes, a place that's not so lonely.

ALEX: A place that's not so lonely. Who might be there?

DON: Friends, family . . . mostly family.

ALEX: Mostly family.

DON: My parents and my sister.

ALEX: Seems like you're missing your parents and your sister.

DON: Sometimes.

ALEX: I'd like to hear more about your parents and sister.

DON: What do you want to know?

ALEX: I guess I'd like to hear the things you think are most important.

DON: Well, I haven't seen them for a while.

ALEX: A while?

DON: About 6 months.

ALEX: So, it's been about 6 months, since . . .

DON: The big fight.

ALEX: The big fight?

DON: Yes, my fight with Dad.

ALEX: (waits for client to continue)

DON: The fight where he kicked me out . . . or I left . . . I'm not real sure.

ALEX: Kind of a mutual thing, huh?

DON: Yes. I guess I just needed some space, but I really wasn't ready for quite this much. Besides, I get concerned about Anna.

ALEX: Anna?

DON: My sister.

ALEX: So you're concerned about your sister Anna?

DON: Yes, having to deal with my parents and their drinking. It's a lot for a 13-year-old.

ALEX: So, tell me more.

DON: Well, you probably know the story. Mom and Dad go out and drink and then come home and pick on us kids. I used to take most of the heat, but since I moved out, I'm sure they're doing it to Anna.

ALEX: So let me get this straight. You are calling with a couple of concerns. First, you are kind of missing contact with your family since you haven't seen them for 6 months. And secondly, you are wondering how your sister is coping with your parents' drinking since you left.

DON: You got it.

ALEX: Anything else?

DON: I guess not.

ALEX: Seems like you are thinking about changing this situation.

DON: I'm not liking the way things are.

ALEX: So is this call the beginning of changing things, or are you also doing other things to change this situation?

DON: Well, I wrote my folks a letter, but I didn't mail it.

ALEX: You wrote your folks a letter?

DON: Yes, I worked on it a long time.

ALEX: What do you think you'll do with it?

DON: I might mail it. I might deliver it in person. I might throw it away.

ALEX: You do have a lot of options.

DON: I do, don't I?

ALEX: Seems like it.

DON: You know, now that I have written it out, I could probably even talk to them directly about it.

ALEX: Is that what you want to do?

DON: I'll have to think about it.

ALEX: Well, you seem like a thoughtful person. I have a sense that you'll figure out what to do next.

DON: Well, it's time to do something. I'll just have to decide what.

ALEX: Is that something that you want my help with?

DON: Not right now I don't think.

ALEX: Okay? Sounds like you're on the way to solving this one.

DON: I think maybe you're right.

ALEX: Anything else to talk about with me?

DON: Not right now.

ALEX: Feel free to call back if you want to keep thinking out loud, if you're looking for a referral someplace, or whatever.

DON: Thanks. I will.

ALEX: Good luck, Don.

? Assess your understanding of responding to thoughts and feelings by taking this brief quiz.

Alex gently steers Don toward a positive, transactional, and forward-looking orientation. To do this, Alex uses deliberate responses that maintain the centrality of Don's message. An effective social worker learns communication and listening skills to respond to clients in ways that balance respect for their views while moving them forward toward resolutions.

SPECIAL ISSUES IN RESPONDING

Certain actions by clients deserve special consideration; they call for thoughtful responses by social workers. Experienced social workers learn successful ways to respond to clients' feelings, anger, silence, trauma, questions, and feedback.

Responding to Feelings

Identifying and expressing feelings benefits everyone. Feelings provide clues about where we stand on things and information about what works. Expressing feelings allows us to be close to and validated by others. The consequences of not expressing feelings include loss of information, sense of isolation, projection of emotions into situations where they don't fit, and even physical and emotional illnesses (Johnson, 2014). When social workers assist clients in accessing their feelings, they empower clients with new information, acceptance, and a sense of control.

Identifying Feelings

Sharing thoughts and describing feelings are very different experiences. For example, running into an old friend at a conference is an observable event that may engender an entire constellation of feelings, from surprise to joy to awkwardness. We can readily share our thoughts about the event by remembering and reporting. But when describing the associated feelings, we may be plagued by their ambiguity. For some of us, expressing feelings is more difficult than describing thoughts. As we try to articulate how we feel about the event of running into an old friend, we may struggle with the task.

With some people, talking about feelings is easy. They relate comfortably on the affective level, expressing feelings directly, articulately, and automatically. But more consistently, clients express feelings nonverbally through facial expressions, voice tone, body posture, and choice of words. Social workers prepare to respond to a client's affect by learning to identify the multiple ways people express feelings and by understanding the cultural implications of such expressions.

Verbalizing Feelings

As clients describe the events in their lives, the associated feelings show up, either tumbling out verbally as part of the reporting of events or surfacing in nonverbal behaviors. Feelings vary in intensity—from mild to strong, and from barely noticeable to preoccupying. When social workers hear clients expressing feelings, they respond with verbal reflections to identify the feelings and their intensity. Social workers make

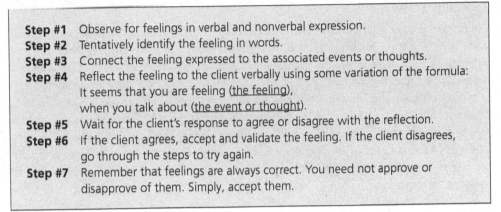

Step #1	Observe for feelings in verbal and nonverbal expression.
Step #2	Tentatively identify the feeling in words.
Step #3	Connect the feeling expressed to the associated events or thoughts.
Step #4	Reflect the feeling to the client verbally using some variation of the formula: It seems that you are feeling (the feeling), when you talk about (the event or thought).
Step #5	Wait for the client's response to agree or disagree with the reflection.
Step #6	If the client agrees, accept and validate the feeling. If the client disagrees, go through the steps to try again.
Step #7	Remember that feelings are always correct. You need not approve or disapprove of them. Simply, accept them.

Figure 7.4
Constructing a Reflection of Feelings

educated guesses about a client's feelings and invite clients as experts to either validate or correct these perceptions.

By following a simple strategy, social workers use reflective skills to identify feelings (Figure 7.4). First, workers scan the client's information and behavior for the feeling. Second, they tentatively attach a descriptive label to the feeling. Third, workers enhance the client's understanding of the feeling by connecting it with the precipitating event or behavior. Clients benefit from information that links feelings to thoughts. For example, a social worker may say the following:

- It seems like you're feeling proud of things you've accomplished to this point, especially your success in parenting.
- I may be detecting a note of sarcasm when you talk about the possibility of your promotion.
- I'm sensing a glimmer of hope when you describe your new approach.
- Look's like you're really angry that the state cut back your funding.
- Seems hopeless since each time you complain to the police, nothing seems to change.

As workers offer hunches about what feelings clients may be experiencing, they make their suggestions tentatively. Workers are actually guessing when they reflect a client's feelings. Only clients know for sure whether the worker's hunch accurately reflects their emotional experiences. Social workers must check out their perceptions. In the subjective world of feelings, only clients can know for sure!

Notice that nowhere in the process of accessing and expressing feelings do workers directly ask, "How do you feel?" Experienced social workers will tell you that the most likely response to "How do you feel?" is an honest "I don't know." Right now, ask yourself the question "How do I feel?" There is nothing like direct questioning about feelings to send every emotion you are experiencing running for cover. Many of us just go blank or struggle to find the right words. Pursuing feelings directly from clients often obscures them, rather than bringing them out. Social workers nurture feelings forward with hunches and observations rather than chase them with probing questions.

Validating Feelings

Clients are always right about their feelings. Each human being is the sole expert about how he or she feels. Feelings don't have to make sense; they are entirely personal and subjective experiences. And importantly, feelings do not mandate behavior. Consider this dramatic example. Even when a father reveals to his social worker that he has hostile feelings about his son, he has done nothing wrong unless he acts on those feelings. In fact, by expressing these feelings, he is actually doing something right. In doing so, he creates the opportunity to take charge of his feelings rather than have his feelings lead him toward problematic behavior. Social workers acknowledge even these feelings, reinforce the client's trust in sharing, and work quickly to enable the client with the capability to make other choices.

Responding to Anger

Predictably, anger is expressed in many social work encounters. Challenging situations can lead to frustration, disappointment, pain, and sadness—all feelings closely associated with and sometimes expressed by anger. When we hurt, we lash out. When clients hurt, social workers are frequently the targets. Self-confident social workers encourage and validate clients' expression of anger even when it volleys directly toward them. Additionally, workers respond to expressions of anger as opportunities to look for other associated feelings and information.

We each have our own degree of comfort with expressing and responding to anger. When clients express anger, social workers respond as they respond to any other feeling they observe: They reflect the feeling to heighten clients' awareness and invite them to clarify their responses:

- You seem angry . . .
- I can see you are upset . . .
- Makes you mad, huh?

Practitioners connect the feeling to the associated events in ways such as the following:

- You seem angry when you talk about the way the media put down your neighborhood.
- When I mention Child Protective Services, I can see your anger.
- Seems to me that you're upset about my suggestion to get information from your probation officer.

Finally, social workers recognize, accept, and validate feelings of anger. They accept the feeling as okay, even good to express, with phrases such as the following:

- I can understand how this makes you angry. I appreciate that you trusted me enough to share that.
- Feels good to get angry sometimes.
- Go ahead, talk about it. It's okay to be mad.

Generally, when people express anger, this outward expression reflects internal pain. Often, people respond to their own experience of pain by defending their vulnerability with anger. Social workers reach beyond the expression of anger to identify and reflect a client's internal turmoil and pain rather than simply leaving this emotion at the surface level:

- You look angry, but it seems to me you feel sad.
- Makes you mad to feel so helpless, doesn't it?
- I'd probably be fighting back, too, if I felt so vulnerable.

Workers respond to anger with the same empathetic, reflective, and informative style used to respond to all feelings.

Sometimes, when clients express anger toward social workers, their anger contains a specific message. In other words, the anger is not misplaced or symbolic of internal pain, but the client is actually upset at something the worker is or is not doing. Maybe the social worker is trying to get too close too fast. Maybe the worker is missing the point or not responding in ways that show understanding and empathy. Maybe the worker is falling prey to prejudices and stereotypes and not seeing clients for who they really are. Here, too, nondefensive responses clarify feedback:

- So, you're upset with my questions?
- You're angry because I interrupted you?
- In your view, I'm just another social worker who doesn't understand your situation?

Anger communicates important information. Workers examine clients' anger for the feedback it provides.

Responding to Silence

In responding to silence, remember the rule in communication: "One cannot not communicate" (Watzlawick et al., 1967, p. 49). Even silent clients tell us things about themselves. Consider these possible meanings of silence: "I don't want to be here." "It's hopeless." "Leave me alone." "I don't trust you." "I don't trust words." "You might think you are in control, but you can't make me talk." "I don't understand a thing you're saying." "I can't deal with this right now." "I need time to think this over." Listening to silence and omissions is critical because "what interviewees avoid saying is as important as what they do say. Not talking is a special way of talking" (Kadushin & Kadushin, 1997, p. 214).

Silence is ambiguous; so, in responding, the worker's empathy and imagination come into play. Social workers formulate hunches about what clients mean by considering contextual elements, nonverbal cues, and the client's characteristics. If a client is involuntary, a lack of trust and the need for some control is likely. If a client is adolescent, withdrawal from and resistance to adults is age appropriate. If the client smiles blankly, a polite lack of understanding may be evident. If a client has suffered oppression or abuse, silence might reflect a sense of powerlessness. If the client is a recent immigrant, language and cultural differences may show up in silence. Moreover, in some cultures, silence infers respect. Workers make their best determination about what clients are saying with their silence, verbalize it, and wait for clients to modify the guess to a more accurate view.

Social workers respond verbally to a client's silence, phrasing their responses in ways that invite clients to talk. Social workers may say any of the following:

- Must be tough for you to be here just because someone told you that you had to come.
- Kind of seems hopeless to try again on something that you've been trying to deal with for so long.
- I can understand how it might be hard to trust a stranger, especially an older person like me. Take your time. Only tell me things when you are ready.
- Is this making sense to you? Could I ask you to explain what you hear me saying?
- ¿Comprende usted? ¿Habla usted inglés?

Whether clients respond verbally or nonverbally, workers continue to converse, providing clients with ample opportunities to talk.

Responding to Trauma

Most social workers will see clients who have experienced trauma. Community-based surveys reveal the pervasiveness of trauma in people's lives, with estimates of between 55 percent and 90 percent of adults having experienced at least one such event (Fallot & Harris, 2009). Nearly two out of three children endure adverse childhood experiences with traumatizing effects (Redding, 2003). Effectively responding to clients who are coping with traumatic events requires worker sensitivity and patience.

Sometimes, social workers know about clients' traumatic experience because the event itself precipitates the referral. At other times, the actual traumatic event is undisclosed, but clients present with symptoms such as depression, anxiety, or substance abuse. Trauma affects each person differently; there is no single way to cope. Clients who are traumatized may respond to workers with silence, unable to find the words or trust workers enough to share their experiences. Or clients might assume a defensive posture and use anger for protection. Social workers can utilize the skills described in the previous sections for guidance on how to respond to silent or angry clients.

More than simply saying the right words, workers concentrate on creating and maintaining a safe and nonjudgmental atmosphere. Workers allow space for survivors of trauma to share their stories whenever they feel ready, and workers also let clients withhold disclosure if they so choose. The skills of inclusive therapy work well here (O'Hanlon, 2003). This approach explores ambivalence by responding to clarify what clients are saying while giving them permission to change or to stay the same. Workers may say any of the following:

- So, you are thinking that this is a person you might be ready to trust, and then again it might be best to take it more slowly.
- I hear there are some other things that you would like to tell me, and I'm here to listen now or whenever you feel the time is right to do so.
- It seems that you want to let go of some of that anger and do that at a pace that still helps you feel protected.

Note the worker's lack of pressure to force progress on the client. Instead, the worker clarifies the client's options to take action, take no action, or take action later when the client feels more ready. Trauma disempowers. The key to responding to a survivor of trauma is giving control, choice, and autonomy back to the client (Guarino et al., 2009).

Importantly, workers recognize that clients have learned to interact in particular ways to feel safe (Guarino et al., 2009). So, whatever clients are doing to cope is likely adaptive and possibly, but not necessarily, the best option at the present time. Social workers should be patient. Healing from trauma occurs in the context of an authentic and nurturing relationship. Workers should provide that environment, creating a secure space for clients to share.

Responding to Questions

Clients ask questions, too. Frequently, clients have questions about the social worker's credentials, the agency's procedures, or what the worker is saying. Questions are good signs. They often indicate a developing partnership in which clients feel free to assert their needs and express their curiosity. When clients actively take charge of eliciting information, they exercise their power. Workers encourage clients' power by acknowledging their rights to information and by providing appropriately direct and honest answers.

Certain questions require cautious responses. Frequently, clients seek advice with questions: "What would you do if you were in my situation?" "So which one of us is right?" "What should I do?" Social workers who fall prey to this invitation to be experts find themselves trapped by the dependencies they create in clients. An empowering response recognizes the client's need for assistance that is evident in the advice-seeking question, yet returns the responsibility for solutions to the partnership. Social workers can say any of the following:

- I know you'd like me to give you the answer. Trouble is, I don't have it.
- I appreciate your confidence in me, but this must be a tough issue or you would have solved it without me.
- Maybe when I know you and your situation better, I can let you know what I think, but right now, you know a lot more than I do about what is going on.
- I don't know who's right. Probably you both have valid points.

Social workers always respond to questions but may choose responses that respect the client's expertise.

Responding to Feedback from Clients

As social workers, we benefit from candid appraisals by clients. Clients know best what helps and what does not. Asking clients to make comments concerning both us and the practice process functions as an empowerment strategy. This means accepting clients' positive commentaries as well as their negative perceptions of who we are as people and professionals.

Social workers learn skills to accept feedback. They prepare themselves for nondefensive listening. They respond with appreciation and enthusiasm to feedback from clients such as the following:

- I appreciate your honesty in telling me when I'm off base.
- Thanks for trusting me enough to share that with me.
- I appreciate you saying how much you enjoy coming here. I think we make a good team, too.

- So, you think I'm not understanding your point of view. I'm glad you let me know. What's the piece you think I'm missing?
- I can understand how it might be difficult to talk to a man about this. How can we make it easier?

Client feedback orients the professional relationship and defines the direction of the work.

Responding to Larger Client Systems

Generalist social workers respond to client systems of all sizes. At all levels of practice, workers respond to clients to elicit their views and to validate their feelings. Practice with any client requires a worker's one-with-one conversational ability. Dialogue with larger client systems places workers in a matrix of conversations.

When practitioners work with larger client systems, they must balance the rights of individuals with the rights of others. This ethical challenge raises numerous questions. For example, is it acceptable for one person within the client group to be the spokesperson? Does everyone need to contribute equally? What if people disagree? How does the social worker respond to each individual member of a system, yet respect the functioning of the group? Two skills—facilitating discussion and respecting existing functioning—provide answers to these questions.

Dialogue with larger client systems places workers in a matrix of conversations.

Facilitating Discussion

Social workers coordinate traffic when responding to multiperson client systems. They actively involve themselves with the client group to influence "who talks when about what." Social workers guide the interaction so that only one person talks at a time, members listen and respond to one another, all members have opportunities to express their views, and the contributions of all members receive respect. To accomplish this, social workers use a variety of methods.

Workers model effective communication by responding in ways that make the thoughts and feelings of all participants more concrete. Workers frequently summarize the group's discussion, highlighting areas of agreement and clarifying options. When others interrupt, contradict, or let one person monopolize, social workers take more active roles. When more than one member talks at once, social workers may say any of the following:

- I love people who talk, but I need it one at a time so I can take it all in.
- I see you both have information. Who wants to start?
- Whoa. There is a lot of enthusiasm here. Good! I want to hear what each of you has to say.

Or social workers may respond nonverbally and

- attend to the person who was first talking through eye contact and body posture and then immediately turn to elicit the view of the person who was interrupting at the first available pause;
- acknowledge the member's desire to contribute with a hand gesture that holds back the person's contribution temporarily and then wave them on to share when possible.

When people's different views lead to conflict, workers may say any of the following:

- You both have interesting views. I guess there's more than one way to look at this situation.
- You know, no two people see the same thing the same way. You both may be right.
- Well, that's two ways to look at it. Anyone have another way?
- It's great when people disagree. It always gives you more options.

When one member monopolizes, workers recognize the mutual responsibility of the talking and the silent members by responding as follows:

- Thanks for all the information. You're really working hard here. Maybe somebody else should take it for a while.
- Well, I think I understand your views. I'm going to need everyone's opinion for this to work. Who's up next?
- You really have a good grasp of the situation. What can the rest of you tell me?
- That was a bold move to go first, and now you get to relax and listen while the others talk.

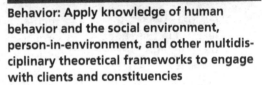

Engagement

Behavior: Apply knowledge of human behavior and the social environment, person-in-environment, and other multidisciplinary theoretical frameworks to engage with clients and constituencies

Critical Thinking Question: Generalist practitioners work with a variety of client systems, including groups. How are the communication skills used by social workers to engage clients in group, organization, and community settings similar to or different from those they use with individual clients?

Social workers respond in ways that show appreciation of contributions yet redirect interactions. Workers validate contributions, encourage participation, and organize the flow of information.

Respecting Existing Functioning

When one member of a client system says more or less than another, this does not mean that social workers must intervene. Workers trust that systems have their own style of relating. How each system member contributes may actually draw on the strengths of the system. Some client systems work best with a combination of talkers and listeners, up-front doers and behind-the-scenes planners. For example, within a given family, a parent who spends more time with the child concerned logically has more to contribute when describing events.

Formal client systems, such as organizations, likely have prescribed interactional processes. With such clients, workers show respect for the organization's structure and practices. For example, if an organization decides through a consensus process that a certain committee will speak for the group, rights of individuals are still ensured. As long as the system operates in a way that respects the contributions of all its members, workers have no reason to interfere.

? Assess your understanding of special issues in responding by taking this brief quiz.

LOOKING FORWARD

Articulating situations means detailing challenging issues from the client's perspective and placing these events in environmental context. Using the skills of proactive responding, workers are able to add future, transactional, and positive dimensions to understanding the problems clients face. Workers mix and match many client-centered responses to help clients express their thoughts and reveal their feelings about problems, goals, and potential solutions. Prepared practitioners also use strategies to talk cooperatively with clients who are angry, silent, curious, or evaluative. Generalist social workers combine the skills appropriate for working with individuals with workers' capabilities to elicit information and balance contributions when working with larger system clients.

To discover the available strengths within clients and their environments, workers first help clients define desired goals. Chapter 8 presents processes that can be used to align workers with clients' motivations and assist clients to describe positive outcomes in order to focus the search for relevant resources.

Evaluate what you learned in this chapter by completing the Chapter Review.

8

Engagement: Defining Directions

LISA F. YOUNG / SHUTTERSTOCK

It's the second Tuesday of the month, and members of the Northside Network are gathering for their monthly brown-bag luncheon. Established less than 3 months ago, the Northside Network is a consortium of human service agencies with representatives from all over the Northside community. Network members are quickly discovering that, in spite of the differences in the services that each provides, they really have much in common. As part of the same community, they confront similar community problems and draw from the same selection of resources and opportunities to serve clients.

During the first two meetings, members of the group get to know one another, and they organize a structure to guide the functioning of the group. Now, it is time to look ahead. Members have yet to decide on a specific purpose for the Network. Miriam Andovich calls the meeting to order, part of her role as facilitator, and she guides the group to develop a coherent direction for action.

Miriam works in the AIDS prevention project at the Northside Alliance for Family Health, and today, she is the facilitator for the

Northside Network—a role that rotates among the group's members. Miriam shifts her focus to the group as a whole and uses many of the same generalist practice skills to facilitate its functioning as she uses with clients in the AIDS prevention project. Miriam suggests that the group begin today's work with a brief structured experience she calls the Network News. She asks that each member take 2 minutes to update the others about newsworthy events at their agencies. Miriam believes that for the group to decide where they are going, they should first establish where they are.

One by one, workers describe current issues affecting the agencies they represent. Tony Marelli announces that the Addictions Recovery Center has new funds for in-school prevention programming, but so far, no schools have applied. Mark Nogales describes his organization's concerns about a reduction in participation by county residents in the programs of the County Mental Health Center. Kay Landon notes that the Family Support Program is seeking funds to hire interpreters and bilingual staff. Andrea Barry describes the frustration workers in the Family Preservation Program are experiencing in helping clients locate low-cost housing. The waiting lists for public assistance housing are growing, and low-cost private rentals are virtually nonexistent. All Network members contribute their own perspectives on what's happening in the Northside community.

As members report, Miriam writes their comments on large sheets of paper mounted on the wall behind her. Next, she asks, "What are our common concerns?" As members offer their ideas, Miriam responds in ways that encourage interaction, summarize and clarify what members say, and guide members to synthesize ideas. Soon, similar opinions about "getting rid of so many restrictions to services" and "simplifying intake processes" lead the members to identify the umbrella issue of accessibility of services as an apparent unifying theme. Miriam sums up the group's direction by saying, "So, our purpose will be to increase the accessibility of our services for both urban and rural county residents." A quick poll of the members confirms this common purpose. Members act to make their consensus an official agreement, or "contract," by proposing it as a formal motion, approving it with a unanimous vote, and recording the transaction in the minutes.

Identifying accessibility as the central issue focuses the group's discussion. Ideas surface concerning community education about available services, services at no cost to clients or based on clients' abilities to pay, better transportation for clients to reach agencies, staff and community training on cultural sensitivity, more in-home services, and the need to examine restrictive eligibility requirements for various programs. Members acknowledge each idea's merit but agree that choosing specific "solutions" right now is premature. No one can say with certainty what poses significant barriers or what actions will have the greatest influence on service accessibility. Members will need a more detailed assessment to determine what activities will do the most good.

Before adjourning, several members volunteer to participate on a committee to develop a community resource assessment plan. Implementing this assessment, members will discover which factors currently enhance accessibility and which create obstacles. The more complete assessment information will then contribute to the members' efforts to develop a workable and concrete plan of action.

Miriam's interaction with the Northside Network illustrates how a practitioner assists a community-based organization to define a direction for its work. The same processes apply to practice at other system levels. Both clients and social workers participate in developing a mutual direction. Clients bring their own **motivation**, sense of destination, and rights to self-determination. Social workers balance their respect for client privileges with their own vision of what could be. Clients benefit from this early effort to define a mutual purpose.

This chapter describes how social workers and clients define a direction for their work. It also examines priority issues that may arise and require an immediate response. Agreeing to a common purpose for the relationship activates client participation and directs the search for relevant resources.

TRANSFORMING CHALLENGES INTO DIRECTIONS

Defining a direction describes the process of negotiating a mutually agreeable purpose or preliminary goal. It logically precedes other actions taken by workers and clients to assess resources or develop an intervention plan (Figure 8.1). In other words, workers

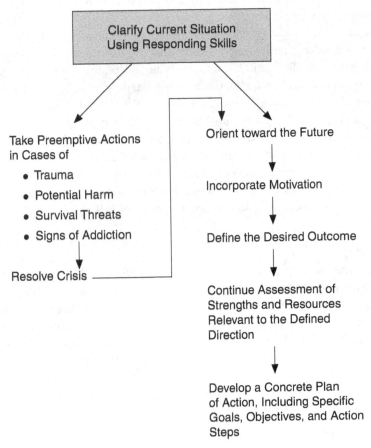

Figure 8.1
The Process of Defining Directions

and clients postpone setting very specific goals at this early juncture in lieu of establishing a more global expectation about the outcomes of the work. This beginning agreement about the purpose of the relationship guides the dialogue toward gathering enough information to frame a concrete intervention plan with more specific goals and objectives—a plan informed by a goal-focused assessment.

Strengths-oriented social workers recognize the benefit of a vision of the future, so they move quickly to define directions with their clients. Often, clients begin the dialogue at intake by describing what they hope to achieve. In the case of individual or family clients, a practitioner might come to an agreement with the client within a few short minutes of beginning the initial interchange. In contrast, the diversity of perspectives in larger client systems will likely require more dialogue before participants can negotiate an agreed-on direction. With client systems at any level, workers may need to nudge clients beyond describing only their present difficulties toward considering future possibilities about how things should be.

Reshaping a report of a challenging situation into a clear direction informs social workers and their clients in several ways. First, clients are most likely to achieve outcomes that they can clearly envision (Walter & Peller, 1992). Second, workers learn what clients want, an important context in which to view the information clients offer. For example, understanding a client's overall purpose helps determine the significance of problematic events and also to identify resources for building a solution. And finally, pausing to consider a preliminary sense of direction gives a generalist social worker time to explore the transactional dimensions of the situation, thereby broadening the field of potential solutions at all system levels.

Social work values come into play when defining directions with clients. The core social work values of client self-determination and autonomy guide social workers to respect the wishes of all clients, even those whose capabilities are limited by disability or crisis. How much a social worker should respect a client's choice depends not so much on client characteristics but more on whether the decision will harm the client or anyone else. Risks associated with any action need to be fully explored and disclosed before clients have full rights to self-determination. Ethical practitioners minimize the risk of underserving clients by overrespecting clients' autonomy (Austin, 1996). Social workers consistently implement social work values, but they balance this by recognizing the client's capacity for making decisions in times of crisis or inability.

> *Strengths-oriented social workers recognize the benefit of a vision of the future, so they move quickly to define directions with their clients.*

Orienting Forward, Not Back

Clients most often want to change their present situation. Solution-oriented social workers urge clients to go beyond simply identifying what they want to change in order to project in detail how they would like to be. Setting overall goals directs helping relationships away from describing problems and toward constructing solutions, from *what is* to *what will be*. Social workers assist clients in visualizing what they want by shifting the conversation from what is not working to the more empowering view of a desirable outcome that clients can achieve.

Observe the dialogue in which Vanessa, a social worker in the state's Child Protective Unit, responds to focus Kim toward the future.

VANESSA: I understand that you are here to talk about ways to stop hitting your son when he talks back.

KIM: That's right. He'll report me for child abuse if I do it again.

VANESSA: Okay. If you're not going to hit your son when he talks back, what do you see yourself doing instead?

KIM: I guess I'll do nothing.

VANESSA: By doing nothing, do you mean that you will allow him to talk back while you just stand there and ignore him, or will you just walk away? What exactly are you hoping to do?

KIM: I'm not really sure. I know I can't hit him. I'll get in trouble. He's getting too big, and it doesn't help anyway. I really wish he just wouldn't talk back. Then I wouldn't have to do anything.

VANESSA: Seems like you're telling me that the first step will be to ignore your son or walk away when he talks back, but in the long run, you'd really like to have him talk with you more respectfully.

KIM: That's right. How can I do that?

VANESSA: I'm not sure right now, but it does give us a general direction to move in. We probably need to start by getting more information about what's going on with you, your son, and your situation before we can figure out specific ways to help you and your son talk together more respectfully.

In this example, Vanessa and Kim quickly determine a positive direction for their work. Notice how Vanessa facilitates this task by responding in ways that enable Kim to maintain control of the general purpose of the relationship while, at the same time, gently reorienting Kim away from describing current dilemmas and forward to look at future solutions.

Framing the Search for Resources

Outcomes that clients can imagine and describe concretely contribute significantly to success. If clients can see it, they are more likely to go there. Solution-focused practitioners prompt clients to visualize how they would like their lives to be different and then work with clients to locate the skills and opportunities available to make that happen (De Jong & Berg, 2013). Social workers learn where to steer the focus of a more comprehensive assessment after the client's desired outcome is clearly articulated.

You can see how helpful defining a concrete outcome can be in framing an assessment process by considering the previous example of Kim and Vanessa. Knowing what Kim wants leads Vanessa to focus directly on those resources Kim has to help her talk with her son more respectfully. Vanessa can now ask Kim about exceptions, times when she either walked away before hitting her son or was able to discuss issues with him in a calm manner. Recognizing an exception or a resource is possible only in the context of how Kim wants things to be. Defining a purpose is prerequisite to discovering what might help to meet it. Chapters 9 and 10 outline specific strategies and suggest tools for assessing client strengths and environmental resources relevant to a clearly defined direction. Chapter 11 details the process of analysis and planning.

Integrating Transactional Dimensions

Setting very specific goals before developing an ecosystemic understanding undermines a generalist approach and may lead to blaming clients for problems that are not within their sphere of control. Planning too quickly can overemphasize clients' responsibilities to make changes while underestimating the potential of social and physical environments to hold solutions. In other words, we may be asking clients to change themselves (because that is now what we know most about) while ignoring the possible benefits of modifying the context.

Reconsider the previous example. What if Kim's unemployment or fears for her son's safety in the neighborhood adds a sense of desperation to her parenting? What if the community's discrimination against Vietnamese immigrants or the housing authority's policy of refusing housing to families without credit histories contributes to an underlying tension in the household that triggers aggression in any difficult interaction? If, early on, a social worker and client set goals that narrowly focus on changing the client's behavior, significant transactional elements may go undetected as possible targets for change. Completing a broader ecosystemic assessment before establishing more concrete goals and plans of action gives flexibility and adds a generalist focus to the process.

? Assess your understanding of transforming challenges into directions by taking this brief quiz.

CONSIDERING CLIENT MOTIVATION

Some social workers summarily dismiss unsuccessful outcomes with a simple, "This client isn't sufficiently motivated." This attitude fails to consider the notion that all behavior is motivated, including seemingly "unmotivated" behaviors such as disinterest in service plans, **resistance** to change, or withdrawal from service. Simply, client behavior, like all human behavior, is motivated toward some end, even if it is not in the direction social workers anticipate.

Simply, client behavior, like all human behavior, is motivated toward some end, even if it is not in the direction social workers anticipate.

Helping professionals have traditionally defined motivation as an individual attribute, something that clients have or do not have, something they bring or fail to bring to the change process. Contemporary social work reconceptualizes motivation as a transactional concept rather than a personal trait. To understand motivational elements, workers examine interactions between the client system and the social worker, as well as clients' transactions with the environment. Once assessed, social workers then take actions to help clients align their motivation with their goals.

Enhancing Client Motivation

Social workers share responsibility for stimulating motivation. When clients reveal little motivation, social workers respond by helping clients consider their desires for change. A stages-of-change model frames workers' assessments of clients' readiness for change (Prochaska & DiClemente, 1983). The skills of **motivational interviewing** offer concrete strategies to help clients resolve ambivalence about change and energize client motivation to participate in the process (Miller & Rollnick, 2013).

▶ Watch this video that illustrates how social workers are responsible for developing a client's motivation for change. What responses work best to engage the client? www.youtube.com/watch?v=67l6g1l7Zao

Stages of Change

Sometimes positive life changes occur quickly, without any apparent effort. Things just happen to propel us forward. In contrast, planned change, such as that which occurs in social work practice, likely progresses in a more methodical manner. Prochaska and DiClemente (1983) first conceptualized a stages-of-change model that continues to be applied in social work practice today.

The original model identified five stages of change, beginning with precontemplation (not thinking about a change) and progressing through contemplation (thinking about making a change), preparation (making plans to achieve a change), action (implementing plans), and maintenance (working to sustain the change). Over time, as this model has been applied, a sixth phase of change described as relapse has been articulated to acknowledge the likely reoccurrence of and recovery from problematic behaviors.

"Starting where the client is" means honoring a client's current level of readiness for change. When clients hesitate, social workers guide them to explore their preferences about change, to consider the potential benefits, and to identify the risks or losses that may be involved. Practitioners work to motivate clients, collaborating with them to progress cooperatively through the stages of change and to achieve desired goals.

Motivational Interviewing

Motivational interviewing provides tools for social workers to enhance a client's commitment to change efforts. Cooperative dialogue that guides clients to explore and resolve their ambivalence about change is the centerpiece of motivational interviewing (Miller & Rollnick, 2013). Dialogue strategies include open-ended questions, affirmations, reflections, and summaries, all with an emphasis on helping clients consider their thoughts and feelings about the impact of potential changes in their lives (Rosengren, 2009). Workers hone in on a client's "change talk," responding to what clients say about their desire to change, their ability to change, the potential benefits of change, and their recognition that change is necessary. Social workers may also suggest what changes to make and how clients might proceed, but only when clients show receptivity to suggestions. If clients show resistance to these ideas, workers should immediately fall back into a reflective posture.

Motivational interviewing strategies work effectively in many fields of social work practice. Scholars have described and evaluated their application in working with alcohol-involved older adults (Hanson & Gutheil, 2004), in settings with mandated substance abuse clients (Linhorst, Kuettel, & Bombardier, 2002), and in counseling juvenile sex offenders (Patel et al., 2008). Van Wormer (2007) suggests that a motivational interviewing approach provides a "framework with wide application across the spectrum of social work practice" (p. 21). Lewis and Osborn (2004) advocate an integrated application of motivational interviewing and solution-focused counseling to build motivation for change and to identify the strengths and resources available to achieve goals.

Building momentum for change is not the responsibility of the client alone. Workers share the challenge of aligning clients' motivation and expectations with the goals and tasks of change. By accepting clients' current levels of readiness for change, exploring their ambivalence and beliefs about the potential for change, and matching the pace of intervention to ensure client cooperation, workers circumvent the pitfalls of client resistance and empower clients to move forward in ways that match their readiness, confidence, and resources.

Motivating Clients Who Have Given Up

Many clients need a motivational boost to succeed, having learned that despite their best efforts, their attempts fail. Life has convinced them they are helpless. Researchers have observed this phenomenon of learned helplessness, documenting that a prolonged lack of success results in a lack of motivation to continue to try (Abramson et al., 1978; Seligman, 1975).

Clients in oppressive situations are most vulnerable to experiencing this state of learned helplessness. Social structures disenfranchise these clients and block them from their rightful share of societal resources. Workers can counteract learned helplessness in four steps by

- listening to and validating the client's frustrating experiences,
- framing an achievable direction,
- expressing belief in the worker's and client's abilities to reach the desired outcome, and
- searching for resources to effect sociopolitical change.

Recognizing Feelings of Hopelessness

Oppression defines the everyday lives of many people. To motivate clients who are oppressed, social workers must first recognize and validate the reality of oppression as clients tell their stories. To offer **hope**, workers can also share what they know about how other clients were able to overcome their **hopelessness** and achieve their goals. In the context of mutual aid groups, shared testimonials about successful problem solving by group members often inspire others to feel hopeful.

Visualizing Positive Outcomes

Workers help clients who feel hopeless define a positive direction. Clients benefit from looking ahead, as looking ahead provides an optimistic context in which to view their present difficulties. Research documents that setting goals increases motivation. Bandura's long-standing research on self-efficacy describes a relationship between feelings of self-efficacy, motivation to achieve a self-prescribed goal, and gains in performance (Bandura, 1997, 2002, 2006, 2008; Bandura & Cervone, 1983). In other words, people make progress when they have clear visions of where they are going, participate in defining the direction, and believe they can achieve their goals.

Expressing Hope and Optimism

To motivate a client who feels hopeless, workers bring hope to the situation. Underlying the worker's efforts to instill hope is the worker's belief that the client can achieve. Assumptions that all clients have strengths and recognition of the transactional and transitory nature of challenges contribute to expectations that positive changes can occur, even for clients who initially view their situations as hopeless. A worker's optimism that a client can succeed is contagious.

Aligning Worker and Client Motivations

Because all human behavior is motivated, we can conclude that clients and workers alike bring motivations to the professional relationship. When workers and clients unite to move in the same direction, this alliance itself becomes a powerful resource in the process. Each validates the sense of purpose in the other. Each contemplates and initiates actions toward the desired outcome. Each has an investment in reaching a common destination. But when workers and clients are heading in different directions, even the most vigorous efforts of one can be neutralized by the energetic efforts of the other. Before clients and workers forge a path ahead, they need to talk enough about where they are going to agree on a mutual direction.

Collaborating with Clients Who Resist

Considering the motivations of clients leads us to look at resistance. Social workers who see resistant behaviors do not blame clients; instead, workers try to figure out how the resistance makes sense. Clients may be sending messages that they have other goals or that environmental obstacles are too great. Behaviors that look uncooperative on the surface merit careful attention. They indicate important information about clients, social workers, and the environments in which they operate.

Resistance Is Motivated

Resistance from clients is to be expected. Certainly, client resistance makes sense in view of the ecosystems perspective. Human systems evolve in ways that represent their best attempts to master their current situations. Why would clients readily change behaviors that have logically developed and provided them with stability and equilibrium? Change will disrupt the expected norm and may not be better or may be even worse than the current difficult situation. Clients are right to suspect change.

Look more closely at the assertion that clients resist. Do we mean that clients are resisting changes, or do we mean that clients are resisting what social workers want them to do? If social workers want to go in one direction and clients want to go in another, who is resisting whom? In his work as a family therapist, de Shazer (1989) refers to resistance when he says, "Attributing blame to either party of an interaction is theoretically unsound. Such a split between members of a system inevitably creates imaginary opposition. But clinically, both therapists and clients are in it together" (p. 231). Resistance indicates a lack of synchrony between clients and social workers; it likely reveals clients' motivation to move in a different direction.

Resistance Is Communication

Resistance often communicates a message that social workers are overstepping their partnership agreements. In other words, at times, clients may rebel against the directions that workers propose simply because they don't want to be told what to do. Any parent experiences those periods in children's lives—for example, the "terrible twos" and adolescence—in which no matter how right parents are, they're wrong. Social workers are not parents to clients. Rather, they are partners with them. When clients respond with resistance, social workers cooperate by clarifying just where clients want to lead them.

Cooperating with Resistance

Reconsider the framing of social work relationships as collaborative partnerships and incorporate the assumption of client expertise; then, the notion of client resistance will melt away. When clients want to go in directions other than those workers choose, empowering practitioners yield and let clients lead the way. Clients have the privilege to resist based on their rights to self-determination. Social workers respect and cooperate with clients who resist. Resistance clearly demonstrates that clients have power! Why would empowering social workers want to invalidate such an expression?

Social workers respond to clients' expressions of resistance in ways that clarify, organize, and encourage. Workers may say any of the following:

- I have the sense that you are not agreeing with me. Please help me understand where I'm off base.
- I keep trying to pull the discussion back to our prepared agenda; however, it seems like this group wants to move in a different direction. I'd like to understand more clearly where you're headed.
- I'm confused. Earlier, I understood that you wanted to protest how the worker at the public aid office is treating you, and now I'm hearing you say that you want to leave well enough alone. In which direction are we going?

Clients have the privilege to resist.

Each response acknowledges that social workers have a part in creating resistance. Each response also demonstrates how workers go with the flow by turning the responsibility for defining the direction back to the client.

Overcoming Environmental Resistance

Even when clients have a high level of investment and see their outcomes as very desirable, their investments may falter under the burden of environmental constraints. Social workers may misread clients' behaviors as resistance in these situations when actually, other factors may be thwarting clients' efforts. Clients' access to the resources needed for successful goal achievement may be limited; or the practicalities of service delivery, such as transportation, costs, and location, may be prohibitive. Social workers and clients maintain creativity in aligning interpersonal and service delivery resources to overcome these very real environmental barriers. Workers may need to target social or environmental impediments to clear the way for the clients to invest fully in the process.

Consider the example of Twyla, who sporadically attends a mothers' support group. The worker's initial impulse is to confront Twyla for her lack of commitment to the group. However, a closer assessment reveals the nature of Twyla's "resistance." In discussing the issue, Twyla describes her husband's anger over her attendance, her difficulty in locating child care, and the undependable car that she drives. Each one of these environmental factors interferes with her attendance at group meetings. In view of these obstacles, even Twyla's sporadic attendance demonstrates a great deal of motivation to participate. To increase Twyla's attendance, the worker needs to help her resolve the issues of child care, transportation, and her husband's attitude.

Motivating Larger Systems

Work with larger systems builds on the motivation of individual members. In large client systems, the key is to activate maximum involvement by as many members as possible. In the example of the Northside Network that opens this chapter, all members will report the group's activities to their own colleagues to generate enthusiasm and receive additional input. They will also update their supervisors, administrators, and boards of directors about the Network's activities to retain their agencies' official sanctions. Each agency will want assurances that the goals of the Network mesh with its own particular mission. A good fit in terms of goals and agreement with the methods chosen will motivate agencies to support the Network's efforts.

Nominal Group Technique

Sometimes, workers define directions with large client systems by using structured processes. **Nominal group technique** is a formal strategy that motivates participants and combines their efforts in setting directions. This quick and efficient process works best with six to nine people (Toseland & Rivas, 2012). However, it can easily be adapted to work with larger organizational and community groups by running the process several times and combining the results.

Nominal group technique offers a way of generating information about a specified issue, eliciting responses from participants by using a round-robin strategy, discussing the ideas participants contribute, and, finally, establishing priorities through a mathematical rank-ordering process. Using this technique includes the following steps:

1. Before the process begins, prepare a clear statement of the issue or problem to which the group will respond.

2. Provide a copy of the statement for participants and ask them to list their responses without conferring with each other.

3. Have participants share their responses one at a time. Record each response so that all participants can view the list of responses. This is a brainstorming strategy in which participants simply report their responses without discussing them or evaluating them. Participants may add new ideas that occur to them during this step.

4. Beginning with the first item on the list and proceeding in order, discuss each item to eliminate the overlap among ideas and to clarify the meanings of the responses.

5. Ask participants to select a predetermined number of items from the list that they consider most important. This step reduces the number of items from which participants select their top priorities.

6. Finally, ask participants to rank-order the items they consider in the top five, using 5 for the highest ranked item and 1 for the lowest. Record the ratings for each item and calculate the total points assigned to each. Ideas receiving the highest point totals are the ones the group identifies as most important.

Nominal group technique has important advantages as a decision-making process in that it always yields a conclusion, considers several alternatives, and encourages participation and discussion. As a planning tool, nominal group

 Assess your understanding of client motivation by taking this brief quiz.

process accommodates the motivation of each individual member, thereby activating a widespread commitment to the group's direction.

COOPERATING WITH MANDATED CLIENTS

Clients mandated to receive services are involuntary participants in social worker–client relationships. They are pressured by legal authorities to work with a practitioner they haven't chosen to deal with problems they may not believe are important, real, or anybody's business but their own. The majority of clients served in child welfare agencies, probation offices, delinquency intervention programs, and many types of mental health services approach these services involuntarily.

Equalizing power within the helping relationship is a major challenge for social workers in forming partnerships with involuntary clients, especially those clients who are members of oppressed population groups. Seeking to increase involuntary clients' experiences of power when someone else is in charge requires the worker to take direct actions that restore clients' feelings of control. So practitioners move quickly to frame a positive experience, to reconfigure the relationship for collaboration, and to define a mutual direction in which the client's goals are primary.

Constructing Workers' Expectations

Previously, we discussed the powerful role that expectations play in human interaction. Without reflective consideration, three damaging presuppositions likely invade a worker's thinking about mandated clients: (1) they are "bad" people, (2) they won't cooperate no matter what I do, and (3) they will be unsuccessful. All of these assumptions are likely untrue. In working with mandated clients, workers must carefully prepare their expectations to construct an atmosphere conducive to collaboration.

Regarding mandated clients as "bad" people obviously violates the social work principles of nonjudgmentalism and acceptance. This posture also fails to apply an ecosystemic understanding that orients workers to examine not just the person but the person in the situation as the focus of inquiry. This vision of where the problem is located—in the person or in the situation—is a key element in encouraging involuntary clients to cooperate with services. Rooney (1992) describes this as the contrast between the deviant/pathological perspective (the problem is within the individual) and the structural perspective (the problem is within how the individual relates to the environment). Workers who demonstrate their belief in a structural perspective will most likely achieve collaboration with involuntary clients.

Research has also shown that mandated clients can achieve success equal to or greater than the outcomes of voluntary clients (Burke & Gregoire, 2007). Mandates to change may actually act as powerful motivators for clients to confront issues that they have ignored or been unable to face without assistance. Workers do best when they recognize the feasibility of a successful outcome, communicate this expectation to clients, and anticipate clients' cooperation to set the helping relationship on a positive course.

Assessment

Behavior: Select appropriate intervention strategies based on the assessment, research knowledge, and values and preferences of clients and constituencies

Critical Thinking Question: Many social work clients are involuntary service recipients. How does this circumstance affect the social work process, especially the selection of intervention strategies?

Structuring a Working Partnership

Mandated clients enter social work relationships convinced that the practitioner and the mandating referral source are functioning as one. Consequently, the feelings of power-lessness and resentment a client experienced with legal authorities transfer immediately to the worker. The client perceives the initial structure of the helping relationship as one-sided—with the client on one side of the relationship and the worker and mandating authority partnered on the other. For workers to initiate a collaborative relationship, they must take action to restructure this initial configuration by talking directly about the worker–client relationship.

Distinguishing Worker Roles

In many respects, working with mandated clients makes social workers involuntary participants as well. Workers acknowledge this reality and discuss it openly with their clients. The purpose of this discourse is to shift how the client perceives the role of the worker in relation to the referral agency—the "common" outside force. Social workers must draw boundaries between themselves and the coercive referral source to find the common ground on which to build partnerships with clients. To this end, workers carefully articulate their own roles in relation to those of the client (as differentiated from those of the referral source), clearly define the client's privileges in the relationship with the worker, and ascertain the client's motivation and goals to recenter the relationship on the client's needs and aspirations.

Workers can expect a certain amount of resistance from involuntary clients, initially in terms of acknowledging that a problem exists and then in response to worker-initiated change attempts. Workers with nonvoluntary clients must weigh the use of the legal authority to force cooperation against the risk of increasing the client's sense of powerlessness.

> Watch this video on social workers' work with mandated clients. What are the rights and limitations on those rights of clients who are mandated to treatment in terms of confidentiality?

> *In many respects, working with mandated clients makes social workers involuntary participants as well.*

Articulating Client Roles

Recently stripped of power, involuntary clients may withhold information to gain some sense of control. Direct talk about power issues can reopen communication. Workers should move quickly to identify just what power clients do hold by providing answers to questions such as the following:

- What, realistically, do clients control?
- What privileges do clients have within the boundaries of the client–worker relationship?
- What are the potential sanctions clients may experience for self-disclosure?
- What are the consequences for clients who refuse to participate?

Discussing the client's legal situation clarifies the expectations affecting both clients and practitioners. Mandated clients benefit from descriptions of how the work will proceed, from the generation of a realistic array of options and choices that may work under the circumstances, and from active participation in defining objectives and tasks (Rooney, 1992).

Defining a Motivating Direction

Involuntary clients enter professional relationships compelled by someone else's decision—the motivation to participate is external; yet, these clients are not without their own motivation. At a minimum, mandated clients want to get someone off their backs, regain control over their lives, or prove that they don't need anybody's help. Social workers openly accept these underlying goals of mandated clients as reasonable and focus on what clients can do that will result in their freedom and independence.

Motivational congruence between clients and workers is a key factor in achieving successful outcomes (Rooney, 1992). When clients' goals vary from those set by authorities, workers respond to shape a mutual agenda. Social workers may say any of the following:

- I believe it when you say that you don't need to be here. What do you think you need to do to convince the Child Protective Unit that you can handle things?
- You're absolutely right. No one can tell you what to do. I certainly don't intend to. What is it that you think we need to be doing?
- It looks like we're stuck together for at least five sessions. Is there something you would like to work on because you're here anyway, or do you just want to wait it out?

Initially, practitioners may accept a client's goal to escape the legal entanglement precipitating the mandate. Consider a simple example. When the court forces parents to use social work services to control their daughter's truancy, the worker accepts the family's goals of getting court and school officials off their backs. When the social worker explores how to make that happen, the family's roles and responsibilities become apparent. Defining an initial direction in terms of how others will change may motivate an involuntary client. As the work continues, the social worker refines this direction by helping clients discover actions within their control to take as a means to change how others respond.

? Assess your understanding of working with mandated clients by taking this brief quiz.

TAKING PRIORITY ACTIONS

Certain situations demand immediate action by social workers. When clients' safety is uncertain, others are at risk, basic survival needs are unmet, or clients are emotionally overwhelmed by recent events, social workers may choose to take charge. This doesn't mean that social workers strip clients of their control; however, it does mean that social workers ensure the welfare of everyone concerned. Recent trauma and crises, large-scale disasters, self-destructive behaviors, abuse, threats toward others, immediate needs for food or shelter—these are all situations that direct social workers to seek guidance from their colleagues and supervisors and take definitive actions.

Responding to Trauma and Crises

Trauma is a sudden occurrence that requires specialized and immediate attention. When environments overwhelm, people need help quickly. Traumatic crisis temporarily overloads people's abilities to cope. Experiencing violence, unexpected death, significant loss, natural disaster, or war can leave people floundering. To respond, social workers lend their support and guidance until clients can reconnect with their own abilities to take charge.

In the context of trauma, social workers provide clients with the essentials to restore safety and a sense of well-being. Research shows that **psychological first aid** works best to assist these clients (WHO, 2011). Psychological first aid involves attending to clients' immediate needs by listening to and acting on their concerns, validating expressed feelings, offering information about what is happening and what clients can expect, and connecting clients to existing supports. Workers avoid probing questions; they do not ask clients to describe or make sense out of what has occurred.

Consider this example of a social worker's response to a crisis in a school. When all members of a family perish in a tragic house fire, Georgia Betts, the school social worker at Northside Elementary where all three of the family's children attended, deftly implements the school district's crisis management plan. Georgia convenes a meeting of school personnel, including teachers, administrators, counselors, cafeteria staff, maintenance workers, and bus drivers. Each of these people participates in the everyday functioning of the school and directly interacts with students. Georgia knows that many of these people have strong relationships with students and will play significant roles in helping the students cope with this tragic event. They will respond to students' questions and concerns in the context of carrying out their normal routines. In this crisis, they will also be asked to observe and identify students who may require additional individual assistance.

At this meeting, Georgia reviews the crisis response plan that instructs school personnel to "listen, protect, and connect" to help students cope (U.S. Department of Education, 2008). Georgia recognizes that many at this meeting are profoundly affected by this loss, so in her review of the crisis plan elements, she also takes the opportunity to assist those gathered using the methods the plan suggests. She "listens" as school personnel share their thoughts and feelings, and she responds with empathy to validate their feelings of sadness. She does not ask probing questions or seek information that participants do not volunteer. During this sharing, Georgia observes who is most affected by the loss and those most nervous about doing the right thing for students. After the meeting she will talk individually with persons she has identified as most vulnerable and follow up to monitor how they are coping. Next, Georgia moves to "protect" those gathered by answering any direct questions about the tragedy. She normalizes their emotional responses, encourages them to maintain their typical school routines, and delineates what else the community is doing to assist those affected. Finally, Georgia describes how the school staff can "connect" with her for additional guidance and reminds them of the employee assistance available if they would like confidential, professional help. She encourages teachers and staff members to talk with each other and to seek the support of their loved ones. Georgia's response to the school personnel models how she wants them to assist students. She listens to their concerns, protects them to restore feelings of safety, and connects them to natural and, if necessary, professional supports.

Ethical and Professional Behavior

Behavior: Make ethical decisions by applying the standards of the NASW *Code of Ethics*, relevant laws and regulations, models for ethical decision-making, ethical conduct of research, and additional codes of ethics as appropriate to context

Critical Thinking Question: Ethical social workers sometimes take charge of clients in situations requiring priority actions. How is "taking charge" ethical considering the social work principles of client self-determination?

Best Practices in Responding to Trauma

Social workers play active roles in responding to the aftermath of trauma. Immediate responses help clients cope well initially and may work to prevent posttraumatic stress disorder (PTSD), an emotional disturbance precipitated by the crisis that can endure into the future. Symptoms associated with PTSD include intrusive thoughts, emotional distress, physiological discomfort, and functional impairment. Research generally agrees that to minimize the potential of PTSD development, clients must quickly begin to feel safe, have periods of calm, find hope, and connect to others in their familial and social networks (WHO, 2011). Immediate physical and emotional support predicts better outcomes as do activities in which clients contribute to their own assistance or help others in their communities. All of these actions constitute psychological first aid and exemplify the current best practices in responding to trauma. Social workers take direct actions to stabilize clients who experience crises with an eye toward restoring control to clients as the urgency subsides.

Responding to Large-Scale Disasters

Social workers and other mental health providers are on the frontlines in responding to community crises, including natural disasters, such as flood, earthquake, hurricane, tornado, or fire; acts of terrorism; epidemics; industrial disasters; school shootings; or workplace violence. These catastrophic events precipitate large-scale relief efforts requiring the deployment of a full spectrum of emergency responders. Social workers are well equipped to meet such challenges.

Most organizations and communities have already developed emergency plans to implement when disaster strikes. However, when such a plan doesn't exist, or it poorly fits the situation, social workers activate the existing resources of the community. First, workers locate key community members in the various subsystems of the community—churches, schools, social agencies, clubs, businesses, and neighborhood organizations—that are already functioning to support community members. Having identified key leaders, workers educate these members about the dynamics of the trauma and the locations of necessary resources. These community members, in turn, provide support in the various contexts in which they are already operating.

A Generalist Perspective

The generalist perspective frames a comprehensive social work response to a community disaster. At the microlevel, workers supply immediate assistance to survivors. As members of a disaster response team, social workers provide psychological first aid to persons directly affected. Empathic listening, reassurance, information, concrete assistance, and casework services are the activities that best fit the needs of people distressed by sudden tragedy. Practitioners recognize that, in the initial aftermath of the event, people more often need post-disaster support and assessment for referral rather than intensive trauma debriefing and psychotherapy. Research shows that immediate psychological debriefing may actually have long-term adverse effects on recovery (Robbins, 2002; Scurfield, 2002).

Social workers also *help the helpers* by talking with paramedics, firefighters, police officers, National Guard personnel, forensic technicians, morticians, and disaster relief workers. This mezzolevel activity addresses the needs of first responders and their organizations. Frontline emergency responders often require counseling after their immediate work is complete in order to mitigate the effects of secondary trauma. After their deployment to a disaster assignment, emergency personnel often experience emotional health issues, including problems with coping and symptoms of posttraumatic stress. Even family members of disaster survivors and crisis responders not directly involved may experience these trauma-induced symptoms. This notion of secondary trauma requires social workers to offer help to helpers and their families as well as attend to their own needs for self-care. Similar to their response in

Social workers are among the first responders in disaster relief efforts.

first hand trauma, practitioners take the lead with clients as to how to help, offer facts and information to counteract misconceptions, activate natural support networks on the client's behalf, and break down the issues facing the client into discrete units to dispel the overwhelming nature of the problem.

At the macrolevel, social work professionals play key roles in planning, policy formulation, coordination, and evaluation. Many social workers affiliate with national or international agencies in the forefront of disaster management and operations, such as the American Red Cross, International Red Cross and Red Crescent Societies, the World Health Organization, and the U.S. Federal Emergency Management Agency (FEMA). In addition, social workers participate in disaster drills sponsored by local public health agencies or community safety and preparedness teams (North & Hong, 2000). These teams provide leadership in coordinating networks of service providers in the three major phases of the disaster—pre-warning preparation, the disaster event, and the recuperative efforts in rebuilding the community (Galambos, 2005). Social workers also implement disaster research protocols to assess damage, identify populations at risk, and delineate safety, health, and mental health needs. As policy analysts, social work professionals assist in improving disaster service policies and procedures by evaluating services delivered during a trauma to assess how well the response met the physical and mental health needs of various constituencies such as survivors, witnesses, and emergency responders.

Responding to the Threat of Suicide

At some time in their careers, most practitioners will work with a client who considers committing or actually commits suicide (Freedenthal, 2008). Statistics show that over 38,000 persons committed suicide in 2010 (CDC, 2012). These data further suggest that for every death by suicide, as many as 25 suicide attempts occur.

Although suicide is not confined to any one particular group, a statistical analysis does show certain trends with respect to race, gender, and age. Although accounting for only 1 percent of all suicides, the rate of suicide among American Indian/Alaska Native adolescents and young adults (23.2 per 100,000) is slightly higher than that of non-Hispanic Whites (22.9 per 100,000), who account for about 83 percent of all suicides (Crosby et al., 2011). Further, a review of data confirms a gender difference, showing suicide rates to be higher among men when compared with women. Although more women attempt suicide, men are 4 times more likely to commit suicide (CDC, 2012). Data also reveal that the highest rate of suicide is among those 75 years of age and older (Crosby et al., 2011).

Data show a trend toward an increased incidence of suicide and attempted suicide among persons ages 15 to 24; suicide is the third leading cause of death in this age group (CDC, 2012). Suicide is also the seventh leading cause of death among children ages 5 to 14. Studies on suicide among gay, lesbian, and bisexual youths indicate that the rate of suicide for these youths is slightly higher than that for heterosexual youths the same age (DeAngelis, 2002). Proctor and Groze's (1994) research discovered that this risk could be mitigated by positive functioning in the areas of self-perception, family interactions, and social relationships. More current research validates the protective role of family acceptance for gay, lesbian, bisexual, and transgender (GLBT) youths in reducing the likelihood of such negative health outcomes as depression and suicide ideation and attempts (Russell et al., 2011; Ryan et al., 2010). This research demonstrates that it is not a homosexual identity itself, but the social response of homophobia and victimization that places GLBT youths at risk.

The threat of client suicide looms over all clinical social workers. After watching this video, what can case manager Mark Henick tell you that will assist you with clients considering suicide? www.youtube.com/watch?v=D1QoyTmeAYw

Recognizing Risks

Although complex biological, psychological, and social factors trigger suicide attempts, psychiatric disorders, including depression, alcohol abuse and dependence, anxiety disorders, eating disorders, or personality disorders are present in 90 percent of persons who complete suicide (Gangwisch, 2010). Personality characteristics such as hopelessness, aggression, and impulsive behavior are also associated with higher risks for suicide. In addition, the American Association of Suicidology indicates associations between suicide attempts and personal or family history of suicide, stressful life events, problems at work, family turmoil, social isolation, lack of social support, purposelessness, and a history of physical or sexual abuse (AAS, 2010).

Certain behaviors give warning that someone is contemplating suicide (AAS, 2014; Gangwisch, 2010). Indicators of acute risk for suicide include explicit suicide ideation such as threatening suicide, seeking the means to commit suicide, or uncharacteristically talking or writing about death. Additionally, sudden changes in behaviors such as withdrawal and isolation from others; an increased use of alcohol or drugs; lethargy or agitation; risk-taking and reckless behaviors; expressions of feeling anxious, purposeless, trapped, or hopeless; and changes in mood are all possible warning signs.

Although any of these signs may alert social workers to possible suicidal thinking, no one sign is definitive. Many of these behaviors correlate with other issues as well, and some may indicate no problem at all. Studies about suicide inform practitioners about trends and signs, but only clients are experts on what they are really thinking. When workers suspect suicidal thinking in clients, they consult with their supervisors and get further information from clients to assess the actual risk.

Box 8.1 Social Work Safety: A Policy–Practice Connection

Social work is risky business. In an NASW survey, many social workers reported significant incidents of violence and other safety concerns including "violence from adult clients (41%), vandalization of their vehicles (35%), car accidents while in the field (34%), physical assault from non-clients (32%), and fear of the neighborhoods in which they work (28%)" (Whitaker & Arrington, 2008, p. 15). These results reinforce earlier findings by Ringstad (2005) that 14 percent of social workers had endured physical assaults and 62 percent felt psychological aggression during the previous year. Violence against social workers has occurred for a long time, but trends indicate a dramatic increase (Newhill, 2003; Jayaratne et al., 2004). Additionally, results of studies in the United Kingdom, Denmark, South Korea, and Canada suggest that violence against social workers is an international issue (Nho & Choi, 2009; MacDonald & Sirotich, 2005; Rasmussen et al., 2013; Winstanley & Hales, 2015).

Employment within institutions such as correctional, inpatient, and school settings places workers at highest risk (Ringstad, 2005). Public sector workers, especially young males, experience higher levels of violence than do females or those in private practice (Jayaratne et al., 2004). The shift from institutional care to community-based services has placed many higher-risk clients in less controlled settings. Understandably, social workers may find themselves in threatening situations. Clients with mental illnesses, those lacking skills in anger management, and persons with substance addictions likely experience escalating emotions yet have limited ability to screen behavior or maintain control. Workers in child protection and domestic violence frequently enter homes where anger is mounting and violence occurs. Social workers are handy targets for those who feel they are wronged, misunderstood, ignored, or looking for someone to blame for situations spiraling beyond their control.

Home visits place social workers in environments where they have limited control, possibly in neighborhoods with high crime rates. However, outreach workers can take steps to mitigate the risks of home visits. Allen and Tracy (2008) suggest notifying the agency about schedules and plans for return, taking a cell phone with emergency contact numbers, and—when possible—working in pairs or teams. The power of partnership builds confidence in one's safety and offers concrete assistance if necessary. In predictably volatile situations such as removing a child from a home or accessing belongings for someone moving to a domestic violence shelter, workers may alert and access law enforcement as needed.

Social workers cannot control clients, but they can influence how clients respond (Shields & Kiser, 2003). Keys to de-escalating client situations include understanding clients' motivations, validating clients' feelings, clarifying clients' perspectives, and negotiating aspects of the situation where clients have legitimate influence, all the while remaining clear and direct about nonnegotiable aspects. When clients get angry, workers acknowledge clients' rights to express feelings before helping clients recognize alternative actions. When workers sense danger, they should trust their instincts and take immediate actions to protect themselves; subsequently, workers should debrief and seek support for dealing with traumatic events (Lyter & Abbott, 2007). Social workers entering potentially treacherous situations should be prepared with facts. What is their role in this situation? What power and authority do they have? What rights do clients maintain in the specific circumstances? What choices do clients have in cooperating? When workers know their roles and act within the limits of their powers, they are more likely to gain client cooperation.

Safety is not the sole responsibility of the social work practitioner. Agency safeguards must be in place. Ethical administrators develop protocols to mitigate risks to workers, create an organizational culture of safety, provide safety training annually, and develop systems for immediate assistance in times of crisis (NASW, 2013). Responsible employing agencies educate workers about inherent risks, implement safety procedures, provide training on de-escalating conflict, and support those who express concerns about clients (Lyter & Abbott, 2007).

Taking Action

When social workers sense that a client is contemplating suicide, they directly discuss their concerns with the client. Workers may say any of the following:

- Are you thinking about harming yourself?
- Are you telling me that you're considering suicide?
- I heard you mention killing yourself. Are you really thinking about that?
- I'm noticing several changes in the way you are handling things, sort of like you are giving up. What are you trying to tell me?

Many workers hesitate to pose these questions, fearing that such direct discussion will foster suicidal behavior; however, this is not the case. By directly talking with clients about what they are hearing and seeing, a social worker gives clients permission to talk openly about any self-destructive thoughts.

In discussing suicidal thinking with a client, social workers strive to assess the seriousness of the client's threats. The most important factor for determining the potential of a suicide threat is the individual's plan. Workers should consider several important behavior indicators in conducting a risk assessment for suicide:

- Is the client expressing thoughts of suicide (suicidal ideation)?
- Are these thoughts related to current stressors in the client's life?
- Does the client have a viable suicide plan?
- Has the client identified a lethal means of suicide?
- Is there a likelihood that the client will carry out the suicide plan?

Risk of suicide is greater when plans are detailed and specific, and when the methods chosen are lethal and readily available. In response to a client who is seriously contemplating suicide, social workers quickly involve support systems for themselves and for the client. Within their own professional support systems, workers seek the advice and counsel of their supervisors, colleagues, or consultants to gain outside perspectives and receive emotional support. Social workers consider whether the client requires hospitalization or, as an alternative, whether to activate the client's natural support system to prevent the suicidal act. Sometimes the worker and the client enlist friends or family members to accompany the client at all times until the client's self-destructive feelings pass. This strategy is sometimes referred to as putting the person "on watch." Whatever choices social workers make, they ensure that clients are not left alone with their suicidal thoughts and feelings of hopelessness.

Careful documentation of all questions posed to the client and the client's responses, points of every consultative conversation, and details of the follow-up plan are all measures of risk management protection against liability and malpractice.

Responding to Threats Toward Others

Sometimes social workers learn that clients are planning violent actions toward others. Clearly, when clients threaten violence, they reveal their frustration, stress, and sense of limited options. Ultimately, practitioners will work to help clients alleviate their anger and expand their vision of possible solutions. But first, workers must intervene to prevent potential harm.

Violence is not in the best interests of clients or society. Actions derived from the principle of protection of human life supersede all other obligations (Dolgoff et al., 2008). If social workers truly believe that clients will commit violent acts, they are ethically and legally bound to prevent clients from carrying out their plans. Workers strictly adhere to the agency's procedures for reporting the potential harm.

Discussing violent thoughts and feelings with a client tests a social worker's ability to remain nonjudgmental. This is not to say that social workers maintain a permissive attitude toward violent acts. Instead workers discuss the client's thinking openly and neutrally. In this way, workers can encourage continued sharing, relieve pressure, and introduce other less dangerous options for coping. Even if a client persists in planning violence, this open discussion of violent impulses allows workers to assess the reality of what the client may do and supplies information on which to build preventive responses. Similar to dealing with potential suicide by clients, workers seek supervisory support and consider using inpatient services.

Duty to Warn

Under most circumstances, social workers keep what they hear from clients confidential, but in the case of potential violence, social workers function as agents of social control. In these situations where there is a **duty to warn**, confidentiality is abridged. When clients threaten others, workers take charge and document their actions carefully (Madden, 2003; NASW, 2005a). A landmark court decision made in California, *Tarasoff v. The Regents of the University of California* (1976), set the stage for legislative initiatives and court decisions in other states. This decision stipulates that

> When a therapist determines, or pursuant to the standards of his profession should determine, that his patient presents a serious danger of violence to another, he incurs an obligation to use reasonable care to protect the intended victim against such danger. The discharge of this duty may require the therapist to take one or more of various steps, depending upon the nature of the case. Thus it may call for him to warn the intended victim or others likely to apprise the victim of the danger, to notify the police, or to take whatever other steps are reasonably necessary under the circumstances. (Ca. 3d 425, 431)

Under *Tarasoff*, four criteria invoke the worker's duty to warn: (1) an imminent threat of violence exists; (2) the threat is believable and explicit, not vague; (3) there is evidence of the foreseeability of the client carrying out the threat; and (4) there are particular identifiable persons, not a general group or category of people. However, legal obligations vary from state to state, as many states have enacted specific duty-to-warn laws—some mandated, some permissive, and some with no statuary standards (NASW, 2008b). The various duty-to-warn statutes and laws differ in how they define foreseeable and imminent threat, specify the mandate of social workers to report to law enforcement officials, and stipulate the process for notifying intended victims. Options for discharging the *Tarasoff* duty to warn include warning the intended victim or relatives, notifying local law enforcement agencies, or initiating voluntary or involuntary commitment. Although warning potential victims raises questions about confidentiality, practitioners who uncover threats of violence in their assessment should report the threat to avoid liability should the threat be carried out.

Proceeding under duty to warn compels social workers to act legally and ethically. Duty to warn necessitates a thorough assessment of the client's threats and history of threats or violent behavior and consultation with supervisors, appropriate crisis response team members, or agency attorneys. Additionally, the social worker needs to provide verbatim documentation of the client's threats and thorough documentation of the worker's observations and decision-making steps leading to notification. At first glance, duty to warn may seem contrary to principles of empowerment. However, consider the consequences of allowing clients to commit acts of violence. Ultimately, if clients harm others, both clients and those they harm lose power to determine the courses of their lives.

Duty to Protect

Duty to protect takes on new meaning in the post-9/11 era. The Patriot Act (Uniting and Strengthening America by Providing Appropriate Tools Required to Intercept and Obstruct Terrorist Acts) was signed into law in October 2001. Under the office of Homeland Security, the Patriot Act extends enforcement of protection against terrorist attacks to include threats to both persons and property. Title II, Sections 213 and 215, allows agents of the FBI to access certain business records (which legal experts define as including medical and psychological records) without warrant, subpoena, or release of information. Furthermore, this provision prohibits practitioners from notifying their clients that the FBI requested or obtained these case records, that the client is under investigation by the FBI, or that they have released confidential information.

The ethical issues associated with this particular definition of duty to protect are numerous. The secrecy associated with the abrupt removal of client records without consideration of privileged communication, privacy, and confidentiality abridges the trust relationship between practitioners and clients. This legal mandate may necessitate social workers, psychologists, and other counseling personnel to inform clients about the limits of confidentiality with respect to national security and intelligence activities by federal officials (Mansdorfer, 2004).

Responding to Child Maltreatment

When social workers suspect that children are being abused, they take appropriate actions to ensure the children's safety and prevent further harm. **Child maltreatment** takes many forms, including physical abuse, neglect, emotional abuse, and sexual abuse. *Child Maltreatment 2013* (USHHS-ACYF, 2015) reports that child protection agencies confirmed reports that 679,000, or 9.1 of every 1,000 children in the United States, experienced some form of child abuse or neglect. About 1,520 children died as a consequence of maltreatment. Social workers most likely to deal with these issues are those in child protective services working under mandates to investigate reports of potential abuse or those working in hospital settings. Even social workers in other practice settings encounter clients in situations in which abuse is occurring. Therefore, all practitioners need to know about how to identify abusive situations and how to respond.

Recognizing Signs of Abuse

Social workers may become aware of child abuse in several different ways. Sometimes workers hear reports of events directly from children or parents that describe harsh discipline, events, or "accidents," which prompt workers to obtain further details to assess the child's safety. At other times, social workers observe physical evidence of abuse in the form of bruises, scratches, burns, or other injuries. Many times, they hear about abusive events from people outside of the client's family, such as friends, extended family members, or neighbors.

Some evidence of abuse is more subtle. Research provides assistance in identifying risk factors, including domestic violence, unemployment, single parenthood, illness or developmental disabilities, preterm birth, history of intergenerational abuse or family violence, social isolation, parental stress and/or aggression, and addiction (Freisthier et al., 2006; Rodriguez, 2010; Wulczyn, 2009). Although not all states collect data on alcohol and drug involvement, available data indicate alcohol is involved in 8.8 percent and drug abuse in 20 percent of substantiated cases of child maltreatment (USHHS-ACYF, 2015). Additional studies show an association between alcohol abuse and recurrent incidents of child maltreatment (Laslett et al., 2012).

Children may show behavioral signs that indicate they are being abused, including such diverse personal actions as aggression, self-destructive behaviors, retreat, or withdrawal (Powell, 2003). How children relate to adults also provides clues to abuse. Children may demonstrate fear of physical contact or affection, extreme dependence and attachment, and excessive attention to parental needs. Children who are abused sometimes reveal problems in social functioning, such as difficulties in learning, even though they have no apparent learning deficits; lack of concentration and low energy at school; depression; impulsive behavior; or noncompliance. On a cautionary note, all of these behaviors can result from a variety of experiences—in and of themselves, none are absolute indicators of abuse or neglect.

Taking Action

Social workers do not immediately assume that families with these characteristics are experiencing family violence. Yet, workers are cautious not to overlook signals of abuse. When practitioners fail to notice abuse, they unknowingly contribute to it. When social workers detect issues of abuse, the safety of the person being abused takes priority.

Social workers seek more information when they suspect abuse. In some instances, they may need to see family members separately to encourage them to speak openly and freely, and to protect vulnerable family members from reprisals by abusive members. Workers proceed cautiously when persons who are abused and perpetrators are present at the same interview because revealing information could precipitate retaliation. Children need reassurance about what will happen to them and their family members. Workers carefully refrain from making judgmental comments about perpetrators after the abuse is reported because the child may have ambivalent emotions of anger and affection about the person involved. As workers respond to information about abuse, they recognize their important role in comforting and protecting those threatened.

Reporting Suspected Child Abuse

Statutes, case law, and administrative regulations and procedures vary from state to state. Although all states have **mandatory reporting** laws that require social workers and other designated professionals to report instances of child maltreatment, these laws offer general guidelines rather than specifying those conditions that warrant reports (Goldman et al., 2003). States also differ on the actual reporting process—whether reports are by phone or written document and with whom reports are filed. Typically, a state department is charged to provide child welfare services, including prompt investigation and follow-up services with families as their situations require.

Responding to Elder Abuse

Although data are not collected systematically, estimates of the prevalence of **elder abuse** and exploitation indicate that in the United States, between 1 and 2 million adults age 60 and older are mistreated annually (NCEA, 2005). Findings of a recent randomized national telephone survey indicate that 11 percent of older adults interviewed reported experiencing some type of mistreatment within the past year (Acierno et al., 2010). More specifically, study findings indicate prevalence rates for specific types of mistreatment reported to authorities include 4.6 percent for emotional mistreatment, 1.6 percent for physical mistreatment, 0.6 percent for sexual mistreatment, and 5.1 percent for potential neglect. The first national incidence study uncovered an "iceberg effect" (NCEA, 1998). These researchers concluded that reported cases of elder abuse represent the "tip of the iceberg," whereas the majority of incidents are "hidden" or not disclosed to authorities. Elder abuse continues to be a hidden problem as estimates indicate that only 1 in 4 incidents of elder abuse, excluding self-neglect is reported (NCEA, 2005). Current research indicates a disproportionately large number of reported incidents of elder maltreatment involve older adults who are physically or cognitively frail (NCEA, 2012; Wiglesworth et al., 2010). Relatives, including spouses and adult children, are the most likely perpetrators of domestic elder abuse.

Reporting Suspected Elder Abuse

Whereas all states have passed legislation that authorizes adult protective services, not every state has established reporting laws that designate certain professionals as mandatory reporters of the abuse of adults who are dependent, as defined by age or mental or physical disabilities (Jirik & Sanders, 2014; NCEA, n.d.; Stiegel & Klem, 2007). Only some reporting laws designate penalties for noncompliance. States vary as to which agencies take responsibility for receiving and investigating reports of elder abuse and the abuse of other dependent adults. Designated agencies include units of state human service departments, local social service agencies, and law enforcement officials.

Several factors complicate both identifying and reporting elder abuse. Many older adults, particularly those who are frail, are homebound and away from public scrutiny. Additionally, older adults may be reluctant to bring charges when a family member or loved one on whom they rely has committed the abuse. They may believe they themselves are to blame, or they may be concerned that reporting will ultimately lead to a nursing home placement. Social workers may also experience dilemmas in weighing an older adult's competency for self-determined decision making and their own duty to protect a client's safety and well-being.

Responding to Intimate Partner Violence

Violence within marital or couple relationships, sometimes called **intimate partner violence**, also requires priority action. Abuse may be physical, psychological, sexual, or economic. Practitioners use caution in working with families in which such violence is happening for fear that changes in any part of the family system may escalate the occurrence of violence. With families experiencing violence, social workers deal with safety issues first, before addressing other concerns. Findings from the National Intimate Partner and Sexual Violence Survey suggest that violence is a serious public health issue for women (Black et al., 2011). Of the women surveyed, 35.6 percent reported intimate partner violence during their lifetime, as compared with 28.5 percent of the men surveyed. In the United States, about 42.4 million women have experienced intimate partner violence in their lifetime. Other studies indicate that parental involvement in partner violence leads to increased risk for children becoming the objects of aggressive parenting and other forms of child abuse (Damant et al., 2010; Goddard & Bedi, 2010; Jouriles et al., 2008).

Research identifies a number of factors associated with increased risk for couple violence (Capaldi et al., 2012; CDC, 2015; Stith et al., 2004). Rates of violence are greater among cohabiting couples than among married couples. Younger couples are more at risk than older couples. Experiencing abuse as a child predicts domestic violence, either as a victim or as a perpetrator. Partner abuse occurs in all socioeconomic groups; however, prevalence is greater in situations of poverty, unemployment, or underemployment. Finally, substance abuse increases the risk for intimate partner violence.

When workers believe that violence is occurring, they may need to meet separately with those at risk to elicit honest information in a secure setting and take immediate action to minimize further harm. An extensive knowledge of community service networks helps workers ensure the safety of persons threatened by domestic violence. Many communities have domestic violence programs that coordinate multilevel services because these clients are likely to require legal assistance, court protection, transitional housing, financial resources, and counseling support. Whether these services are relevant to a client depends on the degree of the community's cultural competence (Pyles & Kim, 2006).

Responding to Survival Needs

All human beings have universal needs for food, shelter, warmth, and sleep. Struggling to meet these basic needs blocks people's abilities to accomplish anything else. This has implications for social workers as they prioritize actions. For example, helping a client return to school to achieve the goal of obtaining a GED before dealing with a client's homelessness and needs for food and shelter makes no sense. Even when empowerment-oriented social workers recognize that a client is lacking the necessities for survival, such as housing, nutrition, and medical needs, they focus on stabilizing the essential supports before working on other issues. Competent social workers in any field of practice need to know about the support services in their communities that provide immediate shelter, food, and financial assistance to network clients for life-sustaining assistance.

Responding to Signs of Addiction

Substance abuse and dependence accompany many situations that challenge clients' abilities to cope and frequently preempt their capabilities to address other concerns. Sometimes persons' substance use contributes to situational or chronic dissatisfaction with life. With chronic alcohol or other drug use, however, physiological changes take place and are associated with a person's ability to function effectively.

Not all people who use substances abuse or are dependent on substances. For example, over 50 percent of Americans age 12 or older indicate that they drink alcohol (SAMHSA, 2014). The 2013 National Survey on Drug Use and Health (SAMHSA, 2014), a large-scale random sample survey, found that 21.6 million Americans, or 8.2 percent of the population age 12 and older, were classified as experiencing substance dependence or substance abuse. According to the 2013 survey on substance use, "adults aged 21 or older who had first used alcohol at age 14 or younger were more likely to be classified with alcohol dependence or abuse than adults who had their first drink at age 21 or older (14.8 vs. 2.3 percent)" (p. 85). Recent surveys have shown that over 8.2 million children live with at least one parent who abuses or is dependent on alcohol or an illicit drug (SAMHSA, 2009). Nearly 14 percent of children 5 years of age and younger lived with a parent who was substance dependent.

According to the *DSM-V*, substance-related and addictive disorders occur when individuals exhibit behaviors indicative of impaired control (American Psychiatric Association, 2013). Characteristically, the preponderance of associated behaviors such as difficulties at work and/or relationships related to substance use, tolerance, continuing to use in the face of danger, cravings, or withdrawal symptoms distinguishes the severity of substance use disorders. The physiological roots lie in the biochemically based reward system of the brain, further anchored by conditioned responses and patterns of positive and negative reinforcement.

A worker who discovers that clients are using drugs or alcohol discusses this openly to determine the extent of the involvement and the impact of use. If clients show signs of addiction, they will probably need assistance from drug treatment programs before continuing to work toward other goals. Even when confronting substance abuse, social workers seek balance to respect a client's right to self-determination, securing the client's cooperation in making referrals for drug and alcohol assessment and treatment. All treatment for addiction requires motivation and participation by clients to be successful. Although social workers may support a client through the process of seeking treatment for addiction, as much as possible, workers activate the client's capabilities for accessing treatment services. Sometimes social workers recognize that the addiction is disabling and the client is unable to acknowledge the need or activate personal resources for change. At these times, social workers contact members of a client's natural support network to arrange treatment.

> **?** Assess your understanding of taking priority actions by taking this brief quiz.

LOOKING FORWARD

Defining directions represents a turning point in the partnership of clients and workers. By agreeing on preliminary goals, the partners focus assessment processes to determine what to do next. During this goal development process, workers align themselves and their efforts to match client readiness and enhance clients' motivations. Even clients mandated by courts to receive services and those seen as "resistant" bring their own motivations and ideas about what they would like to change. By cooperating with clients' perspectives and desires, workers are able to forge agreements with clients to work toward mutual purposes. Exploring current needs and potential goals also reveals whether workers need to take priority actions to prevent immediate harm or cope with crises. Articulating situations and defining directions clarify "where the client is" and begin to define where they are going.

The processes of the dialogue phase set the stage for implementing the discovery processes of searching for strengths, assessing resource capabilities, and planning interventions. In the discovery phase, social workers and clients generate new information, consider resources available within clients and their environments, and frame possible solutions. Identifying strengths, the topic of Chapter 9, initiates these discovery processes.

Evaluate what you learned in this chapter by completing the Chapter Review.

9
Assessment: Identifying Strengths

BLEND IMAGES / SHUTTERSTOCK

Even clients in the toughest situations reveal resiliency and resources to strengths-focused social workers. When social workers acknowledge these strengths, they cement working relationships with clients and energize the process with possibilities. However, the process of identifying strengths in clients is not simple. So accustomed are we to detecting problems, we may overlook indicators of client strengths as they pass right before us.

Read the following excerpt about Chad as he describes what prompted him to seek assistance at the Northside Addictions Recovery Center. Assess your ability to identify Chad's strengths.

Two weeks ago, I felt like I couldn't go on—that's when I decided to call you. I'd just been laid off, and the kids were driving me crazy. I could feel it creeping in—that craving for a drink. I've been sober for 18 months now, but I still think about it every day. Both of my parents had the same problem, and at Alcoholics Anonymous, they say it's hereditary. Maybe there's no escaping it, and I'll die young just like they did. I've needed a drink so bad that I can't stay home, especially with the kids getting on my nerves. I called my friend in to take care of the kids, and I hit the pavement, putting in applications all over town—14 to be exact. I don't think any of them will pay what my accounting job paid, but I still can go back and be a mechanic or even be a waiter again, at least temporarily. I don't know what I'll be doing, but I have to do something. I just can't sit around. I'll go crazy. My brother tells me I'm running away from my problems. What do you think?

If you are a problem-focused practitioner, you might agree with Chad's brother. You might think that Chad fits the description of a multiproblem client. After all, he is the adult child of two alcoholics, a recovering alcoholic himself who is craving a drink, recently unemployed, and frustrated with his children.

Switch your focus to recognize Chad's strengths. Do you notice the fact that he lost his job two full weeks ago and still hasn't had a drink? Do you realize that he is already on the move to getting another job, has actually put in applications, and has a wide range of skills to draw on, including abilities as an accountant, a mechanic, and a waiter? Do you recognize his social support—a friend to take care of his children and a brother to talk with about his issues? Do you acknowledge that he has overcome the adversity of growing up in an alcoholic family? This is only the beginning of the list of strengths that Chad reveals in these few statements.

If you can recognize Chad's strengths, congratulate yourself on your own strengths. You are well on the way to becoming an empowering practitioner. This chapter equips practitioners with the knowledge and skills to identify and utilize client strengths in the practice process.

Acknowledging client strengths helps social workers sustain empowering relationships with clients and builds momentum for constructing effective solutions.

INFUSING A STRENGTHS PERSPECTIVE

The strengths orientation shifts the way social workers view and respond to clients. Strength-focused workers assume client competence and expect to discover client system strengths. To infuse a focus on strengths, practitioners must understand the diverse and contextual nature of strengths and know where to look for strengths in client systems.

What Are Strengths?

To many of us, our strengths are obvious. We recognize them easily and use them to manage our lives and realize our goals. Readily identified strengths include natural talents, acquired capabilities, and skills demonstrated in daily life. However, not all strengths are so apparent. Strengths may surface more subtly as cultural attributes, as coping responses in difficult times, or as luck in achieving goals.

Policy Practice

Behavior: Apply critical thinking to analyze, formulate, and advocate for policies that advance human rights and social, economic, and environmental justice

Critical Thinking Question: A significant policy trend in social work is toward prescriptive models of managed care. In what ways does the managed care environment affect the ability of social workers to promote clients' rights and implement a strengths perspective?

Generalist social workers develop skills to identify strengths relevant for each level of client system—individual, family, group, organization, neighborhood, or community. By looking diligently and creatively for anything that may be useful in activating confidence and achieving goals, workers may discover client strengths in personal histories, interpersonal interactions, organizational culture, social connectedness in neighborhoods, community infrastructures, and interfaces with the larger social environment.

The Contextual Nature of Strengths

What may be an asset for you may be a deficit for others; conversely, what may work for you may have no benefit to someone else. For example, the ability to bring patience, persistence, and a sense of accomplishment to a repetitive task may benefit a person who assembles nuts and bolts in a developmental training program, but these same talents may constrain a worker with a temporary employment agency, which demands quick adaptation and flexibility to learn new tasks on a daily basis. Strengths are relative and embedded in their situational contexts.

A transactional view helps social workers discover strengths in how client systems' abilities mesh with their situations. For example, members of many ethnic groups draw considerable support from extended family networks, leading social workers to explore family resources in their work with clients from these groups. However, whether the extended family is functioning supportively differs with each unique client. To understand the resources of a particular client's situation, workers consider questions such as the following:

- What is actually happening in this client's situation?
- Are extended family members present?
- Are they involved with the client's family?
- Does the client believe that involvement of extended family members helps or interferes?

Workers bring knowledge about potential strengths to each encounter, but only clients can define what is working for them.

Workers bring knowledge about potential strengths to each encounter, but only clients can define what is working for them.

Why Identify Strengths?

Identifying client strengths has many advantages. Most important, accentuating strengths highlights possible resources for achieving goals. A focus on client strengths also contributes to the process in other important ways. Specifically, identifying strengths solidifies the client–social worker partnership, functions as a generally enhancing intervention, and increases clients' motivation to invest in the process.

Acknowledging Strengths to Build Partnerships

Examine the relationships in your own life. In which of these relationships do you experience equality? Of course, you've probably identified those relationships in which you feel that you have something to offer, in which others recognize the potential of your contributions. To engage clients as contributing partners, workers communicate their understanding that clients have resources to offer to the process. Identifying and acknowledging their strengths invites clients into professional relationships as collaborators.

Building productive relationships requires a degree of openness as well as a sense of equality. Clients often withdraw when social workers narrowly focus on problems. Revealing more and more of what is going wrong increases clients' feelings of vulnerability and heightens their defensiveness. When the defensive walls go up, exchanges of information dry up. A worker who balances gentle and accepting explorations of challenges with recognition of strengths encourages clients to bring along feelings of success and power as they explore areas of vulnerability.

Acknowledging a client's strengths early in the developing partnership becomes especially important in cross-cultural relationships. Obvious cultural differences cast doubts on the abilities of clients and workers to relate successfully. Typically, clients wonder how these differences will affect their relationships with social workers. Questions include the following: Will the worker operate from a value base that devalues the client's worldview, choices, or lifestyle? Will the worker see cultural differences as threatening or something to change to move the client into the mainstream? Is the worker informed enough about the client's culture to place information in a cultural context?

Recognizing Strengths as a General Intervention

The perfect solution for a particular issue requires a carefully tailored, specifically designed strategy that fits the unique circumstance of each client system. Although there may be several potential solutions to any one dilemma, no universal strategy fits every situation. However, certain actions that social workers can take likely give any client system a general boost. Accentuating client system strengths is one of those actions.

Assuming that client systems have resources postures attention toward strengths. Presumptions of client strengths prompt social workers to enter each working relationship wearing magnifying glasses to notice strengths, helping to create an empowering atmosphere in which good things exist and other good things are possible. Identifying what clients are doing right enhances their feelings of esteem and amplifies their sense of power. A sense of hope and optimism facilitates workers' and clients' thoughts that change and success are possible—a belief that can become a reality in the context of their work together.

> Watch this video overview that discusses how the strengths and solution focus is essential for empowering social work practice. What are the advantages of using a strengths/solution-focused approach? www.youtube.com/watch?v=ZhfOWQ5E3m8

Identifying Strengths as a Motivational Tool

People change when they are motivated to change and when they believe they have the capabilities and resources to do so. This axiom leads us to conclude that client motivation and confidence comprise essential ingredients for success. Discovery and affirmation of a client's strengths leads clients to recognize their persistence and desire for change, key elements to build a client's motivation for success (Rosengren, 2009).

A strengths-oriented approach to social work heightens clients' sense of competence, hope for the future, and motivation for change (Saleebey, 2009). Offering compliments to acknowledge strengths and resources heightens clients' motivation and stimulates connections to their capabilities. Experienced practitioners indicate that people stretch to prove the truth of compliments but recoil to defend against criticisms. Workers who comment on client strengths keep clients stretching toward success.

Balancing Strengths and Challenges

Talking about strengths does not mean that workers ignore information clients provide about problems. Some "problem talk" is essential to start where the client is, understand the nature of the client's motivation, and gather information about the client's aspirations. Interestingly, even problem talk frequently contains clues about strengths and potential solutions. Clients need to unload their difficulties before opening their eyes to more positive views.

Typically, clients let social workers know if workers move too quickly to identify strengths and possible solutions. Clients have not yet said all they have come to say; they think the worker hasn't heard enough about the situation to competently lead the way forward. They question the shift in direction and work harder to convince the worker that their problems are difficult. Only after clients have exhausted their stories and experienced the worker's understanding are clients ready to shift in the direction of strengths and solutions. Then workers can redirect the focus of conversation by summarizing and clarifying the client's perspective, asking if there is anything else, and seeking permission to move in a more positive direction. Social workers may say any of the following:

- I'm hearing that this marriage has changed in the last few months, that you don't seem to find much time to be together, and when you are together, you don't seem to have much to talk about. Is there anything else? If not, I'd like to find out more about those times before when your marriage was working the way you wanted.
- I guess "support group" isn't a very accurate name for what seems to be happening in the group right now. You all seem to agree that you are beginning to pull back, share less about what you are really thinking and feeling, and you don't know clearly what you want out of it yet. Am I hearing you right? Well, that's one good thing—we seem to have consensus about that. What else do we have that we might build on?
- We all agree that the Council is getting bogged down on defining homelessness. However, several agency representatives to the Community Housing Council have clearly outlined the problems associated with lack of affordable housing, limited shelter space, and the complex referral process. Is this the common ground we're looking for to move our efforts forward?

When workers move too quickly to accentuate strengths, clients think workers are missing the point or minimizing their issues. To keep pace with client readiness, social workers directly acknowledge the significance of problems before tilting the conversation toward strengths. The rest of this chapter details knowledge and skills essential for detecting and accentuating client strengths. Specifically, the sections that follow addresses looking for strengths in general functioning, in the context of challenges, in cultural contexts, and in coping with adversity.

Highlighting Strengths

Social workers find client strengths when they are prepared to look for them. Familiarity with research about human resiliency provides workers with background information about what might be helpful. Knowledge about the unique capabilities of specific cultural groups also puts workers on alert for identifying strengths. Recognizing clients' capabilities builds confidence, motivation, and feelings of power. To identify general strengths, workers keep many questions in mind, for example:

- What are the outstanding qualities of this client?
- In what ways does the client demonstrate power?
- How and with whom does the client successfully build alliances?
- What special or unique characteristics distinguish this client from others?
- What skills does this client system have to connect to its environment?
- What resources support the client?
- In what ways does the client contribute to the social and physical environments?
- How has the client been able to adapt to changes?

These questions consider the qualities that characterize the competence of any human system in its environmental context. Individuals, families, groups, organizations, and communities all draw on internal and environmental resources to adapt and progress.

Strengths in Individuals

Workers locate an individual's personal strengths by exploring cognitive, affective, physical, and cultural attributes. Intelligence, problem-solving skills, and creativity are important cognitive resources. Affective strengths may include positive feelings of self-worth, abilities to identify and express emotions, hopefulness, optimism, and sensitivity. Special physical talents, athletic skills, an attractive appearance, endurance, and good health are all physical qualities that benefit individual functioning. And one's cultural identities may be a source of pride that contributes to a positive sense of self and belonging. Additionally, spirituality serves as a reservoir of strength, as "it can provide emotional consolation, inspiration, guidance, structure and security. It can foster personal responsibility, identity, respect for ethical codes, meaningful ritual, and community building" (Gotterer, 2001, p. 188). Each of these personal strengths contributes to individual well-being and also enhances interpersonal interactions.

Interpersonal strengths are evident in an individual's natural support network. They include rewarding relationships with immediate family members and extended family support. Friends, neighbors, employers, teachers, ministers, rabbis, and other spiritual leaders—all may provide important resources for individual well-being. An individual's abilities in building social alliances such as good communication skills, warmth, trustworthiness, and commitment underlie successful interpersonal relationships.

Rewarding connections to community, institutional, and recreational resources can also function as strengths. When people are aware of available resources and feel privileged to access them, they are positioned well to build productive connections to the environment—an important source of sustenance for individual functioning.

Strengths in Families

No one single formula guarantees a family's success. Families have different styles due to structure, membership, cultural influences, ethnic heritage, and a host of environmental variables. However, 25 years of research by Beavers and Hampson (1990, 1993) showed trends in family interaction that benefited families, including abilities to negotiate differences, clear communication of individual preferences, respect for each other's choices, and feelings of togetherness among family members. Observing the interactions of a competent family reveals "a group of individuals who are spontaneous, enjoy each other, and are allowed clear and direct expression of feelings, attitudes, and beliefs" (1990, pp. 30–31).

Collecting information from more than 10,000 family members from every state in the United States and more than 22 countries, Olson and colleagues (2013) report remarkable cross-cultural similarities with respect to family strengths. Reinforcing the conclusions of earlier studies, they found that factors contributing to family satisfaction and resilience include appreciation and affection, commitment, positive communication, time together, spiritual well-being, and the ability to cope with stress and crisis.

Notice that none of this research about family competence offers evidence that it is necessary in families for there to be two heterosexual, married, or biological parents—or even children, for that matter. No one type of family typifies the only model capable of positive family functioning. Families representing many structures and lifestyles can work together for the benefit of all family members. The nature of a family's interactions and the support that each member gives and receives define a family's health.

Strengths in Groups

In successful groups, each member contributes to the group's overall functioning and, in return, receives the benefits of group membership. To accomplish this balance, groups require the strengths of clearly understood goals, effective communication among members, distributed power, appropriate decision-making procedures, conflict resolution skills, and cohesiveness (Johnson & Johnson, 2013). Competently functioning groups also have similar relationships with their environments, accessing and contributing resources in reciprocal exchanges.

Other qualities of group interaction that constitute strengths depend on the group's specific purpose. For example, a task group draws on particular skills of its members that are most relevant to the task at hand. A support group benefits from members' abilities to articulate feelings and demonstrate empathy. A social action group depends on members' feelings of power and their connections to powerful resources in the community at large. A successful committee finds strengths in efficient operating procedures and diversity among members to stimulate creativity. Social workers discover group strengths by examining the individual qualities of members, the dynamic interaction among members, and the group's relationship to its environment.

Strengths in Organizations

Larger social systems, including human services agencies and other organizations, also demonstrate strengths. For example, in a social service agency, we may discover talented employees, a good training program, a dedicated volunteer pool, supportive and active clientele, a motivated and dedicated board of directors, a sound program evaluation system, or lucrative relationships with community foundations.

Organizations draw on the strengths of their missions, reputations in the community, family-friendly personnel policies and practices, sound financial management, well-maintained facilities, and receptive administrators. Competent organizations efficiently meet their purposes while ensuring the well-being of their workers, honoring employee perspectives in decision making, and respecting the diversity of their workforce (Johnson & Rhodes, 2010). When faced with critical issues such as corporate expansion or downsizing, organizations can rely on their strengths to see them through difficult periods of change.

Strengths in Communities

A community's strengths include an appreciation of its diverse population, shared community values and standards, timely and deliberate response to community problems, and availability of resources. Strengths are also found in well-maintained infrastructures, adequate transportation systems, affordable housing, equitable tax levies, committed office holders, and a sound economy. A community that provides resources, services, and social connectedness to meet residents' needs and activates its citizens to participate in city government, community projects, and long-range planning has the resources in place to resolve upcoming issues. The adaptive capacities of resilient communities draw on networks of resources to equitably support all community members (Norris et al., 2008).

Assessing a community's strengths uses processes similar to those used to explore the resources of other systems. Social workers inventory the community's assets and audit its capacity for development. To respect diversity, workers remain open to culturally specific clues to community strengths. For example, murals in Latino communities may signal strengths in a community, both in terms of the content they present and the process by which they develop community identity (Delgado & Barton, 1998). Workers assess both what the community gives to its members and how members contribute to the community in return.

Solution-Focused Dialogue

Asking about what is working, in addition to fleshing out what is not, seeks readily available information about possible strengths and solutions. Social workers may say any of the following:

- So, what have you been doing to try to solve this?
- What works, even for a little while?
- What are you learning about your situation?
- Is there anyone who seems able to cope with what's going on? What are they doing?
- Are there ever times when things just seem to be going better for no apparent reason?
- What have you discovered about yourself as you work on this issue?
- Do you remember a time when this problem didn't exist? Tell me what was going on then.

Assessment

Behavior: Collect and organize data, and apply critical thinking to interpret information from clients and constituencies

Critical Thinking Question: During assessment processes, empowerment-oriented social workers emphasize client and constituent strengths. What knowledge and skills are most effective in identifying the strengths that clients and constituencies bring to the change effort?

Each of these questions moves clients beyond ruminating about problems by expanding the focus of the dialogue toward solutions.

Many social workers have shifted from problem-centered to solution-centered dialogue with clients (DeJong & Berg, 2013; deShazer et al., 2007; Walter & Peller, 1992, 2000).

Box 9.1 Service Users' Involvement: A Policy–Practice Connection

A strong belief that clients should remain in charge of social service decisions related to their situations (and, therefore, their lives) provides a major impetus for the empowerment-oriented service user's movement in England, Ireland, and other western European nations. Persons involved in this movement, which promotes service–user autonomy in decision making, include self-described mental health system survivors, older adults, persons with learning difficulties, and persons with disabilities (Evans, 2004; Omeni et al., 2014; Patterson et al., 2014; Ross et al., 2014; Soni et al., 2014; Valokivi, 2004). Initially focused on promoting personal control, many service–user movements have now begun to expand their activities to affect larger system change. Shaping Our Lives, an example of one British organization in this movement, draws on the expertise of persons with disabilities to influence policy and program research, planning, and evaluation (Turner, 1997). Reflecting an understanding of empowerment as both a personal and a political process, service users set specific goals, including advocating personal decision making and control, creating responsive programs and services, redressing discrimination and social injustice, and promoting social change.

Closer to home, Weiman and colleagues (2002) describe the consumer-led transformation of one social service agency located in a midwestern urban community in the United States. This not-for-profit community-based agency provides day programs, community employment, and residential support for individuals with intellectual disabilities. Training personnel with a curriculum based on empowerment philosophy and principles, particularly listening and responding as mentors to "clients as experts," fostered changes in the organizational culture of the agency. Staff in training were afforded hands-on opportunities to put mentoring principles into practice through their work with consumer groups. One such consumer group, We Can ... Speak Out!, convened a conference open to any community member to

learn the process of speaking for oneself, hosted forums for congressional candidates, and participated in voters' rallies. Participants' experiences have been so powerful that they initiated and achieved a change in their agency designation from "consumers" to "individuals" and now sit on a committee to screen all applicants for employment at the agency.

As a policy directive, the service–user movement presses for clients to be involved in research efforts, not simply as participants, but as full partners in control of the research process. In the United Kingdom, many private and public funders of social research now stipulate service–user involvement as a requirement of funding. According to Fisher (2002), the benefits of user-controlled research lie in "the possibility of technical enhancements to the processes of defining the research 'problem,' in ensuring that appropriate data are sought and are accessible, in defining outcome measures, and in recognizing relevance during analysis" (p. 310).

Consumers of social services now play increasingly prominent roles in developing policies, defining practice priorities, and serving as research partners. Genuine service user power has important benefits for enhancing service delivery at every level. Based on the work of Beresford and colleagues (2001), the following questions help evaluate the authenticity and inclusiveness of initiatives that involve service users:

- Are agency publications and documents *available* to clients?
- Are the contributions of service users *acknowledged and respected* by agency staff?
- Are the views and contributions of service users regarded as *equal and valued*?
- Are service users *included* in all aspects of policy development and service delivery decisions?

Infusing empowerment theory into the day-to-day practice of social work honors the voices of clients by ensuring meaningful roles for service users in policy, practice, and research.

From an evidence-based perspective, solution-focused interventions demonstrate effectiveness in a broad array of settings (Franklin et al., 2012; Gingerich & Peterson, 2013). From a generalist perspective, a **solution-focused dialogue** applies to numerous fields of practice and across all system levels. For example, Schott and Conyers (2003) discuss the application of a solution-focused dialogue to microlevel work in psychiatric rehabilitation, noting philosophical similarities such as recognizing clients' expertise, capacities, and strengths; emphasizing solutions and potentials for change; and fostering a sense of optimism. In relation to mezzolevel work with groups, Cohen and Graybeal (2007) demonstrate that when workers model solution-focused dialogue to facilitate group discussion, group members respond likewise. Applied to groups, this orientation to dialogue is helpful in such processes as agreeing on a shared purpose, focusing on solutions rather than problems, envisioning a different future, identifying small actions that lead to personal and collective goals, and evaluating progress. Finally, Bloor and Pearson (2004) detail a macrolevel application of a solution-focused approach to organizational change. They adapt solution-focused dialogue to facilitate discourse on change by identifying organizational strengths and capacities and describing the preferred outcome; on solutions by clarifying how the organization will differ, how people inside and outside the organization will recognize these differences, and what goals and objectives are priorities; and on strategies by identifying action steps leading to solutions.

Conversational strategies to discover client strengths and potential solutions guide social workers to (1) create an atmosphere conducive to possibilities, (2) look for **exceptions** to the occurrence of the problem, (3) survey clients' information for **incremental steps** in the direction of goals, and (4) search for **transferable skills** and solutions. Additionally, all of these applications reflect the perceptual shift from helplessness to control.

Creating a Solution-Saturated Atmosphere

Myriad influences affect the atmosphere and tone of transactions between clients and social workers. Solution-focused social workers deliberately tend to the climate of their working relationships to instill confidence, optimism, and the idea that success is inevitable. Positive assumptions enhance this atmosphere significantly. When practitioners assume that clients have competence, believe that challenges are transitory, and recognize that clients have coping skills that they have demonstrated in the past and will do again in the present and the future, workers promote hope and orient clients toward viable solutions.

A social worker's skills can ensure a success-saturated climate, creating a respectful environment in which people experience their potential. Knowing that language frames meaning, social workers choose words carefully to reveal their assumptions that clients can and will succeed. Giving direct compliments works well, and nonverbal messages also contribute to a positive atmosphere. Workers can show their optimism through direct feedback, emotional expression, gestures, and tone of voice as they convey expectations for successful outcomes.

Knowing that language frames meaning, social workers choose words carefully to reveal their assumptions that clients can and will succeed.

Searching for Exceptions

Sometimes problems entrench clients; it seems like everything is going wrong, and nothing is going right. However, "nothing always happens; nothing is always the same" (deShazer, 1985, pp. 161–162). This concise statement alerts social workers to look for exceptions, for indicators of when things are going well or when difficulties abate, even if only briefly. To search for exceptions, workers may say any of the following:

- What is happening on those days when things seem less impossible?
- So, most of the time you feel down. What about the other times?
- The residents raise a number of concerns about the recent deterioration of the neighborhood. What continues to be positive about the neighborhood?
- So, these signs of worker burnout have been going on for almost 6 months. What was different at the agency before things started going wrong?

The way the "exceptions question" works is simple. Workers "focus on the who, what, when, and where of exception times instead of the who, what, when, and where of problems" (DeJong & Miller, 1995, p. 731).

Detecting Incremental Steps

Probably the strengths most often missed by both workers and clients are resources that are just developing. Often, clients are experimenting with new behaviors to overcome their current problems. Workers explore these attempts to discover times when clients feel hopeful and identify those changes that hold clues about what might work. "What are you doing to try to solve this problem?" is a good question for social workers to ask.

Success builds one step at a time. Clients may be capable of accomplishments that are not in and of themselves enough to resolve the current difficulties; nevertheless, they may be steps in the right direction. For example, in trying to overcome an early rift that has divided it into subgroups, members of a support group may demonstrate excellent listening skills. Although recognizing that the support group is not fully accomplished in resolving conflicts, the worker helps members notice that their abilities to listen are essential strengths for negotiating resolutions.

If workers and clients can decide where they are going, they can survey the current situations for signs that clients are moving in the right direction. To discover incremental steps, workers first help clients define a direction toward goals (a process presented in Chapter 8). Second, workers guide clients to identify times when they believe they are inching in that direction. Workers may say any of the following:

- What is the first thing you will notice when things are getting better? Does that ever happen now?
- If this problem disappeared overnight, what would clue you in when you woke up in the morning? Do you remember a time when that thing was happening?
- So, you want everybody on both sides of this blended family to talk openly about how they think things should be organized. I've noticed that everyone has done that here today. Could we talk about how that happened so that we might help it continue?
- When the community and school linkage project began, only a few parents were actively involved. Since that time, the project staff has worked to increase the roster of parents. How can we maximize on this effort?

Sometimes clients cannot describe where they want to go or even what the first step might be. They need opportunities to observe themselves in action to discover if they are making any progress or having any success. In such situations, workers direct clients to examine the events between meetings to notice what is happening that clients would like to see continue.

Searching for Transferable Skills

Even when people are experiencing problems, not everything is likely going wrong. Clients often show abilities in domains of their lives unaffected by their problems. These transferable skills are abilities that they can generalize to resolve the problematic situation at hand. Consider the mother who is short-tempered with her child but who shows great patience and restraint in caring for her aging father. Clearly, the skills and tolerance in both caregiving situations have similarities. The capability is transferable from one relationship to the other. Recognizing success in one situation may help generate solutions in another.

Or, at another system level, consider the example of a community that quickly activates considerable resources in times of a natural disaster such as a flood, tornado, or hurricane but isn't drawing on those same assets to resolve the ongoing crisis in a neighborhood plagued by high crime rates, crumbling streets, and deteriorating housing stock. Strengths demonstrated in one aspect of community functioning hold promise for resolving challenges in other areas of need.

> **?** Assess your understanding of the strengths perspective and solution-focused dialogue by taking this brief quiz.

RECOGNIZING CULTURAL STRENGTHS

Each of us draws strength from a variety of sources. We feel strong when we have a clear sense of who we are and where we fit into our world. Likewise, we sense our strengths when we are secure that others support our ideas and we can count on the backing of people around us. These elements are potentially present in the various cultural identities we hold.

Recall that culture is an attribute of any group of people, though **cultural identity** has been most frequently applied to describe membership qualities in racial or ethnic groups. Beyond race and ethnicity, cultural diversity also references age, social and economic class, color, ability, sex, gender identity, sexual orientation, immigration status, political ideology, religion, regional affiliation, national origin, and personal background. A group's cultural characteristics provide members with affirmation of values and beliefs, guidelines for appropriate behavior, models of customs and traditions, strategies to solve problems, and inspiration to survive difficulties. As such, recognizing cultural strengths may unleash powerful internal and external resources on a client's behalf.

Recognizing cultural strengths may unleash powerful internal and external resources on a client's behalf.

The Challenge of Activating Cultural Strengths

Acknowledging cultural strengths reveals a worker's acceptance of diversity and bonds cross-cultural relationships. So, what is it that makes us overlook valuable cultural resources that clients possess? Is it our discomfort with differences that encourages us to emphasize how we are similar to our clients, steering us to ignore those differences that we sense may threaten the bonds of professional relationships? Are we so accustomed to looking at cultural identities as the roots of prejudice and stereotype that we choose instead to gloss over rather than accentuate and celebrate our cultural diversity?

Most likely, our reluctance to utilize cultural strengths stems from the difficulty of achieving cultural competence in practice. Some scholars suggest that cultural competence represents more of a theoretical ideal than an achievable reality in social work practice (Johnson & Munch, 2009). The range of cultural differences among people is enormous. Scores of distinct cultural groups define society in the United States. How could any of us possibly know the unique strengths and capacities that characterize each of these different groups? And even if we become well educated on various cultures, how well does this knowledge actually fit the unique person we are trying to understand? Individual differences among people within the same cultural groups undermine our best attempts to apply cultural knowledge. Activating clients' cultural strengths requires critical understanding of the complexity of cultural identity, recognition of the political implications of cultural categories, and highly developed skills to access cultural resources.

A Closer Look at Cultural Identity

Watch this video and apply critical race theory to the story of the featured individual. What does she know that social workers should learn about the social construction of race, ethnicity, and privilege? www.youtube.com/watch?v=D9lhs241zeg

On its face, cultural identity may seem to be a simple concept. We automatically categorize the people we meet into groups. At first introduction, we notice whether a person is male or female, Black or White, old or young. Our minds just work that way, sorting and organizing the information we receive to make sense out of our worlds. But what do these quick assessments of others really tell us about what this person has to offer? Not much! Several issues confound our efforts to draw quick and accurate conclusions about someone's cultural attributes based on a glance. They include the social construction of cultural categories, the multicultural nature of an individual's identity, and the standpoint of the observer.

Cultural Categories

Categorizing people into cultural groups, even to study them, carries significant risks. Describing people by cultural identity subjectively sorts people by a selected cultural characteristic such as race, possibly ignoring other influential cultural identities such as gender, age, and economic status. Such narrow focus contributes to the evolution of stereotypes. Categorical grouping poses special risks when one is considering race and ethnicity. Many scholars reject the scientific reality of race altogether, pointing out that race is a concept unsupported by evidence of biological similarities and differences; instead, race is a socially constructed idea that serves to perpetuate racism (Chisom & Washington, 1997; Coleman, 2011). Using ethnicity as an organizing concept bears the same risks, offering the possibility of describing one ethnic group as superior to another ethnic group in some meaningful way. Moreover, who holds the privilege of deciding who is a member of which group—the observer or the observed?

Multiculturalism

Multiculturalism presents another dilemma for the social worker trying to incorporate clients' cultural strengths into practice. Each human being sits at the intersection of multiple cultural identities, backgrounds, life experiences, and perspectives. Some parts of one's cultural identity may be more prominent or useful in certain situations, while other culturally influenced characteristics may be more salient in other circumstances. Some aspects of one's cultural identity may bring privilege, while others may place one at risk of oppression.

Reflecting on the complexity of cultural identity, Daniel (2008) argues the need for a shift in social work perspective from a liberal pluralism (different cultures are equally acceptable) to a critical multiculturalism (each of an individual's many cultural identities has differential impact on life experience). Daniel charges the profession to recognize the linkages among cultural identities, privilege, power, and access to social resources. A life course approach allows individuals to identify what's important in their own sociocultural history (Elder, 1998). For example, "for African American families these influences may include among others African traditions, conventional American (Eurocentric) expectations, [and] popular culture movements" (Dunlap et al., 2006, p. 119).

Standpoint of Observer

Another challenge to a worker's cultural competence is best understood through the view of **standpoint theory**. Standpoint theory says that the way we evaluate the world cannot be separated from the point at which we observe it (Swigonski, 1993). Our social-cultural-political location determines what we do or do not see, how we interpret what we see, and the value or importance of what we notice. Our own cultural identities unavoidably affect how we understand the cultural attributes of others. That which social workers perceive as right or wrong, health or dysfunction, strength or weakness carries the imprints of the worker's own cultural and ethnic background. A social work practitioner's standpoint may blind the worker to resources that may be obvious to others, including clients' cultural strengths.

Observer standpoint holds particular importance for antioppressive social workers. By virtue of their power, dominant cultural groups enjoy privilege to prescribe mainstream cultural values and beliefs, thereby setting societal standards and norms, a concept known as hegemony (Mullaly, 2002). As a result, members of diverse cultures viewed through this dominant lens risk harsh judgment by others, their strengths obscured or underestimated. Practitioners working to avoid these pitfalls must recognize their privilege, critically reflect on their own cultural identities, acquire extensive understanding of their own biases and presuppositions, and develop sensitivity to the perspectives of others.

The Critical Use of Research About Cultural Groups

Contemporary social work practice demands an evidenced-based approach. Guided by social work research and best practices, accountable professionals engage diverse clients, assess client functioning, and implement relevant intervention strategies. The evidence generated by social work research can sensitize workers to notice previously undetectable client resources. However, the same challenges of cultural classification, multiculturalism, and observer standpoint also complicate the effective use of social work research. Social workers using research-based knowledge to understand client cultural strengths must do so carefully by critically analyzing research quality, appropriately applying research findings, and elevating each client's unique perspective.

Knowledge generated by social work research is only as good as the quality of the research itself. To assess quality, workers consider the rigor of the research design, the validity of research outcomes, and the applicability of the research conclusions. (See Chapter 15 for more extensive coverage of the use of evidence in social work practice.) Applying research studies about cultural groups requires even greater scrutiny. Relevant questions include the following: Which are the cultural group or groups being studied? What are the characteristics or boundaries that define group membership (who's in and who's out)? What other cultural group memberships of those being studied may function as intervening variables, possibly undermining the validity of any conclusions drawn? The ethical use of findings from studies about cultural groups requires careful analysis of who is studied, by whom, in what way, and for what purposes.

Diversity and Difference in Practice

Behavior: Apply and communicate understanding of the importance of diversity and difference in shaping life experiences in practice at the micro, mezzo, and macro levels

Critical Thinking Question: What may function as strengths for clients in the face of their diversity may be viewed as a deficit in another context. How does this statement apply to understanding how diversity shapes life experiences and expectations?

For workers to apply social work knowledge ethically and effectively, they must first ascertain the relevance of research for a particular client situation. How well does the knowledge fit? In what context is the evidence generated, and are the conclusions drawn transferable to the client context at hand? What are the political implications of using this knowledge? Does the use of the knowledge pathologize client behavior or explain circumstances in a nonjudgmental way? How does this information benefit the work? Research-based information becomes a resource only when it leads social workers to the unique strengths of each specific client.

The oppressive use of expertly derived cultural knowledge can silence a client's voice and override the reality of a client's unique cultural experience (Weick, 1999). What research claims is true about a cultural group may or may not apply to a specific individual sharing membership within that group. Learning about the worldviews and experiences of various cultural groups alerts workers to possibilities, but to avoid stereotyping, workers should maintain caution in zealously applying general information to any client's specific situation.

Ethnic Group Strengths

Similar resources characterize many ethnic groups in the United States, including African Americans, Latinos, Asian Americans, and Native Americans (Lum, 2004). These attributes include the centrality of family, support of the extended family and kinship network, clear vertical hierarchy in families, and the importance of religion and spirituality. Many of these qualities differ from predominant Euro-American characteristics of independence, autonomy, egalitarianism, and rationality. This contrast demonstrates the need to learn about various racial, ethnic, and cultural groups. The sections that follow highlight some of the ethnic group strengths noted in the cross-cultural literature. As you read, maintain a critical stance to reflect on the ethical use of this social work knowledge in practice.

African Americans

Those persons identifying as Black currently account for about 14 percent of the total population in the United States (Rastogi et al., 2011). Historically, differences distinguishing African American culture from the cultural majority were framed as deficits, a perspective that functioned to perpetuate racism. A more contemporary look reveals these same differences as potential sources of strength (Wright & Anderson, 1998). Major strengths that social workers are likely to discover when working with African American clients include those involving family such as extended family support, adaptability of family roles to fit changing circumstances, and informal adoption processes; those involving values such as a strong work ethic, a high priority placed on educational achievement, and the importance of children; and those involving the centrality of church, spirituality, and community in African American life (Billingsley, 1992; Boyd-Franklin, 1992; Hill, 1997).

Strengths of African American clients become most visible when viewed through an Africentric perspective. The Africentric worldview emphasizes five principles: group above self, respect for self and others, responsibility for self and community, reciprocity, and authenticity (Utsey et al., 2003). An Africentric perspective places high value on collective responsibility, flexible family roles, the importance of kin and fictive kin, interdependence of individuals with their environment, and the integration of spirituality in daily life (Manning et al., 2004). Competent work with African American clients suggests "that a greater value be placed on socioemotional factors such as support, caring, loyalty, religion, and spirituality, and less focus on socioeconomic indices to assess family stability" (Barnes, 2001, p. 450). Practitioners working with African Americans should remain alert for resources available within family, social, and community networks.

Intergenerational kinship bonds are among the potential strengths of African American families.

A survey on religion in the United States indicates that compared with other ethnic groups, Black Americans are more likely to report religious affiliations. However, reflecting the trend in the United States, 19 percent of Black Americans under 30 years of age report no religious affiliation (Sahgal & Smith, 2009). Nonetheless, with nearly 80 percent of African Americans indicating that religion is very important in their lives, the overall strength of religious orientation suggests that ministers and the church community may function as essential community resources for African Americans (Bliss et al., 2008; McNeal & Perkins, 2007; Moore & Miller, 2007). Jang and Johnson (2004) note that highly religious African Americans experience a greater sense of control and social support than those who are less religious.

The **intersectionality** of race and class differentiates the African American experience. Middle-class African Americans have a much different life experience than African Americans who are poor. Economically stable African Americans frequently exhibit bicultural abilities, demonstrating competence in code switching, effectively adapting their behaviors to fit into both Black and White cultural contexts (Day-Vines et al., 2003).

General knowledge about cultural strengths frames areas for workers to explore, leaving clients to fill in the details of their life experiences. McCullough-Chavis and Waites (2004) offer cultural genograms as a helpful tool that effectively steers clients toward topics that are likely to yield benefits. (See Chapter 10 to learn how to construct and use genograms.) In using **cultural genograms** with African American families, they suggest structuring the discussion on five areas of potential strengths identified by the social work literature: family member role flexibility, extended family functioning, caregiving for children and others, spirituality, and family beliefs and traditions. Using this method, generalized social work knowledge is not stereotypically applied; rather, it is fine-tuned by client expertise.

Non-Hispanic White Americans

"White" is a general term used to describe many diverse American ethnic cultures. According to the U.S. Census Bureau, "White" refers to a person having origins in any of the original peoples of Europe, the Middle East, or North Africa (Humes et al., 2011). For example, it includes people who describe themselves as Irish, German, Italian, Lebanese, Arab, or Moroccan. In the 2010 census, 64 percent of those responding identified as White Americans, a decrease from the 69 percent reported just 10 years earlier. White Americans are the slowest growing ethnic group in the United States, and their numbers are expected to fall below 50 percent of the total population by the year 2043 (U.S. Census Bureau, 2012).

Because of its dominant group status, White Americans are sometimes excluded from discussion of American ethnic groups. In keeping with its cultural privilege of defining mainstream American culture, the "White way" is assumed to be the "American way." Cultural values favoring independence, autonomy, personal achievement, egalitarianism, and rationality—touted as mainstream American values—do represent values attributable to many White Americans, especially those who trace their roots to western European countries (Hodge, 2005). However, these values sit in stark contrast to values embraced by other groups classified as White Americans, including those with family origins in eastern Europe, the Middle East, and northern Africa.

Similar to other ethnic groups, persons categorized as White Americans represent a diverse group of people. Contrast your views of someone who traces his or her heritage to the colonial United States with your views of a Bosnian refugee who more recently immigrated to the United States to escape religious and ethnic persecution. The Bosnian emphasis on the centrality of family and extended family, reverence for elder family members, neighborliness, and interconnectedness within community show clear differences from mainstream American values that favor competitiveness, individuality, and the desire for personal space (Snyder et al., 2005). Social workers helping to improve the lives of Bosnian Americans should draw on the strengths of interpersonal relationships rather than work to achieve differentiation and individual success.

Arab Americans

Cultural identities such as gender, religion, age, national origin, and degree of assimilation into American culture are likely to be more influential in defining a person's cultural attributes than one's identity as White. Consider the example of Arab Americans. The term "Arab" is linguistically derived, referring to people who originate in cultures where Arabic is the dominant language (Abu-Ras & Abu-Badur, 2008). Arab Americans are a fast-growing heterogeneous immigrant group with members coming to the United States from the Middle East and North Africa, including Palestine, Iraq, Jordan, Lebanon, Egypt, Syria, and Turkey (Asi & Beaulieu, 2013). Arab Americans are generally well educated as compared with other Americans. Forty percent of Arab

Americans have graduate degrees, and 24 percent have postgraduate degrees, compared to 17 percent and 10 percent of the general population in the United States, respectively (Arab American Institute, 2011).

Two key qualities distinguish members within this ethnic group—their degree of acculturation and religion (Graham et al., 2008). Historically, Arab Americans immigrated in two waves (Abu-Ras & Abu-Badur, 2008). Primarily from Syria and Lebanon, the first group came to the United States from 1887 to 1920. Most members of this group of immigrants identified themselves as Christians. Arab Americans tracing roots to this first migration are likely fully assimilated, native-born Americans for the last two generations. Their Christianity fits readily with the dominant Judeo-Christian perspective in the United States, opening a pathway for easy integration into mainstream culture and community institutions. Many members of this group identify themselves simply as White, which indicates the high degree of acculturation and possibly functions as a defense against the prejudice frequently directed at those identified as "Arab" in current society in the United States. Social workers assessing resources available to these Arab Americans may discover their strengths through the lens of dominant cultural values.

The second wave of Arab immigration began in the 1970s. These immigrants came from countries throughout the Middle East, mostly to escape the Arab–Israeli conflict and civil war. The majority are Muslim, a religious identity that separates them from mainstream culture and places them at risk of discrimination in the larger society (Abu-Ras & Abu-Badur, 2008; Love, 2009). Arab Americans who are followers of Islam ascribe to a value set that is very different from that of European Americans. Hodge (2005) notes the cultural themes of community, connectedness, consensus, and interdependence as differentiating Muslims from other Americans for whom separateness and self-determination are guiding philosophies. Hodge also recognizes the elements of centrality of spirituality, respect for community rights, and emphasis on self-control as strengths for Muslims. Social workers striving to identify the strengths of Arab Americans need information derived directly from clients about their values, the length of time their families have lived in the United States, their religious practices, and the degree to which a spiritual orientation guides their daily lives.

Latino Americans

"Latino" and "Hispanic American" are terms used to characterize as one group the many cultures of Spanish descent. Latino Americans trace their ancestors to places such as Mexico, Puerto Rico, Cuba, other Central and South American countries, and even parts of the southwestern United States that were formerly Mexican territory. The common Spanish language heritage and categorical grouping by the U.S. government gathers these diverse cultures into a single category. Currently, people of Hispanic origin comprise the largest ethnic minority group in the United States, accounting for about 16 percent of the total population, which is a 43 percent increase since 2000 (Ennis et al., 2011). The size of this population group will likely double by 2060, from 53.3 million in 2012 to 128.8 million in 2060, when projections indicate people of Hispanic-Latino origin will constitute one-third of the total population (U.S. Census Bureau, 2012).

Strong family relationships and connectedness within the community comprise key elements of Latino cultures. Reflecting the core Latino values of collectivism and communal orientation, family and community interdependence function as protective factors against distress for Latino Americans and offer potential resources for social workers engaging Latino clients (Furman et al., 2009). Alert social workers will recognize that these values contradict the dominant philosophy of individualism and autonomy embedded in the U.S. social welfare system, a system that privileges personal responsibility over collective solutions. Competent social work practice with Latino clients may require solutions that vary from prescribed practices.

Mexican Americans

Mexican Americans represent the largest Latino group in the United States (Ennis et al., 2011). In contrast to more assimilated ethnic groups, many Mexican Americans continue to maintain core values and traditions typical in Mexico, possibly due to language usage, recent arrival in the United States, residence in predominately Mexican American neighborhoods, and proximity to Mexico. This lack of assimilation into mainstream culture in the United States may function as a strength for Mexican Americans. For example, research by Marsiglia and colleagues (2001) found that middle school children who indicate a strong sense of pride in their Mexican American identities were less likely to abuse substances such as alcohol, marijuana, and tobacco when compared to Mexican American children who took less pride in their ethnic identity. Interestingly, while the same conclusion held true for African American adolescents in the study, the opposite was true for those who identified as non-Hispanic Whites, a group for whom pride in ethnic identity predicted more frequent substance use.

Mexican Americans frequently share the family tasks of child care, financial responsibility, and problem solving within extended family networks that may include godparents and members of other families (Morales & Salcido, 1998). Contradicting an "outside" view, many Mexican American families distribute power more equitably in marital relationships than the male-dominated cultural stereotype indicates (Falicov, 1996). Mexican Americans claim a high degree of spirituality, usually identifying as Catholics. With Mexican American clients, the spiritual domain may be a starting point for change.

Other Latino Cultures

Similar to Mexican Americans, Puerto Rican and Cuban Americans show strengths in extended family support, respect for older family members, strength generated from spiritual beliefs, and a tendency toward cooperation over competition (Bernal & Shapiro, 1996; Garcia-Preto, 1996; Weaver & Wodarski, 1996). Regardless of these similarities, resist the temptation to group all Latino cultures together or risk overlooking varying political realities and subtle cultural differences that distinguish these groups and individuals from each other within each group. Consider the contrast between a Puerto Rican American and a Mexican American. Persons from Puerto Rico enjoy citizenship status in the United States. They can come and go between Puerto Rico and the continental United States freely. At some point in the distant or near past, Mexican American families moved to the United States from a different country, successfully completing or avoiding a complex and lengthy immigration process. Unfairly, even those Mexican Americans who are native born or those who are officially documented still face the stereotype of "illegal" and may be subject to local harassment based on profiling.

Asian Americans

The culturally diverse groups described together as Asian Americans combine to form the fastest-growing ethnic groups in the United States. Demographers project that the size of the Asian American population in the United States will more than double by 2060, increasing from 15.9 million in 2012 to 34.4 million in 2060 (U.S. Census Bureau, 2012). Similar to those cultural groups clustered as Latino, the description "Asian American" is also a broad category applied to various peoples who trace their origins to countries such as the Philippines, China, Vietnam, Korea, Japan, India, Laos, Pakistan, and Cambodia. It is worth noting that the countries from which Asian Americans originate contain 60 percent of the entire population of the world (Population Reference Bureau, 2014). In-group diversity within such an enormous category is inevitable, leaving workers to cautiously apply any conclusions about "Asian American" cultural traits. As Jo (2004) notes, "the category of Asian does not work as conveniently or neatly as it has been used" (p. 19).

Unlike other ethnic groups in the United States, many Asian Americans are not as likely to suffer from negative stereotypes of dysfunction. Rather, they are branded as a "model minority," an overgeneralized myth of unilateral brilliance and success (Jo, 2004). The model minority image has its drawbacks, as does any group stereotyping. It obscures individual differences and diminishes assistance to Asian Americans whose lives do not mirror the myth. Lorenzo and colleagues (2000) identify the depression, withdrawal, and social problems of Asian American adolescents that sometimes lie beneath the model minority image. And the minority status peripheralizes members of this group from the societal mainstream (Oyserman & Sakamoto, 1997). The model minority image does, however, reflect a general awareness of strengths potentially present in Asian American clients.

Similar values among Asian American cultures spring from their worldviews embedded within Eastern philosophy (Ross-Sheriff & Husain, 2001). Family unity; support for family members, particularly in times of crisis; and strong informal support networks such as churches, clubs, and family associations are strengths frequently mentioned as common among Asian Americans. The social work literature shows general agreement that Asian American and Pacific Islanders have strong values favoring reciprocity of kindness and helpfulness in relationships (Ho, 1987). They value concern for others over individual well-being and emphasize family loyalty with unquestioning respect for parents (Fong & Mokuau, 1994). Other commonly identified Asian values include preserving family honor and avoiding shame (McLaughlin & Braun, 1998; Nakanishi & Rittner, 1996). The quest for harmony in all human relationships can function as a powerful resource to compel Asian American clients toward cooperative resolutions (Browne & Broderick, 1994). Ethnic-sensitive social workers withhold their tendency to push Asian American clients toward self-assertion in a cultural context where group interests supersede individual benefits and solutions lie in collaborative endeavors.

Native Americans

The U.S. government, as part of developing federal American Indian policy, conceptualized the broad category of Native American. Legislation in the 1800s, designed to establish a reservation system and delineate Indian rights, defined as one group many disparate tribal nations of distinctive languages, customs, and character (Schaefer, 2012). People counted as members of the demographic category of American Indians and Alaskan Natives number about 2.9 million, or about 1 percent of the population in the United States (Norris et al., 2012). Other names applied to this cultural group include First Nations Peoples or Indigenous Peoples, names chosen to more accurately reflect the historical status of and diverse cultures contained within this demographic category. Currently, more than 500 distinct Native nations exist, and six have populations of more than 100,000: the Cherokee, Navajo, Choctaw, Mexican American Indian, Chippewa, and Sioux.

Many differences distinguish Native American nations, though some common values and resources may be present. Yellow Bird (2001) identifies strong affiliation with tribal identity, generosity, and sharing as important values among many First Nations Peoples. These values are evident in community problem solving, tribal closeness, and the sharing of labor, resources, and child care responsibilities among family, extended family, and tribal members (Blount et al., 1996). Native Americans respect the wisdom and leadership of elders (Weaver & White, 1997). Peaceful coexistence with natural forces shapes Native American spirituality, and spiritual leaders may play significant roles (Yellow Bird, 2001). Social workers who overlook extended family, tribal, and spiritual resources likely will miss opportunities to help. Identifying and developing tribal community strengths rather than using an individualized approach may be the best intervention to benefit Native American clients (Brown & Gundersen, 2001).

Two major factors differentiate cultural identities among people described as Native American (Dykeman et al., 1995; Grimm, 1992). First, distinctive differences in values and traditions are associated with various tribes. This diversity may be rooted in the unique ways that each nation relates to its specific natural environment (Yellow Bird et al., 1995; Yellow Bird, 2001). Second, Native Americans show much variation in degree of assimilation into mainstream American culture; most now live away from reservations. Native Americans who live on reservations have significantly different experiences from those who have relocated to urban centers such as New York, Los Angeles, San Francisco, Minneapolis, Seattle, or Phoenix.

Many American Indians draw strengths from tribal traditions, traditions embedded in family narratives and tribal myths. Such stories passed on by Indian elders emphasize respect for others over personal achievement and "the interdependence of the family, clan, and tribes, rather than on personal gain or wealth" (Garrett, 1993–1994, p. 20). Storytelling is a universal expression of group history and culture, useful both in educating students to be culturally competent and also as a method for eliciting the cultural realities of members of any social group (Carter-Black, 2007). Social workers may consider asking Native American clients to tell stories about their heritage in order to discover strengths residing in their histories.

Strengths in Cultural Group Memberships

Variations in ethnicity are not the only qualities that distinguish cultural groups. Categories based on gender, sexual orientation, age, religion, abilities, and life experiences also shape our understanding of human functioning. Used effectively, such understanding can frame social workers' interactions and assessments; used without reflection, this "knowledge" can stereotype and oppress cultural group members. Competent social workers can accurately identify the unique strengths available in members of any defined group, including women; persons identifying as gay, lesbian, bisexual, or transgender; older adults; people with religious affiliations; and people with disabilities.

Women

Females comprise slightly more than half of the population in the United States (Howden & Meyer, 2011). Women's presence in the labor force has expanded dramatically over the last several decades, yet women are shortchanged in the market place. Even though their wages have increased, in 2012, women earned only about 81 percent of wages earned by men (BLS, 2013). In 2013, about 30 percent of all female-headed households had incomes below the poverty level (DeNavas-Walt & Proctor, 2014). Poverty and other issues affecting women, such as homelessness, domestic violence, inadequate child care provisions, and depression, have at their core social and economic inequities.

Feminism adds a perspective on the strengths of women as survivors of patriarchy, inequalities, and oppression (Simon, 1994). Hanmer and Statham urge a view of women "as active, resilient, and enduring actors in their own behalf rather than as sorry objects of other people's words or actions" (as cited in Simon, p. 171). Women discover self-worth in their abilities to survive oppression as they confront issues of their choosing in their own ways. The consciousness raising and social action groups typical of the women's movement in the mid- to late twentieth century are example feminist strategies that draw on the traditional strengths of women to affiliate (Cohen, 2003). Such groups helped women develop a sense of their own power arising from identifying common objectives and developing alliances with others.

Socially constructed ideas of what it means to be feminine or masculine define what is regarded as appropriate qualities in women and men. From this socially constructed perspective, to be feminine means one is interdependent, peaceful, egalitarian, emotional, nurturing, and concerned about others; this sits in contrast to masculine tendencies to be independent, rational, decisive, achievement oriented, aggressive, and concerned about rights and responsibilities. Western culture has traditionally assigned characteristics associated with masculinity a superior status. Although masculine characteristics support the patriarchal values of rugged individualism, competition, and the work ethic, they fall short in promoting cooperation, communication, and interpersonal relationships. This brand of sexism devalues feminine traits and masks the feminine strengths of both women and men. Nurturance, emotional investments in others, cooperation, and communication skills are elements that support self-growth, strengthen families, enhance interpersonal relationships, and promote "caring" structures within neighborhoods, organizations, communities, and society. These qualities are strengths for social workers to acknowledge in both women and men.

Women and the Intersectionality of Cultural Identity

Not only does sexism constrain a woman's opportunities, but her ethnic identity, age, and socioeconomic class also intersect with gender, potentially creating multiple layers of oppression. For example, women of color experience high rates of poverty and homelessness. From their perspective, these injustices are more likely related to racism, classism, and ethnocentrism than to sexism, factors ignored by traditional feminist perspectives (Gutiérrez & Lewis, 1998). **Institutional racism**, not sexism, is the most critical factor in their experiences of oppression (Lum, 2004). Likewise, age intersects with gender as older women disproportionately experience poverty, confronting ageism as well as sexism. In a self-exploration of her own cultural identity, Torres (2003) describes the vulnerabilities associated with her multiple cultural identities, reflecting on her experiences defined by the categories of gender, age, Hispanic, minority within the larger Hispanic culture, immigrant, and nonnative English speaker.

In spite of multiple oppressions, strengths abound in women's abilities to survive and "leverage political power" (Lum, 2004, p. 111). An exploratory study by Aguilar and Williams (1993, as cited in Lum) revealed the strengths manifested by women of color, including hard work, pride in accomplishments, significant support systems, spirituality, optimism, self-motivation, and persistence. Contributing factors included personal, family, and community resources such as "education and skills, family support and stability, personal strengths, ethnic/racial pride, and community and professional commitment" (p. 31). To show respect for women's abilities, social workers acknowledge the strengths women reveal when facing social injustice (Black, 2003).

Gay, Lesbian, Bisexual, and Transgender Individuals

All social work practitioners will interact with clients and colleagues who are gay, lesbian, bisexual, or transgender. Data from a recent survey shows that 3.4 percent of adults in the United States identify as gay, lesbian, bisexual, or transgender (Gates & Newport, 2012). Likely, these figures underestimate the number of members of these cultural groups, since "an estimated 19 million Americans (8.2%) report that they have engaged in same-sex sexual behavior and nearly 25.6 million Americans (11%) acknowledge at least some same-sex sexual attraction" (Gates, 2011, p. 1). After much political and judicial activism, the U.S. Supreme Court in 2015 reviewed and overturned all state-initiated bans on same-sex marriage. Justices instructed state and local governments to grant marriage licenses and privileges to same sex couples. Despite these recent gains in achieving civil rights, efforts to achieve equality have fallen short of goals. Gays, lesbians, bisexuals, and transgender individuals still face considerable legal and cultural discrimination by governments, at work, in social interactions, and in the marketplace.

Of course, the strengths of gays and lesbians mirror those of other people. They derive strengths from personal qualities, interpersonal relationships, and connections within their communities. But acknowledging and asserting a homosexual orientation in a homophobic society requires unique struggles, creative adaptations, and the ability to take risks. To function successfully in both gay and straight communities, gays and lesbians inevitably learn to be bicultural (Lukes & Land, 1990).

Many gays and lesbians demonstrate considerable strengths in achieving developmental milestones. Developmental processes are complex for gays and lesbians because they must grow into an identity that is not socially sanctioned, a process not faced by heterosexuals (Russell et al., 2011; Ryan et al., 2010). Gays and lesbians show strengths in recognizing and accepting a sexual identity that varies from the dominant norm, in coming out to others, in maintaining committed partnerships without widespread social approval, and in asserting their identities in politically unaccepting environments. At each developmental phase, gays and lesbians must resolve their own personal ambivalence and risk social rejection—unjust dilemmas imposed by a homophobic society but, nevertheless, situations that elicit assertion, creative adaptation, and personal strength.

> ▶ Watch this video and consider the story of Scott Turner Schofield's journey to a congruent gender identity. Note the strengths he developed to cope with oppression of persons who identify as transgender.
> www.youtube.com/watch?v=TWubtUnSfA0

Although frequently overcategorized as one cultural group, persons who are gay, lesbian, bisexual, or transgender have very different life experiences from one another. Being gay, lesbian, or bisexual refers to one's sexual orientation, whereas transgender refers to one's identity as male or female. A gay or lesbian identity describes who you love. Gender identity describes who you define yourself to be. Similarities among members of these groups spring from the shared experiences of social exclusion, legal discrimination, and oppression. Ethical social work requires a broad-based acceptance and understanding of sexual and gender diversity along with skills to activate the strengths of these clients.

Growing up gay or lesbian challenges children and adolescents to embrace an identity that risks bullying and oppression, a situation not faced by heterosexuals (Sullivan, 1994). Gays and lesbians reveal their strengths in asserting their sexual orientations, in coming out to others, and in maintaining committed partnerships where there is limited social sanction.

Creating a family that varies from the traditional norm is challenging, although many gays and lesbians do so successfully. Ainslie and Feltey (1998) note that lesbian couples tend to be independent, self-reliant, assertive, and more flexible in defining gender role expectations, suggesting "the possibility of a very positive childrearing environment in lesbian families" (p. 329). Their study also concludes that children in lesbian families show acceptance of differences and express a high degree of social consciousness about issues such as racism, sexism, and nonviolence. Abilities in community organizing and political activism also typify the power that social workers discover in many gay and lesbian clients (Newman, 1994).

Working successfully with clients who are gay, lesbian, bisexual, or transgender requires workers to reject negative value judgments rooted in oppressive cultural norms, to explore their own biases and homophobic tendencies, and to openly dialogue with others about sexuality. Research shows that social workers who want to achieve a gay-affirming practice should interact frequently with gay and lesbian friends and family, attend workshops that teach skills for working with gay and lesbian clients, and reflect on their own thoughts and feelings about sexual orientation (Crisp, 2006). Similarly, frequently interacting with persons who are transgender, acquiring relevant skills, and taking time for personal reflection may help social workers use affirming practices with transgender clients.

Older Adults

Recent census studies in the United States predict that the number of adults 65 years and older will increase from 44.7 million in 2013 to about 98 million by 2060 (USHHS-AoA, 2015). The subgroup of those 85 years of age and older is currently 40 percent larger than it was in 1900. Projections indicate that this age group will increase from 5.9 million in 2012 to 14.1 million in 2040.

People often associate growing older with sensory loss and changes in mobility; however, for most older adults, these changes are neither as cumbersome nor as apparent as many imagine. Successfully coping with a lifetime of events, older adults often show signs of resilience, both physically and emotionally. This realization is enculturated in beliefs by Asian and Pacific Islanders, who see older adults "as family decision makers and the keepers of family and cultural wisdom" (Browne & Broderick, 1994, p. 254). As people grow older, they accumulate life experiences, gain perspective, and amass the knowledge of a lifetime.

Standardized needs-based assessment processes often overlook the strengths of older adults. In response, Kivnick and Murray (2001) have developed a life strengths interview guide. Key questions orient workers to ask clients to describe a typically good day, consider what has contributed to their current level of confidence and pride, note the ways in which they help others, share what lessons life has taught them about how to cope, and list people most significant in their lives. Social workers also encourage older adults to talk about their past interests and occupations (Kivnick & Stoffel, 2005). Reminiscing provides older clients with opportunities to retell their life stories and gives social workers opportunities to assess clients' strengths, resiliencies, and coping skills.

Religious Affiliations and Spirituality

Although there is public outcry about the decline of values and religion, relative to other countries in the world, religion remains integrated into the culture of the United States (Chaves, 2011). Studies of religious affiliations note several trends, including increases in religious diversity and in those reporting no religious affiliation (Pew Forum, 2008a). However, even those without religious affiliations may pray, believe in God, attend services, and self-identify as "spiritual but not religious." Research on religious beliefs and practices suggests that 75 percent of Americans pray regularly and that 56 percent believe religion is very important (Pew Forum, 2008b). Additional findings indicate that 92 percent of Americans believe in God, with 71 percent absolutely certain of the existence of God. As compared with other subgroups in the United States, African Americans are more likely to define themselves as religious or somewhat religious. For many people, even those not affiliated with a religious denomination, religion and spirituality wield significant influence, fostering strength, resilience, and meaning in life (Askay & Magyar-Russell, 2009; Bhul et al., 2008; Koenig, 2009, 2012; Purnell & Andersen, 2009).

Although specific beliefs and practices vary considerably, religious affiliation and spirituality have similar resources to offer. Affiliating with a community of faith provides a network of personal relationships and concrete support in times of need. In African American churches, research reveals a "haven where children can learn about their heritage from other African Americans who valued and nurtured them" (Haight, 1998). As in other non-Western traditions, the interconnectedness within community is implicit in Hinduism, as the interdependent social body is a manifestation of the sacred order or Hindu dharma (Hodge, 2004). Community is also a common theme among the various traditions of Islam (Hodge, 2005). Within the Muslim community, individualistic Western values such as self-reliance and autonomy are subordinate to "group success, community development, interdependence, and consensus" (p. 161).

Commitment to a faith can initiate a sense of purpose, renewal, and hope for the future. Specifically, "spiritual beliefs and practices strengthen the ability to withstand and transcend adversity" (Walsh, 1999a, p. 38) and are virtual wellsprings for healing and resilience (1999b). Compassion, love, and forgiveness—themes in most religions—contribute to personal and interpersonal healing. Common beliefs, stories of the faith, holy days, and ritual celebrations forge a sense of communal identity. Religious commitment may encourage concern for the welfare of others and, for some, foster a zeal for redressing social injustices.

Social workers need to expand their base of knowledge about cultures to become familiar with the diverse religious and spiritual traditions of those with whom they work. Specifically, social workers can

- increase their awareness of spirituality in themselves and their clients,
- respect differences resulting from religious diversity,
- clarify points of religious bias and the implication of this bias for practice,
- appreciate the significance and meaning of religious metaphors, and
- identify the resources of other professionals who have sensitivity and skill for working with particular aspects of religious diversity.

Persons with Disabilities

The U.S. Census Bureau estimates that about 37.5 million people in the United States of all ages and not living in institutions, or about 12.1 percent, have a disability (Erickson et al., 2014). Many persons with disabilities face challenges in accomplishing life tasks. For example, 28.4 percent of all those between 18 and 64 years of age with disabilities had incomes below the poverty line in 2012. Not only do physical and/or mental conditions limit their opportunities, but according to the **social model of disability**, social context imposes restrictions as well (Barnes & Mercer, 2004; Graf et al., 2009; Oliver, 1996, 1997; Woodcock & Tregaskis, 2008). Stigma, interpersonal degradation, and social marginality lead others to underestimate the capabilities of persons with disabilities as they successfully fulfill meaningful social roles.

Competent social workers recognize that people with physical, cognitive, and psychological disabilities also demonstrate abilities. "A collaborative approach to practice with people with disabilities must be founded on the fact that they are people first and disabled second" (Gilson et al., 1998, p. 194). Just like other human beings, individuals with disabilities draw strengths from their own personal resolve, positive self-images, aspirations, priorities, creativity, supportive relationships with family members and friends, successful rehabilitation, and use of adaptive devices.

A strengths perspective of persons with disabilities focuses on capabilities and indicates that the locus of issues is within the transactions between persons and their physical and social environments, noting environmental limitations in addressing the needs of those with disabilities. The focus for intervention shifts from what's wrong with the client to what can change in the environment that will allow a unique client's strengths to surface. Progressive legislative mandates—such as the **Americans with Disabilities Act (1990)**, which legislated removal of architectural, transportation, and communication barriers—are examples of environmental changes that can ensure the full participation of persons with disabilities in community life.

Clients as Resources for Understanding Cultures

A general knowledge of culture and ethnicity sensitizes practitioners to the diversity of potential resources within various population groups, but, even among people with similar cultural identities, workers remain cautious about overgeneralizing. "The capacity for individualizing the client within a specific cultural matrix is the genius and the challenge of effective cross-cultural social work" (Green, 1999, p. 92).

Luckily, as practitioners work to activate clients' cultural strengths, they have key respondents with them in the same room. Clients themselves provide the best information about their cultural strengths and resources. When social workers bring general cultural awareness, openness to differences, and good listening skills, along with permission for clients to be themselves, workers learn how to relate competently to clients in their cultural contexts.

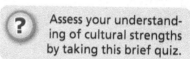

Assess your understanding of cultural strengths by taking this brief quiz.

UNCOVERING STRENGTHS IN ADVERSITY

Since the advent of psychoanalysis, helping professionals have searched the past to account for why things have gone wrong in the present. In this view, the scars of trauma and adversity can accumulate to overwhelming proportions. Strengths-oriented social workers acknowledge that in spite of adversity, somehow people continue on their way. Over time, clients who have experienced victimization become survivors. Surviving difficulties such as oppression, violence, or family disruptions takes courage and strength. Practitioners working with survivors of adversity will discover skills, abilities, and resources when exploring their clients' success in making it this far.

Surviving Oppression

Members of some cultural groups share similar histories and experiences with respect to oppression. Oppression occurs "when a person is blocked from opportunities to self-development...not because of individual failure, but because of his or her membership in a particular group or category of people" (Mullaly, 2002, p. 28). **Racism**, **sexism**, **ageism**, **ableism**, **heterosexism**, **regionalism**, and **classism** are all various forms of oppression. Each form of prejudice and discrimination denies members of a particular group access to their fair share of society's resources, violating human rights and principles of social justice.

Consistent with the mission of their profession, social workers commit to fighting oppression. Workers intervene at the macrolevel to create changes in social policy, helping to ensure universal access to social and economic resources. They also develop their micropractice skills to identify and eradicate their own tendencies to perpetuate oppressive practices in relationships with clients, including microaggressions. Preventing oppression is the goal, but until achieving the ideal of social justice, practitioners will likely interact with many clients coping with oppressive forces. Seeking to empower clients, social workers look beyond the damage that oppression may have caused to applaud the strengths that these same clients have brought to bear in handling injustice.

Workers intervene at the macrolevel to create changes in social policy, helping to ensure universal access to social and economic resources.

Successful Coping Skills

When denied access to societal benefits, people learn to cope in other ways. They group together for support and political power. They help each other out in times of need. They find ways to take advantage of the limited opportunities available. They create informal systems to circumvent the need to access existing discriminatory formal institutional processes. Clear examples of adaptive responses to oppression are evident in the resources developed by African Americans and Native Americans.

"African Americans have a history of drawing upon inner and extended family resources to survive from one generation to the next, no matter what the obstacles and indignities" (Franklin, 1993, p. 37). The strong extended family network present in many African American families has roots in their African heritage and has endured as a response to slavery, threat, and oppression (Boyd-Franklin, 1992). Informal adoption practices exemplify another way that African American families have developed their own resources to operate outside of the institution of the formal child welfare system. A strong connection to history by African American clients draws on the legacy of their cultural identity and their success even in the face of the past abuse of slavery. To bring out these strengths, Franklin suggests asking African American clients to describe the survivors known to them in their own family histories and guide them to search for these same qualities in themselves.

Native Americans have endured many injustices at the hands of the U.S. government. Their separate and unequal treatment is evidenced by a history of extermination, forced residence on reservations, and mandatory assimilation of Native American children into the cultural mainstream. Clustered on reservations offering little economic opportunity, Native Americans have experienced high rates of unemployment, poverty, infant mortality, and reduced life expectancy. Yet, their unique status as federal wards rather than state citizens has led to creative survival strategies. Not subject to state regulation, nearly 200 tribes have successfully launched gambling operations on their reservations. This economic development has produced many benefits for tribal members. Mortality rates have also decreased. Although subjected to oppression, these Native American tribes have found ways to thrive.

Practice-Informed Research

Behavior: Apply critical thinking to engage in analysis of quantitative and qualitative research methods and research findings

Critical Thinking Question: A strengths-based social worker might believe that a person's victimization frequently leads to the development of resilience and strengths. How can a social worker test this hypothesis by using qualitative or quantitative social work research methods?

Other cultural groups have also responded to oppression with creative survival strategies. The women's movement of the 1960s and 1970s advanced the cause of women's rights. This political movement was fueled by the power of women and their allies joining together. Older Americans are also asserting their political power through associations such as the American Association of Retired Persons (AARP). Persons with disabilities have also responded to social exclusion with community activism that has led to legislative changes and political gains.

Responding to Clients Who Are Oppressed

Members of oppressed groups have likely overcome difficult odds. Oppressed clients may benefit from exploring the ways they accomplished this. To do so, workers acknowledge clients' feelings of oppression and then urge them on to describe the ways they have coped with unfair treatment. Workers may say any of the following:

- I know you're right that it's not easy to be an African American in a racist community, but somehow you seem able to cope. How is it that you manage so well?
- It does seem like the school picks on you because you're different. Are there other gay students that you know that seem to get by? What are they doing to cope?
- I agree that this neighborhood doesn't seem to get the same services that the rest of the city gets. I'm so impressed with the way all of you work together, pool your resources, and find ways to cope in spite of the neglect. What do you think we can do to advocate with city officials for better treatment?

In each example, the worker does not underestimate the devastating impact of social injustice, but neither does the worker ignore that clients are making it in spite of the adversity.

Surviving Violence

Many social work clients have experienced various forms of violence, including intimate partner violence, war, natural disaster, or political upheaval. Such trauma can be devastating. But each survivor of such an event has found ways to get through each day in spite of the difficult circumstances. Social workers can assist these clients by first helping them unload their pain and then by directing clients' attention back to their capabilities and survival strategies.

Domestic Violence

Persons victimized by domestic violence or intimate partner violence require immediate social work assistance to ensure their safety and to provide medical services, emotional support, and legal advocacy. But even with an effective response to the crisis event, a client who experiences such intimate violence may continue to have adverse consequences as he or she moves on with life. Being violated by traumatic events tests one's personal strength. Clients who have survived incidents of such violence in the near or distant past have already passed the test.

Danis (2004) notes several strengths developed by women who have experienced abusive relationships, including risk-assessment skills, persistence in working to resolve their relationships, loyalty to and protectiveness of their children, supportive informal helping networks, and spirituality. Social workers with survivors of domestic violence listen carefully to survivors' stories to discover what resources they have used to cope and survive. Key to transcending intimate violence is the restoration of power and choice (Peled et al., 2000). Many women in these situations already demonstrate the power to cope, as evidenced by their positive self-regard and refusal to accept blame for the abuse (Hensley, 2002).

War

Veterans returning from overseas wars suffer significant effects from the horror and stress of war-related activities. Posttraumatic stress disorder (PTSD) and traumatic brain injury (TBI), along with other physical injuries, are frequent consequences of the war zone experience (DOD, 2007). Many veterans also experience disruption in family and community relationships on their return home. Yet, each returning soldier has a survival story that illustrates how he or she has drawn on significant skills and resources in the process.

Certainly, responsible social workers screen for difficulties that veterans may be facing, but strength-based practitioners also recognize the significant accomplishments of coping with such dire circumstances. The 2007 Report of the Department of Defense Task Force on Mental Health questions the current system of health care for veterans, citing its use of the disease-based medical model as possibly a poor fit for the psycho-social symptoms experienced by many veterans. Reacting to this report, Wheeler and Bragin (2007) suggest that "it is time for social work to bring its methods of inquiry to bear on the development of and advocacy for culturally informed, strengths-based, biopsychosocial approaches to work with veterans" (p. 299).

An empowering social worker's task is to bring the strengths of veterans to the forefront. Research shows that social support from family, friends, and other veterans may be significant resources for veterans' reintegration postdeployment (Laffaye et al., 2008). Other strengths that social workers may discover in veterans include maintaining a positive view of life, recognizing purpose in life, showing ability to achieve intimacy in relationships, and framing the war experience as some kind of beneficial life lesson (Fournier, 2002).

Forced Migration

All immigrants face the stress of adapting to a new culture. Refugees who are forced from their homes by **forced migration** related to violent political upheaval or devastating natural disasters such as hurricanes, typhoons, or drought confront challenges beyond the expected cultural adaptation required of those who voluntarily migrate. Many refugees have little time to prepare for the events that dislodge them from their homes. Escape from the situation usually involves fear, anxiety, and witnessing traumatic events. Many refugees spend months or even years in temporary camps or shelters that offer subsistence living standards and are frequently rocked by food shortages, water scarcity, and disease.

The evidence is compelling. In one study, more than 70 percent of refugees fleeing political violence in Sri Lanka reported being hurt in their homeland through physical abuse, emotional trauma, and torture (Weaver & Burns, 2001). Another study revealed that Vietnamese parents who had endured refugee camps raised children more prone to violence than expected compared with normative data (Spencer & Le, 2006). Social workers are challenged to counteract the negative consequences associated with forced migration by recognizing the less salient characteristics that reveal client strengths.

Where do social workers look for strengths in refugees? Using teachers' observations of refugee children, one study directs workers to recognize that students who were refugees may act with unusual respect and also to notice that their parents will likely become involved immediately in any issues affecting their children (Szente et al., 2006). Other experts direct the search for resilience toward exploring each phase of the refugee's migration, including the reasons for leaving the home country, experiences in transit, and the resettlement experience in the new community (Pine & Drachman, 2005). Through this careful retracing of the refugee's path, a strength-focused social worker can highlight the adaptive mechanisms used by the refugee during each phase and consider how these demonstrated abilities may benefit the refugee in resolving current challenges.

Diversity in Survivors' Experiences

Workers acknowledge that there is no right way to respond to violence but recognize that survivors draw on their own developed strengths as they cope. Social workers should remain alert to the different ways that people from various cultures cope. "Too often, the active coping strategies of clients who have little social power are misinterpreted as passivity and giving up" (Holzman, 1994, p. 95). Although workers may readily see strengths in clients who are survivors, not all clients are ready to openly acknowledge that they have gone on. On a cautionary note, workers should not move too quickly to point out the successful ways clients are coping. Clients may first need to experience a worker's empathy and understanding before being able to benefit from a worker's admiration.

Surviving Family Disruption

The impact on children of families that experience disruption is a contemporary issue that receives much attention, giving rise to such support groups as Adult Children of Alcoholics (ACOA). Many helping professionals trace the difficulties adults experience to childhood roots in dysfunctional family functioning. In some ways, we are all affected by the dynamics of our families of origin. Each of us develops in unique familial and other social contexts. Each of us carries the impact of these interpersonal systems with us. Each of us also makes choices about how we respond to these influences. Think about your own life, the ways your family has affected and is affecting you, and the choices that you make in response.

Strengths-oriented social workers acknowledge the inevitable power that families have over children, yet also realize that all persons develop ways to cope. "Care should be taken not to assume that each person who was abused as a child will necessarily be under extreme distress as an adult" (Busby et al., 1993, p. 338). "Strength can emerge from adversity" and result in resiliencies that promote well-being (Wolin & Wolin, 1993, p. 15). Workers certainly empathize with difficult past family experiences, but they also press clients further to explore how clients have responded to historical events. Workers may say any of the following:

- Growing up in an alcoholic family does leave its mark, and I see that you have a good job, a nice home, and people who care about you. How have you managed all of this?
- It must have been terrifying to know that your father was determined to commit suicide. What did you do to overcome that fear and anxiety?
- Growing up in your family meant that you had to grow up fast, almost like you never really got to be a kid. What ways have you found to relax and have fun now that you are in charge of your own life?

? Assess your understanding of uncovering strengths in diversity by taking this brief quiz.

Workers do not underestimate the difficulty of childhood abandonment, neglect, or trauma, nor do they undervalue the strengths survivors have developed in response.

LOOKING FORWARD

Implementing a strengths perspective means shifting focus with clients to highlight their capabilities and successes along with identifying their problems. A social worker's ability to identify strengths springs from a general understanding of what constitutes adaptive human system functioning in individuals, families, groups, organizations, and communities. Practitioners implement solution-focused dialogue skills to maximize the possibility of uncovering strengths and potential solutions. By critically applying social work research, workers can hone in on strengths potentially possessed by members of various ethnic and cultural groups. Social workers also remain alert for the emergent strengths evident in those who have faced and overcome historical adversity.

Clients do not stand alone in mustering their capabilities to meet their challenges. They also have the resources of their social and physical environments. Chapter 10 describes additional assessment processes for social workers to discover what clients' environments might offer to achieve goals.

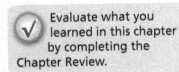

Evaluate what you learned in this chapter by completing the Chapter Review.

Assessment: Assessing Resource Capabilities

MICHAELJUNG/FOTOLIA

When you consider moving into a house, you want to see more than one room. No matter how impressed you are with the first room you see, you still want to explore the entire house—the other rooms, the attic, the basement, the yard. You may even want to stroll around the neighborhood. Because you know that the ambience of one room alone does not define the experience of living in the whole house, you ask to see it all. Life in one room responds to and affects the rest of the house, the yard, and the neighborhood, just as life in the entire house, yard, and neighborhood responds to and affects life in one room.

Clients may not lead social workers around to the "other rooms, yards, or neighborhoods" of their lives unless workers ask for a tour. A generalist **assessment** does more than articulate clients' and constituencies' situations and identify their strengths; it assesses the resource capabilities of client systems. Regardless of the level of the client system, an assessment of resources at all system levels broadens the area of potential solutions. When social workers guide clients to look beyond their immediate situations to explore contextual systems more thoroughly, they discover new information, resources, and opportunities. Discoveries enable social workers and clients to decipher the relationships among events and identify untapped, yet accessible, resources.

An empowering generalist assessment goes beyond simply listing client and environmental resources. The inquiry of assessment, itself, creates change. As a result, social workers move cautiously through this discovery phase to explore and respond productively. The choices clients and social workers make about what to explore begin to shape the possibilities for the solutions they will frame. The processes used in exploring set expectations for clients' involvement in change. With its emphasis on collaboration, this process activates clients to take charge of their own inquiry and builds momentum in their support networks to sustain changes.

This chapter discusses ways that clients and workers evaluate resources available to clients and constituencies in their environments. An assessment of available resources leads practitioners and clients to distribute their change efforts wisely, selecting strategies that draw on existing client strengths and activate accessible environmental resources.

EXPLORING RESOURCE SYSTEMS THROUGH ASSESSMENT

Assessment clarifies "what is the matter" and leads to decisions about courses of action to undertake. Importantly, the assessment process also defines the nature of the working relationship between client and practitioner. Even when clients look for workers to take charge, empowering practitioners move to establish equal partnerships as they, together with clients, gather information and define the direction for change. Throughout the discovery phase, workers continue to construct empowering relationships with clients as they mutually assess the situation at hand and determine where the relationship is going.

Social workers and clients assess resource systems to discover assets not causes or reasons, focusing on areas of competence in client–environment transactions. Assessment clarifies three facets of these transactions: (1) clients' unique capacities, capabilities, and potential; (2) environmental characteristics and resources; and (3) changes that need to be made to enhance transactions (Labassi & Maluccio, 1986). In the spirit of empowerment, assessment is a process for discovering resources. Like strengths, resources are relative, identifiable only in context. The actual ways clients interact with their social and physical environments determine what functions as resources for them. To complete an assessment, the partners explore broadly for resources that may be present in the environment, in the interactions of clients with others, and even in other challenges that clients are facing. Considering environmental contexts is also pivotal in understanding the sources of client stress as well as in identifying resources for framing solutions.

In the spirit of empowerment, assessment is a process for discovering resources.

Recognizing Environmental Resources

Social workers often locate resources in clients' physical and social environments. For individuals, environmental resource systems may include family, friends, neighbors, co-workers, supervisors, classmates, teachers, social groups, school, church, social agencies, organizations, and the community. For a nonprofit organization, contextual resource systems may include consumers, funding bodies, foundations, professional organizations, local colleges, and other agencies in the service delivery network. For any human system, regardless of size, environmental resources are essential for survival and well-being.

Furthermore, considering environmental contexts is pivotal in understanding the sources of client stress as well as in identifying resources for framing solutions. Contextual social work practice involves "practice both with and within context" (Fook, 2002, p. 143). This idea means that in developing practice strategies, social workers must emphasize context, work simultaneously with all players within and outside of the client system, and develop transferable knowledge for practice across different contexts. In other words, social work practice encompasses the understanding that "physical and social environments are deeply implicated in patterns of social opportunity and constraint, and it is essential that social workers be able to read them in this way" (Kemp et al., 2002, p. 20).

> Watch this video and identify skills the social worker uses to collaborate. What else should the worker do to conduct an ecosystems assessment that discovers environmental resources? www.youtube.com/watch?v=IfdApaOlt4E

Every part of our lives contributes to or hinders our ability to maneuver successfully through life. Consider your situation as an example. What in your environment facilitates your work? Likely you are reading this book as part of a social work class. Does the instructor frame this information in such a way as to enhance your understanding? Do you have classmates with whom you will discuss this material to augment your comprehension? Do you have children for whom your spouse, partner, or friends provide child care so that you can study? Do you have a quiet place to read—the school library, your own room, or a picnic table in the park? The presence or absence of these supportive resources has a lot to do with your success in completing your studies.

Look further, and you will also discover other systems that provide resources. How is it that you find yourself in this classroom? Is your family providing financial support? Are you receiving government loans or grants to pay expenses? Are you getting scholarships from community organizations, your church, or the college to defray your costs? Are you working to pay your own way so that your place of employment is a resource to guarantee your education? Does your ethnic or cultural identity place a high value on educational achievement? The presence or absence of these environmental resources influences whether you have the opportunity for academic success and a career as a social worker. Resource systems—from personal support networks to institutional systems—contribute to even the simplest transaction. Recognizing resources requires awareness of environmental contexts, sensitivity to cultural differences, and openness to a broad range of possibilities.

Turning Challenging Situations into Resources

Certainly, not all aspects of ecosystems are resources per se. A comprehensive assessment frequently leads to a different kind of discovery—the discovery of other problems or challenges—but challenges can actually be resources rather than additional constraints. The key is how workers respond. Disempowering responses stack the newly found problems on the others already described. Visualize how this leads to stigmatizing clients with labels such as "multiproblem" or to ascribing blame for "who is causing what." Contrast this response with a more empowering perspective that suggests that recognizing common links among challenging events provides new insights about situations and expands options for change. Notice in the example that follows how an ecological assessment uncovers additional challenges yet enlarges the arena of potential solutions.

An African American woman, Latasha, consults with a social worker about her feelings of depression. Latasha shares her frustration and disappointment in not securing a job in law enforcement despite her obvious qualifications and credentials. Broadening the search for resources to local law enforcement agencies reveals a new challenge—a pattern of discriminatory hiring and promotion practices with respect to women and people of color. Discovering this additional challenge of institutional sexism and racism links Latasha's depression, her unemployment, and the discriminatory hiring practices. Latasha's options for change now expand beyond the personal realm to include political and legal strategies for confronting the discrimination. Latasha's exercise of political power is now an option—an avenue to restore her sense of personal control and relieve her depression.

Collaborating to Search for Resources

Social workers guide clients through an exploration of resource systems, but who or what guides social workers? Environmental contexts are enormous. A thorough examination of inside realms, outside environments, and the relationships between systems and their contexts literally goes on forever. After all, while you are examining any system, it remains dynamic, everchanging, and constantly evolving, even in response to the discovery process itself.

Take care, however, not to fall prey to the trap of certainty that classic diagnosis or categorical labels invite. Merely labeling behavior oversimplifies complex dynamics of human interactions and tends to limit options. Amundson and colleagues (1993) advocate a questioning and tentative attitude rather than a precise and expert posture to maintain an empowering frame during assessment to avoid "the temptation to enact our privilege, to impose upon others normalizing standards or to be blinded to diversity by the 'professional' certainties of our practice" (p. 111).

This advice leads social workers to offer their reflections in tentative and thought-provoking ways and encourage clients to do the same. Workers purposefully share their thoughts to stimulate new interpretations, develop usable theories, and suggest possible directions in ways that encourage mutual discourse. However, rather than stating the certainties, social workers offer hunches and possibilities with phrases such as the following:

- I wonder if . . .
- Is it fair to say that at this time . . .
- I have a hunch that I'd like your opinion about. Have you ever considered . . .
- I'm noticing that Hector's legal problems started at the same time your father died. From your point of view, does it look like . . .

- As I've listened to the Task Force's discussion, I believe that at this time, you've identified three major areas to consider for action . . .
- There may be more, but I seem to hear two different ways of interpreting this situation.

Social workers' insights may, indeed, "unstick" client systems. However, for clients to remain in charge of meaning, social workers phrase their comments in ways that level authority and invite a client to support or disagree with their hypotheses. In recognizing a client's expertise, social workers do not abandon their theoretical knowledge and practice wisdom. Instead, reflective practitioners recognize that the authority of their knowledge has the potential to disempower clients. As Hartman (1992) advises: "We need not discard our knowledge, but we must be open to local knowledge, to the narratives and the truths of our clients . . . to honor and validate our clients' expertise" (p. 484). To define the scope of a comprehensive assessment, practitioners rely on clues from clients. Through this process, workers and clients maintain an informed perspective on what to assess and the ability to screen for what else they need to know.

Adding Viewpoints

All clients enter social work services with their own particular views of their situations. No matter how openly social workers and clients talk, what clients know and report, or what social workers hear and deduce is but a small part of the available information. Soliciting the viewpoints of others provides fresh perspectives and adds indispensable heterogeneity to the information base. Clients and social workers access alternative views by bringing in significant others and collecting information from other professionals.

Bringing in Significant Others

Rather than just talking about what happens in particular environments, social workers and clients have options for inviting others from that environment to present their views. For example, certain situations lead logically to involving others within the client's ecosystem. When practitioners work with young children, older clients who are frail, or persons with severe developmental disabilities or chronic illnesses, it makes sense to include persons most intensively involved in caregiving roles. A client's cultural background also may provide practitioners with clues about other significant people to involve.

Accessing information directly from collateral resource systems has several advantages. More than simply contributing alternative views, it provides clients with direct access to new information within the supportive atmosphere of the social work relationship and affords social workers a clear view of clients in transaction with significant others. Bringing in others begins the process of activating the natural support network on behalf of clients and involves those who are likely to experience effects as client systems change. Also, involving others affords clients opportunities to witness the motivations, resources, and strengths of social supports. This information will be important as clients and social workers attempt to shift the functioning of the ecosystem into patterns that help clients reach desired goals.

Contacting Other Professionals

Many clients are involved with more than one type of formal system, so additional perspectives may be available from psychiatrists, psychologists, physicians, nurses, teachers, ministers, and other helping professionals. Choosing which of these perspectives to access depends on several factors. First, those resources clients consider most significant and acceptable clearly direct these choices because clients themselves control the flow of information between professionals. Additionally, if the social worker and client anticipate that a particular helping system may be a future target for change, this may be a particularly good time to initiate contact, assess, and involve that system. Finally, social workers and clients may discover needs for more information or additional evaluations. Depending on the client's situation, it may be appropriate to consult with physicians, psychologists, occupational therapists, addiction specialists, urban planners, or a myriad of other professionals and organizations.

The way practitioners access information from other professionals makes a difference. Without exception, to legitimate communication with others about clients, social workers must obtain clients' permission or informed consent, as documented by a signed release of information. This means clients themselves decide whether to give social workers permission to gather information from significant others, records, or other professionals. Clients need to know who is being contacted, what information is sought, why the information is required, and what consequences result if they refuse to permit the contact. Practitioners discuss possible sources of information in consultation with clients and, when feasible, encourage clients to handle the arrangements. When clients discuss, arrange, and follow through on gathering additional information from other professionals, they assume their rightful roles and responsibilities in this process.

Assessing Through Observation

The client system, itself, is an important resource for generating new information. Think about it. Any client system's functioning is a dynamic demonstration of its ability to draw on internal and environmental resources. Clients and workers can use this to their advantage by designing ways to observe clients in action.

Observations by Clients

Frequently, social workers and clients are operating on vague generalities that require "all or nothing" solutions rather than concrete data that can lead to a more client-specific approach. In these situations, social workers and clients construct observations to objectify and update assessment information.

Consider the following example. Tanya confides to Kennedy Brown, the social worker at OPTIONS—an agency providing services for older adults—that her father, Reginald, has lost his ability to take care of himself. "All or nothing" thinking leads Tanya directly to the single option of placing her father in a nursing home. A new understanding emerges when Tanya observes and charts what Reginald still does for himself as well as what she does for him. With all or nothing thinking, nursing home placement was a fait accompli. Considering more objective observations leads Tanya and Kennedy to redefine the situation and select viable options from community-based services to promote Reginald's independence by maintaining him in his home.

Notice, in this example, how Tanya observes not only what Reginald is unable to do but also what he can still do for himself. Strengths-oriented workers check their tendencies to suggest that clients go out and observe only their problems. What kind of effect can you predict if clients observe "the problem" and learn everything that they can about it? Instead, imagine asking clients to review their situations for times when things are going well. Which is the more productive observation—the focus on problems or the focus on exceptions? What do clients discover as they watch the successful parts of their experiences? Consider these examples:

Social workers who are self-aware identify the dynamics of their own responses to differentiate those provoked by personal issues from those triggered by clients.

- When a neighborhood group believes the city council is not listening to them, selected group members can attend council meetings to see who the council does heed and what approaches these other people use.
- When domestic partners who are both employed disagree on who is doing more housekeeping, a structured observation not only provides objective data but also clarifies the extent of household tasks necessary if the couple chooses to renegotiate their distribution.

Observations by Workers

Observing our own reactions to clients and observing how clients interact with others provides additional information. Specifically, workers monitor their own responses, clients' interactions with others, and the interactions within multiperson client systems.

As social workers, we learn what responses to expect in ourselves as we relate to clients. To learn about clients, we ask ourselves about our own thoughts, feelings, and reactions. For example, do we look forward to meetings with clients? Do we feel hopeful or invigorated? Do we distance ourselves or become angry? Do we feel an urge to "take care" of clients? Do we call clients to remind them of appointments, give them rides back and forth, or tell them what to do rather than discuss possibilities? Social workers who are self-aware identify the dynamics of their own responses to differentiate those provoked by personal issues from those triggered by clients. To remain objective, social workers strive to keep personal responses separate and share their observations about clients constructively.

The potentially rich information embedded within direct interactions prompts social workers to invite significant others to meetings with clients. Consider Robert, a client in the community-integrated employment program of the Area Association for People with Disabilities. Robert complains to his case manager that his sister, Barbara, always rifles through his personal belongings. Robert agrees to the worker's suggestion that they invite Barbara to talk with them together. When Barbara explains that she is only separating the laundry, a clearer picture emerges. By observing the interaction between Robert and his sister, the worker discovers a pattern of caretaking in which Barbara seems to assume Robert isn't capable—Barbara leads Robert into the office, tells him where to sit, and answers all questions directed to her brother. The worker also notes that Robert's passive response validates his sister's view and encourages her seemingly controlling behavior. These observations provide resources for developing a plan for working out the conflict between the siblings.

Working with multiperson client systems offers workers a firsthand view of the system's structures and interactional patterns. Consider the assessment information available to a social worker from observing a community action group. The worker discovers the group's power structure by noting who speaks and who agrees with the speaker. When the group seeks volunteers to form a steering committee, indigenous leaders come forward, prodded by those who recognize these members as natural choices. By observing who initiates conversations, who contributes the most, who has the last word, and toward whom members look when it's time to respond the worker discovers clues about who is in charge. Subsystem boundaries and member alliances are apparent in seating arrangements, who arrives at the meeting together, who supports whose ideas, and who shares common concerns. The worker can determine the extent of the group's development by observing members' abilities to function as a team in planning activities, the degree of respect shown in how well members listen to one another, and the level of agreement about the group's goals. Direct observation provides concrete assessment information about group structures, process, and development in addition to revealing the strengths of various members.

> **?** Assess your understanding of exploring resource systems through assessment by taking this brief quiz.

ORGANIZING ASSESSMENT BY USING A 5-POINT ECOSYSTEMS SCHEMA

Social workers use frameworks drawn from theories about human system behavior and theories of change to organize the search for resources. Some assessment frameworks apply to human systems at all levels, whereas others are specific to particular situations. The ecosystems framework introduced in Chapter 2 is an example appropriate for generalist practice because it flexibly applies to any system level.

This ecosystems framework organizes the search for resources into a simple 5-point schema. Applying this strategy, practitioners begin by clearly identifying the focal system. From there, the framework guides workers and clients to explore what happens inside this system, what happens outside this system, how the inside and the outside of the system connect, and what happens as the system progresses through time. Applying this framework to any client system produces a dynamic explanation of its functioning in context and uncovers available resources (Figure 10.1).

An ecosystems assessment is a multifaceted description of client system functioning in context. Social workers combine respectful listening with clarifications, summaries, selective questions, and validating feedback to access information framed by the questions below.

Identify the Focal System

- Who are the system's members?
- What characteristics define their membership in the system?

Inside the System Structural Dimensions: Closeness

- What are the subsystems?
- Who supports whom?
- Are members close to one another or isolated?

Structural Dimensions: Power

- What is the system's hierarchy?
- Who is in charge?
- Who makes decisions?
- Who enforces decisions?
- Do members function autonomously or interdependently?

Figure 10.1 (continued)
Ecosystems Assessment Framework

Interactional Dimensions

- How do members communicate?
- Do members talk directly to one another or do they route messages through third parties?
- Do members offer constructive feedback to one another?
- What are the rules and norms for behavior?
- Does everyone share responsibility?

Biopsychosocial Dimensions

- Are members physically healthy?
- What are the special physical abilities and needs of members?
- How do issues of development and maturation affect the functioning of the system?
- How do members feel?
- Do members share their feelings openly?
- How do members think?
- Do members share their own thoughts and respect the contributions of others?
- What are the individual strengths of various members?

Cultural Dimensions

- What are the various cultural influences?
- Do common cultural identities bind members together?
- How do cultural differences influence the relationships within the system?
- What are the predominant beliefs and values of members?
- Are there cultural influences on communication?

Spiritual Dimensions

- What spiritual and/or religious traditions influence the system?
- How do system members define spiritual concepts?
- What meanings evolve from spirituality?
- What spiritual strengths are present?
- What resources are available through connections with religious or spiritual communities?

Outside the System

- What systems are influential in the environment of the focal system? Consider from among the following depending on the level of the system:
  - Family and extended family members
  - Friends, neighbors, natural support networks
  - Neighborhood, community
  - Organizations, groups
  - Social agencies
  - Social institutions
  - Economic systems
  - Government bodies
  - Policies, laws, regulations
- How are these influential systems connected to one another?
- What are the influences of the physical environment?
- What potential resources exist that the system currently does not access?

Figure 10.1 (continued)

Inside and Outside Connections

- Does the focal system's boundary tend to be open or closed?
- What information flows across this boundary?
- Does the system acquire necessary resources from the environment?
- What does the system contribute to the environment?
- Are some members more connected to the outside than others?
- Does the system have power in relationship to outside systems or is it overpowered by environmental demands?
- What outside systems provide stability?
- What outside influences tend to disrupt the system's functioning?
- What is the system's view of the larger environment? Does it see it as threatening or friendly?
- How is the system's cultural identity viewed in the larger environment?
- Is the system at risk of discrimination or oppression?

Movement through Time

- What is the expected development of the system?
- What physical, psychological, emotional, cognitive, moral, and systemic transitions are occurring at this time?
- How is the system handling these transitions?
- What nodal events characterize the system's development?
- How did the system respond to these nodal events?
- Does the system flexibly adapt to meet the needs of members?
- Does the system flexibly adapt to changing environmental demands?
- Were there times in the past when the system worked the way members would like?
- What development changes are expected in the near future?

Figure 10.1 (continued)

Practice Example: Franklin Courts

The following example demonstrates how applying the ecosystems framework organizes the activities of Damon Edwards and the residents of Franklin Courts to assess the situation in the housing complex.

The residents of Franklin Courts are angry. During a routine preschool screening, six children living at the low-income housing complex tested positive for lead contamination. The media reports that parents demand action! The housing authority says only that "we will look into it." Damon Edwards, a social worker in the outreach and advocacy services division of the Neighbors United Neighborhood Development Program, is also "looking into it." Fiona Grant, the grandmother of one of the six children, called Damon to discuss the situation. Damon already knows Mrs. Grant from his work with the youth recreation program. She is a powerful and energetic resident of Franklin Courts. Damon is pleased that Mrs. Grant sees him as a resource. Damon

Assessment

Behavior: Apply knowledge of human behavior and the social environment, person-in-environment, and other multidisciplinary theoretical frameworks in the analysis of assessment data from clients and constituencies

Critical Thinking Question: In the Franklin Courts case example, social worker Damon Edwards applies an ecosystems view informed by his knowledge of the bio-psycho-social dimensions of human behavior to structure his assessment. What characteristics of this ecosystems schema make it a good fit for an assessment from a social work perspective?

doesn't know what he will find in his meeting with the residents that Mrs. Grant promises to gather. However, he has a way to look at the situation that will give him a sense of what's going on and direction for ways he might contribute. Damon applies an ecosystems framework to ensure a generalist approach to assessment.

What's the Focal System?

As always, Damon first identifies the focal system. In this situation, he knows that he will work with a group system. Mrs. Grant was acting on behalf of all the concerned residents. This, coupled with the urgency of the issue at hand, the common goal of the residents, and the fact that residents are already beginning to function in a collective manner, indicates that group action will be a likely strategy for success.

Identifying the group of residents as his client allows Damon to continue to frame his approach. He will need to look inside the group, at its membership, to discover its resources. He will also need to look outside the group to understand environmental opportunities and constraints. Damon doesn't yet know the kinds of linkages this particular group of residents has to resources in the community, but, certainly, exploring these connections will be important. Finally, Damon will examine the group's process and organizational structure. Theory informs him about effective group development. Damon's task will be as much to encourage the growth of the group itself as it will be to work toward the group's goals.

What's Inside the System?

At the first meeting of the Franklin Courts group, Damon discovers that the crisis of the high lead levels in the children and the potential for further lead contamination has indeed activated the residents of Franklin Courts. Twenty-four adults attend the meeting; three other residents are babysitting so that other parents can attend. Much is happening inside the group. Certain members have taken leadership roles. Mrs. Grant is obviously the spokesperson. She convenes the meeting and seems to be in charge of the agenda. When the group adjourns, Mrs. Grant, along with three other influential group members, volunteers to meet with Damon to plan and bring back recommendations to the group's next meeting. Also, smaller groups are beginning to form around specific issues of concern. The parents of the six children need to arrange immediate specialized assessment of their children's health. Several other residents want to press for an investigation into the source of the contamination and prevent further exposure. Damon quickly sees the possibility for task-oriented subcommittees to work concurrently in multiple directions rather than having the whole group continue its debate over what specific outcome to seek first.

What's Outside the System?

Outside of the group, not too much is happening yet to address the concerns of the Franklin Courts residents. Despite the housing authority's promise to look into the lead contamination, the residents have heard nothing from them. The media have expressed interest but have not yet provided extensive reports. On a positive note, the doctor who discovered the problem is sympathetic and willing to support the group's action. And, of course, because the group called Damon, the resources of Neighbors United are accessible to them.

How Does the Inside Connect to the Outside?

Damon sees the group's relationship to the community as a resource to develop. Certainly, the group's connections with other systems need strengthening. For example, somewhere in the city's administration, the housing authority is accountable to a higher office; the Franklin Courts group would benefit from a strong relationship with whomever this might be. Making this important link will increase the group's power in working with the housing authority. Damon also considers the doctor and the media as resources the group should continue to activate.

How Does the System Move Through Time?

Observing the group's developmental progress shows that it is maturing naturally in a productive way. The way the group itself organized child care during group meetings concretely demonstrates its positive development. Damon can build on the group's robust beginning. He will strive to clarify and cultivate the evolving structure and interaction of the group to maximize collaboration among members. Damon is beginning to understand the group's potential and direction.

Focusing on the residents' group as the client system, looking at its resources inside and out, assessing the group's transactions with its environment, and tracing the group's progress as it develops through time—all facets of an ecosystems assessment—contribute to Damon's broad view of what is happening with this particular group. The ecosystems framework offers a way to conceptualize the group throughout the entire process, from assessing the situation to implementing strategies for change.

> Watch this video as you consider that a generalist social work approach requires an ecosystems perspective. What elements of the analysis that these clients do reflect an ecosystems perspective?

Ecosystems Assessment Questions

In addition to the 5-point ecosystems schema, a more robust assessment expands this framework to elucidate client system functioning in context. In this regard, ecosystems assessment questions solicit clarifying information about human system functioning. The following sections detail questions for assessing structures, assessing interactions, assessing thinking and feeling, assessing cultural influences, assessing spiritual dimensions, and assessing the physical environment. Answers to these questions construct a contextually based, comprehensive view of clients' situations.

Ecosystems Questions: Assessing Structures

Recall that the structural perspective on human systems examines the configuration of the ecosystem—the arrangement of interactions between the client system and its physical and social environments. The two most important structural elements are power and closeness or, in systemic terminology, hierarchies and boundaries. Assessing the hierarchies and boundaries of the client's ecosystem leads social workers and clients to understand which components may constrain the client and which hold resources for change.

Who Has the Power?

By definition, the success of an empowering social work process depends on clients gaining a sense of power and control. Identifying where the power currently lies is essential to this effort. Even when clients temporarily feel powerless, those persons or systems that contribute to powerlessness are potential sources of power. In other words, if you know where the power is, you know where client systems can get it. An assessment of the ecosystem identifies sources of power.

Consider the following example. A homeless family temporarily stays with a distant relative while waiting for an opening in a rent-subsidized housing complex. But policies at the city's housing authority require that families living in public shelters receive priority in renting available units. Although this policy has merit, it holds this homeless family hostage, leaving them only the alternative of moving from their temporary living arrangement into an overcrowded and understaffed shelter to become eligible for placement. Clearly, the housing authority and its policies have the power. Assessing this power distribution helps the worker and the family generate new strategies, which range from advocacy with the department to political strategies to initiate policy changes at the state level.

Another place to look for power is in the client system itself. Sometimes clients do exercise power and competence in certain areas of functioning but feel inadequate in others. For example, the neighborhood group that can organize a neighborhood watch program likely has many of the resource capabilities necessary to lobby a school board to institute cultural sensitivity training for teachers to meet the challenge of discriminatory educational practices and harsh discipline of ethnic minority students. When the answer to "where is the power?" is "with the client," the emphasis shifts from using the identified power in one area to meet the challenge in another. Workers and clients contemplate the following questions to discover power resources:

- Who or what has power?
- How does the client access it?
- Who or what can help the client gain power?
- What might get in the way?
- What power resources does the client already possess?
- What will the client do with the power?

What Connections Are Working?

Alliances within and between systems are important sources of support and assistance. Assessing who is close to whom, what resources clients use successfully, and what supports are already available to clients defines areas of the client's functioning to maintain, strengthen, and develop. For example, the existence of a supportive extended family is a resource for an individual client seeking a job. Extended family members may be willing to increase their support and provide child care, financial assistance for specialized training, transportation to fill out job applications, or encouragement during the stressful time of applying, interviewing, and waiting for a job offer. Existing connections are likely to be resources that social workers and clients can expand.

Assessing existing connections may also reveal that the client's boundaries are currently too open to other forces but, if redefined, have the potential to become resources. For example, consider Craig, a divorced father who has custody of his three children. Acknowledging the importance to his children of a strong relationship with their mother, Karen, Craig agrees to an open visitation policy whereby Karen can visit the children in his home whenever she chooses. When Craig and his social worker review the assessment information, they find that Craig has trouble establishing rules and enforcing discipline with the children, and Karen's unpredictable visits complicate this difficulty. Assessing this information identifies the need to renegotiate this boundary—to close it up somewhat—to maintain the relationship with the children's mother as a resource, yet fit her visits into an effective routine for the household.

A boundary assessment identifies how connections are working for the client. The answers to questions about boundaries supply information about the client's alliances with people and resources. Questions to consider include the following:

- What significant connections does the client have?
- Are these relationships functioning effectively?
- Could these connections serve as resources to address the client's current situation?
- What connections might need to be changed for them to function as resources?
- What might prevent the client from renegotiating these connections?

What Connections Are Missing?

When assessing how clients connect with others, the connections they lack also become evident. Just as open boundaries allow access to resources, closed boundaries block clients from obtaining resources. A lack of connection to interpersonal and community resources forces clients to meet all their needs on their own, a situation that is likely to deplete their energies rather than sustain their sense of power. Factors preventing a client from connecting to resources include insufficient information, inaccessible resources, financial constraints, ineligibility, transportation needs, suspicion, and fear.

Consider the example of Marian, a woman who feels powerless to have friends, spend time alone away from home, or buy anything for herself without permission. Marian feels trapped by the rigid control and physical power exerted by her husband, Doug. However, a comprehensive exploration of her ecosystem also reveals that Marian is unaware of the nearby domestic violence center, believes that she is not eligible for the woman's support group at her church, and no longer maintains contact with her own family of origin because they don't like Doug. All these components of Marian's ecosystem—her husband Doug, the domestic violence program, the church group, and her own family of origin—have the potential to be resources of power.

Think about the options created by identifying the missing connections. The worker recognizes that Doug is pivotal in this issue. He is disconnected from the social work endeavor and possibly from understanding Marian's situation. Obviously, if Doug changes his behavior toward Marian in ways that respect her freedom, she will gain a sense of power. The worker can connect Doug to Marian by inviting him to participate in the social work process. Even if the dynamics of this marriage are such that Doug chooses not to change or refuses to join the effort, outside sources of support such as the domestic violence program, the church, and her family may function to give Marian resources for survival should she decide to confront or leave Doug. Assessing Marian's world locates disconnections from these sources of power and identifies options for initiating empowering connections.

Questions that uncover missing connections include the following:

- Who is significant to the client system but uninvolved and might be invited to join the effort?
- What potential resources are present that the client might consider in new ways?

- What resources does the worker know about that the client doesn't?
- What is blocking the client from connecting to resources that might help?

Ecosystems Questions: Assessing Interactions

An assessment of interactions examines how people and their environments relate and evolve. Remember that human systems behave in ways that seek harmony and balance. What happens in a client system somehow is adaptive in its context. The interactional perspective leads us to contemplate just how things make sense.

Is This the Way Things Should Be?

Many times, changes that seem unnatural are actually naturally occurring events and transitions in human system development. Examples of life-stage changes are Erikson's (1963) stages of psychosocial development, Carter and McGoldrick's (1989) family life cycle, Papernow's (1993) stages of stepfamily development, and the natural evolution of groups reported by many authors (Johnson & Johnson, 2013; Schriver, 2015). Knowledge that these changes are expected and desirable is a resource that social workers have available to share with clients.

Consider the example of the social worker hired to consult with a delinquency prevention agency. The agency recently received funds to develop a case management system to coordinate services for first-time offenders and attempt to divert them from prosecution by the juvenile justice system. Assessment reveals that for 2 months, the four-member team worked cooperatively, but, just when they seemed to be getting comfortable with each other, their meetings began to erupt with conflict. The social worker assesses the conflict and recognizes the disequilibrium that naturally evolves in a group as it forms. By helping the team learn conflict-resolution skills to continue its natural development, the worker assists team members to translate their differences into creative resources for developing the new program. To recognize natural transitions, workers and clients consider questions such as the following:

- What physical, cognitive, and psychological transitions are occurring in members of the client system?
- Do family life cycle transitions apply? Group development transitions? Organizational development transitions?
- Is the event or behavior expected based on the client system's stage of development?
- What changes need to occur to facilitate a smooth transition?

What Have We Got to Lose?

The question "What have we got to lose?" considers the consequences of change. Recall the ecosystems view of dysfunction. Even behavior initially seen as problematic may be working adaptively somewhere else in the client's ecosystem. As an example, consider the boy whose academic failure at school activates his parents to sit with him in the evening to help with homework, to visit his teacher to confer about his learning difficulties, and to advocate with the school board to hire a reading specialist for the district. Clearly, the boy's behavior is a resource in connecting him to his parents and connecting his parents to the school system.

What would happen if the boy's behavior suddenly improved? These resources might be lost, leaving him isolated and unnoticed. Consider what life will be like if the problem is resolved, exploring both the positive and negative consequences of change. In this way, workers can assess the potential effects problems have in the system. This information provides insight into how the system is balanced and what changes might occur as solutions develop. To consider how difficulties affect a client's situation, workers contemplate the following:

- How is the system responding to the situation?
- Is there anything good that happens as a result?
- What solutions has the client attempted?
- What else will change when the client overcomes the difficulty?

Ecosystems Questions: Assessing Thinking and Feeling

Human beings think and feel. We respond not only to the structure and functioning of the social systems in which we participate but also to the ways we interpret what happens in these various contexts. An assessment of thinking and feeling results in a clearer understanding of the cognitive and affective factors that influence human behavior.

What Do You Think?

Assessing how the client system functions in its ecosystems context offers new ways to think about events. Typically, clients bring a particular theory about what is going on to the social work relationship. An assessment of thinking processes sheds new light on these previously fixed notions and theories. When social workers and clients reframe and reconceptualize, they generate many new ways to explain situations. Generating alternative ideas and hypotheses leads to multiple options for change. Questions that disclose aspects of thinking include the following:

- What explanations does the client system offer? Do all members of the client system hold the same view?
- Does the client hold notions that, if reframed, would incorporate new possibilities?
- How might changes in thinking lead to changes in behavior?

Assessment provides opportunities for clients to tell their stories.

How Does It Feel?

Assessing feelings supplies intuitive hunches about whether social workers and clients are on the right track. Feelings play a prominent role in how people regard themselves, others, and their situations or problems. Feelings also come into play as people consider different options for resolving their issues. Responses to feelings can be affirming or restraining. Feelings can be a source of energy for change; unattended, they

ROB MARMION/SHUTTERSTOCK

can be obstacles. Accessing affective responses taps into clients' motivations, comfort, and spontaneity. Questions that uncover dimensions of feelings include the following:

- What clues do verbal and nonverbal messages offer about the feelings the client is experiencing?
- In the case of multiperson client systems, are the emotions members express similar or different from one another?
- In what ways are feelings affecting thinking?
- How does the synergy of emotions amplify or diminish the energy available to invest in solutions?

Ecosystems Questions: Assessing Cultural Influences

The cultural identities of any particular system influence the way it interacts with other systems. The cultural influences internalized by various system members contribute to diversity within a given social system. A complete assessment of an ecosystem requires an exploration of cultural elements.

What About the Big Picture?

One aspect to consider in assessing cultural influences is to examine critically how clients fit into the larger picture. Because not all racial, ethnic, gender, or other cultural groups currently receive equal access to the resources of society, the relationship of the culture of the client system to the macrosystem deserves special consideration. Social workers overlook powerful influences when they fail to recognize oppression and discrimination. Helping clients adapt to an environment marked by prejudice and injustice disempowers. Instead, ethical practitioners craft macrosystem interventions to redress injustice. Assessing cultural influences raises the critical consciousness of social workers and clients to the impact of discrimination and oppression and serves as a catalyst for social action and social change. To understand the sociopolitical influences on client systems, workers and clients consider questions such as the following:

Assessing cultural influences raises the critical consciousness of social workers and clients to the impact of discrimination and oppression and serves as a catalyst for social action and social change.

- In what ways do prejudicial attitudes such as racism, sexism, ageism, classism, ableism, heterosexism, and regionalism affect the client's circumstances?
- What roles do discriminatory practices, procedures, and policies play in the client system's situation?
- How has oppression directly and indirectly blocked the client's access to power?
- What strengths can the worker and client discover in the ways the client adapts to experiences of discrimination and oppression?

How Does the System Fit Together?

Culture also affects the internal functioning of each client system. One qualitative study voiced the views of immigrant clients and their social workers in emphasizing the importance of the workers' abilities to see cultural identity as multifaceted. Workers respond to clients' overlapping roles in ways that acknowledge the uniqueness of individuals rather than their salient cultural membership (Russell & White, 2001). Simply applied, even members of the same immigrant family are culturally distinct, possibly leading to the assessment of family conflict as a cross-cultural issue. The stress ethnic group members experience as the result of living in two cultures is called sociocultural dissonance

(Chau, 1989). A similar dynamic occurs in the blending of stepfamilies with conflicting lifestyles (Visher & Visher, 1996). And, certainly, cultural differences are likely to exist among members of larger group, organizational, and community systems. For both clients and workers, cultural information functions as a resource to help externalize issues rather than personalize conflicts. To understand the role of culture, workers consider answers to questions such as the following:

- What different cultural perspectives are operating?
- Do these cultural perspectives agree or conflict with one another?
- Are factors such as the reasons for and experiences of immigration involved?
- In what ways are intergenerational perspectives a factor?
- To what extent does the experience of living in two cultures result in sociocultural dissonance?

Ecosystems Questions: Assessing Spiritual Dimensions

Although historically included as an important dimension of assessment, practitioners have often considered spirituality superfluous to the secular domain of practice. However, when we consider spiritual dimensions, we discover that spiritual beliefs are integrated into every aspect of clients' thoughts, feelings, and day-to-day life and activities (Gotterer, 2001). With respect to social work in health care, the accrediting body for health care, the Joint Commission, requires spiritual assessment as a standard of care (Hodge, 2006).

Spirituality, according to Canda and Furman (1999), "relates to a universal and fundamental aspect of what it is to be human—to search for a sense of meaning, purpose, and moral frameworks for relating with self, others, and the ultimate reality" (p. 37). Spirituality may be experienced as either a part of or separate from organized religion. Although some people may identify particular spiritual concerns, spirituality is the essence of human life.

Research indicates that spirituality is a vital force for dealing with issues related to life transitions, stressors, trauma, and other personal and familial difficulties. For example, one qualitative study of people with a background of addiction and incarceration found that although nearly 70 percent of the respondents didn't have an affiliation with a religious denomination, almost everyone identified spirituality as a dominant force for coping with stress and adversity in their lives (Redman, 2008). Washington and colleagues (2009) report their action research project that explored the resources drawn upon by older African American women who were transitioning from homelessness. In this study, women demonstrating the highest levels of motivation and self-efficacy in the face of adversity were the most likely to report drawing on the deeply rooted resources of their faith as a way to maintain their sense of hope and optimism. Based on a cross-sectional survey exploring the life experiences of older adults living in rural communities, Yoon (2006) found that respondents reporting higher levels of spiritual values were less likely to evidence depression. These researchers all stress the importance of faith communities as sources of strength and support for clients and including spirituality in assessment.

To identify dimensions of spirituality, Hodge (2001) recommends an anthropological approach to assessment—basic questions to initiate conversations about spirituality and interpretive questions to understand in more depth the ways in which spirituality influences emotion, behavior, beliefs, a sense of communion with the Ultimate (for some, God); sense of right, wrong, guilt, and forgiveness; and insight or intuition. Considerations in the initial framework include familial traditions with respect to religion and spirituality, the value placed on spirituality by the family, the impact of nodal life experiences on development, and the strength of spirituality in one's current stage of life.

Ecosystems Questions: Assessing Physical Environments

The final piece to consider in assessing human systems is the influence of physical environments on client functioning. Workers may not have opportunities to view personally their clients' homes, places of work, or neighborhoods and, furthermore, may neglect to inquire about what these settings are like. Deficiencies, obstructions, lack of privacy, and other environmental factors can all contribute to the stress clients experience. The physical environment plays an important role in group dynamics, too. Arrangement of physical space, lighting, and ventilation all make a difference in how group members interact. Immediate environments profoundly influence human behavior and interaction (Saleebey, 2004). Physical environments can augment or restrict client functioning and, therefore, are important factors to assess.

Have You Looked Around This Place?

Consider the situation of Deanna, a client who seeks assistance to balance her budget. Deanna's caseworker carefully evaluates Deanna's competencies in budgeting and is pleased to see that Deanna has appropriate math skills, demonstrates a good awareness of frugality, and organizes her bills effectively. But when the worker visits Deanna at home, the major issues are much clearer. The old apartment building in which Deanna lives clearly needs maintenance. The windows are not sealed properly, the thermostat is broken, and nearly every faucet leaks. The assessment of Deanna's physical environment leads the social worker to the resources of the city building inspector, the apartment owner, and the utility company in helping Deanna with her budgeting problems.

In assessing physical environments, workers and clients can discover resources and constraints. To weigh the effects of the client system's physical environment, workers ask questions such as the following:

Research-Informed Practice

Behavior: Use and translate research evidence to inform and improve practice, policy, and service delivery

Critical Thinking Question: Practitioners apply social work research through all phases of practice. Identify ways research findings inform assessment in various fields of social work practice.

- In what ways does the client system's physical environment enhance or curtail its ability to function?
  - How does the client system respond to the stress that results from factors in the physical environment?
  - What modifications to the physical environment would be helpful to the client system? Which are most realistic to pursue?
  - Who has the decision-making authority to ensure that these modifications will be made?

? Assess your understanding of using a 5-point ecosystems schema to organize assessment by taking this brief quiz.

Box 10.1   Assessment: A Research–Practice Connection

Creating a plan for action, based on a comprehensive assessment, is a collaborative project connecting clients' desires and ideas with social workers' professional knowledge and expertise. As part of their responsibility in assessment and planning processes, competent practitioners consider what the social work research says about what might be going on and what might help. Imagine you are working with an African American adolescent who is identifying himself as gay. He is dealing with a homophobic school environment and contemplating coming out to his family. What does social work research tell you to consider, to avoid, to suggest, and to do?

Based on their review of the literature, Morrison and L'Heureux (2001) advise practitioners to assess the adolescent for risk of suicide and self-injurious behaviors. They note higher suicide risks in youths who come out at an early age, have a history of sexual or physical abuse, exhibit nonconformity to traditional gender stereotypes, and report emotional and psychological conflict about their sexual orientation. In addition, Morrison and L'Heureux recommend examining the client's microsystem to assess both risk and protective factors. They note the increased risks associated with "homophobic and heterosexist attitudes in teachers, peers, religious leaders, and family members" (p. 43). They also identify a decrease in self-destructive behaviors when gay, lesbian, transgender, and transsexual (GLBT) adolescents are connected to affirming environments, including community services that provide support to the GLBT community.

Research conducted by Merighi and Grimes (2000) found that the coming-out process for an African American youth may have key similarities to development of a gay identity in other ethnic groups. In their work to compare the coming-out process for African, European, Mexican, and Vietnamese American gay males, ages 18 to 24, the researchers discovered that all participants "described the importance of preserving and upholding strong family relationship as a salient factor in their decision to come out" (p. 39). In this case, social work research leads social workers to generalize the coming-out experience across cultural differences, emphasizing family response as a core assessment area for working with gay adolescents from any cultural and ethnic background.

Understanding expected milestones for gay identity development is another useful planning framework, one that offers support in normalizing some of the client's feelings. Flowers and Buston (2001) offer such a model based on their examination of 20 retrospective accounts of male gay identity formation during adolescence. This qualitative study suggests that adolescent gay development can be understood by examining salient themes as these adolescents progress through phases "defined by difference, self-reflection and inner conflict, alienation and isolation, living a lie, telling others, and wholeness and integrity" (p. 51). As a social worker informed by research, you can identify your client as thinking about moving to the telling-others phase and help prepare him for possible fallout as a consequence of telling others, including parental rejection.

Social workers wishing to empower clients are careful in their use of social work research to understand their clients. Applying research to assessment and planning neither replaces careful listening to clients as they describe their thoughts and feelings nor supplants the need for comprehensive assessments of clients' unique situations. Clients' unique understandings of their own situations deserve the same consideration as information from research. Research simply provides clues for workers and clients that can guide assessment and planning activities and provide insight into possible intervention outcomes.

USING ASSESSMENT TOOLS

Assessment tools are also useful in structuring the search for resources. Specifically tailored to the purposes and characteristics of client systems, they include such diverse instruments as written questionnaires, standardized psychological tests, visual diagrams, behavioral checklists, role-plays, games, toys, dolls, and community resource assessment instruments.

Assessment tools help to describe situations and identify strengths, stimulate discussion, and facilitate sharing of diverse viewpoints in multiperson systems. By using these tools, workers can screen for issues requiring immediate attention, establish baseline information against which to measure subsequent change, and meet agency **record-keeping** requirements. Because assessment tools mediate conversations between clients and social workers, they are particularly useful for clients who experience difficulty expressing their thoughts and feelings directly. For example, children who have been sexually abused frequently find it easier to express their experiences by drawing pictures, playing with dolls, or telling stories rather than candidly speaking about their personal experiences with sexual abuse. Assessment tools, including computerized forms, provide an intermediate step—a way to be close in a mode that allows a safe distance. Assessment tools may be essential with larger systems to ensure that all those involved have a voice. Formalized procedures such as surveys, polls, and forums can access a broad base of information for assessment.

The following section describes assessment tools that may fit a client's situation, including **social histories**, **genograms**, **eco-maps**, culturally sensitive assessment, and **social network maps**, as well as group, organizational, neighborhood, and community assessment frameworks.

Social Histories

A social history organizes information about the history and current social functioning of individuals and families. Additionally, this standardized report describes the congruence between a client's needs and the formal and informal resources currently available. The exact format varies with the requirements of the practice setting. Some agencies use outlines to structure detailed narrative reports (Figure 10.2). Others use fill-in-the-blank forms that require brief comments in each of several categories. In general, social histories organize demographic data as well as information about personal history and life events. Social histories include information about (1) the client system; (2) the client's concerns, needs, and associated problems; and (3) strengths and limitations of the client in context (Johnson & Yanca, 2010). As an alternative to traditional social history models, Kivnick and Murray (2001) detail a life strengths interview model. Questions expand to focus on assets such as strengths and abilities, values and interests, cultural beliefs and practices, contributions, and protections and supports. Extending assessment to include assets shifts attention to a pool of valuable resources that can be drawn on to minimize deficits and expand the base of strengths. Essentially, clients' stories reveal their core identities, connectivity with others, and priorities, as well as the contexts of their lives.

To complete a social history, workers may choose to structure interviews to match the social history format. Other times, they facilitate conversations with clients that permit the information to flow naturally. Here, the social history outline serves as a checklist to ensure that all necessary information has been included. Either way, workers inform clients that they are completing a social history and detail how the information will be used.

Social histories, as completed written products, are invaluable resources. For example, in a nursing home, various members of the staff, including the social worker,

Client:

Worker:

Date of Report:

1. Identifying information: (preferred name, address, phone, date of birth)
2. Referral information: (source of referral; reason for contact, including challenges faced and previous attempts to resolve; other professional or indigenous helpers currently involved)
3. Individual functioning: (developmental status; current physical, cognitive, emotional, psychological, and interpersonal capabilities; areas of need)
4. Cultural functioning: (race/ethnicity; primary language and languages spoken; significance of cultural identity, cultural strengths, experience of discrimination or oppression)
5. Family information (names, ages, involvement with client, including spouse/partner, parents, siblings, children, and extended family members)
6. Family interaction: (extent of support, family perspective on client, client perspective on family, and relevant family issues)
7. Natural support network: (significant relationships—names and nature of involvement)
8. Physical environment: (housing situation, financial stability, transportation resources, neighborhood)
9. Nodal events: (situation and client's response to deaths of significant others, serious losses or traumas, significant life achievements, other events)
10. Education: (dates, places, and years of education completed; accomplishments, degrees, and credentials)
11. Employment: (current job, type of work, lengths of employment, previous experience, skills, and special training)
12. Medical history: (birth information, illnesses/accidents/surgery, medications used, family medical and genetic issues, physical limitations, diet, alcohol and drug use)
13. Religion: (denomination, church membership, extent of involvement, spiritual perspective, special observances)
14. Social activities: (interests, clubs/organizations, preferred recreation, travels)
15. Future plans: (client's perspective on current situation, goals, personal and environmental resources to meet goals, constraints to goal attainment)

Figure 10.2
Family History Outline, Individual Client

activity director, dietician, physician, and/or family liaison may use the social history as a reference in planning or coordinating services with the resident. Clearly, this indicates the need for accuracy and clarity in the finished product. Sheafor and Horejsi (2014) say that good social history reports are brief, simple, useful, organized, confidential, and objective. In addition, they should be relevant and should focus on client strengths.

Genograms

Genograms visually represent family chronology (Hartman, 1978, reprinted in 1995; McGoldrick & Gerson, 1985, 1989). As schematic diagrams, genograms provide

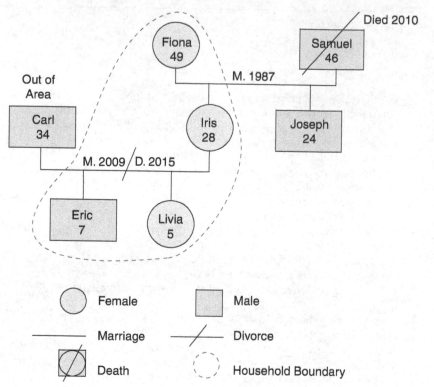

Figure 10.3
Genogram of Fiona Grant's Family

A genogram illustrates family structure and relationships. Genograms list family members in at least two generations, including their names, ages, and dates of marriages and divorces. Workers and clients can also annotate genograms with other information to meet their specific purposes.

summaries of information about context, including family history, marriages, deaths, geographic locations of family members, family structure and roles, and demographics (Figure 10.3). Completed genograms look somewhat like family trees, especially when they include information about several generations. Workers and clients annotate genograms to communicate information about "the sources of nurturance, stimulation, and support that must be available in the intimate and extended environment to make possible growth and survival" (Hartman, p. 113).

By highlighting familial information, genograms aid our understanding of relationship patterns, transitional issues, and life cycle changes. To gather information for genograms, workers ask clients to share family stories and traditions. Adding chronological information about nodal family events furnishes additional information about family transitions and identifies points where families have coped with change over the course of time. To incorporate diversity, one can add critical dimensions to genograms by including ancestral histories and generational narratives about race, age, gender, mobility, and socioeconomic status. Consistent with the strengths perspective, genograms can reveal the patterns of family strengths over time and highlight exceptions to family legacies considered problematic. Genograms are also useful for honoring diversity, identifying multiple cultural influences, tracing intercultural blending through the generations, and emphasizing the unique cultural history and intergenerational cultural legacies of any family (Lim & Nakamoto, 2008; McCullough-Chavis & Waites, 2004).

Practitioners in numerous fields of social work practice consider genograms essential for assessment. For example, in aging services, social workers construct genograms with older adults to facilitate life review. Practitioners working in medical settings can employ genograms to trace patterns of health and wellness or identify potential sources of family support. With respect to child welfare services, genograms can be used to trace adoption histories or record foster care placements and short-term, in-home family preservation services. Finally, in relation to services for immigrants and refugees, social workers can create genograms with clients to trace migration experiences and discern the nature of transnational connectedness and support.

Eco-Maps

As visual representations, eco-maps graphically picture the ecological context of the client system (Hartman, 1978, reprinted in 1995; Hartman & Laird, 1983). Eco-maps focus specifically on the major systems with which clients are involved to visually depict their relationships with these systems. In other words, eco-maps portray transactions between the client and other systems: the exchange of resources, the nature of system relationships, the permeability of boundaries, and connections to the social service delivery system and other contextual supports. To construct an eco-map of a family system, Hartman recommends placing the client's household in the middle of the eco-map and adding contextual or environmental systems with which the client interacts to the parameters of the map. Lines connecting the various systems portray the nature of the relationship and the direction in which energy flows (Figure 10.4).

A generalist application of the eco-map of a larger system places a group, organizational, or community client at the center and maps the larger systems' transactions with related systems. Constructing eco-maps with multiperson system's, whether families, groups, organizations, or communities, can stimulate interaction among members as they explore both the highlights and challenges of their circumstances, offering insights about interpersonal dynamics and connections to networks of supports. Comparing the eco-maps of various constituents or subgroups can offer insight into differing experiences and perceptions of members.

In addition, there are other benefits of constructing eco-maps. As a tool for identifying available resources, existing constraints, and possibilities for new connections, workers and clients can use eco-maps as a basis for constructing plans of action. Also, comparing the "before" and "after" intervention, eco-maps can graphically demonstrate changes in the relationships between the client and other social systems. Moreover, by fostering collaboration, constructing an eco-map with clients demonstrates that social workers want to understand clients' unique circumstances rather than search for their inner faults. In essence, eco-maps externalize problems and diminish blame.

Culturally Sensitive Assessment

For individual and family assessment that is sensitive to cultural differences, social workers augment traditional models of assessment that are more individualistically focused

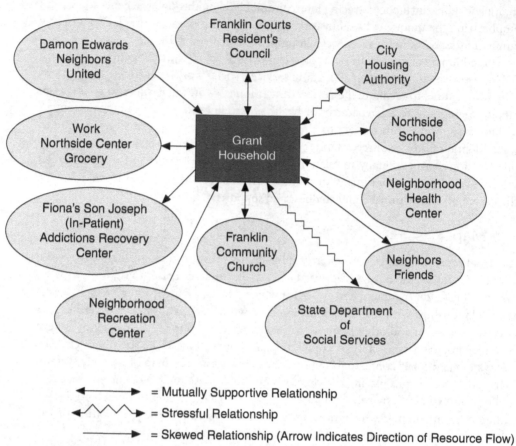

= Mutually Supportive Relationship

= Stressful Relationship

= Skewed Relationship (Arrow Indicates Direction of Resource Flow)

Figure 10.4
Eco-Map of Fiona Grant's Household

An eco-map illustrates a human system in context. It identifies significant environmental systems and describes the nature of the relationships. Constructing eco-maps helps clients clarify environmental resources and constraints.

with collectively focused models that begin by exploring the influences and resources in the macroenvironment. Using the person-in-family-in-community model, social workers assess clients in the context of their families and social systems. To apply this model, social workers assess cultural influences in six areas. They

1. identify the family's place of origin and the continued influence of their societal background;

2. explore the family's affiliations with their ethnic community and their attitudes toward social services;

3. determine in which community and family organizations, including ethnic social organizations, the family holds memberships;

4. detail the family's formal and informal roles, expectations for family members' behaviors, decision-making and power structures, and change agents;

5. analyze the subgroup structures in the extended family and their influence on family dynamics and family members; and

6. examine how individual family members are influenced by family roles, obligations, and responsibilities (Fong, 1997).

Social Network Maps

Social network maps are tools for assessing social support that pictures a client's social support networks and quantifies the nature of support from the client's point of view (Tracy & Whittaker, 1990). To implement this technique, clients first identify members in their support network, including immediate family or household members, extended family, friends, and neighbors, as well as more formal organizations such as work, school, clubs, church, and other services. Then, by using a sorting technique and responding to specific questions, clients describe how they perceive the support they receive from others. Social network mapping assesses

- who provides social support,
- kinds of support available,
- gaps in relationship resources,
- opportunities for reciprocal exchanges,
- presence of negativism and stress that produces criticism,
- barriers to using available resources, and
- priority of social support in relation to other challenges.

Group Assessment

The defining element of any group is its purpose. Group assessment, therefore, focuses on the "fit" between a group's functioning and its purpose. The purposes of client groups vary from those focused on support or therapeutic treatment to those organized for skill development, task completion, or social change. Areas of group functioning to explore include group culture, cohesion, norms, communication, leadership, decision making, controversy, and conflict.

Framework for Group Assessment

Effective groups share common qualities, such as productive communication, good listening skills, appreciation of member diversity, distributed leadership, participatory decision-making procedures, and skills for managing controversy. Similar to other human systems, a group's interaction must be assessed in its context to create a comprehensive view, including the group's goals and resources, interaction patterns, and relationships with various environmental systems.

Group Goals and Resources

- Identify the purposes of the group.
- Determine members' motivation to meet the group's purposes.
- Inventory group members' resources to achieve purposes.
- Explicate the values, beliefs, and cultural affiliations of group members.
- Characterize group consciousness about relevant issues.

Group Interaction

- Measure group cohesion and communication effectiveness.
- Assess members' respect for differences in perspectives and opinions.
- Identify prevailing group norms.
- Describe the group's decision-making processes.
- Assess the distribution of power and leadership within the group.
- Consider the group's ability to manage conflict and controversy.

Group–Environment Relations

- Describe the matrix of environmental systems that influences the group and individual members.
- Determine the accessibility of environmental resources.
- Analyze the impact of race, class, gender, and other cultural identities on group interaction.

Organizational Assessment

An organization is a formal group that joins together to make use of collective resources and skills to achieve a common purpose or goal. Social workers implementing **organizational assessments** may consider an organization as a client, as a context for social service delivery, or as a target for change.

Framework for Organizational Assessment

Like any social system, organizations may be assessed by considering their internal characteristics and the demands and resources of their environments.

Organizational Goals and Structures

- Identify the mission, purpose, goals, and history of the organization.
- Describe the organizational governance and decision-making structures.
- Define the perspectives or principles that guide leadership and managerial staff.
- Characterize the organizational culture and membership and/or constituencies.

Organization–Environment Relations

- Detail the economic, political, demographic, fiscal, cultural, legal/governmental, and technological environments of the organization.
- Characterize the fit between organizational purpose with tasks and the needs and resources of the environment.
- Describe the opportunities and threats posed in the environment.
- Identify relevant policy issues that impact organizational functioning.

Organizational Competence

- Describe how the organization evaluates its achievement of its purpose and goals, and how the organization uses that feedback to enhance effectiveness.
- Assess the organizational capacity for innovation or change.
- Identify mechanisms for strategic planning and continuous quality improvement.
- Characterize the organizational strengths and weaknesses.

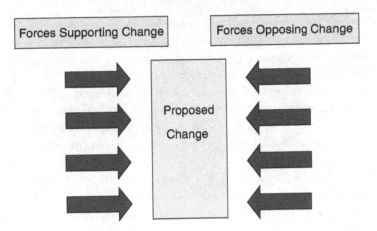

Figure 10.5
Force Field Analysis
Social workers apply force field analysis to evaluate the countervailing factors that support or oppose change, including forces such as stakeholders, funding, polices, and other contingencies.

Force Field Analysis

A creative problem-solving technique developed by Lewin (1951), **force field analysis** applies to organizational assessment, community development, and strategic planning. This strategy is based on the theory that forces within a system either drive toward or restrain change. Either removing restraints or enhancing those forces currently driving toward solutions fuels change (Bargal, 2000; Pippard & Bjorkland, 2004). Force field analysis is useful for understanding forces that promote or block change and then creating strategies to strengthen forces that promote change and reduce those forces that create barriers. Analysis of the forces identified provides insight into power dynamics, stakeholders who are opponents and those who are allies, and weighing the pros and cons of potential actions (Figure 10.5). Steps for implementing a force field analysis are

1. describe the situation, framing the target for change;
2. delineate the forces that support the change;
3. delineate the forces that oppose the change, including those that could either restrain or block change;
4. assign weights to each force identified based on their relative influence;
5. develop a plan of action, including goals, objectives, and strategies to enhance or diminish forces;
6. implement the plan;
7. assess progress toward achieving objectives and viability of strategies; and
8. evaluate outcomes.

Neighborhood and Community Assessment

Needs assessment differs from **asset mapping**. Social workers and planners conduct needs assessments to document problems, identify unmet needs, and establish priorities

▶ Watch this video as you consider that generalist social wokers require skills in assessing communities. How can social workers use community asset mapping as a culturally competent assessment tool?
www.youtube.com/watch?v=wYP0U9Tj1Y8

for service and resource development. Asset mapping in a community or neighborhood, on the other hand, involves assessing capacities, resources, and assets. This includes taking an inventory of the individual, associational, and institutional capacities (Kretzmann & McKnight, 1993). In contrast to the traditional community "needs" assessment, a community asset inventory focuses more on what a community has than on what is missing. This shift in emphasis away from community problem solving toward community capacity building positions localities to implement asset-based community development strategies.

A comprehensive neighborhood or community assessment includes information gathered through a variety of methods (Kettner et al., 1985). **Community surveys** include questionnaires administered face to face or mailed to a representative sample of the community population to solicit opinions and collect data about community life. **Key informant studies** involve structured interviews, surveys, or **focus groups** with individuals identified as having expertise on the subject under study. **Community forums** are open scheduled meetings held to solicit the views of a broad representation of community members. **Telephone surveys** are conducted over the phone with members of representative households. **Statistical indicators** profile the community using a collation of census data, demographic and population statistics, and social and economic indicators.

Framework for Community and Neighborhood Assessment

Social workers find community studies useful for inventorying sources of strengths and assessing community competence. A community assessment is also useful for assessing distinct neighborhoods within a larger community. The assessment includes such elements as a community or neighborhood profile, an inventory of assets, and an audit of the capacity for development.

Community Profile

- Summarize the history of the community.
- Describe the geographical and jurisdictional boundaries of the community.
- Explicate the dominant values, traditions, beliefs, and standards of the community.
- Characterize the relationships among community members.

Community Inventory of Assets

- Prepare a demographic profile of the community population.
- Describe the political/power, economic, religious, education, social welfare, and criminal justice institutions.
- Inventory the talent and resource pool of community members.
- Inventory the resources in the health and human services delivery system, including its agencies, programs, and volunteer initiatives.
- Describe the housing, transportation, and recreational resources of the community.

Community Audit of Capacity for Development

- Delineate the strengths of the community.
- Identify the major community problems.

- Evaluate sources of oppression and discrimination.
- Evaluate the degree to which the community resources meet the needs of its members.
- Assess community competence: How well does the community respond to resident needs? In what ways do community members contribute to the well-being of the community? How does the community relate to other communities and the region?

Focus Groups

Originated by sociologist Robert K. Merton as a strategy for qualitative research, focus groups also have merit as a strategy for gathering information for macrolevel assessment and planning (Kramer et al., 2002). Focus groups typically involve 6 to 12 participants in a 1- to 2-hour discussion session that is recorded. Although participants share an interest or affiliation, they may or may not know each other. Implementing a focus group strategy includes (1) *preparing*, to define the purpose, identify and recruit participants, develop open-ended questions that will elicit discussion, and arrange for a comfortable setting for the focus group meeting; (2) *implementing*, to facilitate the process in a way that builds trust and elicits different points of view; and (3) *reporting*, to summarize the sessions, analyze and interpret the themes, and disseminate the results.

As a macrolevel assessment strategy, focus groups have utility for generating ideas, gathering feedback, and helping discern the respondents' opinions, beliefs, and attitudes. For example, Wright and colleagues (2010) report using focus groups to elicit social workers' perceptions about organizational factors that strengthened or deterred their imple-

mentation of family-centered practice strategies. After further analysis, the challenges identified by focus group respondents can be translated into an organization's strategic plan by specifying strategic objectives, action steps, timelines, and outcome measures. To gather information about factors deterring educational achievements of children in foster care and recommendations for organizational changes, Zetlin and colleagues (2010) conducted focus groups with caregivers, school liaisons, and agency advocates. Analysis of key themes revealed numerous issues identified by each stakeholder group as well as the lack of communication and coordination among the constituents. Among the recommendations generated was to establish an interagency task force that included caregivers and youths in the foster care system in addition to child welfare and education professionals.

Assessment

Behavior: Select appropriate intervention strategies based on the assessment, research knowledge, and values and preferences of clients and constituencies

Critical Thinking Question: Social workers consider various issues when choosing the right assessment tools to understand client situations and appropriate intervention models. How might the choices social workers make about assessment tools and intervention strategies reflect their work toward social justice?

Tools as Resources for Empowerment

Empowerment-based assessment uses tools to discover resources. These tools do not produce products that diagnose or categorize clients and herd them into particular intervention initiatives. Instead, workers use assessment tools to enrich, motivate, and inform clients. Before implementing any tool, practitioners fully explain it, including its administration and purpose. They also share results and discuss implications with clients (Figure 10.6).

 Assess your understanding of using assessment tools by taking this brief quiz.

- What is the purpose of the tool?
- Is the tool a good fit for the unique circumstances of the client system?
- What is the cost in terms of time, effort, and money?
- Are clients fully informed about the tool's purpose and procedure? Do they give their consent to participate?
- Does the tool require special training or certification to administer?
- What is the client's role?
- Will clients see and discuss the results?
- Will the proposed tool provide useful information or does it merely attach a label to the client's behavior?
- How will the results be used?
- Does the tool provide reliable and valid information?

Figure 10.6
Considerations in Using Assessment Tools

RECORD-KEEPING

In many ways, records are resources for clients, social workers, agencies, and even the social work profession. Records provide a coherent and organized database for assessment. Records, like maps, are resource guides. It's hard for people to know how far they've come, unless there's a record of where they started. Likewise, it's hard for people to know which turn to take if they don't have some sense of their destination. A well-constructed record provides concrete evidence of change, information for assessment, and indications for future action.

Ethical and Professional Behavior

Behavior: Use technology ethically and appropriately to facilitate practice outcomes

Critical Thinking Question: When viewed merely as paperwork, record-keeping can easily be devalued as unimportant in practice. However, electronic record-keeping can function as a tool for critical reflection about practice effectiveness. How can social workers synthesize and narrate relevant information in case records in ways that stimulate critical reflection about their work?

Records serve as the basis for individual reflection, supervisory discussion, and peer consultation. Agency administrators aggregate data from records to evaluate current programs and plan for the future. Usually, agencies are accountable to funding bodies for grant-funded service provisions. Accurate records support statistical documentation and provide measures of quality assurance. In addition to this accountability function, records provide the requisite documentation for billable hours in submitting claims to third-party payees, including insurance providers and governmental funding bodies such as Medicaid and Medicare. These payees often require the inclusion of key treatment words that justify claims. Finally, effective social work records facilitate practice and program evaluation research. This section examines several facets of record-keeping, including the role of recording, types of recording techniques, and ethical and legal issues associated with record-keeping.

Recording

Recording assists social workers and clients in numerous ways. By keeping track of contacts, activities, and plans, records aid memory. By organizing relevant information and

- Avoid all derogatory labels (for example, ethnic or racial slurs)
- Demonstrate gender sensitivity
  - Use generic terms to describe people including words such as "mail carrier," "service person," "chairperson," etc.
  - Use the phrases "he or she," "his or her," or "them"
- Maintain nonjudgmentalism
- Refrain from using jargon or slang
- Use concrete descriptions rather than diagnostic labels, generalizations, or subjective wording
- Use active voice
- Proofread your final draft by reading aloud

Figure 10.7
Tips for an Appropriate Writing Style

arranging priorities, records ensure continuity. By carefully documenting case activities, records detail productivity and provide an essential component of professional liability risk management. When their clients give permission or when legal constraints mandate, records enhance a worker's ability to share accurate information with other professionals. Significantly, records offer legal protection to workers because they concretely document professional activities.

The purpose of record-keeping is to objectively document what you did and why you did it. Rather than being a mundane, tedious activity, effective recording is a useful analytic tool. Writing reports requires us to cluster ideas, develop themes, and organize our thoughts. Writing clarifies our thinking. Whereas statistical records document case activities, descriptive case records individualize accounts of process, impressions, and plans. Records form a baseline against which to measure change.

Valuable records contain objective facts and relevant case-related information and documents, such as letters and releases of information. When we communicate with others via written documents, our documents make a significant impression. Poorly prepared documents detract from their content and may not be taken seriously. People evaluate our ideas by scrutinizing the document's format, presentation of ideas, grammar, and style. Some social service administrators consider written communication skills a top priority in their list of qualifications for prospective employees. Factors such as a pleasing format, clear and effective presentation of ideas, correct grammar, and a style that is ethnically sensitive and nonsexist establish credibility (Figure 10.7). Effective social workers prepare records carefully.

The purpose of record-keeping is to objectively document what you did and why you did it.

Types of Recording Formats

Social work records are prepared for a diverse audience, including colleagues, supervisors, third-party payers, clients, and court officials. Some records summarize information about goals, objectives, activities, and outcomes; others narrate a detailed account of progress toward goals. Some records are abbreviated, using outlines, checklists, or abridged forms; others incorporate extensive documentation details. Some records are written to comply with court mandates and/or contractual stipulations; others are kept to meet agency standards. The purposes of the record dictate its format, content, and style.

Note Taking

Good records begin with gathering accurate information. Some circumstances require **note taking**. For example, factual data such as names of family members, committee members, birth dates, meeting times, or specific follow-up tasks may be difficult to remember without a written record. Typically, asking clients for permission to take even limited notes reduces their defensiveness. Effective requests include the following:

- I'd like to keep these details straight. Is it all right with you if I take a few notes?
- Does anyone object to my taking notes during our discussion so that we have a record of our decisions?
- This is a pretty long form to fill out. Do you want me to read the questions to you? Do you want to read along with me? I could give you a blank form and you could just tell me the answers and I'll write them down. What do you think would work best?

There is pressure to remember detail, yet a need to take notes in ways that have minimal effect on the process. By involving clients, social workers convert note taking from a display of expert authority into an empowering strategy. Taking only selective notes during actual meetings with clients requires conscientious social workers to record notes soon after. Noting even a few details enhances the accuracy of recollection in completing formal reports.

Activity Logs

Probably the most widely used style of record is a simple and organized **activity log** of contacts between workers and clients. This type of record is most useful in keeping the worker and client focused on relevant tasks and forms a database for worker and agency accountability. Although the content of these records varies across practice settings, most include information about client goals, activities completed, future plans, people involved, and time invested. Examine the activity log of Rita Garcia, a social worker with the state's Child Protective Unit, who uses this record to document her work with Opal Zander (Figure 10.8). Although they do not offer detailed accounts of her activities, Rita's logs keep her on task and remind her of the sequence of important events when she presents court testimony. She also uses her logs to organize follow-up details.

Process Recording

A **process recording** reviews contacts with clients by including descriptive, specific details. More often found in educational than paid employment settings, process recording applies to any system level, builds self-awareness, refines assessment skills, and supports learning to work effectively with direct service clients and in policy practice (Black & Feld, 2006; Medina, 2010). Process recordings support social workers in becoming reflective practitioners and enhance their conscious use of self. Consonant with the strengths perspective, social workers can modify process recordings to incorporate commentary on client strengths. Process recording goes beyond formal written reports to include audio- and video-recording, and in-session and one-way mirror observations by others.

Content for properly prepared written process recordings includes the verbatim dialogue, comments on the social worker's reactions and feelings, analyses and interpretations of the transactions, and the supervisor's comments. Process recordings need to

Worker: Rita Garcia		Client: Zander Family	
Date	Time Contact	Task/Activity	Action Required
6/19	.25-Call from Smith/DCS	Requested emergency placement for Zander children—4 siblings	Find home for sibling group
6/19	.25-L. Jones-Confirmed Jones will provide foster placement for all four kids		
6/19	.50-Smith/DCS	Discussed disposition of case-Smith will pursue court action	
6/19	1.50-Zander children	Provided transport to Jones' home	Call Jones 6/20
6/20	1.75-Opal Zander	Intake: Discussed procedures and requirements. Set goals for family reunification	Schedule joint meeting with team 6/21 (Families United office, 10:30)
6/21	2.25-Team meeting	Set visitation and determined plan of action including (1) moving out of boyfriend's house into transitional housing, (2) secure employment to achieve financial independence	Zander will contact Northside Shelter and the Women's Resource Center

Figure 10.8
Sample Activity Log

be written immediately. To organize process recording, one can divide legal-size paper into three or four columns or on a computer, format recording columns using a landscape setting to align the paper horizontally. Practitioners evaluate their experiences in the interviewer's column, and supervisors provide constructive feedback in the instructor's comments column. Examine the process recording completed by Rita Garcia as she worked with Opal Zander toward the goal of increasing Opal's employability (Figure 10.9).

Summary Recording

A **summary recording** such as progress notes, intake summaries, and referral reports is more typical of the record-keeping requirements of day-to-day social work practice. Frequency and format depends on agency policy, stipulations of accrediting bodies, government regulations, and grant requirements. Typically, effective summary recordings include basic identifying client information consistent with agency protocols, an overview of the session's goals and accomplishments, a summary of progress, and follow-up plans. Content

Client: Opal Zander	Date: 7/12-(Individual Session # 8)	Interviewer: R. Garcia
Verbatim Account	Interviewer's Response	Analysis
I called the GED center.	Oh?	Opal's taking the initiative. Want to keep my responses minimal while supporting her efforts.
I can start anytime. They call it "study at your own pace."	Good!	
Not going to cost me any money. They've even got a bus token deal.	Mmhmm . . .	
And, something called a resource center for women like me.	For women like you . . .	Emphasizing Opal's connection with other women in program to increase its appeal.
I think so. I said, "I'm nervous and I've been having some hard times." And, then the lady I was talking to said, well I could try it out. So, I've been thinking . . . (pauses a bit)	Yes?	
Well, I've been thinking about whether I should wait until I get the kids back or start now. I even made this list to decide (list shows lots of pluses).	Looks like you're thinking about starting pretty soon.	Emphasizing Opal's efforts in thinking this through. But did I jump in too soon with this?
The way I see it, I've got some time on my hands right now. And, this GED program gives me a chance to do something positive. I sure need that. And, maybe I can make some friends, like we talked about last time, at that women's center.	I'm really impressed with how you're taking charge.	Opal sees she's making a difference; can build on this for parenting, too. How could we connect this with reunification goals?

Figure 10.9
Excerpts from a Process Recording

focuses exclusively on the client rather than on the worker's responses and reactions. Summary content describes outcomes thematically rather than in step-by-step details.

Ethical and Legal Issues in Record-Keeping

Records document courses of action. However, sharing this information with clients and other professionals raises numerous ethical and legal issues, as does the use of computers for record-keeping.

Electronic Records

Although computers streamline the processing and sharing of information and facilitate the collection of data, ethical issues abound. Because the computerized databases maintained in social work practice are likely to contain an abundance of confidential information, safeguards to maintain security and to preserve confidentiality are vital. For social workers in health and mental health settings, ensuring confidentiality for health records is the law. The Health Insurance Portability and Accountability Act of 1996 (HIPAA) stipulates legal regulations and mandated compliance procedures to ensure the privacy of electronic protected health information (NASW, 2001b, 2004a, 2005b). Security measures regulate access to databases through the use of passwords and other "locked file systems," monitor access to information available on computer networks, and rigorously protect the privacy of information on the computer screen. Professionals ensure that stored computerized information is as safe as the records stored in their locked filing cabinets and that records on their computer screens are as private as the records in their files.

Clients' Access to Records

The NASW *Code of Ethics* (1999) indicates that clients should have reasonable access to their records. Specifically, the code indicates that social workers should provide clients with reasonable access to official records that concern them and, when sharing this information with clients, should protect the confidentiality of other persons noted in the records. Clearly, this code upholds clients' rights to access their records.

Several pieces of federal legislation also champion clients' rights to access their records. For example, the Federal Privacy Act of 1974 (Public Law 93-579), the Freedom of Information Act, and the Family Educational Rights legislation of 1974 (FERPA, also known as the Buckley Amendment) specify guidelines with respect to accessing records from educational institutions and from other federally funded or administered programs. HIPAA sets standards for those practicing in the field of health care. These codes, laws, and guidelines prescribe the principle; agency policies and procedures furnish detailed directions as to how clients can access their records.

Social workers need to keep in mind the effect of reading the written reports as they prepare clients' records. Workers always write records with the understanding that the records could be read by clients or various third parties. In preparing compliance reports with respect to mandated clients, practitioners disclose only information specific to the requirements of the referral agencies. Although some professionals struggle with the implications of fully sharing their written impressions with clients, research findings indicate that the quality of records as well as relationships with clients improve when clients have access to their records (Gelman, 1992).

 Assess your understanding of record-keeping by taking this brief quiz.

LOOKING FORWARD

Social work assessment includes both content and process. With respect to content, an ecosystems-derived assessment inquires beyond the individual sphere to understand client functioning in context. A good assessment not only identifies client problems but applies a strengths orientation to locate client strengths and environmental resources. As a process, assessment becomes empowering to the extent that it contextualizes the issues that clients face and locates resources to achieve desired goals. In contrast, assessment processes that elevate social workers' expertise or reduce client situations to stigmatizing labels undermine clients' progress.

Social workers and clients have many ways to access assessment information. Workers can use theoretically derived structured conversations, such as the ecosystems assessment framework. Assessment tools such as genograms, eco-maps, social network maps, and community asset audits as well as evidence-based inventories, standardized psychological tests, and behavioral checklists can supplement assessment conversations with clients. Ethically accessing the viewpoints of significant others and other involved professionals may help in the assessment. Clients and workers can design their own observations to generate new perspectives and add a behavioral dimension to assessment. Professional social workers keep precise written records that become assessment resources. Accurate and timely records offer opportunities for reflection and contain data to measure client progress over time.

An organized assessment of client needs and resources indicates possible actions to include in a plan for change. Framing solutions, the subject of Chapter 11, takes planning further. To frame solutions, social workers and clients clearly articulate goals, consider multiple levels of intervention, develop strategies to achieve desired changes, and concretize their ideas into a coherent action plan.

Evaluate what you learned in this chapter by completing the Chapter Review.

11

Assessment: Framing Solutions

LISA F. YOUNG / SHUTTERSTOCK

During assessment, generalist social workers discover abundant information about what is available, what enhances, and what constrains client systems. Assessment processes often generate such a wealth of information that workers and clients must pause to sift through and organize these discoveries into a coherent plan before taking action. To plan solutions, social workers and clients work collaboratively to address such questions as: What exactly are we trying to accomplish? Who needs to be involved? What are we going to do? There is no single correct answer to any of these questions. Even when we know exactly where we want to go, we can probably plan many routes to get there.

Framing solutions means planning, that is, transforming assessment material into manageable strategies for change. From a generalist social work perspective, planning can be complex because a generalist sees multiple options for solutions at each system level. However, when approached in a thoughtful and organized fashion, generalist planning is never a "dead end." Other possible approaches or other aspects of the situation always are amenable to change.

This chapter describes how social workers and clients develop comprehensive plans of action. Successful completion of a comprehensive plan of action prepares social workers and clients with an explicit guide for their interventions.

COLLABORATIVE PLANNING PROCESSES

A plan of action describes what social workers and clients hope to accomplish and how they intend to do it.

A plan of action describes what social workers and clients hope to accomplish and how they intend to do it. A complete plan contains several components. It has **goals** and **objectives**, possible targets for change, various strategies designed to reach those goals and objectives, a timeline, and evaluation guidelines. **Action plans** delineate activities that specify what social workers and clients will do, with whom, in what locations, and when. The more concrete the plan, the greater the likelihood of accomplishing its purpose. The more flexible the plan, the more the partners can tailor it to changes that occur during its implementation.

The ecosystems perspective naturally leads workers and clients to construct multidimensional plans. Siporin (1975) sums this up succinctly, saying that a comprehensive action plan is "multitarget, multilevel, and multiphasic in its design" (p. 259). Siporin elaborates, describing a plan's many component parts, including

- broad goals and concrete, measurable objectives;
- a prioritization of objectives into immediate, intermediate, and long term;
- strategies to use and actions to take to meet objectives;
- time frames for implementation;
- identified targets for change;
- an inventory of necessary resources such as finances, programs, or staff;
- clear division of responsibility for actions among the client system, social workers, and others;
- evaluation criteria and procedures;
- processes for altering the plan; and
- a defined point of resolution.

Pulling together such a detailed plan of action requires the full participation of both clients and social workers. They openly discuss the information they have discovered, reexamine their goals, and mutually generate ideas about how to accomplish them. Both clients and social workers actively invest in planning processes, but each brings different expertise and plays a different role. Clients are experts on what they want and on what they are willing to do. Social workers contribute technical skills for constructing plans and knowledge of resources for implementing them.

Client Expertise in Planning

Clients bring significant expertise to the planning process. They are *content experts*—they know what they want. They are *motivation experts*—they can describe what they are willing to do. They are *skill experts*—they can demonstrate their own capabilities.

Clients have ultimate power over a plan's acceptability. Social workers may suggest, but clients have the right and the responsibility to say what they can and will do. They can give the "thumbs up" or "thumbs down" on the proposed plan. Clients maintain the privilege of selecting the outcomes and strategies they desire. Collaboration guarantees that plans are relevant to what clients want, and the involvement of clients ensures that the very process of constructing an intervention plan activates clients toward its achievement.

Plans as Motivators for Action

Good plans motivate clients. They incorporate client-centered goals—statements of outcomes desired by clients. To respect self-determination and activate clients' participation, goals and strategies must naturally emerge from the collaborative efforts of workers and clients. Workers help clients clarify and operationalize their chosen goals in ways that retain the motivational quality of these goals. Goals and plans motivate clients when clients assume their ownership. To "own" their plans, clients need to see them as relevant and participate in their construction.

Worker Expertise in Planning

Workers are both technical and resource experts in the planning process. As *technical experts*, practitioners apply planning models to organize goals and ideas for change into coherent action plans. To do so, workers listen carefully to what clients want and help break down these goals into workable units. In other words, workers translate vague, abstract goals into measurable and attainable objectives. Practitioners also guide clients to articulate fully specific strategies in ways that clarify the roles of clients and workers, determine who else should be involved, set time frames, determine evaluation criteria, and specify a schedule to review progress. In planning, workers are technical experts who work with clients to design a framework that will accommodate the content of clients' situations and aspirations.

Workers are also *resource experts* in the planning process. Practitioners keep informed about what resources might be available beyond the social work relationship. In essence, effective social workers are resource directories, serving as vital links to other resources in the community. Informed social workers help clients consider possible options available in other programs, other persons to access who have relevant skills, and even indigenous community resources that are outside of the formal network of social services.

Issues Affecting Collaborative Planning

As much as possible, workers strive to develop action plans that reflect what clients themselves want to do and are hoping to accomplish. However, three factors affect a worker's ability to collaborate in this way with all clients. These factors include the participatory ability of the client, powerful forces outside of the social work relationship system, and other people who will be affected by the plan.

Assessment

Behavior: Develop mutually agreed-on intervention goals and objectives based on the critical assessment of strengths, needs, and challenges within clients and constituencies

Critical Thinking Question: Social workers and clients collaborate to construct goals, objectives, and action plans. What are the similarities and differences in the mutual roles that workers and clients play in this process?

Participatory Abilities of Clients

Sometimes, the particular challenges of clients limit their abilities to participate fully in planning (Linhorst et al., 2002). Those with overwhelming physical, cognitive, or emotional challenges may be currently unable to define where they are going, what they are willing to do, or what skills and abilities they can contribute. When this is the case, workers use their best judgment to make choices based on their awareness of the client's situation and what they believe to be the client's best interest. Workers also call on others in the client's life to assist with this process. If the client has a significant natural support system of family and friends, it is likely that they have already been involved in other parts of the process and can continue to participate in planning.

Even when involving other persons in planning, workers strive to ascertain what the client wants. For example, if the planning concerns medical treatment for a hospice patient who is physically unable to participate, any advance directives previously expressed to workers, family members, and friends should be in the forefront of the planning process. For clients who are differently abled or too young to comprehend the process fully, workers still include them and encourage them to express their views.

Outside Influences on Involuntary Clients

Not all clients are free to plan changes that they want. Involuntary clients frequently come encumbered with predetermined goals and limits on their options. For example, a client may be participating in an alternative counseling program to avoid prosecution. Or a parent may want to regain custody of children placed in foster care and be court-ordered to resolve personal issues and acquire parenting skills. In these cases, the social worker and client must consider the mandates of others. The participation of those representing such outside forces can be direct, such as ordering specific activities or treatments; or it may be indirect, allowing workers and clients to develop their own plans subject to review and approval. In either case, workers accept the responsibility of incorporating into the plan the view of whatever authority is requiring the social work intervention.

When social workers accept involuntary clients, they agree to work within the boundaries set by the mandating agent. That does not necessarily mean that clients and social workers have no influence. Social workers should not ignore their implicit power. Those in authority have shown their trust in the worker enough to believe that social work expertise is what is necessary to facilitate change. Why else would they have ordered the client to work with the social work practitioner? If workers believe that clients would benefit from a different strategy or a plan, they may choose to advocate new orders. In this way, social workers balance the desires of the client with the orders of authorities in developing plans that are compatible and agreeable to both.

Considering Significant Others

Social workers consider the perspectives of others even when clients are voluntary. If the client is a 15-year-old youth who wants to move out of the house, the views of the legal guardian are pivotal. If the client is one partner in a committed relationship, social workers use their expertise to anticipate the impact of the proposed plans on the other partner and discuss this view with the client. With the client's permission, workers may even go so far as to invite the partner's direct commentary on the developing plan. Since changes in the client will inevitably affect people in relationships with the client, the success of the plan ultimately depends on the cooperation that clients receive from those around them.

Planning with larger systems also considers the potential effect of the plan on others. For example, if the client system is a task group in the community, the foresighted worker encourages group members to seek the opinions of their constituents before implementing the plan. If the client is a social agency, the practitioner encourages agency staff to explore the impact of their proposed changes on the social service delivery system in the community network. Generalist social workers always keep in mind that they do not work with clients in isolation. Effective plans meet the client's goals, but good planning also anticipates and accounts for the responses of others.

Planning in Multiperson Systems

Planning means reaching agreement on what clients and social workers will do to accomplish their goals. This may not be such a difficult task for social workers and individual clients, who each have defined roles and clear areas of expertise for the process. But for client systems with two or more members, planning takes on an additional dimension of negotiation. In other words, members of the client system must agree on what they seek and the methods they are willing to use. Dealing with differences, resolving conflicts, and facilitating decision making are additional skills necessary for planning with multiperson client systems.

Social workers function as facilitators in group planning to ensure the best efforts of the client system and, as much as possible, give each member a voice in the plan. Practitioners facilitate planning in groups of many sizes and types—couples, families, support groups, task groups, case management teams, program units in organizations, boards of directors, and community planning councils, to name just a few. Each group may benefit from a different kind of decision-making process depending on its particular needs, goals, and characteristics.

> ▶ Watch this video as you consider that empowerment-oriented social workers collaborate with clients to develop action plans. What is the social worker's role in helping a group create a collaborative action plan?

Decision Making in Groups

Group planning has advantages. It has profound effects on members, including encouraging higher motivation to achieve, increasing commitment to implement the decision, and initiating changes in behavior and attitudes (Johnson & Johnson, 2013). Groups have more resources than any one individual and can actually generate new perspectives and possibilities as members interact with one another. But combining the resources of individual group members also has drawbacks. Effective group decision making takes more time, requires a significant level of group development and maturity, and depends on effective and respectful interpersonal communication among members. Workers facilitating group planning processes may need to help groups develop and learn how to make decisions before actually formulating action plans.

Johnson and Johnson (2013) classify group decision making into several types. Some types ultimately leave decisions in the hands of a single powerful group member. Three examples of individual members tapped to make decisions include members who are in designated authority roles, those respected as experts on the particular issues at hand, and those nominated to poll other members and make decisions based on the input they receive. Sometimes groups vest this same kind of decision-making power in a subgroup such as an executive planning committee or a team of experts chosen from among the group's membership. At other times, the whole group makes decisions democratically by averaging the opinions of all members or by voting, thereby leaving the decision to the majority. Each of these styles—decision making by single members, subgroups, or the group as a whole—may be appropriate, depending on the unique qualities of the group and the decision to be made.

Consensus

When group members have the time and necessary skills, **consensus** decision making may be the most productive (Johnson & Johnson, 2013). Consensus decision making draws on the concept of the group as a social system. It activates all members to contribute to a mutual decision. Consensus does not imply total agreement among members. Rather, consensus decisions meld the variety of views and opinions held by those participating in the process. Although at times difficult to achieve, consensus results in creative decisions that garner participants' support for implementation, draw on their collective resources, and enhance future decision-making effectiveness.

? Assess your understanding of collaborative planning processes by taking this brief quiz.

GOALS AND OBJECTIVES

Ethical social workers practice with purpose directed toward achieving clients' goals. Early in their dialogue with social workers, clients describe a preliminary direction for the work. This sense of purpose guides the assessment process and defines what may function as resources.

Now, in planning, workers and clients reconsider this original purpose in light of the assessment information; they translate this initial purpose into a set of realistic goals and concrete objectives. Therefore, as a beginning step in their planning tasks, clients stop, reflect on where they are, and focus clearly on a point in the future where they would like to be. This point of focus is the goal toward which clients and social workers plan a path of objectives and related activities.

Ethical social workers practice with purpose directed toward achieving clients' goals.

Differentiating Goals and Objectives

Articulating goals is the prelude to preparing objectives and designing specific intervention activities. Setting goals is a process whereby clients consider the outcomes they hope to achieve. Goal setting is a necessary first step before identifying specific objectives that may lead to goal attainment. For simplicity, we define goals and objectives as having distinct meanings. *Goals* are broad, general statements of what clients want to accomplish. They express the desired outcomes, ideal conditions, or long-term aims of the helping relationship. Goals are not necessarily measurable. In contrast, *objectives* are explicit statements of concrete changes desired by clients in their behaviors or situations. Objectives are readily observable and measurable. Objectives are the smaller incremental achievements required to reach goals. Workers and clients may set many objectives to achieve a single goal.

Considering Goals

A goal is a simple concept, but how do social workers and clients actually develop goals? When there are a variety of issues, which one gets attention first? Can practitioners and clients work on several goals at once? What steps translate current difficulties into attainable outcomes? Should goals be long term or immediate? Specific or global? Practitioners answer these questions differently depending on their own practice philosophies and the characteristics of their clients.

What Goals Should Clients Set?

Goals that client systems pursue vary greatly. Based on the work of Goldstein (1973), five types of goals include

1. obtaining some concrete goods or services, or needed resources such as financial assistance, employment, health care, or housing;

2. making important life decisions, resolving crises, relieving immediate distress, or removing barriers to change;

3. modifying structures in social systems such as a family, an organization, or a community by changing communication patterns, interactional behaviors, or roles and rules;

4. pursuing "foresight goals" or fulfilling some future aspiration through rational planning; and

5. recognizing the basic value of growth and change, and seeking social work services to realize their fullest potential.

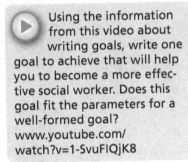
Using the information from this video about writing goals, write one goal to achieve that will help you to become a more effective social worker. Does this goal fit the parameters for a well-formed goal? www.youtube.com/ watch?v=1-SvuFIQjK8

Social workers maintain flexibility to match their strategies and styles of work with the goals toward which clients strive.

How Far Ahead?

Goals describe what we hope will happen in the future; but how far ahead do we look? Social workers maintain flexibility between a long-term outlook as a general guide and a short-term view that clearly defines achievable tasks. A balance of long-term goals with discrete short-term steps keeps the relationship moving successfully forward while ensuring that each step leads in a productive direction.

Reflect for a moment on how you set goals for yourself. Do you have some general ideas about where you would like to be in the future? A 5-year plan? A 10-year plan? As you make daily decisions, do you take small steps in the general direction of your aspirations? Are you a social work student looking ahead to professional practice? What intermediate goals and objectives will you be accomplishing as you move toward your professional career? Likely, you have a clear goal to pass the final exam in this class, but your choice of a field of social work practice may remain vague until you explore the possibilities revealed in further course work and field experiences.

As we progress through a series of accomplishments, we assess, reassess, and decide where to go next. Sometimes we change direction. This same process works for clients, too. Clients benefit from the long-distance look ahead that long-term goals provide, but they also need a clear sense of interim steps.

How Many Goals?

Clients may desire many goals simultaneously. However, setting too many diverse goals may give the partners no direction at all. When clients have a lot they want to accomplish, social workers facilitate a sequential approach to help clients organize and set priorities for issues and goals. Focusing on a reasonable number of goals facilitates their attainment. Social workers encourage clients to think broadly and optimistically about the future but guide them to move in one direction at a time.

Translating Goals into Objectives

Goal setting, as part of the planning process, functions as the initial step toward specifying concrete objectives. Practitioners should formulate objectives in meaningful and realistic ways by considering objectives from many perspectives. Effective objectives are

- steps toward goals,
- explicit and operational,
- realistic and attainable,
- discrete and time-limited,
- observable and measurable, and
- acceptable to both clients and workers. (Siporin, 1975)

The following paragraphs describe these attributes of objectives in further detail.

Steps Toward Goals

How can client systems achieve their goals? Each objective provides a part of the answer to this question. Although possible objectives are numerous and far ranging, those chosen as part of an action plan have one thing in common—each has the specific intent of moving client systems closer to their eventual goals. Objectives are not set to achieve random successes. Instead, they are focused attempts to chip away at the space between where clients are and their goals of where they would like to be. Workers and clients consider two general kinds of objectives:

1. Small positive steps in the direction of goals
2. Removal of obstacles in the path toward goals

By continuing to achieve one step at a time and to remove each obstacle encountered, clients ultimately arrive at their desired goals.

Consider the example of a social worker facilitating a community task group whose members seek the goal of economic development for their deteriorating neighborhood. After a comprehensive assessment of the neighborhood, the social worker and task group are able to specify several objectives

Evaluation

Behavior: Critically analyze, monitor, and evaluate intervention and program processes and outcomes

Critical Thinking Question: In planning, workers and clients develop plans that include goals, objectives, and action steps. How are action plans useful for evaluating client outcomes and practice interventions?

that will help them work toward this goal. They set objectives to accomplish small positive steps, including obtaining the designation of a free enterprise zone for the neighborhood, negotiating with the city council for property tax relief for new businesses, and accessing low-interest loans for neighborhood businesses from a local bank. But other objectives are also necessary to remove identified barriers, including the negative image of the neighborhood and the high rate of crime. Setting additional objectives to enhance the neighborhood's image as an historic district through a public relations campaign, to increase police patrols, and to institute a neighborhood watch program will be steps toward removing these obstacles. As illustrated by this example, carefully developed objectives either take a direct step toward achieving goals or removing a potential obstacle.

Explicit and Operational

A comprehensive set of objectives that considers changes in clients and their environments may involve many persons and projects. Therefore, stating objectives in as precise and exact a manner as possible is essential. Clearly stated and mutually understood, objectives are prerequisites to establishing a common understanding and building consensus about courses of action. Frequently, failures to achieve objectives result from miscommunication. Making objectives explicit and understandable from the beginning effectively reduces this margin of error.

Clients and social workers collaborate to identify goals for change.

AUREMAR/SHUTTERSTOCK

Objectives function as bridges from goals to the activities implemented to reach goals. In other words, objectives break down broad goals into small enough achievements that it begins to be obvious what actions social workers, clients, and others will take to accomplish their purposes. In the previous example of the community task group, the concrete objective to receive low-interest bank loans for neighborhood businesses already implies specific tasks. Obviously, the group will need to designate certain members to contact banks, business owners, and interested entrepreneurs about this project. Explicit objectives state the desired change and the direction of change in terms of specific target behaviors—who will accomplish what. In this example, the task group members will convince local banks to grant low-interest loans to neighborhood businesses. Workers and clients can quickly operationalize well-formed objectives into clearly defined strategies and action steps.

Realistic and Attainable

Success builds on success. Clients need objectives that are realistic, given their present capabilities, readily available opportunities, and potentially accessible resources. This does not imply that clients should settle for less than they desire. It simply means that workers and clients should construct and prioritize objectives in such a way that each is possible to achieve and each achievement makes the next objective easier to accomplish. Objectives that, under present circumstances, require too big a leap or too much change set up clients for failure and disillusionment. For example, when a client who is unable to read sets an objective to pass a high school equivalency exam, disappointment is likely. Instead, when the worker helps this client set realistic incremental objectives of enrolling in an alternative high school and beginning to work with a tutor, the objective to pass the equivalency test becomes more achievable.

Structuring success into a plan of action is essential for maintaining client motivation and facilitating empowerment. Experiences with success lead to feelings of self-efficacy and beliefs in competence to achieve certain levels of performance (Bandura, 1997, 2002, 2006, 2008, 2012). Clients who perceive themselves as competent are likely to persist and exert greater efforts in their pursuit of goals. Conversely, clients who perceive themselves as ineffective may be reluctant to engage in change, may expect failure, and may view failures as evidence of personal deficiencies. Workers have responsibilities to work with clients to set attainable objectives, thereby instilling a sense of confidence and control in effecting desired outcomes.

When clients experience success and view themselves as causal agents of the outcome, they approach future events with feelings of hopefulness. In other words, accomplishments empower clients with confidence and hope. Zimmerman (1990) states that "learned hopefulness suggests that experiences that provide opportunities to enhance perceived control will help individuals cope with stress and solve problems in their personal lives" (pp. 72–73). Experiencing or perceiving a lack of control over events or outcomes may evoke expectations that events in the future are out of reach and beyond control, resulting in symptoms of helplessness (Seligman, 1975). Setting and accomplishing realistic and attainable objectives initiates a chain of success that leads to hope, increased competence, and feelings of power and control.

Discrete and Time Limited

Setting realistic objectives means taking small steps. Continuing success means dividing goals into objective units that are discrete enough to accomplish one step after another. For example, Sean, a client with profound intellectual disabilities, may be overwhelmed by the singular objective of learning to brush his teeth. But when the worker breaks this objective into the discrete accomplishments of Sean picking up his toothbrush, applying toothpaste, wetting the brush, placing it in his mouth, and moving the brush across his teeth, success is now within reach. Sean and the worker can now focus on one objective at a time and celebrate each success as it occurs.

Redefining objectives as mini-objectives also opens up options of working on objectives sequentially (achieving one objective after another) or concurrently (attempting several objectives at one time). Sean, in the previous example, will likely benefit from a sequential approach. A task group, such as the one in the example about working on economic development, has members that can work simultaneously and efficiently in several directions at once and therefore can use a concurrent approach. Achieving each small step, whether sequentially or concurrently, leads to quantum leaps as clients see results, experience success, and gain confidence. Research supports that "self motivation can be best created and sustained by attainable subgoals that lead to larger future ones" (Bandura & Schunk, 1981, p. 587). Feeling satisfied with their achievement of one objective, clients gain a sense of mastery and tend to persist in their change efforts.

Workers and clients also incorporate time considerations when formulating discrete objectives, usually by selecting objectives that can be achieved within a few weeks. If clients cannot accomplish an objective quickly, the objective is too broad or too long term. Workers and clients should break it into smaller sequential objectives. When meeting at designated intervals, such as once a week, workers and clients can easily consider what new objectives to complete by the next time they meet. Quick accomplishments relieve immediate pressures and posture client systems toward further advancements.

Observable and Measurable

In response to the press for accountability and for the evaluation of practice effectiveness, objectives serve an important function in assessing goal achievement. Objectives concretely articulate the path toward goals. Reaching various objectives provides a series of interim markers for checking progress and affirming success on the way to desired goals.

Well-formed objectives express desired outcomes in both behavioral and quantitative terms. To imagine an objective that is behavioral, envision what the outcome will look like. Ask yourself whether you and someone with you would agree on what you are seeing. If both you and the other observer would be likely to describe what you are observing in a similar way, then this observation could be set as a behaviorally observable outcome. If you can "see" when an objective is achieved, it is behavioral.

Objectives are measurable when they state specifically to what extent and how often the events or behaviors will occur. For example, when a family sets the objective to resolve differences through negotiation rather than conflict, they could evaluate the achievement of this objective by noting each time differences arise and recording the interaction that follows. Behaviorally observable and measurable objectives assist in evaluating outcomes.

Acceptable to Client and Worker

To be effective, any objective must relate to a particular client system, reflecting its strengths, distinct capabilities, current situation, and goals. Too often, workers clone somewhat standard objectives from one case plan to another without considering how a specific client would like to proceed. Rubber-stamp objectives do not account for a particular client's goals and values. They cannot replace objectives developed collaboratively and tailored to address a client's unique needs.

Effective objectives directly relate to changes that clients believe will improve their situations. Even when workers envision social or environmental changes as beneficial for clients, ethical social workers recognize the clients' privilege to select goals. Social justice cannot be achieved at the expense of people who are oppressed. Consider the example of the worker who wants to change the state's policy on distributing public assistance, knowing that it will help a specific client who is a single mother receiving benefits. To set this objective, the client needs to understand clearly the implications of this macrolevel approach for her own situation to determine whether she wants to address her individual goals in this way. The product and process of this strategy must be something that this client truly believes is new, improved, or enhanced her own life. Ethical social workers do not use a client as a springboard to larger issues that are of more concern to them than to the client.

Workers also consider whether clients can achieve their objectives without infringing on the rights of others or without coercing change in nonconsenting players. From a generalist perspective, implementing change activities usually involves others in addition to the client system. Even if people are not directly involved in the work, changes in the client system will likely affect others around the client. Social workers maintain professional ethics when they evaluate the potential impact of achieving the client system's objectives on the rights of the client and the rights of others.

? Assess your understanding of goals and objectives by taking this brief quiz.

CONSTRUCTING ACTION PLANS

Understanding goals and objectives prepares social workers and clients to develop action plans. Designing action plans with clients at any system level is a deliberate and careful process involving sequential steps. For example, Figure 11.1 illustrates this process in planning with organizations. Plans build on the assessment information gathered and outline procedures for accomplishing purposes. To develop a relevant and workable plan of action, workers and clients complete the following steps:

1. Set positive and clear outcome goals that fit what clients want and that draw on assessment information.

2. Write concrete and achievable objectives.

3. Prioritize objectives.

4. Generate possible intervention strategies using the broad perspective of generalist practice.

5. Specify tasks, responsibilities, and actions necessary to meet objectives.

6. Determine intervals and methods to review and modify the plan.

Clarifying Outcome Goals

Plans build on the assessment information gathered and outline procedures for accomplishing purposes.

As the beginning step in constructing action plans, workers and clients clarify goals. They consider what they have learned about clients' situations and capabilities during the assessment process in preparation for framing clear goals. Workers ensure that clients formulate goals in positive terms, stating what clients want and will be doing rather than what they don't want or will be avoiding.

Reorienting Problems to Outcomes

Social workers often help clients reorient their self-described problems into a vision of a desired outcome or solution. In other words, workers help turn clients around from looking back at their problems to facing forward and describing what their lives will be like when they have reached the solution.

Stated in positive language, goals reflect aims to enhance or strengthen, not to remediate or reduce. For example, an individual experiencing stress about a recent job loss may state a goal of obtaining other employment. Likewise, a family that seeks counseling because of concern about the constant yelling and bickering among family members may state a goal of finding new ways to resolve differences. Neighborhood residents distressed about gang activity may state the broad goal of creating a safe neighborhood.

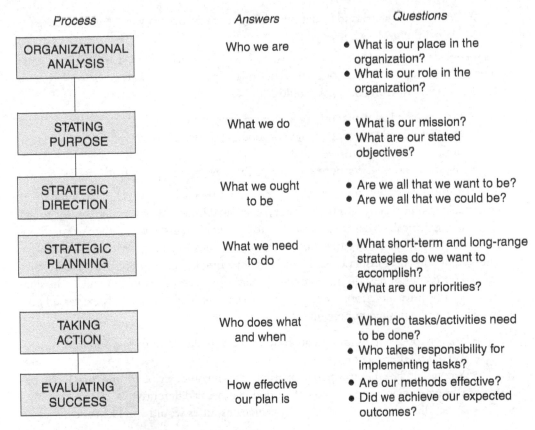

	Process	*Answers*	*Questions*
	ORGANIZATIONAL ANALYSIS	Who we are	• What is our place in the organization? • What is our role in the organization?
	STATING PURPOSE	What we do	• What is our mission? • What are our stated objectives?
	STRATEGIC DIRECTION	What we ought to be	• Are we all that we want to be? • Are we all that we could be?
	STRATEGIC PLANNING	What we need to do	• What short-term and long-range strategies do we want to accomplish? • What are our priorities?
	TAKING ACTION	Who does what and when	• When do tasks/activities need to be done? • Who takes responsibility for implementing tasks?
	EVALUATING SUCCESS	How effective our plan is	• Are our methods effective? • Did we achieve our expected outcomes?

Figure 11.1 Organizational Process Planning
Strategic planning exemplifies one planning process used with organizational clients. This type of planning is a systematic and interactive process used to realize long-term organizational objectives through the construction of short-term action plans. The process involves broad-based participation to examine organizational potential, set goals and priorities, and create a detailed plan of action for implementing the organization's vision for the future.

Based on a presentation, *Visioning the Future: Organizational Strategic Planning* by B. L. DuBois (April 1993).

In each example, the worker helps the client system transform what has been into what will be.

Consider the example of Nate Hardy, a social worker with the Northside Development Association. Nate's primary client system is the Northside community itself. He works with various formal and informal groups in the community to meet his agency's mission of improving the quality of life in Northside. In the process of setting positive goals with a neighborhood group, Nate Hardy does two things. He strives for concreteness to describe the current concerns of the neighborhood residents, and he works to reorient residents to consider the future.

To understand concerns concretely, Nate uses responding skills:

- When a resident says, "I'm unhappy," Nate may respond by inquiring, "With whom?" or "About what?"
- When another member of the neighborhood group says we are "falling apart," Nate can respond with, "What are you noticing that leads you to this conclusion?"

- When a neighborhood leader says "things can't go on this way," Nate can ask, "What things? In what way?"

As the residents answer Nate's questions, each will begin to offer a clearer view of what they are seeking. But these concrete views of the present are likely to be replete with visions of what is wrong or what should stop. Nate is likely to learn that

- the first resident wants others to stop ignoring his opinion,
- the second resident of the neighborhood group wants group members to stop arguing among themselves, and
- the indigenous leader hopes to change the way the city budgets its money.

Each of these assertions begins to hint at goals, but they all stop short of defining them concretely and positively. On the contrary, each goal indicates what clients want to get rid of, not specifically what they would like to have happen instead. In other words, these tentative goals focus on negative outcomes (what needs to change) rather than positive ones (what will occur instead). Social workers encourage clients to positively frame their desired outcomes by describing what will be happening rather than what will be missing.

To set positive directions, Nate responds to each resident's negatively expressed goal to convert it to a positive statement by saying the following:

- So, if people stop ignoring you, how would you like them to respond instead? What will they be doing?
- You would like the group to stop arguing. Can you describe for me how it will be when group members handle their disagreements differently?
- What differences in the way the city allocates funds would you like to see?

Nate's continued prodding to consider the future leads each resident to visualize a positive outcome:

- I want this group to include my ideas in their neighborhood development plan.
- I want the group to negotiate decisions cooperatively.
- I would like to see the city adopt new procedures that access citizen's views at each step of the budgeting process.

Notice how Nate helps these residents construct visual descriptions of what they would like in their futures. Walter and Peller (1992) call this process movie making. A concrete and positive vision of goals is most effective.

Building on Positive Momentum

Not all clients who seek social work services experience situations characterized as problematic. Many others, after a strength-oriented assessment process, may see their situations in a new light. In these cases, goals set in planning may be to encourage something to occur more often or to stabilize an already improving situation. For instance, a newly formed stepfamily may discover that their increased expression of negative feelings is actually a good sign. It indicates that the family is becoming closer, blending together in a more intimate way. They may set goals to learn more about common transitions in stepfamilies to help them anticipate and resolve challenges likely to arise as the new family blends two distinct lifestyles and traditions into one.

Setting positive directions for goals is a straightforward affair when clients are optimistic and recognize existing strengths or recent improvements.

- When a woman says "Things have gotten better since I called you," the worker responds to identify what is working by asking, "What have you noticed that is better?"
- When a couple agrees they "feel hopeful," the worker asks for more details by asking, "What is happening that contributes to this feeling?"
- When the liaison from the agency says, "We want to continue to make consensus decisions," the worker reflects and highlights the goal by saying, "I hear you saying that I am here to help you stabilize your abilities to make consensus decisions."

In each of these examples, the worker continues to clarify what works so that the worker and client can set definitive goals that maintain and strengthen current productive functioning.

Sorting Out Possibilities

Translating problems into positive goals for the future is only one part of an effective goal-setting process. To ensure coherent goals, social workers also help clarify information by ordering it logically. Because too many goals may confuse the direction of the work, social workers assist clients in articulating what is most important to them. Helpful ways for social workers to organize information include two seemingly opposite skills. The first involves arranging complex and integrated information into separate compartments. The second involves grouping similar information around common themes.

Creating Discrete Units

The technique of creating discrete units means taking issues that are complex and separating them into component parts to consider them one piece at a time. In contrast to the approach of clustering, which works to resolve several related issues at once, partializing takes seemingly insurmountable challenges and breaks them down into achievable units. Partializing relieves pressure on client systems and sets the stage for deciding which first step is likely to have the greatest impact on subsequent successes.

Grouping by Similarity

In contrast, social workers can look for similarities among various issues. By finding the threads that run through several issues, social workers ascertain themes that have multiple ramifications. Clustering these issues leads to setting selective and efficient goals, the achievement of which can have multiple benefits. A mother's overprotectiveness, a son's anxious withdrawal, and a father's depression may all spring from the threat of the surrounding neighborhood. Identifying this central theme may lead to neighborhood change strategies or the family's move to a new location. Addressing this common issue brings relief to each of the family's members. Organizing issues coherently facilitates the planning process.

Writing Effective Objectives

Writing effective objectives is the heart of a good case plan. Well-formed objectives embody the realistic hopes of what clients will accomplish. Good objectives are rooted in concrete information about what clients need and the strengths and resources with which they have to work. Outcome objectives clearly lay out "who will achieve what when." They function as guides and give us markers to indicate if we are getting somewhere or if we need to reevaluate what we are doing and try another way.

Measurable objectives include a number of components. According to Sheafor and Horejsi (2014), a good intervention objective answers a five-part question:

- Who . . .
- will do what . . .
- to what extent . . .
- under what condition . . .
- by when?

This simple formula provides a useful tool for conceptualizing objectives. Applying it results in objectives that are specific, achievable, and measurable. Consider the following examples of objectives:

- Denise will receive a passing grade in math by the end of the semester.
- Fernando will secure a teaching job within the next month.
- The Patterson family will resolve each disagreement that arises in the next week by using the *stop, listen, and compliment* approach.
- Each administrative staff member of Neighbors United will access a community action grant within the next fiscal year.
- The task group will successfully persuade the city council to implement gang prevention activities within 3 months.

Notice how each objective offers complete information, yet does so simply and clearly. To ensure that they are writing objectives in a meaningful way, workers can evaluate each objective by using the following criteria:

- Is it active? Does it say what someone will achieve?
- Does it specify one discrete accomplishment rather than many?
- Does it include a time frame for completion?
- Can you observe, measure, and evaluate it?
- Do the social worker, client, and other participants understand it and what their particular part of it is?
- Is it easy enough to accomplish, yet significant enough to make it worth the effort?
- Are both client and worker comfortable with it?
- Does it fit with agency practices and social work ethics? (Sheafor & Horejsi, 2014)

Clearly written objectives lead clients directly to the goals they seek.

Determining Measures

The true test of whether an objective is a concrete enough outcome to guide actions is whether the partners can measure its achievement. Realistically, if clients and workers are to know that they have been successful, they must be able to identify concrete achievement criteria for each objective in the action plan.

For example, consider the efforts of the Child Welfare Division of Northside Prevention Services. The Division has set an objective to increase child safety within the community during the next year. Measurable criteria for achieving this objective include the following:

- The reported incidence of child abuse will decrease by 25 percent over the same time period from last year.
- Fifty percent of residents responding to a random telephone survey will indicate they would report child abuse if they suspect it.
- The Public Health Department will report a 50 percent reduction in child injuries from poisoning and household accidents in the 3 months after the home safety campaign.

Determining ways to measure the attainment of objectives focuses the efforts of all involved in implementing the plan.

Prioritizing Objectives

After articulating objectives, clients and social workers examine them to establish priorities. This process assigns preference to certain objectives in light of critical needs and resource availability. Clearly, protecting a client's safety, relieving distress, and meeting basic human needs are always priority actions. But beyond addressing these immediate needs, setting priorities poses a number of value decisions. Social workers and clients develop priorities by considering motivational factors, the likelihood of success, and the work that might have the greatest or most widespread effect. Logical sequencing may be inherent in the objectives themselves, since some things have a natural order. Questions that may help clients rank priorities include the following:

- Which objectives are most motivating to the client?
- Which will most likely lead to success?
- Which issues are most pressing?
- What does the client want to do first?
- Is there a logical order in which to proceed?
- Is anyone at risk?
- Are priority actions necessary?

Clients have privileges to define the priorities. Social workers have responsibilities to identify risks and take necessary actions to ensure the safety of clients and others.

Screening Generalist Intervention Strategies

Generalist social workers think broadly. Even though workers encourage clients to focus narrowly on concrete outcomes, they broaden clients' perspectives to recognize multiple strategies to achieve these goals and objectives. Systemically oriented social workers acknowledge and act on the principle that changes in one part of the system create changes in other parts of the system. This means that workers and clients can aim anywhere in their related ecosystems—inside or outside of the social work relationship system—to create changes in the direction of desired outcomes.

Policy Practice

Behavior: Apply critical thinking to analyze, formulate, and advocate for policies that advance human rights and social, economic, and environmental justice

Critical Thinking Question: Generalist social workers develop strategies that may include interventions at many system levels, including the level of social policy. What questions should social workers consider to determine whether a specific social policy should be a target for change?

Considering multiple system levels as targets for change adds the generalist perspective to the planning process. During assessment, workers and clients trace the transactional nature of issues. As a result, they discover numerous locations toward which to direct their efforts, specifically, toward client systems, related environmental systems, or the transactions between systems. Interventions at any level may produce the desired change. Synchronizing actions at many system levels, sequentially or in concert, may have the greatest impact.

Relating Outcomes to Locations for Change

Deciding on goals and objectives and locating places to direct attempts at change are companion processes. Considering what you want to accomplish has implications for where you need to work. Considering the places to which you have access to work has implications for the kinds of activities that are possible. Once clients articulate the outcomes they desire, planning how to reach those goals can begin in either place. In other words, workers and clients consider two general questions: What resource systems are available, and how might they contribute to reaching the goal? Or, conversely, what are the steps to take, and what locations are possible for achieving those steps? Each question starts from a different place but ends up with a realistic plan.

Monkman (1991) presents a framework of broad outcome categories for both persons and their environments that illustrates the relationship between outcomes desired and locations for attempting changes. Each outcome category correlates with a specific system level or possible target for change.

Outcomes for Persons	
Survival outcomes	Obtaining and using resources defined as basic necessities for life activities
Affiliation outcomes	Forming close personal relationships or support systems
Growth and achievement	Expanding contributions to one's self and others
Information and skills	Increasing knowledge to acquire proficiency to deal effectively with life situations
Environmental Outcomes	
Informal resources	Accessing extended kin and friendship networks for support, affection, advice, and services
Formal resources	Accessing services from membership organizations and associations
Societal resources	Accessing resources found in social institutions
Expectations	Seeking redefinition of normative behavior and changing role expectations by persons or institutions in the social environment
Laws, policies, customs, and rules	Seeking change by governing and legislative bodies and in administrative rules

Box 11.1 Planning in Aging Services: A Policy–Practice Connection

In 2013 in the United States, 44.7 million, or about 1 in 7, people were 65 years of age or older (USHHS-AoA, 2014). Projections indicate that the number of people over the age of 65 in the United States will double by 2060. Those older than 85 will likely triple, increasing to 14.1 million. The number of centenarians (people 100 years of age and older) has doubled since 1980. The population group older than 65 is also becoming more diverse. The percentage of older adults described as members of minority population groups is expected to rise from 21 percent in 2013 to 28.5 percent in 2030. Demographers anticipate the fastest rate of growth among Hispanic Americans, which will result in a projected 153 percent increase in Hispanic Americans older than 65 by 2030. Projections also indicate that the number of older adults who are foreign born will increase to 16 million by 2050 (Treast & Batalova, 2007, as cited in Choi, 2015). The dramatic increase in the number of people who are 65 years of age and older focuses social work attention on developing policies that will accommodate the needs of older Americans (Bakk et al., 2014; Choi, 2015; Robinson et al., 2012; Rogers et al., 2013; Ruggiano, 2012; Smith et al., 2013).

Developing and implementing effective social policies to meet the needs of those 65 and older is complicated by the diversity and complexity of issues they face. Older adults of any age can be vigorous and healthy, or they may be dependent and physically or cognitively frail. Most older adults live independently or with assistance in the community, but some require the supports offered in specialized care settings. Although the rate of poverty among people older than 65 is lower than that of the general population, people in this age group tend to live on fixed incomes and face the challenges of rising costs in health care, energy, housing, and long-term care. For example, the average annual out-of-pocket cost for health care in 2013 was over $5,000 (USHHS-AoA, 2014).

Policy change is a critical component of addressing the needs of older Americans. Among the policy principles specifically identified by the NASW (2008a) are

- expanding gerontological content in social work programs;
- advancing policies that promote productive aging and that support death with dignity;
- strengthening policies that address the service needs of all older people and protect vulnerable older adults;
- advocating a full complement of funding options for services that meet the biopsychosocial needs of older adults and their caregivers;
- promoting a comprehensive continuum of health care for older adults; and
- involving older adults and caregivers in the design and evaluation of policies, programs, and services.

The dramatic change in the numbers and proportion of people aged 65 and older have profound implications for the infrastructures of social policy that support the full range of services for older adults. Members of the National Association of Social Workers, in their roles as policy makers, can give legislative testimony about the needs of an aging population and participate in drafting and implementing social policies that are responsive to the issues faced by persons in this cohort group.

The particular goals that clients seek lead workers and clients around the ecosystem to gather resources, forge new connections, or make necessary changes. Since clients' problems do not arise in isolation of their situations, solutions also are contextually based. As clients focus on the objectives necessary to achieve their goals, the places they must direct their efforts become more obvious. For example, a teenage girl who wants to improve her academic performance may choose strategies that lead her to school to learn what teachers want from her, to her family to negotiate a quiet space and time away from chores in which to complete homework, to her social group to locate a study partner, and to her own self to increase her persistence in completing tasks. Each one of these systems influences her current functioning and can contribute to her goal of improved academic performance. The goals and objectives that clients set lead logically to the locations to consider for solutions.

Choosing Targets for Change

For each client system, there are four general locations to consider as targets for change:

- The client system
- Subsystems of the client system
- Environmental systems in the context of the client
- Transactional systems or the connections between clients and their environments

A change in any one of these areas of functioning may result in the achievement of clients' goals. Generalist social workers and their clients frequently use a multi-faceted strategy by selecting and combining many targets for change into a unified approach.

Reconsider the example of Nate Hardy and his client system, the Northside community. In open forums, the community has set an objective to increase the availability of low-cost housing. Now, in beginning to formulate strategies, Nate and interested community members are scanning the resource systems of the neighborhood to determine where to direct their efforts at change. To facilitate this effort, Nate charts out the following ideas and locations for change to present for the citizens' review.

Client System

- Create a community newsletter that lists and compares costs of available rentals to encourage competition and lower rents
- Establish an annual festival to celebrate the history of the neighborhood and its current cultural diversity as a way to increase cohesion and affiliation among residents

Subsystems

- Organize a new group of community members with home-building and repair skills to volunteer to fix up currently uninhabited homes
- Initiate a program with the Northside Vocational High School to remodel abandoned homes as educational projects and sell them at cost to neighborhood residents

Environmental Systems

- Modify the local banking practices of lending only for new construction projects
- Change city ordinances that limit the number of "unrelated" persons in the same household to allow friends to live together and reduce housing costs through sharing

Transactional Systems

- Organize a tenant's rights group to attend city council meetings and advocate for new rent control ordinances
- Obtain a federal grant to build scattered subsidized housing units throughout the neighborhood

All the options Nate lists are strategies involving different parts of the Northside community and its environment. Any one strategy works toward the goal of increasing available low-cost housing in the neighborhood. Choosing a combination of these approaches offers even greater possibilities for achieving a broad-based impact.

All client systems have component parts and environments that offer possible locations for change. Consider a family system. A worker could facilitate changes in the ways the family makes decisions. Another possible change could be in how the parents relate, which, in turn, would affect the rest of the family. How much extended family support the family uses, how parents and children relate to jobs and school, and how society views this family in terms of culture, race, socioeconomic status, and lifestyle all contribute to what is happening with this family, and all also hold potential for how this family might change. When considering the places to intervene, clients and social workers look broadly to consider changes at many system levels.

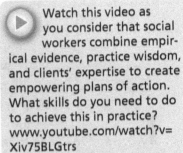 Watch this video as you consider that social workers combine empirical evidence, practice wisdom, and clients' expertise to create empowering plans of action. What skills do you need to do to achieve this in practice? www.youtube.com/watch?v=Xiv75BLGtrs

Choosing Effective Strategies

To determine what strategies to implement requires a careful organization of available information and options. Workers can use many methods to generate options. Frequently, workers compile written lists with clients to ensure that they comprehensively consider everything that is necessary. Some record-keeping procedures require such lists of identified strengths, needs, and possibilities for change.

Brainstorming

A helpful method to use in considering strategies is **brainstorming**, which generates discussion among many individuals to frame multiple potential solutions. In brainstorming, workers and clients list as many ideas as they can imagine without any evaluation of which would be best. The free-flowing nature of this process unleashes creativity and cooperation. This strategy is especially useful in planning with multiperson client systems because it encourages all to participate in the planning process with no fear that their ideas will be criticized.

Matching Resources and Needs

Matching resources available to client needs is another effective approach for developing intervention strategies. For example, Cowger and Snively (2002) recommend charting information to include client system strengths and needs on one side and environmental system resources and obstacles on the other. In this way, the partners delineate the strengths and resources available with respect to the challenges presented. Note how this charting emphasizes the transactional nature of client issues, highlighting possible strategies in the environment as well as those targeting changes in the client system itself.

Cowger and Snively's (2002) framework illustrates how the organizational processes chosen influence the planning that follows. This charting method focuses on both clients and environments and builds on strengths in the process. Consider the differences in the plan that would result from a procedure focusing only on a client's failures or inadequacies. How the partners organize the information makes a difference. Social workers help clients organize information in ways that motivate, encourage, and predict success. The questions to ask when matching challenges with resources include the following:

- What strengths and abilities does the client demonstrate in one area of functioning that might transfer to dealing with the challenge?
- What untapped resources are present in the environment to meet the client's defined needs?
- What does the client need that the worker can provide directly or access for the client?
- What resources need to be expanded or developed?

Answering all these questions orients workers and clients to the resources they currently have to meet objectives and to other resources that might be necessary. Social workers also evaluate the usefulness of potential social service resources to choose effective strategies (see Table 11.1).

Table 11.1   Schema for Assessing Resources

Criteria	Description
Relevance	Does the resource offer services that are congruent with the client system's identified needs?
	Will the resource meet the client system's goals?
Availability	Will the resource be available when the client system requires it?
	Is there a waiting list?
	Do certain circumstances qualify for a quick response?
Accessibility	Is the office located on convenient travel routes?
	Does the resource offer services in the client's language? Sign language?
	Are the facilities accessible to those with disabilities?
Eligibility	What are the guidelines for receiving this service? Are there income, location, age, or other qualifiers?
Applications	Is there a formal application process? Who needs to fill out what form? What time frame is imposed on the application process?
	Are supporting documents required?
Fee	Is there a sliding fee scale?
	If fees are involved, has the client system been informed of the fee schedule?
	Will the client realistically be able to pay for the service? Under what circumstances can the fee be waived?
Feasibility	Considering all of the aforementioned factors, is this a viable resource?

Emphasizing Client Strengths

The most empowering plans build on client strengths. To discover strength-oriented options, workers and clients ask themselves two questions:

- What are clients doing right that they should continue to do; in other words, what should they reinforce and strengthen?
- What strengths and resources of clients or their social and physical environments apply to the current situation?

Enhancing existing strengths and matching resources to needs are steps toward building action plans that clients can approach with feelings of confidence and expectations of success.

Enhancing existing strengths and matching resources to needs are steps toward building action plans that clients can approach with feelings of confidence and expectations of success.

Incorporating Resources of Social Workers

Good action plans also anticipate what workers can bring to the process. What do workers know? What can workers do? To what resources do workers have connections? Some needs that clients bring may require these types of resources for successful resolutions, but be cautious here. Empowering social workers recognize the need to hold their own resources in check so as not to encourage dependency on the part of clients. Workers do not develop strategies that place themselves in central roles and leave the clients as passive observers. The best strategies place clients in charge and use workers' resources and skills as supplemental tools. Clients need as many opportunities as possible to experience their own effectiveness and to affirm their expertise.

Weighing Costs and Benefits

Not all available strategies are equal. It is likely that no perfect solution exists; there are pros and cons to each possibility. Before composing definitive objectives, workers and clients weigh the costs and benefits of each proposed strategy. Pertinent questions include the following:

- Is there an advantage to using one resource rather than another?
- What are the costs of each approach in terms of time and money?
- Are there possible hidden costs?
- Are some strategies easier to implement than others?
- What are the potential risks or consequences?
- Do certain combinations work better than others?
- Is there a logical order for proceeding? Should one approach be implemented first and another held back and used only if necessary?
- Should accessing multiple resources be gradual or simultaneous?
- Do clients think that certain strategies will work better for them than others?
- Which options are best based on the worker's practice experience?
- Does practice evaluation research offer suggestions about approaches?

The answers to these questions lead clients and workers to choose strategies that have the greatest likelihood of success.

Delineating Tasks and Responsibilities

Some strategies are so simple and direct that the way to achieve them may be obvious. At other times, additional specification is necessary so that all people involved know their roles and responsibilities in completing the task. Consider the example of a task group on gang prevention. To achieve their objective of influencing the city council to adopt their recommendations, the task group needs to complete more detailed planning. Tasks and responsibilities assigned may include having one member call the city clerk to reserve a place on the council meeting's agenda. In addition, another member will arrive at the meeting early to save a block of chairs so that task group members can sit together and be seen as a cohesive political unit. Someone will call the local newspaper to guarantee news coverage. The social worker will write a news release incorporating the group's recommendations to distribute to the representatives of the media. Delineating these specific roles and responsibilities ensures a coordinated effort in implementing the objective.

Setting Reviews and Evaluations

Effectively written objectives define intervals for reviewing progress. Because they specify time frames, workers and clients naturally will stop to review how they are doing at those times. Each review offers workers and clients an opportunity to proceed as planned or to make modifications.

Some social delivery systems structure intervals for review in their program procedures. For example, school social workers are very familiar with the Individual Education Plan (IEP), which is an annually updated plan outlining the program tailored for a student with special educational needs. To accommodate unanticipated events, rapid improvements, or changing needs, each IEP also offers opportunities to reconvene the planning body, if necessary. Good planning requires periodic reviews and flexibility to modify plans as necessary.

Contracting

The concept of **contract** underlies all phases of the social work process. Simply, a contract specifies the terms of service to which the client and social worker agree. Although formal contracts usually refer to the explicit agreements that social workers and clients forge to operationalize action plans, an implied contract secures the social worker–client relationship from the initial contact to the last. Contractual agreements vary from assumed to explicit. Clients and workers may operate under either an informal understanding or a more formal written contract. The formality of the contract varies depending on the preferences of both the worker and the client, and agency policy.

Clarity is essential for a contract's success. Workers ensure that all parties involved in the contract clearly understand what they are agreeing to do and hoping to achieve. The most effective contracts have flexibility, incorporate the views of clients, and concretely define the next step.

The Evolving Contract

Describing the contract between social worker and client as evolutionary makes sense in terms of the developmental nature of

Assessment

Behavior: Select appropriate intervention strategies based on the assessment, research knowledge, and values and preferences of clients and constituencies

Critical Thinking Question: In theory, the phases of engagement, assessment, intervention, and evaluation are distinct, but in practice, they often overlap and occur simultaneously. How is each of these four phases of practice reflected in preparing an intervention action plan?

the social work process. The social work contract evolves through phases of agreeing to work together to agreeing to assess the situation to agreeing to the plan for change. Contracts also evolve in the context of work with groups. Members originally contract with themselves and the worker for their own individual purposes, but they change this contract to incorporate more group-centered content as they begin to function as part of the group. What members are working on, how they view themselves, and what seem possible change as the work continues.

The contract changes as the professional relationship and focus of the work progresses over time (Table 11.2). Initially, workers and clients agree to meet and form a working alliance—the **contract for relationship**. The initial dialogue leads to clarity about purpose and defines a direction for the partners to explore the situation further—the **contract for assessment**. Discovering available resources leads to an explicit plan to accomplish the concrete goals defined—the **contract for change**. When social workers and clients achieve their desired outcomes, they agree to dissolve the relationship—the **contract for resolution**. At each point of contracting and recontracting for their work together, social workers and clients have opportunities to redefine their collaboration.

Contracting for Change

When social workers and clients agree to a comprehensive plan of action, this constitutes a contract for change. Contracting for change details the agreement between the client and social worker about roles and responsibilities with respect to such features as goals, objectives, strategies and activities, and methods and timing of evaluation. Creating an action plan clearly lays out the work that a client system and social worker will do. Forging an agreement to proceed with the plan is a contract for change. There is evidence that social work contracts for change, especially those that state objectives explicitly, enhance practice effectiveness. Contracts also give practitioners measurable criteria on which to base their evaluations of success.

Contracting as an Empowering Process

Contracting with clients has benefits beyond a simple clarification of current status and future direction. Contracts emphasize client participation, facilitate communication,

Table 11.2 The Evolving Contract

Phase	Type of Contract	Description
Dialogue phase	Contract for relationship	Agreement to form a working partnership to define direction
	Contract for assessment	Agreement to further explore the situation and assess the resources available
Discovery phase	Contract for change	Agreement to a plan of action to activate and expand resources and opportunities
Development phase	Contract for resolution	Agreement to conclude the client–social worker relationship

improve commitment, foster a sense of autonomy and self-determination, and provide a framework for reflecting on outcomes.

Each time that social workers and clients renegotiate their working agreement, clients experience their power in the relationship. They have an opportunity to control what happens next. Renegotiating the contract also explicitly gives clients permission to change the direction of their work. It can rebalance the power when a social worker's expertise has encouraged the client to settle into a dependent pattern in their relationship. Explicitly discussing the evolving contract contributes to sharing power with clients over the course of the relationship.

> **?** Assess your understanding of constructing action plans by taking this brief quiz.

LOOKING FORWARD

Goal-directed planning focuses on achieving desired outcomes, the ultimate measure of success. Some people question whether this emphasis on goals and end points represents a culturally biased view. Are concreteness and goal achievement Western precepts that ignore significant intangibles, such as relationship and process variables? Can purposeful change be guided by a process vision of relating how you want to relate and approaching challenges in a deliberately ethical and proactive way?

Framing solutions means planning how client systems and workers intend to reach their goals. Planning accomplishes important tasks. It clarifies what the client is seeking, considers what aspects of the client system hold possibilities for solutions, and determines strategies necessary to succeed. The culmination of the planning process is a concrete action plan. Mutual planning produces a synergistic solution that reflects the expertise of both clients and workers. In the upcoming development phase, clients and workers implement the plan, evaluate its effectiveness, and wrap up their work together in a way that maintains progress. Chapter 12 describes the consultancy, resource management, and educational roles that workers play in intervention processes.

> Evaluate what you learned in this chapter by completing the Chapter Review.

Intervention: Activating Resources

NATASA ADZIC/SHUTTERSTOCK

Donna Lester is the mother of 8-year-old twin boys whom the Child Protective Unit at the State Department of Social Services recently determined were beyond Donna's control. Donna herself initiated the chain reaction that led to the removal of her children by asking the local police department for help. The police then called in the Child Protective Unit. Donna's boys were placed in foster care, activating Jon Allen's role as a case advocate in the Foster Care Program at Northside Family Services.

Jon understands why some people see Donna as having little potential, as her challenges are considerable. Her intellectual disability, unstable financial situation, and recent separation from an abusive and alcoholic boyfriend on whom she still periodically depends for assistance could label Donna as "chronic" or "multiproblem." But Jon's strengths-oriented assessment reveals Donna to be "multitalented" as well. Donna recognizes when she needs help. The call to the police is clear evidence of that. She succeeded in getting her boyfriend to move out and is no longer subsidizing his alcoholism, something she learned through her participation with Al-Anon. Donna is also extremely nurturing to her children, emotionally expressive, and loving. She's proud of her excellent cooking skills and demonstrates a good sense of nutrition. Donna's needs are significant, but she is not without personal and social resources.

Donna is adamant that she wants her sons to return home as soon as possible. With this goal in mind, Jon and Donna develop a plan of action that targets three key objectives: to use effective and positive parenting methods, to stabilize her financial situation through employment, and to increase her abilities to function independently of her abusive boyfriend. These forward-looking objectives frame the work ahead.

Jon's work with Donna details how social workers activate the resources of clients and their environments. To activate means to mobilize, energize, charge, stimulate, excite, arouse, start, trigger, and prompt. Notice the unifying thread of meaning in these words. Activating is a beginning, a "jump start," not a lifelong commitment. Activating resources means to take what is available within clients and their ecosystems and get it going. It does not mean to take care of, do for, drag to, control, fix, or treat. Jon and Donna partner to get things moving and keep things going in the direction of goals.

Jon and Donna meet twice a week. At one meeting, Jon spends time with Donna alone to review her situation, discuss her options, encourage her progress, and plan specific activities for the week—small steps toward the outcomes she desires. He uses a solution-focused approach to boost Donna's self-esteem, develop her sense of power, and maintain her motivation. He listens to her story, highlights her successes, congratulates her on progress, and designs readily achievable tasks.

During the second meeting of each week, Jon and Donna work to improve Donna's parenting skills. Originally, Jon referred Donna to parenting classes at his own agency, but when Donna's difficulty with reading stifled her ability to keep up with the other parents in the class, Jon advocated for a more individualized approach. He proposed that the agency fund Donna's access to an online program using videos to demonstrate positive parenting. Jon's assertion that Donna has a right to receive these educational services in a way that she can understand, as guaranteed under the American with Disabilities Act, strengthens his recommendation to approve the purchase. Jon follows up on Donna's progress in parenting as he monitors her weekly visits with the boys. He sits back, allowing space for Donna to test out her new skills, and records his observations so that he and Donna can discuss them later and determine the next steps for improvement.

Working with Donna and the boys exclusively is not enough. To increase productive transactions with others in her social environment, Jon also works with Donna "to fill in her eco-map," as he and Donna name this activity. During assessment, they had drawn Donna's social and community support network as it existed. Now, during their meetings, they pull this eco-map out and target various connections to reinforce or change.

At Jon's suggestion, Donna meets with her TANF (Temporary Assistance to Needy Families) worker to determine how her sons' foster care placement may affect her benefits. When Donna discovers that as long as her children return to her home within 90 days, her payments will be uninterrupted, Jon and Donna accelerate their efforts to achieve a return home within that time frame.

Donna is already working with an employment counselor as required to receive TANF benefits. When Jon transports Donna to one of these meetings, he joins in the discussion, and the three of them agree employment in the food service industry seems like a good fit. To increase her credentials, Donna decides to take a certification course in food handler safety at the Northside Community College. Recognizing Donna's difficulty with reading, Jon helps connect her with the Office of Students with Disabilities. They provide her with the services of a reader to manage course materials and successfully pass the certification exam. With this endorsement in hand, Donna locates a job in the cafeteria of the local middle school—an opportunity that fits her skills and involves hours that will eliminate the need for child care.

To work toward the objective of independence from her ex-boyfriend, Donna continues to attend Al-Anon meetings and begins to participate in some of the program's family social events. Donna also makes new friends with some of the people she meets at work. This expanding social network gives Donna better options when she feels the need for emotional support or recreation.

Each of these activities contributes to Donna's successful achievement of her objectives. The online parenting class, Jon's individualized observations and suggestions, and Donna's persistence in learning new parenting skills increase her effectiveness as a parent. Donna's new job stabilizes her financial situation. Jon's support, respect, and activities to build Donna's self-esteem, along with Donna's newly developed network of friends, increase her confidence to function independently. With these objectives accomplished, the goal to return the boys home is within reach.

Generalist social workers draw on an array of skills for working with both client systems and their environments. Workers use strategies to accentuate and develop client system strengths, introduce potential changes in the ways clients do things, renegotiate the transactions of client systems with their environments, and modify environmental systems. These are mutual tasks in which clients and social workers play complementary roles.

Generalist social workers draw on an array of skills for working with both client systems and their environments.

Despite the diversity of human systems, certain social work practice skills have universal application. All clients, from individuals to communities, benefit from a social worker's interest, encouragement, and organized approach. Clients at all levels respond to an increased sense of power and new ways to look at their situations. All clients benefit from productive connections to resources, relevant information, and newly acquired skills. Generalist social workers can facilitate these benefits as they carry out their roles associated with consultancy, resource management, and education. Throughout their work, practitioners use strategies for maintaining progress, developing power, changing perspectives, managing resources, and educating (Figure 12.1).

This chapter explores how social workers and clients intervene to activate resources for goal achievement. It describes the processes and skills workers use to implement action plans in ways that respect, motivate, and empower clients. By using these intervention processes, social workers increase clients' power and efficient use of available resources.

MAINTAINING PROGRESS IN ACTION PLANS

During the development phase, social workers consult with clients and others to keep moving as directly as possible toward goals. Workers maintain a positive, yet objective, stance on progress to monitor and facilitate the process of the work. To efficiently structure activities during this phase, practitioners draw on the plan that workers and clients have previously framed. To promote effective processes, workers intervene in ways that

Maintaining Progress
- Implementing Action Plans: facilitating a productive, goal-seeking process; reviewing and updating plans as necessary
- Enhancing Interactions: encouraging participation; responding to clarify situations, refine goals, and locate resources; building alliances among participants
- Sustaining Motivation: validating client's views and feelings; providing nurturance; expressing optimism

Developing Power
- Promoting Leadership: asserting client privileges in the relationship; acknowledging leadership abilities
- Recognizing Choices: enhancing agency by recognizing existing options; locating areas of client's control
- Locating Genuine Options: expanding resource networks; overcoming oppressive conditions
- Magnifying Strengths: responding to highlight strengths; recognizing incremental steps

Changing Perspectives
- Offering Feedback: reflecting client actions; examining behavior with respect to goals
- Creating New Concepts: reframing; offering metaphors
- Reconstructing Narratives: externalizing; co-constructing; generating multiple interpretations
- Changing Behaviors: considering new ways to do things; experimenting with behavior change

Managing Resources
- Linking Clients with Resources: locating resources; maximizing client administration of resource network
- Client Advocacy: developing power within the service network; using professional influence on client's behalf
- Maximizing Clients' Rights: implementing a social justice agenda; ensuring clients' due process rights

Educating
- Teaching: modeling; role-playing; structuring educational experiences
- Sharing Information: sharing professional expertise; self-disclosing

Figure 12.1
Generalist Skills for Activating Resources

enhance the achievements of the client system and maintain the client's motivation toward the goal.

Implementing Action Plans

Social workers keep the plan in the forefront of the development phase. The **action plan** prescribes what social workers and clients do when they are together and frames activities to accomplish between meetings. In those instances when the work gets somewhat off-track, social workers use the plan to review progress and redefine directions. Social workers need not rigidly enforce previous agreements. Plans are flexibly implemented and can be modified, yet they structure coordinated efforts for approaching challenges in goal-directed ways.

Collaborating on Actions

The combination of in-meeting activities and between-meeting tasks keeps clients and workers actively moving toward goals. Each meeting provides direct opportunities to activate client resources. Social workers and clients generate new perspectives and review progress. Clients and workers use meetings to plan additional activities for each to implement. Between meetings, clients may experiment with new behaviors, observe the impact of change attempts, or connect to necessary resources. Social workers may investigate untapped community resources for their potential use, advocate with other systems, or consult with supervisors on a client's progress.

Over the course of time, as clients demonstrate their abilities to do more, social workers do less. As clients become proficient in accessing their own resources, workers modulate from being active interveners to becoming more reflective facilitators. Enduring solutions are those clients discover within themselves and in the ways they manage their own worlds.

Enhancing Interactions

During the development phase, dialogue and discovery skills remain important. Clients continue to benefit from articulating thoughts and feelings, observing progress, and locating relevant strengths and resources. Workers strive to maintain focus, sustain participation, stimulate support, and handle differences.

Maintaining Focus

Prior to the development phase, workers and clients agree to an action plan, complete with concrete objectives and definitive activities. With this information in mind, workers guide clients to "stay on course." For example, workers may say any of the following:

- I'm pleased to hear that your job is going well—I'm wondering if you had a chance to call your ex-wife like we talked about last week.
- I thought we were here to talk about your marriage and whether you wanted me to refer you to a marriage counselor. So far, all we're talking about today is problems with the kids. Would you like to talk about the referral, or have you changed your mind?
- We certainly do have fun whenever this group gets together, and now we have some work to do. Who wants to report on their committee assignment first?

In each example, notice how practitioners encourage clients to discuss activities that are current. Social workers facilitate continuity by focusing conversations on the tasks at hand.

Workers also encourage clients to talk about one relevant issue in depth before moving on to another. Shifting from issue to issue often evades dealing intensively with associated feelings, whereas holding to focus allows deeper exploration of more difficult subjects (Shulman, 2012). When workers allow clients to skip around, clients may sense that workers are either uncomfortable or don't feel competent to handle troublesome topics. Workers do not attempt to force clients to talk about particular issues; nevertheless, workers should demonstrate that they can handle tough discussions if clients choose to share.

Larger systems multiply the difficulties that practitioners may experience in keeping the work on track. To focus many people at once, workers rely less on their own interactional skills and more on structured processes. Examples include using written agendas, handouts, questionnaires, audiovisual materials, structured experiences, minutes of previous meetings, and mailings between meetings. Initiating more formal meeting procedures and using tangible materials can keep large groups focused on their purposes.

Encouraging Participation

Multiperson systems work best when they function in ways that allow all members to participate. Families, groups, and other larger systems activate more resources when each member feels free to contribute. This does not mean that every member must contribute equally to each interaction; instead, each member's ideas and expertise merit consideration in light of the issues at hand. People need assurance that they have rights to their views, the privilege to express them, and the trust that others will listen to and respect their ideas even when others disagree. In structural terms, members require some degree of power within the system's hierarchy and enough space to feel free to assert their opinions. Social workers intervene directly with clients to achieve this differentiated and respectful type of structure.

Social workers have many ways to ensure that all group members contribute. To coordinate conversational traffic, one might comment:

- Well, I've heard three opinions. Just two more to go. Who's next?

To ensure that group members hear each contribution, one might inquire:

- Could I ask you to tell me what you just heard Ryan say? Seems like you might have missed it.

To help members accept and appreciate divergent opinions, practitioners can point out the potential benefits of differences with comments such as the following:

- I really don't think that one of you has to be right and the other wrong. You're probably both right. You're two different people. You're bound to see things differently, and that's okay; it gives us more to work with.

With each of these responses, workers encourage the participation of all group members.

Additionally, social workers can use more formal approaches. Conversations dominated by one subgroup or members talking only with the worker hamper effective group functioning and require direct action by the worker. Implementing a structured experience disrupts this uneven pattern of participation. For example, the social worker could begin a meeting by individually inviting each group member to share. Dividing the time available into equal blocks safeguards time for exploring each member's ideas. Structuring interactions unleashes dormant resources.

Stimulating Support Within Client Systems

With simple responses, workers can encourage support among group members. For example, highlighting similarities among members builds alliances:

- I guess the adults in this family see things in the same way.
- I noticed the three of you were nodding in agreement when Geena was talking.

Additionally, articulating underlying expressions of affection solidifies connections between group members:

- I'm seeing you express a strong commitment to working things out with Sharon when you say that.
- All this worry, concern, and nagging seems like love to me!

Recognizing alliances contributes to clients' feelings of support and power, encourages self-confidence, and increases abilities to risk changes.

Physical arrangements contribute to alliances as well. Within a meeting, workers can purposefully arrange seating to encourage closeness. For example, perceptive practitioners create seating arrangements that remove physical barriers to interactions. Commonly, social workers intervening with family systems place parents together and children separately to facilitate the cooperative development of a parenting team and a supportive sibling subsystem.

Careful assignment of tasks and activities may also stimulate new alliances. For example, to develop new subsystems of previously disconnected members, group leaders can implement exercises requiring subgroup activities. Likewise, community workers organize various task groups to involve individual members with each other more intensively.

Paradoxically, holding a separate meeting for selected subgroups within a client system is a powerful strategy for creating alliances. At the community level, consider the impact when the worker convenes a meeting between leaders of four rival factions within a neighborhood organization. The effective alliance among leaders of these conflicting groups increases the respective power of each subgroup and of the entire neighborhood. When working with a family on strengthening parental authority, weigh the benefit of conducting a separate interview with parents. Meeting with parents separately draws a symbolic generational boundary by discussing parenting while at the same time giving them an opportunity to talk about their own relationship.

Handling Differences

Inevitably, differences of opinion arise when systems have more than one member. When topics spark heated debate and divisive conflicts, workers can maintain collaboration among group members by asking each to represent the opposing view or summarize what others are saying (Johnson & Johnson, 2013). This exercise facilitates listening to alternative views and builds on the unique contributions of each.

For example, consider this interaction at an interdisciplinary staffing. The facilitator intervenes in a potentially antagonistic disagreement by saying the following:

I'm hearing several interesting and different perspectives. I guess that's the beauty of bringing people from different disciplines together. To make progress toward some kind of agreement, though, we need to make sure that we are listening to everyone's input. It would probably help if we stopped for a minute and summarized the views we're hearing from each other to make sure that we're all contemplating the same set of options before we move on.

Notice how this social worker shapes the way the team members communicate rather than simply adds information that could fuel the debate.

Intervention

Behavior: Critically choose and implement interventions to achieve practice goals and enhance capacities of clients and constituencies

Critical Thinking Question: If all human behavior is motivated, then there cannot be "unmotivated" clients. How might this understanding of motivation help practitioners work through client resistance, inaction, and lack of follow-through so that clients can resolve their issues through the intervention process?

Sustaining Motivation

Social workers enter clients' lives at vulnerable times—times when clients need support. During times of change, clients are even more likely to be unsure of themselves. Although workers try not to foster dependency in clients, neither do they abandon clients. Instead, they motivate clients with genuine support, acceptance, and caring. Workers encourage clients as they risk new behaviors, experience setbacks, and celebrate successes. To sustain clients, workers strive to validate clients' experiences, reassure them about the uneven nature and the sometimes slow pace of change, respect their uniqueness, and provide emotional support.

Validating the Client's Reality

To maintain their efforts, clients need to know that someone else understands their experiences. The need for validation becomes especially important when clients are oppressed and see workers as unfamiliar with their particular stressors. For example, workers can demonstrate cross-cultural empathy by "openly identifying and discussing institutionalized racism, discrimination, or economic disparities which can minimize clients' feelings of self-blame and helplessness and foster racial pride and identity" (Gibson, 1993, p. 391). This discussion cements the working relationship and opens up conversation about potentially discordant issues.

Another way that workers can validate clients is to **normalize** their experiences. Considering a behavior in its environmental context means that workers convey their belief that, in these particular circumstances, most people would respond similarly. In other words, the client's behavior makes sense in context, especially in terms of the gender, lifestyle, and ethnic identity of the client. Normalizing does not mean minimizing. Saying that many people may have a similar experience does not diminish how tough the situation may be.

Accepting the Nature of Change

Change occurs erratically. Sometimes clients leap forward. At other times, they stabilize or return to old ways. Resistance to change is a natural part of development; all human systems tend to maintain the comfort of habitual patterns in the face of changing situations. When things do change, humans take breaks to restabilize before they continue on. It's natural for clients to slow down progress that is occurring, back up, and do it the old way again to find a sense of security before moving ahead. Introducing the notion of expected setbacks normalizes the process of change. Workers require patience to accept a client's pace and pattern of change. Clients benefit when workers demonstrate enthusiasm for even the smallest incremental changes and remain optimistic when change is slow.

Respecting Uniqueness

No two client systems change in the same way, have the same set of resources or constraints, or magically respond to the exact same strategy. Social workers take caution in applying "standard techniques" or "cookbook interventions" that fail to acknowledge the unique qualities of a particular client system. Certainly, social workers' general practice wisdom, knowledge of special populations, and use of best practices contribute to their effectiveness. But even the most tried and true, research-supported strategies likely need modifications to suit specific situations.

Respecting uniqueness means that social workers also acknowledge their differences from clients. Saying, "I know exactly how you feel" denies the reality of differences. To ask the client, "I guess I'm not really sure. How do potential employers in this area respond to someone who has recently immigrated?" shows respect by honoring the client's first-hand expertise. Openly discussing and accepting differences transforms potential barriers into working alliances.

Matching the Client's Cultural Experience Social work strategies work best when they fit clients's worldviews and cultures. One such example is the traditional Hawaiian family conflict resolution process known as *ho'oponopono*. Hurdle (2002) summarizes ho'oponopono as a clearly defined structured process in which a leader convenes all family members for a structured conversation. In this process, the leader enforces rules that limit emotional expression and conflict, assists family members to discuss the problem and its impact, and encourages all members involved to ask for forgiveness from each other and consider restitution. "The formal nature of the ritual lends an aura of solemnity and importance to the process, which is crucial to many forms of traditional healing . . . [and is] reflective of the integration of spirituality with healing in many indigenous cultures" (p. 189).

Providing Emotional Support

Workers provide emotional support in two basic ways. First, workers compliment clients on the changes they have made and give them credit for these changes. Second, workers can directly provide powerful emotional support by sharing feelings about their experiences of working with clients. Sharing these feelings enhances the worker–client relationship and adds new considerations to the work. However, rather than serving the worker's own personal needs, Shulman (2012) cautions that any feelings expressed by the worker should relate to the purposes and functions of the professional interaction.

> **?** Assess your understanding of generalist intervention skills for maintaining progress in action plans by taking this brief quiz.

DEVELOPING POWER

People feel their own power when they become aware of their expertise, resources, and gifts. People have a sense of control when others respect their views. People feel powerful when they connect to the power of others. Empowerment-based strategies provide

People feel their own power when they become aware of their expertise, resources, and gifts.

clients with information, offer options and opportunities to make decisions, and help to build social support networks. Empowerment requires that workers help clients develop power by promoting leadership, recognize choices by locating genuine options for solutions, and shape competence through cultivating strengths and abilities.

Promoting Leadership

All human systems benefit from capable leadership. Consider social work practice with a community. Embedded community leaders can help achieve broad-based participation in a change effort. The more diverse community constituents get involved, the greater the likelihood of success. Indigenous community leaders likely already exist and probably have a following among community members. Community-level practitioners seek to identify and ally themselves with those leaders who have expertise for the task at hand and represent the views of key constituencies. Social work research shows that in African American communities, indigenous leaders are likely to be ministers or leaders in the church (Bliss et al., 2008; McNeal & Perkins, 2007; Moore & Miller, 2007). In Native American communities, elders may provide leadership and hold sway over tribal members (Yellow Bird, 2001). Persons with existing power in the community can wield influence quickly and stimulate activism among community members.

Watch this video as you consider that the empowerment method requires social workers attend to a client's experience of power. What strategies does the social worker on the video use to help the client recognize his power to change his situation? www.youtube.com/watch?v=z0z5KFAiMJE

Developing leadership competencies not already present constitutes an alternative method of promoting leadership. At the microlevel, this intervention may take the form of helping individuals gain skills in assertiveness, supporting parental authority in decision making, or encouraging group members to take charge of accomplishing tasks. At the mezzolevel, organizations can implement consensus planning models, elevating the voices and developing the leadership potential of all stakeholders. At the macrolevel, skills in public speaking, legislative testimony, and social networking propel people into leadership roles in social and policy change efforts. Ethical and effective leadership elevates the individual power of a system's leaders and other system members as well.

Facilitating Choices

Clients frequently feel powerless, believing that events are beyond their control. Social workers counteract this immobilizing assumption by helping clients recognize those elements of a situation that could realistically change. Clients experience their own power when they see opportunities to make new choices in situations where they previously saw no options.

The power to make choices benefits us all. For example, persons experiencing intimate partner violence benefit from recognizing that they have the choice to leave or stay in the abusive relationship (Peled et al., 2000). What will work to minimize the violence and protect everyone involved? Only the client has the expertise to evaluate the risks and benefits of this decision. Social workers may ask the following:

- What are you thinking that you would like to do?
- In deciding to stay, what actions can you take to help you feel safer?
- How can you best protect your children?

- What choices do you feel are available to you?
- If you were to leave the relationship, what resources and supports would you need to be successful on your own?
- What are you hoping will happen in the long term as we move forward?
- What do you need from me to help you get where you want to go?

The social worker's task is to ensure that the means are available for clients to have realistic choices about how to resolve their difficulties. There is no choice for a client in a violent relationship if the client sees no way out. Clients frequently lack information about what resources are available or how to activate them. At other times, gaps and barriers in service delivery or regressive social policies deny access to needed services. Social workers are most effective when they help clients to articulate genuine possibilities, support clients' freedoms to choose among the options available, locate necessary supports to facilitate clients' decisions, and advocate for additional resource development.

Shaping Competence

When social workers accentuate client strengths, they enhance a client's sense of power. Empowerment-based practitioners recognize the personal, interpersonal, and contextual strengths present in the functioning of any client. Such strengths may include optimism, creativity, motivation, individual talents, cultural identities, networks of support, competent relationships, community resources, and accessible social service options. Even in apparently desperate circumstances, people likely demonstrate strengths in how they cope with their challenges. Social workers discover client strengths by listening closely to what clients are saying, noticing how clients are handling problems, and highlighting the ways in which clients are succeeding. The strategy of a "positive asset search" describes this continual scanning for resources in personal, interpersonal, and contextual systems (Ivey et al., 2014).

Existing client strengths provide a foundation for further competence development. Strength-focused social workers help clients enhance currently productive interactions rather than intervene as if clients are doing nothing right. This skill, when applied in family therapy, is known as shaping competence (Nichols & Schwartz, 2001). For example, when a family social worker notices that a conflicted family has one member who acknowledges and reflects the opposing view expressed by another, the worker moves quickly to compliment this understanding. Helping family members develop their abilities to see other members' perspectives may lead to a reduction in conflict and an increased ability to negotiate differences.

The strategy of shaping competence adapts readily to client systems other than families. For example, place yourself in the position of a worker facilitating a support group and observing the responses of various members to one member's crisis. Your comment that you are impressed with a particular group member's ability to empathize without giving advice will likely influence other members to follow suit. In this way, you are able to guide the group toward a pattern of supporting each other's strengths without undermining the members' existing capabilities. Shaping competence acknowledges client systems' available expertise while fine-tuning the use of their resources to achieve desired changes.

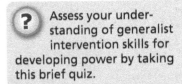
Assess your understanding of generalist intervention skills for developing power by taking this brief quiz.

CHANGING PERSPECTIVES

How we behave depends on how we perceive and interpret events. When we have an experience, we think about it, determine what it means, and behave accordingly. If our perceptions or interpretations change, changes in behavior follow. To bring about a perspective shift, workers may offer feedback that assists clients to step back and look at their situations in more productive ways. Identifying and challenging troublesome thoughts and beliefs may produce desirable changes in behavior. Workers can use metaphors or narrative strategies to help clients reframe their experiences. A change in thinking can also originate at the behavioral level. A client's "experiment" to investigate the effects of different behaviors might produce results that lead clients to change their previous thinking.

Offering Feedback

By offering effective **feedback**, workers urge clients to reflect on their behaviors and choose how they want to act. Practitioners witness firsthand how clients interact in a professional relationship. As a result, social workers can assess

- how client systems approach challenging situations,
- what skills clients bring that work for them,
- the ways clients build relationships and involve others in seeking solutions, and
- which parts of the ecosystem help or hinder the progress.

Additionally, workers observe a client's level of trust, ability to articulate ideas, awareness of feelings, patience, persistence, sense of humor, and creativity. Social workers are well positioned to disclose their perceptions about clients by offering carefully constructed feedback.

Constructing Feedback

Examine the following examples of feedback:

- Could I give you some feedback? I just observed you talking to your daughter about her curfew for a full 5 minutes without yelling. I wonder what's working.
- I have an observation if you are ready for it. It seems to me that each time this agency has a funding crisis, the response is to expect workers to do more for less. It just happened this week when the board of directors decided to eliminate two positions, redistribute the workload, and freeze salaries.
- It's so encouraging to work with someone who takes risks like you. Just now, when I suggested we try something new, you immediately thought of three possibilities.

Notice how the carefully framed feedback of these practitioners draws on the following principles for constructive feedback:

- Describes rather than judges behavior
- Shares perceptions rather than offers advice
- Identifies specific current behaviors rather than recalls incidents from the past

- Reports positive behaviors as well as points to improve
- Keeps pace with the client's readiness

When workers offer feedback neutrally, clients can figure out their own reactions to the information. Because workers give feedback about specific behaviors rather than about the "person" of the client, clients have opportunities to behave in new ways that more clearly match their intent.

Confronting in a Supportive Way

Can you decide what you want, do something to obtain it, and end up getting it? If you can, you are, at least in this one instance, interpersonally effective. When clients articulate the intent of their behaviors, workers can observe and determine which behaviors net intended results and which miss their marks. Workers use this approach to highlight successful behaviors as well as those that may need changing.

To confront effectively, workers help clients articulate their actions in three parts—intent, behavior, and outcome. As workers carefully trace with clients the sequence of intent to behavior to outcome, clients often decide to behave differently. Consider the example of support group member Tom who has grown tired of the way that fellow group member John monopolizes the conversation. Tom responds by disagreeing with everything that John offers, leaving other group members withdrawn and disinterested. When Tom complains that nothing seems to work to stifle John, the worker can lead Tom to see his own involvement by analyzing his behavior as follows:

- The *intent*—Tom wants John to be less active and other group members to say more.
- The *behavior*—Tom argues with what John says.
- The *outcome*—the whole group revolves around John's issues and Tom's disagreement with John.

So, is Tom getting what he wants?

Workers use a **confronting** strategy selectively, usually after establishing a significant, respectful relationship and in an atmosphere of support. In observing and reporting their observations of clients' social effectiveness, workers do not need to blame or accuse but simply to reveal patterns for clients to review and take action.

Creating New Concepts

The way we respond to a situation may have more to do with the way we interpret it than the actual event itself. "Look on the bright side" may sound like a naive approach, but the benefits of a positive outlook are well established. Workers can help clients experience events in helpful ways by modifying thoughts and beliefs, using reframing, or offering metaphors.

Modifying Thoughts and Beliefs

Human behavior does not occur in isolation but rather as part of a sequence of events. When we have an experience, we respond cognitively, deciphering what the experience means. These interpretations activate emotional responses and trigger the resultant

Review this video and identify what helps people change behavior. What are the implications for social work practice? www.youtube.com/ watch?v=I5d8GW6GdR0

Engagement

Behavior: Use empathy, reflection, and interpersonal skills to effectively engage diverse clients and constituencies

Critical Thinking Question: Feedback is a means for social workers to communicate professional judgments to help clients view their situations in more productive ways. When would communicating feedback to clients not be constructive?

behavior. Behavior changes if a part of the sequence changes. If we alter what we think about a situation, both the way we feel about it and how we respond behaviorally will likely change also. Such is the premise of **cognitive behavioral therapy** (**CBT**), a widely used, evidenced-based approach in clinical social work (Beck, 2011).

There is no one correct way to think about any particular event. When several people witness the same event, each individual has an idiosyncratic interpretation of what has happened and what it means. Thoughts are contextual, that is, they are rooted in the social and physical environments in which they occur. People think the way they think based on their past experiences, cultural beliefs, assumptions, and biases. The way we think about an event one day isn't necessarily how we will interpret it the next day. The question is not so much whether what a client believes about events is right or wrong. Instead, the social worker helps the client to ponder whether the belief frees the client to behave in desired ways.

Working with thoughts becomes especially important with persons who have experienced trauma. Traumatic experience can lead people to catastrophic thoughts in response to relatively benign events. Fear, anger, and defensiveness can be functional when someone is threatened. But such thoughts are likely to interfere with daily functioning when traumatized people respond with suspicion and distrust to even positive social overtures. Social workers can help clients identify precipitating thoughts, then examine those thoughts for their validity in the current context, and finally generate alternative understandings to trigger desired behavior changes (Corcoran, 2006).

Reframing

Clients who feel as if they are not getting anywhere benefit from views that they may, after all, be up to something constructive. **Reframing** examines a situation previously perceived as negative and takes a new look, describing it as somehow positive, functional, or useful. Toseland and Rivas (2012) describe the effect of using this strategy with groups, noting that once group members emphasize the positive attributes of a situation, they are more likely see ways to address the negative aspects.

One way to reframe behavior is to consider the view that the response determines the meaning (Walter & Peller, 1992). Even apparently problematic behavior may be up to something good. Consider the following examples. The group member who monopolizes is helping other members avoid dealing with difficult issues. The boy who constantly tests his dad's authority is succeeding in getting his dad closely involved. The depressed adolescent has discovered ways to elicit the support and nurturance of family and friends. The employee who files grievance after grievance is clarifying and developing the agency's policies and procedures. When social workers introduce the question "What's good about it?" they acknowledge that human behavior is likely functional in some way. Identifying how the behavior functions helps locate what clients need and directs the work toward meeting those needs in more constructive ways.

Using Metaphors

Another way to reframe situations is to describe them in the form of a **metaphor**. Consider the parents frustrated with their child's slow progress in learning to read. When the social worker places this situation in the context of the traditional fable "The Tortoise and the Hare," it transforms the behavior from lagging behind to steadily improving. The previous description stimulates feelings of anxiety and impatience. The metaphor helps parents recognize success and be optimistic.

Metaphors are ambiguous, letting clients make their own interpretations. This ambiguity makes metaphors particularly suitable for describing and working with feelings. When social workers and clients seek to articulate feelings, workers use wording such as the following:

- You feel as if you are out on a limb.
- So it's kind of like you're just drifting in the middle of a lake, not really getting anywhere.
- Seems as if you've hit rock bottom.

Building on these same metaphors, social workers can offer hopeful directions such as the following:

- Well, maybe it's time to edge back toward the trunk.
- So as you are drifting, what do you see that catches your interest?
- Now that you're at the bottom, at least there's only one way to go—what's the first thing that needs to happen to pick yourself back up?

Metaphors reorient perspective and affect the way clients think, feel, and respond to their problems.

Using Narrative Strategies

A narrative approach offers another way for clients to reexperience their situations. **Narrative strategies** draw from a social constructionist perspective, a theoretical view that postulates people behave in ways consistent with what they believe is true rather than in keeping with some concrete reality to which we all subscribe. When we experience an event, our response is not directly related to the event itself; rather, our response is determined by the way in which we interpret the event. For example, imagine walking into a room where people are talking and laughing. When you arrive, the conversation stops as one person turns to greet you. What does this mean? Were the people talking about and making fun of you, so when you entered the room, the greeting was an alert to the others to stop? Or was the break in the conversation and greeting a sign of respect to invite you into the interaction? Or was the conversation already wrapping up and its ending not associated with you at all? The situation remains ambiguous, the meaning left to our interpretation. The way we interpret the event determines whether we experience it as an insult, as a compliment, or as having no significance at all.

This interpretation of experience sits at the core of the narrative method and represents the primary focus for intervention. How we interpret events is shaped by our sense of self (do we have confidence about our identities, or do we have doubts about our place in the world?), our previous experiences (what have our life experiences taught us?), and our belief systems (what do we believe to be true about people and the world in general?). Beliefs about ourselves and our worlds comprise the stories of our lives—the "narrative" as articulated in the narrative approach. In implementing a narrative strategy, social workers help clients take charge of their stories in ways that emphasize their strengths, experience their pride, and prepare them to narrate their way into a more desirable future.

Implementing a narrative strategy requires social workers to facilitate three activities during assessment and intervention—collaboration, reflexivity, and multiplicity (Laird, 1995). *Collaboration* requires a specific focus on and respect for a client's experience rather than an externally accepted reality. *Reflexivity* means that social workers use responding skills that allow clients to view their stories more objectively—skills that separate stories out for mutual reflection by both clients and workers. *Multiplicity* is accomplished by simply generating multiple ideas and interpretations. Both clients and workers contribute to this brainstorming. The more options clients have for viewing and interpreting their current story, the more opportunities they have for choosing empowering meanings to guide its future development. Social workers may assist in generating multiple interpretations of events but must affirm clients' privilege to author their lives (Freeman & Couchonnal, 2006).

Several techniques support a narrative approach. With individuals and families, workers can draw genograms to identify the "cast of characters" over the generations and have clients narrate significant tales about the various family members. Workers respond by identifying positive themes and strengths demonstrated over the years. Groups can construct their stories by using journaling (Brower, 1996). In this approach, group members keep independent logs of their responses to the group and select log entries to read at group meetings in order to contribute to "a narrative that gives their group experience coherence, history, rules, myths, and meaning" (p. 342). Considering even larger systems, Saleebey (1994) says that we can analyze individual client narratives for implications about potential mezzo- and macrolevel interventions. People can rewrite history. The narrative method helps clients do just that, by repunctuating their lives with experiences of power, success, and possibility.

Clients with a history of trauma may benefit from a narrative approach. Experiencing trauma can lead to a tragic life story that includes victimization, violence, fear, and anger. The client as victim is a theme that frequently remains pervasive in the lives of those with traumatic backgrounds. Social workers react to these difficult life stories with sensitivity and acceptance, yet they gradually begin to "read between the lines" of the trauma narrative and respond in ways that help clients construct a more empowering outlook. The story of victimization is also a story of survival. What did clients do to cope? What strengths did clients bring to bear that led to their survival? What were the shining moments of resilience, peace, or maybe even joy? How did clients make that happen? Workers help clients restory their lives around these events so that clients can move forward buoyed by the narrative of their successful fight for survival rather than remain bogged down with a story imposed on them by a perpetrator.

Externalizing

Narrative strategies have the advantage of **externalizing** or separating the story of someone's life from the actual person. In other words, the story sits as external to the person and can be modified or directed by the person, an important distinction for people whose lives seem centered around a problematic theme. Social work resists this kind of stigmatizing labeling of someone's life, as evidenced in the preference for "person-first" language such as using the description of a "person with a disability" rather than a "disabled person."

The process of separating people from their problems defines the therapeutic process of externalization (White, 1989). Madsen (2007) describes a four-step process for externalizing and reexperiencing problems. First, establish a supportive alliance with the client and create a safe space conducive to sharing intimate thoughts and beliefs. Second, help people talk about their problems as a separate entity—as something external to themselves. Third, assist clients to renegotiate their relationships with their problems, helping them recognize the ways in which they do influence the problem, which gives rise to ideas about how to manage the problem more effectively. The goal here is to look for unique outcomes, those times when people feel most in control of their problems. Highlighting areas of control leads clients to question negative story lines related to failure and frustration and see new themes related to determination, resilience, and steady progress. Finally, workers help clients use what they have learned to take actions reflective of these emerging story lines of strength and survival.

Trying Out New Behaviors

In many ways, action plans represent carefully designed "experiments" for change. Experimentation always yields productive results. A "success" moves clients toward desired outcomes, and a "failure" provides valuable information to guide future actions. Small-scale experiments, designed by workers and clients and implemented between meetings, can help clients discover the best ways to initiate and sustain desirable changes. To derive maximum benefit, each experiment should be mutually constructed, carefully implemented, and comprehensively evaluated (Figure 12.2).

Constructing Experimental Activities

Social workers and clients have an array of possible activities from which to choose when constructing experiments. Four options include conducting observations, connecting and disconnecting, maintaining productive actions, and taking small steps toward goals.

Observations   Observations are cautious experiments used to gather additional information. They ask for no direct change by the client system but often produce change because observing one's own or someone else's behavior frequently has impact. Workers ask clients to observe when good things are happening or those times when problems are not occurring to decipher what might contribute to these successful events. For example, managers in an organization might observe closely when employees show regular attendance and positive attitudes to understand what might be working to make that happen.

Connecting and Disconnecting   Clients can experiment with change by connecting to new people and resources or by disconnecting from previous relationships. For example, members of an adolescent group working to disassociate from gang membership may agree to keep away from areas of gang activity and refrain from talking with known gang members. These same group members may each also agree to choose a new person to eat lunch with in the school cafeteria to begin new peer relationships to replace their previous gang associations.

Maintaining Productive Actions   Encouraging clients to repeat productive actions is another useful technique. Consider the example of Nancy and her client Jerome. Jerome is a

Types of Activities
- Information gathering through observation
- Connecting to and disconnecting from persons, groups, services, and situations
- Maintaining and repeating productive behaviors
- Taking small steps in the direction of goals

Construction
- Determine client's willingness to participate
- Generate possible activities in mutual discussion
- Select activities based on:
  —Relevance to goals
  —Likelihood of success
  —Client's motivation to complete

Implementation
- Define as experimental
- Keep it clear, concrete, and simple
- Define roles of all participants
- Secure agreements to follow through
- Repeat agreement to ensure understanding

Follow-up
- When activity is completed:
  —Discuss outcomes
  —Access information from all members involved
  —Accept differences in perspectives
  —Validate each participant's perceptions
  —Highlight specific strengths and skills clients demonstrated in the activity
  —Note variations in expected outcome to detect unanticipated solutions
  —Construct follow-up activity
  —Encourage increased responsibility by client in constructing the next activity
- When activity is not completed:
  —Discuss obstacles
  —Determine how to overcome obstacles
  —Consider taking a smaller step
  —Implement the same activity
- If client chose not to complete activity:
  —Determine source of resistance
  —Change activity to match client's current motivation
  —Update client's outcome goals to ensure that worker and client are moving in the same direction

Figure 12.2
Guidelines for Between-Meeting Activities

social worker who questions his choice of profession because he frequently feels depressed and burned out. Recently, Jerome told Nancy about his angry outburst in an interdisciplinary team meeting when the group refused to consider changing the case plan of a client with whom he was working. Knowing that Jerome shows incredible patience and acceptance in his work with his clients, Nancy suggests that Jerome imagine the interdisciplinary team members are his clients at a mezzolevel rather than conceptualizing them as professional colleagues. In other words, Nancy asks Jerome to experiment with transferring his skills in a successful area of functioning to test their benefits in another.

Taking Small Steps   Taking a small step toward the goal is an experiment worth trying. Well-defined objectives in a comprehensive action plan will clearly indicate the options for these small steps. When taking direct steps toward goals seems risky, social workers reassure clients that each step is only experimental. Once the results are in, clients can choose to repeat the action, take another step, or return to the previous ways of behaving. It only makes sense to test out a new behavior and evaluate its impact before committing to doing things differently.

Implementing Activities

Some refer to these types of experiments as homework assignments or directives. Imagine your response to someone assigning or directing you to do something. Social workers circumvent resistance by framing these activities clearly as experiments and collaborating with clients to develop them. The social worker might say, "Are you interested in trying a little experiment?" "So those are my ideas, what do you think?" Clients are more likely to implement experiments that they help construct and agree to complete. To encourage follow through, the social worker might say, "So we agree. You'll try this out and next week let me know what happened."

A well-designed experiment has several components. It describes *who will do what when*. The experiments are concrete, simple, and easily understood by clients and workers. With multiperson systems, all members need to understand what they are agreeing to do and know their particular responsibilities. Useful experiments also specify the time frame for completion and describe how to evaluate the impact. When experiments are relevant, clear, and collaboratively constructed, they are likely to produce the best results.

Following Up

To complete a successful experiment, workers lead clients through a step-by-step process that evaluates the results. Workers may ask the following questions:

- Tell me the details. How did you carry it out?
- Did you implement the experiment as constructed, or did you vary it? What led you to make these changes?
- What happened? Did it turn out like you expected? Did something unexpected happen?
- What did you learn that might help us decide what to do next?

When clients fail to follow through on completing assignments, workers also pursue additional information by asking the following:

- So what got in the way? Was there no opportunity, or did you decide it wasn't something you wanted to do? Did you understand what you were supposed to do?
- Are you willing to try to complete it again, or do you think we're off base here?
- What would you like to do instead?

Assess your understanding of changing perspectives by taking this brief quiz.

Well-designed experiments actively involve clients in the process. When workers sequence experiments one after the other, they gradually pull back from the task in ways that increase clients' responsibilities for their development and implementation. Activating resources in this way prepares clients to function independently of the social worker.

MANAGING RESOURCES

To manage resources, social workers and clients collaborate to locate realistic options, make appropriate connections, and take steps to ensure that clients are successful in accessing resources.

All human systems, from individuals to communities, need environmental resources to sustain their functioning. During assessment, workers explore the various connections that clients have with their environments to see what works and should be reinforced, to detect what is not working and should be modified, and also to recognize what is missing and should be established. To manage resources, social workers and clients collaborate to locate realistic options, make appropriate connections, and take steps to ensure that clients are successful in accessing resources.

Linking clients to necessary resources casts generalist social workers in the roles of brokers, advocates, mediators, activists, and catalysts. To play these roles effectively requires workers to know what the social delivery system has to offer, to learn current eligibility requirements for supportive services, to recognize indigenous resources that communities may possess, and to participate in resource development projects. Chapters 13 and 14 further explore a generalist approach to managing resources at the mezzo- and macrolevel client system levels and in the context of professional relationships.

Linking Clients with Resources

Peer groups are a source of support for practicing new behaviors.

Accessing resources confronts social workers with a common question: How much help do they give to clients in this process? The empowering answer is: As much as is necessary and as little as is needed to be effective. Workers are supplemental in helping clients make connections. Whether workers simply inform clients about resources or take more direct actions, they consistently work for clients to understand the process by which clients might access the same resources without professional assistance. In linking clients with other services, social workers choose methods to match the current capabilities of clients with an eye toward increasing clients' own resource management skills.

Consider Denise VanDeViere, an aftercare worker for Northside

ANDRESR/SHUTTERSTOCK

Hospital, and her client Cassie Carter, who is recovering from a serious head injury. Denise and Cassie have agreed that Cassie will apply for Social Security Disability Income (SSDI). To assist Cassie in this endeavor, Denise has a continuum of options varying from the most supportive to least involved, including the following:

- Denise will call Louise Campbell, a caseworker she knows at Social Security (SS) to arrange an appointment. She will also gather the appropriate medical documentation to demonstrate Cassie's eligibility, pick up Cassie, and accompany her to the appointment.
- Cassie will call Louise, mention that Denise has suggested the call, and arrange the appointment. Denise will gather the necessary medical records, pick up Cassie, and accompany her to the appointment.
- Cassie will arrange the appointment, sign appropriate forms for release for information, gather up her medical records, and meet Denise at the SS office. Denise will guide Cassie through the application process and advocate only as necessary.
- Denise will give information to Cassie about SSDI and the application procedures. Cassie will make the necessary arrangements to go to SS, apply for the assistance, and report the results of her efforts to Denise at the next meeting.

Each option leads to the same outcome—Cassie applies for SSDI. But each option draws differently on the resources of the client and social worker. The best choice is the one in which clients feel confident in their abilities to succeed, use as much of their own capabilities as possible, and learn additional skills for the future. Considering these issues, Denise and Cassie decide that Cassie will make the necessary arrangements, that both will ride the bus together so that Denise can help Cassie learn to use the public transportation system, and that Cassie will do the talking at the SS office unless she directly seeks the assistance of Denise.

This video illustrates that the core component of empowerment-based social work is the ability to refer clients to other services to access essential services. How does the social worker leverage clients' rights and preferences when linking the client with resources for which the client may qualify?

Client Advocacy

Even when informed about helpful services, clients may experience unexpected obstacles or a lack of responsiveness, a situation that calls on practitioners to add their professional power to ensure a successful connection through **client advocacy**. "Client advocacy is built upon a philosophy that seeks to protect, enforce, and ensure clients' *rights, entitlements, resources, services*, and *benefits*" (Schneider & Lester, 2001, p. 152). Although ideally designed to respond to clients' needs, the social delivery network is in reality economically strapped, short of staff, and bureaucratically complex. Frequently, clients need a social worker's voice to traverse the bureaucratic red tape in order to access services for which they are eligible. A social worker's advocacy in networking resources and services is frequently essential to meet the needs of clients.

Intervention

Behavior: Negotiate, mediate, and advocate with and on behalf of diverse clients and constituencies

Critical Thinking Question: Social workers often advocate on behalf of their clients to traverse the bureaucratic maze of the social service delivery network. What benefits can clients derive from participating in or at least observing client advocacy efforts?

Box 12.1   Natural Helping and Self-Help Resources: A Research–Practice Connection

Self-help groups and natural helping networks are valuable supports to client systems, yet these resources are often unidentified and underused by social workers. Self-help groups provide opportunities for participants with similar issues "to gain support and recognition, obtain information on, advocate on behalf of, address issues associated with, and take control of the circumstances that bring about, perpetuate, and provide solutions to their shared concern" (Segal, 2008, p.14). Likewise, natural helping networks are an important source of empowerment, including power over oneself to take control of addictions, cope with emotions and power in relation to the sociopolitical environment to take charge of care decisions, ensure accommodations for disabilities, deal with social stigma, and confront structural barriers (Hardina, 2004; Segal, 2008). Not only beneficial to individual functioning, informal resources are also integral to neighborhood resilience and community competence (Breton, 2001). Contemporary research documents the value of self-help and natural helping across cultures (Mok, 2005).

Just how much support and assistance do people access from their natural support networks? Even among groups in which the utilization of formal support services is low, research shows that people tap into the resources of natural helping networks such as family members, friends, and neighbors (Patterson & Marsiglia, 2000). Williams and colleagues (2001) investigated perceived supports and barriers to the use of social and health services in communities plagued by violence. They discovered that language and cultural barriers interfere with access to formal services, although all groups studied, including African Americans, Latinos, and Vietnamese residents, identified various faith communities as significant sources of support.

Does natural support differ among cultural groups? By using a qualitative research design, Patterson and Marsiglia (2000) studied community-based natural helping networks within the Mexican American community in the southwest United States. They interviewed 12 persons identified by community members as natural helpers and compared their responses with those from previous studies conducted with European American respondents. Similarities led the researchers to conclude that natural helping may be a cross-cultural phenomenon. Natural helpers in these cultural groups implemented combinations of task-related or facilitative roles, depending on the requirements of the situations. Interestingly, "the more polarized gender socialization process that is typically associated with Latinos and Latinas did not emerge" in the study; male natural helpers in their sample "used the facilitating style of helping more than women did" (p. 29).

What about the effectiveness of self-help groups? Mirroring the results of studies conducted in the United States, Mok's (2005) research on self-help groups in Hong Kong showed that participating in self-help groups contributed to participants' perceptions of personal and interpersonal empowerment. Respondents indicated that since joining the self-help group, they were more positive, hopeful, decisive, and competent in problem solving. With respect to interpersonal skills, they reported believing they had made gains in their ability to relate to and get along with others. Although many agreed that participating in self-help groups could be a vehicle for addressing social policy issues related to health, welfare, and housing, this awareness did not necessarily prompt group members to take action.

Research suggests that social workers should value the involvement of nonprofessional helpers and view informal support systems as legitimate resources for clients. Informal supports are likely to be a good cultural fit for clients and to remain intact in clients' systems long after the professional social work relationship ends.

The way in which social workers advocate for their clients makes a difference. Clients such as those with chronic mental illnesses, intellectual disabilities, substance addictions, or major health issues such as AIDS may have long-term needs for advocacy and will benefit from developing key advocacy skills. "There can be no empowerment without participation or, at least, presence and observation. By modeling this behavior, the client learns to become an active consumer/participant" (Klein & Cnaan, 1995,

p. 205). All clients benefit more from working with, rather than by being worked on by, social workers.

Maximizing Clients' Rights

Clients have rights to resources in their communities and to those available within the social service delivery system. However, sometimes, restrictive policies, guidelines, or procedures block clients' attempts to obtain services to which they are rightfully entitled. When interpretations of rules and regulations deny clients access to programs and services, they have rights to fair hearings, appeals, and due process.

Fair Hearings and Appeals

Clients' rights include their right to **fair hearings and appeals** when access to services has been denied or when case decisions negatively affect clients' benefits. Most programs and services stipulate processes for fair hearings and appeals as integral components of agency policies and procedures.

The appeal process often involves an objective hearing officer, external to the agency, to review the claims. In other instances, the hearing officer may be the administrator in charge of the program subject to the appeal. Social workers need to be familiar with their own employers' fair hearing and appeals policies and procedures as well as those in agencies to which they refer to protect their clients' rights. When a client decides to appeal decisions, the worker advocates directly or links the client to a concerned professional who can represent the client's position. Fair hearings and appeals are not to be discouraged. If the agency has determined eligibility and followed procedures within its specified guidelines, then the client benefits from knowing this. Conversely, if the agency has not interpreted or implemented procedures accurately, then the agency personnel need to know how to proceed differently in the future.

Procedural Due Process

Procedural due process protects individuals' rights in administrative proceedings with respect to fair hearings and appeals. Due process ensures a fundamental fairness, that is, a fair opportunity to dispute or challenge administrative decisions. Key features of procedural due process involve clients' rights to

- details concerning the administrative decisions or actions, including the rationale;
- information about any statutory or regulatory provisions that stipulate clients' benefits and rights to services under question;
- information about grievance and appeal rights and procedures;
- present their case before an impartial review panel or hearing officer;
- consult legal counsel and/or advocates;
- cross-examine decision makers; and
- receive a written report about the final judgment in a timely manner after the hearing.

Social workers are not lawyers, but the advocacy practice of social work requires workers to know about laws, the judicial process, and available legal resources.

Intervention

Behavior: Negotiate, mediate, and advocate with and on behalf of diverse clients and constituencies

Critical Thinking Question: Clients have rights to appeals and fair hearings in adverse administrative decisions. What are the consequences of not informing clients of their rights to due process?

? Assess your understanding of managing resources by taking this brief quiz.

EDUCATING

Clients and social workers sometimes select educational strategies. New information often leads to novel solutions. Learning strategies include role-playing, implementing structured curricula, and modeling. Workers also share information with clients by offering relevant professional knowledge and appropriately disclosing personal information.

Teaching

Like all effective social work practice, educational endeavors begin where the client is. With respect to teaching, this means identifying the learner's objectives and learning style. Collaborative educational efforts involve both the facilitator and learners in all aspects of educational processes, from identifying learning needs and goals to evaluating learning outcomes. **Collaborative teaching** transforms educational processes so that learners become consumers rather than simply recipients of education. Possible educational experiences include role-playing and structured training experiences.

Role-Playing

Role-playing develops interpersonal skills. For example, when a client complains that an employer never listens, the worker may suggest a role play. First, the client describes the behaviors of the employer to guide the worker's portrayal. Then the partners play out the scenario, discovering information about the client's approach, hypothesizing possible responses and feelings the employer may be having, and exploring the client's perspective on what might work best. Role-playing provides an arena for trying out new behaviors without risking the consequences of failure.

Role-playing also works with groups. Either structured experiences using scripts or unstructured experiences in which members choose roles for more extemporaneous interaction can test out new behaviors or generate creative ideas. Group members may play another person's role to increase their empathy for and understanding of the other person's position. Playing roles that require group members to represent views they themselves do not hold is particularly useful in developing skills in task groups, in teaching them to elucidate alternatives, and in reaching consensus in group decisions.

Structured Training Experiences

Curriculum-based learning strategies or **structured training** experiences work best with some clients. Many agencies have training manuals, do-it-yourself skill development books, or online training modules for clients to use. Detailed skill development programs are packaged and offered commercially for nearly every kind of interpersonal development. Many social work groups focus on developing interpersonal skills such as anger management, assertiveness, or job interview skills. Examples of other educational topics include managing stress, dealing with caregiving issues, developing a strategic plan, working on a team, negotiating, and effective decision making.

As with any educational experience, material should be culturally sensitive and geared toward the learning objectives, levels, and learning styles of the participants

Collaboratively, educators and learners
- Assess the learning needs
- Identify the learning outcomes, that is, what knowledge or skills or attitudes will be achieved through the training
- Identify various types of learning experiences necessary to achieve learning outcomes such as existing curricula, role plays, films, speakers, lectures, or simulations
- Screen proposed learning strategies for cultural appropriateness
- Sequence the training agenda for a single session or schedule for multiple sessions
- Implement the training sessions
- Evaluate the learning outcomes and the methods used

Figure 12.3
Developing Training Modules

(Figure 12.3). Cultural variations do exist in learning styles. Successful educational programs also consider participants' schedules to determine the best time frames and build in supports for attendance such as child care and transportation.

Technical supports for educational programming are expanding rapidly. For example, web-based transmission connects multiple learning sites. Interactive teleconferences allow participants to interface with well-known experts. Video recording technology allows participants to record activities, play it back, and evaluate their responses. Computer-based programmed learning takes advantage of individualized instruction and immediate feedback.

Modeling

How many of us have heard a parent say, "Do as I say, not as I do"? How many of us have followed this advice? Unavoidably, social workers find themselves as models for clients on how to cope, communicate, and relate. Social workers acknowledge their responsibility as role models by monitoring their own behaviors to check for consistency with what they are saying.

Based on the social learning model developed by Bandura (1986, 1997), **modeling** promotes behavioral changes through the observation, imitation, and vicarious experience of the gains the modeled behavior attains. In social work practice, modeling occurs when clients observe adaptive coping strategies, competent problem-solving skills, and effective patterns of communication exhibited by others. Being chosen as a model depends on perceived similarities between the model and the observer (Bandura). In other words, in the context of social work, the more clients identify with workers, the greater the likelihood they will learn through modeling.

Teaching by modeling works simply. If social workers want clients to listen to one another, workers must first demonstrate their own abilities to listen to what clients are saying. If a social worker wants clients to assert themselves, the practitioner responds enthusiastically when clients disagree with the worker's view. If social workers want clients to show patience, workers demonstrate how they expect change at a realistic and incremental rate. If practitioners discover they themselves are unable to do what they are asking from clients, workers reexamine their own expectations.

Sharing Information

One resource accessible to all clients is the social worker. The personal and professional characteristics of social workers, including genuineness, trustworthiness, and amiability, are influential factors. Additional characteristics include the worker's professional knowledge and skills, including the depth of their understanding of relevant issues and the breadth of their practice experience. To use influence effectively as an intervention, social workers develop their professional reputations, their knowledge about the specific challenges that clients face, and their skills in sharing expertise and self-disclosing.

Offering Professional Knowledge

Clients are experts, but acknowledging client expertise does not strip practitioners of their own. Social workers often offer clients theoretical information, practice wisdom, and research knowledge. The information shared should be consistent with the agreed-on contract, connected to the client's immediate concerns, and within the area of the worker's expertise.

Workers show caution when using their expertise, so as not to undermine clients' expertise. The most empowering way to share expertise is by responding to the client's request. Notice the style and kinds of expertise workers offer in the following examples:

- So, you're interested in what I know about stepfamilies. I did just read some research the other day that said parenting works best when both parent and stepparent discuss together what to do with children, but then the biological parent actually implements what they decide. Research reports that children are much more likely to accept the authority of the biological parent.
- It might help you decide what to do if I shared some information about what we generally see happen when someone first moves into our facility. Are you interested in that?
- I'm impressed with your interest in what we've learned about how foster children adjust to placement. Our observations support your experience as a foster parent; frequently, children do have difficulty eating and sleeping for the first few days.
- I've completed the research you requested, and I have located six foundations that are possible sources of funds for transitional housing.

Each example draws on some piece of the social worker's knowledge base—practice experiences, knowledge of human behavior, theoretical frameworks, or research outcomes. Each comment either responds to what the client seeks or asks permission from the client to continue. None of these examples presents the worker's expertise as absolute, but instead as a piece of information that *might* be helpful or *might* somehow explain. Clients can glean from it what they will. When these workers share their knowledge, they do so as participants in the process rather than as all-knowing and all-seeing expert professionals. Social workers selectively use their expertise to inform, not to impress.

Sharing expertise requires cultural competence. Cultural awareness gives clues to how workers should present information, since people from different cultures tend to differ in their styles of learning. Varying cultural attitudes toward authority also have implications for the approach that workers might choose in sharing expertise. Finally, workers carefully screen the information they offer to ensure that the content is a "cultural fit."

Self-Disclosure

Social workers are people, too. They have lives, relationships, families, jobs, successes, setbacks, embarrassments, and dreams. Sometimes, social workers choose from among their own personal experiences to share something that may benefit clients. However, **self-disclosure** works best when it is brief and infrequent. Workers screen personal information to ensure that it is relevant to clients' situations. For example, workers may share the following:

- I remember what a difficult time I had when my father died.
- I overcame my fear of talking in front of people by taking a speech class at a community college.
- I remember feeling so inadequate my first day on this job. I even got lost in the parking ramp that day.
- My husband and I fight sometimes, but we've learned what works for us is to take breaks, think about it, and come back to talk again in an hour or two.

Workers differentiate between self-disclosing and giving advice. Advice says, "This is how you ought to do it." Self-disclosure says, "This is what it is like for me. I don't know whether this is helpful to you or not. You'll have to decide for yourself." Workers can self-disclose most effectively by identifying the information as a personal sharing and acknowledging that it may or may not be useful to the client. This frees clients to respond in whatever ways they choose (Figure 12.4).

> **?** Assess your understanding of educating by taking this brief quiz.

Before self-disclosing, workers carefully screen information to keep their personal sharing professional by asking themselves the following questions:

1. What experiences have I had that may offer new information or a different perspective or demonstrate empathy?
2. Is this information relevant to the client's situation at this particular time?
3. Do I have a close enough relationship with the client to share personal information? Will personal sharing confuse or inhibit the client?
4. Is it culturally appropriate to disclose this information?
5. What is my motivation in sharing this information? To build the relationship? To inform? To impress?
6. In what way do I expect the client to respond to this information? To see new possibilities? To understand that we have similar experiences?
7. What is the best way to offer this information neutrally? Will the client experience this as advice, contributing to feelings of inadequacy or failure?
8. Can I share this information briefly enough to maintain the focus on the client's issues rather than my own personal life?

Figure 12.4
Checklist for Self-Disclosure

LOOKING FORWARD

Activating resources again tests the worker's ability to do enough, but not too much, for a client. Empowerment-oriented social workers temper their expertise out of respect for client self-direction and determination, taking actions to keep the plan in focus and sustain client motivation. To augment a client's experience of competence, workers use strategies to build confidence and encourage clients to oversee their own development. Practitioners work consistently to help clients recognize and increase their own power to affect current events, become aware of new opportunities, increase use of available resources, and strengthen knowledge and skills related to reaching goals. Social workers and clients collaborate as they implement plans of action.

In an ideal world, efficiently and creatively working with what is available would be enough, but all social workers and clients confront situations in which they wish there were other options. The attempt to locate resources sometimes reveals gaps in service delivery and limited opportunities for clients. Simply dealing with existing resources is not adequate for meeting current and changing needs.

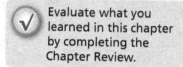

Evaluate what you learned in this chapter by completing the Chapter Review.

To respond to this resource scarcity, social workers strive to enrich environments. Chapter 13, Creating Alliances, describes how workers increase the available pool of resources by creating new connections among clients both within the service delivery network and in clients' natural support networks.

13

Intervention: Creating Alliances

ELISE AMENDOLA/AP IMAGES

When the social work team of Consuela Diaz and Darrell Foster arrives at the community center, they feel as if they are late. The members of the Community Action Council are already talking among themselves, handing out various task group reports, and compiling an agenda for the official meeting. Marvella Harvey, chairperson of the Council, is talking to some members about the Council's new advocacy program, through which the Council represents the interests of citizens in their dealings with city officials, law enforcement officers, and state political representatives. Other members talk excitedly in small groups, pull out additional chairs from the storeroom to accommodate the overflowing crowd, or snack on the coffee and cookies that someone has supplied. The workers see that the group has taken on a life of its own.

As social workers for the Northside Development Association, Consuela and Darrell worked with the Community Action Council from its inception as an informal group of interested citizens. Earlier in their work with the Council, Consuela and Darrell played facilitative roles in the group's operation, guiding the Council through various phases of organization, assessment, and analysis to create a comprehensive plan of action. But now, the plan is in motion, and so are the members of the Council. Both Consuela and Darrell recognize the signs. This group is sensing its power and learning to wield it. It's time for the two workers to take another step back. They greet the members of the Council and take seats on the side of the room.

After Marvella calls the meeting to order, Consuela and Darrell observe firsthand the abilities the group has developed. The members organize their interaction productively, actively seek each other's views, listen closely to one another, welcome differences of opinions as stimulating options rather than threats to unity, and focus on their goals. They even wrap up the meeting by posting a concrete list of the activities that each task group will complete by the next meeting. The members of the Community Action Council can see where they are, plan next steps, and know they have the capabilities to achieve their goals.

Clearly, the Community Action Council is activated—keeping in touch with its resources, feeling its power to make changes, and demonstrating the skills to do so. Do you sense the momentum building in this group? Do you notice how the group seems to be taking over the process of reaching its own goals? This client system is on the move! It is this kind of movement that social workers seek as they work to create and activate alliances.

This chapter discusses the activities of social workers and clients to build productive alliances in their respective environments. Social workers who facilitate alliances for their clients and for themselves will generate resources for service delivery and construct supportive environments for practice.

DEVELOPING ALLIANCES THROUGH SMALL GROUPS

When you add 1 + 1, what do you get? In the world of math, the answer is obviously 2. But in the world of empowering social work, 1 + 1 = 3! Think about the social worker–client system relationship as an example to understand this "new math." When you add the resources of the social worker to the resources of the client, you have two resources with which to begin. But as the social worker and client work together, a third resource emerges: the synergistic resource created through a collaborative **alliance**. The possibilities for resource-generating alliances exist beyond the social worker–client relationship. Social workers support clients' efforts to build productive connections with others.

Clients can benefit from many types of alliances, including those with other clients who have similar concerns, supportive relationships within their natural support networks, alliances between clients and their service providers, organizational **coalitions** among agencies providing services, and the worker's own alliances within the professional network of support(see Figure 13.1).

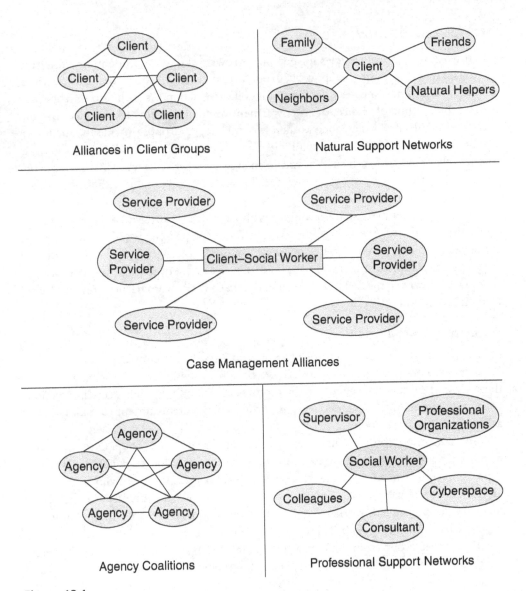

Figure 13.1
Types of Alliances
A generalist perspective reveals many ways that clients can benefit from alliances. Clients experience support from other clients with similar concerns, from people in their natural support networks, and from enhanced connections with potential community service providers. Support is also available from mezzo and macro connections among service providers and within the social worker's own professional service network.

All people benefit from supportive relationships with others. Such relationships contribute to feelings of confidence and security. Good relationships have synergy; they actually become resources—stimulating ideas, feelings, and experiences impossible for any individual to create independently. Social workers facilitate the development of alliances through their use of groups such as **mutual aid** groups, **self-help groups**, and natural support networks.

Groups and Empowerment

Social work groups are vehicles for personal growth, skill development, and environmental change. Through group work, group members may acquire new perspectives, support one another, and also join forces for collective action. As such, group work may well be the method of choice for empowerment-oriented social work practice (Breton, 2002, 2006; DuBois & Miley, 2014; Mullender et al., 2013). Groups provide the forum for people to develop skills in critical thinking, receive information and validation, and organize a power base from which to advocate change in larger social systems. Group work characterizes the social work profession's tradition of empowerment with those persons who are oppressed.

Group work characterizes the social work profession's tradition of empowerment with those persons who are oppressed.

In groups, members share resources with each other rather than depend primarily on the social worker's skills and expertise. From the perspective of empowerment, groups are vehicles for changing "oppressive cognitive, behavioral, social, and political structures or conditions that thwart the control people have over their lives, that prevent them from accessing needed resources, and that keep them from participating in the life of their community" (Breton, 2004, p. 59).

Facilitating Group Functioning

Social workers have responsibilities to maximize the benefits of the group process. Workers use core generalist skills to (1) conceptualize and initiate the group, (2) develop the system of mutual aid essential to the group's success, and (3) mediate the interactions among group members and between the group and its environment to maintain and achieve the group's purpose.

Social workers complete many tasks to initiate an effective group. Often, workers decide on a group approach based on contacts with several individual clients who are expressing similar needs. At other times, the ideas for groups come from social issues identified by the worker or suggestions from indigenous community leaders. Once the group is envisioned, workers engage in other pregroup activities that include taking steps to launch the group. These activities include developing a proposal, receiving sanction for the group from the sponsoring organization, accessing and screening potential members, and orienting members selected to the purpose and process of the group (Corey et al., 2014).

As the group begins, social workers as facilitators develop the system of mutual aid that characterizes the group approach. To accomplish this, workers direct members' interactions toward one another, help members respond to what other members are saying, foster the development of respectful and functional group norms, and highlight members' common characteristics and concerns. This phase of group work is the formation stage, a time when the group takes on its own unique identity. During this time, members begin to sense the power of the group alliance and recognize their place in the structure of the group.

Finally, to achieve the purposes of the group, social workers keep members on task, network appropriate resources and information to members, and help members implement goal-directed activities. Key skills for social workers during this phase of group operation include resolving conflicts, facilitating decision making, and stimulating creativity. For groups to be empowering, workers teach and model these skills so that members themselves can take responsibility for the group's interaction and success. Demonstrating an important skill in group facilitation, social workers do not control the process or evaluate what the group members have done. Instead, as group facilitators, social workers encourage the members themselves to interact and reflect on their own experiences.

Mutual Aid in Groups

Small groups provide opportunities for enhancing mutual aid among clients; clients help themselves by helping each other. "The group is an enterprise in mutual aid, an alliance of individuals who need each other, in varying degrees, to work on certain common problems" (Shulman & Gitterman, 2005, p. 21). Workers facilitate interactions among members and stimulate processes that activate members' contributions to each other.

Watch this video that shows how groups experience power when the members develop a system of mutual aid. What does the social worker do to develop a mutual aid system in which group members help each other rather than relying on the social worker to help each member individually?

Mutual Aid Processes

Nine qualities of mutual aid processes empower group members (Shulman & Gitterman, 2005). *Sharing data* provides group members with opportunities to benefit from the knowledge and resources each member contributes. The *dialectical process* involves point-and-counterpoint discussions in which members articulate and synthesize divergent views. The abilities of some members to begin to talk about "taboo subjects" lend courage to others to do the same. Importantly, mutual exchanges also foster the sense of "all being in the same boat." There is solace in knowing that others have similar experiences. *Mutual support* flows through individual members as well as the group as a whole and has reciprocal effects. Lending support to others benefits both the givers and the receivers. However, caring in and of itself is not enough to facilitate change. *Mutual demand* confronts the need to make changes and holds members accountable for taking action. *Individual problem solving* occurs when work in the group moves back and forth between specific cases and general issues. *Rehearsal* is a role-play strategy for practicing new behaviors in a context where support and feedback can increase members' confidence in their abilities to change. Finally, there is *strength in numbers*. United with others, people will take actions that they dare not or cannot do alone.

Several examples illustrate the power of these alliances. In the context of the strengths perspective, Lietz (2007) describes mutual aid in a group of single mothers. Shifting the focus from problems encountered as single parents, the group worker asked the members to take leadership responsibility for a session by presenting a parenting strategy that had worked well for them. Although initially nervous about making a "minipresentation," they were energized by the support they gave each other, were highly invested in the group process, and wanted to continue on to other topics at the conclusion of the series. Knight and Gitterman (2013) detail the benefits of support and encouragement realized through mutual aid by persons experiencing bereavement. In another example, Wood (2007) explicates the initiatives that sprang from participants' experiences in a mutual aid support group for women with HIV. After they identified the anxiety they all felt upon first coming to the clinic, they coordinated volunteers to create a more hospitable environment, including redesigning the arrangement of furniture in the waiting room and staffing a daily welcome committee with members from the group who reached out to newcomers to the clinic. Finally, Roe-Sepowitz and colleagues (2009) detail their work with adolescent girls in a juvenile correctional facility. Specifically, the psychoeducational support group provided a context for learning about the impact of being exposed to trauma and talking about connections with their own lives. Feedback provided by the participants testified to the support they gained from the mutual aid process and generated ideas for additional topics they wanted to discuss in the future.

Self-Help Groups

Workers are not always pivotal in constructing empowering groups. Self-help groups develop when individuals with similar concerns or problems join together to be helpful resources for one another. The caring that occurs in self-help or mutual support groups creates an empathic environment for exchanging ideas and providing relevant information, offers strategies for coping and problem resolution, and empowers group members to confront troubling issues (Segal, 2008). A study of 253 self-help groups in Kansas found that these groups had developed networks of connections with local professionals and alliances with related local, state, and national organizations, lending both credence and stability to these resources for support (Wituk et al., 2000).

These groups usually form around common concerns or problem areas such as substance abuse, mental illness, intimate violence, grief issues, divorce, stepparenting, family caregiving, and health and wellness concerns. Typically, peers, who are participating group members themselves, facilitate the mutual support groups. Examples of nationally organized self-help groups include Alcoholics Anonymous, Parents Without Partners, and the National Alliance for the Mentally Ill. Not only do these groups provide mutual exchange and support, but they often have a political agenda as well, seeking to change public attitudes and laws that affect their constituencies.

Based on a review of empirical studies focusing specifically on self-help groups for persons with addictions, Moos (2008) explicates four essential characteristics of effective self-help processes. First, strong connections with others typically provide a measure of control over deviant behavior associated with addiction. The interpersonal relationships that are central to self-help groups; the groups' orientation toward goals that promote personal growth, responsibility, and spirituality; and unambiguous expectations for and monitoring of substance abstinence are all characteristics that support exercising control over addictive behaviors. Second, members of self-help groups model abstinence behavior and provide support for adopting their strategies. The third component of effective self-help involves reinforcements for involvement in substance-free social activities, including sponsoring newcomers to self-help group activities. Finally, demonstrated effects of participating in addiction-oriented self-help groups include increases in self-efficacy, in motivation to maintain sobriety, and in coping strategies that promote abstinence. Self-help group

Diversity and Difference in Practice

Behavior: Apply and communicate understanding of the importance of diversity and difference in shaping life experiences in practice at the micro, mezzo, and macro levels

Critical Thinking Question: Self-help groups are a source of social support for individuals who share common concerns and interests. What contributions do peers-helping-peers strategies provide to persons from diverse or minority population groups for understanding issues of oppression and marginalization?

organizers and facilitators can incorporate these characteristics into their programming and as measures of program effectiveness.

Working with Self-Help Groups

Participating in self-help groups often magnifies clients' experiences of empowerment (Cheung et al., 2005; DeCoster & George, 2005; Mok, 2004). These groups provide emotional and **social support**, concrete assistance, a forum for learning new skills, and a base of power for collective action. The self-help group members, by definition, help each other. The peers-helping-peers strategies of self-help are empowering because members are active participants in group discussions and activities rather than passive recipients of services.

Results of studies about the effectiveness of self-help groups provide evidence of these empowering effects. Munn-Giddings and McVicar (2007) conducted a qualitative study to gather feedback from family caregivers who had participated in self-help groups in the southeast region of England. Key themes identified by respondents included the benefits of participating with a group of people facing similar circumstances in reducing their feelings of loneliness and isolation, of experiencing validation of their own experiences, and of gaining insight and practical ideas that helped with day-to-day caregiving challenges. This study concluded that self-help group experiences were a complement to rather than a substitute for professional alliances. Another study reveals the impact of opportunities for learning from others on the personal empowerment of participants in breast cancer self-help groups (Stang & Mittelmark, 2009). Facets of empowerment included increasing awareness about the potential for personal control in managing recovery, gaining objective knowledge about the disease and treatment, and learning from each other.

Because of their potential role for providing clients with support and connections to others with similar difficulties, social workers develop skills for linking clients with self-help groups. To draw on these resources, social workers

- develop a file that contains descriptions of the self-help resources,
- identify the key participants in local self-help groups,
- discuss the benefits of self-help groups with clients,
- give clients up-to-date information or brochures about the self-help group, and
- provide clients with specific and accurate information about meeting times, locations, and contact persons.

Self-help groups provide the social support necessary to empower participants.

PHOTO PASSION/FOTOLIA

Self-help groups are part of a natural helping system within any community that supports the well-being of its members. When social workers draw on the resources of self-help groups, they help strengthen the client's sense of belonging to a community.

Social Action Through Group Work

Whereas mutual aid in groups supports individual change, **social action** in groups generates activities that aim toward mezzo- and macrolevel changes. Sometimes, workers and clients initiate **social action groups** for the sole purpose of mezzo- and macrolevel change. At other times, social action emerges from the processes of mutual aid through which group participants identify the interconnections between personal difficulties and public issues. In either instance, participating in social action groups is often a pathway to a heightened sense of competence (Arches, 2012; Breton, 2004, 2006; Donaldson, 2004; Staples, 2004, 2012).

One example describes the movement from mutual aid to advocacy and resource mobilization in work with Latino and African American mothers in a community mental health center setting (Gutiérrez, 1991). The center ran a series of groups over a 9-month period. The initial group was a *support group* to address the concrete issues the women identified. The second group was a *skills-building group* focused on improving parenting. The group was designed to deal with issues the women identified in a supportive group atmosphere. At the group members' request for continued involvement, the graduates of the first skills-building group became *mentors* for women who joined an open-membership parenting group. From this experience, the fourth group, a client-led *social support and social action group*, evolved. When educational concerns were a recurrent theme, the group took action to invite a representative from the local school board to their meeting. When the results of this conversation did not address their concerns, they initiated discussions with an attorney, who spearheaded a class action suit related to the lack of special education services in the community.

Another example describes work with a group for mothers whose children were enrolled in a day care program. Liddie (1991) used strategies that increased self-esteem and autonomy. Their intentional orientation toward empowerment placed the group members in charge of decisions about the group's activities—the agenda, guest speakers, meal preparation and cleanup, social and educational events, attendance at day care board meetings, and discussions with local politicians. Several interesting projects resulted from their increased self-confidence and their collaborative efforts in identifying common issues and strategizing action plans. Group members successfully organized a contingent of 500 community members to demonstrate at city hall about their objections to cuts in day care funding. The group also arranged meetings with the day care staff to express their desires to develop more mutually beneficial working relationships. What began as a support group for mothers developed into a vehicle for addressing issues in the community and with the day care center. What began as women questioning their own worth and even denying their own strengths evolved to situations in which women experienced firsthand their individual and collective accomplishments.

Natural Support Alliances

People may overlook the significant support they receive from social ties such as their relationships with family members, friends, and colleagues, and their associations with churches, schools, and clubs (Table 13.1). However, support networks play an essential role in social functioning and are a potential resource in the social service delivery network.

Table 13.1 Social Support Networks

Informal Systems	Membership Systems	Professional Systems
Spouses	Churches and synagogues	Social workers
Partners	Informal social clubs	Mental health practitioners
Children	Clubs	Educators
Parents	Associations	Clergy
Siblings	Civic organizations	Lawyers
Extended family	Fraternities and sororities	Doctors and nurses
Friends	Athletic teams	Dieticians
Neighbors	Parent-teacher associations	Speech therapists
Classmates	Unions	Psychologists
Co-workers	Fraternal and social organizations	Elected officials
	Recreational memberships	
	Art and music groups	
	Hangouts (bars, the mall, supper clubs)	
	Mutual-aid groups	

Social Support

Social support includes those exchanges in our social networks that provide the tangible and intangible resources of assistance and support. Family members, friends, neighbors, acquaintances, colleagues, self-help group members, and professionals are all potential sources of social support. As part of the communities in which they are embedded, these persons who form "insider" natural support systems are particularly helpful because they have firsthand knowledge of the culture, strengths, and social needs of the community and its members (Eng et al., 2009). Conversely, a lack of social support and a sense of social isolation often magnify the difficulties people experience, diminish their sense of competence, and reduce the pool of resources that contributes to solutions.

Research findings from numerous fields of practice underscore the significance of social support in protecting, moderating, and buffering the effects of crises and in contributing to people's resiliency in the face of ongoing stress. For example, research confirms that communities of faith offer significant sources of social support, contributing to resilience and well-being in *aging services* and *end-of-life care*. Nelson-Becker's (2005) study of the role of religious coping discovered that older adults gained a sense of purpose from the social support they received through their own interactions with others in faith-based activities and strength and guidance through their contacts with spiritual leaders. Nelson-Becker (2006), focusing on the resilience of older adults in hospice care, uncovered the significance of continued contact with friends and neighbors as a source of connectedness and support. Another study in the field of aging services demonstrates that access to networks of support reduces both loneliness and the need for care (Sintonen & Pehkohen, 2014). In the context of the fields of *addictions* and *mental health*, research confirms the significance of social support for women's

Social support includes those exchanges in our social networks that provide the tangible and intangible resources of assistance and support.

completion of addiction treatment programs and reveals that the respondents' perception of emotional and material support is critical (Lewandowski & Hill, 2009). Furthermore, for persons with serious mental illness, the availability of social support, the size of their social network, and their engagement in daily activities all play critical roles in the recovery process (Hendryx et al., 2009). Woody and Woody's (2007) *family services*–centered research on the impact of social support on the parenting experiences of low-income African American mothers revealed the significance of social support in African American families. The study showed significant connections among experiences of social support, parent satisfaction, and success and effectiveness as parents. Finally, research focusing on social support in relation to *immigrant and refugee services*, underscores the impact of cultural differences on interpreting the meaning of social support (Stewart et al., 2010). Chinese immigrants and Somali refugees identified four types of social support—characterizing support offered by both formal and informal sources—information, concrete assistance, emotional support, and affirmation. However, the Chinese immigrants tended to define support in terms of the concrete assistance, whereas given different cultural and religious influences, the Somali refugees characterized their experiences more holistically, including the financial, psychological, and moral aspects of support. In spite of these categorical differences, both groups identified significant connections between social support and health and well-being.

Social support, by definition, involves connections with others. However, connections with others alone do not guarantee experiences of social support. Boutin-Foster's (2005) research on the significance of social support for health outcomes uncovered respondents' perceptions of problematic interactions, such as the intrusive nature of too many phone calls, emotionally charged conversations, unsolicited advice-giving rather than listening, and meddling in decisions and care. Derived from pessimistic views about social connections, learned social helplessness can lead to not developing and maintaining social support networks (Ciarrochi & Heaven, 2008). One contextual analysis of social support categorizes supports as (1) insufficient as absent because of death, (2) unavailable or present but unable to provide resources or support, and (3) dependent, that is, requiring considerable assistance themselves because of illness, disability, or addictions (Simpson, 2008). Clearly, the quality and nature of relationships makes a difference. Support occurs when relationships are based on reciprocity, mutuality, and shared power in an atmosphere where people can offer what they have to give and receive the resources they seek.

Social support may provide resources for clients, yet workers should not expect naturally supportive networks to solve all dilemmas. Social support networks play a significant role; however, they are best considered as complementary to rather than a substitute for professional social services. The strength of social support may be culturally based. Culturally responsive social workers recognize that extended family and community networks play a significant role in some cultures and geographic regions.

Workers' Roles in Encouraging Social Support

A person's social support network usually develops naturally, but workers can also encourage these networks to develop purposefully. Workers can participate in designing physical environments that create opportunities for interaction. They can also teach clients social skills to prepare them for new relationships. Finally, workers can access **natural helpers** in the community directly to ally them with clients who need support.

Designing Environments   Our physical surroundings either enhance or inhibit the potential for developing social relationships. Opportunities for social contact, the proximity of people to each other, and the appropriateness of space for group interaction all influence the formation of groups and other social networks.

The physical design of space—whether homes, offices, meeting rooms, apartment complexes, residential facilities, neighborhoods, or communities—affects the number of social exchanges people make, and likewise, the chances they have for becoming friends. Social workers can participate in designing spaces that support the development of social relationships and also in modifying the existing environments to promote social interactions.

Enhancing Interactional Skills   The advantage of physical environments that support social interactions is lost if people have not had an opportunity to develop their skills in relating to others. In the context of professional relationships, social workers have opportunities to observe clients in action in an up-front and personal way. Workers' experiences with client systems offer information about how clients interact. Social workers draw selectively from this reservoir to provide feedback to clients about their skills.

When social workers notice positive qualities of clients' interpersonal skills, they compliment them for the client's benefit. Clients who recognize their own interpersonal skills and abilities carry confidence into relationships with others. Workers say things such as the following:

- It's always good to talk with you. You have such a good sense of humor, and we all appreciate a good laugh.
- That's what I like about you! You listen so carefully when people talk, and you are so good at understanding how they feel.
- I appreciate your honesty about your feelings toward the Child Protective Unit. It is so much easier to relate to people who are up front about their views.
- I admire the way you follow through. People can always count on you to keep your commitments to them.

Friendships are based on mutuality and exchange. Friendships are most likely to flourish in the context of shared interests, activities, and projects rather than concentrated efforts at "being friends." Enabling the development of social support networks requires creative use of clients' interests and existing connections. For example, social workers could encourage clients interested in the outdoors to join a hiking club or a group interested in environmental causes, clients with school-age children to volunteer to assist with school activities or participate actively in school-based organizations, or clients who, by their age, qualify to take part in their community's programs for seniors.

Activating Natural Helpers   All communities contain natural helpers, people known in their neighborhoods, workplaces, schools, or faith communities who function effectively on their own and who provide resources and support to others around them. Practitioners who focus their work in a particular community gradually become aware of people who play central roles as indigenous helpers. Indigenous leaders may reveal themselves through their community leadership and voluntarism, or social workers can discover their presence gradually as they hear about their activities in conversations with community members. Research in Hawaii describes the inclusion of indigenous Hawaiian helpers in a professional helping process (Morelli & Fong, 2000). Kupana elders, from whom all tradition is conveyed within the extended family, have proven to be effective healers when participating in a substance abuse treatment program for women. In this culturally sensitive model, Kupana provided child care, taught women Hawaiian ways and values, and participated in the traditional deep therapy process known as *ho'oponopono*.

> **?** Assess your under-
> standing of developing
> alliances through small
> groups by taking this brief
> quiz.

CASE MANAGEMENT: CLIENT–SERVICE ALLIANCES

Case management creates and strengthens alliances among service providers and with clients. A popular, contemporary approach for networking health care and social services, case managers coordinate relevant resources involved with a particular client system. The current shift to social policies and funding protocols that endorse case management strategies ensures that case management will retain its pivotal role in the delivery of services (Roberts-DeGennaro, 2008). This section defines case management, describes its purpose, presents a case example, details case management activities, and examines key issues associated with the urgency to contain costs and the propensity to "manage cases" rather than provide effective service.

Overview of Case Management

Case management, as defined by the Case Management Society of America (2010), is "a collaborative process of assessment, planning, facilitation, care coordination, evaluation, and advocacy for options and services to meet an individual's and family's comprehensive health needs through communication and available resources to promote quality, cost-effective outcomes" (p. 8). Case managers in social work settings coordinate the delivery of health, behavioral health, and other human services for clients who face complex situations and who need to access multiple services, plan for continuity in service provisions, seek fiscal accountability, and ensure service effectiveness. Their activities encompass work with case management clients and family caregivers, with various aspects of the delivery system itself, and within the arena of policy practice.

Origins of Case Management

One can trace the impetus for case management to six factors: deinstitutionalization, decentralization of services, clients with multiple needs, fragmentation of services, the nature of informal social supports, and the press to contain costs in the face of limited funds and scarce resources.

- *Deinstitutionalization* is the trend to provide community-based rather than institution-based services. This means that clients with multiple challenges must sustain their ability to live independently by locating appropriate services among the complicated array of community-based programs.

- The trend toward *decentralization* intensifies the need for coordinating services among multiple community-based service providers.
- Without the benefits of case management, clients with *complex issues and multiple needs* must somehow piece together a "patchwork" of resources for themselves. Often, they must access services from multiple providers, many of whom have never communicated with one another.
- The constraints of the requirements for services—including geographic boundaries, age restrictions, income guidelines, and categorical eligibility stipulations—*fragment* the delivery of social services. This fragmentation complicates the tasks of coordinating services and determining for which services clients are eligible.
- *Social support networks* can either enhance or reduce the positive effect of formal services. Case managers can play a unique role to ensure that formal and informal resources reinforce each other, maximizing the benefits of each.
- The *press to contain costs* and *conserve scarce resources*, while still meeting the needs of clients, requires the efficient processes that case management offers (Moxley, 1989).

Expanding Role for Case Management

Largely as a result of these trends, case management is rapidly acquiring a reputation as a major social work practice strategy with clients who have multiple needs. Case management is used extensively in the fields of mental health; addictions; developmental disabilities; health care; rehabilitation; corrections; public welfare; child welfare; and immigrant and refugee, family-based, and aging services. Within this array of fields, public, private not-for-profit, and private for-profit agencies all provide case management services. Case management is the exclusive domain of some of the agencies; others offer case management services as one of several programs and services. Increasing numbers of generalist social workers will be employed as case managers or, at least, in practice settings that use case management for the delivery of programs and services.

The Purpose of Case Management

There are considerable variations among the case management models used in almost all social work fields of practice and social work settings. The common denominator of all case management models is their function to facilitate clients' use of services and to coordinate a continuum of client-centered care. Focusing on improving social service delivery and promoting client competence, effective case management involves a variety of activities that link clients to services, coordinate service delivery, and advocate policy responsiveness—emphasizing its micro-, mezzo-, and macrolevels of intervention. The purpose of case management is explicated through tasks that relate to clients, service delivery, and policy practice.

Client-Focused Microlevel Tasks

- Access and contract for services
- Identify services needed
- Monitor and evaluate service effectiveness
- Educate clients and caregivers about resources and services

- Make referrals
- Initiate case finding activities
- Conduct risk assessments
- Support caregivers

Service Delivery Mezzolevel Tasks

- Coordinate services
- Identify gaps and barriers to ensure a continuum of care
- Create service alliances
- Evaluate programs
- Engage in quality assurance activities
- Advocate for needed services

Policy Practice Macrolevel Tasks

- Advocate funding
- Support policy responsiveness
- Engage in legislative testimony
- Support prevention programs
- Participate in community planning
- Deliver public awareness and education campaigns

Scan these tasks to note their general themes. Some relate to initiating, planning, implementing, and evaluating services with a particular client. Others relate to the service delivery system itself—coordinating, evaluating, and containing costs, as well as revamping existing services and creating new ones. Finally, policy practice focuses on influencing social policy and securing funding. These tasks apply to case management care for diverse client populations served in a variety of settings and fields of practices.

Case Management Activities with Clients

Watch this video that shows that case management is an essential activity in social work practice. What is the social worker's role in working with clients to access necessary services and supports?

Case managers rely on generic social work processes to carry out their case management activities, from forming partnerships to ending the work. However, case managers individualize each case management plan to specific clients to ensure quality and continuity of client-centered care for each client. Core functions include case finding, networking, assessing needs, planning, contracting, linking, advocating, monitoring, and evaluating outcomes. This section highlights three major case management activities—linking clients with resources, planning in case staffings, and client advocacy.

Linking Clients with Resources

Case managers are consummate information specialists. They offer technical assistance with respect to availability, benefits, eligibility requirements, application procedures, and other vital information about resources. By providing relevant information, case managers guide clients through the maze of the service network to assist them in acquiring suitable resources. With a base of knowledge about social service resources and eligibility requirements, effective case managers use several strategies for linking clients with resources, including the following:

- Making appropriate referrals
- Working effectively on multidisciplinary and interdisciplinary teams
- Participating competently in interagency collaborations
- Monitoring and evaluating service effectiveness

Planning in Case Staffings

Interdisciplinary staffings, a common planning strategy among service providers, coordinate work with client systems. Joint planning efforts synchronize services and avoid unnecessary duplications.

For empowerment-oriented social workers, the key issue in case staffings is ensuring an active role for clients. Many times staffings exclude clients, ostensibly so that professionals can "talk more openly." Carefully examine what this position reveals about professionals' communication with clients and the long-range effect of denying clients direct access to key information about their own situations. Decision-making processes that exclude clients usurp informed consent. Empowerment-based social work practice places clients genuinely in control over what happens in their lives by guaranteeing their participation in case staffings!

Social workers play various roles at case staffings. Sometimes they function as information givers, talking directly about their views of the client's situation. They may also be facilitators, guiding the group's interaction in such a way that clients have opportunities to offer their perspectives and other participants hear and respect what clients say. At other times, staffings require workers to switch their level of focus from their client to the interdisciplinary helping system itself. When focusing on the way the helping system functions, social workers support the effective development of the team. For example, a worker can facilitate a sense of rapport, nonjudgmental openness, and equal distribution of power by listening carefully and by encouraging participants to voice their opinions.

For empowerment-oriented social workers, the key issue in case staffings is ensuring an active role for clients.

Client Advocacy

Case managers as advocates use their influence to compel the social service delivery system to be more responsive to clients. Client advocacy activities include negotiating with referral agencies on behalf of clients, educating clients about their rights to access services, and teaching clients advocacy skills. Questions to evaluate the necessity for initiating advocacy activities include the following:

- Is the resource *available*?
- Is the resource *accessible*?
- Is the provider willing to make the necessary *accommodations*?
- Will the resource be *adequate*?

Rather than directing the advocacy process, case managers are most empowering when they support clients to advocate for themselves. **Client-driven advocacy** places clients in roles that control advocacy activities, leaving corollary roles for social workers to support clients' actions (Moxley & Freddolino, 1994). As initiators, clients define their own needs and select activities to address them. To facilitate this role, social workers as mentors model ways to solve problems, teach skills for dealing with institutions and bureaucracies, and suggest ways to network with others. Clients as implementers act on their own behalf, whereas social workers as coaches guide clients in their advocacy activities. Clients determine whether they should continue, modify, or halt their advocacy activities. Through their support role, social workers bolster clients' advocacy efforts and back their decisions. Clients as educators inform professionals about what they want to achieve, how they want to achieve it, and what they are willing to accept from a provider, telling the social worker when to act as the client's representative in mediating disputes. This client-driven model of advocacy does more than help clients gain access to services. It also underscores self-determination in decision making and honors the resources and competence of clients.

Case Management Activities Within the Delivery System

Case managers also work with other professionals in the delivery system itself, both to coordinate the work of various programs and professionals involved with particular clients and to build a more responsive social service delivery network.

Coordinating Services

As clients' interests are of primary concern in case management, the purpose of coordinating services is to ensure that services are responsive to clients' needs. In coordinating services, the case manager reviews the service provisions to ensure that their goals are congruous, that the services delivered correspond with the agreed-on plan, and that opportunities exist for service providers to communicate. As service coordinators, case managers, to promote empowerment, ensure that clients are involved in *all* aspects of the planning. Factors that impede coordination include turf issues, competition among service providers, disagreements about priorities and intervention strategies, and the lack of a common vision for the plan. Given these factors, case advocacy takes on heightened significance in the coordination service function of case management to ensure client access to needed services.

Relating to Other Professionals

Sometimes, connections between clients and potential resource systems need to be modified. In these situations, workers use skills to enhance the relationships of clients with resource systems. This requires a sorting out of responsibilities between client systems and larger system helpers. Clarifying roles reduces conflicting messages to the client, prevents overlaps in service delivery, and alleviates turf battles among various service providers. When clients renegotiate their connections to larger systems, they can shift the distribution of power—getting larger systems to work for them rather than on them.

The way in which social workers approach other systems has an impact on the ensuing success. Representatives of resource systems are people, too. They respond to the same respectful treatment, appreciate the same consideration, and need the same validation as clients. Effective social workers empower environmental systems as well as clients in their work to reach clients' goals.

Building Responsive Networks of Services

Case management is no panacea for an inadequate social service delivery system that is badly in need of structural reform and financial investment. Even the best plans are inadequate when resources are unavailable or inaccessible. Case managers are in key positions to build more responsive networks of social service. Case managers play integral roles in identifying gaps and barriers in resource availability and in ensuring quality of care of referral services and referring agencies through provider feedback and consumer satisfaction surveys. The range of resources available needs to be congruent with the care needs of the community population. In sum, a prime function of case managers is to advocate changes within the delivery system to make its services more appropriate, adequate, and accessible.

Case Management as Policy Practice

Three major activities associated with the policy practice function of case management include conducting public awareness and community education campaigns, designing community supports, and engaging in public policy advocacy.

Public Awareness and Community Education

The intent of public awareness campaigns is to heighten the visibility of programs and services by educating the general public and other service providers about available programs. Case finding, a more focused activity of these campaigns, directs outreach efforts toward those who are likely to need the services the information is promoting. Case managers hope that, through the early identification made possible by public awareness initiatives, their work with clients can prevent problems of a greater magnitude.

Public awareness and community education initiatives include public speaking engagements, newspaper articles, brochures and pamphlets, and fund-raising campaigns. Contacts with key people in the community, such as indigenous leaders, clergy, visiting nurses, teachers, day care providers, lawyers, and physicians, often play a key role in this work, too. The client's first contact for assistance is often not with a social worker but, instead, with a community member or professional who is in a position of acting as a "bridge" to appropriate programs and services.

Implementing Community Supports

Case managers in all fields of practice are in unique positions to identify gaps and barriers in service provisions as well as to lend vision to designing and implementing a full continuum of community supports that is guided by the principle of least restrictive alternatives. They draw on research findings from community needs assessments, service delivery evaluations, and quality assurance activities to better understand the unmet needs in the community's network of health and human services. Case managers, then, may participate as informed members of community planning task forces or coalitions comprised of municipal managers, representatives of funding bodies, and other agency administrators established to develop proactive plans that address community needs.

Policy Advocacy

The **policy advocacy** activities of case managers include initiatives related to program expansion, funding, prevention services, and standards of care. Typically initiated through legislation, administrative code, or judicial rulings, public social policies generate the programs and services that enroll case management clients. In these policy development situations, case managers may be called on to offer testimony that supports new or continuing service programs. Case managers also advocate for funding to fully support those social service programs as well as advocate for funding research on the effectiveness of case management activities to increase the array of evidence-based and best practice case management models. Although case managers acknowledge the need and advocate for a service continuum that is front-loaded with prevention-oriented services and resources, too often in a tight fiscal environment, funding is more likely directed to intervention rather than prevention services. Finally, professional membership organizations in many fields of social work practice adopt *standards of care* that offer guidelines for practitioners in case management settings. As members of these organizations, case managers themselves are in positions to provide significant input into the development of standards concerning client rights, legal considerations, ethical obligations, cultural competency, case management processes, and collaboration with other professionals.

Workers' Resources for Case Management

Social work knowledge and generalist practice skills support case management activities. Effective case management builds on a sound base of knowledge about the consumers, such as key developmental issues, cultural backgrounds, and the community context. A resourceful case manager also knows about relevant programs and services—their eligibility requirements, costs, restrictions, application procedures, and availability. Being prepared with information helps workers coach clients to deal more successfully with service providers.

Case managers use skills to build relationships, communicate effectively, and work efficiently. Skills in listening are essential for relating to clients and working with colleagues. Gathering and conveying information to clients and with others in the social service delivery network is also pivotal to competent case management. When communicating with others, case managers need to have "facts in hand," respond to messages in a timely fashion, and craft succinct, yet informative, responses. Time management skills help case managers balance countless demands such as responding to crises, coordinating the activities of multiple service providers, and meeting deadlines. Effective organization is the key. Marking appointments, meetings, forms to fill out, calls to make, deadlines, and follow-up work on a daily calendar effectively organizes a workload.

Case Management in Action: A Practice Example

Like other case managers, Kennedy Brown finds he is dealing with issues at all system levels. His responsibilities lead him to work with service providers, as well as with clients and their families.

When Sarah Martin calls to inquire about the availability of community-based services for her parents, Kennedy Brown hears a familiar story. As a case manager for OPTIONS, a Northside agency that provides services and programs for older adults, Kennedy recognizes the need for environmental supports as people become frail. Sarah's parents, Ida and George Palmer, are both 75. Until recently, they were able to maintain their normal routine, living in their own home, tending their yard, enjoying the neighborhood children, watching television, and reading. However, when Sarah visited with her parents the day before, her mother confided that she had been keeping a nightly vigil for several weeks, guarding against George's wandering off during the night. Sarah was shocked to learn that her father, who always seemed so chipper when she visited, had been declining for some time and that her mother had been protecting their "secret." Sarah reports that Ida, although sick with exhaustion herself, is committed to caring for George. After all, they've been married for 55 years.

Sarah feels torn. Both she and her husband have full-time work, and their children have numerous work, school, and family commitments; however, she knows she must do something. The question Sarah poses to Kennedy Brown says it all: "Are there any services in our community that can help my parents?" Kennedy Brown sets up a meeting with Sarah and her parents to discuss their situation more fully and determine a course of action that will support the Palmers.

Kennedy Brown's meeting with his new clients uncovers multiple concerns. Sarah and her parents concur that for George and Ida to remain in their own home, they will need supportive services as soon as possible to meet George's physical needs and to assist Ida in her caregiving role. Together, they begin to generate some options:

- Medical evaluation at Northside Hospital's specialized program for older adults
- Meals on Wheels
- Homemaker services for assistance with household chores
- Afternoon Out respite program

Additional issues may surface after addressing the Palmers' immediate needs. Long-term goals will likely include expanding the family's understanding about disease processes and aging, as well as coping with their grief over George's declining health. For example, Sarah and her mother may want to join a caregiver support group or enroll George in OPTIONS' Adult Care Center. Kennedy knows that depending on their assessment, the interdisciplinary medical team might recommend that George participate in the university-based research project to test the effectiveness of a new drug used to treat Alzheimer's disease.

Kennedy's work with the Palmers also means working with the resource network. Kennedy will convene meetings of service providers who will work with the Palmers, and he will attend meetings of providers that focus on general issues of the client population he serves. Case managers are generalists, simultaneously working with microlevel clients; operating at the mezzolevel to coordinate service provisions, enhance interagency cooperation, identify gaps in services and problems with delivery, and increase the efficient use of scarce resources; and at the marcolevel of policy practice.

Critical Issues and Ethical Dilemmas in Case Management

Although many clients benefit from case management services, this area of practice is also laden with critical issues and ethical dilemmas, including the following:

- Who's in charge of decision making?
- What are the implications of **managed care** for the delivery of social services?

Behavior: Make ethical decisions by applying the standards of the NASW Code of Ethics, relevant laws and regulations, ethical conduct of research, models for ethical decision-making, and additional codes of ethics as appropriate to context

Critical Thinking Question: In many ways, case management is actually care management. What are the ethical obligations of social workers to their clients in a managed care environment?

- Who needs to know and who actually has permission to receive information about a particular client?
- Can clients access the services they want, or do they have to settle for what they can get?

Who's in Charge of Case Management?

Who is responsible for making decisions? The client? The client's family? The case manager? The team of service providers? The representative of the funding body? The case monitor? The empowering answer to these questions is that workers and clients collaborate in assessing what they need and agreeing on what is to be done.

When working with clients whom society labels dependent or dysfunctional—such as those who are frail, poor, uneducated, in ill health, or who have chronic mental illness—case managers may fall into the trap of beneficence. The more practitioners manage decisions for clients, the less involved clients are likely to be. Denying client autonomy in decision making disguises control as care.

Issues of autonomy become more complicated when individuals rely on the support of others to exercise their chosen options. Furthermore, the "right" decision for the client may not be the best decision for family members or, for that matter, the taxpayers. An ecosystems perspective considering the client in social context helps case managers and clients generate solutions that fit their circumstances.

Managed Care

Managed care is a means for determining the type of behavioral, health, and mental health services provided and for regulating the costs of these services. Lauded by some as a strategic way of controlling costs, managed care is criticized by others as provider-driven care regulated by restrictive cost-controlled policies rather than by concern for consumers of health care.

For the most part, services controlled by care management organizations have been located in the private sector, particularly those services reimbursed by private health insurance carriers. As more government entities strive to contain costs, public sector services are contracting with managed care groups to oversee the allocation of entitlements. People question whether the safety net historically provided by public sector services will be lost when for-profit managed care companies restrict or deny service claims. In some cases, already overburdened voluntary agencies are called on to provide services without remuneration for those clients denied access to public sector services.

Managed care has widespread implications for service delivery. For example, because cost is central to decision making in managed care systems, guidelines for the approval of evidence-based treatments emphasize cost containment (Bolen & Hall, 2007). Legal, ethical, professional, and financial issues arise that call into question the appropriateness of a managed care environment for social work professionals and their clients, including quality of client care, limitations placed on professional judgments, protection of client confidentiality, regulation of preferred providers, and the capricious abridgement of service plans.

Box 13.1 Case Management: A Research–Practice Connection

Case management is a prominent casework method applied in the fields of child welfare, mental health, substance abuse, and aging services. Much research has been conducted on the utility and effectiveness of case management models and methods in helping clients access the complex array of services available within the social service delivery network.

To study the experience of clients receiving substance abuse services through a strengths-based case management model, Brun and Rapp (2001) conducted a qualitative study that focused on the experiences of 10 individuals. They posed questions to ascertain clients' perceptions about the strengths-based approach and to compare their responses to the principles of strengths-based case management. Results indicated that strengths-based work was valued by the clients who participated but that not all clients accepted the worker's focus on strengths. Some reported they were reluctant to accept strengths-based feedback because it made them feel vulnerable. Clients also saw value in some kind of reflection on problems, at least problems related to substance use. Clients with addictions cited the quality of the professional relationship with the worker as significant in helping them make productive life changes.

Results of studies focusing on clients with a history of addiction demonstrate the effectiveness of case management with respect to client outcomes. For example, Corsi and colleagues (2010) evaluated outcomes for 149 African American and Hispanic clients addicted to crack who participated in a strengths-based case management program. Six-month follow-up data indicate participants had reduced their use of drugs and alcohol and showed an improvement on overall mental health indicators and employment outcomes.

The potential benefits of including a peer consumer advocate on the case management team was the focus of research by Nwakeze and colleagues (2000). Studying how case management services affected soup kitchen guests, these researchers compared the results of an individual case manager model with the results of a team-based approach that allied a case manager with a paraprofessional peer helper functioning as a peer consumer advocate. Pre- and postservice interviews with clients and service providers were conducted with 86 participants to track clients' progress. Findings indicated that the presence of a peer advocate likely contributed to more follow-up by clients related to keeping appointments with the case manager, connecting clients to more service referrals, and accessing entitlements and services. The partnership of the client and peer advocate freed the case manager to focus on interaction within the professional service network, which was useful in "screening clients for eligibility before referring them to a given service and remaining updated concerning which community providers were open to new clients" (p. 33).

In another field of practice, mental health, Johnson (2000) adds to the understanding of what works in case management with a qualitative study of families of 180 people with chronic and persistent mental illness. Participants were socioeconomically and ethnically diverse. By analyzing interviews with various family members, Johnson identified three key themes to guide the development of case management services. First, results confirmed earlier studies that a family's response to a member with a mental illness varies depending on ethnic identity. The need for a culturally differentiated approach is clear. Second, with respect to a collaborative approach, Johnson concluded that "family members want (and deserve) to be treated as team members by the professional community" (p. 132). Finally, family members emphasized consensus among team members, religious faith, and connections with support groups using a self-help model as factors contributing to competence in coping with family members with chronic and persistent mental illness.

Preserving Confidentiality

Confidentiality issues abound in case management. Even when clients have signed **release of information forms**, the basic quandary is determining who exactly has permission to know what when. For example,

- To what extent does the release of information detail the precise circumstances of sharing information?
- How much information must the case manager share to initially secure service provisions?
- Are all service providers privy to all of the confidential details, or is sharing of information selective, based on relevance and the desires of the client?
- If the client chooses to limit disclosure, will providers, likewise, limit or even refuse to provide services?
- If a client signs releases early in the case management process, does this cover new information revealed during the course of service delivery, or is it necessary to secure updated releases?
- What are the implications for confidentiality if case managers enter confidential information into the managed care database?
- Can we assume confidentiality if case management services are provided under mandated auspices such as an entitlement program, Medicaid, public child welfare, or the criminal justice system?
- What confidentiality issues are raised if case management team members who are present during a case review are not involved with the particular client?
- Does sharing information with multiple providers negate the client's right to claim legal privilege?

Case managers and clients should clarify the rules of confidentiality before clients choose to disclose sensitive information and revisit issues about disclosure periodically to keep pace with the changing base of information.

Accessing Services

In the face of limited funds and rising costs, case managers must be ingenious financial managers to stretch their budgets to meet clients' needs. Caps on spending drive case managers to create plans that work effectively for the least amount of money. Gatekeeping secures the road to fiscal accountability, but does it guarantee clients' rights? Denying access to services often means that clients have to settle for services that are least expensive and available rather than being able to secure the best fit for what they want and need.

To resolve the ethical dilemma posed by being gatekeepers as well as advocates, case managers must define their role as serving a population group rather than an individual client. Case managers, as stewards of community resources, must take seriously their fiduciary responsibilities to allocate resources responsibly. Additionally, they need to participate in social and political actions to enlarge the pool of resources available to potential consumers.

? Assess your understanding of case management by taking this brief quiz.

ORGANIZATIONAL ALLIANCES FOR SERVICE DELIVERY

Even beyond the immediate context of the client, social workers build professional alliances that will have indirect benefits for clients. The organization-to-organization connections forged within interagency coalitions strengthen working relationships among service providers, reveal areas that require resource development, and provide muscle to influence political and legislative action. Finally, the connections that social workers make with each other and other professionals provide support and stimulation that will ultimately benefit clients through workers' feelings of support, increased motivation, and fresh ideas.

Professional organizational alliances expand opportunities to enhance social functioning, improve social service delivery practices, develop comprehensive community-based services, and create avenues for changes in social policies. Federal programs, state bureaucracies, community service networks, multiservice agencies, and coalitions of **nongovernmental organizations** (**NGOs**) are professional alliances in which social workers and clients might find necessary resources. But for the uninformed, these potential resource networks can be tangled webs that frustrate, disappoint, and disempower. To avoid this tangle and to function effectively as service brokers, social workers educate themselves about resource systems. They learn about the policies, eligibility requirements, referral procedures, and appeal processes of the systems that may be important to their clients.

An effective way to learn about other programs and to increase the effectiveness of the network itself is through creating service delivery alliances. Social workers use a variety of strategies to connect with other service organizations. These strategies include forming intergovernmental alliances, building interagency coalitions, developing effective working relationships with other professionals, working on **teams**, and leading meetings.

Professional organizational alliances expand opportunities to enhance social functioning, improve social service delivery practices, develop comprehensive community-based services, and create avenues for changes in social policies.

Participating in Nongovernmental Organizational Alliances

Exemplars of professional collaborations are found in coalitions of national and international nongovernmental organizations. NGOs are legally constituted, nonprofit, voluntary organizations created by private persons or organizations. NGOs exclude government representatives from membership. Although independent from direct government control, as "people organizations," NGOs may work in tandem with the world's governments to resolve problems or to accomplish specific goals of the NGO.

Many international NGOs serve in a consultative capacity in concert with the United Nations on humanitarian issues. They are reputedly outspoken advocates on such issues as human rights, refugee resettlement, social programs and policies, sustainable environments, the alleviation of poverty, and peace efforts, to name a few (Healy, L., 2001; Reichert, 2006; Smith, 2003). "The IASSW [International Association of Schools of Social Work] and IFSW [International Federation of Social Workers] are making efforts to strengthen their consultative status as NGOs. NASW is now a member of Interaction, a coalition of more than 150 U.S.-based development agencies that engages in advocacy on global issues" (Healy, 2008, p. 486). In addition to preparing position statements on advocacy issues, some NGOs may assume a more operational role in designing and implementing relief efforts or social, educational, and economic development projects. Often, to achieve their goals, NGOs join with other organizations to strengthen their initiatives.

Building Interagency Coalitions

Interagency coalitions form as a way for agencies with common interests and concerns to leverage more power by working in concert to achieve agreed-on outcomes. Representatives of the agencies come to some agreement about how they can work on a joint initiative to address a particular community issue or an aspect of social service delivery. Several conditions are necessary for building successful coalitions among agencies. Each agency must participate on a voluntary basis, retain its autonomy, share common goals with other potential coalition members, and discern the benefits of participating in the coalition.

Those leading the effort toward interagency collaboration draw on numerous skills for the outcome to be successful. Leaders create an appropriate climate, forge members' commitment to the purpose of the collaboration, envision a positive outcome, mediate conflicts effectively, and build consensus among members. An effective leader simultaneously maintains a vision of the whole alliance while understanding the intricacies of the constituent parts.

Interagency coalitions benefit from a broad base of ownership and a diverse pool of expertise. Working with other agencies distributes the costs and responsibilities of new ventures among the coalition members. Successful collaborative efforts are likely to improve the overall communication and linkages between and among agencies. Coalitions also present a united front, with more power to influence decision makers, legislators, the media, and the general public.

Bringing together a variety of stakeholders, collaborative practice creates multifaceted approaches to complex social problems (Lawson, 2008). Effective collaborations require stakeholder partners to share power and authority, mediate conflicts, identify common interests for action, establish trust, share resources, and take responsibility for actions and outcomes (Claiborne & Lawson, 2005).

Working on Teams

Social workers implement teamwork skills to activate professional alliances and to collaborate effectively with other professionals. Effective teamwork is essential for maximizing the expertise of various professionals (Abramson & Bronstein, 2008). When the components of a service delivery system are working as a team, clients benefit from the harmonious operation of helping systems. Teams comprise persons who share a common purpose, contribute their expertise to the work at hand, and collaborate to achieve some mutually agreed-on outcome. Professionals often work in teams to design programs and services, plan community action efforts, and develop social action strategies. Teams also convene to coordinate work with individual clients or families when several professionals are involved. Efficient team meetings require responsible preparation, effective organization, economical use of time, and respectful participation by team members. Effective team members have listening skills, respect for differences, and the abilities to manage conflict and build consensus. Among the elements of effective teamwork are

- specification of team purpose and goals;
- agreement on norms for team relationships and communication patterns;
- defined roles and task assignments for team leaders and members;
- adoption of decision making, conflict resolution, and problem-solving models;
- provisions for feedback on team processes and evaluation of the team products; and
- acknowledgement of the place and limits of the team in the context of the organization or coalition.

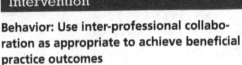

Intervention

Behavior: Use inter-professional collaboration as appropriate to achieve beneficial practice outcomes

Critical Thinking Question: Social workers are integral members of multidisciplinary teams and interagency coalitions. What unique perspectives and expertise do social workers bring to these organizational alliances?

Leading Effective Meetings

Well-conducted meetings begin with a stated purpose, follow an agenda, and complete business within the specified time. Effective meeting facilitators help participants articulate short- and long-term objectives and delineate clear expectations for the tasks to be accomplished between meetings by individuals, officers, standing committees, ad hoc committees, or staff members. The person leading the meeting also takes responsibility for focusing discussions, encouraging participants to contribute their perspectives, and guiding the discussion toward decisions and actions.

Agendas structure meetings by listing the order of business and specifying items for discussion and action. An agenda serves as a physical reminder of the purpose of the meeting. Typically, it identifies the date and time of the meeting and lists items of business, including committee reports, carryover or "unfinished business," topics under "new business," and specifies points the group will need to act on through discussion, consensus, or a formal vote. Tips for conducting effective meetings include the following:

- Developing an orderly agenda
- Sending out timely meeting notices, including minutes from the last meeting and the agenda for the upcoming meeting
- Arranging the meeting space to ensure comfort and participation
- Reviewing the agenda before the meeting begins
- Welcoming participants as they arrive
- Pacing the meeting to complete tasks within the agreed-on time
- Drawing upon listening skills and skills to facilitate discussion
- Acknowledging the accomplishments of the participants

Conducting and concluding meetings requires careful preparation on the part of the meeting facilitator. Effectively concluding meetings is critical for maintaining motivation and progress toward goals. Several strategies for ending meetings include the following:

- Reviewing the agenda and the actions taken
- Identifying follow-up tasks and assignments

- Reviewing the agreed-on decisions
- Setting the date, time, and location for the next meeting
- Identifying action items for the next meeting's agenda
  - Seeking feedback and suggestions from participants regarding process and progress
  - Thanking group members for their input and participation

Assess your understanding of organizational alliances for service delivery by taking this brief quiz.

To the extent that formal meetings are conducted effectively, participants are likely to continue to invest their time and effort.

PROFESSIONAL SUPPORT NETWORKS

Social workers frequently ally themselves with other professionals for support. Supportive professional relationships are usually available within the worker's immediate organizational environment. These relationships are a worker's best ally to avoid **burnout**. Beyond the agency setting, the resources of professional memberships and connections via computers can also stimulate a worker's professional development and provide a web of support.

Alliances Within Organizations

Work settings provide important alliances to support social workers as people and as practitioners. A "one-step removed" perspective offers a fresh look when workers are stumped. Sometimes the client–social worker relationship falls into unproductive patterns, failing to work efficiently toward goals or to envision a broad range of solutions. In these situations, the social worker has several options for assistance. Supervisors provide seasoned expertise and a more objective look at the information workers bring. A review by a team of peers offers a synergistic resource arising from group interaction. Consultants can provide a technical view and offer specific information that is unavailable in the worker's knowledge base or particular practice setting.

Supervision

Most social workers, especially beginning practitioners, function in settings that provide ongoing supervision. **Supervision** may consider either tasks or relationships. The objective of task-focused supervision is to develop skills for efficient and effective job performance and accountability, whereas the objective of relationship-focused supervision is to develop skills necessary to competently and ethically serve clients. In its most effective form, supervision accomplishes three purposes: (1) to structure practice by asking workers to report and critically reflect on their work with client systems, (2) to provide a support system to reinforce and encourage their work, and (3) to create a forum to identify workers' strengths and set goals for professional development.

Supervisory roles include serving as educators, consultants, mentors, colleagues, administrators, and gatekeepers. In their teaching and consulting roles, social service supervisors help their supervisees integrate theory with practice to develop practice skill competencies related to their particular agency setting. As mentors and colleagues, supervisors model professionalism and encourage confidence in the supervisees to develop their own practice approaches and style. Supervisors function as administrators and ethical gatekeepers; they set standards and evaluate performance. In these evaluative roles, supervisors conduct performance evaluations, troubleshoot ethical dilemmas, and judge the suitability of the supervisee for social work practice. Principles for empowerment-oriented supervision related to these supervisory roles include the following:

Educators and Consultants

- People learn best when learning involves positive satisfaction and when they are actively involved in the learning process.
- Supervision for learning requires recognizing the different needs of supervisees at different points in their professional development.
- Opportunities to choose assignments, to acquire new knowledge, and to practice new skills are gifts of educational empowerment.
- Professional development in social work is a partnership investment between the supervisor/educator and the supervisee/learner.
- Educationally oriented supervision should be based on the resources and needs of the developing social work practitioner.

Mentors and Colleagues

- Opportunities to reflect on one's own practice effectiveness, to receive critical feedback to improve performance, and to celebrate successes are gifts of empowerment supervision.
- A commitment to good social work practice guides one's motivations and actions in offering and receiving supervisory feedback.
- A focus on strengths and accomplishments cushions stress and reduces the likelihood of burnout.
- Respectful and collegial interactions in the supervisory relationship are keys to developing professional competence for social work practice.

Administrators and Gatekeepers

- Evaluation should be a collaborative endeavor, one in which mutual support and collegial review sustain continual improvement of practice competencies.
- Supervisees have the right to receive objective, unbiased, justified, fair, and not prejudicial appraisals of their performance.
- Supervisors have a responsibility to offer constructive guidance in correcting any noted performance deficiencies.

Peer Review

Frequently, social workers participate as members of teams that provide professional support. There are many advantages to **peer review**. Presenting a client's situation to the team compels the worker to organize information coherently. The questions that team members ask often reveal information gaps for the worker and client to fill. Team members may also notice similarities between the situation presented and experiences with clients of their own and may offer suggestions on what they have tried with success in these other situations. Finally, the careful review afforded by the peer consultation process accentuates for clients the importance of their situations.

Consultation

The complexity of human behavior extends beyond the knowledge base of any single professional. Sometimes workers and clients need more information for a comprehensive assessment, or they need specific expertise to implement an intervention strategy. In these cases, workers seek the assistance of consulting specialists. Useful outside perspectives may include consultants who are psychologists, neurologists, dieticians, attorneys, indigenous healers, or clergy. For macrosystem clients, these specialists may be economists, demographers, urban planners, engineers, or sociologists. **Consultation** usually moves beyond the worker's organizational setting and requires the worker to gain the client's explicit approval and written permission to do so.

Antidotes to Burnout

High job stress combined with few rewards and minimal involvement in decision making have profound repercussions for professionals (Maslach & Leiter, 2008). When workers lack a sense of control, have overbearing workloads and unreasonable amounts of paperwork, experience insufficient collegial and supervisory support, and receive little recognition for their accomplishments, their work environments become hotbeds of burnout. These work conditions are likely to intensify workers' feelings of immersion in the physical, social, financial, and psychological problems of their clients (Maslach, 2003). Similarly, long-term exposure to suffering and trauma without adequate workplace and personal support results in what Figley (1995) calls **compassion fatigue** and what others identify as **vicarious trauma** (Pearlman & Saakvitne, 1995) or secondary trauma (Bride, 2007; Bride et al., 2007). When accumulating demands exceed workers' tolerance, the likelihood of burnout and compassion fatigue increases dramatically. As a result, practitioners' personal and professional sense of power dwindles along with their practice competence.

In effect, compassion fatigue and organizational burnout take their toll on workers, clients, and the delivery of social services. Maslach (2003) cites research-based evidence of three dimensions of burnout among human service workers: a sense of emotional exhaustion, detachment, and ineffectiveness. Practitioners experiencing burnout become less objective, less positive, less creative, and less concerned about their clients. The aftermath can also include dogmatic thinking as well as rigidly bureaucratic behavior. Other research findings note an association between burnout and issues with physical health (Kim et al., 2011). All these consequences are polar opposites of empowerment-based practice.

Ethical and Professional Behavior

Behavior: Use supervision and consultation to guide professional judgment and behavior

Critical Thinking Question: Worker burnout negatively impacts the quality of client care and the expression of genuine concern for clients. What proactive steps can practitioners, supervisors, and agencies take to reduce job stress and worker burnout?

▶ Watch this video that emphasizes that long-term survival as a social worker requires that you take care of yourself to avoid burnout. What will you, as a social worker, do for self-care? www.youtube.com/watch?v=vJ5fqsWskkE

Self-Care and Compassion Satisfaction

Empowerment-based social workers function best when their work environments empower them as professionals, support a focus on strengths, and encourage their efforts to collaborate with clients as partners. Work settings designed to cushion stress involve employees in decision making, compliment their success, and enhance their self-efficacy, competence, and sense of professional empowerment.

Conclusions based on the social psychology of compassion supports this view as Radley and Figley (2007) advocate a paradigm shift away from avoiding the negative consequences of compassion fatigue toward promoting the protective factors associated with **compassion satisfaction**. Radley and Figely argue that "given that empathic practitioners will face negativity, our profession requires a constant source of inspiration that increases our positivity" (p. 211). Their model incorporates three elements for doing so: (1) increasing positive affect through caseload variety, appropriate time off, and supportive networks within the workplace for dealing with difficult client issues; (2) expanding professional knowledge, networks of social support, and activities that promote physical health and well-being; and (3) extending investments in **self-care**—both through cultivating enriching after-work activities and creating more effective avenues of support within the workplace. As key elements of compassion satisfaction, promoting emotional and physical self-care through activities such as adopting work management strategies, clarifying professional roles, seeking social supports, engaging in professional development, and generating sources of renewed energy all foster practitioner empowerment (Lee & Miller, 2013).

Self-Care and Organizational Support

Measures to counter burnout and enhance compassion satisfaction, thereby reducing emotional exhaustion, the negative effects of stress, and incidences of burnout, include strategies within one's own personal domain, through supervision, and in organizational settings. Personal and professional strategies focus on promoting self-care and nurturing positive affect. The psychological capital associated with optimism, hope, resilience, and a sense of efficacy is significant for mediating workplace issues and stress (Lee & Miller, 2013; Luthans et al., 2008; Schwartz et al., 2007). Actions for individuals that build psychological assets and buffer the effects of stress include the following:

- Fostering positive affect associated with optimism and hope
- Employing effective stress management techniques
- Participating in activities that promote physical health and well-being
- Learning to reframe situations to focus on the positive
- Creating opportunities to spend time with family and friends
- Finding time for recreation
- Ensuring opportunities to immerse oneself in hobbies, community projects, and other activities through which one can experience a sense of achievement and joy
- Developing strategies for changing the topic if you find yourself ruminating about work
- Talking with your supervisor about work-related stress
- Recognizing that learning to deal effectively with work-related stress is an important part of the social work experience

Evidence indicates that supervisory relationships also play key roles in buffering the effects of stress, nurturing positivity, and modifying management practices to be more supportive of frontline workers (Kim & Lee, 2009). Actions for supervisors include the following:

- Providing positive feedback and supervisory support
- Fostering conditions that promote optimism and creativity

- Facilitating open communication
- Encouraging collegiality
- Creating an empowering climate in the work environment

Finally, self-care extends into ensuring an organizational climate that demonstrates a commitment to the care and keeping of employees (NASW, 2008d). Van Breda (2011) suggests that characteristics of the workplace can promote resilience among employees and buffer risks. Agencies and organizations create a climate of empowerment by

- ensuring appropriate organizational supports for programs and services,
- creating a workable bureaucratic environment,
- offering flexible scheduling,
- setting work load requirements at a manageable level,
- promoting an organizational culture that focuses on strengths,
- incorporating collaborative decision-making processes,
- honoring achievements and celebrating success, and
- fostering respectful collegial relationships.

Professional Memberships

Social workers augment their immediate networks of support through their affiliations with professional associations such as the National Association of Social Workers (NASW) and other special interest organizations. These affiliations enhance professional identity, provide opportunities to exchange ideas, and encourage professional growth through conferences, publications, newsletters, and funding for research. Professional organizations also create opportunities for interdisciplinary coalitions and alliances, thus solidifying a united force for policy and legislative advocacy at the local, state, and federal levels.

Nearly 150,000 social work professionals hold membership in the NASW, the world's largest social work professional association (NASW, 2012). Full membership in the NASW is contingent on graduation from a baccalaureate or master's degree program accredited by the Council on Social Work Education (CSWE). Students in these programs also qualify for membership at a reduced rate. Associate membership is available to human service providers with other educational backgrounds.

The NASW has 56 chapters, one in each state and in Washington, D.C., New York City, Puerto Rico, the Virgin Islands, and Guam, and there is an international chapter that serves members in Europe and other parts of the world. Special interest groups within the NASW—such as the National Committees on Minority Affairs; Lesbian, Gay, and Bisexual Issues; and Women's Issues—provide opportunities to emphasize the diverse views of the association's members. To support its membership, the NASW develops standards for various fields of practice, endorses a code of ethics, sponsors local and national conferences and workshops, publishes numerous books and journals, and advocates on Capitol Hill and in state legislatures.

In addition to the NASW, numerous other professional organizations and special interest groups provide support to social workers. Like the NASW, these groups shape professional identity, set standards and monitor practice, provide opportunities for the exchange of ideas and collective endeavors, and foster interdisciplinary relationships. Many publish journals and newsletters (see Figure 13.2).

American Association of Industrial Social Workers

Baccalaureate Program Directors (BPD)

Child Welfare League of America (CWLA)

Commission on Gay Men/Lesbian Women

Council on Social Work Education (CSWE)

International Association of Schools of Social Work

International Federation of Social Workers (IFSW)

International Council on Social Welfare

National Network for Social Work Managers

National Federation of Societies of Clinical Social Work

National Association of Puerto Rican/Hispanic Social Workers

National Association of Oncology Social Workers (NAOSW)

National Indian Social Workers Association

National Association of Black Social Workers

National Association of Social Workers (NASW)

North American Association of Christians in Social Work

The Society for Social Work Administrators in Health Care

Figure 13.2
Examples of Professional Organizations

Colleague Assistance

Support cushions the effects of stress, provides a reduction of isolation, guarantees a sense of connection with others, and assuages the effects of burnout. In addition to providing for collegial exchange, professional social support networks offer a safety net for professionals who experience difficulty with stress, drug addiction, or alcohol abuse. Estimates indicate that at least 20 percent of social work practitioners experience drug addiction or alcohol abuse (Peebles-Wilkins, 2008). Consequences of social workers' difficulties with alcohol and other drugs extend beyond the personal into their professional interactions with clients and colleagues (Siebert, 2005).

The NASW (2008c) policy statement on Professional Impairment recommends lending assistance through programs organized by local NASW chapters. **Colleague assistance programs** offer peer support and encourage workers troubled by psychological stress or chemical dependency to seek professional assistance.

Alliances Through Technology

Alliances to support social workers go beyond the macrosystem level into the virtual world of technology. A rising global awareness coupled with advances in communication technology give social workers stimulating new alliances to explore in the "megasystem" of the international arena. The concept of the megasystem expands our consciousness to consider accessing and sharing resources at the international level through technological advances. It also begins to explore the relevance of the "person:global" environment.

New and emerging technological advances in the electronic age broaden the possibilities for social workers to create alliances with other professionals around the world (Giffords, 2009; LaMendola, 2010). Beyond email and listserv discussion groups, the online world of Web 2.0 now includes social networking sites, blog posts, instant messaging, video conferencing, and user-generated web content (wikis) to name a few. Although there are many advantages to creating alliances with other professionals via cyber connections, the use of this technology by social workers is rife with ethical issues with respect to boundary issues, privacy, and confidentiality (Hill & Ferguson, 2014; Houghton & Joinson, 2010; Reamer, 2013; Strom-Gottfried et al., 2014). Because the propensity to share personal information appears to be the norm, social workers must take cautionary measures not to expose confidential information related to their professional work by posting either photographs or narratives about clients, colleagues, or agencies. In this type of alliance, as in all other alliances, social workers should be mindful of standards of professional comportment and ethics.

? Assess your understanding of professional support networks by taking this brief quiz.

LOOKING FORWARD

Clients have more power when they are buoyed by others in their family, community, and social service network. Mutual aid groups for clients provide support and a springboard for social action. Natural support networks sustain people through tough times and offer opportunities for contributing to the well-being of others. Case management activities team workers and clients with others for a concentrated change effort. At the mezzolevel, networks of agencies and organizations lay a grid for coordinated work that benefits many clients.

Social workers themselves profit from the same experience of empowerment through alliances in the context of their relationships with colleagues and other helping professionals. In this way, they model effective behaviors for clients, encourage empowerment of staff through worker-led peer support groups, create innovative programs, and stimulate social and political action. Workers can also access professional associations and technical resources to fuel their work.

Working within the context of the delivery system frequently reveals gaps in services and limited opportunities for clients. Simply dealing with existing resources does not adequately meet current and changing needs. To respond to this scarcity, social workers strive to increase available resources through social action and community development. Chapter 14, "Intervention: Expanding Opportunities," describes these macrolevel strategies to improve policy and legislation, neighborhoods and communities, and other social institutions.

✓ Evaluate what you learned in this chapter by completing the Chapter Review.

14

Intervention: Expanding Opportunities

SASCHA BURKARD/SHUTTERSTOCK

All human systems—individuals, families, groups, organizations, and communities—depend on internal resources and environmental opportunities to survive, develop, and change. The interconnections among micro-, mezzo-, and macrosystems give generalist social workers many intervention options to expand opportunities and work for social change. Think back on some of the practice examples presented in earlier chapters. Damon Edwards and Nate Hardy are two social workers who operate principally with larger systems in ways that ultimately benefit individuals. Damon Edwards facilitates changes in community policy through his work with the residents of Franklin Courts. By successfully changing the city's response to the crisis of lead contamination, Damon and the residents' group will improve the quality of life for the people of Franklin Courts. These policy changes at the community level will benefit other public housing residents in the city as well. Also consider the example of Nate Hardy of the Northside Development Association. His work to increase the availability of low-cost housing has far-reaching benefits for the entire Northside community. Typical of larger system interventions, many people draw from changes made and resources developed at the macrolevel.

Even those workers whose practice focuses primarily on microlevel clients demonstrate concern for expanding opportunities at other system levels. For example, Andrea Barry, who works in family preservation services, is active in the child welfare lobby in her state. Mark Nogales, who works in the field of mental health, represents his agency on a panel of providers who are planning a more coordinated service network for persons with chronic mental illness. Paul Quillin, a social worker in a family agency, is writing a grant to fund a family life education project to implement in the local school district. Kay Landon and Karen McBride, both outreach health care providers, serve on their state NASW chapter's political task force. Each of these generalist social workers puts ecosystems principles into action by working simultaneously on issues in personal and public domains.

This chapter identifies options for creating environmental change and offers concrete strategies for social workers and clients to work together to expand opportunities. Whether working directly with mezzo- or macrolevel client systems or looking broadly for options to assist microlevel clients, all generalist social workers consider macrolevel strategies to expand opportunities.

OPPORTUNITIES: KEYS TO EMPOWERMENT

Expanding opportunities in the social structures of society is both ethical and effective social work practice for generalist social workers. Generalist social workers are simultaneously clinical and political. As policy practitioners, generalists fulfill the profession's mandate for social justice, and the NASW *Code of Ethics* (1999) charges social workers to extend opportunities and resources to all citizens, particularly those who are disenfranchised and oppressed.

To meet these ethical responsibilities in the broader society, generalist practitioners develop expertise in modifying social and physical environments, drawing on existing community resources, linking clients with natural helping networks, and creating new resources (Acevedo-Garcia et al., 2008; Kemp, 2010; Kemp et al., 2002). Generalist social workers remain committed to the core purposes of the social work profession when they return to their social function of linking people with needed resources, solidifying the network of available resources, and involving themselves in community education and community development. However, many obstacles exist to locating resources for clients. Among these are constraints in social institutions, economic policies, political practices, ideologies, and the legacy of history. All social workers strive to overcome the risks of these environmental obstacles to enhance environmental opportunities for their clients.

Empowerment and Opportunities

Expanding opportunities means promoting client self-sufficiency through social, economic, educational, and political change. It also means eliminating discriminatory barriers that deny access to resources. The NASW *Code of Ethics* (1999) stipulates,

"Social workers should act to expand choice and opportunity for all persons, with special regard for vulnerable, disadvantaged, oppressed, and exploited persons and groups" (Section 6.04b). To expand opportunities in ways that facilitate empowerment, generalist social workers and clients implement strategies that enhance clients' sense of mastery as well as their participatory or political competence. This includes activities that expedite clients' access to services by maximizing their rights and removing obstacles in social service delivery. Likewise, at the community level, workers team with clients to expand public services such as transportation, affordable housing, social service outreach, and community education. Most important, social workers assertively advocate social change to provide institutional supports in the sociopolitical environment.

Policy Practice

Behavior: Assess how social welfare and economic policies impact the delivery of and access to social services

Critical Thinking Question: Empowerment-oriented social workers advocate for resources in the socio-economic-political environment. How does the lack of resources for vulnerable client population groups perpetuate oppression and social injustice?

An economically and socially stratified society distributes its wealth unequally and systematically denies opportunities for some people to participate in decisions about resource allocations. The lack of resources coupled with the lack of power to affect decisions about the distribution of resources perpetuates oppression. For those persons who are powerless or oppressed, choices are limited and, too often, control over opportunities and resources rests with the actions of "others." Social workers must be cautious to avoid being one of those "others" who are limiting their clients' choices. Empowerment-oriented social workers maximize clients' involvement in efforts to influence social policy decisions. Clients take their rightful place in controlling their own opportunities through

- collective action to achieve a just balance of power targeting socioeconomic, political, and structural systems change;
- awareness of political responsibilities, recognizing that socioeconomic and political forces shape people's lives and a class-stratified society creates problems for members of marginalized classes;
- consciousness of the right to have a voice and to exercise that voice;
- recognition of their own competence, trust in their knowledge and abilities, and, in turn, acknowledgment of their competence by others; and
- use of different sources of power—personal, collective, and political—to produce desired results (Breton, 1994).

Empowerment in Groups and Communities

Group and community methods are particularly important for addressing issues of powerlessness with those who have experienced oppression (DuBois & Miley, 2014; Everett et al., 2007; To, 2007). The group is a means by which members of vulnerable populations can offer one another support and camaraderie, both of which are essential to begin a process of social action.

Group intervention is a prelude to critical consciousness. Developing a critical consciousness involves a process of learning to perceive and question social, economic, and political contradictions and take action against oppression. For Freire (1993, 1997), the development of critical awareness, or **conscientization**, transforms people from a naive state to critical consciousness. Freire views critical education as a form of networking knowledge. Praxis, or the combination of reflection and action, is a central theme. Critical learning and thinking generate power within individuals, whereas the process of critical education—reflecting on one's reality, critically examining the world, and engaging in dialogue with others—leads to collective action for social change.

Consciousness-raising is the process of developing a heightened sense of awareness and increased knowledge about oppression and its effects. Consciousness raising and self-awareness are key components of empowerment at the individual and the interpersonal levels. Individuals who experience similar issues can join, develop a critical consciousness about their status, and believe that their collective voice can influence change. This same critical consciousness is a prerequisite to collective action and social change. Thus, empowerment-based practice through work with groups and communities addresses issues of oppression at the personal or interpersonal level and institutes corrective actions at the collective or social policy level.

Consciousness-raising is the process of developing a heightened sense of awareness and increased knowledge about oppression and its effects.

Identifying Resource Shortages

The network of social service delivery agencies, organizations, and private practitioners offers significant resources for its clientele. However, given the diversity of human problems and social issues, the ever-changing needs of human systems, and the complexities of organizational structures, it is no surprise to discover that gaps and barriers exist in the panorama of services and resources in most communities. Figure 14.1 offers guidelines for analyzing needs and availability of resources in a community's human service delivery system.

Part I Continuum of Needs
1. Identify health and human service needs
2. Delineate the service needs of special populations and ethnic minorities
3. Describe the patterns of needs among various population groups

Part II Continuum of Services
1. Inventory informal and formal support services
2. Describe the program parameters and eligibility requirements for each service
3. Describe the structures and opportunities for interagency planning and collaboration
4. Characterize the service delivery network as comprehensive or fragmented, driven by client needs or resource availability

Part III Gaps and Barriers in the Service Delivery System
1. Assess unmet needs of target population groups in the service delivery system
2. Identify gaps in service delivery
3. Assess physical and social barriers to accessing services
4. Evaluate the effectiveness of the service delivery network as a coordinated system

Figure 14.1
Framework for Human Service Delivery System Analysis

Mobilizing Resources

To fill gaps and overcome service delivery barriers, generalist social workers mobilize resources in the private and public arenas. Social workers exercising the role of mobilizer assemble people and organizations and marshal their combined energies to achieve mutual goals. Mobilizers bring together diverse constituencies, open lines of communications, develop a common agenda, clarify the direction of goals, and outline strategies for action. By responding to mobilization strategies, clients can become influential political forces.

Educating the Public

Mindful of the importance of educating citizens about a wide range of subjects—including social issues, social policy development, and the availability of social service resources—social workers disseminate information through community education. Generalist social workers recognize the impact of community education strategies, including such diverse outreach activities as media promotions, television and radio appearances, public service announcements, newsletter mailings, educational brochures, staffing information booths at community fairs, speaking engagements, and video productions. Community education promotes a broader use of social services and raises community consciousness about issues of concern to social workers and the population groups with whom they work.

Writing Grant Proposals

Often, the burning question with respect to creating opportunities through innovative social service programs is, "Where will we get the money?" Agencies face tough choices in expanding service delivery. They can economize within the current budget, switch the program's emphasis from established programs to new services, or expand the agency's funding base. Although any of these financial strategies can yield money for new programs, acquiring new sources of funding through grants frequently gains top priority. When agencies receive grants for new programs, they expand resources rather than simply shift them around.

Preparing proposals for grant funding requires the same kind of thinking generalist social workers apply to working with client systems, including conducting assessments, developing plans that incorporate measurable objectives, implementing strategies, and evaluating outcomes. Before any part of the writing process begins, grant writers research funding bodies that might be interested in their idea. In preparing the grant application, grant writers want to prepare the narrative, develop the budget, and structure the administration of the project in accordance with the guidelines stipulated by the funder. When the proposal is submitted, it enters a competitive review process.

Typical parts of grant proposals for demonstration projects or new programs include the following:

- A *literature review* that presents the theoretical foundation of the proposed program followed by a *needs assessment* that details the background of the identified problem. The literature review describes the problem as addressed in professional journals, reports, and other relevant documents and discusses what approaches other programs have already tried. The needs assessment section answers why

Box 14.1   Social Service Delivery Network: A Policy–Practice Connection

Reflecting a conservative trend, current public policy limits agencies' abilities to respond to the social service needs of communities. Budget cuts, retrenchments of services, and competition for scarce resources characterize social service delivery systems at all levels. Simply, "there is no national social policy addressing the need, significance, and role of social services in the United States" (NASW, 2011b, p. 281). Other issues also contribute to the gaps and barriers in service delivery. DuBois and Miley (2014) detail them as follows:

- Fragmentation of services results from ineffective or inefficient planning for programs and services. Clients frequently experience fragmentation when they are involved with multiple providers. Lack of coordination, conflicting recommendations, and confusing rules, regulations, and procedures create unnecessary burdens with which clients must contend.

- Agency turf battles ensue when agencies protect their service territories and exert their domains of authority. Competition for clients and funding, and therefore survival, complicates cooperative working relationships among service providers and delimits coordinated planning in the overall delivery of services.

- Social triage classifies clients as "treatable" or "untreatable" and, therefore, judges clients as either qualified or unqualified for particular programs and services. Triage too often responds to the pressures of insufficient funding by attempting to sift out those persons who would least likely benefit from the provision of services.

- Privatization is the trend toward decreasing the spectrum of public sector social services, encouraging instead the development of services in the private sector. At issue is the likelihood of differential services—those for the rich and those

for the poor, those for persons with adequate health insurance, and those for persons without insurance benefits.

- Service accessibility is fundamental. Transportation and child care constraints, fees for services, limited times for appointments, waiting lists, and the lack of multilingual professionals seriously limit resource accessibility.

The NASW (2011b) policy statement "Social Services" identifies principles to guide policy analysis and development in an effort to redress limitations in the current social service delivery network:

- Universal access to and voluntary usage of social services

- Comprehensive services, including a continuum of services for both short- and long-term needs in public and private venues

- Informed consent that supports clients' self-determination

- Simplicity and efficiency of procedures and administrative regulations to create transparent systems of accountability

- Stakeholder involvement in establishing social service delivery network policies and priorities

- Planning and evaluation processes that include social work practitioners, managers, community members, and consumers to ensure accountability

- Advocacy activities to promote social justice

Responding to the social justice mandate of the profession, social workers take on leadership roles with respect to influencing and implementing equitable social policies. Social policy changes at the national, state, and local levels will be necessary to shape the philosophy, scope, regulations, and funding necessary to improve the social service delivery network in the United States.

this proposed program is significant and innovative, and how it will address the needs identified.
- Next, the grant proposal identifies the *goals and objectives* the proposed program aims to achieve. Framed as measurable outcomes, this section establishes an evaluative baseline from which to assess program effectiveness and impact.

- A third section of the grant proposal specifies the *program activities* that have been designed to meet the stated goals and objectives. This section of the proposal answers questions about what will be done and how it will be carried out. Included in this section is a discussion of the significance or innovativeness of the proposed project or program. In other words, it delineates the "who, what, when, where, and how" related to implementing the program.
- The *evaluation plan* typically includes a timeline; describes data collection procedures, names those responsible for collecting the data, and details the methods to be used for analyzing the data; and specifies who will receive the final report.
- Grant proposals explicate a *budget* for the program proposal, including a budget justification. The budget also notes sources of additional revenue and in-kind matches, as well as line-item expenditures. In short, the budget section describes why the proposed program costs what it does (Gitlin & Lyons, 2014).

Successful grant writers follow the instructions for preparing the grant application "to the letter" and consult with designated staff from the funding organization for clarifications.

> **?** Assess your understanding of opportunities as keys to empowerment by taking this brief quiz.

COMMUNITY CHANGE

All of us live and work within communities. As community residents, we draw on the opportunities that our communities offer and, in turn, contribute to its economic, political, educational, social, and cultural resources. How well a community supports life within the community and the extent to which its members enrich community life attests to the competence of the community. The nature of this reciprocal exchange between a community and its members determines its need for change and further development. At times, forces such as a weak economy, restrictive federal and state policies, prejudice and discrimination toward special population groups, and limited health and social service resources mitigate the competence of neighborhoods and communities (Breton, 2001).

How well a community supports life within the community and the extent to which its members enrich community life attests to the competence of the community.

These external and internal forces become targets of change as generalist social workers focus their efforts to enhance community competence. Practitioners who apply their generalist skills to macrolevel systems as community practitioners can initiate work with community and organizational leaders to strengthen social network bonds, expand the availability of resources, foster sociopolitical changes, and redress issues of social injustice. With the trend toward applying community-based models in a variety of fields of practice, such as family, mental health, faith-based, and aging services, social work leaders call for direct practice workers to prepare themselves for a community-based approach (Weil, 2005). The purposes of community practice include

- improving the quality of life,
- extending human rights,
- advocacy,

> ▶ Watch this video that illustrates that, for a generalist social worker, intervention at the community level uses the same processes applicable to the microlevel of practice. What actions do these community leaders take that reflect the phases of engagement, assessment, and intervention in working with communities?

- human social and economic development,
- service and program planning,
- service integration,
- political and social action,
- social justice (Weil & Gamble, 2005, p. 126).

Generalist Processes for Working with Communities

Empowerment-based social workers tailor the same generalist processes for working with individuals, families, and groups to structure their community change efforts. These processes, detailed throughout this text, are easily applied to community work and include the following:

- *Forming partnerships* with community residents, local governmental officials, and other community leaders
- *Articulating situations* that interfere with the competence of the community
- *Defining* the purpose and direction of strategies for community change
- *Identifying* relevant community strengths
- *Assessing* community resource capabilities
- *Framing solutions* to address community challenges and unmet needs by planning strategies to facilitate change
- *Activating and mobilizing* existing community resources—people, services, and support base
- *Creating alliances* among and between formal and informal community structures
- *Expanding opportunities* in community institutions through advocacy, policy changes, and resource development
- *Recognizing and measuring the successes* of community involvement in the organizing effort
- *Integrating and stabilizing the gains* made within the social networks and sociopolitical structures of the community

Working with Communities Through Organizing

Diversity and Difference in Practice

Behavior: Present themselves as learners and engage clients and constituencies as experts of their own experiences

Critical Thinking Question: Minority communities have a history of using self-help traditions to address community needs. How can generalist social workers who do not share the minority status of target communities strengthen their effectiveness in their professional organizing efforts?

Community organizing is a method generalist social workers use to bring together people from a community who share common interests and goals for addressing social problems through collective action. As community organizers, social workers promote the interpersonal and political development of constituency groups and facilitate change at the neighborhood, community, and societal levels. Community organizers today initiate many of the same activities they have in the past. They bring diverse constituencies together to dialogue about commonly held issues, bridge differing agendas, promote grassroots leadership development, develop a critical consciousness, and encourage collective action.

Community organizers in the new social movement arena, like their historic counterparts, question the status quo. They call for reexamining the assumptions that stabilize social structures and the societal values that perpetuate them. Furthermore, they draw on research-based evidence to inform their practice and promote community change.

Community Organizing in Minority Communities

Minority communities have a long history of activating informal supports of families and neighbors, as well as formal networks of churches and fraternal organizations, to meet individual and community needs through self-help programs. To redress institutional racism, confront oppression, and secure civil rights, professional organizers build on the self-help traditions in minority communities. Rivera and Erlich (1998) summarize important qualities for organizers to achieve success in racially and culturally diverse communities. In addition to sharing similar cultural and racial characteristics with the community with which they are working, organizers

- are familiar with the culture of the community, including its values, belief systems, and traditions;
- possess linguistic competence in language style and subgroup slang of the ethnic community members;
- convey collaborative leadership styles;
- are adept in analyzing the power dynamics, mediating influences, and economic relationship between the ethnic community and the wider community;
- bring practice wisdom and professional knowledge about the record of success and failures of organizing activities;
- are skillful in using conscientization and empowerment strategies in disenfranchised communities;
- are capable of analyzing the psychological makeup of the community;
- understand the dynamics of organizational functioning and decision making;
- are adept at evaluating community problems and trends and involving community members in participatory research;
- are skillful administrators in planning, developing, and managing programs; and
- recognize their own abilities, intentions, and limits.

Working with Communities Through Development

In contrast to community organization, which focuses on community structures and functions, community development generalist practitioners focus on the sociopsychological functioning of a community. **Community development** enhances community competence by increasing the involvement of citizens in community life. Lane and Henry (2004) assert that "community development—as an empowering, participatory, 'bottom-up' process of change—has considerable potential also, to contribute to the prevention of crime and violence" (p. 209).

People Require Opportunities: A Practice Example

To understand the impact of community development, consider two very different scenarios that explore how Raymond meets his needs in ways that match what the community environment has to offer. First, think of Raymond as a young man who is really moving up in the world. His success in working security has led to his position in sales.

His skill in sales has shown the top brass his growing abilities in management. Clearly, Raymond is a natural leader who has opportunities to exercise and develop his potential. Less than a year ago, Raymond was just another poor kid from the wrong part of town. Fifteen years old, confined by poverty, and intimidated by the roving gangs in his Northside neighborhood, Raymond looked as if he had no future. There seemed to be no way out. But then "opportunity" fell into his lap when Terrence introduced him to the War Lords.

Raymond knew about the War Lords before he became acquainted with Terrence. The War Lords were one of three gangs that roamed and ruled Raymond's neighborhood. Raymond thought that the gangs had always been a part of his neighborhood, but his mother told him that the gangs showed up recently, just when people thought things couldn't get any worse. But the gangs made it worse, or so Raymond's mother said.

Raymond had his own ideas about the War Lords—they were his ticket out. Before the War Lords, Raymond felt trapped. Now, Raymond felt a sense of belonging and some control over his life. Running with the War Lords, he was enjoying money from illegal ventures, the safety of tough and loyal friends, and the power of gang membership. Raymond believed his mother didn't really understand the realities of life when she said that she trusted her faith, hard work, and family to get her "somewhere." After all, that somewhere was a cramped unit of public housing in a neighborhood that came under siege each time the sun went down.

From the outside looking in, joining a gang doesn't make much sense. But Raymond's view of life holds little promise elsewhere. Like all human beings, Raymond seeks emotional and economic security, the freedom to develop his abilities, and the chance to be a success. The way Raymond sees it, the War Lords provide the only path to those goals. Although gangs are certainly antisocial and threatening, viewed from another perspective, they provide what their members perceive as plausible opportunities for security and success. Given other genuine choices, Raymond may be able to avoid the lure of gang membership. Social workers have responsibilities to create those choices. The press for social justice compels workers to develop opportunities, particularly for those who, like Raymond, are disenfranchised and oppressed.

Now, imagine a different scenario for Raymond's story, one in which other opportunities are available, Raymond has choices, and the neighbors have hope. Here, too, Raymond is really moving up in the world. His good work as a cashier at Northside Center Grocery has led to his new position as night manager. His position as night manager pays more than running the register and gives Raymond opportunities to show the store manager his talents in public relations and the quick way he masters new responsibilities. He is developing marketable skills, building a good job record, and making money, too. Raymond is beginning to feel as if he has some control over his life. Just one short year ago, Raymond didn't see a future for himself. Stuck in a deteriorating Northside neighborhood with no money and no plans, even joining a gang had started to seem like his only real option. But that was before Northside Center opened and Raymond discovered he has some real choices.

A community development effort generated the original idea for Northside Center. After receiving a parcel of land, city leaders polled residents in Raymond's neighborhood for ideas about what to do with the property. Results revealed an overwhelming need for convenient neighborhood businesses and services, as families had to travel long distances just to take care of basic needs like buying groceries, filling prescriptions, and doing laundry. Community groups, social agencies, and city leaders combined their efforts to make the neighborhood's dream a reality in the opening of Northside Center, a small mall with a grocery store, a pharmacy, and a laundromat.

Start-up businesses were just the beginning. Last summer, business expanded to include a farmer's market. A startling success, the market drew customers and vendors from all parts of the city and the surrounding rural areas, bringing together people who otherwise would be leading totally separate lives. Northside Center also added a community service agency that coordinates neighborhood social services and recreational activities and provides local residents with information and referral services. It was at the drop-in center that a group of neighbors initiated plans for a watch program to deter gang activity.

Developed as a partnership of local businesses, city leaders, social service agencies, and community members, Northside Center does more than bring the convenience of groceries, medicine, and laundry back to the neighborhood. It expands opportunities for employment, builds relationships among neighbors, and reconnects the Northside neighborhood to the larger community. Raymond is reaping the benefits of this new opportunity, too. He has a job and plans for the future.

Empowerment and Community Development

Empowerment-oriented community development incorporates two core strategies: "promoting the participation of community members in the change process with a focus on self-initiative and providing technical assistance to enable leadership development" (Zippay, 1995, p. 263). Clearly, it is important to organize *with* members of a community in a collaborative sense, rather than *for* them in a patriarchal sense. Community members participating in development efforts acquire a critical consciousness about the needs of the community as a whole and the benefits of collective action. Community practitioners facilitate indigenous leadership, provide leadership development training, and apply a range of strategies to enhance community capacities (Austin et al., 2005; Franco et al., 2007; Harvey et al., 2007; Ohmer, 2007; Wiktuk et al., 2007).

 Assess your understanding of community change by taking this brief quiz.

SOCIAL WORK AS A POLITICAL PROFESSION

Social work by nature is a political profession. Today, most social work professionals work in direct practice settings. At first glance, direct practice seems separate from a macrolevel practice approach that requires a distinct political emphasis. However, policy practice is readily integrated into a microlevel service context. Long (2002) notes that social workers can politicize their direct practice by

- making the connections between the "personal and political";
- considering common needs and issues among clients for policy change action;
- critically evaluating practice theories and models for their tendencies to maintain privilege and social injustice; and
- reviewing organizational policies and procedures for issues of equity, justice, and inclusive participation.

Community forums provide a venue for social action.

Social workers use the political strategies of consensus building, compromise, negotiation, and even conflict to resolve inequities in the allocation of social welfare services and to achieve social justice. Methods to achieve the profession's mandate for social justice draw from divergent political, economic, and social ideologies.

Our perception of problems as either personal or public, how we assign blame and responsibility, and our preferences for change strategies all depend on our political ideals. At the societal level, social welfare policy and social change activities are shaped by the tension among general factions representing the liberal, conservative, and radical perspectives. Although social workers are not expected to adopt a singular viewpoint, clarifying their particular ideological and political positions is essential to professional practice.

No one political ideology represents the social work position. Social workers' duties of social control often conflict with their pursuits of social reform. Although we may be tempted to forge our ideas about social policy into one political mold, the dialogue that results from contradictory conservative, liberal, and radical political perspectives generates creative tension, clarifies positions, and revitalizes the social work profession.

Policy Development

In committing to social justice and expanding opportunities, social workers use the information they accrue to make policy concerns an integral aspect of their professional practice.

Throughout their careers, generalist social work professionals discuss policy issues, and social workers, on their own and collectively through professional associations like the NASW, are in positions to frame public policy and debate the consequences of policy directives. Direct service practitioners have at their fingertips key information about social problems gleaned from their frontline experiences. They also have ideas about causes of and solutions to those problems. Because of their close proximity to consumers of social services, workers witness the intentional and unintentional effects of policies on social service delivery in general and their clients in particular. In committing to social justice and expanding opportunities, social workers use the information they accrue to make policy concerns an integral aspect of their professional practice.

Policy Analysis and Change

▶ Watch this video as you consider that direct servicer practitioners recognize the influence of policy on practice and the need for policy change. How does the social worker use her macrolevel consultancy role to initiate a policy change?

Social **policy analysis** involves studying and evaluating those public policies that are intended to address citizens' needs or to redress identified social problems. Generalist social workers monitor legislation or other forms of policy during its development to analyze its intent and anticipate its potential consequences. During the phase of policy development, workers can offer

Part I Policy Specification
1. Detail the history of the policy under study and related policies
2. Describe the problems that the policy will redress
3. Identify the social values and ideological beliefs embedded in the policy
4. State the goals of the policy
5. Summarize the details of the policy regarding implementation, funding, eligibility criteria, and other stipulations

Part II Policy Feasibility
1. Identify projected outcomes of the policy
2. Discuss the political and economic feasibility of the policy
3. Characterize the support or dissent for the policy
4. Assess the ramifications of the policy for the existing health and human service delivery structures

Part III Policy Merits
1. Assess the effectiveness and efficiency of the implementation of the policy
2. Weigh the social costs and consequences of the policy
3. Evaluate the differential effects of the policy on diverse population groups
4. Judge the merits of the policy

Figure 14.2
Framework for Policy Analysis

critical data to shape the direction of the policy. After the implementation of a policy, social workers can assess its actual impact on targeted populations, measure the degree to which it achieves its goals, examine its short- and long-term consequences, evaluate its social implications, and determine its cost-effectiveness.

As policy analysts, social workers examine the social, economic, political, and global variables evident in the process of formulating policies; study the values and preferences that those policies reflect; and analyze the legalities as well as the costs and benefits of implementing the policies. Many authors propose comprehensive models for policy analysis (Chambers & Bonk, 2013; Gilbert & Terrell, 2013; Karger & Stoesz, 2014). Figure 14.2 highlights the major components of a policy analysis.

Policy Practice

Behavior: Assess how social welfare and economic policies impact the delivery of and access to social services

Critical Thinking Question: Empowering social workers believe that clients' voices should be heard in developing social policies and agency policies. Identify meaningful ways for clients to speak in their own voices in policy development processes.

Consumer Participation in Policy Development

As identified stakeholders in social welfare policy and agency services, social workers and their clients must find meaningful ways to participate in the policy process—from clarifying issues to setting priorities to formulating, implementing, and evaluating policies. Empowerment-based practice presupposes that consumers will be directly involved in developing policies at all levels—from those of local agencies to those of national organizations and the federal government.

Many opportunities exist for active citizen participation (Woodford & Preston, 2011). Broad-based constituent involvement in strategic planning, community forums, brainstorming sessions, and consumer advisory groups are all mechanisms for involving a variety of interested parties, including clients, in policymaking. Interested individuals and public-interest groups contact political leaders to share information and experiences about a policy issue.

Agency Policy and Consumer Participation

Consumers' participation in developing agency policy safeguards their rights as clients, secures the relevancy of program services, and holds agencies accountable to their constituencies. Individual consumers who participate in policy development benefit from the self-growth, increased feelings of personal control, and networks of cooperative relationships that develop. Factors that increase the likelihood of consumers' successful participation include a clear mandate for their participation, a power base from which to assert their right to participate, and recognition of their legitimacy as spokespersons.

Social service consumers influence organizational development by being involved in

- defining service delivery procedures and setting agency policies,
- participating in program evaluation,
- influencing the direction of strategic planning,
- presenting testimony on proposed social policy and legislative changes,
- helping in fundraising activities,
- identifying new areas for service initiatives,
- participating on staff and administrative hiring committees, and
- serving on advisory committees and boards of directors.

? Assess your understanding of social work as a political profession by taking this brief quiz.

Involving clients in making policy decisions requires that social workers provide technical knowledge rather than direct the process. For example, workers support effective group decision making to analyze the situation, refine goals and objectives, and develop plans of action. Workers and clients function as partners, recognizing the benefits of shared decision making.

SOCIAL ACTIVISM AND SOCIAL ADVOCACY

Accessible and equitable resources in society's social, economic, educational, and political institutions directly affect persons' ability to achieve an optimal level of social functioning. Social activism is a strategy used by generalist social workers to redress the inequities that result from differential social status, resource distribution, and power. The NASW *Code of Ethics* (1999) makes clear the expectation that social workers will use social and political action as a means to guarantee access to resources and opportunities for all persons. To ensure fair access to existing rights, entitlements, and resources, generalist practitioners work toward creating opportunities in macrolevel systems through social action, advocacy, lobbying, and legislative testimony.

A Heritage of Social Reform

Social action and social advocacy permeate the early history of the social work profession. Seeking to address social problems associated with industrialization, urban overcrowding, and immigration, settlement house workers utilized their research and community organizing skills to initiate social change. Even the micro-oriented Charity Organization Society recognized the effects of environmental conditions and focused attention on public issues such as unemployment and housing and their impact on individuals.

Throughout the twentieth century, many professionals carried on this tradition of social action and social reform. Among the most noteworthy is Bertha Capen Reynolds, a social activist and advocate who instilled in her students and colleagues the necessity for political activity, social advocacy, and other pursuits of social justice. Writing about social casework, Reynolds (1951) described it as helping "people to test and understand their reality, physical, social and emotional, to mobilize resources within themselves and in their social environment to meet their reality or change it" (p. 131).

With the recent trend toward privatization of social work services, some people question whether activism remains central to social work practice. Many social workers say, "Yes!" A study of activism among social work professionals found that social workers who identify strongly with their profession are likely to reflect social work's heritage of social action (Reeser, 1991).

To ensure fair access to existing rights, entitlements, and resources, generalist practitioners work toward creating opportunities in macrolevel systems through social action, advocacy, lobbying, and legislative testimony.

Promoting Social Action

A strong commitment to social justice, egalitarian values, and the ability to take risks are professional ingredients that prompt social workers to social action. Successful social justice advocates

- build relationships with stakeholders and other constituents that revolve around a common interest in a social justice or human rights issue;
- reach consensus about optimal solutions that address the need or problem;
- broaden the base of support within the larger community context;
- mediate differences with adversaries to arrive at an acceptable negotiated outcome;
- draw upon web-based technologies and social networking tools to educate and engage widespread support and involvement; and
- apply empowerment principles of civic engagement, citizen participation, collaboration and partnership, coalition building, and social advocacy.

Advocacy Role

Closely related to social justice, generalists' advocacy activities can be applied in the micro-, mezzo-, and macrolevel practice arenas. **Client advocacy** directs social workers to collaborate with clients to influence how social systems respond to a client's attempt to gather resources. Activities illustrating a client advocacy approach include educating clients on their rights, negotiating with agencies on behalf of clients, and teaching advocacy skills to clients. As seasoned social workers begin to see similar constraints

Watch this video as you consider that success as an advocate requires that a social worker become influential. How does a social worker develop influence within an organization to lay the groundwork for effective advocacy on behalf of a client?

and frustrations in the experiences of many clients as they seek to connect with specific resources, they respond by expanding their efforts from case advocacy to **cause advocacy**. Arguing for more effective services for clients and educating the general public on an issue are examples of cause advocacy activities focused on larger system change.

Advocates work to achieve social justice by empowering people to speak out and exercise their influence to correct inequity. Achieving social change through advocacy that empowers requires the active partnership of citizens who are vulnerable or disenfranchised with professionals who recognize the public issues inherent in personal troubles. Advocates speak on behalf of clients and encourage clients to speak for themselves when situations deny their rights and entitlements.

Advocacy efforts can focus either on protecting the interests of individual clients or on the general issues of collective causes. As you recall from Chapter 12, client advocacy refers to working on behalf of one's client or client group to obtain needed services or social welfare entitlements. In contrast, class or cause advocacy seeks to redress collective issues through championing social reform and developing responsive social policies.

On the surface, these two types of advocacy seem separate and distinct in purpose and action. Indeed, client advocacy is usually associated with microlevel practice, whereas cause advocacy is an important component of macrolevel practice. Yet, it is often the experience of microlevel work that provides the impetus for macrolevel change. There is an essential relationship between micro- and macrolevel practitioners in successful advocacy efforts.

Essential to empowerment-based advocacy is the continual involvement of stakeholders. Workers who ignore the potential and power of clients as resources in social action waste resources and risk alienating those who are in the best position to inform the process. To involve clients in advocacy efforts, workers provide them with pertinent information, use consciousness-raising strategies to help clients understand the impact of the sociopolitical and economic systems on their situations, ensure client access to existing agency services and entitlements, and argue with decision makers for expanded client entitlements and new services. Importantly, workers help them organize into groups to push for their rights and entitlements en masse because supportive alliances of people with similar concerns provide a sense of power. With the increased prominence of technology, advocates can take advantage of the Internet and cyberactivism (Hick & McNutt, 2002; McNutt & Menon, 2003, 2008).

Designing Advocacy Interventions

The knowledge, skills, values, and processes of generalist practice apply to a social worker's advocacy efforts regardless of the particular system targeted for change. In designing case or cause advocacy interventions, social workers consider numerous variables, including the following:

- At what social system level do advocates *define the problem*? For instance, does the problem reflect a personal need, a relationship difficulty, a social service delivery gap, an interorganizational conflict, or an inequitable social policy?
- What is the *objective* of the intervention? For example, is the purpose of the advocacy effort to entitle clients to available services or to expand the pool of resources?

- What is the *target system* for the advocacy intervention? In some situations, this may be the advocate's own agency, another organization, or a social institution. Advocates evaluate the positive or negative nature of their relationship with decision makers in the system targeted for change.
- What *sanction*, right, or authority does the worker have to intervene in a targeted system? Legal rights, judicial decisions, and client entitlements all provide leverage for advocacy efforts.
- What *resources* are available? Sound advocacy requires resources such as the worker's professional expertise, political influence, credibility, and negotiating skills as well as clients' expertise and supports.
- How likely is it that the target system will be *receptive* to the advocacy effort? Typically, when target systems consider the advocacy legitimate, reasonable, or lawful, they are more receptive to negotiating change.
- What *level of intervention* is necessary to achieve the desired outcome? Different levels include policy changes, procedural or administrative modifications, and alterations in discretionary actions taken by management or staff.
- Who is the *object of the advocacy* intervention? Depending on the cause, individuals with whom the advocate intervenes may range from the direct service worker, to an agency administrator, to a regional organization, to a legislative body.
- What *strategies or modes of intervention* are appropriate to achieve the desired objectives? Advocates may assume roles as adversaries, negotiators, or collaborators. They use a variety of intervention techniques such as mediating disputes, building coalitions, negotiating differences, and exchanging information.
- What can advocates *learn from the outcomes* of prior advocacy efforts? Advocates glean information from both their successes and failures (McGowan, 1987).

Legislative Advocacy

Pressing for change in public policies requires advocacy in the context of legislative activities. In today's political and economic climate, everything generalist social workers and their clients do is affected by legislation and social policies. Ortiz and colleagues (2004) note that legislative casework involves the intersection of policies and social work practice. They call for an increased presence of social workers in this policy arena. The dearth of funding, the glut of problems, and the competition among programs make legislative advocacy skills vital to everyday practice. Strategies and skills for **legislative advocacy** include **legislative analysis, lobbying**, and **legislative testimony**.

Legislative Analysis

Numerous pieces of legislation interest social work professionals, including diverse laws related to child welfare, health care reform, education, public welfare, mental health, and emergency relief services. Social workers focus on five areas to analyze legislative proposals: substantive issues, committee structure, fiscal requirements, political dimensions, and support and opposition relative to the legislative initiative (Kleinkauf, 1981).

Policy Practice

Behavior: Identify social policy at the local, state, and federal level, that impacts well-being, service delivery, and access to social services

Critical Thinking Question: Legislation and social policies undergird all aspects of social work in every field of practice. What can social workers do at the state and federal levels to create policy agendas and set funding priorities to address the unmet needs of disadvantaged client population groups, to redress gaps and barriers in the public welfare system, and to promote prevention services?

To *analyze substantive issues*, legislative advocates consider the status of current laws and regulations, extent of proposed changes, constituency affected, potential ramifications, and inherent social work value issues. Because proposed legislation is assigned to specific *legislative committees* that hold hearings, social workers identify the members of relevant committees and ascertain their positions on social work issues. The *fiscal analysis* of the proposed legislation reviews the results of the findings of the committee about potential cost of implementation. Social workers ensure that sound fiscal analysis considers human as well as monetary costs. Estimating the likelihood that a bill will gain enough support to pass means scrutinizing its *political status*. This involves reviewing the way in which it was initiated, surveying the position of key legislators, and evaluating plans that support its passage. Social workers identify which governmental agencies are affected, list those individuals and systems that *support or oppose* the bill, and summarize the major points of their positions. By thoroughly investigating these key areas, workers can evaluate a bill's chances for passage and estimate the impetus for mobilizing political action to support or oppose it.

Lobbying

Lobbying is any political activity that seeks to sway the plans of lawmakers and government officeholders for legislative and public policy. Lobbyists attempt to persuade lawmakers to draft legislation favorable to their special interest positions.

Professional staff lobbyists employed by the NASW carry out many of the lobbying functions for the social work profession. The Educational Legislative Action Network (ELAN) serves as a communication and action network for the congressional districts of the NASW's various chapters. Another NASW-sponsored initiative, Political Action for Candidate Election (PACE), tracks the voting records of legislators and promotes political awareness and lawful action by the NASW membership.

The NASW (2009a) presents a *Lobby Day Tool Kit* that includes a time frame calendar, sample fact sheets, and activities to help social workers prepare for grassroots lobbying activities. Examples of lobbying steps include the following:

1. Determine the issues and policies to lobby and assess the degree of support expected from elected officials and policy makers for these policies.

2. Prepare a packet of information and talking points for training the lobbying volunteers and for educating targeted officials.

3. Schedule personal or group meetings with elected officials in locations convenient to the offices of the elected officials.

4. Present a cogent case that both argues for the policy and anticipates the questions that will likely arise.

5. Follow up with personal acknowledgements and thank you notes and include additional printed information that furthers the request for support.

6. Evaluate the process and the outcomes of the lobbying activities.

Lobbying activities include understanding the needs and issues of constituent groups, prioritizing action steps, providing evidence and expertise to legislative decision makers, building coalitions of groups with common interests, and becoming involved in political processes.

Recent lobbying agenda and legislative advocacy issues addressed by social workers through their professional state and national affiliations with the NASW focus on various public policy initiatives. Examples include support for the Social Work Reinvestment Initiative, the Strengthening Social Work Workforce Act, loan forgiveness for social workers and training for child welfare workers, affordable access to health care and health insurance, affordable housing through rental vouchers, the development of infrastructures to prevent child deaths resulting from child abuse and neglect, the promotion of the civil and human rights of disenfranchised population groups, and access to behavioral health treatment by military veterans and service personnel.

Legislative Testimony

At **public hearings** sponsored by legislators or public officials, social workers and their clients can ask questions about newly proposed or adopted policies and express opinions on important social issues. Public hearings are often mandated by law. Additionally, if one has not been scheduled, the general public may demand a hearing to discuss controversial issues.

When presenting testimony before legislative committees and at public hearings, clients and social workers may share written or oral statements about their own experiences and expertise. More often than not, clients who tell their own stories have the most powerful effect on lawmakers. Speaking in their own voices from their own experiences and on their own behalf, clients can effectively address the merits of particular social service programs and the probable impact of proposed bills. Jackson-Elmore (2005) conducted a key informant study of 12 states to learn about sources of information state legislators relied on for policymaking decisions. Findings indicated that state legislators from various communities regarded feedback from local grassroots organizations as important. What was most appreciated was direct personal contact by individuals and organizational representatives, particularly constituents. This research provides evidence that involving clients in legislative testimony and action is, indeed, a valuable strategy.

To maximize the desired impact of legislative testimony, social workers follow these guidelines:

- Research pending legislation for public policies of importance to social workers and their clients, including the history of the bills, sponsorship, current status, and passage through committees.
- Assess the sociopolitical and economic context of the proposed legislation to determine the points of support, influence, and opposition and analyze the proposal with respect to social work values and ethical preferences related to social justice and human rights.
- Prepare a cogent and factual position paper or professional presentation for various stakeholders, such as legislators, other elected officials, and supportive colleagues.
- When giving the testimony, represent the needs of clients and constituents.

- Be prepared to respond to questions from an informed knowledge base.
- Follow up with legislators and elected officials by providing any additional information or documentation they requested.

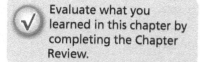
Assess your understanding of social activism and social advocacy by taking this brief quiz.

When social workers prepare written testimony, their finished documents should be clear and understandable, free of jargon, and based on facts and logic.

LOOKING FORWARD

There can be no client empowerment without opportunities to meet needs and fulfill aspirations. This axiom of empowerment coupled with the social justice mandate of the social work profession prompts social workers to participate in macrolevel change efforts. Increasing available resources in clients' personal, interpersonal, organizational, and societal domains affords options and accords power for resolving challenges. Practitioners seek to mobilize existing societal resources for maximum benefit, educate the public about social issues, and pursue grants to expand service delivery. They also work with communities to assist with organization and development. Social work is a political profession. Social workers aim to achieve social equity and more responsive social institutions through policy development, social action, and legislative advocacy. Social workers and clients join together in collective energies to ignite social reform and achieve community enrichment.

Evaluate what you learned in this chapter by completing the Chapter Review.

How effective are the resources used and the strategies implemented in satisfying the client's expressed goals and meeting social work imperatives? Chapter 15, "Evaluation: Recognizing Success," explores evaluation and research processes that are useful for assessing the practice effectiveness. Only when clients recognize their success and determine how it was achieved do they truly increase their power.

15

Evaluation: Recognizing Success

MANDY GODBEHEAR / SHUTTERSTOCK

Are clients achieving their goals? Is our work with clients making a difference? Are we selecting the most effective and efficient practice techniques? Does the practice research support our selection of intervention strategies and program delivery models? These are important questions that social workers and clients ask themselves throughout the development phase of the intervention process. Social work evaluation and **research** answers these questions and provides information to enrich future attempts. In empowerment-based social work, the purpose of evaluation goes beyond simply measuring outcomes and processes. It also affirms the accomplishments made by clients and confirms the effectiveness of social service programs and social policies. The phrase "recognizing success" frames evaluation of client outcomes as a process that empowers by highlighting the positive achievements of clients.

Certainly, the emphasis on recognizing success does not diminish the accountability function of measurement in **practice evaluation**. Social workers do need to acknowledge that not all strategies lead to successful solutions. If social work programs and practices fall short of their stated programmatic outcomes, their utility should be questioned, and if the level of client goal achievement does not satisfy their expectations, clients may lose confidence. Monitoring activities during a social work intervention affords opportunities to make necessary changes. Ongoing review and evaluation allow workers to modify their approaches and give clients opportunities to redirect their efforts.

Because research is central to all generalist practice, social workers require literacy in research terminology as well as basic research and evaluation design to understand published studies and conduct practice evaluation. For example, workers implement **evidence-based practice** and continuously evaluate their own practice to increase the effectiveness of their work with clients and contribute to the knowledge base of the profession. Additionally, practitioners participate in more global projects to evaluate programs within their agencies. Some social workers practice as research specialists, evaluating theories, approaches, and methods to contribute their scientific findings to the knowledge base of social work and to develop **best practices**.

This chapter examines the methods social workers use to contribute to the research base of the profession and evaluate their own practice. Competency in conducting research and evaluation as well as in applying the results defines research literacy for accountable social work practice.

SOCIAL WORK RESEARCH AND EVALUATION

Research was paramount to the work of early social work pioneers. At the turn of the twentieth century, settlement house workers documented adverse societal conditions through research studies that ultimately led to legislative and social policy reforms in child labor practices, housing, sanitation, and juvenile courts. In that same era, principles of social investigation and "scientific charity" guided the casework of charity organization societies' friendly visitors. Throughout the remainder of the twentieth century, practitioners continued to apply research methods to address social problems and to use evaluation techniques to demonstrate the effectiveness of social work practice.

Today, social workers continue the tradition of integrating research and evaluation into their practice. Consider the various ways that the generalist social workers featured in previous chapters can carry out research and evaluation projects.

- Mark Nogales conducts a needs assessment to determine whether there is a need for more community-based services for persons with chronic mental illnesses. Mark gathers information from clients and their families, mental health advocates, human service practitioners, employers, and other key informants to document gaps in services and identify the types of services most needed.
- Megan Camden compiles client outcome data for a research project authorized by the Veterans Administration. The purpose of the research is to test and establish best practices and evidence-based treatment approaches for military veterans who experience PTSD.
- Kay Landon routinely administers client satisfaction surveys to access clients' perceptions of the quality and usefulness of the home health services they receive.

- Paul Quillin prepares a paper for publication on his empirical research about the relationship between degree of parental involvement and level of children's self-esteem.
- Karen McBride, along with four of her clients, participates in a regional study, the purpose of which is to identify the characteristics of practitioners whom clients perceive as most empowering. As a research participant, Karen uses process recording to document her actions and behaviors; her clients complete research surveys to evaluate Karen's approach.
- As a research consumer, Tony Marelli reads professional journals and attends conferences to learn about evidence-based strategies and best practices that he can apply to his addictions recovery work.
- Damon Edwards collects data on the incidence and severity of the lead poisoning problem at Franklin Courts and prepares a position paper to influence the housing authority's action on lead abatement.
- Rita Garcia uses single-system case monitoring designs to help clients in the family reunification program evaluate their progress and identify areas that require further work.
- OPTIONS, the agency for which Kennedy Brown works, is a lead agency in the State Department of Aging Services' case management pilot program. OPTIONS will implement an innovative assessment component that directs workers to seek specific information about clients' preferences for the delivery of home-based services—including how, when, and by whom. An agency that is not implementing the new component will serve as the control. After a 6-month period, researchers will evaluate the data to determine whether increased personal choice results in a lower rate of nursing home admissions.
- In his work with the Northside Development Association, Nate Hardy prepares a cost–benefit analysis of a public–private partnership between the city and owners of apartment complexes in the community. His findings lend Nate support to influence the city council to consider his proposal to increase the availability of low-income housing through a viable alternative to costly new construction.

These examples illustrate how generalist social workers participate in a variety of research and evaluation activities in their day-to-day practice. Social work professionals, as active researchers, develop and test the theory base of their practice and contribute to the growing body of evidence-based best practices through their own research activities.

Integrating Research and Practice

Social work practice and research are interdependent. The practice arena offers many opportunities to engage in evaluation. Research, in turn, is an important tool for conducting ethical and effective practice. The reciprocal functions of informing practice and evaluating practice highlight the integration of social research and social work practice.

Informing Practice

Social research informs social work practice—a solution-seeking function. Social work requires research-based knowledge to understand human behavior as well as social processes and social problems that differentially affect client systems. Practitioners make numerous professional judgments in their day-to-day practice activities. As such, their decisions and actions need a firm foundation of research evidence rather than merely intuition and untested assumptions. Furthermore, being competent in reading and understanding research studies that inform practice requires a level of research literacy.

Evaluating Practice

Similarly, *social work practice generates social research*—a knowledge-building function. Held accountable for their actions by clients, agencies, and funders, social workers evaluate the changes made by clients, the effectiveness of specific intervention strategies, and the overall outcomes of programs and services. To demonstrate accountability, social workers evaluate these various components of their practice to determine whether client systems' situations improve during the course of social work interventions. In this way, social work research expands the knowledge base of practice and provides a way to evaluate practice effectiveness.

Client Involvement in Research and Evaluation

Within the domain of social work research and practice evaluation, the effect of professionals "objectively" studying clients is particularly insidious, as research and evaluation done *on* rather than *with* people creates an exclusive base of knowledge that privileges the views and values of expert professionals. Ristock and Pennell contend that from a political perspective, the traditional researcher as expert approach perpetuates a power imbalance that privileges the researcher rather than the researched, imposing thinking or conclusions that ultimately serve the interests of the dominant group (1996, as cited in Altpeter et al., 1999). Identified variously as **action research**, participatory action research, community action research, or empowerment evaluation, this belief supports the notion that clients are not only qualified to be but should be involved in all steps of the research and evaluation process, from identifying the research question through collecting **data** and analyzing the results. In this way, professional practitioners regard themselves as facilitators of the processes as they work in partnership with clients.

Evidence-Based Practice

With its roots in evidence-based decision-making in medicine and other health care professions, evidence-based practice is increasing in prominence in social work practice internationally (Gambrill, 2008; Regehr et al., 2007; Thyer & Myers, 2011). The evidence-based practice approach applies to all fields of social work practice, including mental health, criminal justice, child welfare, and aging services. Additionally, it extends to all facets of generalist practice, including work with individuals, families, groups, organizations, and communities, and in policy practice.

Gibbs and Gambrill (2002) define evidence-based practice as "the conscientious, explicit, and judicious use of current best evidence in making decisions about the care of clients" (p. 452). Social workers who adopt evidence-based practice incorporate salient research about the efficacy of interventions into their decision-making processes (Jenson & Howard, 2008). Evidence-based practice is a process that combines research-documented practice, ethical considerations, and clients' preferences to inform service delivery at all system levels from individual treatment to policy practice and to create linkages among practice, policy, and research (IASWR, 2008; SWPI, 2010).

> Watch this video as you consider that using evidence-based practice is required for accountability as a professional social worker. What does the social worker do to maintain a collaborative partnership with the client when suggesting an evidence-based practice?

Steps for Evidence-Based Decision Making

In essence, evidence-based practice is a process of informed decision-making. Applying this approach follows five structured steps:

1. Frame an answerable question about the practice need.
2. Collect evidence that addresses the question.
3. Appraise the validity and generalizability of the research evidence.
4. Apply the evidence, considering the practitioner's expertise and the unique characteristics of the client.
5. Evaluate the effectiveness of this evidence-based decision-making process. (Straus et al., 2011)

Answerable Questions

Developing an explicit, answerable question is critical for all types of research. With respect to evidence-based practice, well-framed questions are more efficient in directing the search for answers toward relevant research studies. Social workers are likely interested in a range of topic areas, including effective methods and assessments, prevention, factors related to risk and resilience, costs, potential drawbacks, and harm (Gambrill, 2006). Effective questions delineate the specific parameters of the information needed to obtain answers.

Tracking Down Evidence

Although the steps in evidence-based practice seem straightforward, locating research evidence requires sophisticated information literacy skills, including knowing *where* to locate such information and knowing *how* to use effective search strategies. Well-defined search terms are critical when searching for scholarly articles, exploring electronic databases, or identifying web-based information.

With the increased popularity of evidence-based approaches, more resources are being developed, many of which are available online (see Table 15.1). One such resource is the Campbell Collaboration, an international nonprofit organization that reviews and synthesizes research about interventions and public policies in social, behavioral, and educational arenas. Research teams conduct and disseminate systematic reviews through a meta-analysis of research studies on interventions and public policies in social welfare, criminal justice, and education. The primary focus is on disseminating information about policy and practice effectiveness as well as **variables** that influence outcomes.

Table 15.1   Selected Organizational Resources for Evidence-Based Practice

California Evidence-Based Clearinghouse for Child Welfare
Campbell Collaboration
National Initiative for the Care of the Elderly
Social Care Institute for Excellence
SAMHSA Guide to Evidence-Based Practices
Swedish Institute for Evidence-Based Practice

These reports are available to policy makers as background for their decision-making, to practitioners for selecting research–practice methods, to researchers for accessing databases of meta-analyses, and to the general public for ensuring accountability.

Critically Appraising Evidence

Critical appraisal involves assessing the authority of the research and determining whether the research findings are relevant to the situation about which we have the question. The Institute for the Advancement of Social Work Research (IASWR, 2008) categorizes research studies according to the following hierarchy: "surveillance data, systematic reviews of multiple intervention research studies, expert opinion/narrative reviews, a single intervention research study, program evaluation, word of mouth/media/marketing, and personal experience" (p. 2). Underlining the importance of consumer involvement, the Social Care Institute for Excellence in London incorporates evidence provided by consumers, family members, and volunteers, in addition to knowledge from practitioners, organizations, policy implementation, and research (Pawson et al., 2003, cited in Johnson & Austin, 2008).

Applying the Evidence

To apply the research-based evidence to a particular facet of practice, social workers use "critical thinking skills, sensitive interpersonal skills, insights into personal and contextual factors, awareness of political and power issues and a strong value base" (Plath, 2006, p. 70). Considerations include similarities and differences between the research, the specifics of the practice question, and the potential effects of any modifications. In other words, social workers must critically evaluate the particulars of the practice context as well as the details of the research evidence. Plath cautions social workers not to accept research at face value and not to automatically generalize the findings to different contexts.

Evaluating Effectiveness

As with the application of any strategy, practitioners are more likely to make improvements to a process when they assess its effectiveness. Evaluating each step of the process creates a cycle of continuous quality improvement. Examining how closely strategies and programs replicate the research findings provides a measure of fidelity. For example, the Substance Abuse and Mental Health Services Administration (SAMSHA) has developed fidelity scales, which are essentially goal attainment scales to assist agency personnel in assessing how closely their programs adhere to SAMSHA's specifications for the evidence-based model.

Implications for Social Work Practice

Evidence-based practice has many benefits as well as indicators for caution. An evidence-based research approach to social work practice enhances the scientific foundation of the social work profession and legitimizes practice strategies. The increased emphasis on evidence-based practice calls for increased skills related to understanding, interpreting, and conducting research. Although social research often focuses on redressing social problems (public issues), Bolen and Hall (2007) warn against examining only individual-level variables (private troubles) to develop evidence-based practice models.

Given the standard for practice accountability in the NASW *Code of Ethics* (1999), it makes sense to select practice strategies, initiate programs, and develop policies based on high-quality research evidence. Improvements in the quality of social work practice follow from the feedback loops embedded in practice evaluation. With respect to notes of caution, social workers could fall into a trap of privilege in relation to expertise in research unless they are committed to involving clients as full partners in analyzing and selecting strategies that are most appropriate to the client's situation.

Improvements in the quality of social work practice follow from the feedback loops embedded in practice evaluation.

Ethics in Research

As with other aspects of social work practice, ethics influences the ways practitioners conduct social work research and evaluation. Practitioners are responsible for designing and carrying out research and evaluation both knowledgeably and ethically (Anastas, 2008). This includes considering diversity in each aspect of the research process. Relevant ethical principles include

- *Informed consent*—Subjects give their consent to participate only after researchers fully disclose the purpose of the research or evaluation, what it entails, and its potential effects or consequences.
- *Confidentiality*—Researchers ensure the privacy of clients' responses.
- *Anonymity*—Researchers carefully guard the identity of the respondents.
- *Voluntary participation*—Clients' involvement in research and evaluation is strictly by their choice. Researchers never coerce respondents into participating.
- *Objectivity*—Researchers conduct studies and report results impartially.
- *Careful research design*—Researchers construct designs that are unobtrusive so as not to conflict with practice priorities.
- *Accurate reports of findings*—Researchers report their findings accurately to avoid misrepresenting the data.

Guidelines for ethical research endeavors are set forth clearly in the NASW's *Code of Ethics* (1999) with respect to obtaining voluntary and written **informed consent** from participants without

Ethical and Professional Behavior

Behavior: Make ethical decisions by applying the standards of the NASW *Code of Ethics*, relevant laws and regulations, models for ethical decision-making, ethical conduct of research, and additional codes of ethics as appropriate to context

Critical Thinking Question: Ethical principles for research include informed consent, confidentiality, anonymity, voluntary participation, objectivity, careful research design, and accurate reporting of findings. What guidelines does the NASW *Code of Ethics* delineate regarding ethical practice in research?

any penalty for refusal; informing participants about their rights to withdraw from the research project at any time; protecting participants from distress, harm, danger, or deprivation as a result of participating in the research; and safeguarding the confidentiality of participants. Following ethical guidelines for research not only protects clients' rights but also ensures the integrity of the results.

Research-Informed Practice

Research, in its broadest definition, is a method of systematic investigation or experimentation. In the context of social work, research both informs practice and adds to the knowledge base of the profession. Social workers conduct research to test theories about human behavior and the social environment and to document evidence of the effectiveness of intervention strategies. Generalist social workers require a base of research literacy that includes knowledge about the research process, research terminology, and related ethical issues. They need this knowledge to both critically analyze research studies and to conduct formal research for purposes of practice evaluation, program development, and policy analysis.

The Research Process

Research is a meticulous and organized process that follows a logical progression of steps. Most often, research includes these interdependent steps:

1. Specifying the research problem
2. Reviewing the professional literature
3. Relating the research problem to theory
4. Formulating a testable hypothesis
5. Selecting the research design
6. Gathering data
7. Analyzing the data
8. Interpreting the results
9. Identifying implications for practice
10. Preparing the research report

The research process begins by identifying a problem and formulating a hypothesis. *Problem identification* evolves from a general concern or curiosity. From a general interest, the researcher narrows the field of study to formulate a researchable question. Through a *review of the literature*, the researcher locates and studies research related to the research question to determine the status of knowledge and viewpoints about this and similar problems. The researcher then explores the *relationship of the research problem* to theory, examines alternative theories, and formulates the problem into a testable hypothesis by expressing the problem in precise terms. A *hypothesis* is a tentative statement of the relationship that exists between two variables, such as the social work intervention and the client outcome. Sometimes, **hypotheses** specify the nature of the relationship between independent and dependent variables.

Conducting research also involves designing the research plan for collecting, analyzing, and interpreting the data. The *research design* conceptualizes the sequence of strategies necessary to test the hypothesis and details the methods for gathering and analyzing data. *Gathering data* is the process of systematically collecting information pertinent to the research question. A researcher may locate data in existing data or generate original data through observations, surveys, interviews, tests, or experiments. *Data analysis* uses techniques such as scaling, graphical presentations, or statistical manipulations to examine and evaluate the data. *Data interpretation* gives meaning and understanding to the research results. The researcher is then in a position to infer or project the *implications* for practice of the research findings and suggest subsequent courses of action. Finally, researchers compile their findings in *research reports* and disseminate the information through publications or presentations. The empowerment-oriented practitioner–researcher must be sensitive to client participation throughout the research process.

The empowerment-oriented practitioner–researcher must be sensitive to client participation throughout the research process.

Research Terminology

Research has a vocabulary of its own. Explaining all the nuances of social work research and practice evaluation is beyond the scope of this chapter. The following sections briefly highlight fundamental concepts relevant to a beginning understanding of research. Understanding these basic concepts is the foundation for research literacy. For in-depth information, consult a specialized book on social work research and statistics (Neuman, 2012; Rubin & Babbie, 2014; Weinbach & Grinnell, 2015).

Variables

Research variables are concepts that vary in ways that can be observed, recorded, and measured. Examples are variations in behaviors among different client systems or in the behaviors of the same client system at different points in time. Research variables may also be differences among types of social work interventions or variations within a single intervention. Practice evaluation research examines the relationship between the variables of the social work intervention and the client outcomes to monitor and evaluate a client's progress and to guide decisions about a social worker's method.

Independent Variables

Social work researchers typically designate the intervention as the **independent variable**. As such, the intervention is the causal, or influencing, variable that affects change. For example, consider a home visitor prevention program that offers support and child development information to new parents. The home visitor program is the independent variable when evaluating whether the program reduces the incidence of child abuse and neglect in a community. Likewise, the program is the independent variable when measuring participants' increased knowledge of infant care.

Any social work intervention may itself have numerous variations. For instance, an intervention can vary in type, intensity, and length of time. The home visitor program can offer in-home visitation by a trained volunteer twice a week for 6 months or once a week for a year; or parents may or may not attend parenting skills classes conducted by a child development specialist in conjunction with the visitation component; or the program may involve all new parents or only those defined as being at risk. Consequently, research practitioners make conscious choices about which interventions to select, how to arrange and implement them, and over what period of time to administer them.

Dependent Variables

The outcome of the intervention—that is, changes in the incidence, severity, or degree of the targeted problems, solutions, or changes in the client system's behaviors, attitudes, or feelings—*depends* on the intervention. Hence, the problem or behavior being measured is called the **dependent variable**. The primary goals of many home visitor programs are to reduce child abuse and neglect and enhance parenting effectiveness. In this instance, two variables—the incidence of abuse and the level of parenting skills—are dependent variables. Carefully formulated research designs accurately measure changes in the dependent variable. Clearly, positive change in the dependent variable is the goal of social work intervention and is of utmost importance in practice evaluation.

Intervening Variables

Frequently, researchers are unable to conclude that the outcomes are entirely the result of the action of the independent variable. Sometimes, other factors interject their influence. These factors are **intervening variables**. An intervening variable is any other variable that inadvertently affects the outcome, either positively or negatively. Suppose, in the home visitor program, that the reports of child abuse decrease over time. Evaluators should question whether the home visitor program is solely responsible and consider other possibilities for this positive outcome. Examples of intervening variables may be a lower birth rate, an improved economic climate in the community, or the increased availability of affordable child care. Researchers strive to design research studies in ways that, insofar as possible, control for the effects of intervening variables.

Graphing the Variables

In social work research, the relationship between the influencing and resulting variables is framed in terms of X and Y. X denotes the independent variable, or the influencing intervention; Y denotes the dependent variable, or the resulting change. To represent data pictorially, the researcher locates the independent variable (X) on the horizontal axis of a graph and places the dependent variable (Y) along the vertical axis. The graph plots the relationship between the independent (X) and dependent (Y) variables. Each point on the graph represents the position at which the X and Y variables intersect. In this way, the graph portrays the effect of the intervention on the direction of change, either positive or negative.

Hypotheses

Hypotheses state the connection between the independent and dependent variables. A hypothesis is a tentative statement of the relationship between these two variables. In practice evaluation, the variables are the intervention variable and the outcome variable. Simply, the research hypothesis in outcome assessment states that if X (the intervention) occurs, then Y (the outcome) results. In the example about the home visitor program, one hypothesis postulates that if a community implements a home visitor program (X), then the incidence of child abuse and neglect (Y) will decrease. Another possible hypothesis states that new parents who participate in the program (X) are likely to follow up with well-baby appointments (Y) and immunization schedules (Y) at a higher rate than nonparticipants. The research process subjects the hypotheses to tests or comparisons to either prove or disprove the supposition that a relationship exists between the intervention and outcome variables. Here are several examples of hypotheses:

- If the Acme company sponsors on-site child care provisions, then workers' absenteeism will decrease.
- Foster parents who complete the intensive training program are less likely to experience placement disruptions.
- The incidence of residential burglary will decrease after implementation of the neighborhood watch program.
- Julie's score on the self-esteem scale will increase as she participates in counseling.

Measurement

In evaluating practice effectiveness, researchers assign meaningful labels or numeric values to the observations made and the data collected about client progress and the intervention methods. **Measurement** is an objective process by which the evaluator collects data. One uses measures to assess the status, or the "what is," of the object under study or to evaluate the value of the "what should be." In terms of the relationship between evaluation and measurement, one measures first and then uses the measures to assess or evaluate. For example, researchers can label the degree of achievement of client goals on a continuum from fully achieved to unachieved, or they can calculate actual behaviors into percentages. Likewise, workers can evaluate interventions by classifying successful or unsuccessful attempts or by simply counting the number of sessions.

Reliability and Validity

Researchers consider issues of **reliability** and **validity** when choosing measuring instruments such as questionnaires, surveys, structured observations, and diagnostic scales. A measuring instrument is reliable when its measures are similar or consistent over time or with repeated applications. A measuring instrument has validity when it accurately measures the variable it intends to measure.

To be effective, measuring instruments must be both reliable and valid. Reliability and validity are two distinct yet interrelated issues. It is possible for an instrument to be reliable, that is, consistently to result in same measures over time, and not be valid by failing to measure what it is supposed to measure. In short, if a measuring instrument or variable used to represent the concept is not valid, don't bother to test for reliability, as a lack of validity automatically nullifies reliability. Conversely, if a measuring instrument is valid, that is, it measures what it is supposed to measure, then it may prove reliable. Reputable measurement tools have passed appropriate tests and statistical analyses for reliability and validity. Typically, documentation about reliability and validity accompanies published scales.

All social work practitioners should understand the concepts of reliability and validity. First and foremost, social workers, as research consumers, draw on the published research findings of others to guide their practice. In this capacity, social workers consider reliability and validity information to examine the research critically for its accuracy and usefulness. Second, in their role as research practitioners, social workers often develop their own tools for use with various clients and routinely collect data from clients to evaluate client outcomes and practice methods. Well-constructed research designs and reliable and valid data collection instruments are necessary for practitioners to have confidence in their research results. And finally, for the research specialist whose primary function is building theories or conducting practice research, measures of reliability and validity are central to designing research instruments, constructing diagnostic scales, and making statistical inferences.

Qualitative and Quantitative Data Analysis

Social workers collect information, or data, about their clientele. Data are the facts gathered about the client system's situation. The data collected either describe qualities of the variables being studied or measure their quantity. For instance, in conducting a community study on the plight of those who are homeless, practitioners may gather qualitative information through verbal descriptions or written accounts by persons who are homeless or from providers of services to these clients. The data collected in this example are qualitative because they *describe* the conditions of homelessness. If social workers research the effectiveness of shelter programs on reducing the number of homeless families in the community, the data gathered would be quantitative. In this instance, **quantitative data** involve *a numerical measurement* of the homeless population before and after the program's implementation. Both qualitative and quantitative data inform social work practice.

Data and research methods are interdependent. The nature or type of data—whether qualitative or quantitative—dictates the method most applicable for the data analysis. Simply put, if the data consist of words, researchers select qualitative methods; if the data are numeric, researchers select quantitative methods. **Qualitative data** usually result in descriptive analysis, although researchers can still assign numeric representations to the words and apply limited statistical analyses. Examples of **qualitative research** in social work include case studies, document research, surveys, and key informant studies. Researchers may analyze quantitative data mathematically by using more powerful statistical applications. Experimental, quasi-experimental, and other studies involving statistical analysis are examples of **quantitative research**.

The role of hypotheses differs in qualitative and quantitative research. In qualitative studies, researchers can construct hypotheses and make generalizations about the relationship of the independent and dependent variables after collecting and analyzing the data. Quantitative studies are hypothesis-driven studies; in these studies, researchers develop the design to test hypotheses and draw conclusions about specific causal relationships. Each type of research makes a unique contribution to the research base of social work practice.

? Assess your understanding of social work research and evaluation by taking this brief quiz.

CLIENT OUTCOME EVALUATION

A critical component of generalist social work, practice evaluation is a method of assessing client outcomes and measuring the effectiveness of social work strategies. Practitioners and clients assess client outcomes and monitor *progress* to assess what clients *achieve* and to evaluate what programs *accomplish* rather than what they fail to do. Recognizing success during evaluation infuses the strengths perspective into practice.

Table 15.2 General Evaluative Criteria

Criteria	Key Questions
Effectiveness	Was the desired outcome attained?
Efficiency	Was the outcome reached in the most direct way?
Equity	Were the client's rights protected? Were the rights of others ensured?

It increases the client system's energy and motivation for further change, directs the partners to repeat effective strategies, and acts as a catalyst for improving social services. See Table 15.2 for general evaluative criteria.

Client Outcome Assessment

Client outcome assessment involves measuring a client's achievement of goals and the effectiveness of the methods used in the change process. In client outcome assessment, workers simultaneously evaluate the degree of client goal achievement and the effectiveness of the strategies implemented. In short, social workers apply practice evaluation to gain answers to two basic questions: "Were the desired client outcome goals reached?" and "In what ways did the social work methods used contribute to the desired change?" Additional information workers and clients can gain from outcome assessments includes the identification of the client's strengths and resources that contribute to goal achievement, the degree of change, the stability of the change, the unintended or unanticipated consequences of the change, and the efficiency of the change effort.

Evaluation

Behavior: Select and use appropriate methods for evaluation of outcomes

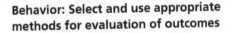

Critical Thinking Question: Social workers are held accountable by their clients, funders, and the public for the achievement of client outcomes. What are the implications of this mandate for professional accountability in the design of client outcomes assessment?

Questions that focus on outcomes include the following:

- To what extent did the client system accomplish its goals?
- Can the changes be attributed to the intervention?
- Are there other factors that can account for the changes?
- Which client strengths and environmental resources were most significant in achieving results?
- Does the situation warrant further intervention?
- In what ways should workers modify their strategies?
- How does this information apply to follow-up work with this client and to work with future clients?
- To what degree was the client system involved in the evaluation process?

In spite of its name, outcome assessment is not a "tag-on" last step in the helping process. Rather, workers conduct outcome assessments in their earliest contacts with clients and repeat these assessments throughout the process. Each time clients and social workers meet, they clarify the current situation, discuss goals and objectives, and examine progress. Each discussion involves a "mini" outcome assessment to evaluate progress and plan the next step.

Outcome assessment has four practical uses in social work. First, it provides concrete, continuous feedback on progress toward goals. This information is invaluable as clients and practitioners refine goals and develop further plans. Second, measuring the level of the achievement of goals and objectives documents outcomes and promotes accountability. Third, results of evaluations provide vital information that social workers can incorporate when planning with other clients. Finally, practitioners use the results of outcome assessment for their own professional development. These four benefits—continuous feedback, accountability, transferability, and professional development—make outcome assessment an essential part of every social worker's professional practice.

Using Standardized Instruments in Practice Evaluation

Social workers, in all fields of social work practice, use a variety of **standardized instruments** or evaluative tools for assessing client needs, measuring client outcomes, and evaluating program effectiveness. With the increased focus on quality assurance and fiscal accountability, clinicians, community organizers, policy practitioners, and administrators respond to the impetus to use standardized measures, including assessment scales, **progress evaluation** instruments, and outcome measurement tools specific to each system level—individuals and families, groups and organizations, and communities and other macrolevel systems. As with any evaluation, the ethical position for social workers involves acquiring informed consent from program participants. To give their informed consent, participants require information about how their confidentiality will be protected and how what they share will be reported.

Individuals and Families

A variety of psychometric tools are available to measure the biopsychosocial, cultural, and spiritual dimensions of human behavior. Standardized measures for individuals include those for initial functional and behavioral assessments, screening for appropriate levels of care, and client outcomes. For example, standardized instruments are used to assess mental competency, mood and depression, self-efficacy, dementia, addiction severity, spiritual needs, caregiver burden, posttraumatic stress disorder, and emotional health. Standardized family scales and inventories include those that assess family self-sufficiency, child abuse potential, family functioning styles, family needs, and marriage and family health and well-being.

Groups and Organizations

At the group and organizational level, standardized instruments are available to evaluate group and organizational climate, communication and relationship patterns, leadership styles, decision-making strategies, and fiscal viability. In addition, specialized instruments are available for social service agencies, including consumer satisfaction surveys, planning inventories, marketing templates, fidelity scales, and other outcome measures related to the implementation of evidence-based model programs. Logic models represent a current trend in social service program evaluations by not-for-profit organizations. These models link program resources/inputs with service activities/outputs and bridge them to client outcome changes and the impact in the larger community.

Communities and Other Macrolevel Systems

A number of evaluative instruments are available for use by community organizers, policy practitioners, and other generalist social workers in the macrolevel arena. Scales and inventories available to measure community functioning include those related to community capacity, civic engagement, community belongingness, community leadership, community participation, needs assessments, and neighborhood asset mapping. Needs assessments and policy impact scales are important tools for policy practice. Other standardized tools for systematic inquiry at the policy level include those for policy analysis and feedback, citizen and stakeholder input, political and economic surveys, and the ecological impact of public policy.

Progress Evaluation

Action plans direct clients' and practitioners' activities during the development phase. Progress evaluation refers to continually monitoring and evaluating the success of the action plan. These plans include well-defined goals, concrete objectives, and specific activities for social workers and clients to carry out to reach the desired outcomes. However, the most comprehensive plan can only suggest strategies that social workers and clients believe have the best possibility of attaining a successful outcome. Throughout the social work intervention, a client and a practitioner periodically take stock of what is happening to determine what is and what is not working. In light of this, the social worker is responsible for participating in the implementation of the plan and also for monitoring, evaluating, and updating the plan.

Throughout the social work intervention, a client and a practitioner periodically take stock of what is happening to determine what is and what is not working.

Monitoring and Evaluating Action Plans

Workers monitor and evaluate action plans as they are implemented to detect positive movement and steer activities in the direction of the desired outcomes. When workers and clients discover success, they stay the course. If a plan is ineffective or unworkable, the worker stops to discuss the situation with the client and revise the plan as necessary. As social workers oversee the implementation of the plan, they look for answers to several evaluation questions:

- Are both clients and workers doing what they have contracted to do?
- Are some parts of the plan working while other parts are running into roadblocks or dead ends?
- What activities have the greatest impact? What activities take a lot of effort but realize a minimal return?
- Is the plan on the right track, or is it falling short of expectations?
- Are clients actively involved in carrying out their part of the plan? If they are not, what is getting in the way?
- Do clients understand their roles, or do they lack confidence that implementing the plan is worth the effort?
- Have clients' goals and motivations changed?

After considering this new evaluative information, workers and clients modify action plans to incorporate recent changes and emerging strengths. Before considering a new approach, workers caution clients not to discard previously planned activities until they have had a chance to be successful. Sometimes, progress is slow and requires patience for success. However, it doesn't make sense to repeat strategies that fail to produce desired outcomes.

Goal Attainment Scaling

Goal attainment scaling (GAS) is an evaluation design that measures client achievement levels. In this evaluation, practitioners use clients' statements of their goals as the criteria for measurement. Thus, GAS is individualized and tailored for each client system. Social workers can apply GAS at all client system levels. Goal attainment scaling is best used as a collaborative process between social workers and client systems (individuals and families, groups and organizations, or neighborhoods and communities) to identify concrete intervention goals and to specify expected outcome levels for each goal. The scale can also be used to monitor and measure progress by setting a time frame for periodic review of goal attainment that reflects realistic time expectations for achieving each goal.

Framed around explicit and measurable goal statements rather than problem areas, goal attainment scaling uses a 5-point scale of predicted levels of attainment. These levels can range, for example, from "much less than expected" to "much more than expected," or from "least favorable outcome" to "most favorable outcome." Similar to a rating scale, the GAS technique uses a rubric or matrix to document client system progress and measure outcome change. The degree of goal achievement or change is typically measured using a 5-point numeric scale that includes a narrative explication of each score. To achieve a quantitative GAS score, social work researchers assign a numeric weight to each point on the scale. Potential outcomes receive numeric values of −2, −1, 0, +1, and +2 for each activity undertaken, where −2 indicates a "less than expected" level of achievement and +2 indicates a "more than expected" level of goal achievement. For each point on the scale, the client specifies a behavioral outcome appropriate to the designated levels of outcome achievement.

Each scale is tailored to measure the expected level of outcome achievement of a particular client system (individual, group, organization, or community). In the case of **program evaluation**, the scale is designed to measure the expected achievement of program or project goals. The advantage of GAS lies in the inherent flexibility and versatility of its subjective design and user-friendly methodology. Conversely, a criticism of the GAS instrument is that it lacks the psychometric properties expected in more objective fixed measurement tools used for client outcomes assessment in clinical settings.

? Assess your understanding of client outcome evaluation by taking this brief quiz.

Table 15.3 illustrates a goal attainment scale for the following case example. The Northside Community Action Council has identified three goals: (1) to form a neighborhood watch program, (2) to demolish abandoned buildings, and (3) to propose an ordinance to limit on-street parking to residents only.

Table 15.3   Northside Community Action Council: Goal Attainment Scale

Goal Attainment Level	Goal 1: Form a Neighborhood Watch Program	Goal 2: Demolish Abandoned Buildings	Goal 3: Establish an Ordinance to Limit On-Street Parking to Residents Only
−2 Much less than expected outcome achievement	No neighborhood support for program	Lawsuits ensue over target properties	Residents object to the proposed ordinance
−1 Less than expected outcome achievement	Participation by a few households	Agreement to demolish but postponed 2 years	Proposed ordinance Defeated
0 Expected level of outcome achievement	Half of the households participate	A scheduled plan for demolition approved	Ordinance considered by city council
+1 More than expected outcome achievement	Household participation and commitment to weekly meetings	Funds for neighborhood rehabilitation and renovation considered	Ordinance passed by city council
+2 Much more than expected outcome achievement	Full neighborhood participation and private security	Full funding for building renovations	Off-street parking lot constructed

SINGLE-SYSTEM DESIGNS

One of the most practical ways for social workers to assess client change and evaluate practice effectiveness is through the use of **single-system designs**. Single-subject or single-case designs, as they are sometimes called, typically involve evaluating and monitoring the effects of interventions on a client system's target problem. The term "single-system" indicates this design applies the same research principles to evaluating interventions in multiperson systems such as families, groups, organizations, neighborhoods, and communities.

To be implemented successfully, single-system designs meet three requirements. They must

- state the change objective in measurable terms,
- evaluate the achievement with reliable and valid outcome measures (that is, the observations, verbal reports, and physiological measures) that produce quantitative data, and
- display the data graphically (Grinnell & Unrau, 2013).

For applications of single-system designs to be empowering, clients must be actively involved in all aspects of design, implementation, data analysis, and interpretation. Empowerment-oriented practitioners take caution to avoid the role of "analytical expert" in interpreting behaviorally driven, single-system outcome evaluations. This collaboration may heighten clients' motivation to change and promote self-direction in change activities.

This video shows how single-system design is a way to assess the effectiveness of practice. What is an appropriate single-system design to evaluate whether the evidence-based practice proposed by the social worker is effective for this client in this situation?

Elements of Single-System Designs

One distinguishing characteristic of single-system designs is the planned comparison of measurements made in a preintervention period with measurements completed during or after the intervention. The periods of time during which observations of the client systems' behavior or evaluation of the client systems' progress occur are called phases. To compare the "before" and "after," practitioners need to understand the concepts of **baseline** and intervention phases.

Baseline Phase

To implement a single-system design, practitioners first establish a baseline. Taken in the preintervention period, baseline measurement involves a series of observations of the naturally occurring frequency of the behaviors under study. Workers measure the behavior that reflects the client's problem or observe the client's situation as it presently exists for a specified period.

Carefully constructed research establishes a baseline measure before introducing intervention strategies. However, ethical researchers consider the detrimental effects of counting adverse behaviors to acquire baseline data with clients who need immediate relief. Sometimes, the choice to gather baseline information gives way to the need for immediate intervention.

Intervention Phase

In a single-system research design, an intervention phase is the phase in which something is done to affect or change the identified target behaviors. As such, the intervention under study may be a single practice technique, a combination of several strategies, or an entire program with multiple components (Bloom et al., 2009). Possible interventions may include such differing practice techniques as marriage counseling, a 12-step program, advocacy, mediation, a support group, neighborhood development, or a community action. Recall that in social work research, the intervention is the independent variable, meaning that it is within the control of the worker and the client. They may apply an intervention, change its intensity, or withdraw it.

Alphabetic Notation

Researchers use alphabetic notation to represent the phases in single-system designs. The letter "A" denotes the baseline or preintervention phase, and subsequent letters designate the intervention phases. So, an AB design indicates a baseline phase (A) followed by an intervention phase (B). Likewise, an ABC design includes a baseline phase (A) that is followed by an intervention phase (B), which in turn is followed by another, yet different, intervention (C). How the baseline and intervention phases are arranged determines the type of single-system research design being implemented.

Types of Single-System Designs

Single-system designs commonly used in social work include case study or monitor design (B design), the basic baseline–intervention design (AB design), and other variations of the AB design, notably, the successive intervention design (ABC design), the withdrawal or reversal design (ABAB design and BAB design), and multiple baseline designs.

Using the B design or the AB design answers the evaluative question: Did the client's situation improve during the course of treatment? The reversal designs are experimental designs and answer the question of causation: Did the client system improve because of social work intervention? Social workers are more likely to seek answers to evaluative questions in their practice by using the B or AB design, as these designs are more practical to implement than the more ambitious experimental designs that require rigorous controls.

Applications of single-system designs include quantifiable measures of frequency, duration, and intensity. Specified in the objectives for behavioral change to either reinforce or substitute target behaviors, these measures apply to all variations of single-system designs. *Frequency* measures the increased or decreased rate of incidence, prevalence, or reoccurrence of the behavior targeted for change. Measures of *duration* assess the length of time the client exhibits the behavior under study, whether increasing the duration of desired behaviors or decreasing the duration of inappropriate behaviors. Finally, *intensity* refers to strengthening the degree or moderating the severity of the target behavior. The intensity of individuals' activities, thoughts, or feelings can be measured at the microlevel. At the macrolevel, the robustness of health indicators, economy, and employment rate are examples of measures of intensity.

AB Design

The AB design is a useful and popular single-system design that social workers use to observe and measure change in target problems. It is simple to apply because it includes only one baseline period (A) and one intervention period (B). In many ways, it is one of the least intrusive evaluative measures in terms of preserving social work practice priorities. It naturally fits into an organized practice process—observing first what is and then implementing and evaluating efforts to change.

In the AB design, workers introduce a single independent variable or intervention technique after the baseline phase. Practitioners monitor shifts in the data from the baseline phase to the intervention phase to determine whether the client's situation is improving. From this information, the practitioner can draw only tentative conclusions about whether the intervention led to the improvement or whether changes were caused by some extraneous event, an intervening variable, or by chance. Despite this limitation, the AB design does provide immediate feedback about the direction of change during the intervention phase. As a result, practitioners and clients can discuss the possible explanations for the change and modify their strategies if necessary.

Consider the following case example that uses an AB design to measure frequency.

The Millwork Company discontinued Mr. Jones' job position, resulting in termination of his employment. His unemployment benefits are insufficient to meet his family's income needs. He wants to find new employment, but he is hesitant to seek other jobs and lacks confidence in his job-seeking and interviewing skills. To feel prepared and confident for a job interview, Mr. Jones role-played a simulated interview with his employment counselor. Together, they analyzed the videotaped interview and noted points of strengths and areas for improvement.

Client System: Individual—Mr. Jones
Target Problem: Hesitancy to Apply for Jobs
Intervention: Videotaped Role Play of a Job Interview

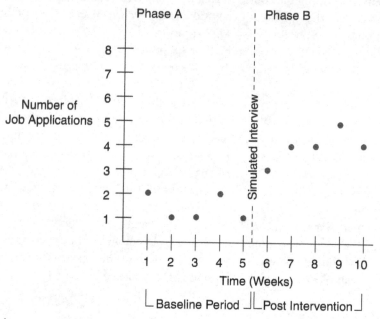

Figure 15.1
AB, or Baseline and Intervention, Design
Evaluation: The number of job applications Mr. Jones placed each week increased after the role play of the simulated interview.

As depicted in Figure 15.1, during the 5-week baseline, or preintervention, phase, Mr. Jones applied for a total of seven jobs. Following the role-play intervention, Mr. Jones significantly increased the number of employment applications, thus demonstrating an increased frequency of the target behavior.

B Design

The B design is often referred to as the case study method or the monitoring design. With this design, clients and practitioners apply an intervention and monitor the client's target problem to see if it is changing in the desired direction. This design does not stipulate taking baseline measurements before implementing the intervention strategy. However, in some situations, practitioners can ascertain a retroactive baseline from pre-existing records or verbal reports from the client system. The lack of a baseline for comparing before and after measures is a significant drawback of this design method, as the design offers no way to decipher what accounts for observed changes.

The following case example illustrates the B design as applied to measuring the duration of a behavior.

Zachary Smith, a 7-year-old second grader has come to the attention of the school social worker because of his disruptive behaviors in the classroom. His classroom teacher, Mrs. Martin, reports Zachary's inability to stay on task and his behavior

Client System: Individual—Zachery Smith
Target Problem: Disruptive Behavior
Intervention: Strength-Based Behavioral Change Model

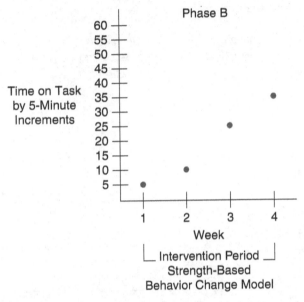

Figure 15.2
The B, or Case Study or Monitor, Design
Evaluation: By the end of the 4-week period, Zachary showed demonstrable gains in on-task time.

that interrupts the learning environment and that she spends more than half her time each day dealing with his behavior. The social worker introduces a strength-based model for behavioral change to Mrs. Martin and coaches her on its implementation. The social worker follows up by periodically monitoring the duration of Zachary's on-task performance over a 4-week period of time.

As Figure 15.2 indicates, Zachary demonstrates overall improvement of the duration of on-task behavior over the 4-week period. In Zachary's situation, given the disruptiveness to the learning environment reported by the teacher, a baseline measure was not advisable. In many ways, this design also measures the effectiveness of the intervention model.

ABC Design

Workers use successive intervention phases after the baseline period when implementing the ABC single-system design. Like the basic AB design, the ABC design establishes a pattern of data in the baseline phase (A), introduces an intervention in the first intervention phase (B), and then adds a different, or perhaps modified, intervention (C). If workers add even more interventions, they label subsequent intervention phases D, E, and so on.

ABC designs apply when practitioners introduce multiple intervention components in sequence or when they modify one intervention in frequency or intensity because it doesn't appear to be working as planned. Because practitioners introduce several interventions during the change process, they are uncertain which specific intervention created the desired effect.

Client System: Community—Kanton
Target Problem: High Unemployment Rate
Interventions: 1. Job Retraining Program
             2. Job Placement Program

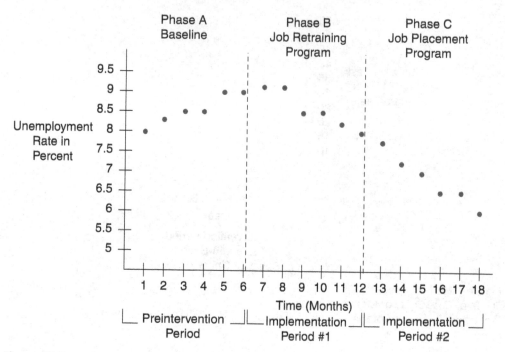

Figure 15.3
ABC, or Successive Intervention, Design
Evaluation: The community unemployment rate steadily decreased as both the job retraining program and the job placement program were being implemented.

The ABC design is used in the following case example showing a measure of intensity in a community context.

For the past 6 months, the Kanton metropolitan area saw a rising unemployment rate as local industry experienced severe cutbacks, subsequent layoffs, and manufacturing plant closings. The Kanton Economic Development Group (EDG) recognized a need for a two-part approach to the problem—a job retraining program and a job placement program. The EDG contracted with the WORK organization (Work, Opportunities, and Resources for Kanton) to design and implement community-based programming for the displaced workers.

Figure 15.3 shows the decreasing unemployment rate over the course of the year as each of the programs was being implemented. In this macrolevel example, robustness of employment in a community is a measure of intensity.

ABAB Design

Simply, the ABAB design is a string of AB designs used to evaluate changes in the same client system after reapplying the same intervention technique. After the initial baseline and intervention phases, the ABAB design adds a second baseline phase, after which workers reintroduce the intervention. They establish the second baseline by discontinuing or withdrawing the intervention for a period of time. Social workers and clients may plan this withdrawal or may simply experience an unexpected pause in the intervention.

The ABAB single-system design is a *reversal*, or withdrawal, design. Logically, we presume that if the target behavior improves during the first intervention phase, reverts when the intervention is withdrawn, and improves again during the second intervention phase, the improvement is likely to result from the intervention. Thus, the ABAB design offers more evidence of the causal effects of the intervention on the behavior or target problems.

Clearly, ethical issues emerge with planned withdrawals of interventions, especially when an intervention appears to be helpful. Concerned social workers question whether clients will suffer unnecessarily if their situation reverts to the preintervention level. After all, the well-being of client systems is a priority concern of social work practice. In some cases, social workers and clients purposely discontinue services temporarily to test whether clients can independently sustain the gains. At other times, an unexpected time-out from intervention caused by either clients' or social workers' circumstances offers an opportunity for establishing the second baseline.

BAB Design

The BAB design is also a reversal design, though it does not establish an initial baseline pattern. Instead, the social worker immediately introduces an intervention (phase B). Later, the worker withdraws the intervention and observes changes in the behavior, establishing a postintervention baseline (phase A). Subsequently, the worker reapplies the intervention (phase B).

Changes in the patterns of data observed and measured during the first intervention period (B), the withdrawal period (A), and the second intervention period (B) provide valuable information about the effectiveness of the intervention on the target problems. If, after the intervention is withdrawn, the behavior gains are lost during phase A and then later improve when the intervention is reintroduced, the social worker can make a stronger inference about the causal influence of the intervention. Again, ethical social workers carefully explore the potential consequences of withdrawing services that appear to be working.

Multiple-Baseline Designs

Another variation of the AB design establishes baselines with and observes changes in multiple clients, in multiple settings, and for multiple target problems. This multiple-baseline design allows social workers to monitor three types of situations. Workers can track (1) two or more client systems that share the same problem and use the same intervention, (2) a client system that experiences the same problem in more than one setting, or (3) a single subject who exhibits more than one problem situation in the same setting.

Evaluating multiple client systems with the same problem allows the practitioner to generalize findings with different clients. A social worker who monitors the effects of an intervention with one client system in two or more settings looks for a generalization of the outcomes within the client's functioning. The multiple-baseline design also allows practitioners to simultaneously evaluate changes in multiple problem situations presented by a single client system.

Practice-Informed Research

Behavior: Apply critical thinking to engage in analysis of quantitative and qualitative research methods and research findings

Critical Thinking Question: In conducting single-system evaluations, social workers need to accommodate the research/evaluation role without violating their service role. What ethical issues emerge when the evaluation mandate collides with practice priorities?

Limitations of Single-System Designs

Single-case evaluations and single-system research designs are gaining a degree of acceptance by social work practitioners as they seek to evaluate practice effectiveness and to contribute to the knowledge base of practice. However, these designs may not fit all practice situations.

Single-case designs measure behavioral change, but not all social workers use behavioral or task-centered models that specify problems in the ways necessary to implement single-case designs. Thus, methodological issues arise in applying single-subject research by those practitioners who use other approaches. To apply single-system designs in these situations, researchers carefully delineate and operationally define client outcome goals in ways that can be measured objectively. Researchers should identify intermediate progress indicators to monitor the achievement of short-term objectives in long-term interventions.

Agencies hold direct service practitioners accountable for assessing client outcomes and evaluating the effectiveness of the interventions they use. Practitioners are also in positions to conduct empirical or experimental practice research. Certainly, research should not intrude on the client–practitioner relationship, nor should research dominate the intervention process.

> **?** Assess your understanding of single-system designs by taking this brief quiz.

PROGRAM EVALUATION

A program evaluation determines the value of the particular program under review. In other words, program evaluation is used to assess the effectiveness of a particular program or service in accomplishing programmatic goals. Moreover, the NASW *Code of Ethics* (1999) sets forth standards for practice accountability. Social workers should not promise what they cannot deliver. Program evaluation provides the tangible evidence required for fiscal responsibility and ethical accountability. Additionally, program evaluation tracks the achievement of programmatic goals and objectives and identifies gaps that need to be addressed in service delivery.

Because many meritorious social programs compete for limited funding, funding agents expect assurances that programs for which they provide money do make a difference. For example, the Substance Abuse and Mental Health Services Administration funds major program initiatives related to drugs and alcohol and mental health. For funding and evaluation purposes, SAMHSA identifies three categories of evidence-based programs: promising programs,

KONSTANTIN SUTYAGIN / SHUTTERSTOCK

For many, graduation marks the achievement of an important personal goal.

effective programs, and model programs. Meeting rigorous standards of research for program evaluation as reviewed by the National Registry of Evidence-Based Programs and Practices (NREPP), model programs, by design, are developed for replication and nationwide implementation.

Program evaluation asks whether the program is accomplishing what it set out to do. Social workers use a number of methods to secure data to discover the answer. Considering each client's outcome and compiling the results help determine whether a particular program has met its goals. Agencies may also administer **consumer satisfaction surveys** to ascertain clients' perspectives on the effectiveness of workers and services. Follow-up surveys of former clients and referral agencies are other sources of valuable information regarding the effectiveness and reputation of a particular program. Periodic reviews of case files by agency staff reveal client progress in relation to the overall program goals and agency mission. Finally, formalized processes such as quality-assurance checks by peers and supervisors provide internal mechanisms for program evaluation. Each method of program evaluation examines services from a different angle. A combination of approaches leads to a more comprehensive view of service delivery.

Program evaluation measures the effects that programs have on the clientele served, the agency organization, and the general public. Examples of researchable questions for program evaluation include the following:

- Does the program cause the desired changes for clients?
- Is the program sensitive to diverse populations?
- Does the program meet the expectations of funding organizations?
- Are the program objectives consonant with the agency mission?
- What are the strengths and weaknesses of the program?
- Is staffing for the program adequate?
- How accessible is the program to potential clientele?
- Does the program alter public attitudes or awareness?
- Does this program continue to satisfy a need in the community?
- Is this program viable?

Program evaluation asks whether the program is accomplishing what it set out to do.

Program Evaluation Design

An evaluation design is a written plan for administering the evaluation study, including ways to obtain information and report results. The evaluation design specifies when to collect data, what data to collect, and how to collect that data. Specifically, it

- describes the role of evaluators;
- determines the feasibility of the evaluation for its costs and congruence with agency protocols;
- prepares the evaluation questions;
- delineates the data collection processes, including the sample and time frame;
- assesses the reliability and validity of the data collection instruments;
- addresses issues of informed consent;
- specifies data analysis procedures; and
- identifies ways to disseminate findings.

Most grant-funded demonstration projects, evidence-based programs, and best practice models provide their own evaluation design, including the standardized instruments, scales, or inventories to be used to evaluate the program; time frames and methodologies for collecting data; and norm-referenced studies for comparative analysis of the findings. The results of these evaluations are often reported to and compiled by a program-specific statistical clearinghouse as further evidence of program effectiveness.

Agency personnel use program evaluation data to make administrative decisions. These research findings provide information that is useful for formulating agency policy, especially with respect to planning programs, developing services, setting priorities, and allocating resources. Program managers also use program evaluation research to identify ways to streamline agency procedures and replicate successful strategies in other program areas.

Consumer Satisfaction Surveys

Program evaluators often poll clients to determine their satisfaction with services. Consumer satisfaction surveys assess clients' perceptions or attitudes about an agency's delivery of services. These surveys solicit clients' views about the relevance of the services received, the extent to which the services actually resolved their presenting problems, and their satisfaction with the social work process. Questions typically posed in client satisfaction surveys include the following:

- Did you feel welcome?
- Did the program meet your needs?
- Did the staff treat you with courtesy and respect?
- Were you actively involved in selecting your goals and objectives?
- Were you satisfied with the services you received?
- Were the services available when you needed them?
- In what ways could the services and staff be more helpful?

Although they are valuable sources of information, client satisfaction instruments measure the subjective experiences of clients. Alone, they are not sufficient to evaluate

Box 15.1 Action Research: A Research–Practice Connection

Through research, we develop theories about social problems, human behavior, and client population groups. From traditional research findings, we acquire information to guide decisions at the levels of policy, program, and direct practice. In contrast, action research contributes practical solutions to everyday problems through its emphasis on stakeholder participation in both action and reflection (Hacker, 2014; Reason & Bradbury, 2008). With respect to expertise in conducting action research, the fundamental principle of action research is that those who experience situations are most qualified to investigate those situations. Given its roots in the work of Freire (1973a, 1973b, 1993) and the outcome potential of social justice through social change, action research is especially appropriate with those who are in some way disadvantaged or oppressed (Johnston-Goodstar, 2013; Patel, 2005; Strier, 2007).

By definition, action research is participatory, builds capacities, and empowers participants and communities (Gutiérrez et al., 1996; Hanley, 2005).

It combines research, education, and action. Research cycles through a series of recurring steps—planning, acting, observing, and reflecting. Critical reflection, similar to conscientization, plays an integral role, as it lends vision to subsequent cycles of planning, acting, observing, and reflecting. The relationship between researcher and participants provides the foundation for successful implementation. They work together collaboratively throughout the process as co-learners, from developing the design, to collecting the data, to implementing plans for change and evaluating the results. Action research gives voice to the participants, reveals their worldviews, affirms their humanity, leads to a heightened critical consciousness, and incorporates elements of reflection and action.

Action research serves many purposes. For example, this research strategy has been applied to give voice to lesbian, gay, bisexual, transgender, queer, and questioning youths in regard to policy changes within their schools (Wernick et al., 2014), to demonstrate the impact of negative community attitudes on people living with dementia and the need for public education and attitudinal change (O'Sullivan et al., 2014), to establish an integrated system of support for minority women transitioning from homelessness (Moxley & Washington, 2012; Washington et al., 2009), and to build international and interdisciplinary community partnerships to address domestic violence (Ritchie & Eby, 2007). Additionally, action research can be applied within the social service delivery network to create changes by providing a forum for service users and stimulating changes in service delivery. For example, Mirzaa and colleagues (2008) report their action research project with key staff and clientele at a center providing support for people with psychiatric disabilities leaving institutional care to live in the community. The purpose of the project was to better understand the experiences of persons with psychiatric disabilities and to develop more response systems of support for community reintegration. Themes identified included the difficulties of living in nursing homes, the participants' perceptions of their need for continued treatment and access to medication, the importance of peer support and a sense of personal control, and access to stable housing and opportunities for participation in community life, such as education and employment. Their vision for seamless, one-stop services through a place they called the Solution Center for Living was an ideal that was difficult to translate to reality because of complexities and turf issues related to the current system of services. However, ongoing dialogue between representatives of the various support agencies and their key stakeholders—the persons with psychiatric disabilities whom they serve—has begun and holds promise for stimulating additional changes within the delivery network.

An innovative application of community-based participatory action research, the qualitative research strategies associated with photovoice supplement written reports with photographs to heighten sensitivity to social justice issues and facilitate social change (Molloy, 2007; Powers & Freedman, 2012). Photovoice has been applied to address a wide range of community issues from immigration experiences to health promotion practices. Participants are integrally involved in identifying the focus issue and photovoice training, are given photo assignments, and take part in the follow-up discussion and analysis based on the array of photos that contextualize their collective perceptions of the focus issue. In essence, "photovoice is designed to empower persons to develop and acquire skills to become advocates for themselves and their community, enabling them to reach out to policy makers and influential advocates" (Hergenrather et al., 2009, p. 688). For example, Mapping Vulnerability, Picturing Place used the photovoice strategy to elucidate the social and emotional experiences of women who immigrated to two small Canadian cities (Sutherland & Cheng, 2009). Photographs of local places that held significance for the women captured detailed memories of their immigration experiences, thus facilitating deeply meaningful discussions and personal transformation. The public display of pictures and associated stories provided an opportunity for community education and prompted social changes that led to more welcoming communities for immigrants.

the quality of services. They are significant from an empowerment perspective, as client satisfaction surveys ensure that clients have opportunities for feedback that can influence agency policies and program development. For example, one adult day service reports crafting a specialized interview process to incorporate the opinions of persons with dementia into the program evaluation process (Carroll et al., 2005). Adding information from the program participants to the responses of family caregivers honors the voices of vulnerable older adults, promotes a measure of independence, and affirms their sense of self-worth.

Empowerment Evaluation

Empowerment evaluation is an alternative approach to the more conventional program evaluation methods. It aims to foster ongoing self-assessments and promote continuous program improvements (Andrews et al., 2005; Conway et al., 2010; Fetterman, 2002). In actualizing participants' self-determination, empowerment evaluation emphasizes participant learning and capacity building. Empowerment evaluation also uses evaluation to influence policy development.

Five facets frame empowerment evaluation—training, facilitation, advocacy, illumination, and liberation (Fetterman, 1996). *Training* refers to teaching program participants to internalize evaluation principles and practices, conduct their own evaluation, become more self-sufficient as evaluators, and create opportunities for capacity building. *Facilitation* characterizes the role of empowerment evaluators as coaches for a process of self-evaluation. As coaches, evaluators offer general direction and guidelines, provide suggestions about process, and help participants create evaluation designs. *Advocacy* refers to assisting disenfranchised people to become empowered through their participation in evaluation processes and subsequent recommendations for program improvements. Advocacy includes both helping others to advocate on their own behalf and advocating on behalf of disempowered groups. Advocacy extends to advocating policy and legislative change as well as economic development. *Illumination* involves promoting insight or framing new understandings of program structures and processes. In this way, program participants acquire confidence in their abilities to assess problems and frame workable solutions. Finally, *liberation,* which is an outgrowth of illumination, refers to the emancipation of one's self and the corollary action of taking charge of one's life. In other words, "empowerment evaluation enables participants to find new opportunities, see existing resources in a new light, and redefine their identities and future roles" (p. 16).

The empowerment evaluation model protects the voices of consumers, customers, and clients from being inadvertently silenced or reinterpreted by professional or managerial voices. By design, empowerment evaluation requires that client systems play a prominent role in all facets of the evaluation process, from defining the focus of the evaluation to interpreting the results.

Watch this video as you consider that empowerment evaluation elevates clients' voices and privileges. What features of the evaluation process described in this video are characteristics of empowerment evaluation? www.youtube.com/watch?v=GEubejt8oUg&noredirect=1

Assess your understanding of program evaluation by taking this brief quiz.

LOOKING FORWARD

Social work research and evaluation support effective generalist practice. Practitioners apply evidence-based strategies, participate in social research, and conduct practice evaluation. Microlevel clinicians can contribute to the knowledge and skill base of the social work profession by evaluating their own practices and monitoring client progress, sometimes using tools such as single-system evaluation designs. Policy makers rely on valid research and careful program evaluations to identify potential enhancements in social service delivery. Program evaluation processes such as empowerment evaluation and action research enlist clients themselves as leaders in design, development, and implementation. These evaluation processes blend social work practice with research and policy activism.

Recognizing client and program successes in social work practice prompts progress in achievement. The process of recognizing success cues the client and social worker as to when it is time to conclude their work together. If clients are sufficiently satisfied with their level of goal achievement, social workers prepare to bring closure to the professional relationship. Chapter 16, "Integrating Gains," explores how social workers and clients wrap up their work together in ways that credit clients with success and stabilize the progress achieved.

 Evaluate what you learned in this chapter by completing the Chapter Review.

Intervention: Integrating Gains

H. TULLER / SHUTTERSTOCK

The rule in personal relationships is that as long as things are going well, the relationships will continue to evolve and intensify. The rule in social worker–client relationships is that even when things are going well, relationships will end. Practitioners work themselves out of a job with each successful practice endeavor. Simply, the common goal of all social work is for client systems to operate independent of the social worker, drawing on their own competence, support networks, and the resources of a just society.

Social work literature sometimes refers to the final step in the social work process as **termination**. However, the word "terminate" has nefarious connotations. Whereas "terminate" does mean "discontinue or conclude," it also evokes more negative undertones associated with death, dismissal, and being fired. Others offer "endings" as an alternative term to use.

Whatever words or phrases practitioners choose, their words should reflect the reality that when workers and clients resolve their professional relationships, they don't encapsulate their work and put it aside. Paradoxically, social work practice "endings" are also beginnings. Clients go on, empowered to incorporate what they have learned into how they continue to cope. Social workers also move on, enriched with yet another professional relationship experience and additional practice wisdom.

Describing this last process as one of integrating gains emphasizes the importance of client growth, development, and change beyond the professional relationship. Within the context of each successful social work endeavor, clients discover the power available from the strengths within themselves and from the resources of their environments. A social worker's task when ending the relationship is to sustain the client's ability to independently draw on and amplify this power. Endings are crucial for the success of the process as a whole. Adept endings help client systems integrate the work of earlier phases, recognize achievements, build a sense of mastery, consolidate gains, and provide a springboard into the future.

This chapter describes what social workers and clients do to resolve their work together in ways that integrate and apply what each has gained from the experience. Social workers end their work with clients in ways that stabilize desired changes and empower client systems to continue functioning competently.

SOCIAL WORK ENDINGS

Generally, three situations define exit points for most client systems (Table 16.1). Workers celebrate with clients who reach their goals, acknowledge the rights of clients to withdraw from services as they see fit, or refer clients to other professionals when necessary. Each type of resolution requires a unique process to end the work in a way that benefits clients and provides workers with information to further their continuing professional development.

Table 16.1　Types of Closure

Categories	Description	Social Work Processes
Completing Contracts	Clients made significant progress or achieved success in the plan of action and no longer need social work services	Preparing for resolution Discussing readiness Reviewing progress Sharing feelings Generalizing outcomes
Closing with Referral	Clients require continued services beyond the contracted work with the practitioner that may involve more specialized provider expertise or agency programming	Acknowledging limited resources Smoothing the transition Tracking clients' progress
Responding to Client Withdrawal	Clients, on their own initiative, conclude the helping relationship	Preparing for early withdrawal Recognizing exiting clues Pursuing mutual resolution

The actions a worker takes at closure vary, depending on the preferences and behaviors of clients and the specific situation. In planning effective closure processes, workers consider many issues, including the following:

- The degree of success that has been achieved so far
- The potential benefits of continuing the work
- The duration and intensity of the relationship with the client
- The resources available to continue the work in this particular setting
- Whether the client is voluntary or mandated
- The client's plans
- The role the social worker may play in the client's life after the closure

Endings also differ depending on the level of client system. Work with individuals and families has a degree of intimacy that may reveal itself in the intensity of feelings during the closure process. In group work, individuals are likely to be facing the loss of relationships with other group members as well as the discontinuation of the relationship with the social worker. Work within organizations and communities may be ongoing rather than short term, thus redefining the closure process as a transition to the next task or project rather than signaling the end of the professional relationship itself.

Completing Contracts

The first and most preferred resolution is when clients have made significant progress toward the goals they have set. Planning for this kind of ending, **completing contracts**, begins early in the relationship with the negotiation of a specific contract for services. Recognizing that it is time to resolve the relationship "according to plan" hinges on the clarity of the observable and measurable outcomes contained in this contract. Resolving a social worker–client relationship by successfully completing the contract is the culmination of a collaborative effort. Both social workers and clients deserve credit. Both benefit from an opportunity to reflect on their work and incorporate what they have learned so that they can apply it to future endeavors. To maximize the benefits of their experience, workers and clients examine where they are, review where they've been, and predict where they are going after their work together ends.

Specific steps in successful resolutions include the following:

- Thorough preparation throughout the entire process, especially in terms of contracting, and periodic reminders of the time-limited nature of the relationship
- Open discussion about the client's readiness for closure, including a concrete evaluation of success, that draws on both client and worker perspectives
- Comprehensive review of the relationship that highlights the client's contributions, significant achievements, and methods used to achieve results
- Mutual sharing of feelings about the relationship and the upcoming closure
- Thoughtful anticipation of the future that projects upcoming challenges and predicts the client's continuing success
- Clear agreement on the point of transition from active to closed, description of how the client accesses additional service if necessary, and discussion of possible follow-up contacts

Preparing for Resolution

Social workers prepare for closures in professional relationships from the beginning of the work. Social workers foreshadow successful resolutions by defining a purposeful and professionally oriented relationship from the outset. They continue to hone the specificity of this purpose as they create action plans with outcomes that clearly indicate when the work is complete.

Throughout the entire process, social workers remind clients of the transitory nature of the relationship by using direct and indirect messages. Social workers may say any of the following:

- I noticed that this is the end of our third month of working together—halfway through the 6-month period that our program permits.
- By my count, this is group meeting number 8 out of 12. Just 4 meetings left in our agreement. I guess that means if there's anything you've been putting off that you'd like to talk about, this might be the time.
- You've been coming up with great ideas about how to proceed. This demonstrates that you are probably ready to handle things on your own.

Social workers intersperse these comments selectively early in the process but interject them more frequently as the ending becomes imminent. By the time only a few meetings are left and clients are clearly finishing up, the discussion of endings becomes central in conversations between clients and workers. Although workers cannot control whether clients choose to drop out of services suddenly, ethical social workers never abruptly withdraw services from clients without an explanation or direction.

Recall the flexibility of the social work contract and how it keeps pace with the current focus of the work during the course of the relationship. Through this continuous renegotiation of the contract, clients clearly experience their power to continue or end the work. These discussions offer clients legitimate exit points, acknowledging their rights to self-determination about how they would like to pursue their goals. Choosing to wrap up their work with the social worker in favor of proceeding on their own may signal that clients are empowered with their own sense of efficacy.

Stopping Short of Goals

Sometimes clients and workers make significant progress yet don't quite attain predetermined goals. Clients may have reached a plateau where continued joint efforts are producing no appreciable benefit. Perhaps the goals were overly ambitious. Maybe the immediate crisis has passed, leaving clients comfortable with where they are and with limited motivation to continue their change efforts. When workers see few possibilities for productivity in future sessions, they may suggest renegotiating the original goals to those outcomes clients have already achieved. In other words, they ask, "Is this good enough?" If clients agree, social workers proceed with closure activities that acknowledge what clients have achieved thus far and suggest that clients may return for additional work in the future.

Intervention

Behavior: Facilitate effective transitions and endings that advance mutually agreed-on goals

Critical Thinking Question: Research indicates that clients withdraw from services for many different reasons. What clues signal a client's intent to discontinue services, and how should social workers respond to this possibility?

Discussing Readiness

Social workers observe carefully for signs that the work is done. They monitor progress toward goals and assess clients' developing abilities to manage independently. Workers are not alone in looking for the end.

As clients near the achievement of their goals, social workers engage them in conversations about their readiness to finish up the work. Periodically evaluating progress in carrying out the action plan is one way that workers measure a client's preparedness for ending the relationship. Workers also keep an eye on other behavioral indicators that clients are moving from interdependent work with the social worker to independent work of their own. Behaviors that signal clients may be outgrowing the need for professional assistance include when clients

- use meetings with the worker as a forum to put forth their ideas about what to do rather than passively seek the worker's suggestions and expertise;
- take the initiative between meetings to modify and improve plans developed with the social worker;
- begin to manage the process of change by organizing their own assessment, analysis, planning, and intervention activities to modify situations they desire to change; and
- acknowledge their own abilities openly, demonstrate confidence, and express optimism.

When workers believe that the time to end the professional relationship is approaching, they share their observations directly with clients. Workers keep the progress toward goals, not the relationship itself, in the forefront of discussions.

Reviewing Progress

Social workers and clients retrace their progress to identify and reinforce client strengths and abilities. Reviewing progress solidifies changes and reinforces clients' sense of achievement. As clients review their progress, they are likely to attribute success or failure to their own efforts or to forces outside themselves. **Dispositional attributions** are those in which clients believe they created the improvement and experience their own competency. **Situational attributions** are those in which clients credit workers or other forces outside themselves with creating the change. When clients make situational attributions, workers get the credit rather than clients. By making dispositional attributions, clients acknowledge their part in creating the change. A review process that encourages dispositional attributions helps clients believe they have the power to sustain change.

Evaluating

Although evaluation is integral to successful work throughout the entire social work process, it functions in a very important way near the end. As part of the closure process, a comprehensive evaluation identifies what worked and clarifies the methods and strategies that the client used most effectively. In effect, engaging in evaluation processes can empower the client with information that might be useful in meeting future challenges and brings a sense of completion to the current work. Evaluative questions that facilitate closure include the following:

- What has been most useful to you throughout the process?
- What would you change about our way of working?
- What changes will you continue to make after our work concludes?

Many techniques are available for evaluating outcomes. Chapter 15 provides an overview of some of these approaches, including single-system design, goal attainment scaling, and qualitative methods. Workers and clients choose evaluation methods that fit their particular situation the best and actively involve clients. For example, clients could compare their support networks at the beginning of the work with their networks as they exist at the end. Imagine the impact on a client of viewing the differences between an earlier eco-map that was sparse with connections and a subsequent one enriched with community and social supports developed during the course of the social work endeavor.

Responding to Evaluations

Both workers and clients benefit from evaluating their work nondefensively. Honest appraisals can be empowering. Openly considering what worked and what didn't gives concrete information on which to build future solutions. To elicit such information, workers ask directly for feedback about their work and respond nondefensively by thanking clients for information, whether it compliments or criticizes.

Some practitioners are reluctant to acknowledge their good work, fearing that they will take away from a client's sense of achievement. However, acknowledging mutual accomplishments should represent no problem for collaborative social work partnerships because both partners have contributed to their success. Social workers accept their part of the credit while continuing to highlight those aspects of the work for which clients deserve praise.

Sharing Feelings

To bring closure to the relationship, social workers and clients share their feelings about completing their work. Practitioners can anticipate the possible range of feelings clients may experience by considering the intensity and length of the relationship, the content of the work, the size of client system, the client's past experiences with transitions, and the reason for ending.

Often, when we think about endings, we think of the feelings related to **grief** and sadness. However, this is not necessarily the case when workers focus on a client's potential mastery, adaptation, and maturation process. Endings can be positive events, reorienting workers from merely empathizing with their clients' feelings of loss at closure to joining clients in their celebrations of success.

Social workers' personal experiences with transitions combined with their sense of competence as professionals and their feelings toward clients influence how they respond as the working relationship ends. In examining their feelings about endings, social workers take into consideration previous reactions to experiences involving separations and transitions and their assessment of their professional involvement with this particular client. Self-awareness helps us differentiate our own experiences from those of

Watch this video as you consider that, when social workers end their relationships with clients, feelings arise in both parties. What feelings expressed by these social workers and clients should be addressed as workers and clients wrap up their work? www.youtube.com/ watch?v=84bE1M6Usz0 our clients, supports a forthright evaluation of our work, and leads to constructive resolutions of our relationships with client systems.

Generalizing Outcomes

Even though closure means that the work is winding down, social workers are not quite finished yet, as there is evidence that the carryover of gains or **generalizing outcomes** is most effective when gains are integrated into everyday functioning.

Accomplishments are more likely to generalize when social workers have helped clients continually focus on relevant issues and situations, as well as practice new skills and behaviors in a variety of situations and settings, and when clients have gained confidence in their own abilities rather than in those of the worker (Toseland & Rivas, 2012). The most enduring work is that which is consistently integrated into the client's functioning throughout the entire process. The increase of community-integrated programs, work with natural support networks, in-home treatment, and policies of deinstitutionalization reflect attempts to make and keep social work practice immediately relevant in clients' natural settings.

Changes also endure when clients not only experience the results of the success but also when they learn the process by which the success has been achieved. To teach process, workers openly collaborate with clients to define problems clearly, complete comprehensive assessments, articulate concrete action plans, and actively implement change strategies. At closure, workers can help clients take knowledge of these processes with them by reviewing the processes implemented and discussing how to apply these processes to issues that may arise in the future.

An important activity in closure is for workers and clients to make connections between what they have done together and how clients might approach upcoming issues.

Stabilizing Success

An important activity in closure is for workers and clients to make connections between what they have done together and how clients might approach upcoming issues. A comprehensive review that emphasizes client strengths facilitates this connection and empowers clients to move on with an objective understanding of their ability to resolve issues on their own. Clients benefit from an appraisal of their strengths and how they might work in the future, but Shulman (2012) cautions workers to avoid reassuring clients who express doubts about their own competence. He adds that even though workers can display confidence in clients, they should stop short of minimizing the difficulties that may lie ahead. Clients transition to independent functioning best with an honest view of their competencies and how these abilities might help them in the future.

To endure beyond the end of a social work process, supportive changes must occur at several system levels. Increases in a client's personal capacity, effective interaction with their family and friends, responsive community organizations and institutions, and socially just policies all combine to reinforce and perpetuate achievements. To experience sustainable and integrative change, clients must return to a different or enhanced environmental system, that is, one flexible enough to embrace and support the changes made. The ethic of change charges social workers to effect long-term contextual change.

Sustainable Change Is Multisystemic   At the intrapersonal level, enduring change occurs in an individual's beliefs, attitudes, and values about self-identify and personal competence. At the interpersonal level, increases in power and support within significant relationships can sustain development. Qualities at the macrosystem level that stabilize changes include community responsiveness to fundamental and critical needs and opportunities for social support and enjoyment. Clients succeed in sustaining positive changes when their contexts nourish and reinforce their success.

Firming Up Social Supports

Clients function most effectively after discontinuing their work with practitioners if they have ongoing support from others. Self-help groups, natural helping networks, clubs, neighborhoods, and churches are places that clients and workers can explore for ongoing support.

Earlier work in which workers helped clients assess and activate resource systems may already leave clients closely involved with supports that will help maintain their stability. To facilitate further access to supports, workers can help clients plan what events will require the support of others, determine ways that they will contact supports if necessary, or even invite significant others into closing sessions.

Celebrations and Ritualized Endings

What traditions does your family have to mark passages, transitions, and achievements? Do you have family gatherings, picnics, suppers, or ceremonies? Do certain family members play particular roles in giving toasts, lighting candles, singing songs, giving gifts, or preparing special food? Are passages recorded in your family albums, books, or other treasures? Individuals and families, as well as other groups, frequently mark normal life passages, milestones, and achievements with rituals and ceremonies. Rituals provide human systems with structured ways to deal with emotions, vehicles for communication, and means to celebrate accomplishments.

Rituals function positively for the endings of social worker–client relationships, providing a definitive transition point for both social workers and clients. Rituals mark progress, celebrate strengths, and anticipate possibilities for the future. By providing a structure for communicating thoughts and emotions about endings, ceremonies help us cope with ambiguous and sometimes contradictory feelings.

In designing meaningful ceremonies to mark endings, workers and clients create experiences that are symbolic of the work's achievements. "Graduation" ceremonies with music, processionals, and diplomas may successfully signify the end of a training group. Collaborating on creating a mural or collage may signify a stepfamily's successful blending into a cohesively functioning unit. Each event integrates the gains of the work completed and clearly indicates the transition in the client system and the professional relationship.

Social workers encourage ongoing support by family members.

MONKEY BUSINESS IMAGES / SHUTTERSTOCK

Looking to the Future

Constructive resolutions look to the future. To encourage competent functioning beyond the relationship, social workers and clients envision plans and future successes as well as anticipate upcoming challenges. Workers inquire how clients will approach potential issues; develop plans for follow-up, including specifying resources for continued support; possibly suggest the idea of a follow-up appointment; or simply acknowledge that recurrence does not represent failure.

Social workers' knowledge of human behavior in general and their experiences with specific clients may allow workers to formulate hunches about what might be coming up. Expected life transitions, particular risk factors in clients' lives, previous patterns likely to resurface—all may be worth mentioning so that clients are not blindsided in their optimism in having accomplished current tasks.

Read the following examples of how social workers help clients anticipate upcoming challenges:

- I have been so impressed with your ability to figure out how to balance giving Hank the freedom to be with his friends with your concerns about the safety of the neighborhood. But I also see that Celia is approaching the age where she will want to do the same. What have you learned from this experience with Hank that you think might help you with Celia's transition to adolescence?
- This neighborhood really did dodge the wrecking ball just in the nick of time. Your abilities to organize, target key people in the city's administration, and generate public support have been amazing. I also recognize that some of the same concerns that prompted the city's actions still exist—the high crime rate, sporadic mainte-nance, and abandoned buildings. Have you thought what you might do with the resources you've developed to head off the city's next move before it happens?
- You really do seem set for now. Your skill in managing all of those services to keep Howard at home is nothing short of miraculous. But we both know that Alzheimer's is a progressive disease. What sort of plans are you making for the future?

Each of these comments reflects workers' confidence in their clients yet indicates the reality that things don't stand still; clients will have to continue to cope as time goes on. Workers can guide clients to apply the skills and processes they have learned to each of these upcoming situations.

Following Up

For successful resolution, workers and clients also clarify exactly where the relationship goes from here. Will there be additional contacts? Should clients schedule a checkup visit for 3 months to monitor whether they are still on track? Will someone from the agency contact clients to check on their continuing progress as part of the agency's outcome evaluation procedure? How will clients access their records if they choose to do so? What if clients really feel the need to contact the worker again—how do they do it? Is it acceptable for clients to get back in touch? Can they call with good news, or are contacts limited to requests for additional assistance? What are clients supposed to do if they coincidentally run into workers in other contexts—at the mall, the grocery store, or the movies?

These questions deserve attention to alleviate clients' concerns about the future. As workers and clients discuss the answers to these issues, they modify their working agreement to formulate a "contract for closure" that specifies how clients will continue without workers and the conditions under which clients or workers may reinitiate contact. Clients need information about policies and procedures for reconnecting to the worker. Clarity about these issues gives clients the information they need to make sound decisions about managing their own resources in the future.

Responding to Clients' Discontinuation of Services

Clients conclude their work in different ways, sometimes earlier than social workers would prefer, which necessitates workers to respond to unplanned exits. Many reasons prompt clients to withdraw from services prematurely—reasons that vary widely, from clients' feelings of disillusionment to their feelings of success and empowerment. Regardless of the reason, workers recognize that clients have the privilege to withdraw from services as they see fit. Even involuntary clients can choose to stop and then experience the consequences for their refusal to continue. One qualitative study about terminations in an adolescent mental health treatment program found that most endings were neither planned for nor announced or initiated by the adolescent clients (Mirabito, 2006).

Many reasons prompt clients to withdraw from services prematurely—reasons that vary widely, from clients' feelings of disillusionment to their feelings of success and empowerment.

Preparing for Early Discontinuation

Practitioners work actively to resolve relationships successfully, even with clients who drop out of services. First, workers structure each meeting with clients in such a way that if clients fail to return, they have still gained something from the work. Second, workers learn to recognize signs that clients are drifting away so that they can invite an open discussion about the direction of the work. Finally, workers follow up with clients who drop out to clarify the status of the relationship, receive feedback on the reasons that clients discontinued the service, and let clients know how to return in the future if they so desire.

The dynamic nature of social work practice demands that workers attend to all facets of the process simultaneously, regardless of the specific phase that time factors may indicate. As social workers, we assess clients as we build partnerships with them; we observe clients change and develop even while we are still discovering what they can do; we continue to build relationships as we implement changes; and we anticipate the end of the relationship even as we are beginning. Preparing for the inevitable ending, workers integrate gains throughout the entire process. To do so, workers consistently guide clients in the direction of their strengths, their goals, and their power. Clients will then leave the work with greater confidence in their abilities, even if they exit prematurely.

"Every session is the first and every session is the last" (Walter & Peller, 1992, p. 140). This statement depicts a here-and-now style of practice and also says that social workers help clients best when they function as if each session could be the last. When workers end each meeting with a summary of the progress made and concretely plan the next step to take, clients leave with a sense of accomplishment and direction that they will keep with them whether or not they return for their next scheduled meeting.

Intervention

Behavior: Facilitate effective transitions and endings that advance mutually agreed-on goals

Critical Thinking Question: Social workers should follow up with clients who unexpectedly drop services. Why is bringing some type of formal resolution and closure to the helping relationship important for both clients and practitioners?

Recognizing Exit Clues

Social workers attend to clients' clues of pending departure. Many times, clients reveal their tendency to discontinue services in behavioral rather than verbal ways. Clients begin to show up late for meetings, cancel sessions frequently because more important events are occurring, or miss appointments altogether. They neglect to carry out activities as planned in previous sessions. Clients may seem inattentive or fail to present important issues during meetings. All of these behaviors may indicate early withdrawal. However, these signals are ambiguous, leaving workers to share their observations and ask clients about their motivation to continue.

When workers see evidence that client involvement is waning, they bring these observations to the forefront. Workers do not accuse clients of hidden agendas. Instead, they convey acceptance and acknowledge that clients have choices to stop early. In the example that follows, notice the worker's up-front, yet accepting, tone in sharing observations with a client who is showing exiting behaviors:

> I'm a little unclear about what's going on. This is the second week you've come late to our appointment. You're also telling me that you really don't have much to talk about, haven't gotten around to completing the "homework" we designed, and you need to leave early today. I'm wondering if you're thinking that we've gone about as far as you want to and you'd like to wrap up or take a break.

Clarifying what clients are saying with "withdrawing" behaviors works whether or not the worker's hunches are correct. If clients are indeed preparing to depart, workers can initiate processes to wrap up the work more productively. If clients are unaware that they are losing focus, a worker's comments may bring them back to task. If clients are indirectly communicating other issues, such as their dissatisfaction with the worker or the present plan, the worker's feedback invites direct discussion and redirection. When workers share their observations that clients are not keeping their commitments to the process, they remind clients they have the privilege to take charge of where the relationship goes next.

Resolving Unplanned Exits

Sometimes workers miss clues that indicate clients are leaving. Other clients leave no clues. When clients simply don't show up for appointments or call and cancel not only the next appointment but the work altogether, the professional relationship is left unresolved. The reasons clients withdraw abruptly vary. Some may feel angry or hopeless. Some may feel that things are good enough. Others may perceive that the worker isn't really interested. Still others may assess that the effort in time, transportation, and other costs does not justify the limited benefits they are receiving. Or totally unrelated factors may interfere.

Good social work requires that practitioners follow up with clients who make "unplanned" exits (Hepworth et al., 2013). Workers have several purposes in doing so, including the following:

- Understanding a client's reasons for withdrawing
- Validating a client's right to withdraw
- Inviting the client back for future work if desired

- Reinforcing any client progress thus far
- Evaluating and improving the worker's own skills in "reading" client messages and resolving relationships effectively
- Clarifying the "open" or "closed" status of clients for agency accountability purposes

Most important, this follow-up contact reassures clients they can feel comfortable in pursuing their goals in their own way and at their own pace. Workers should not leave clients with thoughts that they have somehow done something wrong.

? Assess your understanding of social work endings by taking this brief quiz.

CLOSING WITH REFERRAL

Sometimes, relationships between social workers and clients end before they reach the desired goals. For a variety of reasons, workers may identify the need for **referrals** of clients elsewhere for continued service. This decision may be prompted by the agency's restrictions on length of service or client eligibility, the worker's move to a new position, or the worker's lack of qualifications to continue working with the client's issues that have surfaced. Changes in clients' needs, crisis events in their lives, or lack of continuing progress may also precipitate a referral and subsequent resolution of the professional relationship.

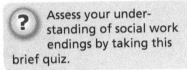

Previous chapters describe processes for linking clients with available resources while clients continue to work with the current agency and worker. But when referring clients at closure, workers attempt to smooth the transition, maintain client motivation, and incorporate any progress achieved so far into the work of the subsequent helping relationship. In closing with clients by referring to another service, workers are simultaneously ending and beginning—wrapping up a phase of the work and orienting clients toward a successful start somewhere else.

Intervention

Behavior: Use inter-professional collaboration as appropriate to achieve beneficial practice outcomes

Critical Thinking Question: Generalist social workers frequently need to refer clients to other agencies and organizations for specialized assistance. In what ways do social workers proactively use their knowledge and skills to ensure that the service delivery network has a full complement of services available?

Acknowledging Limited Resources

When practitioners contract with clients for social work services, they are guaranteeing that what clients appear to need is a good fit for what the agency offers. To honor this agreement, workers monitor three systems—the agency, the client, and the worker. Changes in any of these systems may create a gap between what the client seeks and what the agency or worker can provide. Social workers know that it is time to end the professional relationship with an appropriate referral when these systems are unable to mesh in ways effective to reach clients' goals.

When Client Needs Exceed Worker Limits

Sometimes workers discover that their practice abilities or agency programs can offer clients nothing further. Workers may recognize this situation in their own inability to respond to what clients want or when updated assessment information reveals that clients need something that workers do not have available. Ethical social workers accept their limits and refer clients when the situation moves beyond the worker's role or expertise.

Ethical social workers accept their limits and refer clients when the situation moves beyond the worker's role or expertise.

Discovering the need to refer is not unusual. Some challenges surface more slowly than others. When clients withhold significant information, workers may blame themselves or clients. However, this does not mean that workers are inadequate or that clients have been "lying." Sensitive subjects may require extensive testing of the worker and a trusting, established professional relationship for the client to come forward. Clients are often reluctant to quickly share "what is really happening" in situations that involve alcoholism, drug addiction, sexual abuse, or criminal behavior. When clients have developed enough trust to disclose these issues, workers respond in a trustworthy manner by referring clients to the most appropriate service.

Dale Storonski is well acquainted with the constraints that sometimes lead him to end his work with clients by referring them to others for continued assistance. Dale, a delinquency prevention worker at Northside Youth Services, recently closed a case that provides such an example. Todd, a client referred to Dale after his arrest for shoplifting, continued his illegal activity in spite of their work to focus Todd on more productive activities. When Todd finally admitted to Dale that he was using cocaine daily, Dale explained his inability to work with addiction in his particular setting and referred Todd to the Addictions Recovery Center. In this situation, the indications for referral were explicit. The priority actions necessary for the best interests of this client required Dale to close out his work and refer Todd elsewhere for continuing service.

Service Restrictions

At other times, organizational constraints prescribe endings rather than leaving the actual choice to social workers or clients. Agencies may impose time limits based on guidelines from fund sources or policies about the distribution of services. Managed care policies often delimit the length of service for which the third-party providers will pay. Service restrictions also occur when agency policies target clients in a particular age range, feature time-limited interventions, or emphasize crisis resolution rather than long-term work. Consider a delinquency prevention program that may work only with juveniles under the age of 18 because older clients are no longer at risk of delinquency according to the laws of the particular state. As part of developing a service continuum, the agency can mitigate any disruptions by negotiating working agreements with adult-oriented services to accept referrals when the delinquency prevention program's clients turn 18.

Other organizational stipulations affect the nature and duration of service as well. For example, many workers practice in host settings, where social work services are supplementary to the organization's primary mission. Such organizations include hospitals, schools, prisons, and private businesses. Organizational factors, including discharge from the hospital, the end of the school year, transfer, release of prisoners, or termination of employment, can force social workers to finalize their work quickly. Although social workers can anticipate these endings, they may not represent "natural" conclusions or resolutions. For successful closure with these clients, workers clarify the limits of their services at the outset, negotiate only goals that fit the setting, and provide referral options at closure.

Finally, internal changes in an agency's structure or mission may shift a worker's responsibilities and create other personnel and programmatic changes that affect the continuity of services. Fiscal constraints all too often determine parameters for services. Social workers assess what impact these changes will have on clients and apprise them of what they can expect. When agency practices, guidelines, or changes force clients out before they are ready, ethical social workers build bridges to other assistance to sustain client motivation, safety, and progress.

Implementing Legal Mandates

All social workers are mandated to report incidents that threaten clients' safety or the safety of others. High-risk situations, including child abuse, elder abuse, intimate violence, and potential suicide or homicide, require that workers take immediate steps to secure the safety of those involved. This may entail actions to report concerns to state protective services, local police, or potential victims, or to arrange for clients to be evaluated at community mental health centers. Chapter 8 describes these circumstances and the priority actions that social workers must take to prevent harm.

Moreover, complying with legal mandates may interrupt a practitioner's work with a client. Mandated service providers are likely to have service arrangements that make preexisting services unnecessary or shift previous goals to a secondary importance in the face of the current crisis. In some cases, clients themselves may respond to the worker's actions negatively, feel betrayed or undermined, and refuse to continue the relationship. As a result, a social worker's contract with a client may be preempted by the mandated report of a dangerous situation.

Social workers cannot be swayed by the potential for service disruption in handling such events. A social worker's ethical responsibility to report harm takes precedence over the preference for service continuance. However, workers should also be careful not to abandon clients at these times of crisis. Clients benefit from workers who stay involved for a period sufficient to make the necessary transition. A worker's goals at this time are similar to those in other situations in which the client transfers to a new service provider or withdraws prematurely from service. The worker attempts to consolidate the progress from the work thus far and facilitate the success of the subsequent plan.

As an example, consider the case of Linda, a client who reveals to youth worker Dale Storonski that her grandfather has been sexually abusing her. Dale's mandated report to the Child Protective Unit results in Linda's removal from her grandparents' home and emergency placement in a foster home across town. The web of services offered by the child welfare system usurps Dale's role with Linda, requiring that he close out his work and prepare Linda to work successfully within the new service arena. To facilitate this transition, Dale arranges a conjoint meeting with Linda, her new caseworker, and her foster family to discuss his previous work with Linda and so that he can participate in updating Linda's case plan for implementation under these new circumstances.

Making Referrals

When workers reach the limit of what they can offer, they have an ethical obligation to discuss this with clients openly and to offer clients other resource possibilities. Failure to offer honest information about the worker's or agency's limitations may leave clients feeling like they are being "dumped." To avoid misunderstandings, workers may say any of the following:

- As we discussed when we first got together, the crisis service we offer allows us only 30 days per client. Things seem a little calmer now, but you've told me that you still would like to build on the progress you are making. I have several possibilities for where to go next that I think we should discuss.

• You have been great at figuring out how to deal with the kids and avoid using physical punishment, but now you are asking me for assistance with your marriage, and I don't really feel qualified as a marriage therapist. There are, however, several excellent programs that I could recommend to you.

• I need to let you know that I'll be leaving my position in 3 weeks. I got a promotion, but that moves me out to the regional office. I know we're right in the middle of things, so would you like me to refer you to the new worker immediately so that you don't lose any ground?

• I know that you are still facing a big challenge in confronting the school board about some of its discriminatory suspension policies. But guidelines set by my board of directors prevent me from participating in the kind of protest against the school that you are planning. I do know that the Center for Citizens' Rights has dealt with some similar concerns. Would you be interested in contacting them for continued support?

Notice how, in each example, workers directly acknowledge their limitations, offer honest expectations, reinforce the progress already made, and clearly indicate where clients might go next.

Recognizing Interim Success

Resolving a professional relationship by referring clients elsewhere is not a defeat; rather, it is a step on the way to success. Identifying a more appropriate service clearly moves clients toward the solutions they seek. When making the transition to a new service, workers reflect this perspective by reviewing the client's successes so far in a positive way. So, workers guide clients to discuss their readiness to discontinue, highlight achievements, encourage the exchange of feelings, and anticipate future development.

Smoothing the Transition

Workers have a double dilemma when referring clients to others for continuation of the work. If the work has been successful, clients have probably developed a sense of confidence in the relationship and will be reluctant to transfer. If the work has run into obstacles, clients may be discouraged about continuing with anyone. Recognizing these potential hazards in closing a case by referral, practitioners work carefully on transitions that keep clients moving toward their goals.

Imagine yourself in the role of a client for a minute. You finally take a risk of getting some assistance. Things are going pretty well, that is, until your social worker starts talking about running out of time—something about eligibility and agency policy. What would help you pick up with a new worker where you left off with the old one? Clearly, the transition would be easier if you didn't have to start all over. You would want the new worker to be informed. You would also want the new worker to be someone you could relate to easily. And you might want to circumvent all the red tape that some agencies put you through before you actually get into one of the inner offices or get the direct service worker into your home.

Facilitating Client Control

By following a few simple suggestions, the social worker can assist the client and the referral worker build on the progress already made. For example, it works best to refer clients to another human being with a name, description, and set of qualifications rather than an agency, program, or department. If possible, provide clients with alternatives from which to choose. Inform clients of the entry procedures so that they can navigate those sometimes confusing and uncomfortable beginning processes. Collaborate with clients on how to transfer information and secure their written consent to facilitate the transfer of case records. A referral conference that includes the client, the former worker, and the referral worker allows all of the participants to discuss the work already completed in a format that allows for clarification and questioning. When time or organizational constraints prevent this type of direct transfer, social workers and clients still work cooperatively toward a smooth transition.

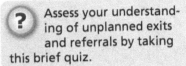

Assess your understanding of unplanned exits and referrals by taking this brief quiz.

WHEN CLIENTS DIE

The realm of social work reflects the human seasons of birth through death. Social workers in medical settings and gerontological services are most likely to experience a client's death. But social workers in other settings may also be confronted with the realities of death. As a result, all social workers need fundamental knowledge about grief and its impact as well as skills to support those who have survived the loss of someone they loved.

Grief

Classic studies of grief by Kübler-Ross (1969) offer a paradigm for understanding the emotional dimensions of our experiences with death and dying. These emotions may include denial, anger, bargaining, depression, and acceptance. More recent research on grief describes the idiosyncratic response of each individual to loss and casts doubt on the abilities of any worker to assess and treat a client's grief accurately by applying a predetermined linear model (Bonanno, 2009). This collaborative approach matches the reality that people may experience only some of the emotions Kübler-Ross identifies, experience these emotions in various sequences, or respond completely differently.

A person's age, gender, health, coping style, cultural background, religious beliefs, previous experiences with death, and availability of familial and social support all contribute to feelings of vulnerability, resiliency, or loss when people die (Berk, 2014; Bonanno, 2009; Nakashima, 2003). Some people may talk readily about their sorrow; others may feel a greater need for privacy and withhold their feelings from the scrutiny of others. Still others may disavow their loss, separating themselves from consciously considering their feelings, feelings that may emerge in other ways such as physical affliction, anger, depression, or acting out behavior. Being able to anticipate the loss provides opportunities to work on unfinished business prior to death.

To respond in a supportive way to those who are grieving, workers accept the diverse methods people use to deal with loss and allow survivors to cope at a pace that

Watch this video that describes the power inherent in one's ability to be vulnerable. What are the implications of vulnerability for working with clients facing end-of-life issues? www.youtube.com/watch?v=AO6n9HmG0qM

fits the person and the situation. Supportive workers extensively use good listening skills, even when clients repeat information; accept both direct and indirect expression of feelings; and encourage adaptive coping strategies. Responsible social workers also update their information on the array of community services available for grief support, including specialty services such as support groups for parents who have lost children, people who have lost partners to cancer, and people who have lost loved ones to violence.

End-of-Life Care

Paradoxically, resilience is an important characteristic when people are at the ends of their lives and holds significance for **end-of-life care**. Resilience involves discovering meaning in life and living a meaningful life that extends beyond the experience of illness. Based on a small-scale qualitative study of older individuals in hospice care, Nelson-Becker (2006) identifies four major themes that reveal measures respondents were taking to come to terms with their terminal illness: (1) redefining self-image, (2) drawing on the strength of religion or grappling with uncertainty of meaning, (3) investing in social relationships, and (4) wanting to maintain independence. In end-of-life care work, social workers provide support for dying well so that clients can engage in living as fully as possible in whatever way they choose. "Dying well is ultimately about living fully and consciously in whatever way one chooses until the moment of death" (p. 88).

Advance Care Planning

Evolving in importance in health care and gerontological social work, **advance care planning** (ACP) involves both advance directives and planning for end-of-life care (Black, 2007). The Patient Self-Determination Act (PL 101-508) requires Medicare and Medicaid providers to ask everyone using their health care services if they have advance directives, such as a living will or durable power of attorney (Csikai, 2008). **Living wills** provide instructions with respect to the application of life sustaining measures. **Durable powers of attorney for health care** are legal documents that assign the responsibility for following directives if individuals are no longer able to make decisions for themselves. ACP also emphasizes holistic long-range planning for end-of-life care (Black). Among the areas of focus are needs in psychological, social, spiritual, medical, physical, and financial domains.

Grieving the Death of a Client

Although experiencing the death of a client certainly differs from enduring the loss of a family member or friend, personal and professional grief have common elements. Emotional responses of workers vary, depending on the unique background and perspectives of workers and clients as well as the nature of their professional relationship. Factors influencing the ways social workers cope with a client's death include their anticipation of the death of the client, their professional preparation for working competently with grieving processes, and their own responses to grief and death. The particular circumstances of the client's death—whether it was sudden, lingering, or marked by suffering—as well as the impact on the client's family and significant others also influence the worker's experience and response.

The recollections of Emily Carter, a Northside Hospital hospice social worker, convey the emotional experience of working with death and dying. She says, "Faces of clients and their stories fill my memory. Knowing them, I've learned about myself. I remember 8-year-old Amanda whose rage was fueled by incurable cancer and fear of loneliness, and her parents whose anguish choked their ability to communicate openly with their daughter. I recall Seth, the plucky 3-year-old boy with leukemia who brought laughter to the hospital unit and bittersweet joy to his parent's heart. And there is Irene, from the skilled care unit, with whom I had worked for several months. We were talking about my going on vacation when she abruptly said, "Let me put on my glasses so I can see your face clearly one more time!" And then we talked about my leaving and her dying. She thanked me for being someone who did not judge her for being angry, someone who would sit with her in silence, someone who would listen to her reminiscing about her past and musing about the future, someone who helped her to discover hope even in the face of sorrow. I remember crying with Irene that day and later grieving her death. Mostly, I remember the power of her affirmation and the meaningfulness of our work together."

Self-awareness and support are key components in handling issues of death and dying. Workers who cope successfully with the deaths of clients are honest in their appraisal of impact. It is not "unprofessional" to grieve the loss of a genuine relationship. Practice settings such as hospitals, extended care facilities, hospice programs, and caregiver support programs frequently develop staff support services to deal with the significant effects of working in situations in which clients die. Beside self-care and institutional support, Strom-Gottfried and Mowbray (2006) recommend that preparation, review and debriefing, and memorial rituals are beneficial supports for professionals working through grief issues.

Death by Accident or Intention

One of the most difficult experiences that workers may confront is when clients die in ways that workers believe might have been prevented. When clients die of drug overdoses, are murdered while participating in gang activity, or take their own lives, workers may be left with guilt that somehow they could have done more or done something different. Shulman (2012) emphasizes the importance of the practice setting in helping workers cope. He offers a three-step model for responding to such events: first, encourage the worker to grieve; second, elicit support from other workers with similar experiences or whose positions put them at risk of the same experience; and finally, refocus the worker toward other clients who still need assistance.

? Assess your understanding of issues of grief and end-of-life-care by taking this brief quiz.

RESOLVING RELATIONSHIPS
WITH LARGER SYSTEMS

Closure skills with larger systems incorporate all those processes already discussed. Workers perform tasks to help members express feelings, evaluate progress, function independently, plan for the future, and maintain progress. But ending the work with

Box 16.1   End-of-Life Care: A Policy–Practice Connection

End-of-life care involves assessment and interventions across the full spectrum of life, including biological, psychological, social, economic, cultural, and spiritual dimensions. Social workers in many fields of practice are involved in end-of-life care (Kramer et al., 2003). Medical social work settings in which social workers are likely to confront end-of-life issues include home health care, hospice services, and hospital units such as the emergency room, oncology, intensive care, pediatrics, and critical care. Social workers practicing in other settings, particularly schools, child welfare, and aging services, are also likely to encounter issues related to death and illness in their day-to-day work.

The psychological, cultural, and social ramifications of death, grief, and bereavement for both social workers and their clients are further complicated by numerous legal and ethical challenges. The NASW (2011a) policy statement on hospice care, for example, identifies several concerns related to end-of-life care:

- Increased costs of hospice services coupled with diminishing rates of reimbursement jeopardize the financial viability of nearly 90 percent of all hospice programs, many of which provide hospice services in rural areas.
- Although more people are receiving end-of-life care through hospice services, the length of time many receive services is less than 2 weeks, thus reducing the benefits families receive from the supports offered through the care of hospice teams.

- Ethnic minorities are underrepresented among those served by end-of-life care programs and services.
- End-of-life care services such as hospice often rely on the presence of family caregivers to provide day-to-day support to the person who is dying, but the geographic mobility of family members and employment obligations of caregivers often create barriers to intensive family involvement.

With respect to empowerment and advocacy, the NASW Standards for Palliative and End-of-Life Care (2004b) calls for social workers to engage proactively in the social and political arenas to ensure that clients have access to needed resources in palliative and end-of-life care.

The principle of self-determination guides social workers in assisting clients with end-of-life decisions. Two factors have played a significant role in ushering in a new era of formalized documentation of personal choice—the legal press for personal involvement in decision making coupled with the financial reality of prolonging life through extraordinary interventions. Social workers play a role in implementing and complying with the legal requirements of advance directives, such as living wills and durable powers of attorney for health care, while ensuring that clients' preferences are heard and honored (Black, 2004, 2010; Baughman et al., 2012; Buchanan et al., 2004; NASW, 2014).

a multiperson client system requires additional actions to stabilize the functioning of the system as a whole and to ensure the continued well-being of its members. Consider the special circumstances of resolving relationships with groups, organizations, and communities.

Small Group Endings

Social workers facilitate small group clients with many different purposes. The specific purpose affects the interaction, development, intensity, duration, and character of the group. To plan appropriately for closure, workers analyze each group's particular characteristics, examine important events that have transpired during the life of the group, and consider where the group and its members will go next.

Whether the group is closed- or open-ended is a significant feature that affects closure activities. A **closed-ended group** meets for a predetermined number of meetings or long enough to reach a desired goal. At closure, the group disbands, and all members leave at once. Conversely, an **open-ended group** continues to meet as some members "graduate." At any given time, a worker may be wrapping up with some group members while simultaneously initiating new members into the group's activities. The different meanings of "ending" in these two types of groups lead workers to facilitate closure activities to fit each situation.

Closed-Ended Groups

Closed-ended groups may work to raise consciousness among people who are oppressed, implement social action strategies in the larger environment, provide mutual aid, or increase members' skills in communication, assertion, parenting, or other areas of functioning. By the time the group moves toward closure, all members have worked together to create a shared experience and history with one another. They have convened simultaneously, learned to communicate and relate with one another, worked collaboratively on common tasks, and now face the reality that the group as a resource will soon cease to exist for them.

The similar experiences of members in closed-ended groups allow workers to steer the focus toward shared concerns. All members will benefit from conversations that review and evaluate the work, share feelings, and look ahead toward how the group's benefits can be integrated into each member's functioning outside of the group. Adapting closure activities to a group client, workers also recognize the additional complexity because each group member is actually ending multiple relationships at once. Members are resolving their relationships with the worker, with each other, and with the group itself. Workers guide members to express their thoughts and feelings concerning each of these relationships as the work ends. Particularly, members should consider that the group as an entity will not exist past closure, leaving them without the group as a resource to fall back on.

Open-Ended Groups

Groups structured in an open-ended style may include treatment groups to modify behaviors, addiction recovery groups, and support groups such as those focused on grief, caregiving stress, or survival after violence. Similar to participation in other groups, members will progress through phases that define their relationship to, comfort in, and work with the group. But because members are entering and leaving the group at different times, each member is constructing an idiosyncratic and unique history with the group—sharing common experiences with some group members but having very little interaction with others. In facilitating closure activities with an open-ended group, workers face a collection of members at various developmental levels with very diverse needs.

Even when only one member leaves an open-ended group, every other group member also experiences the closure, yet this event holds a different significance for each. All group members can benefit from an open exchange of the different perspectives they hold. New members are able to imagine themselves completing their work as they listen to others describe their progress and success. Members who are now leaving can see their own progress more vividly through the eyes of new members. When a member leaves, workers simultaneously wrap up with that member and use the member's success to activate other members who may be only beginning their work.

Session Endings

Each group meeting contains elements of the entire social work process, combining beginning, middle, and ending phases or, in the language of empowering practice, the phases of dialogue, discovery, and development. Beginning phases reinforce the group's cohesion and identify the meeting's goals. Middle phases complete tasks in ways that activate group member resources. Ending phases of a group meeting solidify and integrate the group's success for that session and anticipate the impact on the future work of the group.

Birnbaum and Cicchetti (2000) describe the ending phase of a group encounter as the most neglected part of the session. They propose that successful **session endings** allow reflection on the group's work and its application to members' lives, anticipate the issues and challenges of the upcoming session as a way to create continuity, and ensure that members have a sense of completion, satisfaction, and accomplishment about the work completed. Session endings are most important for an open-ended group because, for some members, this may be their final group meeting.

Resolving Intermember Relationships

When practitioners complete their work with group clients, the worker–client relationship is not the only one to resolve. Members of larger client systems also have relationships with each other—relationships from which members have benefited and on which they have grown to depend. Workers must also provide opportunities for members of multiperson client systems to wrap up their work with each other in ways that acknowledge and support the benefits of relationships among group members.

If you are a proficient math student, you can readily calculate the incredible number of relationship combinations in a client system with many members. In a small group of 5 people, there are 10 dyadic relationships and many small group combinations. In a group of 10 members, there are 45 dyadic relationships and enough subgroup possibilities to boggle the mind. Imagine the complexity of relationships in a large organization or community! Obviously, there is not enough time to resolve all of these relationships individually or even know the significance of each one. To cope with closing these multiple relationships, workers initiate structured processes to meet members' needs in a time-efficient and productive way.

Structured Endings

Workers plan final meetings with larger client systems to provide all members with opportunities to share their thoughts and feelings about the work completed and to consider the future. For example, workers may solicit written feedback from members and present summary information to the group. Practitioners may also use structured experiences in which members take turns responding to similar questions, such as "What was the most important thing you learned?" or "How do you anticipate using what you have learned in the future?"

A rotating dyadic experience in which each group member talks briefly one-on-one with each other group member also offers opportunities for members to wrap up with each other. Workers may leave the topic of these dialogues to the discretion of the members. As an alternative, workers can suggest that members thank each other for the benefits that have accrued based on the relationship or reminisce about positive interactions and events that have occurred in the life of the group.

Endings with Organizations and Communities

Much work with organizations and communities involves face-to-face human interaction with people in various leadership roles, task groups, or teams. Therefore, resolving relationships with these larger client systems draws on the same skills that workers implement with individuals, families, and small groups. But integrating gains in work with mezzo- and macrolevel systems additionally requires substantive changes in organizational or community structures, policies, procedures, and operations. Workers see a larger system's readiness for closure when the system has institutionalized the desired changes by incorporating them into the functioning of the organization or community itself. To wrap up their work, organizational- and community-level workers also strive to support the continuing development of leadership, intrasystem alliances, and widespread collaboration in decision-making.

Institutionalizing Change

To maintain the stability of progress initiated in a larger system client past the point of closure, workers target changes in policies and practices that will endure. A social system's tendency to maintain equilibrium works in favor of sustaining desired changes that become a routine part of the system's functioning.

Consider the example of Damon Edwards, first presented in Chapter 10, as he wraps up his work with the residents of Franklin Courts. The residents have achieved their goals. The children with lead poisoning are receiving medical treatment, the source of the contamination has been discovered, and city work crews are renovating buildings to ensure their safety. To stabilize these changes, the members have also initiated policy changes in the housing authority's code that ensure monitoring of materials used in public housing work projects. Organizing annual blood screenings is another institutionalized accomplishment that will monitor the health of those children already exposed to lead. These embedded changes in policy and practice are institutional changes that will have enduring benefits after Damon and the residents of Franklin Courts complete their work together.

Sustaining Empowered Functioning   The ultimate goal for any level of client system in empowerment-based social work practice is the sustained empowered functioning of the client after the contracted work is completed. Key elements necessary to sustain this empowered functioning in larger client systems include leadership development, collegial collaboration, and consensus-building skills such as negotiation and mediation.

Drawing on the Franklin Courts example, Damon Edwards can work to enhance the leadership of Fiona Grant. Having identified Mrs. Grant's leadership abilities early in

The ultimate goal for any level of client system in empowerment-based social work practice is the sustained empowered functioning of the client after the contracted work is completed.

the work, Damon has always found ways to create plenty of space for her to lead, leaving himself in a consulting role. The group's success has activated Mrs. Grant's motivation further, and she has now expanded her activities to focus on other neighborhood issues. At closure, Damon directly states his confidence in Mrs. Grant's abilities and offers honest feedback on her strengths as he sees them.

To encourage powerful alliances within the group, Damon also helps members establish a resident council that meets regularly to review conditions at Franklin Courts, maintains a presence at city council meetings, and monitors the activities of the housing authority, even after the initial crisis has faded. Developing leadership and maintaining effective structures and alliances will empower the residents to continue their efforts without needing Damon's involvement. Through his work with this council, Damon has also facilitated the development of decision-making skills. Members work toward consensus by accessing each participant's views, respecting differences of opinion, and creating plans that incorporate the strengths of everyone involved.

Ethical and Professional Behavior

Behavior: Use supervision and consultation to guide professional judgment and behavior

Critical Thinking Question: Professional community organizers often work in the communities in which they reside. What issues related to supervision and consultation arise for these macropractice social workers as they transition between resident and organizer and vice versa?

Termination or Transition?

An important consideration in closure activities with organizations and communities is the role that the social worker will play with the system after the point of closure. In organizational practice, the worker is often a member of the client system itself and will continue to be so when the project at hand is complete. In community practice, the worker is likely to have a long-term, ongoing relationship with the community, wrapping up one project and moving on to the next. In these situations, closure will not mark the end of the relationship with the client system; instead, it signifies a change in the worker's role.

For such a transition to be successful, the closure must be clearly understood, and the client system must be able to sustain the desired changes without the continuing efforts of the social worker. Damon Edwards' successful work in supporting Fiona Grant and the resident council as leaders in Franklin Courts allows him to return to his previous role in the Northside Community. He will still interact with the Franklin Courts residents, but he will refrain from doing for them what they can now do for themselves.

To increase clarity about the role changes that occur at these points of transition, macrolevel practitioners discuss them openly. Workers may also use symbolic means to mark the turning point in their involvement. Work with groups, task forces, committees, organizations, and communities has long been known for its use of ritualized endings. Parties, ceremonies to recognize accomplishments, certificates of merit, voting approval of the final committee report, and notifications of grant funding all affirm accomplishments, mark endings, and serve as bridges to new beginnings. In planning closure ceremonies, workers seek to offer members opportunities to reflect on their work together and define their future relationships with each other in addition to wrapping up with the social worker.

? Assess your understanding of resolving relationships with larger systems by taking this short quiz.

ENDINGS ARE BEGINNINGS

Social work clients end relationships with workers in many ways. At times, workers and clients meet their contracted goals and methodically wrap up their work in a way that sustains and celebrates achievements. At other times, clients require referral to another service that is more appropriate to their current needs. Sometimes, clients withdraw from services unexpectedly, leaving workers to resolve the relationship. In some cases, clients die, and workers may cope with grief and loss. Ending the work with larger client systems points workers toward processes that fit the needs of groups, organizations, communities, and their members. Social workers need knowledge and skills to implement appropriate closure processes for each type of ending.

Watch this video that shows how clients frequently want to share their appreciation with social workers as the relationship ends. How do these messages from appreciative clients in this video shape your ideas about who you want to be as a social work professional? www.youtube.com/watch?v=84bE1M6Usz0

An effective closing process does not terminate the client's development. Instead, it represents a shift in responsibility for continued change from the worker–client relationship to the client. Clients are left to stabilize the progress gained, integrate the skills learned, and function independently of the worker. The success of this transition not only rests on discrete closing activities but also requires a process to encourage client self-direction throughout the entire social work relationship. A collaborative social worker–client partnership that develops client strengths, creates productive alliances, and increases opportunities empowers clients with the resources to continue to function competently after the professional relationship ends.

Social workers also move beyond the partnership, enriched by another practice experience. An ending that carefully reviews the process and includes an open exchange of thoughts and feelings offers workers important feedback about their professional skills and interpersonal qualities. The practice wisdom gained by workers from each client stimulates the worker's professional development and benefits future clients.

Evaluate what you learned in this chapter by completing the Chapter Review.

Epilogue

Andrea Barry walked out into the summer evening. She felt energized, enthused, and content, all at the same time. The Northside Network's annual conference always seemed to leave her with feelings of confidence, a sense of support, and something new to try. Following each conference over the past two years, Andrea had experienced similar feelings. It felt good to get together with Northside's other social workers.

The idea to start the annual conference had come up at one of the Northside Network's brown-bag lunches. With each meeting of the Network, members were seeing more clearly that they were all "in this together." In spite of their differences in agency settings and clientele, all workers used similar practice processes. Each Northside social worker also drew resources from the Northside community. What benefited the work of one held potential benefits for them all. It seemed only logical that they should pool their efforts. The annual conference was one way they did that.

The conference was a multidimensional experience. Each member of the Network facilitated a workshop, presentation, or task-oriented session. From Mark Nogales, Andrea had learned about the integration of the strengths perspective into working with clients with mental illnesses. Andrea had also participated in writing a position paper about the need for more low-cost and transitional housing. She really enjoyed the "Tune In, Don't Burn Out" workshop, in which Tony Marelli presented relaxation skills and stress-reduction techniques. She attended a panel discussion that involved several clients discussing what services, approaches, and workers' styles they felt were most helpful. Andrea herself had presented the results of her research on the impact of cultural sensitivity training on worker–client relationships.

But it was the closing ceremony that had left Andrea with the afterglow that she would carry into the evening and back to work tomorrow. Kay Landon was the facilitator. She led those attending through a series of reflections on the work of the past year, an update of current conditions in the Northside community, and a guided fantasy experience of where they could be one year from now. As the experience drew to a close, Kay invited participants to share what being a social worker meant to them. It was Damon Edwards' words that still rang in Andrea's thoughts:

> We are in a beautiful place here. We are social workers. We have the opportunity to know people. Some are people similar to others we might have run into anyway. But many are people that we would never know in any other context. They all fascinate us because each brings his or her own unique way. They are resources to us. They have taught us more about human diversity than we have learned in textbooks.

We are in an important place here. We sit at the crossroads because, as social workers we connect to people at all different levels. We are the elevators of society's people. We pick them up in one place and go with them to where they want to go. We understand the connections and the connectors.

We are in a challenging place here. We weave science and art because social work practice needs spontaneity with precision. Clients aren't simple, and neither are we. And all that is gold does not glitter.

We are in a vulnerable place here. People show us their pain. They share their reality and shake our beliefs. They swamp our perspectives as we work for their goals. And just when we get there, we let them go.

We are in the right place here. Somehow, we've always been on the way. The world has nurtured us, and now we nurture it in return. Just as all universes seek balance, we too work as part of our world's solution. We are naturals. We revel in the opportunities for the world and for us.

References

Chapter 1

Dennison, S. T., Poole, J., & Qaqish, B. (2007). Students' perceptions of social work: Implications for strengthening the image of social work among college students. *Social Work*, *52*(4), 350–360. doi: 10.1093/sw/52.4.350

Dessel, A., Rogge, M. E., & Garlington, S. B. (2006). Using intergroup dialogue to promote social justice and change. *Social Work*, *51*(4), 303–315. doi: 10.1093/sw/51.4.303

DuBois, B., & Miley, K. K. (2014). *Social work: An empowering profession* (8th ed.). Boston: Pearson.

Freeman, M. L., & Valentine, D. P. (2004). Through the eyes of Hollywood: Images of social workers in film. *Social Work*, *49*(2), 151–161.

Hawkins, L., Fook, J., & Ryan, M. (2001). Social workers' use of the language of social justice. *British Journal of Social Work*, *31*, 1–13.

Healy, K. (2001). Reinventing critical social work: Challenges from practice, context and postmodernism. *Critical Social Work*, *2*(1). Retrieved June 8, 2015, from http://www1.uwindsor.ca/criticalsocialwork/reinventing-critical-social-work-challenges-from-practice-context-and-postmodernism

International Federation of Social Workers & International Association of Schools of Social Work [IFSW & IASSW]. (2004). *Ethics in social work, statement of principles*. Retrieved June 10, 2011, from www.ifsw.org/f38000032.html

International Federation of Social Workers. (2014). *Global definition of social work*. Retrieved September 15, 2014, from http://ifsw.org/get-involved/global-definition-of-social-work/

Karger, H. J., & Hernandez, M. T. (2004). The decline of the public intellectual in social work. *Journal of Sociology & Social Welfare*, *31*(3), 51–68.

Maluccio, A. N. (1981). Competence-oriented social work practice: An ecological approach. In A. N. Maluccio (Ed.), *Promoting competence in clients: A new/old approach to social work practice* (pp. 1–24). New York: The Free Press.

Miley, K. K., & DuBois, B. (2005, February). *Social work image: Drawing on the traditions of social work*. Presented at Council on Social Work Education Annual Program Meeting, Anaheim, CA.

National Association of Social Workers. (1981). *Standards for the classification of social work practice: Policy statement 4*. Silver Spring, MD: Author.

National Association of Social Workers [NASW]. (1999). *Code of ethics of the National Association of Social Workers*. Washington, DC: Author.

Olson, J. J. (2007). Social work's professional and social justice projects: Discourses in conflict. *Journal of Progressive Human Services*, *18*(1), 45–69. doi: 10.1300/J059v18n01_04

Reisch, M. (2002). Defining social justice in a socially unjust world. *Families in Society*, *83*(4), 343–354.

Reisch, M., & Andrews, J. (2004). *The road not taken: A history of radical social work in the United States*. New York: Brunner-Routledge.

Schorr, A. L. (1985). Professional practice as policy. *Social Service Review*, *59*, 178–196.

Searing, H. (2003). *The crisis in social work: The radical solution*. Retrieved June 5, 2008, from www.radical.org.uk/barefoot/crisis.htm

Smalley, R. (1967). *Theory for social work practice*. New York: Columbia University Press.

Specht, H. (1983). Policy issues in clinical practice. In A. Rosenblatt & D. Waldfogel (Eds.), *Handbook of clinical social work* (pp. 721–730). San Francisco, CA: Jossey-Bass.

Specht, H., & Courtney, M. E. (1994). *Unfaithful angels: How social work has abandoned its mission*. New York: The Free Press.

Tracy, B., & DuBois, B. (1987, September). *Information model for generalist social work practice*. Paper presented at the meeting of the Baccalaureate Program Directors of Social Work Programs, Kansas City, KS.

Whitaker, T., Weismiller, T., & Clark, E. (2006). *Assuring the sufficiency of a frontline workforce: A national study of licensed social workers*. Washington, DC: National Association of Social Workers. Retrieved June 8, 2015, from http://workforce.socialworkers.org/studies/nasw_06_execsummary.pdf

Zugazaga, C. B., Surette, R. B., Mendez, M., & Otto, C. W. (2006). Social worker perceptions of the portrayal of the profession in the news and entertainment media: An exploratory study. *Journal of Social Work Education*, *42*(3), 621–636. doi: 10.5175/JSWE.2006.200500502

Chapter 2

Abrams, L. G., & Moio, J. A. (2009). Critical race theory and the cultural competence dilemma in social work education. *Journal of Social Work Education*, *45*(2), 245–261.

American Psychiatric Association. (2013). *Diagnostic and statistical manual of mental disorders* (5th ed.). Washington, DC: Author.

American Psychological Association [APA]. (2015). *Stress in America: Paying with our health.* Washington, D.C.: Author. Retrieved May 15, 2015, from www.apa.org/news/press/releases/stress/2014/stress-report.pdf

Anda, R. (n.d.). *The health and social impact of growing up with adverse childhood experiences: The human and economic costs of the status quo.* Retrieved May 20, 2015, from www.nacoa.org/pdfs/Anda%20NACoA%20Review_web.pdf

Anderson, R. E., Carter, I., & Lowe, G. (1999). *Human behavior in the social environment: A social systems approach* (5th ed.). New York: Aldine de Gruyter.

Baines, D. (1997). Feminist social work in the inner-city: The challenges of race, class, and gender. *Affilia, 12*(3), 297–317.

Baines, D. (Ed.). (2007). *Doing anti-oppressive practice: Building transformative politicized social work.* Halifax, NS: Fernwood.

Bartlett, H. (1970). *The common base of social work practice.* New York: National Association of Social Workers.

Booth, J., Ayers, S. L., & Marsiglia, F. F. (2012). Perceived neighborhood safety and psychological distress: Exploring protective factors. *Journal of Sociology and Social Welfare, 39*(4), 137–156.

Bricker-Jenkins, M. (1991). The propositions and assumptions of feminist social work practice. In M. Bricker-Jenkins, N. R. Hooyman, & N. Gottlieb (Eds.), *Feminist social work practice in clinical settings* (pp. 271–303). Newbury Park, CA: Sage.

Carp, J. M. (2010). Resiliency: The essence of survival in chaos. *Families in Society, 91*(3), 266–271.

Carr, E. W. (2003). Rethinking empowerment theory using a feminist lens: The importance of process. *Affilia, 18*(1), 8–20.

Carter, B., & McGoldrick, M. (2005). *The expanded family life cycle: Individual, family, and social perspectives* (3rd ed.). Boston: Allyn & Bacon.

Combs-Orme, T. (2012). Epigenetics and the social work imperative. *Social Work, 58*(1), 23–30. doi: 10.1093/sw/sws052

Cooney, C. A. (2007). Epigenetics: DNA-based mirror of our environment? *Disease Markers, 23,* 121–137.

Corcoran, J., & Nichols-Casebolt, A. (2004). Risk and resilience ecological framework for assessment and goal formulation. *Child and Adolescent Social Work Journal, 21*(3), 211–235.

Cortes, R. T., & Lee, M. (2012). The interaction of genes, behavior, and social environment. *Today's Research on Aging.* Population Reference Bureau. Retrieved May 21, 2015, from www.prb.org/pdf12/TodaysResearchAging27.pdf

Council on Social Work Education [CSWE]. (2012). *Advanced social work practice in trauma.* Retrieved May 20, 2015, from www.cswe.org/File.aspx?id=63842

Daniel, C. D. (2008). From liberal pluralism to critical multiculturalism: The need for a paradigm shift in multicultural education for social work practice in the United States. *Journal of Progressive Human Services, 19*(1), 19–38. doi: 10.1080/10428230802070215

Delgado, R., & Stefancic, J. (2007). Critical race theory. *Humanity & Society, 31,* 133–145.

Delgado, R., & Stefancic, J. (2012). *Critical race theory: An introduction* (2nd ed.). New York: New York University Press.

Diaz Anzoldua, A., Diaz-Martinez, A., & Diaz-Martinez, L. R. (2011). The complex interplay of genetics, epigenetics, and environment in the predisposition to alcohol dependence. *Salud Mental, 34*(2), 157–166.

Elder, G. H. (1994). Time, human agency and social change: Perspectives on the life course. *Social Psychology Quarterly, 57*(1), 4–13.

Elder, G. H. (1998). The life course as developmental theory. *Child Development, 69*(1), 1–12.

Elder, G. H. (2001). Families, social change, and individual lives. *Marriage and Family Review, 31*(1/2), 177–192.

Erikson, E. H. (1963). *Childhood and society* (2nd ed.). New York: Norton.

Felitti, V. J., & Anda, R. F. (2010). The relationship of adverse childhood experiences to adult health, well-being, social function, and healthcare. In R. A. Lanius, E. Vermetten, & C. Pain (Eds.), *The impact of early life trauma on health and disease: The hidden epidemic* (pp. 77–87). Cambridge, England: Cambridge University Press.

Finkelhor, D., Turner, H., Hambry, S., & Ormund, R. (2011, October). Polyvictimization: Children's exposure to multiple types of violence, crime, and abuse. *Juvenile Justice Bulletin.* U.S. Department of Justice, Office of Juvenile Justice and Delinquency Prevention. Retrieved May 21, 2015, from www.ncjrs.gov/pdffiles1/ojjdp/235504.pdf

Finkelhor, D., Turner, H., Ormrod, R., Hamby, S., & Kracke, K. (2009, October). Children's exposure to violence: A comprehensive national survey. *Juvenile Justice Bulletin.* U.S. Department of Justice, Office of Juvenile Justice and Delinquency Prevention. Retrieved May 21, 2015, from https://www.ncjrs.gov/pdffiles1/ojjdp/227744.pdf

Fook, J. (2002). *Social work: Critical theory and practice.* Thousand Oaks, CA: Sage.

Garbarino, J. (1983). Social support networks: Rx for the helping professions. In J. K. Whittaker & J. Garbarino (Eds.), *Social support networks: Informal helping in the human services* (pp. 3–28). New York: Aldine de-Gruyter.

Gergen, K. J. (1994). *Realities and relationships: Soundings in social construction.* Cambridge, MA: Harvard University Press.

Germain, C. B. (1979). Ecology and social work. In C. B. Germain (Ed.), *Social work practice: People and environments* (pp. 1–22). New York: Columbia University Press.

Germain, C. B. (1983). Using social and physical environments. In A. Rosenblatt & D. Waldfogel (Eds.), *Handbook of clinical social work* (pp. 110–133). San Francisco, CA: Jossey-Bass.

Germain, C. B., & Gitterman, A. (1996). *The life model of social work practice: Advances in theory and practice.* New York: Columbia University Press.

Gilbert, S. F. (2009). Aging and cancer as diseases of epigenesis. *Journal of Biosciences, 34*(4), 601–604.

Gitterman, A., & Germain, C. B. (2008). Ecological framework. In T. Mizrahi & L. E. Davis (Eds.), *Encyclopedia of social work: Vol. 1* (20th ed., pp. 97–102). Washington, DC: NASW Press.

Gray, M., & Webb, S. A. (2013). Critical social work. In M. Gray & S. A. Webb (Eds.), *Social work theories and methods* (2nd ed., pp. 99–109). London: Sage.

Greene, G. J., & Lee, M. Y. (2002). The social construction of empowerment. In M. O'Melia & K. K. Miley (Eds.), *Pathways to power: Readings in contextual social work practice* (pp. 175–201). Boston: Allyn & Bacon.

Greene, G. J., Jensen, C., & Jones, D. H. (1996). A constructive perspective on clinical social work practice with ethnically diverse clients. *Social Work, 41*(2), 172–180.

Greene, R. (2010). Holocaust survivors: Resilience revisited. *Journal of Human Behavior in the Social Environment, 20*(4), 411–422. doi: 10.1080/10911350903269963

Greene, R. R., & Cohen, H. L. (2005). Social work with older adults and their families: Changing practice paradigms. *Families in Society, 86*(3), 367–373.

Gutiérrez, L. M., & Lewis, E. A. (1998). A feminist perspective on organizing with women of color. In F. G. Rivera & J. L. Erlich (Eds.), *Community organizing in a diverse society* (pp. 97–115). Boston: Allyn & Bacon.

Hamblen, J. (2013). *What is PTSD?* Washington, DC: National Center on PTSD, U.S. Department of Veterans' Affairs. Retrieved May 21, 2015, from www.ptsd.va.gov/professional /continuing_ed/transcript-pdf/what-is-ptsd.pdf

Harris, P. B. (2008). Another wrinkle in the debate about successful aging: The undervalued concept of resilience and the lived experience of dementia. *International Journal of Aging & Human Development, 67*(1), 43–61.

Heim, C., & Binder, E. B. (2012). Current research trends in early life stress and depression: Review of human studies on sensitive periods, gene-environment interactions, and epigenetics. *Experimental Neurology, 233*, 102–111. doi: 10.1016/j.expneurol.2011.10.032

Hurley, R. A. (2013). *Windows to the brain: Neuropsychiatry of TBI.* Washington, DC: National Center on PTSD, U.S. Department of Veterans' Affairs. Retrieved May 21, 2015, from www .ptsd.va.gov/professional/continuing_ed/transcript-pdf /traumatic-brain-injury.pdf

Hutchinson, E. D. (2005). The life course perspective: A promising approach for bridging the micro and macro worlds for social workers. *Families in Society, 86*(1), 143–152.

Hyde, C. A. (2008). Feminist social work practice. In T. Mizrahi & L. E. Davis (Eds.), *Encyclopedia of social work: Vol. 2* (20th ed., pp. 216–221). Washington, DC: NASW Press.

Kalil, J. A. (2015). Childhood poverty and parental stress: Important determinants of health. *UBC Medical Journal, 6*(2), 41–43. doi: 10.1111/cpsp.12004

Keenan, E. K. (2004). From sociocultural categories to socially located relations: Using critical theory in social work practice. *Families in Society, 85*(4), 539–548.

Kemp, S. P., & Brandwein, R. (2010). Feminisms and social work in the United States: An intertwined history. *Affilia: Journal of Women and Social Work, 25*(4), 341–364. doi: 10.1177/0886/099/0384075

Kolivoski, K. M., Weaver, A., & Constance-Huggins, M. (2014). Critical race theory: Opportunities for application in social work practice and policy. *Families in Society, 95*(4), 269–276. doi: 10.1606/1044-3894.2014.95.36

Kondrat, M. E. (2002). Actor-centered social work: Revisioning "person-in-environment" through a critical theory lens. *Social Work, 47*(4), 435–448.

Kotler, M., Iancu, I., Efroni, R., & Amir, M. (2001). Anger, impulsivity, social support, and suicide risk in patients with posttraumatic stress disorder. *Journal of Nervous and Mental Disease, 189*(3), 162–167.

Lai, B. S., Kelley, M. L., Harrison, K. M., Thompson, J. E., & Self-Brown, S. (2015). Posttraumatic stress, anxiety, and depression symptoms among children after Hurricane Katrina: A latent profile analysis. *Journal of Child and Family Studies, 24*, 1262–1270. doi: 10.1007/s10826-014-9934-3

Lee, J. S., Ahn, Y. S., Jeong, K. S., Chae, J. H., & Choi, K. S. (2014). Resilience buffers the impact of traumatic events on the development of PTSD symptoms in firefighters. *Journal of Affective Disorders, 162*, 128–133. doi: 10.1016/j.jad.2014.02.031

Li, Y., Cao, F., Cao, D., Wang, Q., & Cui, N. (2012). Predictors of posttraumatic growth among parents of children undergoing inpatient corrective surgery for congenital disease. *Journal of Pediatric Surgery, 47*(11), 2011–2021. doi: 10.1016 /j.jpedsurg.2012.07.005

Little, M., Axford, N., & Morpeth, L. (2004). Research review: Risk and protection in the context of services for children in need. *Child and Family Social Work, 9*, 105–117.

Mancini, A. D., & Bonanno, G. A. (2009). Predictors and parameters of resilience to loss: Toward an individual differences model. *Journal of Personality, 77*(6), 1805–1832. doi: 10.1111/j.1467-6494.2009.00601.x

Masten, A. S. (2005). Children who overcome adversity to succeed in life. In B. A. Warren (Ed.), *Just in time research: Resilient communities.* Minneapolis, MN: University of Minnesota. Retrieved June 7, 2011, from www.extension.umn.edu /distribution/ familydevelopment/components/7565_06.html

McGoldrick, M., Carter, B., & Garcia-Preto, N. (2015). *The expanding family life cycle: Individual, family, and social perspectives* (5th ed.). Boston: Pearson.

McGovern, M. P., Lambert-Harris, C., Xie, H., Meier, A., McLeman, B., & Saunders, E. (2015). A randomized controlled trial of treatments for co-occurring substance use disorders and PTSD. *Addiction* (Epub ahead of print). doi: 10.1111/add.12943

Mullaly, B. (2002). *Challenging oppression: A critical social work approach.* Ontario, Canada: Oxford University Press.

National Institute of Health [NIH]. (2015). *All about the Human Genome Project.* National Human Genome Research Institute. Retrieved May 16, 2015, from www.genome.gov/10001772

National Scientific Council on the Developing Child [NCSDC]. (2005/2014). *Excessive stress disrupts the architecture of the developing brain: Working paper 3* (updated ed.). Retrieved June 6, 2015, from http://www.developingchild.harvard.edu

O'Melia, M. (1991). *Generalist perspectives in case coordination.* Workshop presentation at the Association for Retarded Citizens of Rock Island County, Rock Island, IL.

Olatunji, B. O., Ciesielski, B. G., & Tolin, D. F. (2014). Fear and loathing: A meta-analytic review of the specificity of anger in PTSD. *Behavioral Therapy*, 41(1), 93–105. doi: 10.1016/j.beth.2009.01.004

Oquendo, M., Brent, D. A., Birmaher, B., Greenhill, L., Kolko, D., Stanley, B., Zelazny, J., Burke, A. K., Firinciogullari, S., Ellis, S. P., & Mann, J. J. (2005). Posttraumatic stress disorder comorbid with major depression: Factors mediating the association with suicidal behavior. *American Journal of Psychiatry*, 162(3), 560–566.

Putnam, K. T., Harris, W. W., & Putnam, F. W. (2013). Synergistic childhood adversities and complex adult psychopathology. *Journal of Traumatic Stress*, 26(4), 435–442. doi: 10. 1002/jts.21833

Radley, J. J., Kabbaj, M., Jacobson, L., Heydendael, W., Yehuda, R., & Herman, J. P. (2011). Stress risk factors and stress-related pathology: Neuroplasticity, epigenetics and endophenotypes. *Stress*, 14(5), 481–497. doi: 10.3109/10253890.2011.604751

Rodgers, S. F. (2014). Posttraumatic growth. *Encyclopedia of social work* (online version). Washington, DC: NASW.

Rodrigues, A. J., Leão, P., Carvalho, M., Almeida, O. F. X., & Sousa, N. 2011. Potential programming of dopaminergic circuits by early life stress. *Psychopharmacology*, 214, 107–120. doi: 10.1007/s00213-010-2085-3

Ruch, G. (2002). From triangle to spiral: Reflective practice in social work education, practice and research. *Social Work Education*, 21(2), 199–216.

Salas, L. M., Sen, S., & Segal, E. A. (2010). Critical theory: Pathway from dichotomous to integrated social work practice. *Families in Society*, 91(1), 91–95. doi: 10.1606/1044-3894.3961

Salloum, A., Kondrat, D. C., Johnco, C., & Olson, K. R. (2015). The role of self-care on compassion satisfaction, burnout, and secondary trauma among child welfare workers. *Children and Youth Services Review*, 49, 54–61. doi: 1016/j.childyouth.2014.12.023

Sareen, J. (2014). Posttraumatic stress disorder in adults: Impact, comorbidity, risk factors, and treatment. *Canadian Journal of Psychiatry*, 59(9), 460–467.

Sasaki, A., DeVega, W. C., McGowan, P. O. (2013). Biological embedding in mental health: An epigenomic perspective. *Biochemical Cell Biology*, 91, 14–21. doi: org/10.1139/bcb-2012-0070

Saulnier, C. F. (1996). *Feminist theories and social work: Approaches and applications*. New York: Haworth Press.

Schneiderman, N., Ironson, G., & Siegel, S. D. (2005). Stress and health: Psychological, behavioral, and biological determinants. *Annual Review of Clinical Psychology*, 1, 607–628. doi: 10.1146/annurev.clinpsy.1.102803.144141

Schriver, J. M. (2015). *Human behavior and the social environment: Shirting paradigms in essential knowledge for social work* (6th ed.). Boston: Pearson.

Siporin, M. (1980). Ecological systems theory in social work. *Journal of Sociology and Social Welfare*, 7, 507–532.

Sisneros, J., Stakeman, C., Joyner, M., & Schmitz, C. E. (2008). *Critical multicultural social work*. Chicago, IL: Lyceum Books.

Sominsky, L., & Spencer, S. J. (2014). Eating behavior and stress: A Pathway to obesity. *Frontiers in Psychology*, 5, 434. Retrieved May 23, 2015, from journal.fronticrsin.org/article/10.3389/fpsyg.2014.00434/full doi: 10.3389/fpsyg.2014.00434

Sotiropoulos, I., Catania, C., Pinto, L. G., Silva, R., Pollerberg, G. E., Takashima, A., Sousa, N., & Almeida, O. F. X. (2011). Stress acts cumulatively to precipitate Alzheimer's disease–like tau pathology and cognitive deficits. *Journal of Neuroscience*, 31, 7840–7847. doi: 10.1523/JNEUROSCI.0730-11.2011

Sousa, N., & Almeida, O. F. X. (2012). Disconnection and reconnection: The morphological basis of (mal)adaptation to stress. *Trends in Neurosciences*, 35, 742–751. doi: 10.1016/j.tins.2012.08.006

Staufenbiel, S. M., Penninx, B. W., Spijker, A. T., Elzinga, B. M., & van Rossum, E. F. (2013). Hair cortisol, stress exposure, and mental health in humans: A systematic review. *Psychoneuroendocrinology*, 38(8), 1220–1235. doi: 10.1016/j.psyneuen.2012.11.015

Street, A. (2013). *Sexual harassment and sexual assault during military service*. Washington, DC: National Center on PTSD, U.S. Department of Veterans' Affairs. Retrieved May 21, 2015, from www.ptsd.va.gov/professional/continuing_ed/transcript-pdf/military_sexual_trauma.pdf

Talbot, L. S., Maquen, S., Epel, E. S., Metzler, T. J., & Nevlanm, T. C. (2013). Posttraumatic stress disorder is associated with emotional earing. *Journal of Traumatic Stress*, 26(4), 521–525. doi: 10.1002/jts.21824

Teixeira, R. R., Diaz, M. M., Santos, T. V., Bernardes, J. T., Peixoto, L. G., Bocanegra, O. O., Neto, M. B., & Espindola, F. S. (2015). Chronic stress induces a hyporeactivity of the autonomic nervous system in response to acute mental stressor and impairs cognitive performance in business executives. *PLoS One*, 10(3): e0119025. doi: 10.1371/journal.pone.0119025

Thompson, R. A. (2014). Stress and child development. *Future of Children*, 24(1), 41–59.

Tunc-Ozcan, E., Sittig, L. J., Harper, K. M., Graf, E. N., & Redel, E. E. (2014). Hypothesis: Genetic and epigenetic risk factors interact to modulate vulnerability and resilience to FASD. *Frontiers in Genetics*, 5, 1–11. doi: 10.3389/fgene2014.00261

Turner, S. G., & Maschi, T. M. (2015). Feminist and empowerment theory and social work practice. *Journal of Social Work Practice: Psychotherapeutic Approaches in Health, Welfare and the Community*, 29(2), 151–162. doi: 10.1080/02650533.2014.941282

Tyrka, A. R., Burgers, D. E., Phillip, N. S., Price, L. H., & Carpenter, L. L. (2013). The neurobiological correlates of childhood adversity and implications for treatment. *Acta Psuchiatrica Scandinavica*, 128, 434–447. doi: 10.1111/acps.12143

Tyrka, A. R., Price, L. H., Marsit, C., Walters, O. C., & Carpenter, L. L. (2012). Childhood adversity and epigenetic modulation of the leukocyte glucocorticoid receptor: Preliminary findings in healthy adults. *PLoS One*, 7(1), 1–8.

von Bertalanffy, L. (1968). *General system theory*. New York: George Braziller.

Wheeler-Brooks, J. (2009). Structuration theory and critical consciousness: Potential applications for social work practice. *Journal of Sociology & Social Welfare*, 34(1), 123–140.

Williams, C. C. (2002). A rationale for an anti-racist entry point to anti-oppressive social work in mental health. *Critical Social Work*, 2(2), 20–31. Retrieved June 4, 2015, from http://www1.uwindsor.ca/criticalsocialwork/a-rationale-for-an-anti-racist-entry-point-to-anti-oppressive-social-work-in-mental-health-services

Chapter 3

Bem, S. L. (1993). *The lenses of gender: Transforming the debate on sexual inequality*. New Haven, CT: Yale University Press.

Berlin, S. (2005). The value of acceptance in social work direct practice: A historical and contemporary view. *Social Service Review*, 79(3), 482–510.

Biestek, F. P. (1957). *The casework relationship*. Chicago, IL: Loyola University Press.

Briggs, H. E., Briggs, A. D., & Leary, J. D. (2005). Promoting culturally competent systems of care through statewide family advocacy networks. *Best Practices in Mental Health*, 1(2), 77–99.

Cartledge, G., Kea, C., & Simmons-Reed, E. (2002). Serving culturally diverse children with serious emotional disturbance and their families. *Journal of Child and Family Studies*, 11(1), 113–126.

Castex, G. (1994). The function of stereotyping processes: A challenge for practice. In L. G. Gardella, R. Daniel, M. C. Joyner, N. Mokuau, & J. M. Schriver (Eds.), *In memory of Ronald C. Federico: A BPD Festschrift* (pp. 8–16). Springfield, MO: Association of Baccalaureate Program Directors.

Choi, K.-H., & Wynne, M. E. (2000). Providing services to Asian Americans with developmental disabilities and their families: Mainstream service providers' perspectives. *Community Mental Health Journal*, 36(6), 589–595.

Chow, J. C.-C., & Austin, M. J. (2008). The culturally responsive social service agency: The application of an evolving definition to a case study. *Administration in Social Work*, 32(4), 39–63. doi: 10.1080/03643100802293832

Dean, R. G. (2001). The myth of cross-cultural competence. *Families in Society*, 82(6), 623–630.

Dolgoff, R., Loewenberg, F. M., & Harrington, D. (2008). *Ethical decisions for social work practice* (8th ed.). Pacific Grove, CA: Brooks/Cole.

Goldstein, H. (1987). The neglected moral link in social work practice. *Social Work*, 32, 181–186.

Gomez, A. (2002). Measuring the cultural pulse of service providers. *Focal Point: A National Bulletin on Family Support and Children's Mental Health*, 16(2), 13–15. Retrieved July 28, 2015, from www.pathwaysrtc.pdx.edu/pdf/fpF02.pdf

Green, J. W. (1999). *Cultural awareness in the human services: A multi-ethnic approach* (3rd ed.). Boston: Allyn & Bacon.

Hopps, J. G., Pinderhughes, E., & Shankar, R. (1995). *The power to care: Clinical practice effectiveness with overwhelmed clients*. New York: The Free Press.

Huang, L. N. (2002). Reflections on cultural competence: A need for renewed urgency. *Focal Point: A National Bulletin on Family Support and Children's Mental Health*, 16(2), 4–7. Retrieved June 8, 2015, from http://www.pathwaysrtc.pdx.edu/pdf/fpF02.pdf

Johnson, L. C., & Yanca, S. (2010). *Social work practice: A generalist approach* (10th ed.). Boston: Pearson.

Kulis, S., Marsiglia, F. F., Elek, E., Dustman, P., Wagstaff, D., & Hecht, M. L. (2005). Mexican/Mexican American adolescents and keepin' it REAL: An evidence-based substance use prevention program. *Children & Schools*, 27(3), 133–145.

Lee, M.-Y., & Greene, G. J. (1999). A social constructivist framework for integrating cross-cultural issues in teaching clinical social work. *Journal of Social Work Education*, 35(1), 21–37.

Lum, D. (2004). *Social work with people of color: A process-stage approach* (5th ed.). Pacific Grove, CA: Brooks/Cole.

McIntosh, P. (1998). White privilege: Unpacking the invisible knapsack. In M. McGoldrick (Ed.), *Re-visioning family therapy: Race, culture, and gender in clinical practice* (pp. 147–152). New York: Guilford Press.

Miller, O. A., & Gaston, R. J. (2003). A model of culture-centered child welfare practice. *Child Welfare*, 82(2), 235–250.

Napoli, M. (1999). The non-Indian therapist working with American Indian clients: Transference-countertransference implications. *Psychoanalytic Social Work*, 6(1), 25–47.

National Association of Social Workers [NASW]. (1999). *Code of ethics of the National Association of Social Workers*. Washington, D.C.: Author.

National Association of Social Workers [NASW]. (2001a). *National standards for cultural competence in social work practice*. Washington, D.C.: NASW Press.

O'Melia, M. (1998, October). *Proactive responding: Paths toward diverse strengths*. Paper presented at Bacclaureate Program Directors 16th Annual Conference, Albuquerque, NM.

Raheim, S. (2002). Cultural competence: A requirement of empowerment practice. In M. O'Melia & K. K. Miley (Eds.), *Pathways to power: Readings in contextual social work practice* (pp. 95–107). Boston: Allyn & Bacon.

Reamer, F. G. (2008). Ethics and values. In T. Mizrahi & L. E. Davis (Eds.), *Encyclopedia of social work: Vol. 2* (20th ed., pp. 143–151). Washington, DC: NASW Press.

Rosenthal, R., & Jacobson, L. (1968). *Pygmalion in the classroom*. New York: Holt, Rinehart and Winston.

Schlosser, L. Z. (2003). Christian privilege: Breaking a sacred taboo. *Journal of Multicultural Counseling and Development*, 31, 44–51.

Schriver, J. M. (2015). *Human behavior and the social environment: Shirting paradigms in essential knowledge for social work* (6th ed.). Boston: Pearson.

Siporin, M. (1983). Morality and immorality in working with clients. *Social Thought*, 9(4), 10–28.

Siporin, M. (1985). Current social work perspectives on clinical practice. *Clinical Social Work Journal*, 13, 198–217.

Sue, D. W. (2010a). *Microaggressions and marginality: Manifestations, dynamics, and impact*. New York: Wiley.

Sue, D. W. (2010b). *Microaggressions in everyday life: Race, gender, and sexual orientation*. New York: Wiley.

Sue, D. W., & Sue, D. (2013). *Counseling the culturally diverse: Theory and practice* (6th ed.). Hoboken, NJ: John Wiley & Sons.

Sue, D. W., Capodilupo, C. M., Torino, G. C., Bucceri, J. M., Holder, A. M. B., Nadal, K. L., et al. (2007). Racial microaggressions in everyday life. *American Psychologist, 62*(4), 271–286. doi: 10.1037/0003-066X.62.4.271

Sue, D. W., Nadal, K. L., Capodilupo, C. M., Lin, A. I., Torino, G. C., & Rivera, D. P. (2008). Racial microaggressions against Black Americans: Implications for counseling. *Journal of Counseling & Development, 86*, 330–338. doi: 10.1002/j.1556-6678.2008.tb00517

Tillich, P. (1962). The philosophy of social work. *Social Service Review, 36*(1), 13–16.

Trevithick, P. (2003). Effective relationship-based practice: A theoretical exploration. *Journal of Social Work Practice, 17*(2), 163–176.

Walker, J. S., & Cook, J. (2002). Caregivers' perspectives on cultural competence. *Focal Point: A National Bulletin on Family Support and Children's Mental Health, 16*(2), 35–37. Retrieved July 31, 2015, from www.pathwaysrtc.pdx.edu/pdf/fpF02.pdf

Walker, R., & Staton, M. (2000). Multiculturalism in social work ethics. *Journal of Social Work Education, 36*(3), 449–462.

Watzlawick, P., Bavelas, J. M., & Jackson, D. D. (1967). *Pragmatics of human communication.* New York: W. W. Norton.

Weaver, H. (1999). Indigenous people and the social work profession: Defining culturally competent services. *Social Work, 44*(3), 217–225.

Webb, S. A. (2000). The politics of social work: Power and subjectivity. *Critical Social Work, 1*(2). Retrieved June 5, 2015, from www1.uwindsor.ca/criticalsocialwork/the-politics-of-social-work-power-and-subjectivity

Weick, A., & Chamberlain, R. (2002). Putting problems in their place: Further explorations in the strengths perspective. In D. Saleebey (Ed.), *The strengths perspective in social work practice* (3rd ed., pp. 95–105). Boston: Allyn & Bacon.

Chapter 4

Ackerson, B. J., & Harrison, W. D. (2000). Practitioner's perceptions of empowerment. *Families in Society, 81*(3), 238–244.

Baines, D. (Ed.). (2007). *Doing anti-oppressive practice: Building transformative politicized social work.* Halifax, NS: Fernwood.

Breton, M. (1993). Relating competence-promotion and empowerment. *Journal of Progressive Human Services, 5*(1), 27–44.

Breton, M. (1994). On the meaning of empowerment and empowerment-oriented social work practice. *Social Work with Groups, 17*(3), 23–37.

Breton, M. (2002). Empowerment practice in Canada and the United States: Restoring policy issues at the center of social work. *Social Policy Journal, 1*(1), 19–34.

Breton, M. (2004). An empowerment perspective. In C. D. Garvin, L. M. Gutiérrez, & M. J. Galinsky (Eds.), *Handbook of social work with groups* (pp. 58–75). New York: Guilford Press.

Breton, M. (2006). Path dependence and the place of social action in social work practice. *Social Work with Groups, 29*(4), 25–44. doi: 10.1300/J009v29n04_03

Carr, E. W. (2003). Rethinking empowerment theory using a feminist lens: The importance of process. *Affilia, 18*(1), 8–20.

Cocker, C., & Hafford-Letchfield, T. (2014). *Rethinking anti-discriminatory and anti-oppressive theories for social work.* Basingtoke, England: Palgrove-Macmillion.

Cohen, M. B. (1998). Perceptions of power in client/worker relationships. *Families in Society, 79*(4), 433–442.

Fisher, B. J., & Gosselink, C. A. (2008). Enhancing the efficacy and empowerment of older adults through group formation. *Journal of Gerontological Social Work, 51*(1/2), 2–18. doi: 10.1080/01634370801967513

Franco, L. M., Mckay, M., Miranda, A., Chambers, N., Paulino, A., & Lawrence, R. (2007). Voices from the community: Key ingredients for community collaboration. *Social Work in Mental Health, 5*(3/4), 313–331. doi: 10.1300/J200v05n03_04

Gil, D. G. (2002). Challenging injustice and oppression. In M. O'Melia & K. K. Miley (Eds.), *Pathways to power: Readings in contextual social work practice* (pp. 35–54). Boston: Allyn & Bacon.

Gitterman, A., & Shulman, L. (2005). Preface. In A. Gitterman & L. Shulman (Eds.), *Mutual aid groups, vulnerable and resilient populations, and the life cycle* (3rd ed., pp. ix–xv). New York: Columbia University Press.

Goldstein, H. (1987). The neglected moral link in social work practice. *Social Work, 32*, 181–186.

Gummer, B. (1983). Consumerism and clients rights. In A. Rosenblatt & D. Waldfogel (Eds.), *Handbook of clinical social work* (pp. 920–938). San Francisco, CA: Jossey-Bass.

Gutiérrez, L., DeLois, K., & GlenMaye, L. (1995a). Understanding empowerment practice: Building on practitioner-based knowledge. *Families in Society, 76*, 534–542.

Gutiérrez, L., GlenMaye, L., & DeLois, K. (1995b). The organizational context of empowerment practice: Implications for social work administration. *Social Work, 40*, 249–258.

Gutiérrez, L. M. (1991). Empowering women of color: A feminist model. In M. Bricker-Jenkins, N. R. Hooyman, & N. Gottlieb (Eds.), *Feminist social work practice in clinical settings* (pp. 199–214). Newbury Park, CA: Sage.

Hardiman, E. R. (2004). Networks of caring: A qualitative study of social support in consumer-run mental health agencies. *Qualitative Social Work, 3*(4), 431–448.

Hernandez, P., Almeid, A. R., & Dolen-Del-Vecchio, K. (2005). Critical consciousness, accountability, and empowerment: Key processes for helping families heal. *Family Process, 44*(1), 105–119.

Hines, J. M. (2012). Using an anti-oppressive framework in social work practice with lesbians. *Journal of Gay and Lesbian Social Services, 24*(1), 23–39. doi: 10.1080/105538720.2011.611103

Hodge, D. R. (2007). Social justice and people of faith: A transnational perspective. *Social Work, 52*(2), 139–148. doi: 10.1093/sw/52.2.139

Jacobson, M., & Rugeley, C. (2007). Community-based participatory research: Group work for social justice and community change. *Social Work with Groups, 30*(4), 21–39. doi: 10.1300/J009v30n04_03

Kieffer, C. (1984). Citizen empowerment: A developmental perspective. In J. Rappaport, C. Swift, & R. Hess (Eds.), *Studies in empowerment: Toward understanding and action* (pp. 9–36). New York: Haworth Press.

Larson, G. (2008). Anti-oppressive practice in mental health. *Journal of Progressive Human Services, 19*(1), 31–54. doi: 10.1080/10428230802070223

Lee, J. A. B. (2001). *An empowerment approach to social work practice: Building the beloved community* (2nd ed.). New York: Columbia University Press.

Lenrow, P. B., & Burch, R. W. (1981). Mutual aid and professional services: Opposing or complementary? In B. H. Gottlieb (Ed.), *Social networks and social supports: Vol. 4. Sage studies in community mental health* (pp. 233–257). Beverly Hills, CA: Sage.

Leonardsen, D. (2007). Empowerment in social work: An individual vs. a relational perspective. *International Journal of Social Welfare, 16*, 3–11.

Link, B. G., & Phelan, J. C. (2001). Conceptualizing stigma. *Annual Review of Sociology, 27*, 363–385.

Macleod, J., & Nelson, G. (2000). Programs for the promotion of family wellness and the prevention of child maltreatment: A meta-analytic review. *Child Abuse & Neglect, 24*(9), 1127–1149.

Malekoff, A. (2008). Transforming trauma and empowering children and adolescents in the aftermath of disaster through group work. *Social Work with Groups, 31*(1), 29–52. doi: 10.1300/J009v31n01_04

May, R. (1972). *Power and innocence: A search for the sources of violence.* New York: W. W. Norton.

Miley, K. K. (2011, January). *Empowerment social work.* Presentation at St. Ambrose University, Davenport, IA.

Miley, K. K., & DuBois, B. (2004, May). *Ethical preferences for the clinical practice of empowerment social work.* Presented at the Fourth International Conference on Health and Mental Health, Quebec City, Canada.

Miley, K. K., & DuBois, B. (2005, February). *Social work image: Drawing on the traditions of social work.* Presented at Council on Social Work Education Annual Program Meeting, Anaheim, CA.

Miley, K. K., & DuBois, B. (2007). Ethical preferences for the clinical practice of empowerment social work. *Social Work in Health Care, 44*(1/2), 29–44. doi: 10.1300/J010v44n01_04

National Association of Social Workers [NASW]. (1999). *Code of ethics of the National Association of Social Workers.* Washington, D.C.: Author.

National Association of Social Workers [NASW]. (2002). *Pippahpack: Promoting positive youth environments.* Washington, D.C.: NASW Press.

Nelson, G., Lord, J., & Ochocka, J. (2001). Empowerment and mental health in community: Narratives of psychiatric consumer/survivors. *Journal of Community & Applied Social Psychology, 11*, 125–142.

Nicotera, N., & Kang, H.-K. (2009). Beyond diversity courses: Strategies for integrating critical consciousness across social work curriculum. *Journal of Teaching in Social Work, 29*, 188–203. doi: 10.1080/08841230802240738

Parsons, R. J. (2001). Specific practice strategies for empowerment-based practice with women: A study of two groups. *Affilia, 16*(2), 159–179.

Parsons, R. J. (2008). Empowerment practice. In T. Mizrahi & L. E. Davis (Eds.), *Encyclopedia of social work: Vol. 2* (20th ed., pp. 123–126). Washington, DC: NASW Press.

Parsons, R. J., & East, J. (2013). Empowerment practice. In Franklin, C. (Ed.), *Encyclopedia of social work (online).* NASW Press and Oxford University Press. doi: 10/1093/acrefore/9730199975839.013.128

Rappaport, J. (1981). In praise of paradox: A social policy or empowerment over prevention. *American Journal of Community Psychology, 9*, 1–25.

Rappaport, J. (1985). The power of empowerment language. *Social Policy, 17*, 15–21.

Rappaport, J. (1987). Terms of empowerment/exemplars of prevention: Toward a theory for community psychology. *American Journal of Community Psychology, 15*(2), 121–144.

Ryan, W. (1976). *Blaming the victim* (rev. ed.). New York: Vintage Books.

Sakamoto, I., & Pitner, R. O. (2005). Use of critical consciousness in anti-oppressive social work practice: Disentangling power dynamics at personal and structural levels. *British Journal of Social Work, 35*(4), 435–452. doi: 10.1093/bjsw/bch190

Saleebey, D. (2009). *The strengths perspective in social work practice* (5th ed.). Boston: Pearson.

Solomon, B. B. (1976). *Black empowerment: Social work in oppressed communities.* New York: Columbia University Press.

Solomon, B. B. (1987). Human development: Sociocultural perspectives. In A. Minahan (Ed.), *Encyclopedia of social work: Vol. 1* (18th ed., pp. 856–866). Silver Spring, MD: National Association of Social Workers, Inc.

Strier, R., & Binyamin, S. (2010). Developing anti-oppressive services for the poor: A theoretical and organisational rationale. *British Journal of Social Work, 40*(6), 1908–1926. doi: 10.1093/bjsw/bcp122

Swift, C., & Levin, G. (1987). Empowerment: An emerging mental health technology. *Journal of Primary Prevention, 8*(1/2), 71–94.

Tower, K. D. (1994). Consumer-centered social work practice: Restoring client self-determination. *Social Work, 39*, 191–196.

Vojak, C. (2009). Choosing language: Social service framing and social justice. *British Journal of Social Work, 39*, 936–949. doi: 10.1093/bjsw/bcm144

Ward, N. (2009). Social exclusion, social identity and social work: Analyzing social exclusion from a material discursive perspective. *Social Work Education, 28*(3), 237–252. doi: 10.1080/02615470802659332

Washington, J., & Paylor, I. (2000). Social exclusion and inequalities in the United Kingdom. *Critical Social Work, 1*(2). Retrieved July 31, 2015, from www.uwindsor.ca /criticalsocialwork/social-exclusion-and-inequalities -in-the-united-Kingdom

Weick, A. (1980). Issues of power in social work practice. In A. Weick & S. T. Vandiver (Eds.), *Women, power, and change* (pp. 173–185). Washington, DC: NASW Press.

Weick, A., & Chamberlain, R. (2002). Putting problems in their place: Further explorations in the strengths perspective. In D. Saleebey (Ed.), *The strengths perspective in social work practice* (3rd ed., pp. 95–105). Boston: Allyn & Bacon.

Weick, A., Rapp, C., Sullivan, W. P., & Kisthardt, W. (1989). A strengths perspective for social work practice. *Social Work, 34,* 350–354.

Wheeler-Brooks, J. (2009). Structuration theory and critical consciousness: Potential applications for social work practice. *Journal of Sociology & Social Welfare, 34*(1), 123–140.

Whitley, D. M. (2011). Perceptions of family empowerment in African American custodial grandmothers raising grandchildren: Thoughts for research and practice. *Families in Society, 92*(4), 383–389. doi: 10.1606/1044-3894.4148

Chapter 5

DuBois, B., Miley, K. K., & O'Melia, M. (1993, March). *Applying an empowerment process in social work practice.* Paper presented at the Central Midwest Conference on Child Abuse, Moline, IL.

Dunst, C. J. (1993, April). *Empowerment strategies in human services programs.* Paper presented for the Central Midwest Conference on Child Abuse, Moline, IL.

Maluccio, A. N., & Libassi, M. F. (1984). Competence clarification in social work practice. *Social Thought, 10,* 51–58.

National Association of Social Workers [NASW]. (2010). *Social work imperatives for the next decade.* Retrieved October 21, 2014, from www.socialworkers.org/2010congress/documents /2010imperatives.pdf

Saleebey, D. (1992). Introduction: Power in the people. In D. Saleebey (Ed.), *The strengths perspective in social work practice* (pp. 3–17). New York: Longman.

Chapter 6

Abramson, L. Y., Seligman, M. E. P., & Teasdale, J. C. (1978). Learned helplessness in humans: Critique and reformulation. *Journal of Abnormal Psychology, 87,* 49–74.

Association of Social Work Boards. (2012). *Model social work practice act.* Retrieved September 17, 2014, from www.aswb .org/wp-content/uploads/2013/10/Model_law.pdf

Beresford, P., Croft, S., & Adshead, L. (2008). "We don't see her as a social worker": A service user case study of the importance of the social worker's relationship and humanity. *British Journal of Social Work, 38,* 1388–1407.

Berlin, S. (2005). The value of acceptance in social work direct practice: A historical and contemporary view. *Social Service Review, 79*(3), 482–510.

Book, H. E. (1988). Empathy: Misconceptions and misuses in psychotherapy. *American Journal of Psychiatry, 145*(4), 420–424.

Coates, D., Renzaglia, G. J., & Embree, M. C. (1983). When helping backfires: Help and helplessness. In J. D. Fisher, A. Nadler, & B. M. DePaulo (Eds.), *New directions in helping: Vol 1. Recipient reactions to aid* (pp. 251–279). New York: Academic Press.

Cohen, M. B. (1998). Perceptions of power in client/worker relationships. *Families in Society, 79*(4), 433–442.

Corey, G., Corey, M. S., Corey, C., & Callanan, P. (2015). *Issues and ethics in the helping professions* (9th ed.). Belmont, CA: Cengage.

Davies, R. L., Heslop, P., Onyett, S., & Soteriou, T. (2014). Effective support for those who are "hard to engage": A qualitative user-led study. *Journal of Mental Health, 23*(2), 62–66. doi: 10.3109/09638237.2013.841868

Dawson, K., & Berry, M. (2002). Engaging families in child welfare services: An evidence-based approach to best practice. *Child Welfare, 82*(2), 293–317.

Dean, R. G. (1993). Constructivism: An approach to clinical practice. *Smith College Studies in Social Work, 63*(2), 127–146.

Dempsey, I., & Dunst, C. J. (2004). Helpgiving styles and parent empowerment in families with a young child with a disability. *Journal of Intellectual & Developmental Disability, 29*(1), 40–51.

Dunst, C. J. (1993, April). *Empowerment strategies in human services programs.* Paper presented for the Central Midwest Conference on Child Abuse, Moline, IL.

Dunst, C. J., Boyd, K., Trivette, C. M., & Hamby, D. W. (2002). Family-oriented program models and professional help-giving practices. *Family Relations, 51*(3), 221–229.

Dunst, C. J., & Trivette, C. M. (1988). Helping, helplessness, and harm. In J. C. Witt, S. N. Elliot, & F. M. Gresham (Eds.), *Handbook of behavior therapy* (pp. 343–376). New York: Plenum Press.

Fischer, J. (1973). An eclectic approach to therapeutic casework. In J. Fischer (Ed.), *Interpersonal helping: Emerging approaches for social work practice* (pp. 317–335). Springfield, IL: Charles C Thomas.

Fuller, T. L., Paceley, M. S., & Schreiber, J. C. (2015). Differential response family assessments: Listening to what parents say about service helpfulness. *Child Abuse and Neglect, 29,* 7–17. doi: 10.1016/j.chiabu.2014.05.010

Graybeal, C. T. (2007). Evidence for the art of social work. *Families in Society, 88*(4), 513–523.

Gutiérrez, L., Moxley, D. P., Alvarez, A., & Johnson, A. K. (2005). The complexity of community empowerment. *Journal of Community Practice, 132,* 1–3.

Hopps, J. G., Pinderhughes, E., & Shankar, R. (1995). *The power to care: Clinical practice effectiveness with overwhelmed clients.* New York: The Free Press.

Iachini, A. L., Hock, R. M., Thomas, M., & Clone, S. (2015). Exploring the youth and parent perspective on practitioner behaviors that promote treatment engagement. *Journal of Family Social Work, 18*(1), 57–73. doi: 10.1080/10522158.2014.974293

Itzhaky, H., & Schwartz, C. (2000). Empowerment of parents of children with disabilities: The effect of community and personal variables. *Journal of Family Social Work, 5*(1), 21–36.

Ivanoff, A. M., Blythe, B. J., & Tripodi, T. (1994). *Involuntary clients in social work practice: A research-based approach.* New York: Aldine de Gruyter.

Keith-Lucas, A. (1972). *The giving and taking of help.* Chapel Hill: University of North Carolina Press.

Lum, D. (2004). *Social work with people of color: A process-stage approach* (5th ed.). Pacific Grove, CA: Brooks/Cole.

Maluccio, A. N. (1979). *Learning from clients.* New York: The Free Press.

Maluccio, A. N. (1981). Competence-oriented social work practice: An ecological approach. In A. N. Maluccio (Ed.), *Promoting competence in clients: A new/old approach to social work practice* (pp. 1–24). New York: The Free Press.

Meer, D., & VandeCreek, L. (2002). Cultural considerations in release of information. *Ethics & Behavior, 12*(2), 143–156.

National Association of Social Workers [NASW]. (1999). *Code of ethics of the National Association of Social Workers.* Washington, D.C.: Author.

National Association of Social Workers [NASW]. (2005c). *Social workers and psychotherapist-patient privilege: Jaffee v. Redmond revisited.* Retrieved June 9, 2008, from www.socialworkers .org/ldf/legal_issue/200503.asp

National Association of Social Workers [NASW]. (2009b). *Responding to a subpoena.* Retrieved June 6, 2015, from https://www.socialworkers.org/ldf/legal_issue/2009 /200904.asp?back=yes

O'Donnell, J., & Giovannoni, J. M. (2006). Consumer perceptions of family resource center service delivery strategies. *Families in Society, 87*(3), 377–384.

Orme, J. (2002). Social work: Gender, care and justice. *British Journal of Social Work, 32,* 799–814.

Palmer, N., & Kaufman, M. (2003). The ethics of informed consent: Implications for multicultural practice. *Journal of Ethnic & Cultural Diversity in Social Work, 12*(1), 1–25.

Parsons, R. J. (2001). Specific practice strategies for empowerment-based practice with women: A study of two groups. *Affilia, 16*(2), 159–179.

Perlman, H. H. (1957). *Social casework: A problem solving process.* Chicago, IL: University of Chicago Press.

Pinderhughes, E. (1995). Empowering diverse populations: Family practice in the 21st century. *Families in Society, 76,* 131–140.

Pinderhughes, E. B. (1979). Teaching empathy in cross-cultural social work. *Social Work, 24*(4), 312–316.

Proctor, E. K., & Davis, L. E. (1994). The challenge of racial difference: Skills for clinical practice. *Social Work, 39,* 314–323.

Reamer, F. G. (2003). *Social work malpractice and strategies for prevention* (2nd ed.). New York: Columbia University Press.

Rooney, R. H. (1992). *Strategies for work with involuntary clients.* New York: Columbia University Press.

Sakamoto, I., & Pitner, R. O. (2005). Use of critical consciousness in anti-oppressive social work practice: Disentangling power dynamics at personal and structural levels. *British Journal of Social Work, 35*(4), 435–452. doi: 10.1093/bjsw/bch190

Scheyett, A., & Diehl, M. J. (2004). Walking our talk in social work education: Partnering with consumers of mental health services. *Social Work Education, 23*(4), 435–450.

Seligman, M. E. P. (1975). *Helplessness.* San Francisco, CA: Freeman Press.

Shulman, L. (2012). *The skills of helping individuals, families, groups, and communities* (7th ed.). Pacific Grove, CA: Wadsworth.

Simon, B. L. (1994). *The empowerment tradition in American social work: A history.* New York: Columbia University Press.

Trotter, C. (1999, reprinted in 2004). *Working with involuntary clients: A guide to practice.* Thousand Oaks, CA: Sage.

Walker, J. S. (2001). Caregivers' views on the cultural appropriateness of services for children with emotional or behavioral disorders. *Journal of Child and Family Studies, 10,* 315–331.

Weaver, H. N. (2000). Culture and professional education: The experience of Native American social workers. *Journal of Social Work Education, 36*(3), 415–428.

Weick, A. (2000). Hidden voices. *Social Work, 45*(5), 395–402.

Weick, A., & Chamberlain, R. (2002). Putting problems in their place: Further explorations in the strengths perspective. In D. Saleebey (Ed.), *The strengths perspective in social work practice* (3rd ed., pp. 95–105). Boston: Allyn & Bacon.

Woody, D. J., & Green, R. (2001). The influence of race/ethnicity and gender on psychosocial and social well-being. *Journal of Ethnic & Cultural Diversity in Social Work, 9*(3/4), 151–166.

Chapter 7

Balgopal, P. R. (2000). Social work practice with immigrants and refugees: An overview. In P. R. Balgopal (Ed.), *Social work practice with immigrants and refugees* (pp. 1–29). New York: Columbia University Press.

Bandler, R., & Grinder, J. (1975). *The structure of magic.* Palo Alto, CA: Science and Behavior Books.

Behnia, B. (2004). Trust building from the perspective of survivors of war and torture. *Social Service Review, 78*(1), 26–40.

Birdwhistell, R. (1955). Background to kinesics. *Etc, 13,* 10–18.

Dean, R. G. (1993). Constructivism: An approach to clinical practice. *Smith College Studies in Social Work, 63*(2), 127–146.

Diwan, S., Jonnalagadda, S. S., & Balaswamy, S. (2004). Resources predicting positive and negative affect during the experience of stress: A study of older Asian Indian immigrants in the United States. *Gerontologist, 44*(5), 605–614.

Drake, B. (1994). Relationship competencies in child welfare services. *Social Work, 39*, 595–602.

Ekman, P., & Friesen, W. V. (1975). *Unmasking the face.* Englewood Cliffs, NJ: Prentice Hall.

Ely, G. E. (2004). Domestic violence and immigrant communities in the United States: A review of women's unique needs and recommendations for social work practice and research. *Stress, Trauma, and Crisis, 7*, 223–241.

Falicov, C. J. (1996). Mexican families. In M. McGoldrick, J. Giordano, & J. K. Pearce (Eds.), *Ethnicity and family therapy* (2nd ed., pp. 169–182). New York: Guilford Press.

Fallot, R. D., & Harris, M. (2009). Creating cultures of trauma-informed care (CCTIC): A self-assessment and planning protocol. *Community Connections.* Retrieved May 20, 2015, from www.healthcare.uiowa.edu/icmh/documents/CCTICSelf-AsessmentandPlanningProtocol0709.pdf

Guarino, K., Soares, P., Konnath, K., Clervil, R., & Bassuk, E. (2009). *Trauma-informed organizational toolkit.* Rockville, MD: Center for Mental Health Services, Substance Abuse and Mental Health Services Administration, the Daniels Fund, the National Child Traumatic Stress Network, and the W.K. Kellogg Foundation.

Henckens, M. J. A. G., Hermans, E. J., Pu, A., Joels, M., & Fernández, G. (2009). Stressed memories: How acute stress affects memory formation in humans. *Journal of Neuroscience, 29*(32), 10111–10119. doi: 10.1523/JNEUROSCI.1184-09.2009

Johnson, D. W. (2014). *Reaching out: Interpersonal effectiveness* (11th ed.). Boston: Pearson.

Kadushin, A., & Kadushin, G. (1997). *The social work interview.* New York: Columbia University Press.

Knapp, M. L., Hall, J. A., & Horgan, T. G. (2014). *Nonverbal communication in human interaction* (8th ed.). Boston: Wadsworth/Cengage.

Limb, G. E., Hodge, D. R., & Panos, P. (2008). Social work with native people: Orienting child welfare workers to the beliefs, values, and practices of Native American families and children. *Journal of Public Child Welfare, 2*(3), 383–397. doi: 10.1080/15548730802463595

Loftus, E. (1979). *Eyewitness testimony.* Cambridge, MA: Harvard University Press.

McGoldrick, M. (1989). Ethnicity and the family life cycle. In B. Carter & M. McGoldrick (Eds.), *The changing family life cycle: A framework for family therapy* (2nd ed., pp. 69–90). Boston: Allyn & Bacon.

Nakanishi, M., & Rittner, B. (1992). The inclusionary cultural model. *Journal of Social Work Education, 28*, 27–35.

O'Hanlon, B. (2003). *A guide to inclusive therapy.* New York: W. W. Norton.

O'Melia, M. (1998, October). *Proactive responding: Paths toward diverse strengths.* Paper presented at Bacclaureate Program Directors 16th Annual Conference, Albuquerque, NM.

Redding, C. A. (2003). Origins and essence of the study. *ACE Reporter, 1*(1), 1–4. Retrieved May 20, 2015, from www.acestudy.org/yahoo_site_admin/assets/docs/ARViN1.127150541.pdf

Ringel, S., Ronell, N., & Getahune, S. (2005). Factors in the integration process of adolescent immigrants. *International Social Work, 49*(1), 63–76.

Robinson, S. J., & Rollings, L. L. (2011). The effect of mood-context on visual recognition and recall memory. *Journal of General Psychology, 138*(1), 66–79. doi: 10.1080/00221309.2010.534405

Russell, M. N., & White, B. (2001). Practice with immigrants and refugees: Social worker and client perspectives. *Journal of Ethnic & Cultural Diversity in Social Work, 9*(3/4), 73–92.

Stewart, P. (2008). Who is kin? Family definition and African American families. *Journal of Human Behavior and the Social Environment, 15*(2/3), 163–181. doi: 10.1300/J137v15n02_10

United Nations High Commission on Refugees [UNHCR]. (2015). *Global trends: Forced displacement in 2014.* Retrieved from www.unhcr.org/556725e69.html

Wade, C., Tavris, C., & Garry, M. (2015). *Psychology with DSM V update* (11th ed.). Boston: Pearson.

Watzlawick, P., Bavelas, J. M., & Jackson, D. D. (1967). *Pragmatics of human communication.* New York: W. W. Norton.

Chapter 8

Abramson, L. Y., Seligman, M. E. P., & Teasdale, J. C. (1978). Learned helplessness in humans: Critique and reformulation. *Journal of Abnormal Psychology, 87*, 49–74.

Acierno, R., Hernandez, M. A., Amstadter, A. B., Resnick, H. S., Steve, K., Muzzy, W., & Kilpatrick, D. G. (2010). Prevalence and correlates of emotional, physical, sexual, and financial abuse and potential neglect in the United States: The National Elder Mistreatment Study. *American Journal of Public Health, 100*(2), 292–297. doi: 10.2105/AJPH.2009.163089

Allen, S. F., & Tracy, E. M. (2008). Developing student knowledge and skills for home-based social work practice. *Journal of Social Work Education, 44*(1), 125–143.

American Association of Suicidology [AAS]. (2010. *The risk factors for suicide.* Retrieved June 13, 2011, from www.suicidology.org/web/guest/stats-and-tools/fact-sheets

American Association of Suicidology [AAS]. (2014). *Know the warning signs of suicide.* Retrieved September 17, 2014, from www.suicidology.org/resources/warning-signs

American Psychiatric Association. (2013). *Diagnostic and statistical manual of mental disorders* (5th ed.). Washington, DC: Author.

Austin, C. D. (1996). Aging and long term care. In C. D. Austin & R. W. McClelland (Eds.), *Perspectives on case management practice* (pp. 1–16). Milwaukee, WI: Families International.

Bandura, A. (1997). *Self-efficacy: The exercise of control.* New York: Freeman.

Bandura, A. (2006). Toward a psychology of human agency. *Perspectives on Psychological Science, 1*, 164–180.

Bandura, A. (2008). An agentic perspective on positive psychology. In S. J. Lopez (Ed.), *Positive psychology: Exploring the best in people* (Vol. 1, pp. 167–196). Westport, CT: Greenwood Publishing Company.

Bandura, A., & Cervone, D. (1983). Self-evaluative and self-efficacy mechanisms governing the motivational effects of goals systems. *Journal of Personality and Social Psychology, 45*, 1017–1028.

Black, M. C., Basile, K. C., Breiding, M. J., Smith, S. G., Walters, M. L., Merrick, M. T., Chen, J., & Stevens, M. R. (2011). *The National Intimate Partner and Sexual Violence Survey (NISVS): 2010 summary report.* Atlanta, GA: National Center for Injury Prevention and Control, Centers for Disease Control and Prevention. Retrieved September 19, 2014, from www.Vdc .gov/violenceprevention/pdf/NISVS_report2010-a.pdf

Burke, A. C., & Gregoire, T. K. (2007). Substance abuse treatment outcomes for coerced and noncoerced clients. *Health and Social Work, 32*(1), 7–15. doi: 10.1300/J009v30n04_04

Capaldi, D. M., Knoble, N. B., Shortt, J. W., & Kim, H. K. (2012). A systematic review of risk factors for intimate partner violence. *Partner Abuse, 3*(2), 231–280.

Centers for Disease Control [CDC]. (2012). *Suicide: Facts at a glance.* Centers for Disease Control and Prevention, National Center for Injury Prevention and Control. Retrieved August 11, 2014, from www.cdc.gov/ViolencePrevention/pdf /Suicide-DataSheet-a.pdf

Centers for Disease Control and Prevention [CDC]. (2015). *Intimate partner violence: Risk and protective factors.* Retrieved April 12, 2015, from ww.cdc.gov/violenceprevention /intimatepartnerviolence/riskprotectivefactors.html

Crosby, A. E., Ortega, L., & Stevens, M. R. (2011, January 14). Suicides: United States, 1999–2007. *Morbidity and Mortality Weekly Report: Supplement. Health Disparities and Inequalities Report; United States, 2011, 60*, 56–59.

Damant, D., Lapierre, S., Leboss, C., Thibault, S., Lessard, G., Hamelin-Brabant, L., Lavergne, C., & Fortin, A. (2010). Women's abuse of their children in the context of domestic violence: Reflection from women's accounts. *Child & Family Social Work, 15*(1), 12–21. doi: 10.1111/j.1365-2206.2009.00632.x

DeAngelis, T. (2002). New data on lesbian, gay and bisexual mental health. *Monitor on Psychology, 33*(2), 46.

DeJong, P., & Berg, I. K. (2013). *Interviewing for solutions* (4th ed.). Belmont, CA: Wadsworth.

deShazer, S. (1989). Resistance revisited. *Contemporary Family Therapy, 11*(4), 227–233.

Dolgoff, R., Loewenberg, F. M., & Harrington, D. (2008). *Ethical decisions for social work practice* (8th ed.). Pacific Grove, CA: Brooks/Cole.

Freedenthal, S. (2008). Suicide. In T. Mizrahi & L. E. Davis (Eds.), *Encyclopedia of social work: Vol. 4* (20th ed., pp. 181–186). Washington, DC: NASW Press.

Freisthier, B., Merritt, D. H., & Lascala, E. A. (2006). Understanding the ecology of child maltreatment: A review of the literature and directions for future research. *Child Maltreatment, 11*(9), 263–280.

Galambos, C. M. (2005). Natural disasters: Health and mental health considerations. *Health & Social Work, 30*(2), 83–86.

Gangwisch, J. E. (2010). Suicide risk assessment. *Current Medical Literature: Psychiatry, 21*(4), 113–119.

Goddard, C., & Bedi, G. (2010). Intimate partner violence and child abuse: A child-centred perspective. *Child Abuse Review, 19*(1), 5–20. doi: 10.1002/car.1084

Goldman, J., Salus, D., Wolcott, D., & Kennedy. K. Y. (2003). *A coordinated response to child abuse and neglect: The foundation for practice.* Children's Bureau, Office on Child Abuse and Neglect. Retrieved September 21, 2014, from childwelfare. gov/pubs/usermanuals/foundation/foundation.pdf

Hanson, M., & Gutheil, I. A. (2004). Motivational strategies with alcohol-involved older adults: Implications for social work practice. *Social Work, 49*(3), 364–372.

Jayaratne, S., Croxton, T. A., & Mattison, D. (2004). A national survey of violence in the practice of social work. *Families in Society, 85*(4), 445–453.

Jirik, S., & Sanders, S. (2014). Analysis of elder abuse statutes across the United States, 2011–2012. *Journal of Gerontological Social Work, 57*(5), 478–497. doi: 10.1080/01634372.2014.884514

Jouriles, E. N., McDonald, R., Smith Slep, A. M., Heyman, R. E., & Garrido, E. (2008). Child abuse in the context of domestic violence: Prevalence, explanations, and practice implications. *Violence & Victims, 23*(2), 221–235.

Laslett, A. M., Room, R., Dietze, P., & Ferris, J. (2012). Alcohol's involvement in recurrent child abuse and neglect. *Addiction, 107*(10), 1786–1793. doi: 10.1111/j.1360-0443.2012.03917

Lewis, T. F., & Osborn, C. J. (2004). Solution-focused counseling and motivational interviewing: A consideration of confluence. *Journal of Counseling & Development, 82*, 38–48.

Linhorst, P., Kuettel, T. J., & Bombardier, C. H. (2002). Motivational interviewing in a group setting with mandated clients: A pilot study. *Addictive Behaviors, 27*, 381–391.

Lyter, S. C., & Abbott, A. A. (2007). Home visits in a violent world. *Clinical Supervisor, 26*(1/2), 17–33.

MacDonald, G., & Sirotich, F. (2005). Violence in the social work workplace: The Canadian experience. *International Social Work, 48*(6), 772–781.

Madden, R. G. (2003). *Essential law for social workers.* New York: Columbia University Press.

Mansdorfer, J. B. (2004). Psychologists and the patriot act. *National Psychologist, 13*(4). Retrieved June 28, 2011, from http://nationalpsychologist.com/articles/art _v13n4_3.htm

Miller, W. R., & Rollnick, S. (2013). *Motivational interviewing: Helping people change* (3rd ed.). New York: Guilford Press.

National Association of Social Workers [NASW]. (2005a). *Social workers and duty to warn.* Retrieved June 9, 2008, from www.socialworkers.org/ldf/legal_issue/200502.asp

National Association of Social Workers [NASW]. (2008b). *Social workers and "duty to warn" state laws.* Retrieved June 28, 2011, from www.naswdc.org/ldf/legal_issue/2008/200802 .asp?back=yes

National Association of Social Workers [NASW]. (2013). *Guidelines for social worker safety in the workplace.* Washington, D.C.:

Author. Retrieved October 21, 2014, from www.socialwork-ers.org/practice/naswstandards/safetystandards2013.pdf

National Center on Elder Abuse [NCEA]. (1998). *The national elder abuse incidence study.* Retrieved June 8, 2015, from http://aoa.gov/AoA_Programs/Elder_Rights/Elder_Abuse/docs/ABuseReport_Full.pdf

National Center on Elder Abuse [NCEA]. (2005). *Fact sheet: Elder abuse prevalence and incidence.* Retrieved June 8, 2015, from www.ncea.aoa.gov/resources/publication/docs/finalstatistics050331.pdf

National Center on Elder Abuse [NCEA]. (2012). *Abuse of adults with a disability.* Retrieved June 8, 2015, from www.ncea.aoa.gov/Resources/Publication/docs/NCEA_AwDisabilities_ResearchBrief_2013.pdf

National Center on Elder Abuse [NCEA]. (n.d.). *State resources.* Retrieved September 21, 2014, from http://www.ncea.aoa.gov/Stop_Abuse/Get_Help/State/index.aspx

Newhill, C. E. (2003). *Client violence in social work practice: Prevention, intervention and research.* New York: Guilford Press.

Nho, C. R., & Choi, S. (2009). Are social workers safe in their workplace? South Korean managers' views. *Asia Pacific Journal of Social Work and Development, 19*(1), 39–49. doi: 10.1080/21650993.2009.9756052

North, C. S., & Hong, B. A. (2000). Project CREST: A new model for mental health intervention after a community disaster. *American Journal of Public Health, 90*(7), 1057–1058.

Patel, S. H., Lambie, G. W., & Glover, M. M. (2008). Motivational counseling: Implications for counseling juvenile sex offenders. *Journal of Addictions & Offenders Counseling, 28*(2), 86–100. doi: 10.1002/j.2161-1874.2008.tb00035

Powell, C. (2003). Early indicators of child abuse and neglect: A multi-professional delphi study. *Child Abuse Review, 12*, 25–40.

Prochaska, J., & DiClemente, C. (1983). Stages and processes of self-change in smoking: Toward an integrative model of change. *Journal of Consulting and Clinical Psychology, 5*, 390–395.

Proctor, C. D., & Groze, V. K. (1994). Risk factors for suicide among gay, lesbian, and bisexual youth. *Social Work, 39*, 504–512.

Pyles, L., & Kim, K. M. (2006). A multilevel approach to cultural competence: A study of the community response to underserved domestic violence victims. *Families in Society, 87*(2), 221–229.

Rasmussen, C. A., Hogh, A., & Andersen, L. P. (2013). Threats and physical violence in the workplace: A comparative study of four areas of human service work. *Journal of Interpersonal Violence, 28*(13), 2749–2769. doi: 10.1177/0886260513487987

Ringstad, R. (2005). Conflict in the workplace: Social workers as victims and perpetrators. *Social Work, 50*(4), 305–313.

Robbins, S. (2002). The rush to counsel: Lessons of caution in the aftermath of disaster. *Families in Society, 83*(2), 113–116.

Rodriguez, C. M. (2010). Parent–child aggression: Association with child abuse potential and parenting styles. *Violence and Victims, 25*(6), 728–741.

Rooney, R. H. (1992). *Strategies for work with involuntary clients.* New York: Columbia University Press.

Rosengren, D. B. (2009). *Building motivational interviewing skills: A practitioner workbook.* New York: Guilford Press.

Russell, S. T., Ryan, C., Toomey, R. B., Diaz, R., & Sanchez, J. (2011). Lesbian, gay, bisexual, and transgender adolescent school victimization: Implications for young adult health and adjustment. *Journal of School Health, 81*(5), 223–230. doi: 10.1111/j.1746-1561.2011.00583

Ryan, C., Russell, S. T., Huebner, D., Diaz, R., & Sanchez, J. (2010). Family acceptance in adolescence and health of LGBT young adults. *Journal of Child and Adolescent Psychiatric Nursing, 23*(4), 205–213. doi: 10.1111/j.1744-6171.2010.00246

Scurfield, R. M. (2002). Commentary about the terrorist acts of September 11, 2001: Posttraumatic reactions and related social and policy issues. *Trauma, Violence & Abuse, 3*(1), 3–14.

Seligman, M. E. P. (1975). *Helplessness.* San Francisco: Freeman Press.

Shields, G., & Kiser, J. (2003). Violence and aggression toward human service workers: An exploratory study. *Families in Society, 84*(1), 13–20.

Stiegel, L., & Klem, E. (2007). *Reporting requirements: Provisions and citations in adult protective services laws, by state.* American Bar Association Commission in Law and Aging. Retrieved September 21, 2014, from www.americanbar.org/content/dam/aba/migrated/aging/docs/MandatoryReportingProvisionsChart.authcheckdam.pdf

Stith, S. M., Smith, D. B., Penn, C., Ward, D., & Tritt, D. (2004). Risk factor analysis for spouse physical maltreatment: A meta-analytic review. *Journal of Aggression and Violent Behavior, 10*, 65–98.

Substance Abuse and Mental Health Services Administration, Office of Applied Studies [SAMHSA]. (2009). *The NSDUH Report: Children living with substance-dependent or substance-abusing parents, 2002–2007.* Rockville, MD: Author.

Substance Abuse and Mental Health Services Administration [SAMHSA]. (2014). Results from the 2013 National Survey on Drug Use and Health: Summary of National Findings, NSDUH Series H-48, HHS Publication No. (SMA) 14-4863. Rockville, MD: Author. Retrieved July 31, 2015, from www.samhsa.gov/data/sites/default/files/NSDUHresultsPDF-WHTML2013/Web/NSDUHresults2013.pdf

Toseland, R. W., & Rivas, F. F. (2012). *An introduction to group work practice* (7th ed.). Boston: Pearson.

U.S. Department of Education. (2008). Psychological first aid (PFA) for students and teachers: Listen, protect, connect – model and teach. *Helpful Hints for School Emergency Management, 3*(3). Retrieved May 21, 2015, from rems.ed.gov/docs/HH_Vol3Issue3.pdf

U. S. Department of Health and Human Services, Administration on Aging [USHHS-AoA]. (2015). *A profile of older Americans, 2014.* Retrieved June 8, 2015, from www.aoa.acl.gov/Aging_Statistics/Profile/2014/docs/2014-Profile.pdf

U.S. Department of Health and Human Services, Administration for Children and Families, Administration on Children, Youth and Families, Children's Bureau [USHHS-ACYF]. (2015).

Child maltreatment, 2013. Retrieved September 21, 2015, from www.acf.hhs.gov/sites/default/files/cb/cm2013.pdf

van Wormer, K. (2007). Principles of motivational interviewing geared to stages of change: A pedagogical challenge. *Journal of Teaching in Social Work, 27*(2), 21–35. doi: 10.1300/J067v27n01_02

Walter, J. L., & Peller, J. E. (1992). *Becoming solution-focused in brief therapy*. New York: Brunner/Mazel.

Whitaker, T., & Arrington, P. (2008). Social workers at work. *NASW membership workforce study*. Washington, DC: National Association of Social Workers. Retrieved June 20, 2011, from //workforce.socialworkers.org/studies/SWatWork.pdf

Wiglesworth, A., Mosqueda, L., Mulnard, R., Liao, S., Gibbs, L., & Fitzgerald, W. (2010). Screening for abuse and neglect of people with dementia. *Journal of the American Geriatrics Society, 58*(3), 493–500. doi: 10.1111/j.1532-5415.2010.02737

Winstanley, S., & Hales, L. (2015). A preliminary study of burnout in residential social workers experiencing workplace aggression: Might it be cyclical. *British Journal of Social Work, 45*(1), 24–33. doi: 10.1093/bjsw/bcu036

World Health Organization [WHO]. (2011). *Psychological first aid: Guide for field workers*. Geneva, Switzerland: WHO Press. Retrieved May 20, 2015, from whqlibdoc.who.int/publications/2011/9789241548205_eng.pdf?ua=1

Wulczyn, F. (2009). Epidemiological perspectives on maltreatment prevention. *Future of Children, 19*(2), 39–66. Retrieved June 8, 2015, from http://files.eric.ed.gov/fulltext/EJ856313.pdf

Chapter 9

Abu-Ras, W., & Abu-Badur, S. H. (2008). The impact of the September 11, 2001, attacks on the well-being of Arab Americans in New York City. *Journal of Muslim Mental Health, 3,* 217–239.

Ainslie, J., & Feltey, K. (1998). Definitions and dynamics of motherhood and family in lesbian communities. In J. M. Schriver (Ed.), *Human behavior and the social environment* (pp. 327–343). Boston: Allyn & Bacon.

Arab American Institute. (2011). *Demographics*. Retrieved June 25, 2011, from www.aaiusa.org/pages/demographics/

Asi, M., & Beaulieu, D. (2013). Arab households in the United States, 2006–2010. *American Community Survey Briefs*. Washington, DC: U.S. Census Bureau. Retrieved September 22, 2014, from www.census.gov/content/dam/Census/library/publications/2013/acs/acsbr10-20.pdf

Askay, S. W., & Magyar-Russell, G. (2009). Post-traumatic growth and spirituality in burn recovery. *International Review of Psychiatry, 21*(6), 570–579.

Barnes, S. L. (2001). Stressors and strengths: A theoretical and practical examination of nuclear, single-parent, and augmented African American families. *Families in Society, 82*(5), 449–460.

Barnes, C., & Mercer, G. (2004). *Implementing the social model of disability: Theory and research*. Leeds, England: Disability Press.

Beavers, W. R., & Hampson, R. B. (1990). *Successful families: Assessment and intervention*. New York: Norton.

Beavers, W. R., & Hampson, R. B. (1993). Measuring family competence: The Beavers' systems model. In F. Walsh (Ed.), *Normal family processes* (2nd ed., pp. 73–103). New York: Guilford Press.

Beresford, P., Brough, P., & Turner, M. (2001). Where do you stand with service users? *Journal of Social Work, 1*(1), 119–120.

Bernal, G., & Shapiro, E. (1996). Cuban families. In M. McGoldrick, J. Giordano, & J. K. Pearce (Eds.), *Ethnicity and family therapy* (2nd ed., pp. 155–168). New York: Guilford Press.

Bhul, K., King, M., Dein, S., & O'Connor, W. (2008). Ethnicity and religious coping with mental distress. *Journal of Mental Health, 17*(2), 141–151. doi: 10.1080/09638230701498408

Billingsley, A. (1992). *Climbing Jacob's ladder: The enduring legacy of African American families*. New York: Simon & Schuster.

Black, C. J. (2003). Translating principles into practice: Implementing the feminist and strengths perspective in work with battered women. *Affilia, 18*(3), 332–349.

Bliss, M., Oglery-Oliver, E., Jackson, E., Harp, S., & Kaslow, N. (2008). African American women's readiness to change abusive relationships. *Journal of Family Violence, 23*(3), 161–171. doi: 10.1007/s10896-007-9138-3

Bloor, R., & Pearson, D. (2004). Brief solution-focused organizational redesign. *International Journal of Mental Health, 33*(2), 44–53.

Blount, M., Thyer, B. A., & Frye, T. (1996). Social work practice with Native Americans. In D. F. Harrison, B. A. Thyer, & J. S. Wodarski (Eds.), *Cultural diversity and social work practice* (2nd ed., pp. 257–298). Springfield, IL: Charles C Thomas.

Boyd-Franklin, N. (1992, July). *African American families in therapy*. Presentation for the Illinois Chapter of the National Association of Social Workers, Springfield, IL.

Brown, E. F., & Gundersen, B. N. (2001). Organization and community intervention with American Indian tribal communities. In R. Fong & S. Furuto (Eds.), *Culturally competent practice: Skills, interventions, and evaluations* (pp. 299–312). Boston: Allyn & Bacon.

Browne, C., & Broderick, A. (1994). Asian and Pacific Island elders: Issues for social work practice and education. *Social Work, 39,* 252–259.

Bureau of Labor Statistics. (2013). Highlights of women's earnings in 2012. *BLS Reports: October 2013*. Washington, DC: U.S. Bureau of Labor Statistics. Retrieved September 22, 2014, from www.bls.gov/cps/cpswom2012.pdf

Busby, D. M., Glenn, E., Stegell, G. L., & Adamson, D. W. (1993). Treatment issues for survivors of physical and sexual abuse. *Journal of Marital and Family Therapy, 19,* 377–392.

Carter-Black, J. (2007). Teaching cultural competence: An innovative strategy grounded in the universality of storytelling as depicted in African and African American storytelling traditions. *Journal of Social Work Education, 43*(1), 31–50.

Chaves, M. (2011). *American religion: Contemporary trends*. Princeton, NJ: Princeton University Press.

Chisom, R., & Washington, M. (1997). *Undoing racism: A philosophy of international social change* (2nd ed.). New York: People's Institute Press.

Cohen, M. B. (2003). Women in groups: The history of feminist empowerment. In M. B. Cohen & A. Mullender (Eds.), *Gender and groupwork* (pp. 32–40). London: Routledge.

Cohen, M. B., & Graybeal, C. T. (2007). Using solution-oriented techniques in mutual aid groups. *Social Work with Groups, 30*(4), 41–58.

Coleman, S. (2011). Addressing the puzzle of race. *Journal of Social Work Education, 47*(1), 91–108. doi: 10.5175/JSWE.2011.200900086

Crisp, C. (2006). Correlates of homophobia and use of gay affirmative practice among social workers. *Journal of Human Behavior in the Social Environment, 14*(4), 119–143.

Daniel, C. D. (2008). From liberal pluralism to critical multiculturalism: The need for a paradigm shift in multicultural education for social work practice in the United States. *Journal of Progressive Human Services, 19*(1), 19–38. doi: 10.1080/10428230802070215

Danis, F. S. (2004). Domestic violence: An overview. In F. S. Danis & L. L. Lockhart (Eds.), *Breaking the silence in social work education: Domestic violence modules for foundation courses* (pp. 1–8). Alexandria, VA: Council on Social Work Education.

Day-Vines, N. L., Patton, J. M., & Baytops, J. L. (2003). Counseling African American adolescents: The impact of race, culture, and middle class status. *Professional School Counseling, 7*(1), 40–51.

DeJong, P., & Berg, I. K. (2013). *Interviewing for solutions* (4th ed.). Belmont, CA: Wadsworth.

DeJong, P., & Miller, S. D. (1995). How to interview for client strengths. *Social Work, 40,* 729–736.

Delgado, M., & Barton, K. (1998). Murals in Latino communities: Social indicators of community strengths. *Social Work, 43*(4), 346–356.

DeNavas-Walt, & Proctor, B. D. (2014). *Income and poverty in the United States, 2013.* Washington, DC: U.S. Census Bureau. Retrieved September 22, 2014, from www.census.gov/content/dam/Census/library/publications/2014/demo/p60-249.pdf

Department of Defense Task Force on Mental Health. (2007). *An achievable vision: Report of the Department of Defense Task Force on Mental Health.* Falls Church, VA: Defense Health Board. Retrieved June 8, 2015, from http://intransition.dcoe.mil/sites/default/files/MHTFReportFinal.pdf

deShazer, S. (1985). *Keys to solution in brief therapy.* New York: W. W. Norton.

deShazer, S., & Dolan, Y. with Korman, H., Trepper, T., McCollum, E., & Berg, I. K. (2007). *More than miracles: The state of the art in solution-focused brief therapy.* Binghamton, NY: Haworth Press.

Dunlap, E., Golub, A., & Johnson, B. D. (2006). The severely-distressed African American family in the crack era: Empowerment is not enough. *Journal of Sociology & Social Welfare, 33*(1), 115–139.

Dykeman, J., Nelson, R., & Appleton, V. (1995). Building strong working alliances with American Indian families. *Social Work in Education, 17*(3), 148–158.

Elder, G. H. (1998). The life course as developmental theory. *Child Development, 69*(1), 1–12.

Ennis, S. R., Rios-Varges, M., & Albert, N. G. (2011). *The Hispanic population, 2010: 2010 census briefs.* U.S. Census Bureau, U.S. Department of Commerce, Economics and Statistics Administration. Retrieved June 2, 2015, from www.census.gov/prod/cen2010/briefs/c2010br-04.pdf

Erickson, W., Lee, C., & von Schrader, S. (2014). *2012 disability status report: The United States.* Ithaca, NY: Cornell University Rehabilitation Research and Training Center on Disability Demographics and Statistics.

Evans, C. (2004). Reflections on a model of empowered user involvement. *Journal of Integrated Care, 12*(6), 22–27.

Falicov, C. J. (1996). Mexican families. In M. McGoldrick, J. Giordano, & J. K. Pearce (Eds.), *Ethnicity and family therapy* (2nd ed., pp. 169–182). New York: Guilford Press.

Fisher, M. (2002). The role of service users in problem formulation and technical aspects of social research. *Social Work Education, 21*(3), 305–312.

Fong, R., & Mokuau, N. (1994). Not simply "Asian American": Periodical literature review on Asians and Pacific Islanders. *Social Work, 39,* 298–306.

Fournier, R. R. (2002). A trauma education workshop on posttraumatic stress. *Health & Social Work, 27*(2), 113–124.

Franklin, A. J. (1993). The invisibility syndrome. *Family Therapy Networker, 17*(4), 32–39.

Franklin, C., Trapper, T. S., McCollum, E. E., & Gingerich, W. J. (Eds.). (2012). *Solution-focused brief therapy: A handbook of evidence-based practice.* New York: Oxford University Press.

Furman, R., Negi, N. J., Iwanmoto, D. K., Rowan, D., Shukraft, A., & Gragg, J. (2009). Social work practice with Latinos: Key issues for social workers. *Social Work, 54*(2), 167–174. doi: 10.1093/sw/54.2.167

Garcia-Preto, N. (1996). Puerto Rican families. In M. McGoldrick, J. Giordano, & J. K. Pearce (Eds.), *Ethnicity and family therapy* (2nd ed., pp. 183–199). New York: Guilford Press.

Garrett, J. T. (1993–1994). Understanding Indian children. *Children Today, 22*(4), 18–21, 40.

Gates, G. J. (2011, April). *How many people are gay, lesbian, bisexual, or transgender?* Williams Institute, UCLA School of Law. Retrieved June 8, 2015, from williamsinstitute.law.ucla.edu/wp-content/uploads/Gates-How-Many-People-LGBT-Apr-2011.pdf

Gates, G. J., & Newport, F. (2012, October). Special report: 3.4% of U.S. adults identify as LGBT. *Gallup Politics.* Retrieved September 22, 2014, from www.gallup.com/poll/158066/special-report-adults-identify-lgbt.aspx

Gilson, S. F., Bricout, J. C., & Baskind, F. R. (1998). Listening to the voices of individuals with disabilities. *Families in Society, 79*(2), 188–196.

Gingerich, W. J., & Peterson, L. T. (2013). Effectiveness of solution-focused brief therapy: A systematic qualitative review of controlled outcome studies. *Research on Social Work Practice*, 23(3), 266–283. doi: 10.1177/1049731512470859

Gotterer, R. (2001). The spiritual dimension in clinical social work practice: A client perspective. *Families in Society, 82*(2), 187–193.

Graf, N. M., Blankenship, C. J., & Marini, I. (2009). One hundred words about disability. *Journal of Rehabilitation, 75*(2), 23–34.

Graham, J. R., Bradshaw, C., & Trew, J. L. (2008). Social worker's understanding of the immigrant Muslim client's perspective. *Journal of Muslim Mental Health, 3*, 125–144. doi: 10.1080/15564900802487527

Green, J. W. (1999). *Cultural awareness in the human services: A multi-ethnic approach* (3rd ed.). Boston: Allyn & Bacon.

Grimm, L. L. (1992). The Native American child in school: An ecological perspective. In M. J. Fine & C. Carlson (Eds.), *The handbook of family-school intervention* (pp. 102–118). Boston: Allyn & Bacon.

Gutiérrez, L. M., & Lewis, E. A. (1998). A feminist perspective on organizing with women of color. In F. G. Rivera & J. L. Erlich (Eds.), *Community organizing in a diverse society* (pp. 97–115). Boston: Allyn & Bacon.

Haight, W. L. (1998). "Gathering the spirit" at first Baptist church: Spirituality as a protective factor in the lives of African American children. *Social Work, 43*(3), 213–221.

Hensley, L. G. (2002). Treatment for survivors of rape: Issues and interventions. *Journal of Mental Health Counseling, 24*(4), 431–448.

Hill, R. B. (1997). *The strengths of African American families: Twenty-five years later.* Washington, DC: R & B Publishers.

Ho, M. K. (1987). *Family therapy with ethnic minorities.* Newbury Park, CA: Sage.

Hodge, D. R. (2004). Working with Hindu clients with a spiritually sensitive manner. *Social Work, 49*(1), 27–38. doi: 10.1093/sw/49.1.27

Hodge, D. R. (2005). Social work and the House of Islam: Orienting practitioners to the beliefs and values of Muslims in the United States. *Social Work, 50*(2), 162–173. doi:10.1093/sw/50.2.162

Holzman, C. G. (1994). Multicultural perspectives on counseling survivors of rape. *Journal of Social Distress and the Homeless, 3*(1), 81–97.

Howden, L. M., & Meyer, J. A. (2011). *Age and sex composition, 2010: 2010 census briefs.* U.S. Census Bureau, U.S. Department of Commerce, Economics and Statistics Administration. Retrieved June 2, 2015, from www.census.gov/prod/cen2010/briefs/c2010br-03.pdf

Humes, K. R., Jones, N. A., & Ramirez, R. K. (2011). *Overview of race and Hispanic origin, 2010: 2010 census briefs.* U.S. Census Bureau, U.S. Department of Commerce, Economics and Statistics Administration. Retrieved September 21, 2014, from www.census.gov/prod/cen2010/briefs/c2010br-02.pdf

Jang, S. J., & Johnson, B. R. (2004). Explaining religious effects on distress among African Americans. *Journal for the Scientific Study of Religion, 43*(2), 239–260.

Jo, J.-Y. O. (2004). Neglected voices in the multicultural America: Asian Americans' racial politics and its implication for multicultural education. *Multicultural Perspectives, 6*(1), 19–25.

Johnson, D. W., & Johnson, F. P. (2013). *Joining together: Group theory and group skills* (11th ed.). Boston: Pearson.

Johnson, M. M., & Rhodes, R. (2010). *Human behavior and the larger environment: A new synthesis* (2nd ed.). Boston: Pearson.

Johnson, Y. M., & Munch, S. (2009). Fundamental contradictions in cultural competence. *Social Work, 54*(3), 220–231. doi: 10.1093/sw/54.3.220

Kivnick, H. Q., & Murray, S. V. (2001). Life strengths interview guide: Assessing elder clients' strengths. *Journal of Gerontological Social Work, 34*(4), 7–32.

Kivnick, H. Q., & Stoffel, S. A. (2005). Vital involvement practice: Strengths as more than tools for solving problems. *Journal of Gerontological Social Work, 46*(2), 85–116.

Koenig, H. G. (2009). Research on religion, spirituality, and mental health: A review. *Canadian Journal of Psychiatry, 54*(5), 283–291.

Koenig, H. G. (2012). Religion, spirituality, and health: The research and clinical implications. *ISRN Psychiatry, 2012,* Article ID 278730. doi:10.5402/2012/278730

Laffaye, C., Cavella, S., Dreshcer, K., & Rosen, C. (2008). Relationships among PTSD symptoms, social support, and support source in veterans with chronic PTSD. *Journal of Traumatic Stress, 21*(4), 394–401. doi: 10.1002/jts.20348

Lorenzo, M. K., Frost, A. K., & Reinherz, H. Z. (2000). Social and emotional functioning of older Asian American adolescents. *Child and Adolescent Social Work Journal, 17*(4), 289–304.

Love, E. (2009). Confronting Islamophobia in the United States: Framing civil rights activism among Middle Eastern Americans. *Patterns of Prejudice, 43*(3/4), 401–425. doi: 10.1080/00313220903109367

Lukes, C. A., & Land, H. (1990). Biculturality and homosexuality. *Social Work, 35,* 155–161.

Lum, D. (2004). *Social work with people of color: A process-stage approach* (5th ed.). Pacific Grove, CA: Brooks/Cole.

Manning, M. C., Cornelius, L. J., & Okundaye, J. N. (2004). Empowering African Americans through social work practice: Integrating an Afrocentric perspective, ego psychology, and spirituality. *Families in Society, 85*(2), 229–235.

Marsiglia, F., Kunis, S., & Hecht, M. L. (2001). Ethnic labels and ethnic identity as predictors of drug use among middle school students in the southwest. *Journal of Research on Adolescence, 11*(1), 21–48.

McCullough-Chavis, A., & Waites, C. (2004). Genograms with African American families: Considering cultural context. *Journal of Family Social Work, 8*(2), 1–19.

McLaughlin, L. A., & Braun, K. L. (1998). Asian and Pacific Islander cultural values: Considerations for health care decision making. *Health and Social Work, 23*(2), 116–126.

McNeal, C., & Perkins, I. (2007). Potential roles of black churches in HIV/AIDS prevention. *Journal of Human Behavior in the Social Environment, 15*(2/3), 219–232.

Moore, V. R., & Miller, S. D. (2007). Coping resources: Effects on the psychological well-being of African American grandparents raising grandchildren. *Journal of Health & Social Policy,* 22(3/4), 137–148. doi: 10.1300/J045v22n03_09

Morales, A. T., & Salcido, R. (1998). Social work practice with Mexican Americans. In A. T. Morales & B. W. Sheafor (Eds.), *Social work: A profession of many faces* (8th ed., pp. 513–539). Boston: Allyn & Bacon.

Mullaly, B. (2002). *Challenging oppression: A critical social work approach.* Ontario, Canada: Oxford University Press.

Nakanishi, M., & Rittner, B. (1992). The inclusionary cultural model. *Journal of Social Work Education,* 28, 27–35.

Newman, B. S. (1994). Diversity and populations at risk: Gays and lesbians. In F. G. Reamer (Ed.), *The foundations of social work knowledge* (pp. 346–392). New York: Columbia University Press.

Norris, F. H., Stevens, S. P., Pfefferbaum, B., Wyche, K. F., & Pfefferbaum, R. L. (2008). Community resilience as a metaphor, theory, set of capacities, and strategy for disaster readiness. *American Journal of Community Psychology,* 41(1/2), 127–150. doi: 10.1007/s10464-007-9156-6

Norris, T., Vines, P. L., & Hoeffel, E. M. (2012). *The American Indian and Alaska Native population, 2010.* Washington, DC: U.S. Census Bureau. Retrieved September 22, 2014, from www.census.gov/content/dam/Census/library/publications/2012/demo/c2010br-10.pdf

Oliver, M. (1996). *Understanding disability: From theory to practice.* London: Macmillan Press.

Oliver, M. (1997). The disability movement is a new social movement. *Community Development Journal,* 32(3), 244–251.

Olson, D. H., DeFrain, J., & Skogrand, L. (2013). *Marriages and families: Intimacy, diversity, and strengths* (8th ed.). Boston: McGraw-Hill.

Omeni, E., Barnes, M., MacDonald, D., Crawford, M., & Rose, D. (2014). Service user involvement: Impact and participation. A survey of service user and staff perspectives. *BMC Health Service Research,* 14(1), 491. doi:10.1186/s12913-014-0491-7. Retrieved June 1, 2015, from www.biomedcentral.com/1472-6963/14/491

Oyserman, D., & Sakamoto, I. (1997). Being Asian American: Identity, cultural constructs, and stereotype perception. *Journal of Applied Behavioral Science,* 33(4), 435–453.

Patterson, S., Trite, J., & Weaver, T. (2014). Activity and views of service users involved in mental health research: UK survey. *British Journal of Psychiatry,* 205(1), 68–75. doi: 10.1192/bjp.bp.113.128637

Peled, E., Eisikovits, Z., Enosh, G., & Winstok, Z. (2000). Choice and empowerment for battered women who stay: Toward a constructivist model. *Social Work,* 45(1), 9–25.

Pew Forum on Religion and Public Life. (2008a). *U.S. Religious landscape survey, 2008: Religious affiliation. Diverse and dynamic.* Retrieved March 14, 2015, from www.pewforum.org/files/2013/05/report-religious-landscape-study-full.pdf

Pew Forum on Religion and Public Life. (2008b). *U.S. Religious landscape survey, 2008: Religious beliefs and practices. Diverse and politically relevant.* Retrieved March 14, 2015, from www.pewforum.org/files/2008/06/report2-religious-landscape-study-full.pdf

Pine, B. A., & Drachman, D. (2005). Effective child welfare practice with immigrant and refugee children and their families. *Child Welfare,* 84(5), 537–562.

Population Reference Bureau. (2014). *World population data sheet, 2014.* Washington, DC: Population Reference Bureau. Retrieved September 21, 2014, from www.prb.org/Publications/Datasheets/2014/2014-world-population-data-sheet/data-sheet.aspx

Purnell, J. Q., & Andersen, B. L. (2009). Religious practice and spirituality in the psychological adjustment of survivors of breast cancer. *Counseling and Values,* 53, 165–182.

Rastogi, S., Johnson, T. D., Heoffel, E. M., & Drewery, M. P. (2011). *The Black population, 2010.* Washington, DC: U.S. Census Bureau. Retrieved September 22, 2014, from www.census.gov/prod/cen2010/briefs/c2010br-06.pdf

Rosengren, D. B. (2009). *Building motivational interviewing skills: A practitioner workbook.* New York: Guilford Press.

Ross, F., Smith, P., Bying, R., Christian, S., Allan, H., Price, L., & Brearley, S. (2014). Learning from people with long-term conditions: New insights for governance in primary healthcare. *Health and Social Care in the Community,* 22(4), 405–416. doi 10.1111/hsc.12097

Ross-Sheriff, F., & Husain, A. (2001). Values and ethics in social work practice with Asian Americans: A South Asian Muslim case example. In R. Fong & S. Furuto (Eds.), *Culturally competent practice: Skills, interventions, and evaluations* (pp. 75–88). Boston: Allyn & Bacon.

Russell, S. T., Ryan, C., Toomey, R. B., Diaz, R., & Sanchez, J. (2011). Lesbian, gay, bisexual, and transgender adolescent school victimization: Implications for young adult health and adjustment. *Journal of School Health,* 81(5), 223–230. doi: 10.1111/j.1746-1561.2011.00583

Ryan, C., Russell, S. T., Huebner, D., Diaz, R., & Sanchez, J. (2010). Family acceptance in adolescence and health of LGBT young adults. *Journal of Child and Adolescent Psychiatric Nursing,* 23(4), 205–213. doi: 10.1111/j.1744-6171.2010.00246

Sahgal, N., & Smith, G. (2009). A religious portrait of African Americans. *Pew Research: Religion & Public Life.* Retrieved September 21, 2014, from http://www.pewforum.org/2009/01/30/a-religious-portrait-of-african-americans/#overview

Saleebey, D. (2009). *The strengths perspective in social work practice* (5th ed.). Boston: Pearson.

Schaefer, R. T. (2012). *Racial and ethnic groups* (13th ed.). Upper Saddle River, NJ: Pearson.

Schott, S. A., & Conyers, L. M. (2003). A solution-focused approach to psychiatric rehabilitation. *Psychiatric Rehabilitation Journal,* 27(1), 43–51.

Simon, B. L. (1994). *The empowerment tradition in American social work: A history.* New York: Columbia University Press.

Snyder, C. S., May, J. D., Zulcic, N. N., & Gabbard, W. J. (2005). Social work with Bosnian Muslim refugee children and families: A review of the literature. *Child Welfare,* 84(5), 607–630.

Soni, S., Hall, I., Doulton, P., & Bowie, P. (2014). Involving people with intellectual disabilities in the assessment of healthcare professionals. *Advances in Mental Health and Intellectual Disabilities*, 8(6), 362–369. doi: 10.1108/AMHID-04-2014-0011

Spencer, J. H., & Le, T. N. (2006). Parent refugee status, immigration stressors, and southeast Asian youth violence. *Journal of Immigrant Health*, 8, 359–368.

Sullivan, T. R. (1994). Obstacles to effective child welfare service with gay and lesbian youths. *Child Welfare*, 73, 291–304.

Swigonski, M. E. (1993). Feminist standpoint theory and the questions of social work research. *Affilia*, 8(2), 171–183.

Szente, J., Hoot, J., & Taylor, D. (2006). Responding to the special needs of refugee children: Practical ideas for teachers. *Early Childhood Education Journal*, 34(1), 15–20.

Torres, M. N. (2003). To the margins and back: The high cost of being Latina in "America." *Journal of Latinos and Education*, 3(2), 123–141.

Turner, M. (1997). Reshaping our lives. *Research, Policy and Planning*, 15(2), 23–25.

U.S. Census Bureau. (2012). *U.S. Census Bureau projections show a slower growing, older, more diverse nation a half century from now.* Retrieved September 21, 2014, from https://www.census.gov/newsroom/releases/archives/population/cb12-243.html

U.S. Department of Health and Human Services, Administration on Aging [USHHS-AoA]. (2014). *Future growth.* Retrieved June 8, 2015, from www.aoa.acl.gov/Aging_Statistics/Profile/2014/4.aspx

Utsey, S. O., Howard, A., & Williams, O. (2003). Therapeutic group mentoring with African American male adolescents. *Journal of Mental Health Counseling*, 25(2), 126–139.

Valokivi, H. (2004). Participation and citizenship of elderly persons: User experiences from Finland. *Social Work in Health Care*, 39(1/2), 181–207.

Walsh, F. (1999a). Opening family therapy to spirituality. In F. Walsh (Ed.), *Spiritual resources in family therapy* (pp. 28–58). New York: Guilford Press.

Walsh, F. (1999b). Religion and spirituality: Wellsprings for healing and resilience. In F. Walsh (Ed.), *Spiritual resources in family therapy* (pp. 3–27). New York: Guilford Press.

Walter, J. L., & Peller, J. E. (1992). *Becoming solution-focused in brief therapy.* New York: Brunner/Mazel.

Walter, J. L., & Peller, J. E. (2000). *Recreating brief therapy: Preferences and possibilities.* New York: W. W. Norton.

Weaver, H. N., & Burns, B. J. (2001). "I shout with fear at night": Understanding the traumatic experiences of refugees and asylum seekers. *Journal of Social Work*, 1(2), 147–164.

Weaver, H. N., & White, B. J. (1997). The Native American family cycle: Roots of resiliency. *Journal of Family Social Work*, 2(1), 67–79.

Weaver, H., & Wodarski, J. S. (1996). Social work practice with Latinos. In D. F. Harrison, B. A. Thyer, & J. S. Wodarski (Eds.), *Cultural diversity and social work practice* (pp. 52–86). Springfield, IL: Charles C Thomas.

Weick, A. (1999). Guilty knowledge. *Families in Society*, 80(4), 327–332.

Weiman, K., Dosland-Hasenmiller, C., & O'Melia, J. (2002). Shutting off that damn bell: Raising the voices within. In M. O'Melia & K. K. Miley (Eds.), *Pathways to power: Readings in contextual social work practice* (pp. 156–174). Boston: Allyn & Bacon.

Wheeler, D. P., & Bragin, M. (2007). Bringing it all back home: Social work and the challenge of returning veterans. *Health and Social Work*, 32(4), 297–300. doi: 10.1093/hsw/32.4.297

Wolin, S. J., & Wolin, S. (1993). *The resilient self: How survivors of troubled families rise above adversity.* New York: Villard Books.

Woodcock, J., & Tregaskis, C. (2008). Understanding structural and communication barriers to ordinary family life for families with disabled children: A combined social work and social model of disability analysis. *British Journal of Social Work*, 38, 55–71. doi: 10.1093/bjsw/bcl065

Wright, O. L., & Anderson, J. P. (1998). Clinical social work practice with urban African American families. *Families in Society*, 79(2), 197–205.

Yellow Bird, M. (2001). Critical values and First Nations peoples. In R. Fong & S. Furuto (Eds.), *Culturally competent practice: Skills, interventions, and evaluations* (pp. 61–75). Boston: Allyn & Bacon.

Yellow Bird, M., Fong, R., Galindo, P., Nowicki, J., & Freeman, E. M. (1995). The multicultural mosaic. *Social Work in Education*, 17(3), 131–138.

Chapter 10

Amundson, J., Stewart, K., & Valentine, L. (1993). Temptations of power and certainty. *Journal of Marital and Family Therapy*, 19(2), 111–123.

Bargal, D. (2000). The future development of occupational social work. *Administration in Social Work*, 23(3/4), 139–156.

Black, P. N., & Feld, A. (2006). Process recording revisited: A learning-oriented thematic approach integrating field education and classroom curriculum. *Journal of Teaching in Social Work*, 26(3/4), 137–153.

Canda, E. R., & Furman, L. (1999). *Spiritual diversity in social work practice: The heart of helping.* New York: The Free Press.

Carter, B., & McGoldrick, M. (1989). Overview: The changing family life cycle. A framework for family therapy. In B. Carter & M. McGoldrick (Eds.), *The changing family life cycle: A framework for family therapy* (2nd ed., pp. 3–28). Boston: Allyn & Bacon.

Chau, K. (1989). Sociocultural dissonance among ethnic minority populations. *Social Casework*, 70, 224–239.

Erikson, E. H. (1963). *Childhood and society* (2nd ed.). New York: Norton.

Flowers, P., & Buston, K. (2001). "I was terrified of being different": Exploring gay men's accounts of growing-up in a heterosexist society. *Journal of Adolescence*, 24, 51–65.

Fong, R. (1997). Child welfare practice with Chinese families: Assessment issues for immigrants from the People's Republic of China. *Journal of Family Social Work*, 2(1), 33–47.

Fook, J. (2002). *Social work: Critical theory and practice.* Thousand Oaks, CA: Sage.

Gelman, S. R. (1992). Risk management through client access to case records. *Social Work, 37,* 73–79.

Gotterer, R. (2001). The spiritual dimension in clinical social work practice: A client perspective. *Families in Society, 82(2),* 187–193.

Hartman, A. (1978, reprinted in 1995). Diagrammatic assessment of family relationships. *Families in Society, 76,* 111–122.

Hartman, A. (1992). In search of subjugated knowledge. *Social Work, 37,* 483–484.

Hartman, A., & Laird, J. (1983). *Family centered social work practice.* New York: The Free Press.

Hodge, D. R. (2001). Spiritual assessment: A review of major qualitative methods and a new framework for assessing spirituality. *Social Work, 46(3),* 203–214.

Hodge, D. R. (2006). A template for spiritual assessment: A review of the JCAHO requirements and guidelines for implementation. *Social Work, 51(4),* 317–326. doi:10.1093/sw/51.4.317

Johnson, D. W., & Johnson, F. P. (2013). *Joining together: Group theory and group skills* (11th ed.). Boston: Pearson.

Johnson, L. C., & Yanca, S. (2010). *Social work practice: A generalist approach* (10th ed.). Boston: Pearson.

Kemp, S. P., Whittaker, J. K., & Tracy, E. M. (2002). Contextual social work practice. In M. O'Melia & K. K. Miley (Eds.), *Pathways to power: Readings in contextual social work practice* (pp. 15–34). Boston: Allyn & Bacon.

Kettner, P. M., Daley, J. M., & Nichols, A. W. (1985). *Initiating change in organizations and communities: A macro practice model.* Monterey, CA: Brooks/Cole.

Kivnick, H. Q., & Murray, S. V. (2001). Life strengths interview guide: Assessing elder clients' strengths. *Journal of Gerontological Social Work, 34(4),* 7–32.

Kramer, T. L., Jones, K. A., Kichner, M. D., Miller, T. L., & Wilson, C. (2002). Addressing personnel concerns about school violence through education assessment and strategic planning. *Education, 123(2),* 292–204.

Kretzmann, J. P., & McKnight, J. L. (1993). *Building communities from the inside out: A path toward finding and mobilizing a community's assets.* Chicago, IL: ACTA Publications.

Labassi, M. F., & Maluccio, A. N. (1986). Competence centered social work: Prevention in action. *Journal of Primary Prevention, 6,* 168–180.

Lewin, K. (1951). *Field theory in social science.* Westport, CT: Greenwood Press.

Lim, S.-L., & Nakamoto, T. (2008). Genograms: Use in therapy with Asian families with diverse cultural heritages. *Contemporary Family Therapy, 30,* 199–219. doi: 10.1007/s10591-008-9070-6

McCullough-Chavis, A., & Waites, C. (2004). Genograms with African American families: Considering cultural context. *Journal of Family Social Work, 8(2),* 1–19.

McGoldrick, M., & Gerson, R. (1985). *Genograms in family assessment.* New York: Norton.

McGoldrick, M., & Gerson, R. (1989). Genograms and the family life cycle. In B. Carter & M. McGoldrick (Eds.), *The changing family life cycle: A framework for family therapy* (2nd ed., pp. 164–189). Boston: Allyn & Bacon.

Medina, C. K. (2010). The need and use of process recording in policy practice: A learning and assessment tool for macro practice. *Journal of Teaching in Social Work, 30(1),* 29–45. doi: 1080/08841230903479474

Merighi, J. R., & Grimes, M. D. (2000). Coming out to families in a multicultural context. *Families in Society, 81(1),* 32–41.

Morrison, L. L., & L'Heureux, J. (2001). Suicide and gay/lesbian /bisexual youth: Implications for clinicians. *Journal of Adolescence, 24,* 39–49.

National Association of Social Workers [NASW]. (1999). *Code of ethics of the National Association of Social Workers.* Washington, D.C.: Author.

National Association of Social Workers [NASW]. (2001b). *What social workers should know about the HIPAA privacy regulations.* Retrieved June 7, 2011, from www.socialworkers.org /practice/behavioral_health/mbh0101.asp

National Association of Social Workers [NASW]. (2004a). *HIPAA for social work employers and administrators.* Retrieved June 9, 2008, from www.socialworkers.org/ldf /legal_issue/200405.asp

National Association of Social Workers [NASW]. (2005b). *Social workers and HIPAA security standards.* Retrieved June 9, 2011, from www.socialworkers.org/ldf/legal_issue/200504.asp

Papernow, P. (1993). *Becoming a stepfamily: Patterns of development in remarried families.* San Francisco: Jossey-Bass.

Pippard, J. L., & Bjorkland, R. W. (2004). Identifying essential techniques for social work community practice. *Journal of Community Practice, 11(4),* 101–116.

Redman, D. (2008). Stressful life experiences and the roles of spirituality among people with a history of substance abuse and incarceration. *Journal of Religion & Spirituality in Social Work: Social Thought, 27(1/2),* 47–67. doi: 10.1080/15426430802113780

Russell, M. N., & White, B. (2001). Practice with immigrants and refugees: Social worker and client perspectives. *Journal of Ethnic & Cultural Diversity in Social Work, 9(3/4),* 73–92.

Saleebey, D. (2004). "The power of place": Another look at the environment. *Families in Society, 85(1),* 7–16.

Schriver, J. M. (2015). *Human behavior and the social environment: Shirting paradigms in essential knowledge for social work* (6th ed.). Boston: Pearson.

Sheafor, B. W., & Horejsi, C. R. (2014). *Techniques and guidelines for social work practice* (10th ed.). Boston: Pearson.

Tracy, E. M., & Whittaker, J. K. (1990). The social support network map: Assessing social support in clinical practice. *Families in Society, 71,* 461–470.

Visher, E. B., & Visher, J. S. (1996). *Therapy with step-families.* New York: Brunner/Mazel.

Washington, O. G. M., Moxley, D. P., Garriott, L., & Crystal, J. P. (2009). Support and advocacy for older African American homeless women through developmental action research. *Contemporary Nurse, 33*(2), 140–160. doi: 10.5172/conu.2009.33.2.140

Wright, A., Heibert-Murphy, D., & Trute, B. (2010). Professionals: Perspectives on organizational factors that support or hinder the successful implementation of family-centered practice. *Journal of Family Social Work, 13*, 114–130. doi: 10.1080/10522150903503036

Yoon, D. P. (2006). Factors affecting subjective well-being for rural elderly individuals: The importance of spirituality, religiousness, and social support. *Journal of Religion & Spirituality in Social Work, 25*(2), 59–75. doi: 10.1300/J377v25n02_04

Zetlin, A., Weinberg, L., & Shea, N. M. (2010). Caregivers, school liaisons, and agency advocates speak out about the educational needs of children and youths in foster care. *Social Work, 55*(3), 245–254. doi:10.1093/sw/55.3.245

Chapter 11

Bakk, L., Woodward, A. T., & Dunkle, R. E. (2014). The Medicare Part D coverage gap: Implications for non-dually eligible older adults with a mental illness. *Journal of Gerontological Social Work, 57*(1), 37–51. doi: 10.1080/01634372.2013.854857

Bandura, A. (1997). *Self-efficacy: The exercise of control*. New York: Freeman.

Bandura, A. (2002). Social cognitive theory in cultural context. *Applied Psychology: An International Review, 151*, 269–290.

Bandura, A. (2006). Toward a psychology of human agency. *Perspectives on Psychological Science, 1*, 164–180.

Bandura, A. (2008). An agentic perspective on positive psychology. In S. J. Lopez (Ed.), *Positive psychology: Exploring the best in people* (Vol. 1, pp. 167–196). Westport, CT: Greenwood Publishing Company.

Bandura, A. (2012). On the functional properties of self-efficacy revisited. *Journal of Management, 38*, 9–44. doi: 10.1177/0149206311410606

Bandura, A., & Schunk, D. H. (1981). Cultivating competence, self-efficacy, and intrinsic interest through proximal self-motivation. *Journal of Personality and Social Psychology, 41*(3), 586–598.

Choi, S. (2015). Out-of-pocket expenditures and the financial burden of healthcare among older adults: By nativity and length of residence in the United States. *Journal of Gerontological Social Work, 58*, 149–170. doi: 10.1080/01634372.2014.943447

Cowger, C. D., & Snively, C. A. (2002). Assessing client strengths: Individual, family, and community empowerment. In D. Saleebey (Ed.), *The strengths perspective in social work practice* (3rd ed., pp. 106–123). Boston: Allyn & Bacon.

Goldstein, H. (1973). *Social work practice: A unitary approach*. Columbia, SC: University of South Carolina Press.

Johnson, D. W., & Johnson, F. P. (2013). *Joining together: Group theory and group skills* (11th ed.). Boston: Pearson.

Linhorst, D. M., Hamilton, G., Young, E., & Eckert, A. (2002). Opportunities and barriers to empowering people with severe mental illness through participation in treatment planning. *Social Work, 47*(4), 425–434.

Monkman, M. M. (1991). Outcome objectives in social work practice: Person and environment. *Social Work, 36*(3), 253–258.

National Association of Social Workers. (2008a). Aging and wellness. In *Social work speaks: National Association of Social Workers policy statements, 2015–2017* (10th ed., pp. 13–20). Washington, DC: NASW Press.

Robinson, J., Shugrue, N., Porter, M., Fortinsky, R. H., & Curry, L. A. (2012). Transition from home care to nursing home: Unmet needs in a home- and community-based program for older adults. *Journal of Aging and Social Policy, 24*(3), 251–270. doi: 10.1080/08959420.2012.676315

Rogers, A., Rebbe, R. Gardella, C., Worlein, M., & Chamberlin, M. (2013). Older LGBT adult training panels: An opportunity to educate about issues faced by the older LGBT community. *Journal of Gerontological Social Work, 56*, 580–595. doi: 10.1080/01634372.2013.811710

Ruggiano, N. (2012). Consumer direction in long-term care policy: Overcoming barriers to promoting older adults' opportunity for self-direction. *Journal of Gerontological Social Work, 55*, 146–159. doi: 10.1080/01634372.2011.638701

Seligman, M. E. P. (1975). *Helplessness*. San Francisco: Freeman Press.

Sheafor, B. W., & Horejsi, C. R. (2014). *Techniques and guidelines for social work practice* (10th ed.). Boston: Pearson.

Siporin, M. (1975). *Introduction to social work practice*. New York: Macmillan.

Smith, R. J., Lehning, A. J., & Dunkle, R. E. (2013). Conceptualizing age-friendly community characteristics in a sample of urban elders: An exploratory factor analysis. *Journal of Gerontological Social Work, 56*, 90–111. doi: 10.1080/01634372.2012.739267

U.S. Department of Health and Human Services, Administration on Aging [USHHS-AoA]. (2014). *Future growth*. Retrieved June 8, 2015, from www.aoa.acl.gov/Aging_Statistics/Profile/2014/4.aspx

Walter, J. L., & Peller, J. E. (1992). *Becoming solution-focused in brief therapy*. New York: Brunner/Mazel.

Zimmerman, M. A. (1990). Toward a theory of learned hopefulness: A structural model analysis of participation and empowerment. *Journal of Research in Personality, 24*, 71–86.

Chapter 12

Bandura, A. (1986). *Social foundations of thought and action: A social-cognitive theory*. Englewood Cliffs, NJ: Prentice Hall.

Bandura, A. (1997). *Self-efficacy: The exercise of control*. New York: Freeman.

Beck, J. (2011). *Cognitive behavior therapy* (2nd ed.). New York: Guilford Press.

Bliss, M., Oglery-Oliver, E., Jackson, E., Harp, S., & Kaslow, N. (2008). African American women's readiness to change abusive relationships. *Journal of Family Violence, 23*(3), 161–171. doi: 10.1007/s10896-007-9138-3

Breton, M. (2001). Neighborhood resiliency. *Journal of Community Practice, 9*(1), 21–36.

Brower, A. M. (1996). Group development as constructed social reality revisited: The constructivism of small groups. *Families in Society, 77*, 336–343.

Corcoran, J. (2006). *Cognitive-behavioral methods for social workers: A workbook.* Boston: Allyn & Bacon.

Freeman, E. M., & Couchonnal, G. (2006). Narrative and culturally based approaches in practice with families. *Families in Society, 87*(2), 198–208.

Gibson, C. M. (1993). Empowerment theory and practice with adolescents of color in the child welfare system. *Families in Society, 74*, 387–396.

Hardina, D. (2004). Linking citizen participation to empowerment practice: A historical overview. *Journal of Community Practice, 11*(4), 11–37.

Hurdle, D. E. (2002). Native Hawaiian traditional healing: Culturally based interventions for social work practice. *Social Work, 47*(2), 183–192.

Ivey, A. E., Ivey, M. B., & Zalaquett, C. P. (2014). *Intentional interviewing and counseling: Facilitating client development in a multicultural society* (8th ed.). Pacific Grove, CA: Cengage.

Johnson, D. W., & Johnson, F. P. (2013). *Joining together: Group theory and group skills* (11th ed.). Boston: Pearson.

Klein, A. R., & Cnaan, R. A. (1995). Practice with high risk clients. *Families in Society, 76*, 203–211.

Laird, J. (1995). Family-centered practice in the postmodern era. *Families in Society, 76*(3), 150–162.

Madsen, W. C. (2007). *Collaborative therapy with multi-stressed families* (2nd ed.). New York: Guilford Press.

McNeal, C., & Perkins, I. (2007). Potential roles of black churches in HIV/AIDS prevention. *Journal of Human Behavior in the Social Environment, 15*(2/3), 219–232.

Mok, B.-H. (2005). Organizing self-help groups for empowerment and social change: Findings and insights from an empirical study in Hong Kong. *Journal of Community Practice, 13*(1), 49–67.

Moore, V. R., & Miller, S. D. (2007). Coping resources: Effects on the psychological well-being of African American grandparents raising grandchildren. *Journal of Health & Social Policy, 22*(3/4), 137–148. doi: 10.1300/J045v22n03_09

Nichols, M. P., & Schwartz, R. C. (2001). *Family therapy: Concepts and methods* (5th ed.). Boston: Allyn & Bacon.

Patterson, S. L., & Marsiglia, F. F. (2000). "Mi casa es su casa": Beginning exploration of Mexican Americans' natural helping. *Families in Society, 81*(1), 22–31.

Peled, E., Eisikovits, Z., Enosh, G., & Winstok, Z. (2000). Choice and empowerment for battered women who stay: Toward a constructivist model. *Social Work, 45*(1), 9–25.

Saleebey, D. (1994). Culture, theory, and narrative: The intersection of meanings in practice. *Social Work, 39*(4), 351–359.

Schneider, R. L., & Lester, L. (2001). *Social work advocacy.* Belmont, CA: Brooks/Cole.

Segal, S. P. (2008). Self-help groups. In T. Mizrahi & L. E. Davis (Eds.), *Encyclopedia of social work: Vol. 4* (20th ed., pp. 14–17). Washington, DC: NASW Press.

Shulman, L. (2012). *The skills of helping individuals, families, groups, and communities* (7th ed.). Pacific Grove, CA: Wadsworth.

Toseland, R. W., & Rivas, F. F. (2012). *An introduction to group work practice* (7th ed.). Boston: Pearson.

Walter, J. L., & Peller, J. E. (1992). *Becoming solution-focused in brief therapy.* New York: Brunner/Mazel.

White, M. (1989). The externalizing of the problem and the re-authoring of lives and relationships. In M. White (Ed.), *Selected papers* (pp. 5–28). Adelaide, Australia: Dulwich Centre Publications.

Williams, J. H., Pierce, R., Young, N. S., & Van Dorn, R. A. (2001). Service utilization in high-crime communities: Consumer views on supports and barriers. *Families in Society, 82*(4), 409–417.

Yellow Bird, M. (2001). Critical values and First Nations peoples. In R. Fong & S. Furuto (Eds.), *Culturally competent practice: Skills, interventions, and evaluations* (pp. 61–75). Boston: Allyn & Bacon.

Chapter 13

Abramson, J., & Bronstein, L. (2008). Teams. In T. Mizrahi & L. E. Davis (Eds.), *Encyclopedia of social work: Vol. 4* (20th ed., pp. 199–204). Washington, DC: NASW Press.

Arches, J. (2012). The role of groupwork in social action projects with youth. *Groupwork, 22*(1), 59–71.

Bolen, R. M., & Hall, J. C. (2007). Managed care and evidence-based practice: The untold story. *Journal of Social Work Education, 43*(3), 463–479.

Boutin-Foster, C. (2005). In spite of good intentions: Patients' perspectives on problematic social support interactions. *Health & Quality of Life Outcomes, 3*, 52–57.

Breton, M. (2002). Empowerment practice in Canada and the United States: Restoring policy issues at the center of social work. *Social Policy Journal, 1*(1), 19–34.

Breton, M. (2004). An empowerment perspective. In C. D. Garvin, L. M. Gutiérrez, & M. J. Galinsky (Eds.), *Handbook of social work with groups* (pp. 58–75). New York: Guilford Press.

Breton, M. (2006). Path dependence and the place of social action in social work practice. *Social Work with Groups, 29*(4), 25–44. doi: 10.1300/J009v29n04_03

Bride, B. E. (2007). Prevalence of secondary stress among social workers, *Social Work, 52*(1), 63–70. doi: 10.1093/sw/52.1.63

Bride, B. E., Radley, M., & Figley, C. R. (2007). Measuring compassion fatigue. *Clinical Social Work Journal, 35*, 155–163. doi: 10.1007/s10615-007-0091-7

Brun, C., & Rapp, R. C. (2001). Strengths-based case management: Individuals' perspectives on strengths and the case manager relationship. *Social Work, 46*(3), 278–289.

Case Management Society of America. (2010). *Standards for practice in case management.* Retrieved January 7, 2015, from http://www.cmsa.org/portals/0/pdf/memberonly /StandardsOfPractice.pdf

Cheung, Y. W., Bong-Ho, M., & Tak-Sing, C. (2005). Personal empowerment and life satisfaction among self-help group members in Hong Kong. *Small Group Research, 36*(3), 354–377.

Ciarrochi, J., & Heaven, P. L. (2008). Learned social hopelessness: The role of explanatory style in predicting social support during adolescence. *Journal of Child Psychology & Psychiatry, 49*(12), 1279–1286. doi: 10.1111/j.1469-7610.2008.01950

Claiborne, N., & Lawson, H. (2005). An intervention framework for collaboration. *Families in Society, 86*(1), 93–103.

Corey, M. S., Corey, G., & Corey, C. (2014). *Groups: Process and practice* (9th ed.). Pacific Grove, CA: Cengage.

Corsi, K. F., Rinehart, D. J., Kwiatkowski, C. F., & Booth, R. E. (2010). Case management outcomes for women who use crack. *Journal of Evidence-Based Social Work, 7,* 30–40. doi: 10.1080/15433710903175858

DeCoster, V. A., & George, L. (2005). An empowerment approach for elders living with diabetes: A pilot study of a community-based self-help group. The Diabetes Club. *Educational Gerontology, 31*(9), 699–713.

Donaldson, L. P. (2004). Toward validating the therapeutic benefits of empowerment-oriented social action groups. *Social Work with Groups, 27*(2/3), 159–175.

DuBois, B., & Miley, K. K. (2014). *Social work: An empowering profession* (8th ed.). Boston: Pearson.

Eng, E., Rhodes, S. D., & Parker, E. (2009). Natural helper models to enhance a community's health and competence. In R. J. DiClemente, R. A. Crosby, & M. C. Kegler (Eds.), *Emerging theories in health promotion practice and research* (2nd ed., pp. 303–330). San Francisco: Jossey-Bass.

Figley, C. R. (1995). *Compassion fatigue: Coping with secondary traumatic stress disorders in those who treat the traumatized.* New York: Brunner/Mazel.

Giffords, E. D. (2009). The Internet and social work: The next generation. *Families in Society, 90*(4), 413–418. doi: 10.1606/1044-3894.3920

Gutiérrez, L. M. (1991). Empowering women of color: A feminist model. In M. Bricker-Jenkins, N. R. Hooyman, & N. Gottlieb (Eds.), *Feminist social work practice in clinical settings* (pp. 199–214). Newbury Park, CA: Sage.

Healy, K. (2001). Reinventing critical social work: Challenges from practice, context and postmodernism. *Critical Social Work, 2*(1). Retrieved June 8, 2015, from http://www1.uwindsor.ca /criticalsocialwork/reinventing-critical-social-work -challenges-from-practice-context-and-postmodernism

Healy, L. M. (2008). International social work. In T. Mizrahi & L. E. Davis (Eds.), *Encyclopedia of social work: Vol. 2* (20th ed., pp. 483–488). Washington, DC: NASW Press.

Hendryx, M., Green, C. A., & Perrin, N. A. (2009). Social support, activities, and recovery from serious mental illness: STARS study findings. *Journal of Behavioral Health Services & Research, 36*(3), 320–329. doi: 10.1007/s11414-008-9151-1

Hill, K., & Ferguson., S. M. (2014). Web 2.0 in social work macro practice: Ethical considerations and questions. *Journal of Social Work Values & Ethics, 11*(1), 2–11. Retrieved June 9, 2015, from jswve.org /download/2014-1/articles/2-JSWVE-11-1Web%202.0%20in%20 Social%20Work%20Macro%20Practice-pp%202-11.pdf

Houghton, D. J., & Joinson, A. N. (2010). Privacy, social network sites, and social relations. *Journal of Technology in Human Services, 28*(1/2), 74–94. doi:10.1080/15228831003770775

Johnson, E. D. (2000). Differences among families coping with serious mental illness: A qualitative analysis. *American Journal of Orthopsychiatry, 70*(1), 126–134.

Kim, H., & Lee, S. Y. (2009). Supervisory communication, burnout and turnover intention among social workers in health care settings. *Social Work in Health Care, 48,* 364–385. doi: 10.1080/00981380802598499

Kim, H., Ji, J., & Kao, E. (2011). Burnout and physical health among social workers: A three-year longitudinal study. *Social Work, 56*(3), 258–268. doi: 10.1093/sw/56.3.258

Knight, C., & Gitterman, A. (2013). Group work with bereaved individuals: The power of mutual aid. *Social Work, 59*(1), 5–11. doi: 10.1093/sw/swt050

LaMendola, W. (2010). Social work and social presence in an online world. *Journal of Technology in Human Services, 28*(1/2), 108–119. doi: 10.1080/15228831003759562

Lawson, H. (2008). Collaborative practice. In T. Mizrahi & L. E. Davis (Eds.), *Encyclopedia of social work: Vol. 1* (20th ed., pp. 341–346). Washington, DC: NASW Press.

Lee, J. J., & Miller, S. E. (2013). A self-care framework for social workers: Building a strong foundation for practice. *Families in Society, 94*(2), 96–103. doi: 10.1606/1044-3894.4289

Lewandowski, C. A., & Hill, T. J. (2009). The impact of emotional and material social support on women's drug treatment completion. *Health & Social Work, 34*(3), 213–221. doi: 10.1093/hsw/34.3.213

Liddie, B. W. (1991). Relearning feminism on the job. In M. Bricker-Jenkins, N. R. Hooyman, & N. Gottlieb (Eds.), *Feminist social work practice in clinical settings* (pp. 131–146). Newbury Park, CA: Sage.

Lietz, C. A. (2007). Strengths-based group practice: Three case studies. *Social Work with Groups, 30*(2), 73–87. doi: 10.1300/ J009v30n02_07

Luthans, F., Norman, S. M., & Avolio, B. J. (2008). The mediating role of psychological capital in the supportive organizational climate-employee performance relationship. *Journal of Organizational Behavior, 29*(2), 219–238. doi/10.1002/job.507

Maslach, C. (2003). Job burnout: New directions in research and intervention. *Current Directions in Psychological Science, 12*(5), 189–192.

Maslach, C., & Leiter, M. P. (2008). Early predictors of job burnout and engagement. *Journal of Applied Psychology, 93*(3), 498–512. doi: 10.1037/0021-9010.93.3.498

Mok, B.-H. (2004). Self-help group participation and empowerment in Hong Kong. *Journal of Sociology & Social Welfare, 31*(3), 153–168.

Moos, R. H. (2008). Active ingredients of substance use–focused self-help groups. *Addiction, 103*(3), 387–396. doi: 10.1111/j.1360-0443.2007.02111

Morelli, P. T., & Fong, R. (2000). The role of Hawaiian elders in substance abuse treatment among Asian/Pacific Islander women. *Journal of Family Social Work, 4*(4), 33–44.

Moxley, D. P. (1989). *The practice of case management.* Newbury Park, CA: Sage.

Moxley, D. P., & Freddolino, P. P. (1994). Client-driven advocacy and psychiatric disability: A model for social work practice. *Journal of Sociology and Social Welfare, 21*(2), 91–108.

Mullender, A., Ward, D., & Fleming, J. (2013). *Empowerment in action: Self-directed groupwork.* Basingstoke, England: Palgrave-Macmillan.

Munn-Giddings, C., & McVicar, A. (2007). Self-help groups as mutual support: What do carers value? *Health & Social Care in the Community, 15*(1), 26–34.

National Association of Social Workers [NASW]. (2008c). Professional impairment. In *Social work speaks: National Association of Social Workers policy statements 2012-2014* (9th ed., pp. 262-271). Washington, DC: NASW Press.

National Association of Social Workers [NASW]. (2008d). Professional self-care and social work. *Social work speaks: National Association of Social Workers Policy Statements 2012-2014* (9th ed., pp. 267-271). pp. 267-271 Washington, DC: NASW Press.

National Association of Social Workers (NASW). (2012). *NASW annual report 2011-2012.* Retrieved January 6, 2015, from, naswdc.org/nasw/annual_report/2012/2012AnnualReport.pdf

Nelson-Becker, H. (2005). Religion and coping in older adults: A social work perspective. *Journal of Gerontological Social Work, 45*(1/2), 51–67.

Nelson-Becker, H. (2006). Voices of resilience: Older adults in hospice care. *Journal of Social Work in End-Of-Life & Palliative Care, 2*(3), 87–106.

Nwakeze, P. C., Magura, S., Rosenblum, A., & Josephs, H. (2000). Service outcomes of peer consumer advocacy for soup kitchen guests. *Journal of Social Service Research, 27*(2), 19–38.

Pearlman, L. A., & Saakvitne, K. W. (1995). *Trauma and the therapist: Countertransference and vicarious traumatization in psychotherapy with incest survivors.* New York: Norton.

Peebles-Wilkins, W. (2008). Professional impairment. In T. Mizrahi & L. E. Davis (Eds.), *Encyclopedia of social work: Vol. 3* (20th ed., pp. 423–425). Washington, DC: NASW Press.

Radley, M., & Figley, C. R. (2007). The social psychology of compassion. *Clinical Social Work Journal, 35*(3), 207–214.

Reamer, F. G. (2013). Social work in a digital age: Ethical and risk management challenges. *Social Work, 58*(1), 163–172. doi 10.1093/sw/swt003

Reichert, E. (2006). *Understanding human rights.* Thousand Oaks, CA: Sage.

Roberts-DeGennaro, M. (2008). Case management. In T. Mizrahi & L. E. Davis (Eds.), *Encyclopedia of social work: Vol. 1* (20th ed., pp. 222–227). Washington, DC: NASW Press.

Roe-Sepowitz, D. A., Pate, K. N., Bedard, L. E., & Greenwald, M. (2009). Trauma-based group intervention for incarcerated girls. *Social Work with Groups, 32,* 330–341. doi: 10.1080/01609510903092972

Schwartz, R. H., Tiamiyu, M. F., & Dwyer, D. J. (2007). Social worker hope and perceived burnout: The effects of age, years in practice, and setting. *Administration in Social Work, 31*(4), 103–119. doi: 10.1300/J147v31n04_08

Segal, S. P. (2008). Self-help groups. In T. Mizrahi & L. E. Davis (Eds.), *Encyclopedia of social work: Vol. 4* (20th ed., pp. 14–17). Washington, DC: NASW Press.

Shulman, L., & Gitterman, A. (2005). The life model, oppression, vulnerability and resilience, mutual aid and the mediating function. In A. Gitterman & L. Shulman (Eds.), *Mutual aid groups, vulnerable and resilient populations, and the life cycle* (3rd ed., pp. 3–37). New York: Columbia University Press.

Siebert, D. C. (2005). Help seeking for AOD misuse among social workers: Patterns, barriers, and implications. *Social Work, 101,* 65–75.

Simpson, G. M. (2008). A qualitative perspective of family resources among low income, African American grandmother-caregivers. *Journal of Gerontological Social Work, 51*(1/2), 19–41. doi: 10.1080/01634370801967539

Sintonen, S., & Pehkonen, A. (2014). Effect of social networks and well-being on acute care needs. *Health and Social Care in the Community, 22*(1), 87–95. doi: 10.1111/hsc.12068

Smith, R. K. M. (2003). *International human rights.* New York: Oxford University Press.

Stang, I., & Mittelmark, M. (2009). Learning as an empowerment process in breast cancer self-help groups. *Journal of Clinical Nursing, 18*(14), 2049–2057. doi: 10.1111/j.1365-2702.2008.0232

Staples, L. (2004). Social action groups. In C. D. Garvin, L. M. Gutierrez, & M. J. Galinsky (Eds.), *Handbook of social work with groups* (pp. 344–359). New York: Guilford Press.

Staples, L. (2012). Community organizing for social justice: Grassroots groups for power. *Social Work with Groups, 35*(3), 287–296. doi: 10.1080/01609513.2012.656233

Stewart, M. J., Makwarimba, E., Beiser, M., Neufeld, A., Simich, L., & Spitzer, D. (2010). Social support and health: Immigrants' and refugees' perspectives. *Diversity in Health & Care, 7*(2), 91–103. doi: 10.1007/s10903-005-5123-1

Strom-Gottfried, K., Thomas, M. S., & Anderson, H. (2014). Social work and social media: Reconciling ethical standards and emerging technologies. *Journal of Social Work Values & Ethics, 11*(1), 54–65.

Van Breda, A. D. (2011). Resilient workplaces: An initial conceptualization. *Families in Society, 92*(1), 33–40. doi: 10.1606/1044-3894.4059

Wituk, S., Shepherd, M. D., Slavich, S., Warren, M. L., & Meissen, G. (2000). *Social Work, 45*(2), 157–165.

Wood, S. A. (2007). The analysis of an innovative HIV-positive women's support group. *Social Work with Groups, 30*(3), 9–28. doi: 10.1300/J009v30n03_02

Woody, D., & Woody, D. J. (2007). The significance of social support on parenting among a group of single, low-income,

African American mothers. *Journal of Human Behavior in the Social Environment, 15*(2/3), 183–198. doi: 10.1300/J137v15n02_11

Chapter 14

Acevedo-Garcia, D., Osypuk, T. L., McArdle, N., & Williams, D. R. (2008). Toward a policy-relevant analysis of geographic and racial/ethnic disparities in child health. *Health Affairs, 27*(2), 321–333.

Austin, C. D., Des Camp, E., Flux, D., McClelland, R. W., & Sieppert, J. (2005). Community development with older adults in their neighborhoods: The Elder Friendly Communities program. *Families in Society, 86*(3), 401–409.

Breton, M. (1994). On the meaning of empowerment and empowerment-oriented social work practice. *Social Work with Groups, 17*(3), 23–37.

Breton, M. (2001). Neighborhood resiliency. *Journal of Community Practice, 9*(1), 21–36.

Chambers, D. E., & Bonk, J. F. (2013). *Social policy and social programs: A method for the practical public policy analyst* (6th ed.). Boston: Pearson.

DuBois, B., & Miley, K. K. (2014). *Social work: An empowering profession* (8th ed.). Boston: Pearson.

Everett, J. E., Homstead, K., & Drisko, J. (2007). Frontline worker perceptions of the empowerment process in community-based agencies. *Social Work, 52*(2), 161–170. doi: 10.1093/sw/52.2.161

Franco, L. M., Mckay, M., Miranda, A., Chambers, N., Paulino, A., & Lawrence, R. (2007). Voices from the community: Key ingredients for community collaboration. *Social Work in Mental Health, 5*(3/4), 313–331. doi: 10.1300/J200v05n03_04

Freire, P. (1993). *Pedagogy of the oppressed* (new rev. 20th anniversary ed.). New York: Continuum.

Freire, P. (1997). *Pedagogy of the heart.* New York: Continuum.

Gilbert, N., & Terrell, P. (2013). *Dimensions of social welfare policy* (8th ed.). Boston: Pearson.

Gitlin, L. N., & Lyons, K. J. (2014). *Successful grant writing: Strategies for health and human service professionals* (4th ed.). New York: Springer.

Harvey, M. R., Mondesir, A. V., & Aldrich, H. (2007). Fostering resilience in traumatized communities: A community empowerment model of intervention. *Journal of Aggression, Maltreatment, & Trauma, 14*(1/2), 265–285. doi: 10.1300/ J146v14n01_14

Hick, S., & McNutt, J. (2002). *Advocacy and activism on the Internet: Perspectives from community organization and social policy.* Chicago, IL: Lyceum.

Jackson-Elmore, C. (2005). Informing state policy makers: Opportunities for social workers. *Social Work, 50*(3), 251–261.

Karger, H. J., & Stoesz, D. (2014). *American social welfare policy: A pluralist approach* (7th ed.). Boston: Pearson.

Kemp, S. P. (2010). Place matters: Toward a rejuvenated theory of environment for social work practice. In W. Borden (Ed.), *The place and play of theory in social work: Toward a critical*

pluralism in contemporary practice (pp. 114–145). New York: Columbia University Press.

Kemp, S. P., Whittaker, J. K., & Tracy, E. M. (2002). Contextual social work practice. In M. O'Melia & K. K. Miley (Eds.), *Pathways to power: Readings in contextual social work practice* (pp. 15–34). Boston: Allyn & Bacon.

Kleinkauf, C. (1981). A guide to giving legislative testimony. *Social Work, 26,* 297–303.

Lane, M., & Henry, K. (2004). Beyond symptoms: Crime prevention and community development. *Australian Journal of Social Work, 39*(2), 201–213.

Long, P. (2002). Ethical and inescapable: Politicized social work practice. In M. O'Melia & K. K. Miley (Eds.), *Pathways to power: Readings in contextual social work practice* (pp. 55–73). Boston: Allyn & Bacon.

McGowan, B. G. (1987). Advocacy. In A. Minahan (Ed.), *Encyclopedia of social work: Vol. 1* (18th ed., pp. 89–95). Silver Spring, MD: NASW.

McNutt, J. G., & Menon, G. (2003). Electronic democracy and social welfare policy: A look at Internet resources. *Social Policy Journal, 2*(3), 87–91.

McNutt, J. G., & Menon, G. M. (2008). The rise of cyberactivism: Implications for the future of advocacy in the human services. *Families in Society, 89*(1), 33–38. doi: 10.1606/1044-3894.3706

National Association of Social Workers [NASW]. (1999). *Code of ethics of the National Association of Social Workers.* Washington, D.C.: Author.

National Association of Social Workers [NASW]. (2009a). *Lobby day toolkit.* Retrieved June 28, 2011, from www.socialworkreinvestment.org/content/lobbyday.pdf

National Association of Social Workers [NASW]. (2011b). Social services. In *Social work speaks: National Association of Social Workers policy statements, 2015–2017* (10th ed., pp. 280–283). Washington, D.C.: NASW Press.

Ohmer, M. L. (2007). Citizen participation in neighborhood organizations and its relationship to volunteers' self- and collective efficacy and sense of community. *Social Work Research, 31*(1), 109–120. doi: 10.1093/swr/31.2.109

Ortiz, L. P., Wirtz, K., & Rodriguez, C. (2004). Legislative casework: Where policy and practice intersect. *Journal of Sociology and Social Welfare, 31*(2), 49–68.

Reeser, L. C. (1991). Professionalization, striving, and social work activism. *Journal of Social Service Research, 14*(3/4), 1–22.

Reynolds, B. C. (1951). *Social work and social living.* New York: Citadel Press.

Rivera, F. G., & Erlich, J. L. (1998). A time of fear: A time of hope. In F. G. Rivera & J. L. Erlich (Eds.), *Community organizing in a diverse society* (pp. 1–24). Boston: Allyn & Bacon.

To, S.-M. (2007). Empowering school social work practices for positive youth development: Hong Kong experience. *Adolescence, 42*(167), 555–567.

Weil, M. (2005). Introduction: Contexts and challenges for 21st century communities. In M. Weil (Ed.), *Handbook of community practice* (pp. 3–34). Thousand Oaks, CA: Sage.

Weil, M., & Gamble, D. N. (2005). Evolution, models, and the changing context of community practice. In M. Weil (Ed.), *Handbook of community practice* (pp. 117–150). Thousand Oaks, CA: Sage.

Wituk, S., Pearson, R., Bomhoff, K., Hinde, M., & Meissen, G. (2007). A participatory process involving people with developmental disabilities in community development. *Journal of Developmental and Physical Disabilities, 19,* 323–335. doi: 10.1007/s10882-007-9052

Woodford, M. R., & Preston, S. (2011). Developing a strategy to meaningfully engage stakeholders in program/policy planning: A guide for human services managers and practitioners. *Journal of Community Practice, 19,* 159–174. doi: 10.1080/10705422.2011.571091

Zippay, A. (1995). The politics of empowerment. *Social Work, 40,* 263–267.

Chapter 15

Altpeter, M., Schopler, J. H., Galinsky, M. J., & Pennell, J. (1999). Participatory research as social work practice: When is it viable? *Journal of Progressive Human Services, 10*(2), 31–53.

Anastas, J. W. (2008). Ethics in research. In T. Mizrahi & L. E. Davis (Eds.), *Encyclopedia of social work: Vol. 2* (20th ed., pp. 151–158). Washington, DC: NASW Press.

Andrews, A. B., Motes, P. S., Floyd, A. G., Flerx, V. C., & Lopez-DeFede, A. (2005). Building evaluation capacity in community-based organizations: Reflections of an empowerment evaluation team. *Journal of Community Practice, 13*(4), 85–104.

Bloom, M., Fischer, J., & Orme, J. G. (2009). *Evaluating practice: Guidelines for the accountable professional* (6th ed.). Boston: Pearson.

Bolen, R. M., & Hall, J. C. (2007). Managed care and evidence-based practice: The untold story. *Journal of Social Work Education, 43*(3), 463–479.

Carroll, A. M., Vetor, K., Holmes, S., & Supiano, K. P. (2005). Ask the consumer: An innovative approach to dementia-related adult day service evaluation. *American Journal of Alzheimer's Disease and Other Dementias, 20*(5), 290–294.

Conway, P., Cresswell, J., Harmon, D., Pospishil, C., Smith, K., Wages, J., & Weisz, L. (2010). Using empowerment evaluation to facilitate the development of intimate partner and sexual violence prevention programs. *Journal of Family Social Work, 13*(4), 343–361. doi: 10.1080/10522158.2010.493736

Fetterman, D. M. (1996). Empowerment evaluation: An introduction to theory and practice. In D. M. Fetterman, S. J. Kaftarian, & A. Wandersman (Eds.), *Empowerment evaluation: Knowledge and tools for self-assessment and accountability* (pp. 3–46). Thousand Oaks, CA: Sage.

Fetterman, D. M. (2002). Empowerment evaluation: Building communities of practice and a culture of learning. *American Journal of Community Psychology, 30*(1), 89–102.

Freire, P. (1973a). *Education for critical consciousness.* New York: Continuum.

Freire, P. (1973b). *Pedagogy of the oppressed.* New York: Seabury.

Freire, P. (1993). *Pedagogy of the oppressed* (new rev. 20th anniversary ed.). New York: Continuum.

Gambrill, E. (2006). Evidence-based practice and policy: Choices ahead. *Research on Social Work Practice, 16*(10), 336–357.

Gambrill, E. (2008). Evidence-based (informed) macro practice: Process and philosophy. *Journal of Evidence-Based Social Work, 5*(3/4), 423–452. doi: 10.1080/15433710802083971

Gibbs, L., & Gambrill, E. (2002). Evidence-based practice: Counterarguments to objections. *Research on Social Work Practice, 12,* 452–476.

Grinnell, R. M., & Unrau, Y. A. (2013). *Social work research and evaluation* (10th ed.). New York: Oxford University Press.

Gutiérrez, L., Alvarez, R. A., Nemon, H., & Lewis, E. A. (1996). Multicultural community organizing: A strategy for change. *Social Work, 41*(5), 501–508.

Hacker, K. (2014). *Community-based participatory research.* Los Angeles, CA: Sage.

Hanley, B. (2005). *Research as empowerment? Report of a series of seminars organised by the Toronto Group.* New York and England: Joseph Rowntree Foundation. Retrieved June 8, 2015, from www.jrf.org.uk/sites/files/jrf/1859353185.pdf

Hergenrather, K. C., Rhodes, S. D., Cowan, C. A., Bardhoshi, G., & Pula, S. (2009). Photovoice as community-based participatory research: A qualitative review. *American Journal of Health Behavior, 33*(6), 686–698. doi: 10.1525/jer.2012.7.4.34

Institute for the Advancement of Social Work Research [IASWR]. (2008, January). *Evidence-based practice: A brief from the institute for the advancement of social work research.* Washington, D.C.: International Association of Social Science Research.

Jenson, J. M., & Howard, M. O. (2008). Evidence-based practice. In T. Mizrahi & L. E. Davis (Eds.), *Encyclopedia of social work: Vol. 2* (20th ed., pp. 158–165). Washington, DC: NASW Press.

Johnson, M., & Austin, M. J. (2008). Evidence-based practice in the social services: Implications for organizational change. *Journal of Evidence-Based Social Work, 5*(1/2), 239–269. doi: 10.1300/J394v05n01_12

Johnston-Goodstar, K. (2013). Indigenous youth participatory action research: Re-visioning social justice for social work with indigenous youths. *Social Work, 58*(4), 314–320. doi: 10.1093/sw/swt036

Mirzaa, M., Gossettb, A., Chana, N. K.-C., Burford, L., & Hammelab, J. (2008). Community reintegration for people with psychiatric disabilities: Challenging systemic barriers to service provision and public policy through participatory action research. *Disability & Society, 23*(4), 323–336. doi: 10.1080/09687590802038829

Molloy, J. K. (2007). Photovoice as a tool for social justice workers. *Journal of Progressive Human Services, 18*(2), 39–55. doi: 10.1300/J059v18n02_04

Moxley, D. P., & Washington, O. G. M. (2012). Using a developmental action research strategy to build theory for intervention into homelessness among minority women. *Social Work in Mental Health, 10*(5), 426–444. doi: 10.1080/15332985.2012.698957

National Association of Social Workers. (1999). *Code of ethics of the National Association of Social Workers.* Washington, DC: Author.

Neuman, L. W. (2012). *Basics of social research: Quantitative and qualitative approaches* (3rd ed.). Boston: Pearson.

O'Sullivan, G., Hocking, C., & Spence, D. (2014). Dementia: The need for attitudinal change. *Dementia: International Journal of Social Research and Practice, 13*(4), 483–497. doi: 10.1177/1471301213478241

Patel, T. (2005). The usefulness of oral life (hi)story to understand and empower: The case of trans-racial adoption. *Qualitative Social Work, 10*(2), 327–345.

Plath, D. (2006). Evidence-based practice: Current issues and future directions. *Australian Social Work, 59*(1), 56–72.

Powers, M. C. F., & Freedman, D. A. (2012). Applying a social justice framework to photovoice research on environmental issues: A comprehensive literature review. *Critical Social Work, 13*(2), 81–100. Retrieved June 9, 2015, from www1.uwindsor.ca/criticalsocialwork/applyingsocialjusticeframe-workphotovoiceresearch

Reason, P., & Bradbury, H. (2008). Introduction. In P. Reason & H. Bradbury (Eds.), *The handbook of action research participative inquiry and practice* (pp. 1–10). Los Angeles, CA: Sage.

Regehr, C., Stern, S., & Shlonsky, A. (2007). Operationalizing evidence-based practice: The development of an institute for evidence-based social work. *Research on Social Work Practice, 17*, 408–416. doi: 10.1177/1049731506293561

Ritchie, D. J., & Eby, K. K. (2007). Transcending boundaries: An international, interdisciplinary community partnership to address domestic violence. *Journal of Community Practice, 15*(1/2), 121–145. doi: 10.1300/J125v15n01_06

Rubin, A., & Babbie, E. (2014). *Research methods for social work* (8th ed.). Pacific Grove, CA: Cengage.

Social Work Policy Institute [SWPI]. (2010). *Comparative effectiveness research and social work: Strengthening the connection.* Washington, D.C.: NASW. Retrieved June 1, 2011, from www.socialworkpolicy.org/wp-content/uploads/2010/03/SWPI-CER.ExSummary.pdf

Straus, S., Richardson, W. S., Glasziou, P., & Haynes, R. B. (2011). *Evidence-based medicine: How to practice and teach EBM* (4th ed.). Edinburgh, TX: Churchill Livingstone.

Strier, R. (2007). Anti-oppressive research in social work: A preliminary definition. *British Journal of Social Work, 37*(5), 857–871. doi: 10.1093/bjsw/bcl062

Sutherland, C., & Cheng, Y. (2009). Participatory-action research with (im)migrant women in two small Canadian cities: Using photovoice in Kingston and Peterborough, Ontario. *Journal of Immigrant & Refugee Studies, 7*, 290–307. doi: 10.1080/15562940903150089

Thyer, B. A., & Myers, L. L. (2011). The quest for evidence-based practice: A view from the United States. *Journal of Social Work, 11*(1), 8–25. doi: 10.1177/1468017310381812

Washington, O. G. M., Moxley, D. P., Garriott, L., & Crystal, J. P. (2009). Support and advocacy for older African American homeless women through developmental action research. *Contemporary Nurse, 33*(2), 140–160. doi: 10.5172/conu.2009.33.2.140

Weinbach, R. W., & Grinnell, R. M. (2015). *Statistics for social workers* (9th ed.). Boston: Pearson.

Wernick, L. J., Woodford, M. R., & Kulick, A. (2014). LGBTQQ youth using participatory action research and theater to effect change: Moving adult decision-makers to create youth-centered change. *Journal of Community Practice, 22*(102), 47–66. doi: 10.1080/10705422.2014.901996

Chapter 16

Baughman, K. R., Aultman, J., Hazelett, S., Palmisano, B., O'Neill, A., Ludwick, R., & Sanders, M. (2012). Managing in the trenches of consumer care: The challenges of understanding and initiating the advance care planning process. *Journal of Gerontological Social Work, 55*(8), 721–737. doi: 10.1080/01634372.2012.708389

Berk, L. E. (2014). *Development through the lifespan* (6th ed.). Boston: Pearson.

Birnbaum, M., & Cicchetti, A. (2000). The power of purposeful sessional endings in each group encounter. *Social Work with Groups, 23*(3), 37–52.

Black, K. (2004). Advance directive communication with hospitalized elderly patients: Social workers' roles and practices. *Journal of Gerontological Social Work, 43*(2/3), 131–145.

Black, K. (2007). Advance care planning throughout the end-of-life: Focusing the lens for social work practice. *Journal of Social Work in End-of-Life & Palliative Care, 3*(2), 39–58. doi: 10.1300/J457v03n02_04

Black, K. (2010). Promoting advance care planning through the National Healthcare Decisions Day initiative. *Journal of Social Work in End-of-Life & Palliative Care, 6*(1), 11–26. doi: 10.1080/15524256.2010.489220

Bonanno, G. A. (2009). *The other side of sadness: What the new science of bereavement tells us about life after loss.* New York: Basic Books.

Buchanan, R. J., Chakravorty, B., Bolin, J., Wang, S., & Kim, M.-S. (2004). Decision making and the use of advance directives among nursing home residents at admission and one year after admission. *Journal of Social Work in Long-Term Care, 3*(2), 3–12.

Csikai, E. L. (2008). End-of-life decisions. In T. Mizrahi & L. E. Davis (Eds.), *Encyclopedia of social work: Vol. 2* (20th ed., pp. 126–132). Washington, DC: NASW Press.

Hepworth, D. H., Rooney, R. H., Rooney, G. D., & Strom-Gottfried, K. (2013). *Direct social work practice: Theory and skills* (9th ed.). Pacific Grove, CA: Cengage.

Kramer, B. J., Pacourek, L., & Hovland-Scafe, C. (2003). Analysis of end-of-life content in social work textbooks. *Journal of Social Work Education, 39*, 299–300.

Kübler-Ross, E. (1969). *On death and dying.* New York: Macmillan.

Mirabito, D. M. (2006). Revisiting unplanned termination: Clinicians' perceptions of termination from adolescent mental health treatment. *Families in Society, 87*(2), 171–180.

Nakashima, M. (2003). Beyond coping and adaptation: Promoting a holistic perspective on dying. *Families in Society, 84*(3), 367–376.

National Association of Social Workers [NASW]. (2004b). *NASW standards for palliative and end of life care.* Washington, D.C.: National Association of Social Workers. Retrieved June 7, 2011, from www.socialworkers.org/practice/bereavement/standards/standards0504New.pdf

National Association of Social Workers [NASW]. (2011a). Hospice care. In *Social work speaks: National Association of Social Workers policy statements 2012-2014* (9th ed., pp. 187-192). Washington, DC: NASW Press.

National Association of Social Workers [NASW]. (2014). End-of-life decision-making and care. In *Social work speaks: National Association of Social Workers policy statements, 2015–2017* (10th ed., pp. 101-107). Washington, D.C.: NASW Press.

Nelson-Becker, H. (2006). Voices of resilience: Older adults in hospice care. *Journal of Social Work in End-Of-Life & Palliative Care, 2*(3), 87–106.

Shulman, L. (2012). *The skills of helping individuals, families, groups, and communities* (7th ed.). Pacific Grove, CA: Wadsworth.

Strom-Gottfried, K., & Mowbray, N. D. (2006). Who heals the helper? Facilitating the social worker's grief. *Families in Society, 87*(1), 9–15.

Toseland, R. W., & Rivas, F. F. (2012). *An introduction to group work practice* (7th ed.). Boston: Pearson.

Walter, J. L., & Peller, J. E. (1992). *Becoming solution-focused in brief therapy.* New York: Brunner/Mazel.

Glossary

Ableism prejudice against people who have mental or physical disabilities

Absolute Confidentiality social worker's guarantee that client information will never be recorded or shared in any form; rarely offered in actual practice

Acceptance social work principle of positive regard for clients demonstrated by affirming clients' perspectives and valuing what clients contribute

Access to Resources social work principle that guarantees fair access to available alternatives and opportunities

Accountability social work principle involving professional proficiency, integrity, impartiality, responsible use of resources, and utilization of sound protocols in practice and research

Action Plan outlines the session work of social workers and clients and frames activities to accomplish between meetings

Action Plans intervention plans that detail goals, objectives, strategies, responsibilities, and follow-up for reviewing progress

Action Research empowerment-oriented, participatory research method that incorporates elements of research, education, and action to achieve organizational, community, and social change goals

Activating Resources development phase process in which workers and clients collaborate on action plans by mobilizing available resources through consultancy, resource management, and education

Active Listening listening carefully with empathy and respect to understand situations from the client's view

Activist macrolevel resource management role for identifying and rectifying detrimental societal conditions and involving the general public in change efforts

Activity Log style of recording that details the nature of contacts between workers and clients, including client goals, activities completed, future plans, people involved, and time invested

Adaptive Fit all systems evolve to fit the resources and demands of their worlds

Advance Care Planning advance directives and planning for end-of-life care

Adverse Childhood Experiences (ACEs) cluster of experiences—child abuse, neglect, sexual abuse, family dysfunction—associated with life-long health risks

Advocate microlevel resource management role in which workers act as intermediaries between clients and other systems to ensure access to resources and to protect clients' rights

Ageism belief that one age group is inferior to another

Alliance collaborative partnership among individuals, families, groups, organizations, communities, and/or others to achieve support, service coordination, and social change

Allowing Space allowing moments of silence that give clients chances to formulate words to express their thoughts and feelings

Americans with Disabilities Act (1990) progressive legislative mandate to remove architectural, transportation, and communication barriers to ensure the full participation of persons with disabilities in community life

Articulating Situations dialogue phase process in which workers and clients develop a mutual understanding of the situations, placing client situations in environmental context

Assessing Resource Capabilities discovery phase process in which workers and clients survey available and potential resources within the client's ecosystem

Assessment discovery process to clarify presenting issues, identify clients' strengths and potential, and evaluate availability of resources to determine a viable course of action

Asset Mapping assesses capacities, resources, and assets in a community or neighborhood by completion of an inventory of individual, associational, and institutional capacities

Baseline initial measurement of behavior made during the preintervention period

Best Practices practice models confirmed as or considered effective

Biology and Behavior reciprocal interaction between behavior and biology throughout the life span with positive or negative, subtle or dramatic, short- or long-term effects

Biopsychosocial Dimensions biological, cognitive, and affective characteristics of individuals

Boundaries structural concept referring to the degree of closeness between two systems in transaction; defined by proximity, intensity, and frequency of interaction

Brainstorming free-flowing group process to generate, but not evaluate, creative ideas or solutions; frequently used as part of group, organizational, and community planning

Broker microlevel resource management role to assess situations, provide clients with choices among alternative resources, and facilitate clients' connections with referral agencies

Burnout sense of physical and psychological exhaustion resulting from disempowering work environments or becoming overly invested in the job

Case Management process of accessing and coordinating an array of services and supports relevant to a specific client's needs and goals

Catalyst professional-level resource management role through which workers team with colleagues and other professionals to create organizational, policy, and other social change

Cause Advocacy work to achieve social justice in larger social issues by empowering people to speak out and exercise their influence to correct inequity or achieve social change

Child Maltreatment physical abuse, emotional abuse, sexual abuse, neglect of children

Circular Causality reciprocal influences of human systems and their environments

Clarification active way to check understanding of information

Classism prejudice against those in lower economic classes

Client Advocacy provides assistance when clients experience unexpected obstacles or lack of responsiveness in bureaucratic systems; work to secure available resources for clients in microlevel practice

Client-Driven Advocacy clients take on roles that control advocacy activities, leaving corollary roles for social workers to support their actions

Client Outcome Assessment evaluates the degree of goal achievement and the effectiveness of intervention strategies with a particular client system

Clients' Rights legal and ethical privileges guaranteed to those assuming client roles

Closed Systems systems with rigid boundaries, not open to outside influences or resources

Closed-Ended Group group that meets for a predetermined number of meetings or long enough to reach a desired goal; all members begin and end their participation at the same time

Coalition cooperative alliance of agencies or individuals to address a specific issue or need

Cognitive Behavioral Therapy (CBT) counseling approach focused on how thoughts and feelings trigger behavioral responses, targeting changes in thinking as a method to create desired behavioral changes

Collaboration sharing decision-making power in client–practitioner relationships, freeing clients to access their own power resources

Collaborative Partnership cooperative relationships between clients and social workers characterized by shared mutual responsibilities

Collaborative Teaching educational experiences, including role play and structured training designed for learners to become directly involved rather than simply recipients of education

Colleague professional-level consultancy role that provides professional acculturation for other social workers through mentoring, guidance, and support

Colleague Assistance Programs provide support and encouragement for social workers troubled by psychological stress or chemical dependency to seek professional assistance

Community Development enhances community competence by increasing citizens' involvement in community life

Community Forums open scheduled meetings held to solicit the views of a broad representation of community members

Community Organizing method social workers use to bring together people from the community who share common interests and goals; addresses social problems through collective action

Community Surveys questionnaires administered face to face or mailed to a representative sample of the community population to solicit opinions and collect data about community life

Compassion Fatigue involves harboring negative feelings about the helping process due to worker burnout

Compassion Satisfaction involves sustaining positive feelings and inspiration about the demands of the helping process; derived from protective factors such as personal and organizational self-care

Competence ability of human systems to take care of themselves, draw resources from effective interaction with other systems, and contribute to the resource pool of the social and physical environment

Completing Contracts implemented when clients have made significant progress or achieved success in the plan of action and no longer need social work services

Confidentiality social work principle about clients' right to have what they share held in confidence, forming the basis for trustworthy professional relationships

Confronting clarifies three facets of clients' actions: intent, behavior, and outcome

Conscientization development of critical awareness that results in an "aha" experience

Conscious Use of Self expression of the practitioner's own unique personal and practice style

Consciousness-Raising facilitation of an individual's or group's critical awareness of oppression and sensitivity to status, privilege, and relative situation

Consensus melds variety of views and opinions held by those participating in a decision-making process

Consultancy social work function through which workers and clients at any system level confer and deliberate together to develop plans for change and seek solutions for challenges to social functioning

Consultation a process used to acquire perspectives of knowledgeable persons to add depth to assessments or expertise to implement intervention strategies

Consumer Satisfaction Surveys instruments to assess clients' perceptions or attitudes about an agency's delivery of services

Context environment surrounding a particular system

Contract informal or explicit formal agreement that specifies the terms of service to which clients and social workers agree

Contract for Assessment agreement to further explore the client's situation and assess the resources available

Contract for Change agreement to implement the plan of action

Contract for Relationship agreement between the client and social worker to form a working partnership

Contract for Resolution agreement to conclude the client–social worker relationship

Convener mezzolevel resource management role to promote interagency discussion and planning, mobilize coordinated networks for effective service delivery, and advocate policies that promise equitable funding and just service provisions

Core Values of the Social Work Profession service, social justice, dignity and worth of the person, importance of human relationships, integrity, and practice competence

Creating Alliances development phase process that aligns efforts of clients within groups and support networks; develops collaboration among colleagues, supervisors, and professional organizations

Critical Consciousness occurs when one learns to perceive, question, and take action with respect to social, economic, and political contradictions

Critical Race Theory emphasizes social structures and everyday patterns of action as forces behind racism

Critical Theory emphasizes power differentials in social structures and social interactions

Cultural Competence social worker's ability to acquire and utilize extensive knowledge about various cultural groups

Cultural Diversity phenomena of human differences as generated by membership in various identifiable human groups

Cultural Elements the influences of ethnicity and culture on human functioning

Cultural Genograms schematic diagrams that enhance visual representations of family structure and chronology with unique cultural patterns and interactions

Cultural Identity identity associated with membership in racial or ethnic groups, age cohorts, social and economic class, ability, gender identity, sexual orientation, immigration status, political ideology, religion, regional affiliation, national origin, and personal background

Cultural Responsiveness use client perspective–centered practice skills as a method to achieve multicultural competence

Cultural Sensitivity occurs when social workers recognize that the multiple facets of clients' life experiences affect their values and priorities; awareness and acceptance of cultural similarities and differences in cross-cultural relationships

Cultural Uniqueness derives from membership in multiple cultures such as those associated with gender, occupations, clubs and organizations, geographic regions, ethnicity, and religion

Culture quality of all communities of people identified by geographic location, common characteristics, or similar interests, including values, norms, beliefs, language, and traditions

Data information obtained through qualitative (words) or quantitative (numeric) methods for further analysis

Decode Messages interpret messages based on perception of meaning

Defining Directions dialogue phase process in which practitioners and clients articulate a mutual understanding of the purpose of their work together

Dependent Variable known as the outcome variable; denotes changes in the incidence, severity, or degree of the targeted problems, solutions, or changes in the client system's behaviors, attitudes, or feelings

Development Phase practice processes related to *intervention* and *evaluation* to activate resources, create alliances, expand opportunities through resource development, evaluate success, and integrate gains

Dialogue Phase practice processes related to *engagement* of client systems—developing partnerships, articulating clients' situations, and agreeing to a purpose for the work together

Discovery Phase practice processes related to *assessment*; describes how clients and social workers systematically locate relevant strengths and resources with which to build concrete plans for solutions

Dispositional Attributions occur when credit for improvement is attributed to one's own personal competence

Dual Relationships secondary roles of social workers with clients, including friendships, business associations, family relationships, or sexual involvement; may constitute serious ethical violations

Durable Powers of Attorney for Health Care legal document that assigns the responsibility for following directives if the individual is no longer able to make decisions for himself or herself

Duty to Protect provision in the Patriot Act of 2001 extending enforcement of protection against terrorist attacks to include threats to both persons and property and giving broad powers to the FBI to access certain business records, including medical and psychological records, without warrant, subpoena, or release of information and to prohibit practitioners from informing clients of these actions

Duty to Warn legal obligation of professionals to inform potential victims of impending danger, as prescribed by *Tarasoff v. Regents of the University of California*

Eco-Maps diagrams depicting the ecological context of a focal system

Ecosystems Perspective predominant way social workers frame their generalist practice considering the impact of the sociopolitical, economic, and physical environments on human systems

Education social work function that describes the information exchange and educational partnerships of co-learners and co-teachers at all levels of social work practice

Elder Abuse physical abuse, emotional abuse, sexual abuse, neglect, and/or exploitation of dependent adults or adults over the age of 65

Empathy expresses the objective caring and commitment required for competent social work practice

Empowerment personal empowerment refers to a subjective state of mind; political empowerment refers to the objective reality of opportunities and reallocations of power in societal structures

Empowerment as a Concept constructs a framework for understanding the personal, interpersonal, and sociopolitical dimensions of any given situation

Empowerment as a Process describes how practitioners actually approach their work so that clients can procure personal, interpersonal, and sociopolitical resources to achieve their goals

Empowerment as an Outcome end result of recognizing, facilitating, and promoting a human system's capacity for competent functioning

Empowerment Evaluation alternative approach to conventional program evaluation; fosters ongoing self-assessments and promotes continuous program improvements

Empowerment Method a generalist approach social work practice utilizing three phrases of practice: dialogue (engagement), discovery (assessment), and development (intervention and evaluation)

Enabler microlevel consultancy role for engaging individuals, families, and small groups in counseling processes

Encode Messages translate thoughts and feelings into words and actions

End-of-Life Care care that support "dying well"; meets needs in the psychological, social, spiritual, medical, physical, and financial domains

Environment ecosystemic context of any system

Environmental Opportunities ideologies, social institutions, and community supports that foster individual and societal well-being

Environmental Risks ideologies, institutions, or cultural alignments that work against the well-being of certain individuals and therefore society as a whole

Epigenesis biochemical process that regulates cells and their phenotypic expression without altering the genetic instructions

Equilibrium state of balance within a system

Ethic of Advocacy leverages professional resources as a means to champion the rights of individual cases or a cause

Ethic of Antioppressive Practice redresses oppression and social exclusion through liberation, emancipation, and enfranchisement of population groups who are vulnerable and oppressed

Ethic of Autonomy focuses on two dimensions of autonomy—promoting a sense of capability and ensuring independence of undue influence or control by others

Ethic of Care emphasizes the social caretaking role for both individual care and social action

Ethic of Change effects long-term contextual and multisystemic sustainable and integrative change

Ethic of Collaboration creates alliances to join power resources in planned change efforts

Ethic of Contextual Practice practice that occurs both with and within contexts of physical and social environments

Ethic of Critical Thinking engaging in a process of informed action that derives from multidimensional analysis by "thinking outside the box"

Ethic of Critique critically examines and understands sociopolitical-economic arrangements and their impact on defining human identity, beliefs, and interactions

Ethic of Discourse emphasizes the use of language and influence of context in meaning-making about experience and defining place and value in those experiences

Ethic of Inclusion redresses issues of exclusivity in practice processes by working collaboratively with clients in all facets of practice, policy, and research

Ethic of Justice guarantees clients' access to services, opportunities to experience social and economic privilege, rights to due process, voice in policy formulation, and influence on the allocation of resources

Ethic of Politicized Practice emphasizes that social work is inherently political and that social workers have a responsibility to engage in social and political action

Ethic of Power critically uses power to protect human rights and achieve social justice

Ethic of Praxis engages in reflective discourse and a continuous loop of action, reflection, and action throughout social change efforts

Ethic of Respect uses a strategy of cultural naiveté in discovering and respecting people's capabilities and talents

Evidence-Based Practice incorporation of salient research about the efficacy of interventions into decision-making processes about programs and services

Evolutionary Change describes how individuals and other human systems change and stabilize in response to internal and external forces

Exceptions indications that things are going well or that difficulties have abated, even if only briefly

Expanding Opportunities development phase process describing how social workers join with clients to expand societal resources through program development, community organizing, and social action

Externalizing narrative strategy that separates the person from the problem

Facilitator mezzolevel consultancy role for activating participation of constituents in organizational development efforts

Fair Hearings and Appeals venue for appealing decisions that have negatively affected clients' benefits or services

Feedback continuous flow of information between systems actions; or reflective comments provided to others about their behaviors or the results of their actions

Feminist Perspective regards gender as central to social organization, connecting personal issues to political and social forces

Fetal Alcohol Spectrum Disorder diagnostic category that includes the range of effects of alcohol consumption during pregnancy on the child's physical, cognitive, and behavioral development

Focal System identified reference point for analysis or change

Focus Groups qualitative research technique for gathering information about a particular topic from a select group of respondents

Force Field Analysis planning strategy to identify factors that drive or obstruct macrolevel change

Forced Migration migration precipitated by such events as violent political upheaval or devastating natural disasters, including hurricanes, typhoons, or drought

Forming Partnerships dialogue phase process describes how workers and clients define empowering relationships, reflecting the uniqueness of client systems and fitting professional purposes and standards

Frames of Reference perceptions of others and expectations of situations that influence how we process information and interpret events

Framing Solutions discovery phase process describing collaborative, concrete, and generalist methods for workers and clients to develop detailed plans for action

Generalist Social Work multileveled approach through which practitioners work with clients at all system levels, link clients to resources, advocate just social policies and responsive service delivery, and research practice effectiveness

Generalizing Outcomes carrying over gains in one area into other aspects of daily functioning

Genograms schematic diagrams that visually represent family structure and chronology

Genome entire set of genetic material in a cell

Genotype genetic blueprint

Genuineness personal quality of effective workers characterized by authenticity, nondefensiveness, and spontaneity

Goal statement of desired intervention outcome

Goal Attainment Scaling (GAS) type of evaluation design that measures client achievement levels according to a predetermined, incremental scale

Goodness of Fit mutually beneficial balance between persons and environments

Grief emotional response to loss

Health Insurance Portability and Accountability Act of 1996 (HIPAA) stipulates legal requirements and mandated compliance procedures to ensure privacy of health information

Hegemony invisible control over norms held by the majority group

Heterosexism prejudice against people whose sexual orientation differs from that of heterosexuals

Hierarchy distribution of power, status, and privilege among individuals and subsystems in a particular system

Holons systems that are a part of larger systems (environments) and that are composed of smaller systems (subsystems)

Hope visualization of positive outcomes and optimism for the future

Hopelessness disenfranchisement and oppression; leads to the conclusion that failure is inevitable in spite of best efforts

Human Dignity and Worth fundamental social work value that holds all people have the right to respect and consideration, regardless of race, ethnicity, gender, sexual orientation, age, ability, or socioeconomic status

Hypotheses tentative statements about the relationship between the independent (intervention) and dependent (outcome) variables

Identifying Strengths discovery phase process to search for client strengths in interpersonal relationships, community connections, cultural memberships, previous experiences, and current change attempts

Incremental Steps small steps marking progress toward goal achievement as detailed in an action plan

Independent Variable the intervention variable; measures whether the intervention is the causal, or influencing, variable that affects change

Individualization social work principle that reflects treating each client as a persons with distinct differences

Informed Consent a process by which clients grant explicit permission to release specific information to a third party; also consent by subjects to participate only after researchers fully disclose the purpose and potential consequences of the research and evaluation

Institutional Racism ethnic discrimination in institutions that diminishes political power by closing opportunity structures of society

Integrating Gains development phase process that emphasizes the importance of client growth, development, and change as the professional relationship ends

Interaction puts structure of a social system into motion and shows how the system operates as its components respond to and affect each other

Interpersonal Empowerment involves the ability to successfully interact with and influence others

Intersectionality confounding effects of factors such as class, culture, race, ethnicity, and other differences that exacerbate disparities

Intervening Variables previously unknown or predictable factors that influence the outcome of research

Intervention at Multiple System Levels intervention options move beyond individually focused practice to include micro-, mezzo-, and marcolevel client systems and the social work profession

Intimate Partner Violence violence within marital or couple relationships, such as physical, emotional, and sexual abuse or financial exploitation

Involuntary Clients clients participating in social work services as a result of mandates by others; frequently occurs in work related to child welfare, domestic violence, criminal justice, mental health, and substance abuse

Key Informant Studies structured interviews, surveys, or focus groups with individuals identified as having expertise on the subject under study

Legislative Advocacy press for change in public policies in the context of legislative activities

Legislative Analysis critically examines legislative proposals for substantive issues, committee structure, fiscal requirements, political dimensions, and sources of support and opposition

Legislative Testimony formal process for asking questions and expressing opinions at public hearings held about newly proposed or officially adopted social policies

Life Course Theory emphasizes the influences of the socio-cultural-historical contexts on human development

Living Wills legally recognized documents that provide instructions with respect to the application of life-sustaining measures

Lobbying political activities that seek to sway the plans of lawmakers and government officeholders for legislative and public policy

Macrolevel Intervention social change in neighborhoods, communities, and society through such activities as neighborhood organizing, community planning, locality development, public education, policy practice, and social action

Managed Care decision-making process for determining eligibility for behavioral, health, and mental health services

Mandatory Reporting unique state laws that require social workers and other designated professionals to report instances of child maltreatment or elder and dependent abuse

Maternalism unintentional control exercised through overpowering caring behaviors

Measurement a process to assess the current status of the object under study or to evaluate the outcome

Mediator mezzolevel resource management role in which social workers use skills to negotiate differences and resolve conflicts within group and organizational networks

Metaphor ambiguous description that frames situations in new ways, thus inviting clients to make their own interpretations

Mezzolevel Intervention work to create changes within organizations and formal groups, such as task groups, teams, organizations, and the service delivery network

Microaggressions hidden messages of racism and prejudice in everyday verbal and nonverbal communications

Microlevel Intervention work with people individually, in families, or in small groups to foster changes within personal functioning, in social relationships, and in the ways people interact with social and institutional resources

Modeling learning new behaviors and attitudes by observing others

Monitor professional-level consultancy role through which social workers provide support for colleagues to uphold expectations for ethical conduct

Motivation degree of attention and energy within a human system to move in a specific direction

Motivational Interviewing offers concrete strategies to help clients resolve ambivalence about change and energizes client motivation to participate in the intervention process

Multicultural Social Work social work practice with culturally diverse client populations

Multiculturalism multiple cultural identities, backgrounds, life experiences, and perspectives

Mutual Aid process by which group members help themselves by helping each other

Narrative Strategies constructivist strategies that help clients take charge of their stories in ways that emphasize their strengths, experience their pride, and prepare them for a more desirable future

Natural Helpers people known in neighborhoods, workplaces, schools, or churches who function effectively on their own and who provide resources and support to other around them

Needs Assessment formalized macrolevel process to document problems, identify unmet needs, and establish priorities for service and resource development

Nodal Events expected and unexpected life-changing events that disrupts an individual's or system's equilibrium

Nominal Group Technique small group strategy to generate information about a specific issue using a round-robin technique and forum for discussing responses and establishing rank-ordered priorities

Nongovernmental Organizations (NGOs) legally constituted, nonprofit, voluntary organizations created by private persons or organizations that are independent from direct governmental control

Nonjudgmentalism social work principle that requires workers to neither blame nor evaluate others as good or bad

Nonverbal Communication messages accompanying every verbal expression and sometimes standing on their own, including body posture, facial expressions, eye contact, head and body movements, other attending behaviors, voice tone, inflection, and intensity

Nonverbal Responses powerful, yet ambiguous, behavioral messages that communicate through the way we sit, the looks we give, and how we express ourselves

Normalize occurs when practitioners consider behaviors in environmental context, conveying their belief that, in these particular circumstances, most people would respond similarly

Note Taking record of specific details noted during an interview that without notes may be difficult to remember

Objectives statements articulating the specifics of planned action—the who, what, where, when, and how

Objectivity social work principles involved in separating one's own personal feelings from a client's situation, avoiding the pitfalls of bias, labeling, detachment, or overidentification

Open Systems systems with permeable boundaries that facilitate exchange of resources between systems

Open-Ended Group ongoing group focused on a topic or shared concern; new members enter and other members leave at any time as the group continues to meet

Oppression injustice resulting from the domination and control of resources by certain groups at the expense of others as well as entitling favored groups and disenfranchising others

Organizational Assessments compiled and analyzed information about internal characteristics of organizations as well as the demands and resources of their environments

Outreach macrolevel educational role for informing the general public about social problems, describing social injustices, and suggesting services and policies that address issues

Paternalism occurs when preferences and decisions are imposed on clients based on "knowing best" or "knowing what is in the best interest of the client"

Peer Review involves consultation with professional colleagues for the purpose of professional accountability and quality assurance

Person:Environment notation about the interrelatedness of people in transaction with their social and physical environments

Personal Empowerment one's personal sense of competence, mastery, and ability to effect change

Phenotypic Expression observable expression of genetic blueprint

Planner macrolevel consultancy role through which workers collect and assess data systematically, explore alternative courses of action, and recommend changes to community leaders

Policy Advocacy involves legislative, administrative, and judicial initiatives by practitioners related to program expansion, funding, preventive services, and standards of care

Policy Analysis examines the social, economic, political, and global variables evident in public policy initiatives, including inherent values, preferences, costs, and benefits

Posttraumatic Growth positive outcomes emanating from traumatic experiences

Posttraumatic Stress Disorder clusters of symptoms associated with emotional responses to crises and trauma, including intrusive thoughts, emotional distress, physiological discomfort, and functional impairment

Power attained when an individual or group has access to information and societal resources and is thus able to choose actions from many possibilities and act on these choices

Power Blocks deny access to opportunities and thereby undermine competent functioning

Powerlessness pervasive oppression of disenfranchised population groups, individually or in communities, resulting in self-blame, distrust, alienation, vulnerability, and disenfranchisement

Practice Evaluation method of assessing the outcomes and measuring the effectiveness of social work strategies

Praxis cycle of reflection, action, and reflection

Privilege occurs when membership in some cultural groups confers differential and preferential status

Privileged Communication occurs when a social worker is legally prohibited from divulging in court private conversations her or she had with the client

Privileged Groups membership confers status, power, authority, and domination

Proactive Responding dialogue skills used by strengths-focused social workers to encourage clients to articulate their current situation and uncover strengths and resources

Procedural Due Process protects individuals' rights when dealing with governmental bodies

Process Recording contains verbatim account of dialogue with clients, comments on the social worker's reactions and feelings, analysis and interpretations of the transactions, and the supervisor's comments

Professional-Level Intervention addresses myriad accountability and practice issues within the system of the social work profession itself

Program Evaluation outcome assessment used to determine the value of the particular program under review

Progress Evaluation involves continually monitoring and evaluating the success of the action plan

Psychological First Aid attending to clients' immediate needs by listening to and acting on their concerns, validating expressed feelings, offering information about what is happening and what clients can expect, and connecting clients to existing supports

Public Hearings open forums often sponsored by legislators or public officials at which the general public can comment on newly proposed or adopted policies

Purpose of Social Work assess challenges in social functioning, develop skills, and create support for change; link people with resources and services; work toward a humane and adequate social service delivery system; participate in social policy development; and engage in research

Purposefulness occurs when social work relationships are grounded in fulfilling the profession's mission and purpose to improve quality of life and achieve a goodness of fit between persons and their environments

Qualitative Data descriptive information to which researchers could assign numeric representations to the words and apply limited statistical analyses

Qualitative Research describes and analyzes the qualities of variables being studied, such as case studies or key informant studies

Quantitative Data involve a numerical measurement of the object of study

Quantitative Research measures the numeric quantity of the variables being studied that can be subject to statistical analysis

Questioning asking questions to open new areas of information or to follow up for more specific details

Racism ideology that perpetuates the social domination of one racial group by another

Recognizing Success development phase process emphasizing clients' accomplishments and describing numerous ways to measure achievement of goals and evaluate service effectiveness

Record-Keeping maintaining records of practitioner–client interactions that serve as the basis for individual reflection, supervisory discussion, peer consultation, progress evaluation, and quality assurance

Referrals new linkages between clients and service providers or community resources

Reflective Practice continuous process of thinking, doing, and reflecting—a process that incorporates feedback to garner insight and refine actions

Reframing narrative strategy offering new perspectives on clients' situations, reinterpreting them as positive, functional, or useful

Regionalism prejudicial attitudes based on people's geographical origin and/or current residence

Relative Confidentiality legal and ethical requirement that ensures, with few exceptions, that information about clients remains private and confidential within the agency context

Release of Information Form permission form signed by clients allowing workers to disclose case information to a third party

Reliability quality of a measurement tool or process that indicates measures are similar or consistent over time or with repeated applications

Requests to Continue unobtrusive requests that ask clients to continue

Research method of systematic investigation or experimentation to enrich theory and refine practice applications

Researcher professional-level educational role for conducting empirical research and practice evaluation to contribute to the professional knowledge base

Resilience capacity to deal effectively with difficulties

Resistance motivated response by clients to oppose change or to move in a direction different from that of practitioners

Resource Management social work function through which social workers foster connections with resources that clients already use to some extent, facilitate connections with other resources, and develop resources that are not currently available

Respect occurs when social workers regard clients as partners, listen to their opinions, communicate cordially, honor cultural differences, and credit clients as having strengths and potential

Responsive Environment conditions in physical and social environments that offer sufficient resources and opportunities

Restatement response that repeats the client's last few words or a significant phrase

Role Playing rehearsing a scenario to develop interpersonal skills or try out new behaviors

Scholar professional-level educational role to refine knowledge and skills through continuing education, training, and scholarly reading; also to share knowledge through presentations

Self-Awareness knowledge of one's self, including strengths, weaknesses, values, and biases

Self-Care involves attending to personal needs to ensure good health, mental health, and social well-being

Self-Determination social work principle upholding people's rights to make their own life-course decisions

Self-Disclosure occurs when social workers carefully choose from among their own personal experiences to share something of benefit to clients

Self-Help Groups groups of individuals with similar concerns or problems who join together to be helpful resources for one another

Session Endings ending phases of a group meeting that solidify and integrate the group's success for that session and anticipate the impact for the future work of the group

Sexism belief that one sex is superior to the other

Single-System Designs research designs for evaluating the effects of interventions on a client system's target problem

Single-Word Responses one-word responses or utterances can convey attentive, accepting attitude

Situational Attributions occur when credit is conferred to others for creating change in one's situation

Social Action mobilizes clients and professional allies to address organizational, community, and social policy issues; collective action to reallocate sociopolitical power so that disenfranchised citizens can access and contribute to society's resources

Social Action Groups groups mobilized around shared concerns to work toward creating mezzo- and macrolevel changes

Social Constructionism centers on how people construct meaning in their lives, emphasizing social meaning as generated through language, cultural beliefs, and social interactions

Social Histories organize information gathered about past and current functioning through structured interviews or free-flowing conversations with clients

Social Injustice prevails when society infringes on human rights, holds prejudicial attitudes toward some of its members, and institutionalizes inequality by discriminating against segments of its citizenry

Social Justice core social work value prevailing when all members of a society share equally in the social order, secure an equitable consideration of resources and opportunities, and enjoy their full benefit of civil liberties

Social Model of Disability perspective that defines disability as a product of the social and physical environment rather than a personal characteristic

Social Network Maps tools for assessing social support, picturing social support networks, and quantifying the nature of support

Social Policy laws and rules that determine how a society distributes its resources among its members

Social Support networks of personal and professional support that cushion stress, help people cope, and provide material assistance

Social System structure in which interdependent people interact

Social Work profession that supports individuals, groups, and communities in a changing society and creates social conditions favorable to the well-being of people and society

Sociopolitical Empowerment increases access to and control of sociopolitical or structural resources

Solution-Focused Dialogue conversations with clients that create an atmosphere conducive to possibilities, clearly articulating what clients want, and framing incremental steps toward goals

Standardized Instruments published data collection tools with verified reliability and validity standards

Standpoint Theory theoretical perspective postulating that social-cultural-political location determines what we do or do not see, how we interpret what we see, and the value or importance of what we notice

Statistical Indicators profile the community using a collation of census data, demographic and population statistics, and social and economic indicators

Strengths Perspective views people as resourceful with untapped mental, physical, emotional, social, and spiritual abilities and capacities for continued growth

Stress tension resulting from demanding conditions, transitions, and challenging life experiences

Structure refers to the organization of social system at a given point in time

Structured Training consists of curriculum-based learning strategies

Subsystem smaller system nested within larger systems

Summary Clarification clarifies themes or clusters of information

Summary Recording written report that describes interactions thematically rather than in step-by-step detail

Supervision support and oversight of practitioners to develop skills for efficient and effective job performance and accountability, and for competent and ethical services for clients

Systems structures in which interdependent people interact

Teacher microlevel educational role through which workers and clients acquire and use information to resolve current issues

Teams groups of professionals who share a common purpose, contribute their expertise to the initiative, and collaborate to achieve a mutually agreed-on outcome

Telephone Surveys surveys conducted over the phone with selected informants or randomized respondents

Termination discontinuation or conclusion of service delivery

Trainer mezzolevel educational role in which workers function as education specialists for formal groups and organizations

Transactions reciprocal interactions among systems and between systems and their environments

Transferable Skills skills in one area that can be generalized to other situations

Trauma crisis events such as experiencing violence, unexpected death, dramatic loss, or the aftermath of war that affect abilities to cope

Trauma-Informed Perspective considers effects that trauma experienced by clients may have on their current situations

Traumatic Brain Injury (TBI) severe trauma to the brain

Trustworthiness multidimensional personal quality based on clients' perceptions of workers' reliability, honesty, credibility, sincerity, and integrity

Validity quality of a measurement process or tool when it accurately measures the variable it intends to measure

Variables concepts that vary in ways that can be observed, recorded, and measured through research and evaluation

Verbal Utterances brief, affirming verbal expressions such as mm-hmm

Vicarious Trauma experience of secondary trauma resulting from engaging with clients who have experienced trauma-based pain and suffering firsthand; vulnerability to vicarious trauma increases with personal history of trauma

Victim Blaming casts aspersions on society's victim rather than holding society itself accountable for a given social problem

Voluntary Clients participants in social work services who have the privilege to participate freely without coercion, based on their perceived notion that social work assistance will help

Wholeness principle indicating that change in one part of a system precipitates changes in other parts and in the system as a whole

Name Index

469

Subject Index